INTERNET

& e

WEB ESSENTIALS
WHAT YOU NEED TO KNOW

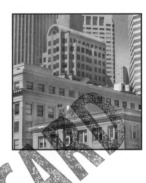

ERNEST ACKERMANN
MARY WASHINGTON COLLEGE

KAREN HARTMAN
MARY WASHINGTON COLLEGE

Franklin, Beedle & Associates, Incorporated
8536 SW St. Helens Drive, Suite D
Wilsonville, Oregon 97070
(503) 682-7668
www.fbeedle.com

Dedication

To Lynn, Karl, and Oliver
—E. A.

To my parents, Roy and Mary Pearce, for giving me that
which has made all the difference: a happy, secure childhood
—K. H.

President & Publisher	Jim Leisy (jimleisy@fbeedle.com)
Developmental Editor	Sue Page
Manuscript Editor	Stephanie Welch
Cover Design	Ian Shadburne
Illustrations	Oliver Ackermann
Production	Stephanie Welch
	Tom Sumner
Marketing Representative	Chris Collier
Order Processing	Krista Hall
	Lois Allison

Rights and Permissions
Franklin, Beedle & Associates, Incorporated
8536 SW St. Helens Drive, Suite D
Wilsonville, Oregon 97070
503/682-7668
www.fbeedle.com

Library of Congress Cataloging-in-Publication Data

Ackermann, Ernest
    Internet & Web essentials : what you need to know / Ackermann & Hartman.
      p. cm.
    ISBN 1-887902-40-6
     1. Internet. 2. World Wide Web. I. Title: Internet and Web essentials. II. Hartman, Karen. III. Title.

TK5105.875.I57 A235 2000
025.04--dc21
                                                      00-044264

Table of Contents

Chapter 9   Successful Search Strategies 267

Chapter 10   Specialized Databases 296

Preface

Internet and Web Essentials: What You Need to Know is designed for
students in a college-level, three-credit Internet course; for students
in a course that uses the Internet; and for people learning on their
own. It gives the reader the skills necessary to use the Internet and a
Web browser in the areas of communicating, accessing and evaluating
resources, and authoring and designing for the Web. The chapters include
a statement of objectives for the learner, clear explanations, activities
that show step-by-step instructions for using necessary software, a list of
important terms introduced in the chapter, and exercises and projects that
give the reader practice using the concepts and tools introduced. Previous
experience with the Internet and the Web isn't necessary to successfully
use and learn from the text. Students in any discipline will find the book
useful. The text is interesting, informative, and accessible.

We've been teaching and writing about the Internet and the Web
for several years. That work and our personal involvement in using and
providing Internet services brings us to the belief that an informed and
discriminating user of the Internet needs to know:

- the basic technology that supports the Internet

- effective means of using the Internet for communication

- how to search for and locate information resources

- how to critically evaluate information from the Internet

- how to produce information that can be effectively shared with others
  on the Internet

- the social, ethical, and legal issues surrounding the use of the Internet
  and the World Wide Web

This book provides the essential information and skills to meet those
needs.

Important Features of the Book

We present the important information about the topics that are essential
to becoming a well-informed user of the Internet. These include basic

Internet technology, connecting to the Internet, using the Internet for communication, using a Web browser, accessing and evaluating information on the Internet, producing and publishing information on the Internet, and a variety of legal and ethical issues associated with using the Internet and the Web. Several of the topics are presented in an integrated manner. Social, legal, and ethical issues, for example, are presented in the context of other topics.

Each chapter begins with an introduction to its topic. This is followed by a list of goals and objectives for the reader and a list of the major topics in the chapter. The text of each chapter includes one or more guided activities or examples: step-by-step instructions learners can follow to enforce and enhance their understanding of the skills and concepts introduced in the chapter. In most cases the activities access sites on the World Wide Web; in some cases we've provided the files needed for the activities on the disk included with the book. Each chapter also contains several short lists of Web resources titled "FYI." A reader can use these as a means to further explore some of the topics introduced. A summary, a list of important terms, and exercises conclude each chapter.

The book includes two appendices and a glossary of the important terms listed in the chapters. The first appendix is an annotated list of search tools, including search engines, directories, virtual libraries, and specialized databases, mentioned in the book. The second appendix is a collection of all the URLs listed throughout the chapters to help guide you to related information—we called them FYIs. Each of these collections serves as reference material.

Both Netscape Navigator and Internet Explorer are used for activities and examples. The browsers are similar enough that using one or the other makes very little difference in most cases. We do point out the differences and give specific and separate instructions for using the features of each when it is important to do so.

Organization of This Book

The book is arranged so that the information presented is reinforced and built on in subsequent chapters. We also have grouped and sequenced information into the topic areas of introduction to the Internet and the World Wide Web and their supporting technologies; communication on the Internet; using a Web browser; searching for, locating, evaluating, and citing information on the Internet and the Web; managing and using Internet information; and preparing and publishing information on the Web. As we stated earlier, social, legal, and ethical issues are presented in the context of other topics.

Here is a view of how the book is organized:

Internet and Web Basics

Chapter 1   "Introduction to the Internet and the World Wide Web."
Issues of etiquette and law; a brief history of the development of the Internet and the Web.

Chapter 2   "How the Internet Works and Getting Connected." Basic
terminology and technology associated with the Internet
and the Web; connecting to the Internet; setting preferences
for email and Usenet.

Internet Communication

Chapter 3   "Communication on the Internet." An overview of the
variety of forms used for communicating on the Internet,
including asynchronous (such as email and Usenet) and
synchronous (such as chat and IRC) forms of communication; effective Internet communication.

Chapter 4   "Electronic Mail." Advantages and limitations of email;
communication issues specific to email; details and examples of using Outlook Express for email.

Chapter 5   "Email Discussion Groups." Essential information for working with and finding email discussion groups; etiquette and
behavior associated with participating in email discussion
groups.

Chapter 6   "Usenet News." Essential information needed for effective
use of Usenet; details of using a news reader; Usenet news
etiquette.

Using the Web as an Information Resource

Chapter 7   "Getting Around the World Wide Web—Using a Web
Browser." Both Netscape and Internet Explorer are covered
in detail; navigating the Web; security and privacy on the
Web.

Chapter 8   "Finding Information on the World Wide Web." Guidelines
for evaluating information needs before beginning to search;
a survey of the different types of search tools, such as
directories and search engines, and guidelines for selecting
the best type of tool for a specific task; content issues
including pornography, free speech, censorship, filtering,
and copyright.

Chapter 9   "Successful Search Strategies." Various facets of search
engine databases, including their construction and features;
several examples of using specific search engines.

Chapter 10   "Specialized Databases." Advantages and characteristics of specialized databases; finding and using specialized databases; examples of finding company and industry information.

Chapter 11   "Selecting, Evaluating, and Citing Information from the Internet." A very important chapter for people interested in using the Internet and the Web for research; deals with important issues related to critically evaluating information content; guidelines for citing information; using the bookmark list to create a bibliography.

Chapter 12   "Managing and Using Information from the Internet and the World Wide Web." Common file types; copyright guidelines; methods for capturing text, images, and data from Web pages and using that information in other applications.

Chapter 13   "Transferring Files Using FTP." File Transfer Protocol; retrieving files using FTP; locating and using software archives; working with an FTP client.

Producing Information and Publishing on the Web

Chapter 14   "Putting Information on the Web." Considers the issues related to putting information on the Web, including Web-page and Web-site design, technologies used to produce Web pages, and putting Web page source files on a Web server; evaluating Web-page design; publicizing information on the Web.

Chapter 15   "Writing Web Pages." The details of using HTML for basic Web pages; using images, colors, and tables; contains an activity that goes through all the steps to create and link Web pages.

Chapter 16   "Enhancing Web Pages." How to make Web pages more useful and valuable; minimizing download time for images; including a variety of media—animated images, sound, and video; including interactive elements through Java, JavaScript, and CGI-type programs.

Chapter Selection

Chapters 1 and 2 are fundamental to the rest of the material in the text. After you've read them you can go through the rest of the material in the order it's presented in the text, or you can focus on any of the major areas individually. If you take the latter path you'll want to deal with a section in its entirety.

The book contains ample material for a one-semester, three-credit course. It can also be used for a shorter eight-week course or as a supplement to a course that uses the Internet.

If the primary focus of the course is communication, then include:

Chapter 1	Introduction to the Internet and the World Wide Web
Chapter 2	How the Internet Works and Getting Connected
Chapter 3	Communication on the Internet
Chapter 4	Electronic Mail
Chapter 5	Email Discussion Groups
Chapter 6	Usenet News
Chapter 7	Getting Around the World Wide Web—Using a Web Browser

If the primary focus is using the Internet for research, then include:

Chapter 1	Introduction to the Internet and the World Wide Web
Chapter 2	How the Internet Works and Getting Connected
Chapter 7	Getting Around the World Wide Web—Using a Web Browser
Chapter 8	Finding Information on the World Wide Web
Chapter 9	Successful Search Strategies
Chapter 10	Specialized Databases
Chapter 11	Selecting, Evaluating, and Citing Information from the Internet
Chapter 12	Managing and Using Information from the Internet and the World Wide Web

If the primary focus is on producing information to put on the Web, then include:

Chapter 1	Introduction to the Internet and the World Wide Web
Chapter 2	How the Internet Works and Getting Connected
Chapter 7	Getting Around the World Wide Web—Using a Web Browser
Chapter 8	Finding Information on the World Wide Web
Chapter 12	Managing and Using Information from the Internet and the World Wide Web
Chapter 13	Transferring Files Using FTP
Chapter 14	Putting Information on the Web
Chapter 15	Writing Web Pages
Chapter 16	Enhancing Web Pages

Chapter 16 contains material that goes more deeply into providing enhancements to Web pages than some readers may want, but it's worth it to read that chapter so you're aware of some of the possibilities.

Supplemental Materials

We maintain a Web site with the URL **http://www.webliminal.com/ essentials** to accompany this book. The Web pages that make up the site contain up-to-date links to all the resources mentioned in the book. We'll be updating the Web pages regularly, so please check the Web site to see what has changed since the book was printed. It's likely that some of the URLs will change because that's the nature of the Web, but the concepts we discuss in the book stay the same.

The disk that's included with the book contains HTML versions of the exercises, the summary, and selected terms from each chapter. They can be viewed with any browser and make it easier to work on the exercises. Some of the activities in the text require files that are also included on the disk. To use the disk, start your computer, put the disk in Drive A, start your Web browser, and type **A:\index.htm** in the location or address field. That opens a Web page that gives instructions and hyperlinks to follow for the other material on the disk.

For teachers using this book an instructor's guide is available from the publisher, Franklin, Beedle & Associates. The publisher can be contacted through its Web site, **http://www.fbeedle.com**, or by phone, 1-800-FBA-BOOK.

About the Authors

As a professor of computer science and a reference and instruction librarian, we've been using the Internet and the World Wide Web for over a decade in our professional work. We have also had the chance for the last five years to teach others about using the Web and the Internet for communication, research, and Web publishing. On top of this good fortune we've also had the chance to write several textbooks that deal in one way or the other with those same topics. This book, we think, is our best effort yet.

Acknowledgments

There are many people to thank for helping us with this project. First, what must be inadequate thanks go to our families. They, more than anyone, have made it possible for us to complete this work. It's more than their helping with specific tasks, such as proofreading, fielding ideas, checking URLs, and doing our share of chores. What is so special is that they allow us the selfish pleasure of writing. Ernie wants to thank his wife Lynn for her help and love. His sons Karl and Oliver have been a constant source of encouragement. Oliver is responsible for the excellent illustrations in the book. Karen wants to especially thank her husband Jack for his ideas, which have prompted creative solutions in many aspects of her work; his unwavering support of all her pursuits; and his enduring faith in her abilities as an educator, writer, and mother. She also wants to thank her daughters Tracy and Hilary for keeping her up to date with new trends, especially MP3.

Our friends, colleagues, and students in Fredericksburg and at Mary Washington College deserve a great deal of thanks. We get a much better view of what's important about using the Internet because of working with them. Special thanks go to Joseph Dreiss, professor of art history at Mary Washington College, who worked very closely with us in the early stages of this project. We would also like to thank Jack Bales for allowing us to use a piece of his writing in an example of citing Web pages in Chapter 11.

Franklin, Beedle & Associates has been a very supportive and cooperative publisher and has helped us greatly throughout this project. We'd like to especially thank Jim Leisy, president; Sue Page, developmental editor; Stephanie Welch, Ian Shadburne, and Tom Sumner, production; Chris Collier; Lois Allison; and Krista Hall.

This book has been through several reviews and we want to thank our reviewers:

Ralph Sanford	Bristol Community College
Judy Scholl	Austin Community College
Ken Shaw	Metropolitan State College of Denver
Nancy Greenwood	St. Charles County Community College
Terryl Kistler	College of San Mateo

We hope you enjoy this book and find it useful. Please send us email to let us know your opinions and suggestions. When you have the time add something to our guestbooks, which are accessible from our home pages at **http://www.webliminal.com/ernie** and **http://www.library.mwc.edu/ ~ khartman**.

Peace.

Ernest Ackermann
Department of Computer Science
Mary Washington College
ernie@mwc.edu
http://www.webliminal.com/ernie

Karen Hartman
James Monroe Center Library
Mary Washington College
khartman@mwc.edu
http://www.library.mwc.edu/ ~ khartman

Chapter 1

INTRODUCTION TO THE

INTERNET AND THE

WORLD WIDE WEB

Let's start right here. You've heard a lot about the Internet and the World Wide Web (WWW) and are interested in learning how they work and how to use them effectively. We'll describe the Web and the Internet, emphasizing the ways people use them for personal or professional communications, accessing and retrieving information, and producing information for others to view on the Web. We will include some background information on how the Internet and the Web developed, and we'll introduce some of the ethical and legal issues related to using the Web and the Internet. We'll also take you through a hands-on activity to introduce you to the World Wide Web.

You'll see that this chapter, and each chapter in this book, begins with a list of goals/objectives. We list these from the point of view of someone reading the book. In other words, these goals/objectives tell you what you can expect to know or understand and what skills you will gain by reading the text and working through the activities and exercises. (You'll find that some chapters naturally have a greater emphasis on concepts and others on skills.) You can use this list to help you find information in the text of the chapter.

Goals/Objectives

- Know the basic concepts of the WWW and the Internet
- Comprehend the significance of the Web as it relates to your professional and personal activities
- Learn about the history and development of the Internet and the Web
- Become familiar with some of the basic issues related to Internet etiquette and proper use

Topics

- Introduction to the Internet and the World Wide Web
- Services and Tools You Use on the Internet and the Web
- The Significance of the Internet and the World Wide Web
- Issues of Etiquette and Law
- How the Internet and the World Wide Web Developed

Introduction to the Internet and the World Wide Web

The reports are appearing everywhere: in the newspaper, on the radio, and on the television news. Go to any magazine display and you'll see the words *World Wide Web* and *Internet* on several of the covers. Your friends and family are telling you about the Web and asking you for your email address. The Internet has caused a momentous change in society, the reports say. The Internet is transforming the way people communicate with each other. It has revolutionized the way people do research and conduct business. It has changed the way research is published and distributed and the way products are marketed and sold.

You keep hearing and reading about all of this, but you want to know what isn't talked about much. You want to know what exactly is the Internet? How does it work? Where does the World Wide Web fit in? How do you get connected? How can the Internet make your life fuller, richer, more productive, and more fun? The aim of this book is to answer all these questions and more. But for now let's begin at the beginning and talk about what the Internet actually is.

The **Internet** is an international collection of computer networks that exchange information according to a fixed set of rules. A network is a group of computers that are linked together so that they can exchange information. The computers and networks on the Internet communicate with each other by exchanging data according to the same rules, even though the individual networks and computer systems may use different technologies. The rules for exchanging information are called **protocols**. Since the Internet is a collection of computer networks on a worldwide scale, this means that your computer can retrieve information from networks throughout the world.

The **World Wide Web** is the collection of information accessible through the Internet. The information is linked together like a web through **hyperlinks**. This information may be any type of content, including text, video, audio, or graphical images. We can refer to these types of information on the Web as **hypermedia**. Each link is specified or written using a ***Uniform Resource Locator***, or ***URL***, which acts as an address for the information. The protocol that's used to exchange information through hyperlinks is called ***HTTP, Hypertext Transfer Protocol***. There's no definite starting point on the Web, and the path you take is your choice. You can move around in many ways: by going backward, forward, up, down, right, or left.

Many people who use the Internet use it for communicating with others through electronic mail. Others use the Internet primarily for research,

> **Fy** TO LEARN MORE ABOUT THE INTERNET AND THE WORLD WIDE WEB
> ~ "Beginners Central"
> http://www.northernwebs
> .com/bc
> ~ "Chapter 1: What is the Internet?"
> http://members.unlimited.net/
> ~kumbach/internet/
> whatsnet.html
> ~ "Getting Started on the Internet"
> http://www.imagescape.com/
> helpweb/welcome.html

employing the vast resources found on the World Wide Web. The World Wide Web has popularized the Internet for tens of millions of people throughout the world. By allowing people to simply click on an image or a block of text and be taken to documents that enrich and expand on the text by incorporating graphics, sounds, and video, the Web has revolutionized the way learning, communication, and commerce are accomplished.

The beauty of the Internet is that it is interactive. People are encouraged to contribute to its development. It doesn't matter who you are, where you live, or what work you do, it's the quality of the communication and interaction that's important. You can send an email message to someone who lives in a different country as easily as to a friend who lives across town. You can search for and read documents that have been placed on the Internet from all over the world. It's a decentralized entity; there is no one company, organization, or government running it, nor is there any control over what information is accessed through it. The Internet, by its very nature, is an evolving and expanding creation.

We'll talk about all of these things in detail later. For now, we're going to provide an overview of the Internet environment by concentrating on the tools and services that make it possible to use the Internet to access and share information. We'll also talk about the social components: those communities of people that use the Internet for communication.

Services and Tools You Use on the Internet and the Web

In this section we'll focus on the tools and services that you'll use on the Internet and the World Wide Web to access, share, and produce information, as well as the tools for communication. The major categories of services and tools we'll consider here are those used for:

∾ Accessing Information

∾ Communicating with Individuals or Groups

∾ Searching For and Finding Information

∾ Creating, Composing, and Authoring Web Pages

Accessing Information

Accessing information means either retrieving information that's available as a Web page or retrieving a file (a collection of information that has a name) by some other means. The two primary ways of accessing information are using a Web browser and using File Transfer Protocol (FTP).

Telnet, a popular means of accessing information before the invention of graphical Web browsers, is still used to access some databases on the Internet and to log in to remote systems.

We explain each technology further here.

Web Browser

The concept behind the World Wide Web was the development of a hypertext networked information system. One of the goals was a uniform means of accessing all the different types of information on the Internet. Since you only need to know one way to get information, you can concentrate on what you want, not how to get it. You access the WWW by using a program called a **Web browser**.

There are several browsers available. The first popular browser was Mosaic, and currently the most popular ones are Netscape Navigator and Microsoft Internet Explorer. Each has its special features and advantages, but they also have a lot in common. We'll use both browsers—Netscape's Navigator and Microsoft's Internet Explorer—in this book. In most cases we'll be able to use one in the same way we use the other. When it's necessary we'll specifically mention the way to use Netscape and the corresponding way to use Internet Explorer.

You move from place to place and item to item on the Web by using a mouse to select and click on a portion of text, an icon, or a region of a map or image. These hyperlinks, or *links* for short, represent information somewhere on the Internet. The browser also includes features that let you save files and print documents you've found on the Web. You can also use it to keep lists of sites and resources you'd like to visit again.

 COMPARING WEB BROWSERS

~ "Browsers: A CNET Topic Center"
http://home.cnet.com/
category/0-3773.html
~ "BrowserWatch-Browser Blvd."
http://browserwatch.internet
.com/browsers.html
~ "Web Browser"
http://www.zdnet.com/
products/filter/guide/
0,7267,1500102,00.html

Some folks stay with the browser that comes with their computer, but you may want to know the different ones available. You may also want to take a look at a comparison of some of the features of the most popular browsers and some that aren't as popular.

FTP

FTP stands for **File Transfer Protocol**. It is the original protocol used to share files among computers with access to the Internet. It works something like this: You use an FTP program as a tool to contact another computer on the Internet. Then you can retrieve a file from that computer or upload a file from your computer. There are thousands of FTP archives containing information in various formats, such as text, data, programs, images, and audio.

Telnet

Telnet allows your computer to log in to a remote computer system and use it as if you were directly connected to it through a computer terminal. Many of the sites that used to be available only through Telnet are now available as Web pages.

Communicating with Individuals or Groups

The widespread use of the Internet has had a significant impact on personal and professional communications. More than 200 million people are connected to the Internet. **Electronic mail**, or **email**, is its most popular use. A significant amount of personal and commercial communication is done through email. A large number of electronic or virtual communities have developed on the Internet because of the ease of both group and individual communications.

Electronic Mail (Email)

This is a basic Internet service that allows individuals or groups to communicate. The communication is **asynchronous**; people don't have to be connected to the Internet at the same time to communicate. Individuals use email programs to read, send, and manage email. Sometimes the program is called an email client or a mail user agent.

Most email programs make it easy to work with text, images, and other types of files that are part of or are an attachment to an email message. Others work best with messages that are only text.

Email Discussion Group

Email discussion groups are sometimes called **interest groups**, **listservs**, or **mailing lists**. Internet users join, contribute messages to, and read messages from the group through email.

Fy COMPUTER-MEDIATED COMMUNICATION

There are two electronic journals dedicated to computer-mediated communication. One, *Computer-Mediated Communication Magazine*, was continuously published on the Web from 1994 to January 1999. The other, *Journal of Computer-Mediated Communication*, has been continuously published quarterly since June 1995. Both of these are rich sources of information on using computer systems for communication.

~ "CMC Magazine Archive"
   http://www.december.com/cmc/mag/archive
~ "Journal of Computer-Mediated Communication"
   http://www.ascusc.org/jcmc

Usenet

Rather than being exchanged between individuals, messages are sent from one computer system to another, each system acting as a Usenet host. All the messages are available to anyone wishing to read them. In this form of group communication the messages are called articles and are arranged into categories called newsgroups. The tool that an individual uses to read, post, reply to, and manage articles is called a **newsreader**.

Internet Relay Chat (IRC), Chat, Instant Messenger, MOO, and MUD

These are used for realtime, or **synchronous**, group discussions. Each of these services has its own characteristics but they operate essentially the same way. People meet on channels which, depending on the service, are also called chat rooms, Buddy Lists, **MUDs** (multiuser dungeons), or **MOOs** (multiuser dungeons that are object oriented). Think of these as virtual meeting places or even virtual communities.

Internet Conferencing

Internet or Web *conferencing* involves two or more participants working together and communicating at the same time. These programs put high demands on network speed and capacity since the exchange of realistic and simultaneous video, audio, and images requires that a great deal of information be transferred in a very short period of time.

Searching For and Finding Information

The Internet and the Web were created to share information. Naturally, then, there are lots of resources available for information on almost any topic. There are several ways to navigate through the Web. If you know the address of the site you want to visit, you simply enter the URL in the field provided. After the site appears, you can browse it by clicking on hyperlinks that you choose. If you don't know the address or URL of a site, you can search for the information you need by using a search tool. Several tools have been developed to meet the challenge of finding specific, appropriate, and relevant information from the vast resources available. These search tools will, in response to the search request you enter, return to your screen a list of hyperlinks that are relevant to your topic. Here's a brief description of the two major types of search tools.

Search Engine

A *search engine* is a collection of programs that gather information from the Web, index it, and put it in a database so it can be searched. The programs that gather the information are called spiders or robots. Each search engine also provides a tool for finding information in its database. The search engine takes the keywords or phrases you enter, searches the database for words that match the search expression, and returns the results to you. The results are hyperlinks to sources that have descriptions, titles, or contents matching the search expression.

Directory

A *directory* is a topical list of Internet resources arranged by subject. You click on the subject category that is likely to contain either the Web pages you want or other subject categories that are more specific. Several directories contain reviews or descriptions of the entries. Directories are for browsing, but they can also be searched. Directories differ from search engines in one major way—the human element involved in collecting and updating the information.

Creating, Composing, and Authoring Web Pages

One of the significant aspects of the Internet is that it makes it relatively easy for us to be producers of information, not only consumers. It virtually invites us to become involved in the production of information and resources for others to use. From the early days of the Internet people have been information providers through email, email discussion groups, Usenet newsgroups, and FTP.

The advent of the World Wide Web has increased the opportunities for making information available to a wide audience and in some ways made it easier and more commonplace. Lots of folks—hundreds of thousands—have personal home pages, pages that tell something about themselves. An example of an excellent personal home page is "Jan's Home Page," **http://jan.redmood.com**, created by Jan Hanford. It seems as if every business, school, periodical, and organization has a Web site. There are also a large number of sites that deal with scholarly, research, or technical topics, some to provide a community service, others created for entertainment or whimsy, and others that give us the daily data of modern life such as news reports, weather reports, sports statistics, and the performance of the stock market. Information quality and presentation varies.

All anyone needs to produce information that's accessible throughout the world is a computer, a program to create Web pages, and a computer system that acts as a Web server.

∿ Web pages are files in which **HTML (Hypertext Markup Language)** is used to specify the format of the Web page, the images to be displayed, hyperlinks, and possibly other elements.

∿ A Web browser interprets the HTML in the file and then displays the Web page. The HTML tags give the browser information about how to display or represent information in the file.

∿ The files have to be placed on a computer that's connected to the Internet and acts as a Web server. The Web page is then available to anyone on the Internet through its URL. The Web page that lists Ernest Ackermann's office hours, for example, is in a file named **offhrs.html** in his home Web directory on the computer whose Internet address is **www1.mwc.edu**. This is reflected in its URL, **http://www1.mwc.edu/ ~ ernie/offhrs.html**.

Fy HELP FOR WEB PAGE AUTHORS AND WEB SITE DESIGNERS
∿ "Web Page Design and Layout" http://dir.yahoo.com/Arts/ Design_Arts/Graphic_Design/ Web_Page_Design_and_Layout
∿ "The Web Design Group's Links" http://www.htmlhelp.com/ links

There are a number of commercial services and Internet service providers that will host a Web site for a monthly fee. The cost usually depends on how much information is required to store the Web page files and how many times per month the Web pages are accessed. Some hosting services are free or available for a small yearly fee. Tripod, **http://www.tripod.com**, allows registered members (there is no cost to register) to use its site as a Web server.

Now that you've been introduced to what types of services are available, let's try a hands-on activity that will demonstrate some of the concepts of navigating the World Wide Web.

In this activity, we'll explore the United States Census Bureau's Web site. The Census Bureau has made most of the 1990 census available online for the public, as well as historical United States population information. Some people are interested in the data to determine demographic information. Business people and economists often need to find out population characteristics to further their understanding of business trends and make intelligent hypotheses regarding projected economic changes. Perhaps you're taking a job or moving to another part of the country and want to know something about the population in that area.

The United States Census Bureau is the most reliable source for this type of information, and its Web site is well-designed and filled with useful information. The activity will give you practice browsing a Web site and will show you how easy it is to use the World Wide Web to find the information you need.

ABOUT ACTIVITIES

The following is the first of many activities in this book. Each activity is divided into two parts: "Overview" and "Details." In the "Overview" section, we discuss what we'll be covering in the activity and enumerate the steps we'll follow. "Details" takes you through the steps, shows you the results we got when we tried the activity, and discusses certain aspects of the particular skill being shown.

Follow the steps, use what's here as a guide, and pay attention to what you see. As you work through this and other activities in the book, appears next to actions that you need to take in order to move through the steps.

Remember that the Web is always changing, and there is a possibility that the results you get may differ from those shown here. Don't let this confuse you. These activities demonstrate fundamental skills that don't change, even though what you see when you follow the steps may look very different.

BROWSING THE U.S. CENSUS BUREAU'S WEB SITE

Overview

We're assuming that you have a browser program set up on your computer and that you have a way of connecting to the Internet.

In going through the steps of this activity, we'll start the browser, explain some of the items you'll see on your screen, and then type in a URL that will take us to the United States Census Bureau's home page. We'll locate a population clock for the United States and browse for census information for a county in Michigan. These are the steps we'll follow:

1. Start the Web browser.
2. Go to the United States Census Bureau's home page.
3. Explore the United States Census Bureau's Web site.
4. Exit the Web browser.

Details

1. Start the Web browser.

You start the Web browser by clicking on an icon or choosing the browser from a menu. You'll need to find the icon on the desktop or select the program from a list of programs you can run from your computer.

If you're using Netscape, locate an icon that looks like one of the following:

Netscape   Netscape   Netscape
Navigator   Communicator

If you're using Internet Explorer, look for an icon that looks like:

Internet
Explorer

Clicking one of these icons starts the Web browser.

Double-click on the icon for the browser.

From here on we'll give the steps for the activity assuming that Netscape Navigator is being used as the Web browser.

A window similar to the one in Figure 1.1 will appear on your screen, although the contents will be different. In this case, the browser brought to the screen the home page for the computer that we are using for this activity. We will use this page as a starting point for this Web exploration exercise.

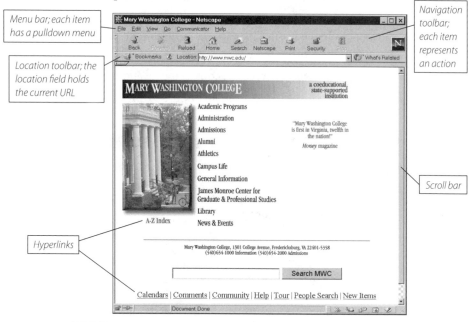

Figure 1.1   A Home Page

If you're familiar with a windowed environment, you should feel very comfortable using a Web browser. You can work with many of the items in this window in the same way as with any other window. The menu commands are listed across the top row. They include:

File   Edit   View   Go   Communicator   Help

The menu bar contains items (such as File, Edit, and Help) that are common to several windowed applications. Each command has a pulldown menu; click on the command and a menu will appear.

The browser's window also has several items in the navigation toolbar, as we point out in Figure 1.1. You can use them to go from one Web page to another, print a Web page, stop the current page that is loading, and so forth. For example, you click on **Back** to go to the previous Web page.

2. Go to the United States Census Bureau's home page.

In order to go to the United States Census Bureau's home page, you need to know what its Uniform Resource Locator, or URL, is. We can assume that you have found the URL in a book or a newspaper article or a friend has given it to you. The URL, **http://www.census.gov**, will be typed in the location field of the browser window. The location field is labeled either Location: or Netsite:.

Use the mouse to point to the location field and click the (left) mouse button.

When you click on the location field, it changes color. You can type a new URL to replace the current one.

Type http://www.census.gov in the location field and press Enter.

After you type the URL in the location field, its label will change to Go to:, as shown in Figure 1.2.

Figure 1.2   A URL Typed in the Location Field

When you press **Enter**, your Web browser sends a request to the Census Bureau's Web server, the computer that makes the U.S. census material available. The server then sends the Web page with the URL **http://www.census.gov** across the Internet to your computer. The United States Census Bureau's home page appears in Figure 1.3.

It's worth noting here that a URL gives us some information about a Web site. The first part of any URL after **http://** is the *Internet domain name* of the computer that hosts the Web site. In this case the domain name is **www.census.gov**. Only U.S. government sites can have a domain name that ends with **gov**, so the URL here indicates that this is a Web site associated with an agency of the U.S. government.

tip TYPING ONLY PART OF A URL

If you're using Netscape Navigator version 2 or later, you don't need to type the complete URL. You can always omit the leading **http://**; simply type **www.census.gov** in the location field. In fact you could even omit **www**. The browser will automatically put **http://www.** in front of any partial URL you type in the location field.

If the URL doesn't start with **http://www**, then you'll have to type in the complete URL. We use the full form in this book so the URLs are complete and will work with any browser. Complete URLs *must* be used when you're creating a Web page using HTML.

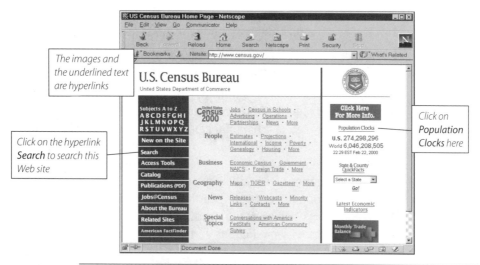

Figure 1.3   The U.S. Census Bureau's Home Page

3. Explore the United States Census Bureau's Web site.

There are many ways to explore the U.S. Census Bureau. Let's start out by simply clicking on a hyperlink that looks interesting. You'll notice in Figure 1.3 the hyperlink **Population Clocks**. By clicking on this hyperlink, we can find out current population statistics for the United States and the world. Let's see what we can find out.

Click on the hyperlink that's entitled **Population Clocks**, as shown in Figure 1.3.

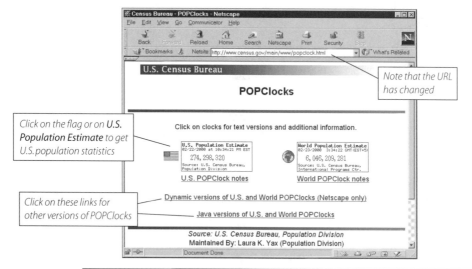

Figure 1.4   Population Clock Hyperlinks

We can find out population statistics for the United States or for the world. Let's try clicking on the one for the United States.

(Do it!) Click on the flag or **U.S. Population Estimate**, as shown in Figure 1.4.

Note the information retrieved in Figure 1.5. This population clock is a projection. This means that the numbers aren't exact, they are estimates. The Census Bureau uses the numbers it has in its databases from the last national census and adds numbers gathered from state and local governments to project a current population. The page shows the time intervals between births and deaths and other related information. One advantage of using a government site like this one for population data is that it provides reliable information. The U.S. Census Bureau stands behind its projections, using scientific data to formulate its predictions and other statistics.

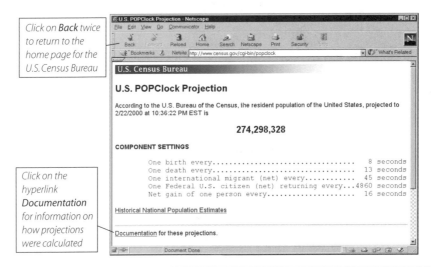

*Click on **Back** twice to return to the home page for the U.S. Census Bureau*

Click on the hyperlink Documentation for information on how projections were calculated

Figure 1.5   The Current Projected Population of the United States

Now let's explore some other areas of the Census Bureau. We want to return to the Census Bureau's home page, pictured in Figure 1.3. You'll need to go back two Web pages. You can do that by clicking on **Back**, in the navigation toolbar, twice.

tip USING BACK AND FORWARD FOR NAVIGATION

Clicking once on **Back** or **Forward** in the navigation toolbar takes you to a Web page you previously visited. If you clicked a hyperlink on a Web page or typed in a URL to get to the present page, then clicking on **Back** will return you to the page you were just at. You can retrace your steps by continuing to click on **Back**. Once you've gone back, you can return to where you were by clicking on **Forward**.

Click on the **Back** icon twice, until you're at the U.S. Census Bureau's home page, as pictured in Figure 1.3.

You'll notice if you look at Figure 1.3 that there is a hyperlink entitled Search. Let's see what the options for searching the Census Bureau's site are.

Click on **Search**.

The browser retrieves the Web page titled "Search the Census Bureau." The form and hyperlinks on this page let you search by word, place, map, and staff. We're going to try a search by map, so use the vertical scroll bar to get the hyperlink Map Search in the browser's window, as shown in Figure 1.6.

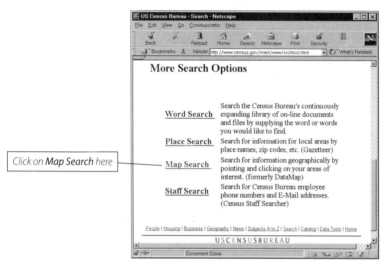

Figure 1.6   Ways to Search the Census Bureau's Site

The hyperlinks we've clicked so far in this activity have been either text links or, in the case of the population clock, icons. Now we'll demonstrate how a hyperlink can be part of a map.

Click on **Map Search**, as shown in Figure 1.6.

A map of the continental United States, Alaska, and Hawaii will appear, as shown in Figure 1.7.

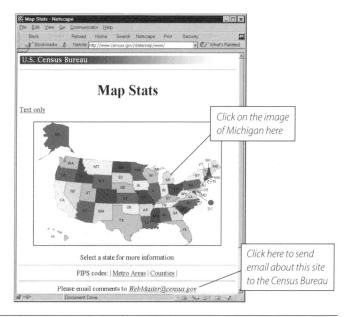

Figure 1.7   An Image Map of the United States

You can click on any state for population information. If you want, you can click on your own state. We'll click on the state of Michigan.

Click on Michigan, as shown in Figure 1.7.

The state of Michigan, with its counties as hyperlinks, is shown in Figure 1.8. Click on any county's shape and you'll retrieve population information about that county. Let's try Washtenaw County.

Click on Washtenaw, as shown in Figure 1.8.

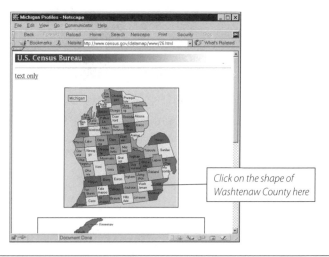

Figure 1.8   Michigan with Its Counties Outlined

The hyperlinks shown in Figure 1.9 all link to census data for Washtenaw County. Let's look at the general population profile for 1996.

 Click on **1996** next to USA Counties General Profile, as shown in Figure 1.9.

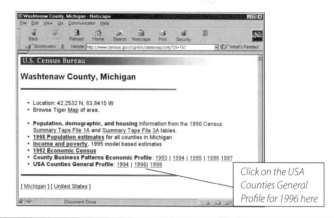

Click on the USA Counties General Profile for 1996 here

Figure 1.9   Washtenaw County Census Information Hyperlinks

A portion of the general population profile for this county is shown in Figure 1.10. Note that the Census Bureau breaks population down into categories such as education level, employment, home owner-ship, and so forth.

*One way to end the browser session is to click on **File** and select **Exit***

Note some of the population categories

*Another way to end the session is to click on **X** in the upper-right corner*

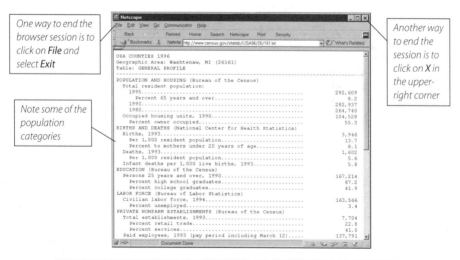

Figure 1.10   Census Profile for Washtenaw County, Michigan

We could spend hours exploring the U.S. Census Bureau's site, but let's stop now so we can talk about some important issues related to the Internet and the World Wide Web.

4. Exit the Web browser.

You can exit the browser in the same way you exit most other windowed applications. Here are two ways that work:

- Click on **File** in the menu bar and select **Exit**.
- Click on the box with an **X** in the upper-right corner of the window.

The window will close, and you will have ended this session with the browser. Make sure your connection is terminated if you are paying by the minute or the hour.

END OF ACTIVITY 1.1

In Activity 1.1 we introduced you to the Web browser and how to get started retrieving information from the World Wide Web by looking at a United States government Web site, the site of the Census Bureau. We'll be covering many more details of using a Web browser later on in the textbook. You may have noticed that some of the Web pages had a hyperlink **text only**; you can use that to bypass the graphic images. When the Internet is busy you'll find you can save time by getting a text-only view. Now that you've had a chance to see how the Web works, let's discuss what impact this information retrieval system is making on individuals and society.

The Significance of the Internet and the World Wide Web

The Internet has made global communication and sharing of information and resources a reality. Since the Web and the Internet are decentralized, there is no way for governments to stop the movement of information or to control the content of what is being published. A panel of federal judges ruling on the Communications Decency Act (6/12/96) stated "As the most participatory form of mass speech yet developed, the Internet deserves the highest protection from governmental intrusion." The development of the Web is significant in that for the first time in history, ordinary people have the ability to publish information and distribute it internationally without having to spend a lot of money. This is possible because the information is distributed in a digital, electronic form rather than in some physical format. Some governments, however, are attempting to control Internet access and the information on the Internet available to the inhabitants of their countries. In addition to being a medium for communication, the Internet is being used in a significant way in research, learning, and commerce.

The Impact on Communication and Learning

The Internet has made electronic mail the most useful and popular of all the services available. Email has made communication between teacher and student, between company president and department manager, and between parent and child informal, cheap, and fast. The interactive element of the Web is highly significant in that people are urged to provide feedback and ask questions. There is an Internet culture that encourages altruism. It is easy for people to share information on the Internet, so they do. For example, the U.S. Census Bureau's site provided hyperlinks for the user to email comments or questions to the Census Bureau staff. This is two-way communication, not like television and other broadcast media, which are one way.

The Internet and the Web are also having a significant impact on the way teaching and learning are being accomplished. Classes and courses are offered through the Internet. By incorporating video, audio, and asynchronous and synchronous communication in these courses, students are guaranteed a rich learning experience without having to spend time in the same real space with others taking the course. Use of the Web for distance education means classes may be taken at a time and place convenient for the student. Use of the Internet for teaching may change the fundamental way higher education and training has been traditionally provided.

The Impact on Science and Research

For scientists and other researchers, the Internet has revolutionized the way information is distributed. Researchers have access to online journal articles and books. A researcher can read an article online the day it is published and send the article to a colleague almost anywhere in the world and receive feedback in minutes, instead of days or weeks. With more publishers making their indexes and other materials available on the Web, whole campuses can have simultaneous access to databases, encyclopedias, dictionaries, and other types of information resources. The United States census is again a good example. Although it is available in book form, thousands of people now have access to it from their computers; no need to travel to a library that has the U.S. census on its shelves. According to the U.S. Census Bureau's Web site, an average of 500,000 people access its pages in one day! Certainly the easy access to this type of information is changing the process of conducting research.

The Impact on Business

The Internet and the World Wide Web are changing the way business is being conducted in the United States and the world. Companies are being transformed in three major ways: increased communication, faster and more personal service, and more effective distribution of products. Most companies have Web sites with information about themselves. Online product catalogs are cheaper and much easier to maintain than paper catalogs. The Web has made it possible for global niche markets to flourish.

The Internet can be good for consumers who can shop around for a better price without leaving their home. Companies can provide personal service by building links with customers. One example of this might be keeping a record of what people have purchased in the past and helping them select what they might like to buy in the future.

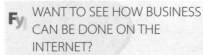

WANT TO SEE HOW BUSINESS CAN BE DONE ON THE INTERNET?

∿ Amazon.com
   http://www.amazon.com
∿ CDNOW
   http://www.cdnow.com
∿ Shopping.com
   http://www.shopping.com/ store

Amazon.com, an online bookstore, has this feature. By keeping track of what you have purchased in the past, Amazon.com selects books that you might be interested in buying now.

The Internet has also transformed the way business is conducted inside companies. The immediacy of email tends to accelerate business decisions. Information becomes quickly available to people. The Internet has also made it easier for people to work at home. Telecommuting has increased dramatically in the past few years, coinciding with the growth of the Internet.

With all this discussion about the impact the Internet is having and will have on our lives, it's important to think about proper use of the Internet. This next section introduces some of the issues related to proper network etiquette.

Issues of Etiquette and Law

The Internet connects networks throughout the world and no one agency controls it. People from many different countries, cultures, and backgrounds use it in an effective way. This diversity, along with the lack of central control, could lead to disorganized anarchy, a lack of concern for the effects of using resources at other computer systems, and an indifference to the feelings, opinions, and concerns of individuals. Any of these effects would be intolerable and would detract from the utility, richness, and vigor of the Internet. It may seem too good to be true, but the users of the Internet generally behave in a way that protects individuals, fosters the sharing of information, and preserves Internet resources. This is because users realize the benefits both to the individual and to the group of maintaining the manner in which the Internet has developed and continues to grow.

Over the years organizations have developed policies, rules, and codes for acceptable behavior. We'll list a few issues here that you'll want to consider as you use the Internet.

Resources and Services

The services and resources on the Internet are generally offered in a spirit of cooperation and sharing. They need to be used in the same manner. In many cases you'll be a guest, accessing resources on a remote computer system. Be a good guest and show respect for the needs and wishes of the host. When you access the Internet you are sharing your local network as well. Transferring large files or Web pages with lots of graphics during peak usage times can put a strain on any network. If you connect to the Internet using a modem, then disconnect when you aren't using the Internet so that you don't block others from accessing it.

> **Fy** GUIDES TO NETIQUETTE
>
> *Netiquette* is the term used to describe rules for proper behavior on the Internet.
>
> ~ "The Net: User Guidelines and Netiquette"
>   http://www.fau.edu/rinaldi/net/index.html
> ~ "Netiquette Home Page"
>   http://www.albion.com/netiquette/index.html
> ~ "RFC 1855: Netiquette Guidelines"
>   http://marketing.tenagra.com/rfc1855.html

Concerns of Individuals

There is strong support for individual rights, feelings, and opinions on the Internet. Its users represent a wide range of opinions and values. Some folks may express opinions that aren't to your liking; some things may be offensive to you. Before making an immediate reply or taking instantaneous action, take some time to consider your response. Treat others with respect and concern.

Copyright

Copyright laws and treaties generally protect material on the Internet. Because something can be copied electronically and is easy to obtain doesn't mean it can be distributed without permission. This applies to text, images, and other types of information. Most information contains a copyright statement indicating that it can be distributed electronically and used for noncommercial purposes.

Commercial Activities

For a relatively long time, in terms of the history of the Internet, commercial activity wasn't allowed. That's not the case now, but the Internet is still not wide open to marketing or commercial announcements. It's technologically possible to send an email announcement of a product or service to thousands of people on the Internet. But that type of activity is usually met with protests, wastes a lot of resources, and generally does more harm than good. Take some time to know the culture and expectations of Internet users before attempting any commercial activities.

The Law

Generally, laws governing espionage, fraud, harassment, libel, pornography, and theft apply to activities carried on electronic networks. Several laws have been passed in the U.S. and other countries that apply specifically to electronic communications. There is a lot of freedom and openness on the Internet, but that doesn't mean the Internet is beyond the rule of law.

Contributing to the Internet

The Internet is a network, and networks are created to share resources. When you have the opportunity to make something available to others on the Internet, do so. This includes helping others with questions, collecting and organizing information, or sharing your resources.

Read on to find out how the Internet got to where it is today; it has been around a lot longer than you may have thought!

How the Internet and the World Wide Web Developed

We've arranged the history of the Internet and the Web according to some of the significant periods of its development.

ARPANET, Department of Defense, 1960s–1970s

In the late 1960s, the United States Department of Defense, through its Advanced Research Projects Agency (ARPA), funded research into the establishment of a decentralized computer network. From the beginning, some of the developers and researchers saw the advantages of a network in which computer systems of differing types could communicate. They also foresaw the development of a community among the users of this network. The network, named ARPANET, linked researchers at universities, research laboratories, and some military labs. The 1970s and the 1980s saw the further development of the ARPANET and the establishment of networks in other countries. There were fewer than 100 computer systems on these networks. The widespread acceptance and implementation of the basic Internet protocols (IP, TCP, and FTP) were crucial to the growth and development of what came to be called the Internet.

Fyi HISTORY OF THE INTERNET AND THE WORLD WIDE WEB
~ "A Brief History of the Internet"
http://www.isoc.org/internet/history/brief.html
~ "Hobbes' Internet Timeline"
http://info.isoc.org/guest/zakon/Internet/History/HIT.html
~ "Net Timeline"
http://www.pbs.org/internet/timeline

NSFNET, 1980s–1990s

In the late 1980s the U.S. National Science Foundation funded the development of a network to connect supercomputer centers in the United States. Many colleges and universities were encouraged to connect to this network, which was named NSFNET. The number of sites increased rapidly; there were over 10,000 sites in 1987 and over 100,000 in 1989. Similar activity, although not on such a large scale, was taking place in other countries as well.

Usenet and Community Networks, 1970s–1990s

Usenet, the Users' Network, originated in 1979 and allowed people to share information in the form of articles arranged into newsgroups. Usenet was developed completely separately from the Internet, but programs and protocols for distributing articles on the Internet became readily available.

A number of commercial networks, some using technologies that weren't adapted to Internet protocols, were started in the 1970s and 1980s. Public access to the Internet has always been an issue during its development. The Cleveland Free-Net, a community-based network, was also developed in the late 1980s to give Internet access to anyone with a computer and a modem.

Commercial Networks and the Internet, 1980s–Today

The development and operation of ARPANET, NSFNET, and several other networks throughout the world were subsidized by government funds. These networks established acceptable use policies, which gave rules for their use and stated what types of activities were allowed on these publicly supported networks. The policies prohibited any purely commercial activities and set the tone for a developing code of network ethics or etiquette. Commercial networks were also being developed, although they could not, under the acceptable use policies, use the transmission links of the public networks. So for some time commercial activity on the major portion of the Internet in the United States was prohibited. In 1988, several commercial networks reached an agreement with NSFNET to allow their email to be carried on NSFNET.

In 1990 ARPANET ceased to exist as an administrative entity, and the public network in the United States was turned over to NSFNET. The Internet was growing at a remarkable rate and was clearly becoming too big for the public institutions to manage or support. It also became clear that the Internet would become an important part of the world's information infrastructure supporting research, education, and commercial activity. In the early 1990s, commercial networks with their own Internet exchanges or gateways were allowed to conduct business on the Internet. In 1993 the NSF created the InterNIC to provide services, such as registration of domain names and directory and database services, and information about Internet services to the Internet community. These services were contracted to the private sector.

Late in 1999 several organizations or companies were given permission to register domain names. Since a site can't be accessed from anywhere on the Internet unless its domain name is properly registered, this marked a change in policy and perhaps direction for the Internet as it moves into a phase where it's viewed as other utilities or services available to the public. The Internet Corporation for Assigned Names and Numbers (ICANN), a nonprofit corporation, was formed to take over responsibility for domain name management, assigning IP addresses and protocol numbers and performing other services formerly contracted by the U.S. government to other organizations.

The 1990s also saw the development of other protocols and software designed to make it easier to access and use the Internet. These include Archie for finding files available through FTP, Hytelnet for contacting sites available through Telnet, WAIS (Wide Area Information Servers) for searching and retrieving items from databases on the Internet, Gopher for accessing information and services on the Internet through a menu-oriented system, and, most notably, the World Wide Web.

The World Wide Web, 1990s–Today

The concept of the WWW is credited to Tim Berners-Lee. The Web was started to provide a single means of access to the wealth of services and resources on the Internet. What made the Web and the Internet itself extremely popular was the ability to access the WWW by using a program called a Web browser. The first popular browser was Mosaic (1993) and it had a significant impact on the growth of the Web and the Internet. Mosaic was the first graphical, easy-to-use interface to the Web.

Traffic on the Internet directly related to the WWW increased at a rate of several hundred thousand percent, and this was accompanied by extraordinary growth in the number of commercial sites connecting to the Internet and the number of Internet service providers. Marc Andreessen, Eric Bina, and others developed Mosaic at the National Center for Supercomputing Applications (NCSA) at the University of Illinois, Urbana-Champaign. Andreessen and others left NCSA to form a company called Netscape Communications Corporation, which continues to develop and market Netscape Navigator and Netscape Communicator. Microsoft Corporation, likely sensing a huge market developing, eventually developed and distributed another popular Web browser, called Microsoft Internet Explorer.

The explosive growth on the Internet and the inclusion of commercial networks and services have been accompanied by an astounding increase in the population of Internet users, including users who are not part of an academic or research community. The Internet is reaching the size and importance of an infrastructure, a necessary underpinning of society. In approximately 30 years the Internet has grown rapidly from a research project into something that involves millions of people worldwide.

Summary

The Internet is, by definition, a collection of networks throughout the world that agree to communicate using specific telecommunications protocols. But this definition doesn't describe what makes the Internet so exciting. The Internet can also be viewed in terms of the people who use it and the ways they communicate with each other to share information and ideas. It is also a place for people to do research, conduct business, and find information that may enrich their daily lives. The major difference between the Internet and other media, such as television, is that it is interactive and provides immediate feedback. We define the World Wide Web to be the collection of information available through the Internet.

While many people primarily use the Internet for communicating, either one-on-one or in groups, the World Wide Web is gaining popularity around the world. Since the advent of graphical browsers like Netscape Navigator and Microsoft Internet Explorer, the hypertext environment on the Web has made it easy for people to access information by simply clicking on a hyperlink. These hyperlinks can connect the user to text files, programs, charts, graphical images, and digitized video and audio files. The possibilities seem endless, and the path you take is your own choice. A Uniform Resource Locator, or URL, represents each hyperlink. Web browsers use these URLs to specify the type of Internet service or protocol needed and the location of the item. For example, the URL for the Web page "POPClocks" (at the U.S. Census Bureau's Web site) is **http://www.census.gov/main/www/popclock.html**. The protocol or service in this case is HTTP, or Hypertext Transfer Protocol, and a Web browser using that URL would contact the Internet site **www.census.gov** and access the file **popclock.html** in the directory named **www**.

There are services and tools on the Internet that help you access information, communicate, search for information, and make information available on the World Wide Web. There are services for asynchronous group communication, such as email discussion groups and Usenet newsgroups, as well as services for one-on-one communication. There is also the opportunity to be involved with synchronous communication through chat groups.

The amount of information on the World Wide Web is growing at such a rate that it is a challenge to know how to find what you need. To help you find resources, a number of search services and tools have been developed. There are two major types of search tools: search engines and directories.

The Internet developed through projects sponsored by governments in the United States and elsewhere to allow researchers to communicate with each other and share results. The initial work began in the late 1960s. There was a tremendous growth both in the number of networks communicating according to the Internet protocols and the number of users accessing the Internet during the 1980s and '90s. There is no central controlling authority that governs the activities on the Internet. However, a number of local laws, acceptable use policies, codes of ethics, and information literacy guidelines are being adopted so that users can use the Internet in a productive and creative way.

Selected Terms Discussed in This Chapter

asynchronous

conferencing

directory

electronic mail (email)

email discussion group

File Transfer Protocol (FTP)

hyperlink

hypermedia

Hypertext Markup Language
   (HTML)

Hypertext Transfer Protocol
   (HTTP)

interest group

Internet

Internet domain name

Internet Relay Chat (IRC)

listserv

mailing list

MOO

MUD

newsreader

protocol

search engine

synchronous

Telnet

Uniform Resource Locator (URL)

Usenet   World Wide Web
Web browser

Exercises and Projects

The following questions concern your connection to the Internet:

1. Do you have to type in a user name when you want to connect to the Internet? What is it? What is your email address?

2. Write down the steps you have to follow to start the Web browser on your computer.

3. What's the name of the Web browser that you use?

4. What Web page is displayed when you start the browser? What is its URL?

5. Start your browser, click on **Help** in the menu bar, and select the item that tells you about your browser. (If you're using, for example, Netscape Communicator, the item to select is **About Communicator**.) What is displayed? Which version of the browser are you using?

6. Is there a person, office, or agency you can contact when you have problems or questions about using your computer or the Internet when you're at school or at work? If so, give the name, email address, URL of the Web page, or phone number of the place you may contact when you have a problem or a question. If there is no help desk or contact group for your organization, assume you're a student at Mary Washington College and start looking for this information at the Web page with the URL **http://inte.mwc.edu**.

7. Most organizations and Internet service providers (ISPs) have a set of policies about proper use and behavior on the Internet and the network you use to access the Internet. Get a copy of the policies for your organization or school; many times it's available as a hyperlink from your organization or school's site.
   a. What is the URL of the policy? If it's not available on the Web then give the steps necessary to obtain a copy.
   b. Most policies give a list of acceptable uses or user responsibilities. List the three that are in your opinion most important.
   c. What sorts of activities are prohibited?
   d. How does the policy address the issue of protecting your privacy and keeping private information about you?

Now let's do a little exploring:

8. Use the same techniques as in Activity 1.1 to find:
   a. the current U.S. and world population.

b. the percentage of the general population that are high school graduates and the percentage that are college graduates for the county where you currently live or where you call home.

9. Going back to the Web site for the U.S. Census Bureau, as in Activity 1.1,
   a. give a synopsis of the documentation or technical description of the U.S. Population Clocks projections.
   b. use the National Historical Population Estimates to find the average rate of increase in the U.S. population for the past five years. How does that compare with the average rate of increase for the years 1976–1980 and 1986–1990?

10. Imagine you are planning a trip to a foreign country or a different state. Start planning your trip by accessing a travel site. Using your browser, type this URL in the location field: **http://city.net/regions**. If no map is displayed on that Web page, click on the hyperlink **Maps**. You'll see a map of the world. Each area is a hyperlink that will take you to a more detailed map. Pick a place and browse until you find some hyperlinks about the place you are going to visit. Write down where you have traveled. When you get to your final destination, write down the URLs and the titles of two Web pages that contain relevant information.

11. Lots of colleges and universities make information available on the Web. They include information about their academic programs, activities, costs, and more.
    a. Go to the home page for Mary Washington College, **http://www.mwc.edu**. Click on the hyperlink labeled **Admissions**, and then click on **Visit MWC!**. That takes you to a Web page with directions to the college. Click on **Print** in the navigation toolbar to print a copy.
    b. Now go to the home page for a college or university that's located near to where you live. If directions to the school are available on the Web, print them out. Write down the steps you took to find the directions.

12. Let's take a look at some multimedia applications on the Web. Type the URL **http://dailynews.yahoo.com/** in the location field of your browser. You will go to the news section of Yahoo!. What's featured at that site? List some photographic, audio, and video information available. Give the URL and title of each. View and/or listen to each, and then write a brief description of each or explain any problems you had accessing any of the items or dealing with the media.

Chapter 2

HOW THE INTERNET

WORKS AND GETTING

CONNECTED

How does the Internet work? What are the basic terms and technical concepts? What happens when an email message, a file, a Web page, or any information is transported from one computer to another on the Internet? What does it mean to be connected to the Internet? What different types of Internet connections are available? We will give answers to these and related questions in this chapter. Starting with an introduction to some of the technical concepts of the Internet, we then go over some fundamental concepts related to using the Internet and the way information is accessed on the Web. With that as a background we'll go over what you need to know to get connected to the Internet and to get ready for email and Usenet.

You may also be wondering whether you need to know all this technical information. There are lots of technical and complicated things we use in daily life without knowing the details of how they work, such as a television, an automobile, or a microwave oven. The difference is that these other items can be thought of as appliances, relatively easy-to-use equipment designed for a specific task. The Internet is different from that; it is a growing, evolving entity. There are many different technologies available. New opportunities and ways to use the Internet come along almost daily. Knowing some of the technical concepts and details makes it easier for you to use and grow with the Internet.

Goals/Objectives

- Gain a general understanding of the technical aspects of the Internet
- Learn the primary terms and concepts associated with using the Internet and the Web
- Learn the key concepts related to getting connected to the Internet
- Learn about your options for getting connected to the Internet
- Know how to set preferences and options to enable email and Usenet

Topics

∾ How the Internet Works: A Quick Introduction

∾ Basic Terms and Concepts

∾ Getting Connected to the Internet

∾ Getting Set for Email and Usenet News

How the Internet Works: A Quick Introduction

When you are connected to the Internet you're able to communicate with others on the Internet through email, Usenet news, and chat; you're able to access Web sites using your browser to browse or search for information. Having the ability to do these things means there's a lot of technology supporting you. This includes hardware: networks, computers, modems, and other devices that make the connection possible. It also includes software such as communication, client, server, and other programs.

Protocols

The Internet is designed so computer systems within one network can exchange information with computers on other networks. The rules that govern this form of communication are called *protocols*. By using the same protocols, different types of networks and computer systems can communicate with each other. Each network and computer needs to have the software and hardware in place to deal with information in the form specified by the protocols.

∾ Two basic protocols used are *Internet Protocol (IP)* and *Transmission Control Protocol (TCP)*. You often see them referred to together as TCP/IP.

IP Addresses and Domain Names

The Internet is a collection of thousands of computer networks, each with its own address. Each network must have its own address so information can be reliably routed from one to another.

∾ Each network on the Internet has a unique address, called an *IP address*, and each of the computer systems making up a network has an IP address, which is sometimes based on the network's IP address.

At a basic level the addresses are numeric, 209.196.179.233, for example. You don't need to memorize the numbers; the addresses can also be specified as names, such as **www.webliminal.com**. This is called an

Internet domain name. Domain names are included in URLs and email addresses. In the URL **http://www.webliminal.com/ internet-today/it-gloss.html** the domain name is **www. webliminal.com**. In the email address **jimleisy@fbeedle.com** the domain name is **fbeedle.com**.

The translation of domain names to IP addresses is handled automatically by the *domain name system*.

A domain name can tell you something about the site you're contacting. Some domain names are geographical and the last two letters are an abbreviation for the country where the net-work is located. For example, the

Fy GETTING MORE INFORMATION ABOUT HOW THE INTERNET WORKS
~ "Chapter 1: What is the Internet?"
http://members.unlimited.net/ ~kumbach/internet/ whatsnet.html
~ "Connected: An Internet Ency-clopedia"
http://www.FreeSoft.org/CIE/ index.htm
~ "20 questions: how the Net works"
http://www.cnet.com/Content/ Features/Techno/Networks
~ "Zen and the Art of the Internet"
http://www.cs.indiana.edu/ docproject/zen/ zen-1.0_toc.html

domain name **www.ee.ic.ac.uk** indicates a network in the United King-dom. Some domain names end in three letters that indicate the type of network. Table 2.1 lists the major types.

Domain Name Ending	Type of Network	Example
edu	Educational, usually a school, college, or university	**www.mwc.edu**
gov	A U.S. government agency	**www.census.gov**
com	Commercial	**www.microsoft.com**
net	A network	**www.earthlink.net**
org	An organization, a nonprofit institution	**www.sierraclub.org**

Table 2.1   Domain Name Clues

A Packet-Switched Network

Using Internet Protocol, a message consisting of at most 1,500 bytes or characters is put into a packet. Each packet has the address of the sender and the address of the destination. You can think of a packet in the same way you think of a letter sent by a postal service.

∿ Packets of characters, like envelopes holding messages, are used to carry information on the Internet.

Using TCP, a single message is divided into a sequence of IP packets. The packets are passed from one network to another until they reach their destination. At the destination the TCP software reassembles the packets into a complete message. If packets are lost or damaged a request is transmitted to resend them. It isn't necessary for all the packets in a single message to take the same route through the Internet or for the same message to take the same route each time it's sent. This notion of a message naturally applies to email, but it's extended to apply to many of the other services on the Internet.

∿ The Internet is a *packet-switched network*.

Emphasis is on transmitting and receiving packets, rather than on connecting computer systems to each other. The packets that make up a single message or file can be sent by different routes from one computer to another. Passing information and implementing the Internet services with packets keeps one system from tying up the networks with a connection dedicated to a single program.

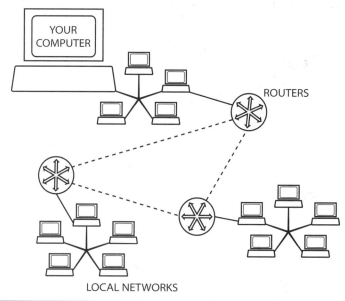

Figure 2.1   A Diagram of the Internet

The networks on the Internet use hardware, devices called ***routers***, to communicate with other networks. The router on a network accepts packets addressed to it and passes on packets addressed to other networks.

∾ Each computer system with a direct connection to the Internet has to have the hardware and software to allow it to work with packets. It's up to the individual computer systems to take care of sending and receiving packets.

The bulk of Internet traffic is carried on high-capacity communication lines that link communication centers throughout the world. These lines are sometimes called the Internet backbone. The lines are leased from major communication companies. Information on the Internet travels from individual users to a local network, and from there (if necessary) to a larger network that provides a connection to another network until the information makes it to the backbone. Then it's carried on these high-capacity lines until it is passed off to a network that passes it to a smaller network, and so on, until it gets to its destination.

Your Internet Connection

Your Internet connection makes your computer part of a network, and that network has a connection to the Internet. Your computer has to have software and hardware installed that makes it possible for information to be transmitted in packets according to Internet protocols. There are lots of variations on your specific type of Internet connection, but it is likely one of two types:

∾ Your computer is directly connected to a network. It has a network card and a cable connecting you to a network. In this case, we say you've got a direct IP connection to the Internet.

∾ You use a ***modem*** to call and connect to a network. Your computer and the network you reach through the phone lines communicate with each other by using software called ***PPP (Point-to-Point Protocol)***. This is called a dial-up IP connection to the Internet.

Now that we know some of the basic technical concepts about how the Internet works, let's look into some of the basic concepts related to using the Internet and the way information is accessed on the Web.

Basic Terms and Concepts

In this section we'll discuss some of the terms and concepts that are important to know about as you're working with the Internet and the Web. We will focus on these topics:

∾ Digital Format

∾ Client/Server

- Hypertext Transfer Protocol (HTTP)
- Hypertext Markup Language (HTML)
- HTML Source for a Web Page
- Information About a Web Page
- Uniform Resource Locator (URL)
- Error Messages

Digital Format

All the information on the Internet is sent, transmitted across networks, and received in a digital format. This has some significant consequences:

- Information is transmitted as electrons and then converted to other forms, such as Web pages or printed pages, at its destination. The person receiving the information has a choice of how to view, save, or manipulate it.

- It is possible to create true multimedia environments and experiences since the different media can be represented in a digital format and a single device (a computer) can present them simultaneously. These environments can be shared concurrently at several locations.

- Questions of distance virtually disappear because electrons travel at rates approaching the speed of light. A more relevant issue is the amount of information, measured in bytes, that can be transported through a network in a given period of time.

- It's possible, and generally relatively easy, to make an exact copy of any file that's accessible through the Internet.

Client/Server

When you start a WWW browser or follow a hyperlink, the browser sends a request to a computer on the Internet. That computer returns a file that the browser then displays. This sort of interaction in which one system requests information and another provides it is called a **client/server** relationship. The browser is the client, and it communicates with another program called a server, which provides the information. It's also common to use the term *client* to refer to the computer that's running the browser, and to call the computer that is supplying the information the *server.*

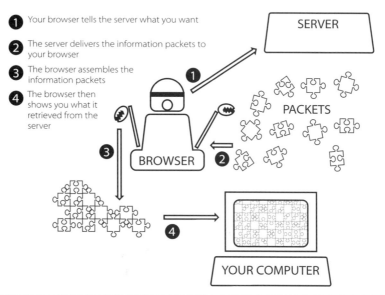

1. Your browser tells the server what you want
2. The server delivers the information packets to your browser
3. The browser assembles the information packets
4. The browser then shows you what it retrieved from the server

| Figure 2.2 | Client/Server: The Browser Is the Client and Receives Packets from the Server |

Hypertext Transfer Protocol (HTTP)

The documents or screens are passed from a server to a client according to specific rules for exchanging information. These rules are called protocols. The protocol used on the WWW is named **HTTP**, which stands for **Hypertext Transfer Protocol**, because the documents, pages, or other items passed from one computer to another are in hypertext or hypermedia form.

Hypertext Markup Language (HTML)

The rules for creating or writing a Web page are all specified as **HTML (Hypertext Markup Language)**. This language provides the formal rules for marking text. The rules govern how text is displayed as part of a Web page. HTML would be used, for example, to mark text so that it appeared in boldface or italics. In order for text or an icon to represent a hyperlink, it has to be marked as a link in HTML, and the URL has to be included. Web pages are usually stored in files with names that end with **.html** or **.htm**.

If the file is written using HTML, the browser interprets the file so that graphics and images are displayed along with the text. Depending on the HTML code in the file, the text is displayed in different sizes and styles and hyperlinks are represented on the page.

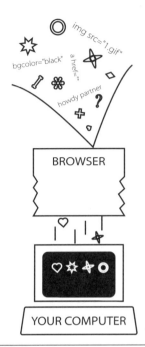

Figure 2.3   The Browser Interprets HTML to Display a Web Page

Here are a few lines to demonstrate what HTML looks like in a Web document.

```
This is a <B>very short</B> example of HTML.
For more examples take a look at the Web page
<A HREF="http://www1.mwc.edu/~ernie/writeweb/writeweb.html">
Writing Your Own Web Pages.</A>
```

A Web browser would display the HTML above as

This is a **very short** example of HTML. For more examples take a look at the Web page **<u>Writing Your Own Web Pages.</u>**

The tags used here are
~   < B > and < /B >
      The text between them is displayed as bold.
~   < A HREF = "http://www1.mwc.edu/ ~ ernie/writeweb/ writeweb.html" > and < /A >
      The text between them is a hyperlink.

HTML Source Information for a Web Page

Having access to the HTML source for a Web page is very useful when you're learning to write Web pages or when you are curious about how something was done on a Web page.

To view the HTML source of a Web page:

1. Place the mouse pointer anywhere in the window that holds the Web page.
2. Click the right, or secondary, mouse button.
3. Select **View Source** from the pop-up menu.

A Web page or document we see displayed by our browser is present on our computer, and the browser has interpreted the source to present the display we see.

Information About a Web Page

Netscape Navigator allows you to view information about a Web page. The information is sometimes useful when you are trying to find when a Web page was last modified. It's also useful to help understand the structure of a Web page.

If you're using Netscape Navigator, to view information about a Web page:

1. Place the mouse pointer anywhere in the window that holds the Web page.
2. Click the right, or secondary, mouse button.
3. Select **View Info** from the pop-up menu.

Uniform Resource Locator (URL)

A *hyperlink* is represented in a specific format called a ***URL***, or ***Uniform Resource Locator***. In Activity 1.1 we pointed out that the URL is displayed just above the content area in a Web browser's window. Each Web page has a URL as its address. For example, the URL for the Library of Congress's Web page "Abraham Lincoln: Internet Resources from the Library of Congress" is **http://lcweb2.loc.gov/ammem/alhtml/alrel.html**.

URLs that point to Web pages all start with **http://** because they are all transmitted according to HTTP. You'll see something different for URLs that access information through other Internet services or protocols. For example, information available by FTP, File Transfer Protocol, uses **ftp://** in its URL. The URL for the NASA collection of space images is **ftp://ftp.jpl.nasa.gov/pub/images**.

You'll find it helpful to think of a URL as having the form:

```
how-to-get-there://where-to-go/what-to-get
```

We will now show you the different parts of a URL so that you have a better idea about the information a URL conveys:

Protocol: Internet protocol to use (*http* is Hypertext Transfer Protocol)	*Internet Domain Name:* Name of the Web server	*File or Directory Name:* Full path name, including directories and file name, of the file holding the information

```
http://www1.mwc.edu/~ernie/glossary/list.htm
```

Most URLs have this format. By indicating which Internet protocol to use, they tell you how to retrieve the information. By naming both the Web server and the file or directory holding the information, they tell you where the page is located. If only a server name is present and not a file name, as in **http://www.loc.gov**, you still retrieve a file; by default, the server passes along a certain file, usually named **index.html**. Sometimes you'll see URLs written without **http://** in front. You can safely omit **http://** when you open a Web page or location by typing the URL into the browser's location field.

Error Messages

As amazing as some computer systems are, they generally need very precise instructions. You have to be careful about spacing (generally there aren't blank spaces in a URL), the symbols used (a slash and a period are not interchangeable), and the case of the letters.

For example, the URL for the frequently asked questions (FAQ) for finding email addresses is **http://www.qucis.queensu.ca/FAQs/email/finding.html**. Replacing email with EMAIL, as in the URL **http://www.qucis.queensu.ca/FAQs/EMAIL/finding.html**, would cause the server to report an error back to the browser. The following would be displayed:

```
404
The requested URL was not found on this server.
```

The error message tells us that part of the URL was correct—the name of the Web server, **www.qucis.queensu.ca**—but that the Web server could not find the file on the server because there was something wrong with the rest of the URL.

A message such as this is called a ***404 error***. You may see this error message if the URL is incorrect. Sometimes you'll also get this error message if a Web page has been removed from a Web server or is no longer available.

There are several other types of error codes you may see as you use the Web. Take a look at "Internet Errors Explained," **http://www.cnet.com/Resources/Tech/Advisers/Error**, for a complete list.

We've discussed quite a few concepts and terms. We'll go through an activity here that

In this activity we'll use Internet Explorer to look at a file that's on the disk included with this book. You can go through the steps in the same manner if you use Netscape Navigator. These activities are meant to demonstrate fundamental skills and concepts.

reviews how to view the HTML source of a Web page. Viewing the HTML source is useful to see how a page is written. It's also useful to look at the source when you're writing your own pages and you want to check the HTML.

VIEWING THE HTML SOURCE
FOR A WEB PAGE

Overview

We're assuming that you've started your browser on your computer and are connected to the Internet.

We're going to take two different views of a Web page:

~ its appearance in the browser window.
~ the HTML source for the Web page.

You can follow the same steps for any Web page. Looking at the source is useful when you want to learn about using HTML to create your own pages.

In this activity we're going to view a Web page that is on the disk that comes with this book. To view the Web page we'll select the item **Open** after clicking on **File** in the menu bar of the browser. You can use Open to view any Web page that's available as a file on your computer or to view a Web page anywhere on the Internet.

These are the steps:

1. Start the Web browser.
2. Insert the disk that comes with the textbook in Drive A: of your computer.
3. Click on **File** in the menu bar of Internet Explorer and then select **Open**.
4. Use Browse to select the file to view.
5. View the Web page with the source file Activity2-1.htm.
6. View the HTML source for the Web page.
7. Follow a hyperlink to another site on the Internet and note technical details.

Details

1. Start the Web browser.

We're going to use Internet Explorer for this activity. If you prefer to use Netscape Navigator, feel free to do so. You'll see that many of the steps we follow are the same.

 Double-click on the icon for the browser, ![Internet Explorer] .

As in Activity 1.1, the browser starts displaying the Web page that's set as the browser's home page.

2. **Insert the disk that comes with the textbook in Drive A: of your computer.**

   (Do it!) Put the disk into Drive A: of your computer.

3. **Click on File in the menu bar of Internet Explorer and then select Open.**

   (Do it!) Click on **File** in the menu bar of Internet Explorer.

   (Do it!) Click on **Open** in the pop-up menu that appears.

   Figure 2.4 shows what you'll see as you click on **File** and select **Open**.

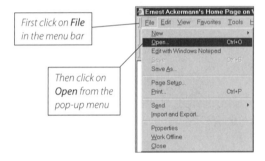

*First click on **File** in the menu bar*

*Then click on **Open** from the pop-up menu*

Figure 2.4   Selecting Open from the File Menu in the Menu Bar

4. **Use Browse to select the file to view.**

   Clicking on **Open** opens a dialog box. Here is where you can type a URL or open a file on your computer. Figure 2.5 shows the dialog box.

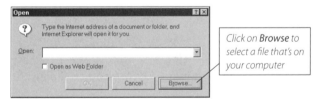

*Click on **Browse** to select a file that's on your computer*

Figure 2.5   The Dialog Box to Open a Web Page with the Browser

   (Do it!) Click on **Browse** in the dialog box.

When you click on **Browse** another window pops up that you can use to access the files on your computer. You'll probably have to go through three of these windows. They all have the same format and look like the one shown in Figure 2.6. In that one you select the

Web page for this activity. As you follow these steps, each window is replaced with another.

(Do it)!   Click on **My Computer.**

(Do it)!   Click on **3 ½ Floppy (A:).**

(Do it)!   Double-click on **Chap2.**

(Do it)!   Double-click on **Activity2-1.htm.**

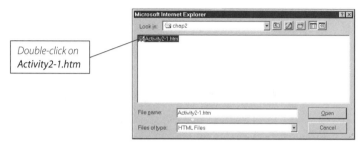

Double-click on
Activity2-1.htm

Figure 2.6   Selecting Activity2-1.htm from the A: Drive

After you select the file, the browser takes you back to the previous dialog box. Figure 2.7 shows what you'll see.

There's just one more step!

*Click on OK to view
the Web page*

Figure 2.7   The Open Dialog Box with the File Activity2-1.htm Selected

(Do it)!   Click on **OK.**

5. View the Web page with the source file Activity2-1.htm.

When you click on **OK** the Web page is displayed in the browser. What you see ought to be similar to what's shown in Figure 2.8. We've labeled some portions of the page that we'll take a closer look at when we view the HTML source.

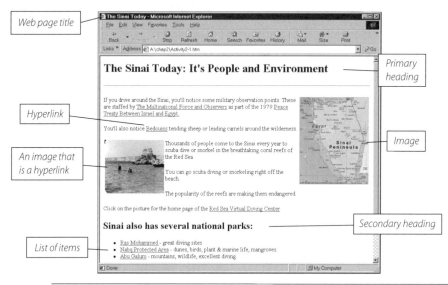

Figure 2.8   The Browser View of the Web Page
with the Source File Activity2-1.htm

6. View the HTML source for the Web page.

Figure 2.8 shows what's produced by the Web browser when it interprets the source in the file Activity2-1.htm. Looking at the source will help us understand some basic HTML tags.

(Do it!)   Click on **View** in the menu bar and select **Source**.

Figure 2.9 shows a portion of the page source. We've pointed out the HTML for the items we've noted in Figure 2.8.

Another way to display the HTML source for a Web page is to put the mouse pointer on the Web page, click the right mouse button, and select **View Source** from the pop-up menu.

```
<html>
<head>
<title>The Sinai Today</title>
</head>
<body bgcolor="#FFFFFF">
<h1>The Sinai Today: Its People and Environment</h1>
<hr>
<p> <img src="sinaip.gif" width="200"
height="246" align="right"> </p>
<p>If you drive around the Sinai, you'll notice some
military observation points.
These are staffed by <a href="http://www.mfo.org/
main.htm">The Multinational Force and Observers</a>
as part of the 1979 <a href="http://www.israel.org/
mfa/go.asp?MFAH00if0">Peace Treaty
Between Israel and Egypt.</a> </p>
```

Web page title

Primary heading

Image

```
<p>You'll also notice <a href="http://
www.interknowledge.com/egypt/sinai/bedouin.htm">
Bedouins</a> tending sheep or leading camels around the
wilderness. </p>
<p>
<a href="http://touregypt.net/vdc/"><img align=LEFT
width=175 height=150 src="scuba.jpg"
border="0" alt="scuba diving in the Red Sea">
</a>
Thousands of people come to the Sinai every year to scuba
dive or snorkel in the breathtaking coral reefs of the
Red Sea. </p>
<p>You can go scuba diving or snorkeling right off the
beach. </p>
<p>The popularity of the reefs are making them endangered.
</p>
<p>Click on the picture for the home page of the
<a href="http://touregypt.net/vdc/">Red Sea Virtual
Diving Center</a></p>
<H2>Sinai also has several national parks:</H2>
<ul>
<li><a href="http://www.interknowledge.com/egypt/sinai/
rasmohammed.htm"> Ras Mohammed </a>- great diving
sites</li>
<li>
<a href="http://www.interknowledge.com/
egypt/sinai/protectedarea.htm">
Nabq Protected Area</a> - dunes, birds, plant &amp; marine
life, mangroves.</li>
<li><a href="http://www.interknowledge.com/egypt/sinai/
abughalum.htm">Abu Galum</a> - mountains, wildlife,
excellent diving. </li>
</ul>
<p>
```

Hyperlink

Image that is a hyperlink

Secondary heading

List of items

Figure 2.9   The HTML Source for the Web Page in Figure 2.8

Here are a few things to note about the HTML we've pointed out in Figure 2.9:

∾ We've written the HTML tags here in lowercase, for the most part, but they may be written in upper- or lowercase.

∾ HTML tags are in brackets, as in < title > and < h1 >.

∾ Most HTML tags are used as a pair surrounding some text as in `<title>The Sinai Today</title>`.

∾ The Web page title—the text that appears in the title bar at the top of the browser window—is in the "head" section marked by < head > and < /head >, and it's the text between the tags < title > and < /title >.

∾ The primary heading of the Web page is marked by an H1 tag as in `<h1>The Sinai Today: Its People and Environment</h1>`.

ᵔ   A secondary heading is denoted by an H2 tag as in `<H2>Sinai also has several national parks:</H2>`.

ᵔ   An image is represented by the img tag as in `<img src="sinaip.gif" width="200" height="246" align="right">`. The tag may include several attributes about the image such as the source (src), which may be a file name or a URL, and the width, height, and alignment of the image.

ᵔ   A hyperlink is represented using an "a href" tag as in `<a href="http://www.interknowledge.com/egypt/sinai/ bedouin.htm"> Bedouins</a>`. A URL is put after href, and the text surrounded by < a href = "*URL*" > and < /a > is a hyperlink.

ᵔ   An image may also be a hyperlink by a combination of the < a href = "*URL*" > and the img tags.
```
<a href="http://touregypt.net/vdc/">
<img align=LEFT width=175 height=150 src="scuba.jpg"
border="0" alt="scuba diving in the Red Sea">
</a>
```

ᵔ   A list of items may be denoted by using the tags < ul > and < /ul > to mark the beginning and end of the list and the tags < li > and < /li > to identify the individual items in the list.
```
<ul>
<li><a href="http://www.interknowledge.com/egypt/
sinai/rasmohammed.htm"> Ras Mohammed </a>- great
diving sites</li>
<li><a href="http://www.interknowledge.com/egypt/
sinai/protectedarea.htm"> Nabq Protected Area</a>
- dunes, birds, plant &amp; marine life,
mangroves.</li>
<li><a href="http://www.interknowledge.com/egypt/
sinai/abughalum.htm">Abu Galum</a> - mountains,
wildlife, excellent diving. </li>
</ul>
```

Close the window that displays the source when you're finished viewing it.

ᐧ   Click on the **X** in the upper-right corner of the window that shows the Web page source.

7. Follow a hyperlink to another site on the Internet and note technical details.

ᐧ   Click on the hyperlink **Bedouins** in the Web page shown in Figure 2.8.

Clicking on the hyperlink causes your Web browser to send a request to a specific Web server for the source of a Web page. When that file is retrieved, the browser displays the Web page.

We know, from the source for the Web page shown in Figure 2.9 and from looking at the address box once the Web page is displayed, that the URL for this hyperlink is **http://www.interknowledge.com/ egypt/sinai/bedouin.htm**. That tells us that the Internet domain name of the Web server is **www.interknowledge.com** and the source for the Web page is in a file named **bedouin.html**.

Now let's consider some of the technical details involved in retrieving and displaying the Web page associated with the hyperlink.

∾ When we click on the hyperlink, the client (your Web browser) attempts to start communicating with the server (the computer at **www.interknowledge.com**) using HTTP. The IP address for **www.interknowledge.com** has to be determined before that can happen. Using the domain name system (DNS), the client first contacts a computer on its network that can be used to resolve IP addresses or determine an IP address that corresponds to a domain name. A query is sent to other computers on the Internet that can provide authoritative information about the IP address associated with a domain name. While this is going on you'll see "Finding site www.interknowledge.com" and "Site found" in the status bar of the browser window. These addresses are saved for short periods of time to speed up retrieval of information in subsequent requests.

∾ Once the IP address is known, the client and the server can communicate using HTTP. Using the portion of the URL that follows the domain name, the client requests a file from the server. The server sends the file to the client. Following the TCP/IP protocols, the file is divided into packets and sent to the client. When the client has received all the packets, communication with the server is terminated.

∾ The browser now begins to interpret the source and display the Web page. In some cases, such as when there is an img tag like < img src = "sinaip.gif" width = "200" height = "246" align = "right" > , the client sends another request to a server for the source for the image.

In many cases all this takes just a few seconds. Pretty neat, huh!?

END OF ACTIVITY 2.1

In Activity 2.1 we went through the steps to view the source for a Web page. We also went over some of the technical details of the process of clicking on a hyperlink and having a Web page displayed. Now that we've gone over fundamental concepts about the Internet and the Web, let's look into getting connected to the Internet.

Getting Connected to the Internet

If you already have Internet access, congratulations! It is still worth your while to read this section to get an understanding of some of the issues involved and some of the alternatives available. If you're reading this because you'll be getting an Internet connection, congratulations! There are lots of good things in store for you.

Here are the major topics we'll cover:

∾ What You Need to Be Connected to the Internet

∾ Selecting an Internet Service Provider

∾ Getting Connected: Two Scenarios

What You Need to Be Connected to the Internet

We will go over the concepts and terms you need to know when you're thinking about getting connected to the Internet. There is more than one way to establish a connection to the Internet, and you'll want to have an affordable connection that meets your needs.

You need a computer or some other digital device that has the software and hardware necessary to implement the TCP/IP and other protocols. Personal computers are the most common device used to access the Internet, but other devices include hand-held digital communication devices, game machines, WebTV, and specially outfitted telephones. There are some differences in the technology used to access the Internet, but the essential concepts are the same. In order to simplify the discussion we'll focus on the details of connecting to the Internet using a personal computer. The necessary software is included on most modern computers or is readily available from the company or organization that provides your network and your access to the Internet.

Your computer needs to include a device—a network card or a modem—that permits a connection to a network that will be providing the Internet services. Either the device comes as part of the computer or you need to obtain a network card or modem to connect to a network. If your school, organization, or company has its own network then you'll probably use a network card. The card—a collection of integrated circuits and chips on plastic—sits inside your computer. It has a cable attached to it that plugs into a wall jack (or similar receptacle) to connect to the network. In this case you're likely to have relatively high-speed access to the Internet.

If you don't have such immediate access to a network; for example, if you want to connect to the Internet from your home, you'll use a device called a modem to connect with a network. (The term *modem* comes from a combination of *mo*dulate and *dem*odulate.) A modem is necessary because the computers on the network only deal with information in digital format and that information needs to be transmitted through an analog, not digital, medium such as an ordinary phone line.

In a typical setup the modem, with dial-up networking software, dials a phone number and the call is answered by another modem which is also connected to a computer. The sending computer has its information modulated from digital to analog format, and the receiving modem demodulates the information so it can be used by the computer it's connected to. Variations on this setup include using a high-speed connection on your existing phone line called a DSL (digital subscriber line) or on a digital communications line called an ISDN (Integrated Services Digital Network) that can be shared by voice telephones, computers, and fax machines; and using a cable modem or WebTV, which connect to the Internet using cable TV lines. Other technologies are being tested and will likely be generally available in the near future.

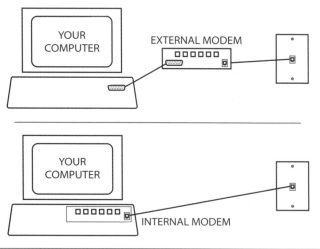

Figure 2.10   A Typical Modem Setup

The speed at which information is exchanged with the Internet depends on the type of connection you have to the Internet and also on

other factors such as the total amount of information being transmitted over a local network or the Internet backbone.

The speed at which information is transmitted across the Internet is measured in bits per second (bps). Bits symbolize the fundamental 1s and 0s that all computers use to represent information. If you have a network card in your computer then you likely have a fast connection to the Internet, possibly in the range of 1.5 to 44 Mbps (M represents million or mega). An ISDN connection typically gives a maximum throughput of 128K (128,000) bps. A DSL connection typically allows for transfer rates between 512 Kbps and 128 Kbps. Modems used with ordinary telephone lines are rated at 56 Kbps, 33.4 Kbps, or 28.8 Kbps. Higher speed access usually costs more. Typical charges (when this book was written) put the cost of access at several hundred dollars per month for Mbps speed, about $50 to $80 per month for DSL or ISDN access, and about $20 per month for access with a modem at 56 Kbps or slower.

The speed of your connection isn't the only consideration. There are limits to the amount of information that can be carried by a network at any instant, and a popular network has the potential for being saturated. Some current uses of the Internet, such as sound or video, require sending and retrieving large quantities of data. Another factor that affects access time is the speed of the connection at the site that's providing the information. Having a 44 Mbps connection doesn't help very much if the information is being provided by a computer with a 28.8 Kbps connection to the Internet.

You have to connect to a network that itself has a connection to the Internet. That network assigns an IP address or domain name to the computer. You may have to select an Internet service provider (ISP).

It seems that the Internet is ubiquitous. It's everywhere, but you still need to become part of a network that has established access to the Internet. Each computer on the network has to have an IP address in order to send and receive packets of information. In some networks the IP address is assigned whenever you log on to or connect to the network. In others your computer is assigned a permanent IP address.

tip

WHEN YOU'RE READY TO GET CONNECTED:

~ Get as much information beforehand as to what type of hardware and software you'll need.

~ Read over the Help information available on your computer. Click on **Help** in the Start menu; select the topic or type in the keyword **Internet**.

~ Be sure to know whom to call for assistance.

~ Invite a friend over who has gone through this before.

The organization that provides the network that you'll connect to for Internet access is called an ***Internet service provider (ISP)***. Sometimes it's up to you to make the choice of an ISP, but not always. The authors of this book work for the same employer and don't have to decide on an ISP where they work, but each has a different ISP for other off-campus activities (such as writing this book!). There are a number of considerations that go into selecting an ISP, and we'll go over them in more detail next. Two major factors that folks often consider are the cost of access and the speed of access.

Selecting an Internet Service Provider

If you're setting up Internet access in your home for work or personal use, you'll have to select an Internet service provider (ISP). The ISP is your link to the Internet, so it is an important choice. You'll want to choose one that provides reliable, convenient, and affordable service. Since you'll be accessing the World Wide Web through this ISP you'll want to be sure they provide PPP (Point-to-Point Protocol) access to the Internet, and you'll also want an email address.

As the Internet has become more popular, it has become easier to find an ISP that can provide you with local service—one you can reach by making a local phone call. There are several large ISPs that provide access to the Internet in virtually every city in the U.S. and Canada, and many cities throughout the world.

Access

The ISP is your link to the Internet. Be sure you can connect to the Internet without delays of long periods of busy signals.
Ask questions about local access. Dial the local number to be sure it's local. Call at different times of the day to see if you get busy signals.

- Can I access my account through a local (toll-free) phone number? Is there an 800-number access? What's the cost for 800-number access?

- How many modems are available in my local calling area? How frequently and at what times are all the modems busy?

If you're planing on using the Internet when you travel then you'll want an ISP with local access available nationwide or worldwide.

- What numbers do I call for access if I'm travelling away from home?

Reliability

Do a little checking into the reliability of services provided by the ISP and the satisfaction of current customers.

- What are the names of references I can contact about your service?

〜 Have you been evaluated and rated by an impartial party? Has your service been compared to others?

〜 What percentage of the time is the network available and functioning properly? What percentage of the time is email available? Usenet?

〜 How do you notify users about times the network or some features won't be available?

Service

Somewhere along the line you'll need some assistance from the ISP or need to report a problem.

Fy SELECTING AN ISP AND GETTING CONNECTED

〜 "Dawn McGatney's Overview Guide to Finding an ISP" http://dogwolf.seagull.net/first.html

〜 "Finding an Internet Service Provider" http://hotwired.lycos.com/webmonkey/guides/web/isp.html

〜 "ISP Finder" http://www.ispfinder.com

〜 "Learn the Net: Getting Connected" http://www.learnthenet.com/english/html/04connec.htm

You'll want to know about getting help by phone and through email and a place on the Internet where you can check to see if others are experiencing problems.

〜 How do I get help when I need it? Is there a toll-free phone number I can call? Do you handle questions or help requests submitted by email? What are the times that I can call and speak to a person about a problem?

〜 What help and software do you provide during the setup process?

〜 Is there online help available? Are problems or notices listed online? Is there a FAQ for this ISP?

Not all problems are technical.

〜 Can I view my account status online? How do we resolve billing problems?

Speed

A faster connection is usually better, provided the cost doesn't become prohibitive. If you're using the access mainly for email or text-based communication then a 28.8 connection is sufficient; otherwise you'll want faster access.

You'll want to know about the options you have for connecting to the ISP's network and its connection to the Internet.

〜 What modem speeds do you support? 28.8, 33.6, 56K? What type of 56K modems do you support? Do you support other types of access?

∾ Describe your (the ISP's) connection to the Internet. Do you have a full T1 (1.5 Mbps) or T3 (44.3 Mbps) connection? (You don't want to deal with an ISP unless they have at least a full T1 connection to the Internet.)

Fees

Some services offer a discount if fees are paid yearly instead of monthly. Some ISPs offer different pricing depending on the amount of time connected.

Be sure you understand the fee structure and don't underestimate how much you'll use the service. Charges for extra time are often at a rate of $1.50 to $2.00 per hour.

∾ Is there a setup fee?

∾ What different pricing plans do you offer? Is there a plan that offers unlimited (no time limit) access? If I choose a plan with limited hours what are the charges for exceeding the limit?

∾ Is there a charge for setting up and maintaining a home page?

Features

Some ISPs offer only basic service—a reliable connection to the Internet. Others also offer Web page space and other services. Be sure the ISP offers Internet connection using PPP (Point-to-Point Protocol). Stay away from access that is only SLIP or TCP/IP. Explore the features available from several ISPs and decide which features are important to you.

∾ Do you provide software to set up my account?

∾ How many different email addresses or mailboxes are available with this account? What is the limit to the amount of email I can keep on the server? Is it possible to forward email?

∾ What email clients do you recommend? Do you provide the software and support for any email clients, Web browsers, or other Internet software?

∾ What clients do you support for Usenet news? Which newsgroups do you have available?

∾ Do you provide space for hosting a Web page? Do you provide software that will help me construct and maintain a Web page?

As you can see there are a number of factors to consider when selecting an ISP. Take the time to consider the alternatives and get some recommendations before you decide which to use. Now that we've discussed selecting an ISP, it's time to move on to getting connected to the Internet.

Getting Connected: Two Scenarios

Here we'll cover two scenarios for getting connected to the Internet, one using a network card and the other using a modem. These match the two types of Internet connections previously mentioned. In both these scenarios we assume you have a computer that uses Microsoft Windows as the operating system.

Scenario I: Steps to Follow

Your company or school has a network with Internet access in the building where you work or in your residence hall.

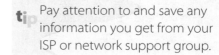 Pay attention to and save any information you get from your ISP or network support group.

∿ Find out as much as possible beforehand about the type of network card you need and the software settings for a proper network connection. If possible, arrange to have a technician on hand or on call for the installation.

∿ Obtain a network card that meets the specifications provided by the people who provide network support.

∿ Have the network card and the network software installed. You may have to do this yourself. The computer will have to be opened to install a network card. Once the card is installed determine if the connection to the local network is working properly. Try to send email to someone on the local network or print a file on a network printer. The exact steps you'll follow depend on the type of network card, the network software, and local matters.

Your computer is directly connected to the network. It has a network card and a cable connecting you to the network. In this case we say you've got a direct IP connection to the Internet.
You may find that the software you've installed handles proper configuration of your Internet connection. If it does then that's all there is to it! If you're not in that happy situation you'll have to deal with the settings yourself. It's not hard; you just have to go through it step by step.

With your computer started, click on the **Start** button, select **Settings**, select **Control Panel**, and then select **Network**. Click on **TCP/IP** and then click on **Properties**. We'll go through the properties you're likely to have to set.

You may have to fill in some key addresses. You'll get the numeric IP addresses and domain names you'll need from your network support center or ISP. Be sure to have those numbers and addresses on hand before you start.

- **DNS Configuration.** Find out whether the DNS (domain name system) will be disabled or enabled. The DNS takes care of translating an Internet domain name to its numeric IP addresses. If DNS is enabled, select that option. Put in the proper host and domain names and carefully enter the numeric IP addresses for the DNS. These are the addresses of the computers on your network that take care of the translations. If these aren't set correctly, you won't be able to retrieve anything from the Internet or view any Web pages.

- **IP Address.** In this panel you assign, if necessary, the IP address for the computer. In some cases the IP address is assigned dynamically each time the computer is started or a user logs on to the network. If your computer has a permanent IP address, and you'll need one if you are going to be providing Internet services such as a Web server, then you'll have to fill in the IP addresses and the subnet mask assigned to the computer. In many cases the subnet mask 255.555.255.0 is used. Be sure to use the proper value; otherwise you won't have a connection to the Internet.

- **Gateway.** If your network uses a gateway to connect to the Internet, you'll have to carefully enter the proper IP address of the system that acts as the gateway. You'll need this to be correct to connect to sites on the Internet through your network.

Scenario II: Steps to Follow

You've decided to set up dial-up access to the Internet from the computer in your home office or from the family computer at home. You've selected an ISP and have a login name and password from the ISP.

- Get a modem that meets the specifications provided by the folks who support the network.

  You'll want the fastest modem you can afford, and one that's supported by your ISP—check with them before buying a modem. You'll also want a modem that can be used for sending and receiving faxes as files, and one that features data compression and error control. If a modem isn't already installed in your computer, get an external modem. It's easier to install and troubleshoot, but it costs a little more. An external modem is connected to your computer by a serial cable that's plugged into a serial port, usually labeled COM 1 or COM 2, on your computer. An external modem also has a power cord to plug into a power outlet. The modem connects to the phone line through a phone wire to a telephone jack. Most modems come with the necessary cables. You can buy longer cables; you may need that if the phone jack isn't nearby.

∿ Follow the installation instructions that come with the modem.

Turn off the power on your computer. If the modem is internal you'll have to take the cover off the computer and plug the modem into a slot in the computer. If the modem is external, connect it to a serial port; plug in the cable to the phone jack and the power cord. Boot the computer. Click on **Start**, **Settings**, **Control Panel**, and then **Add New Hardware**. Follow the instructions; Windows ought to detect the hardware and take you step by step through the installation.

You use a modem to call and connect to a network. Your computer and the network you reach through the phone lines communicate with each other by using software called PPP (Point-to-Point Protocol). This is called a dial-up IP connection to the Internet.

∿ Configure dial-up networking.

Many ISPs supply the software to configure your computer so it has the proper settings for TCP/IP. If you have that software, install it and then test your connection. If you don't have the software, instructions for configuring dial-up networking follow.

∿ Double-click on the icon **Dial-Up Networking**.

Find the dial-up icon on the desktop or click on **My Computer** and select **Dial-Up Networking**. That will open a folder with one or more entries. Each entry in this folder represents a dial-up connection to the Internet.

∿ Double-click on the icon labeled **Make New Connection**.

If that icon isn't present, click on **Connections** in the menu bar and select **Make a New Connection**. This takes you through a step-by-step process where you enter a name for the connection (give any name you'd like) and have the option of selecting a modem from the ones installed or connected to your computer. Clicking on **Next** takes you to a page where you enter the phone number to dial. Then click on **Finish**.

∿ Set the properties for the new connection.

Move the mouse pointer to the icon for the new connection, click once with the right mouse button, and select **Properties**. A set of panels appears. The one labeled General should have the information you just entered. Click on the tab labeled **Server Types**. For Type of Dial-Up Server, select **PPP: Internet, NT, Windows 98**. Don't change the Advanced options. Click on **TCP/IP Settings**. Check the instructions from your ISP to see if you have to set the IP address or DNS address. *Check the instructions again* to see if values have to be entered and that the values you entered are correct. If these aren't right then you won't make a connection to the Internet. Click on **OK**.

∿ Test the connection.

Click on the icon in the Dial-Up Networking folder and then select **Connect** to make the connection. Give the password you need to connect to your ISP. If the sound is turned up on your computer you'll hear a dial tone and then the phone number being dialed. In about a minute or so the modems will connect and begin to communicate. If you have problems call a friend or the ISP for help.

Once you're connected look for a Netscape or Internet Explorer icon on your desktop. Click on it. A browser will start, and a home page will be displayed. Bon voyage!

Getting Set for Email and Usenet News

You'll want to be sure you're set for electronic mail and Usenet newsgroups. You may need to set some IP addresses or domain names if you're going to be using an email client on your computer. An email client is a program that runs on your computer and fetches email from another that acts as an email server. Some examples of email clients are Eudora, Microsoft Outlook Express, and Netscape Messenger. If you're going to be using a Usenet newsreader client then you'll also need to set an IP address or domain name for the system that will serve Usenet news articles to your computer. Microsoft Outlook Express, Free Agent, and Netscape Collabra are examples of Usenet clients.

In addition to setting the addresses or names of the servers, you may have to also configure the clients to include your user name for the server(s), your email address, and your "real name," the name that's different from your email address and is passed along when you post messages.

Email clients sometimes work with two servers. One

tip You probably will not need to set IP addresses or Internet domain names if:

∿ your company or campus has its own network and uses a proprietary email system such as GroupWise or cc:Mail.

∿ you're going to be using a Web-based email system such as Hotmail, **http:// www.hotmail.com**, or Yahoo! Mail, **http://www.yahoo.mail**.

∿ you're going to be using a Web-based newsreader such as Deja.com, **http://www.deja.com**.

server is the computer that handles outgoing email. When you compose and send an email message it is passed to a mail server that specializes in sending out email messages. Sometimes a different computer or server is used to handle incoming email. The incoming server is (hopefully) always on and connected to the Internet. When you check your email, the incoming server transfers any email it has for you to your computer. Outgoing and incoming email are often handled by different protocols; that's why there are two servers involved. Outgoing email is usually handled through SMTP (Simple Mail Transfer Protocol) and incoming mail is handled through POP (Post Office Protocol) or IMAP (Internet Message Address Protocol). Both of these functions or servers can be handled by one computer.

Usenet news is often transported using NNTP (Network News Transport Protocol).

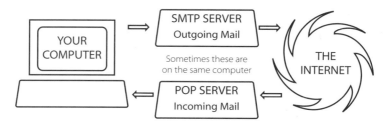

Figure 2.11   The Relationship of Servers and Incoming/Outgoing Email

To demonstrate some of these concepts we'll go through the steps to configure Outlook Express for email and for Usenet news. Outlook Express is a Microsoft product and it's present on most computers that use Microsoft Windows as the operating system. You go through similar steps for other email clients or newsreaders. We'll set the IP addresses or domain name for the outgoing and incoming email servers and the address for the Usenet news server. We'll also set our user name, email address, and real name. You can get to Outlook Express through the browser (click on **Mail** in the navigation toolbar) or click on the Outlook Express icon, which is likely on your desktop. We'll assume that Internet Explorer is started.

Configuring Outlook Express for Your Email

1. **Start the email client, Outlook Express.**

   ∿ Click on **Mail** in the toolbar as shown here.

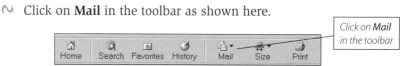

*Click on **Mail** in the toolbar*

This brings up a menu.

～ Click on the item **Read Mail**.

This starts Outlook Express.

2. **Set your name and email address.**
   If your email hasn't been set up through Outlook Express then a program called Internet Connection Wizard will start to take you through the steps of entering the appropriate information for email. We'll go over changing some of this information later.

   ～ Internet Connection Wizard will prompt you for your name. This is transmitted with all outgoing email.

   ～ Then you'll be prompted for an email address. This will be used as the return or reply-to address for all the outgoing email. You'll get the correct email address to use from your ISP or the people that provide network services to your organization.

3. **Set the domain name for incoming and outgoing email servers and the user name you need to log in to the incoming email server.**

   ～ Internet Connection Wizard will then prompt you for the domain names of the incoming and outgoing email servers. You'll need this information from your ISP or the people who provide network services to your organization.

   ～ You'll also need to select the protocol, POP3 or IMAP (choose **POP3** if you don't know), which is used to communicate with the incoming mail server.

   A possible configuration is shown in Figure 2.12.

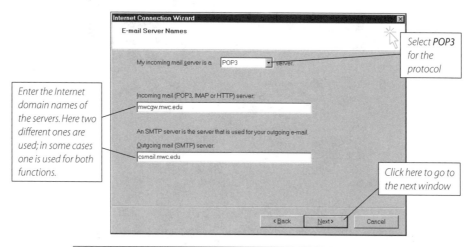

Figure 2.12   Setting the Protocol and the Incoming and Outgoing Servers

↻ Click on **Next** to get to the next window, where you'll fill in the account name and the password.

The account name is the name or term you use to log in to the computer system to check for incoming email. It's usually the same name that's used to connect or log in to your ISP or local network. You can enter the password here too and have the password saved along with the other information for checking and using email. Think twice about doing this. If the computer you're using is going to be shared by other people—a common situation in a public computer lab, in a shared office, or in a shared living space—then you probably don't want the password readily available to anyone using this computer.

↻ Click on **Next** to get to the last window.

If the information you entered is in a proper format, you're all done and Outlook Express will set up email for you on your computer.

↻ Click on **Finish**.

After you click on **Finish** the settings you entered are saved and Outlook Express starts. Figure 2.13 shows an Outlook Express window.

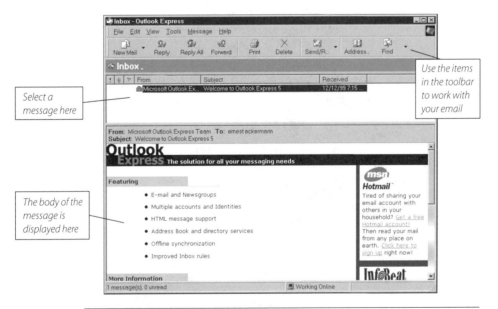

Figure 2.13   The Outlook Express Window

Making Changes to Your Email Settings

There are times when you may want to change your email settings, for example:

 〜 you've made an error in one of the settings

 〜 your organization changes the name of the incoming or outgoing
    mail servers

 〜 you change Internet service providers and have to change some of
    the settings

Here is how you can change the settings:

 〜 Start Outlook Express.

 〜 Click on **Tools** in the menu bar.

 〜 Select **Accounts** from the menu as shown in Figure 2.14.

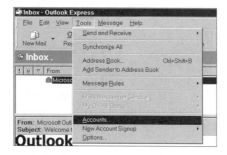

Figure 2.14   Selecting Accounts After Clicking on Tools in the Menu Bar

That opens a window that lists the accounts or email settings for this
computer. Figure 2.15 shows what that may look like. (Be sure to click
on the tab **Mail** to show the list of email accounts.) There's only one
listed.

 〜 Highlight the account information you'd like to change and click on
    Properties.

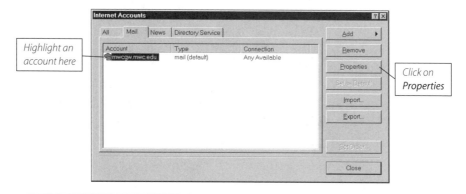

Figure 2.15   The Email Accounts Window in Outlook Express

Clicking on **Properties** opens another window that you use to set or change email settings.

Click on the appropriate tab in that window to set or change some email settings. Figure 2.16 below shows the window after we've clicked on the **Servers** tab.

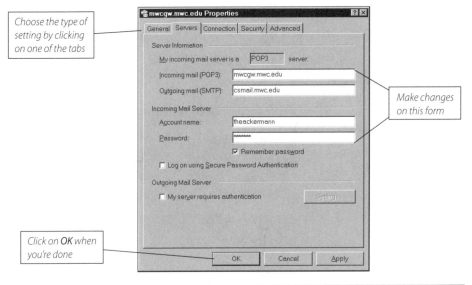

Choose the type of setting by clicking on one of the tabs

Make changes on this form

Click on **OK** when you're done

Figure 2.16   The Servers Properties for Email Settings

∾ Make changes in the forms and click on OK when you're done.

Configuring Outlook Express for Usenet News

1. **Set the user name and the IP address or Internet domain name for the Usenet news server.**

   We'll start the Usenet newsreader that's part of Outlook Express as it is included with Microsoft Internet Explorer. Setting up the newsreader is similar to setting up Outlook Express for email. Internet Connection Wizard will take us through the steps. You'll be able to change or create new settings using Outlook Express in a way similar to changing settings for email. We'll assume that Internet Explorer is already started.

   ∾ Click on **Mail** in the toolbar.

   This brings up a menu.

   ∾ Click on **Read News**.

   This starts Internet Connection Wizard. The first window asks for your name. What you enter here will be sent out with any articles you post to Usenet.

ⁿ Type your name and click on **Next**.

The next window asks for your email address. People who read your articles can use this address to reply directly to you.

ⁿ Type your email address and click on **Next**.

The next window asks for the domain name of the Usenet news server. This server brings the titles of articles to your computer. Your ISP or network support group should provide you with the name of the server. In some cases you'll have to give a login name and password when you access Usenet news. If that's the case then click on the checkbox as shown in Figure 2.17 below.

ⁿ Type in the IP address or Internet domain name of the computer system that runs the NNTP or Usenet news server software.

ⁿ Click on the checkbox if you have to log in to use Usenet.

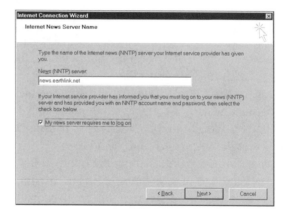

Figure 2.17   Using Internet Connection Wizard to Set the Domain Name of the News Server

ⁿ Click on **Next**.

The next window asks you for your account name and password. The account name is the name or term you use to log in to the computer system to read Usenet news. It's usually the same name that's used to connect or log in to your ISP or local network. You can enter the password here too and have the password saved along with the other information for using Usenet news.

ⁿ Click on **Next**.

This takes you to the last window.

ⁿ Click on **Finish**.

This starts Outlook Express as a Usenet newsreader. We'll talk more about using Usenet in Chapter 6.

Changing the Settings for Usenet News

You can change any of the settings for Usenet news in the same way you make changes in the settings for email.

∾   Start Outlook Express.

∾   Click on **Tools** in the menu bar.

∾   Select **Accounts** from the menu.

∾   Click on the **News** tab in the window that pops up.

This opens another window that you can use to manage or make changes to your Usenet settings.

∾   Click on the tab **News**.

∾   Highlight an account.

∾   Click on **Properties**.

Summary

From a technical point of view the Internet is a collection of thousands of networks, distributed throughout the world, that agree to communicate using certain rules or protocols.

Each site on the Internet has a unique numeric address called its IP address and usually a corresponding name called the domain name. Information is passed around the Internet in packets. Each packet contains the address of the sender and the address of the destination. The packets can take different paths through the Internet. It's up to the software at the destination to receive the packets and reassemble them. The emphasis is placed on the packets, not on the connections between systems. Users generally access sites by giving a domain name; the hardware and software convert a domain name to an IP address.

Many of the services operate according to a client/server model. A program called the client is started on one system and contacts a program called the server at another computer on the Internet. The client sends the commands typed or given by a user to the server. The server sends a reply to the client, and the client presents the information to the user.

All information on the Internet is in digital format. This includes text, programs, charts, images, graphics, video, and audio. When using the WWW you work in a hypertext or hypermedia environment. A Uniform Resource Locator (URL) specifies items, services, and resources. These are used by Web browsers to specify the type of Internet service or protocol to use and the location of the item. The URL for the Web page "Abraham Lincoln: Internet Resources from the Library of Congress," for example, is **http://lcweb2.loc.gov/ammem/alhtml/alrel.html**. The protocol or service in this case is HTTP, or Hypertext Transfer Protocol, and a Web browser using it would contact the Internet site **lcweb2.loc.gov** and access a document named **alrel.html**. The documents on the WWW are called Web pages. These are written and constructed using a language or set of rules called Hypertext Markup Language (HTML).

You can access the Internet by having a direct connection from your computer to a network. This is often the case when your company or campus has a network installed in offices, classrooms, labs, or residence hall rooms. To get connected to the Internet you'll need the proper device to connect to your organization's network and (possibly) the IP address for your computer and for a domain name system. Another way to connect to the Internet is to use a modem to call an Internet service provider (ISP) and gain access through a PPP (Point-to-Point Protocol) connection. In either case you may have to configure an email client and Usenet news client to handle incoming and outgoing email and reading and posting messages to Usenet newsgroups.

Selected Terms Used in This Chapter

404 error	Internet service provider (ISP)
client/server	IP address
domain name system	modem
hyperlink	packet-switched network
Hypertext Markup Language (HTML)	Point-to-Point Protocol (PPP)
	protocols
Hypertext Transfer Protocol (HTTP)	router
	Transmission Control Protocol (TCP)
Internet domain name	
Internet Protocol (IP)	Uniform Resource Locator (URL)

Exercises and Projects

1. What type of connection do you have to the Internet? Who supplies the Internet services? What are the charges for Internet access and who pays them?

2. When you're connected to the Internet, what IP address is assigned to your computer? What's its domain name? You may have to ask your ISP or someone in network support for help in answering this question.

3. Visit the Web site with the URL **http://www.nsrc.org/codes/ country-codes.html**.
   a. Describe what you find at the Web site.
   b. What is the Internet domain name for the Web server that hosts this site?

c. Using the domain name as a guide, state the type of network that hosts this server.

d. Suppose you were to retrieve the Web page with the URL **http:// hotline.pvtnet.cz/utility/nslookup.htm**. In what country is the network registered that hosts that Web site?

4. nslookup is an Internet utility that you can use to find the IP address of a domain name or to find the domain name (if there is one) that corresponds to an IP address. Some sites that make this service available on the Web can be accessed by using these URLS: **http://dns411.com**, **http://www.lasaltech.com/cgi-bin/ nslookup**, or **http://www.virtual.net.au/cgi-bin/nslookup**.

a. Use any of these URLs to find the IP addresses of the following: **www.skills.net.au**, **www.webliminal.com**, **www.library.mwc.edu**, and the Web server of your company or school.

b. Use any of the Web services to find the domain name associated with each of these IP addresses: 204.71.200.170, 198.137.240.91, 194.149.103.180, and the IP address of the Web server for your company or school.

5. If you use an email client, find the name or IP address of the incoming email server and the outgoing email server. If you don't use an email client then describe the email program or service you use for email.

6. Go to the Web page with the URL **http://www1.mwc.edu/ ~ ernie/ cpsc104/emailadl.html**. View the source of the Web page.

a. What is in the Head section? (That's the section marked with the HTML tags < HEAD > and < /HEAD >.)

b. Look at the source for the first occurrence of the HTML tag < UL >. You'll notice that from there until < /UL > several items begin with the tag < LI >. How are those items displayed on the Web page?

c. Suppose we changed the tags < UL > and < /UL > in the source to < OL > and < /OL >. What effect would that have on the way the Web page is displayed? (For help with this one take a look at the Web page "Create a List," **http://builder.cnet.com/ Authoring/Basics/ss05.html**.

7. This exercise requires that you use Netscape Navigator. Go to the Web page with the URL **http://www.webliminal.com/internet-today.html**. View the page information of the Web page using the method described in the section "Basic Terms and Concepts."

    a. When was the Web page last modified?

    b. What's the content length of the document?

    c. What are the URLs of each of the images on the Web page?

    d. What's the size in bytes of each image? (*Hint:* Click on the URL for each image in the "page info" view of the Web page.)

8. Take a look at the document "Chapter 1: What is the Internet?" **http://members.unlimited.net/ ~ kumbach/internet/whatsnet.html**. It's mentioned in the first FYI section in Chapter 1. Using the definitions and concepts described in that document define each of these terms:

    a. domain

    b. backbone

    c. NAP

    d. POP

    e. domain name system

9. The Web site whatis.com, **http://www.whatis.com**, is sometimes useful when you need to know about technical terms. What is its definition of

    a. modem?

    b. router?

    c. protocol?

    d. IP address?

10. Read through "Finding an ISP," **http://hotwired.lycos.com/webmonkey/guides/web/isp.html**.

    a. What does that article say is the difference between AOL and a smaller ISP?

    b. The article lists 10 questions to ask before selecting an ISP. Select three of the questions that in your opinion are the most important. Why are they the most important?

11. Retrieve a copy of "Learn the Net: Getting Connected," **http://www.learnthenet.com/english/html/04connec.htm**.

    a. Outline the steps given in that article for connecting a modem.

    b. What does that article suggest you do if you're using a modem and have call waiting on your phone line?

    c. Follow the hyperlink to the related article "About Modems." According to that article how long would it take to download a 20-second video clip if you were using a modem rated at 57.6Kbps? How long would it take to download a 30-second audio clip with the same modem? Why is there is such a difference between the two times?

Chapter 3

COMMUNICATION

ON THE

INTERNET

*T*he most popular use of the Internet? Communication! It's been that way almost since the Internet began. Soon after the introduction of electronic mail, or email, it became apparent that email was the most popular and one of the most important Internet services. People enjoy, value, and appreciate being able to communicate with others. The communication isn't only chitchat, either. The Internet has become a medium for professional communications, distributing and sharing information related to education, research, business, and other professional areas. There are other types or forms of communication on the Internet too. These include email discussion groups and Usenet newsgroups, and realtime communication such as chat groups and virtual worlds. Each of these has characteristics that make it more appropriate to use in certain situations. The majority use only text (typed words and symbols) for communication, but some allow for audio, video, or images to be part of the communication.

This is the first of several chapters in this book that deal with communication on the Internet. This chapter sets the context for discussion of the individual types of communication. We'll discuss their characteristics, some of the issues involved with using one or another, and matters of etiquette and effective communication. We'll also look at some of the legal and ethical issues that have developed as the result of these types of communication. In the next three chapters we'll discuss some of the individual types in more detail. Since communication is the most popular use of the Internet, it's what you need to know!

Goals/Objectives

- Understand the concepts associated with communication on the Internet
- Know some of the prevalent technologies used for communication on the Internet
- Be able to decide, based on specific requirements, which communication technology is appropriate
- Know how to communicate effectively on the Internet
- Be aware of legal and ethical issues related to the use of communication technologies

Topics

- ~ Communication Technologies
- ~ Effective Internet Communication
- ~ Behavior and Etiquette Guidelines
- ~ Legal and Ethical Issues

Communication Technologies

Communication is one of the most popular services for the hundreds of millions of people throughout the world with access to the Internet. Using the Internet is an accepted (if not preferred) means of communication for personal and professional uses. Furthermore, the Internet supports different ways for people to communicate. Each of the different forms of communication has its own characteristics. Some of these characteristics have to do with the different types of technologies employed and some have to do with the type of social interaction they support. Some forms of communication are used from one individual to another and others for group communication. Some of the technologies or ways of communicating are unique to the Internet—email, Usenet, and chat groups, for example. They have come about because information transmitted on the Internet is transmitted in digital format, and the Internet behaves as if it were a computer network that connects people without regard for distance.

Asynchronous and Synchronous Communication

Internet communication can be characterized in other ways too. Some communication, like email, is **asynchronous**. A message is sent or read without the sender and the recipient participating in the communications system simultaneously.

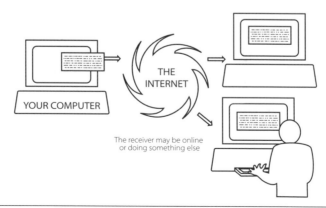

YOUR COMPUTER

THE INTERNET

The receiver may be online or doing something else

Figure 3.1   Asynchronous Communication

For example, you send a message to Chris. Chris may or may not be connected to the Internet when the message is sent. But the message can be read when Chris connects to the Internet.

Synchronous communication, on the other hand, requires all parties involved to be present at the same time. An example of this type of communication on the Internet is an online *chat room*.

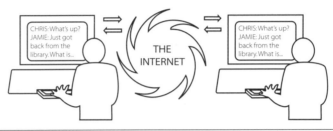

Figure 3.2   Synchronous Communication

For example, you and Chris both are connected to the Internet and are using communications software or are at a Web site that lets each of you send and receive messages in realtime (as it's happening).

Communication Technologies

Here we'll list, briefly characterize, and describe some of the major forms of Internet communication. We'll do this in two groups. This first group—email, email discussion groups, and Usenet news—consists of the most established Internet communications technologies. We discuss them in greater detail in the next three chapters. They're used for personal communications, business uses, and the exchange of scholarly research.

Electronic Mail (Email)

This is a basic Internet service that allows individuals or groups to communicate. A person uses an email program to read, send, and manage her email. The program is sometimes called an email client or mail user agent. Most email programs make it easy to work with text, images, and other types of files that are part of or are an attachment to an email message. Others work best with messages that are only text.

Email is an example of asynchronous communication. It's good for individual or group communication. You communicate with groups either by including a list of recipients in the address of the email or by sending email to an email discussion group. Email is well suited to personal or professional communication.

Email Discussion Groups

Email discussion groups are also called *interest groups*, *listservs*, or *mailing lists*. Internet users join, contribute to, and read messages to the entire group through email. Several thousand different groups exist. An individual group may keep archives of the postings to the group. In many cases, it's more appropriate to think of a group's members rather than a group's archives as a good resource for information.

An email discussion group is an example of asynchronous communication. It's designed for group communication. You communicate by sending email to the address for the group, and the message is automatically distributed to everyone in the group. Some discussion groups focus on professional or research issues, while others are recreational, dealing with personal interests.

Usenet News

Usenet news is a collection of messages called articles grouped into categories called newsgroups. There are thousands of newsgroups, with tens of thousands of articles posted daily. Rather than exchanging messages or articles among individuals, the articles are sent from one computer system, acting as a Usenet host, to another. The tool that an individual uses to read, post, reply to, and manage articles is called a newsreader. Several different newsreaders are available. Usenet has a long history, in Internet terms, of supporting uncensored free speech with little or no central control.

Usenet news is an example of asynchronous communication. It's designed for group communication. An article posted by an individual to a newsgroup is likely to be available throughout the world within a few hours. The topics for newsgroups run the gamut from professional or research issues to a wide variety of recreational topics dealing with special interests.

Realtime, Synchronous Communication on the Internet

Realtime or synchronous communications on the Internet are a lot like the conversations and meetings we have in real space, as part of our daily lives when we're not using the Internet. They're like two or more people talking in a classroom, in the mall, in a meeting, at a sporting event, or at a party. There may be one or several conversations going on at once. Everyone is in the same place and participating some way or other; one or more people are talking, some people are listening, and somebody else is waving trying to get somebody's attention. All of this can be happening at the same time.

If we take those same situations and use the Internet as a communications medium then we call this environment where the communication takes places a virtual meeting place, a virtual room, or even a virtual world.

We'll discuss these types of communication in some detail here.

Internet Relay Chat (IRC), Chat Rooms, MOOs, MUDs, and Virtual Worlds

Each of these services has its own characteristics but they operate essentially the same way. Usually several people participate simultaneously. People meet on channels which, depending on the service, are also called chat rooms, **MUDs** (multiuser dimensions or multi-user dungeons), or **MOOs** (multiuser dimensions that are object oriented). There are thousands of channels covering a wide range of topics. Think of these as virtual meeting places or even virtual communities. People usually converse through text, each person typing a message that's displayed in realtime to the computer screens of all participants. Some of these virtual communities are elaborate three-dimensional environments where participants may construct objects, houses, buildings, and cities.

These synchronous communication forms are designed for group communication but can be used for individual communication. Communication is immediate and lends itself to brief informal comments similar to what one would use in a conversation. The topics run the gamut from business or technical issues to a wide variety of recreational topics dealing with special interests. Some of these technologies, most notably MOOs, have been used for educational purposes.

In order to use any of these services you need to be connected to the Internet, as they all involve realtime communication. Because of the nature of this communication you can't be sure with whom you're communicating so you have to be careful about giving out personal information.

We'll go over just a little history about these technologies before covering each in some detail.

Some History

Ways of chatting or holding realtime group discussions on the computer networks have been around and available for some time. Before the Internet was as commonplace as it is today, computer systems were connected on local networks. These networks often included ways for individuals to communicate with each other.

Many academic networks were supported by computer systems that used the Unix operating system. These systems included a program named **finger** that would tell who else was using a computer system and other programs named **talk** and **write** that were used to communicate with others on the same computer system or network.

Some commercial networks such as the Source, CompuServe, and America Online had a number of online forums or discussion groups available to their customers. These facilities and types of programs were naturally extended across the Internet.

Virtual worlds or group role-playing games were also developed at individual sites and on individual networks. Using Telnet, one of the early Internet services still in use, a person using one computer could log on or sign on to another computer anywhere on the Internet. This was provided, of course, that the person was connected to the Internet and knew the appropriate login names, passwords, and commands. Telnet made it possible for these virtual worlds and group discussions to be open to practically anyone, anywhere in the world, on the Internet.

Fy THE HISTORY OF IRC, MUDS, AND MOOS
~ "Early IRC History"
http://www.the-project.org/history.html
~ "The MUDex"
http://www.apocalypse.org/pub/u/lpb/muddex
~ "MOO-Cows FAQ"
http://www.moo.mud.org/moo-faq

IRC

IRC (Internet Relay Chat) is a popular chat system developed in the late 1980s by Jarkko Oikarinen in Finland. It operates using a client/server model. You use an IRC client on your computer to contact one of several IRC servers throughout the world. You then connect to a channel or chat area provided by the server. Some servers support thousands of channels. There are different channels or chat areas on each network. Each channel has an operator who can be contacted if you need help dealing with someone else in the channel or chat room.

Individuals are known by nicknames that they choose and control the amount of information they make public about themselves.

Everyone on a channel can communicate simultaneously. Whatever one person types is broadcast to everyone in the channel. As you might imagine this can get hectic or confusing. If a large number of people are communicating, the text of the conversations moves too fast to follow. IRC, like other chat technologies, allows users to set up exclusive conversations.

Once you connect to a server you use IRC commands to work with the server. There are lots of commands available. Most folks start with a small set of commands and learn more as they need them. There's quite a lot to learn to become familiar with ways to use IRC and its culture. Here's some basic information to help you when you're starting out.

How IRC Works

Before you can use IRC you'll have to have an IRC client (software) on your computer. You only have to install the client once. From then on you use the client to

~ log on to an IRC server.
~ join a channel (chat group) at the server.
~ communicate with others in the chat group or channel.
~ disconnect from a channel.
~ quit the server.

You'll use IRC commands or the client's menu items or icons to do the items listed above.

Here's a list of some of the basic IRC commands. They all start with a slash, /.

tip Before you jump right in, take the time to get a copy of or make a bookmark to the site "The IRC Prelude," **http://www.irchelp.org/irchelp/new2irc.html**.

IRC Command	Function
/help command	Gives help about a specific command
/list	Lists the channels available in the server
/join #channel	Connects you to a specific channel. Channel names begin with # (the number sign).
/part	Disconnects you from the current channel
/names	Shows the nicknames of the users of the current channel
/nick new-name	Changes your nickname
/who	Gives a list of nicknames of the people on a channel
/whois nick-name	Gives the public information about a specific user
/msg nick-name message	Sends a private message to a specified user
/quit	Quits or leaves IRC

Jargon

The communication is text-based. Over the years a number of special acronyms called jargon and symbols called ***emoticons*** have been developed to foster more expressive and efficient communication. For example, the acronym "lol" means "laughing out loud" and :-(is used to represent a frown. These acronyms and symbols are also used in email and Usenet newsgroups. For terms and jargon that are more specific to IRC take a look at:

- ∾ "How Do I Use Chatspeak?"
 http://www.cnet.com/Content/Features/Howto/Beyond2/ ss01e.html

- ∾ "IRC Terminology"
 http://www.newbie-u.com/irc/terms.html

More Information
Here are two resources to help you become comfortable using IRC:

- ∾ "Internet Relay Chat (IRC) Help," **http://www.irchelp.org**. An excellent resource for beginners and novices.

- ∾ "Tracy Marks' IRC Bookmarks," **http://www.geocities.com/ ~ webwinds/irc/bkirc.htm**. An extensive list of bookmarks to resources about IRC.

Getting Set for IRC
One of the most popular IRC clients for computers using the Windows operating system is mIRC. If you want to try IRC and don't have a client, go to the home page for mIRC, **http://www.geocities.com/ ~ mirc**, and follow the instructions to download and install the client. Get the 32-bit version of the client if you're using MS Windows 95, 98, 2000, or NT. Before you do be sure you have permission to install mIRC on the computer you're using. For other IRC clients check the list on the Web page "AfterNET IRC Network: Files," **http://www.afternet.org/files**.

Web-based Chat

Web-based chat is usually easier to use and more closely moderated that IRC. Most of the major news sources on the Web such as CNN.com and the New York Times on the Web; popular search services such as Excite, Go, Lycos, Snap, and Yahoo!; and other types of Web sites provide chat capabilities. Some sites specialize in providing chat services and others sponsor chat events with celebrities.

In many cases you can use a Web-based chat site without downloading any special software. Sometimes, though, you can download software that makes working with the chat group easier to manage. Some chat sites require that you download particular chat software to participate in the discussions. At Yahoo! Chat, **http://chat.yahoo.com**, for example, you have a choice of not using any special software or using Java-enhanced chat. The chat rooms at ParentsPlace.com, **http:// www.parentsplace.com/ppchat/daily/**, also let you use other chat software such as ichat, a popular chat client. (For more information take a look at the ichat home page by using the URL **http://www.ichat.com**.)

The chat groups or chat rooms, as they're called, are relatively easy to access and available on a wide variety of topics. They all operate essentially the same way. You register at a site and then you can participate in the chat rooms available at that site. In most cases you need to supply your name and email address. Then you choose a login name or nickname and a password. You'll certainly want to be careful about making personal information available to the public. This helps you to avoid, at the least, unsolicited email or, worse, strangers knowing your home address. Many chat sites also let you include a picture, a link to your home page, and other ways to let people know about you. The sites also give you ways of keeping all that private. You may want to check out a Web chat site's privacy policy before you submit any information. For an example, take a look at "Yahoo! Privacy Policy," **http://www.yahoo.com/docs/info/privacy.html**.

Fy WHERE ARE THE CHAT SITES?

~ "The Free Chat Rooms"
http://www.free-chat-rooms.to
~ "The Webarrow Chat Directory"
http://www.webarrow.net/
chatindex/list.html
~ "Ultimate Chat"
http://www.ewsonline.com/
chat

Most of the Web-based chats are text-based but some allow you to include image files, and some allow for audio files and **avatars**. An avatar is an icon, image, or figure that you can use to represent yourself in a chat. Some of the avatars are quite elaborate with three-dimensional attributes and animation. To use these more sophisticated and complex avatars you'll have to select the avatar from a collection at the site or, in some cases, you can create your own. You'll also have to download or purchase software to enable an avatar and if the chat involves audio or video then you may also have to get the hardware and software necessary for that. Some Web sites that host chats with avatars or other exceptional features are:

~ "The Cybertown Palace"
   http://www.cybertown.com/palace.html

~ "Worlds Ultimate 3D Chat Plus"
   http://www.worlds.net/3dcd/index.html

~ "Alpha World"
   http://www.activeworlds.com/tour/alpha.html

Now we'll take a look at a specific Web-based chat site, Yahoo! Chat. We'll start with the home page that lists some of the chat rooms or groups and take a look at the Web page you would use to register at Yahoo! Chat. We'll talk about what you can expect at this popular type of chat site and some of the issues related to using a Web-based chat site, and then we'll leave it to you to explore the site. This chat site, like many other Web-based chat sites, has lots of help available.

The home page for Yahoo! Chat is shown in Figure 3.3. Its URL is **http://chat.yahoo.com**. You follow steps similar to those in Activity 1.1 to access this page.

∿   Start your browser.

∿   Click on the location field.

∿   Type **http://chat.yahoo.com** and press **Enter**.

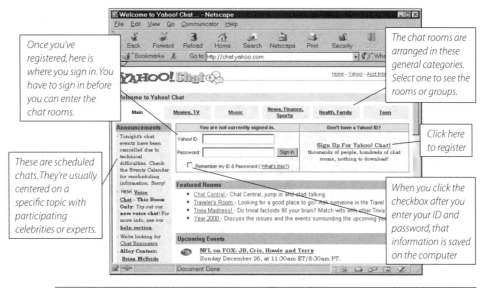

Figure 3.3   The Yahoo! Chat Home Page

If you're interested in using chat, the most important things on the Yahoo! Chat home page may be the hyperlinks to the categories of chat rooms, the specific chat rooms, and the chat events. Before you can enter any of the chat rooms you have to sign on as a registered member. When you register you'll choose a user name and can give other information about yourself—in other words your persona at Yahoo! Chat. By allowing only registered users to access the chat rooms, this server (Yahoo! Chat) can exercise some control over who may use the service. Two reasons for doing this are: the service may deny access to a user who doesn't follow agreed-upon rules or is causing a problem for others; or the service can collect information about its users for marketing purposes. We'll look at registering in more detail shortly.

When you do type your ID and password you can request that the browser remember that information when you click on the button labeled "Sign in." Clicking the checkbox labeled "Remember my ID & Password" means the browser will write your ID and password to this computer. The browser writes what's called a ***cookie***, so that a Web server at yahoo.com can access the information. A cookie is a relatively small amount of information, about as long as a sentence, that a server instructs a browser to write to the client computer. Only a server from the same domain as the server that deposited the cookie can read it. This "remembering" is convenient if you're the only person who uses the computer, but you shouldn't select that option if you're using a public computer. If the computer is public, another person could use it and possibly access Yahoo! Chat using your ID and password, since it's on the computer. Yahoo! uses cookies for other parts of the chat session, but they don't contain sensitive information. They claim that the ID and password cookie is erased when you click on the hyperlink **Sign Out** or when you exit the browser.

Now let's take a look at what we need to do to register at Yahoo! Chat.

ɴ   To register or sign up for the service click on the hyperlink **Sign Up for Yahoo! Chat!**, as in Figure 3.3.

This opens another Web page where you type and submit the required information to sign up for Yahoo! Chat (and other services that Yahoo! offers). Yahoo!, like most services, also asks for information it'd like to have, but doesn't require. A portion of that page is shown in Figure 3.4.

Why register? You'll want to register if you're interested in taking advantage of the services Yahoo! offers such as chat and access to email through a Web page. In exchange for these services you give up information about yourself. Some say it's an exchange of your privacy for the services. It's really less simple than that; you have a choice about some of the information you disclose, and you can make choices about some of the ways you prefer the information to be used.

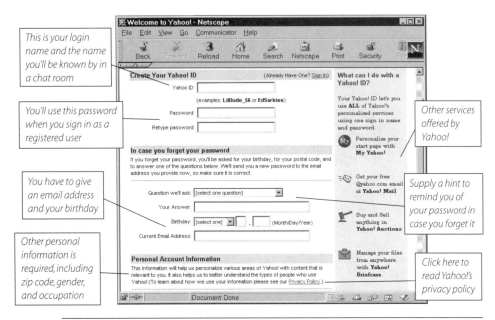

This is your login name and the name you'll be known by in a chat room

You'll use this password when you sign in as a registered user

You have to give an email address and your birthday

Other personal information is required, including zip code, gender, and occupation

Other services offered by Yahoo!

Supply a hint to remind you of your password in case you forget it

Click here to read Yahoo!'s privacy policy

Figure 3.4   The Yahoo! Registration Page

Figure 3.4 shows the registration page for Yahoo! Chat. It is typical of the type of registration page you'll find for a chat service. The ID and password are used to log in as a registered member. You can choose them to be whatever you'd like, but you may have to make more than one choice for an ID if the one you choose is already taken. You must give your email address, gender, and zip code. Most sites require at least that much so that members aren't completely anonymous. You can choose what information you'll reveal to other people who've registered. You do that after registering—click on **Edit/Create Profiles**. Be sure to check the privacy policy before you register so you know how this service will use the information you give it. Yahoo! may also use the email address to send you information, but you can choose to request that it not do that. The last portion of the page contains a link to "Terms of Service." You will have to read and agree to it before you are registered. Take the time to read it so you know what you may or may not do with this service. Once you've filled in the necessary and optional information you choose, a confirmation will be sent to the email address you gave. Once you're registered you can enter a chat session.

Figure 3.5 shows the home page for Yahoo! Chat after you've signed in. You see there are several hyperlinks you can use to select a chat room. Once a group is selected a page pops up that shows the ID of each person currently in the chat room with a message displayed every few seconds. We'll leave looking at individual chat rooms up to you since it

wouldn't be appropriate to show conversations here. There are several
other things to point out and explore. We'll start at the upper right and
go clockwise.

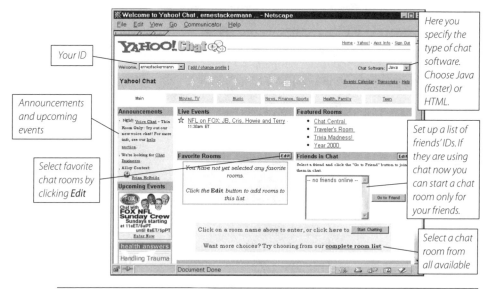

Figure 3.5   The Yahoo! Chat Web Page After You Sign In

You can select either a Java or HTML implementation of the chat
software—that's what you'll be using while you're chatting. The Java (a
programming language) implementation is faster and has more features.
Choose that and when you enter a chat room the Java software will start.

The section "Friends in Chat" displays a list of your friends' IDs when
both you and they are using this service. Click on an ID in the list and
that person is sent a message to join you in a chat. This is a convenient
way to communicate in realtime with your friends. It is essentially the
same as the instant messenger services we'll discuss later. You add or
delete an ID from your list by clicking on the button labeled **Edit** to the
right of "Friends in Chat." People are sent messages letting them know
that you've added them to your list. You can block messages from another
person if they've added you to their "Friends" list and you'd rather not
be on that list.

A link near the bottom of Figure 3.5 takes you to a list of all the
available chat rooms. A little above that is the section "Favorite Rooms."
Using the link Edit you can select names of chat rooms and add them
to this list. (That link is also what you'll use to delete rooms from your
list.)

Announcements and a schedule of live events are on the left. The
announcements tell of changed or new services. The live events are

specially scheduled chat rooms. They often include some expert on a topic or a celebrity. The upper left lists your ID. The link next to it takes you to a page where you can create a public profile about yourself or hide your online presence from others. Think of the public profile as the way you want to portray yourself to others, in other words, your persona. Naturally you won't want to mislead people, and you probably won't want to give out personal information. Any registered user can view the profile.

Some people make regular visits to chat rooms and make friends or acquaintances with other regular visitors. It is natural to call a group of people who regularly get together to communicate using the Internet a *virtual community*.

MUDs

The term MUD (multiuser dungeon) was first applied to a multiuse role-playing game or environment developed in the early 1980s by Richard Bartle and Roy Trubshaw at the University of Essex, U.K. Now the term is used as an acronym for any multiuser domain and to describe any of a class of virtual environments based on some theme (such as a castle or a world) with several participants communicating using (usually) only text in realtime.

Some of these environments are based on competition or (virtual) combat, while more recent versions, such as TinyMUD, are built around cooperation, world-building, and socialization. People usually access a MUD by using Telnet to access a server or by using a MUD client. Using a MUD (MUDding) can be addictive and

BLOCKED BY A FIREWALL?

Some networks use a firewall system, usually a combination of hardware and software, as a security measure. All packets to and from the Internet have to go through the firewall system but certain types of packets are not permitted to pass through. This filtering of packets is often done based on the port number associated with the packet. The port number is used to identify the type of Internet service, such as SMTP with standard port 25, HTTP with standard port number 80, and Telnet with standard port number 23. Many of the MUDs and MOOs use nonstandard port numbers and the firewall on the network you use may not let you contact a MUD or a MOO.

What to do? You can ask the network administrator if some ports may be opened up permitting packets for services that support MUDs and MOOs. If that's not possible then you'll probably have to find another Internet service provider.

consume a great deal of time. (We personally know students who have essentially dropped out of several of their classes and spent most of their time MUDding.) A MUD environment is usually complex with many rooms (in some cases hundreds or thousands) or regions. In addition to providing a rich and complex environment for the people involved in the MUD, these environments have been the focus of several serious studies. They give a glimpse of a society being built by its participants. When you participate in a MUD you enter a fanciful, text-based virtual environment. All the participants have a handle (a name) and a persona. People participate in a MUD by giving commands and communicating and cooperating with others. A good place to start to learn about MUDs and how to connect to them is the Web site "The MUD Connector," **http://www.mudconnect.com**.

Fyi MORE INFORMATION ABOUT MUDS

~ "The MUD Resource Collection" **http://www.godlike.com/muds**, by Lydia Leong is an up-to-date and extensive collection of links. The items are of interest to people interested in MUDding or studying the use of MUDs as a form of computer-mediated communication.

~ "The MUDdex" **http://www. apocalypse.org/pub/u/lpb/ muddex**, by Lauren P. Burka gives an in-depth collection of links to documents for those interested in the development and history of MUDs.

~ "The MUD FAQ" **http://www.mudconnect.com/ mudfaq/index.html**, maintained by Jennifer Smith.

MOOs

In 1990 Pavel Curtis, a researcher at Xerox PARC, became interested in some work that was done that enabled the easy construction of MUDs. The work was a programming language called MOO (MUD Object-Oriented) done by Stephen White, a student at the University of Waterloo. Curtis developed the concepts so that people who were not experienced programmers could develop MUDs customized for a specific purpose. These are called MOOs and have become popular with educators and others involved in computer-mediated communications, training, and distance learning. Curtis developed a well-regarded MOO called Lambda MOO.

Virtual Worlds

MUDs and MOOs are similar since both represent virtual worlds. Because of that we can say that they go further than chat rooms and

IRC in establishing and maintaining virtual communities. The participants not only build and maintain relationships; they also build and maintain objects.

The communication in MUDs and MOOs is all text-based. Other types of virtual worlds include two- and three-dimensional views of the environments, graphical avatars for participants, and realtime audio. We mentioned a few earlier in the chapter. You may want to investigate some of these worlds, but you'll need special software and maybe some additional hardware to participate.

Internet Instant Messenger and Paging Services

There are several services available on the Internet and the Web that will let you know when someone also connects to the same service and will permit you to send a message directly to that person. The message is sent through the service, not by email. In that way these services are like paging or messenger services. You can also use these services to set up chat sessions with one or more people using the service.

Three popular messenger and paging services are AOL Instant Messenger (currently being distributed with Netscape Navigator), the somewhat more established service ICQ (an acronym meant to represent "I seek you") from Mirabilis LTD, and Microsoft MSN Messenger Service. Other software companies are releasing similar products.

Fyi FURTHER RESOURCES ABOUT MOOS

~ A good straightforward introduction to the value and purpose of MOOs is "MOOs, Not Just Cows" **http://www.cas.usf.edu/lis/lis5937/moo.html**, by Ilene Frank. She also describes some of the basic commands in MOOs and gives links to other resources.

~ If you want to try a Web-based MOO use the URL **http://moo.du.org:8888** to access the MOO at Diversity University, **http://www.du.org**.

~ Another source of information about MOOs and links to MOOs is "The Purpose of MOOs" **http://cinemaspace.berkeley.edu/~rachel/moo.html**, by Rachel Rein.

Fyi COMPARING INSTANT MESSAGING SOFTWARE

~ "Fast Talkers: CNET Reviews the Top Instant Messengers" **http://www.cnet.com/internet/0-4023-7-1591649.html**, by Gregg Keizer

~ "Chat Goes to Work" **http://www.zdnet.com/products/stories/reviews/0,4161,2411029,00.html**, by Frank Derfler

The services are very similar and, like some of the other software we've been discussing in this chapter, are free, have good documentation and help, and are relatively easy to install.

∾ You can get AOL Instant Messenger (AIM) through the AIM home page with the URL **http://free.aol.com/aim/**. The online help is part of the software you install on your computer.

∾ ICQ is available through the ICQ home page with the URL **http://www.icq.com**. Online help is available through that Web page and also through the ICQ FAQ, **http://www.icq.com/support/99faq**.

∾ Go to the home page for MSN Messenger Service, **http://messenger. msn.com**, to download the software. You can get help by using the URL **http://messenger.msn.com/support/helphome.asp**.

After you get the software and follow the instructions to install it, you're led through an installation and registration process. With each of the services you select an online name or nickname—the name people will use to contact you. You'll have to supply an email address and other information. You can take steps to protect your privacy by keeping that information hidden from other users of the service. However, you can choose to make information public to all or just to selected registered users. With each service you can construct one or more lists of friends, colleagues, or work groups. Then whenever you sign on, the service checks to see which of the people in your groups is online.

These services offer convenient ways to keep in touch with other people on the Internet. Take a look at the home page for each service. The services are usually not compatible, though. A person registered on one isn't always accessible from another. These services are popular and becoming more so.

Internet or IP Telephony

With Internet or **IP telephony** you simulate a telephone call on the Internet. Ordinary telephone equipment transmits and receives information in analog, not digital, format. Internet telephony converts the sounds of a telephone conversation into a digital format, puts it in packets, and transmits the packets across the Internet. Specialized software, a microphone, a sound card, and speakers or a headset are needed for this. Some of the services let you use a phone number and with others you contact another party using the IP address or domain name of the computer that they use. The main advantage of this technology is that you can make a long distance phone call at a cost lower than telephone rates, and sometimes for free! There are several disadvantages, though. Delays in routing the packets and the speed of your connection may make the conversation choppy with less than desirable sound quality. In some cases the computer's sound card or the IP telephony software doesn't allow for sounds to be transmitted and received at the same time—while you're speaking you can't receive a message. This is like using a CB radio for a conversation. It's adequate in some situations, but not the same as using a telephone. Want to try out a Web-based telephony service? Use the URL **http://www.dialpad.com** to access the home page of dialpad.com. After you register and download the necessary software, you'll be able to make free Internet-to-telephone calls in the U.S.

Internet Pictures and Video

We know that it's possible, and in fact ordinary, to transmit digital images on the Internet. Using a digital camera it's possible to capture images, store them in a file, and then send them across the Internet. With the appropriate hardware, called a video capture card, you can connect a camcorder to your computer and transmit video across the Internet. Some people use special video capture devices to hold video conferences on the Internet. These technologies increase the demands for speed—in computation, display, and transmission—on a computer and the Internet. You remember that it takes a good deal of bytes to represent images and video, and including more detail and colors increases the number of bytes. Some digital cameras produce files that take up about 30KB. A 30-second video needs about 1.8 million bytes. Video transmission on the Internet isn't really considered to be high quality because transmission speed usually limits displays to 15 or fewer frames per second.

In the early 1990s people at Cornell University began to develop software to support video *conferencing* using common personal computers and relatively inexpensive video and audio devices. That research project is now available to the public as CU-SeeMe.

This is an example of synchronous communication. Transmitting images and video lends itself well to personal communication and bringing groups together in realtime for conferences or educational purposes.

Internet Conference

Internet or Web conferencing involves two or more participants working together in realtime. The tools for enabling these conferences include a video-capture card and a camera, a microphone, a sound card, and speakers. This allows for what is virtually face-to-face, audio communication. Participants can also share a common clipboard so all can share images and other information. These programs put high demands on network speed and capacity since the exchange of realistic and simultaneous video, audio, and images requires that a great deal of information be transferred in a very short period of time. Thus it's often necessary that the participants have high-speed connections to the Internet or that they be on a network within a single building or on a single campus for these tools to be used effectively.

Here's how this works. You give the email address or IP address of the person or persons with whom you want to meet. The program sends a message on the Internet to those addresses, inviting them to meet with you. When they agree, the connections are set up so that whatever any of the participants types, says, or brings into view of the camera is displayed at the sites of all the other participants.

This is an example of synchronous communication. It can be used for individual or group communication. Because of the demands this puts on the networks and computer systems necessary to support what is essentially a multimedia conference, these technologies are often used for professional purposes.

The characteristics of each of the communications technologies are summarized in Table 3.1.

Fyi MORE INFORMATION ABOUT TELEPHONY, VIDEO, AND INTERNET CONFERENCING

Internet telephony:
- "Sorting Out Internet Telephony" http://www.zdnet.com/anchordesk/story/story_2113.html
- "internetTelephony" http://www.internettelephony.com

CU-SeeMe:
- "Video Conferencing with CU-SeeMe" http://www.webmec.com/cuseeme
- "CU-SeeMe Frequently Asked Questions" http://support.wpine.com/cuseeme

Internet conferencing:
- "Meeting of the Minds: 4 Net conferencing programs" http://www.cnet.com/Content/Reviews/Compare/Netconference
- "Virtual Meeting Solutions" http://www.infoworld.com/cgi-bin/displayTC.pl?/970602comp.htm

Technology	Individual	Group	Asynchronous	Synchronous (Realtime)
Email	✔	✔	✔	
Email discussion groups		✔	✔	
Usenet news		✔	✔	
IRC and chat	✔	✔		✔
Internet paging services	✔	✔		✔
Internet telephony	✔			✔
Video and audio conferencing	✔	✔		✔

Table 3.1   Characteristics of Types of Communication on the Internet

Having introduced some of the technologies that are used to communicate on the Internet, now we'll go over some guidelines for effective Internet communication.

Effective Internet Communication

We'll discuss effective Internet communication as it relates to the communication technologies that are unique to the Internet—email, discussion groups, Usenet news, and synchronous communication such as chat. Most of the communication in these technologies is done through text.

Differences and Similarities Between Spoken and Traditional Written Communication

Because messages are sent electronically, it is possible to get a response in a matter of minutes or seconds. When we're using synchronous communication the response is immediate. When we're trading comments separated by only a few seconds, Internet communication is similar to spoken communication. It tends to get informal and personal, and that's probably just the way we want it to be. On the other hand, when we're communicating using the written word, we can't show our facial expressions or gestures or express intonation the same ways we would when speaking.

Internet communication is, of course, a form of written communication but it's a different medium from traditional written communication. It isn't bound by the physical limitations of a page of paper; it can be transmitted and received very quickly, and a single message can be sent to a group of thousands of people as easily as it can be sent to one or two people. Since the communication is written communication and it's not done on paper we have to do what we can to make it easy to read and easy to comprehend.

tip You'll have to take full advantage of your writing ability, the jargon and acronyms available, and the generally accepted rules for effective communication in a text-based electronic environment.

Remember the difference between casual communication and business or professional communication. Using the Internet for communication doesn't mean you can be more or less casual than when you're face to face.

There's no substitute for a well-thought-out and well-expressed message. To make your communication most effective you need to write clearly, take into account that people will likely be reading your message on a computer screen, and take full advantage of the medium itself.

Here are some guidelines for effective Internet communication using text:

- Be careful about spelling and punctuation. Follow the same rules you'd use if you were writing a letter or a memo.

- If you want to state something strongly, surround it with asterisks (*) or write it in uppercase, but don't take this too far. Some folks equate items in uppercase letters with shouting. Emoticons or *smileys* were developed to express facial expressions or gestures as part of text-based communication. Take a look at the Web page "Common Emoticons and Acronyms," **http://www.pb.org/emoticon.html**.

- Use a subject header or tag that gets the reader's attention and accurately characterizes what's in the message.

- Make your message as short as possible, but don't make it cryptic or unclear. Most users have to deal with limits on the amount of information they can receive. Keep the body of the message succinct. If you're using email or posting a message to a discussion group or Usenet, limit the message to one or two screens. In some cases—such as using chat—you need to capture someone's attention quickly, and you may be limited to the amount of text you can send in one message.

~ Write relatively short paragraphs and limit lines to 75 characters. Some of the programs you use for email or Usenet wrap long lines at whatever the window margin is set. Others don't do that. Give your reader a break and wrap the lines for them.

> **Fyi** TIPS ON WRITING EFFECTIVE EMAIL
> You can also use the tips for other forms of Internet communication.
> ~ "A Beginner's Guide to Effective Email" by Kaitlin Duck Sherwood, **http://www.webfoot. com/advice/estyle.html**.
> ~ "BUSINESS NETIQUETTE INTERNATIONAL" by Frederick Pearce, **http://www.bspage.com/ 1netiq/Netiq.html**.

~ Include parts—but not all—of an original message when you are writing a reply. Include only the portions pertinent to your reply. You do this to set a context for your message. This takes advantage of a unique feature of Internet communication: it's relatively easy to include your reply within the context of the original message.

Figure 3.6 shows some of the features of using the Internet for communication, along with demonstrating some of the guides to effective communication. This example is of email, but it could be another type of communication. The figure shows working with email using Outlook Express, the email program included with Internet Explorer.

Here are a few things to note about the message:

~ It is a message to a group. Multiple copies are sent by including all the addresses in the header.

~ The subject header is to the point and will get the reader's attention.

~ The message uses the same tone of voice as one would find in an interoffice business memo. The spelling and grammar are correct, but not formal.

~ The message uses asterisks (*) to emphasize a word in the text.

~ The message discloses business information—email address and office phone and fax numbers—but doesn't contain personal information.

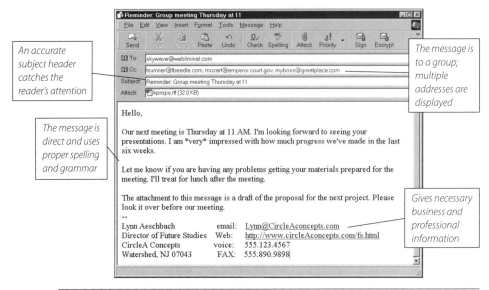

Figure 3.6   An Email Communication to a Group

~ Any of the recipients of the message shown in Figure 3.6 may send
   a reply. When they do they'll need to decide whether to reply to the
   original sender only, Lynn Aeschbach, or to the group.

   Next we'll consider some accepted and appropriate ways to behave or
   act when you're communicating on the Internet.

Behavior and Etiquette Guidelines

Using the special technologies
for communicating on the Internet carries its own set of rules of
etiquette and proper behavior. In most
cases your communication will be using
only text. You need to remember that the recipient will read it without
the benefit of being with you, seeing your expressions, or getting your
immediate and considerate reactions. You need to say what you mean in
a clear, direct, and thoughtful way. In some cases you may not know the
person you're communicating with. Here is a list of guidelines to follow.

Be aware of the risks involved with giving out personal information.
Common sense tells us not to give out personal information, home phone
numbers, or home addresses to people we don't know.
   Since it may be difficult to know with whom you're communicating,
you particularly need to be careful about disclosing personal information.
Children especially need to know about and be informed of the risks
and dangers involved with using the Internet. They need to discuss these
issues with their parents, and they need to understand clearly stated rules

about not giving out any personal information or telling someone where they go to school or play. The Web page "Staying Street Smart on the Web!" **http://www.yahooligans.com/docs/safety**, is a good place to find information about Internet safety issues for children and parents.

Dangerous situations can arise when we develop a relationship with someone through email or a chat group. Most of the communication is through text; we don't get to hear the person's voice or see them. We may see a picture or get a description, but we may never have certain knowledge. You may, for example, be involved in a long series of email messages or have several conversations in a chat room with a person who claims to be your age and gender. The person may even send a photograph. It could be that the person is totally misrepresenting his or her true self. So we need to be very careful about giving out any personal information, and we certainly wouldn't make arrangements to meet the person without having the meeting take place in a public location and without taking other precautions.

The Internet gives us lots of opportunities for learning, recreation, and communication. We don't need to be rude or unfriendly, but we do need to be very careful.

Take some time to consider what you will write.
You'll find you can usually give a better response if you take some time to think about it. Also, if someone writes something that upsets you, don't react immediately. Perhaps you've misinterpreted the original message. Treat others with dignity and respect, as if you were communicating face to face.

Be careful when using humor and sarcasm.
The person reading your message may misinterpret your remarks, and you won't be able to immediately clear up a misunderstanding. When you use the Internet you have the chance to communicate with people throughout the world. The person with whom you are communicating may be from a different culture, may not be familiar with your language, and may have views and values different from yours.

Don't assume the communication is private.
You can never be sure where a copy of the email you write will end up. It's easy to forward email, so the message you send could be shared with others. When you're communicating in a group discussion, remember that everyone in the group may see your messages. Everyone in the group has the chance to read, save, or print your message.

Check the address when you compose a message or reply to a message you've received.
Be sure it's going to the person(s) who ought to receive it. If the original message was sent to a group of people, such as a discussion group or Usenet newsgroup, be sure of the address you use so the reply goes to an individual or the entire group as necessary. It's embarrassing when email is sent to a group but is meant for an individual.

The rules or guidelines above give some useful tips in dealing with some of the issues related to using the Internet for communication. We've mentioned that Internet communication isn't necessarily private, and we'll take a more detailed look at that issue in the next section.

Legal and Ethical Issues

A number of social, ethical, and legal issues have developed related to communication on the Internet. Some of these are related to important personal concerns, such as privacy; some are related to insuring confidential communications, such as **encryption**; and others are related to appropriate business practices. Here we'll discuss:

- Privacy
- Electronic Communications Privacy Act
- Encryption
- Offensive and Abusive Email
- Libel
- Unsolicited and Inappropriate Email—Spam

Privacy

What's reasonable to expect in terms of privacy when you use the Internet for communication?
Your initial response might be that you expect the same protection of your privacy on the Internet as you have in your other dealings in society. Codes of behavior or rules of etiquette have developed on the Internet over the years. Some of these are informal, and others have been codified into policy statements for network use in a company, organization, or school.

In some cases laws have been adopted to provide the same level of protection of privacy for working with electronic media as with any other media. An important point is that privacy as it relates to communication is sometimes defined in terms of the medium. The laws in the United States dealing with communications in printed form, on paper, have needed to be changed to suit electronic communications. We'll cover a few of the important issues related to privacy.

∾ The manner in which communication is implemented on the Internet makes it susceptible to monitoring. We can't assume then that our Internet communications are private.

When you send a message, the message is broken into packets and the packets are sent out over the Internet. The number of packets depends on the size of the message. Each message has the IP address of the sender (your address) and the address of the recipient. Packets from a single message may take different routes to the destination or may take different routes at different times. This works well for the Internet and for you. Packets are generally sent through the best path, depending on the traffic load on the Internet. The path doesn't depend on certain systems being in operation, and all you have to give is the address of the destination.

The packets making up a message may pass through several different systems before reaching their destination. This means there may be some places

> PRIVACY IN THE WORKPLACE: CAN YOUR EMPLOYER MONITOR YOUR ELECTRONIC COMMUNICATIONS? Yes! If you're using an email system owned by your employer, then any email message—or other communication—transmitted by or received by that system belongs to your employer. Decisions in several court cases support the concept that your employer owns and may monitor email or other communications. It's a good idea to check with your employer to learn the company policy and see what practices are followed.
>
> One site to visit for more information about privacy in the workplace is the *Privacy Rights Clearinghouse*. Specifically take a look at "Fact Sheet # 7: Employee Monitoring: Is There Privacy in the Workplace?" **http://www.privacyrights.org/fs/fs7-work.htm**.

between you and the destination where the packets could be intercepted and examined. Since all the systems have to be able to look at the address of the destination, each system could be able to examine the contents of the message.

∾ Some say that sending email is like sending a message on a postcard.

If you're using a computer system shared by others or if the system at the destination is shared by others, there is usually someone (a system administrator) capable of examining all the messages. So, in the absence of codes of ethics or the protection of law, Internet communications could be very public. Needless to say, you shouldn't be reading someone else's email. Most system administrators adopt a code of ethics under which they will not examine email unless they feel it's important to support the system(s) they administer. The truth of the matter is they are often too busy to bother reading other people's mail.

Electronic Communications Privacy Act

One example of a law to ensure the privacy of email is the **Electronic Communications Privacy Act (ECPA)** passed in 1986 by Congress. It prohibits anyone from intentionally intercepting, using, or disclosing email messages without the sender's permission. The ECPA was passed to protect individuals from having their private messages accessed by government officers or others without legal permission. That bill extended the protections that existed for voice communications to nonvoice communications conveyed through wires or over the airwaves. You can, of course, give your permission for someone to access your email. However, law enforcement officials or others cannot access your email in stored form (on a disk or tape) without a warrant, and electronic transmission of your email can't be intercepted or "tapped" without a court order. The ECPA does allow a system administrator to access users' email on a computer system if it's necessary for the operation or security of the system. The ECPA then gives the system administrator the responsibility to allow no access to email passing within or through a system without a court order or warrant. She can and indeed should refuse any requests to examine email unless the proper legal steps are followed.

∾   Although the ECPA makes it illegal for someone else to read your email, the law has been rarely applied.

Encryption

When you send a message by email it's often transmitted in the same form you typed it. Even though it's unethical and illegal for someone else to read it, the message is in a form that's easy to read. This is similar to sending a message written on a postcard through the postal service. Deleting email from your mailbox doesn't necessarily mean that it's gone. On many computer systems email is routinely backed up or saved to tape in case it's necessary to retrieve a "lost" message.

A better way to prevent others from reading your mail is to use encryption to put a message into an unreadable form. The characters in the message can be changed by substitution or scrambling, usually based on some secret code. The message can't be read unless the code and method of encryption are known. The code is called a key. Many messages are encoded by a method called **public key encryption**. If you encrypt a message and send it on to someone, that person has to know the key to decode your message. If the key is also sent by email, it might be easy to intercept the key and decode the encrypted message.

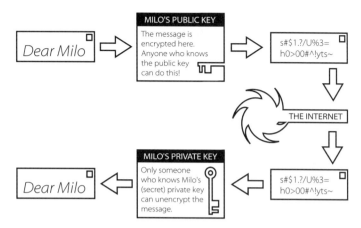

Figure 3.7   Using Public and Private Keys to Encrypt Messages

With public key encryption there are two keys, one public and the other private. The public key needs to be known. To send a message to a friend, you use her or his public key to encrypt the message. Your friend then uses her or his private key to decode the message after receiving it. Suppose you want to send an encrypted message to your friend Milo. He tells you his public key; in fact, there's no harm if he tells everybody. You write the message and then encrypt it using Milo's public key. He receives the message and then uses his private key to decode it. It doesn't matter who sent the message to Milo as long as it was encrypted with his public key. Also, even if the message was intercepted, it couldn't be read without knowing Milo's private key. It's up to him to keep that secret. Likewise, if he wanted to respond, he would use your public key to encrypt the message. You would use your private key to decode it.

Fyi MORE INFORMATION ABOUT ELECTRONIC PRIVACY
- "6.805/STS085: Readings on Privacy Implications of Computer Networks" http://www-swiss.ai.mit.edu/6095/readings-privacy.html
- "EPIC Online Guide to Privacy Resources" http://www.epic.org/privacy/privacy_resources_faq.html
- "The Privacy Pages" http://www.2020tech.com/maildrop/privacy.html

What we've said so far still allows someone to forge an email message. Someone using your name could encrypt a message and send it to Milo. He might think it came from you! Some encryption techniques using private and public keys are used to virtually eliminate the possibility of forgery. When you send a message you use your private key to create an encrypted digital signature. When Milo gets your message he can apply your public key to the signature to verify that it was sent by you, and that the message hasn't been altered.

You can obtain a version of public key encryption software called **PGP**, for Pretty Good Privacy. It's freely available to individuals and may be purchased for commercial use.

There are some restrictions on the use of the encryption software developed in the United States. At the time of this writing State Department regulations prohibit the export of most encryption methods, while other

MORE INFORMATION ABOUT PGP

~ "Introduction to PGP"
http://web.bham.ac.uk/
N.M.Queen/pgp/pgp.html

~ "The comp.security.pgp FAQ"
http://www.cam.ac.uk.pgp.
net/pgpnet/pgp-faq

~ "Where to Get the Pretty Good
Privacy Program (PGP) FAQ"
http://www.cryptography.
org/getpgp.htm

countries allow the export of encryption methods and algorithms. Some people feel strongly that these policies should be changed for the sake of sharing information and for the sake of allowing common encryption of sensitive and business messages, but others don't agree.

~ One issue that needs to be resolved is whether it should be possible for law enforcement or other government officials to decode encrypted messages.

Some argue that because of the need to detect criminal action or in the interests of national security, the means to decode any messages should be available to the appropriate authorities. Others argue that individuals have the right to privacy in their communications. In the United States, the issue has been decided in favor of government access in the case of digital telephone communications. The issue hasn't been settled yet for email or other forms of electronic communications.

Offensive and Abusive Email

Virtually all codes of etiquette, ethics, and policies for acceptable use of networked computer facilities include statements that prohibit sending offensive or abusive messages by email. This is, naturally, similar to the codes of behavior and laws we adhere to in other, everyday communications. One difference between dealing with this sort of behavior on the Internet and other forms of communication, such as the telephone or postal service, is that no one is in charge of the Internet—it is a cooperative organization.

~ If you have a problem with someone at your site, talk with your supervisor, their supervisor, your system administrator, or your Internet service provider about it. If the problem comes from another site, send email to the address **postmaster@*the.other.site***, and talk with the system administrator at your site or your supervisor about it. (You substitute the Internet domain name of the site in question for *the.other.site.*)

Individuals have been arrested and prosecuted for making threatening remarks by email. Civil suits and charges have been filed against individuals in cases of harassment, abuse, and stalking.

Libel

Some libel suits have been filed based on postings to Usenet or some other network. This happens when one person or company feels that another has slandered them or falsely attempted to damage their reputation. Once again, you would expect the same laws or rules for libel in the society at large to be applied to network communications. That's generally the case, but an interesting issue comes up, centering around whether the company or organization that maintains a computer telecommunication system is responsible for libelous or even illegal messages posted there. In the United States the courts have generally drawn an analogy between these systems and a bookstore. The owner of a bookstore is not responsible for the contents of all the books in the store, and likewise, the management of commercial networked systems on the Internet has not been held responsible for all messages on its systems. On the other hand, some commercial network systems claim to screen all messages before they're posted. In that case they may be held accountable for libelous messages. Also, consider that telephone companies aren't held responsible for the speech on their equipment since they fall into the category of a "common carrier." However, television and radio stations are responsible for the content of their broadcasts.

Unsolicited and Inappropriate Advertising—Spam

There was a time—before the late 1980s—when commercial traffic was not allowed on the Internet. Now the use of the Internet for commercial activities is commonplace. It's not unusual for Web pages to carry advertisements. Usenet and email discussion groups developed on the Internet in the late 1970s and early 1980s in an atmosphere free from marketing and advertising. While some (relatively few) Usenet newsgroups and discussion groups tolerate commercial announcements, most are adamantly opposed to any selling or advertising, and unsolicited marketing is met with strong resistance. This resistance has included attempting to have the advertiser dropped by their ISP and flooding the advertiser's mailbox with email messages.

∾ Most users prefer that advertising and commerce be done in clearly identified newsgroups, discussion groups, or Web pages.

Unsolicited commercial email is called **spam**. That term is also applied to an inappropriate commercial posting to newsgroups. The term spamming is used to mean sending a message to many unrelated newsgroups, discussion groups, or individual email addresses. Because email is composed and sent by a computer, it's relatively easy to send several thousand messages in less than an hour. Naturally, it's annoying to get this "junk" email or posting to groups. It's also costly to the person receiving the spam, and, unfairly, not very costly to the person sending the email. Some estimates put the cost of spam at over $30 million per year.

∾   Spam is more than an annoyance; it slows other traffic on the Internet and imposes a cost on the receiver through dealing with the unsolicited commercial email or newsgroup postings at little cost to the sender.

Some legislation dealing with spam is pending in the U.S. Congress, and several states have passed anti-spam laws. Identifying spammers and notifying their Internet service provider is sometimes helpful in dealing with the problem. Several major ISPs have instituted policies that attempt to prohibit spam from their servers (but still it's the ISP's customers that have to eventually pay the bill for that). In 1997 one ISP, EarthLink, successfully mounted a legal challenge against Cyber Promotions, Inc., in order to stop the company from sending unsolicited email to its customers or using the ISP's networks for distributing unsolicited email. In 1998 Cyber Promotions was ordered to pay EarthLink $2 million.

The Coalition Against Unsolicited Commercial Email (CAUCE) is an all-volunteer organization that supports legislative and technical solutions to eliminating spam. Visit its Web site "Join the Fight Against Spam," **http://www.cauce.org**, for more information. The Web site "Get that spammer!" **http://kryten.eng.monash.edu.au/gspam.html**, by Julian Byrne contains lots of information about ways to track down and stop spammers.

Summary

Communication is the most popular use of the Internet, with email topping the list of all the technologies used. Some of the types of communication technologies used also include email discussion groups, Usenet news, chat groups, and IRC. These are unique to networked computer environments and have come into wide popularity because of the Internet. Other technologies, including video and audio conferencing and Internet telephony, are also available on the Internet. They require more multimedia capabilities of computer systems and are more taxing of network resources than the others. They also are adaptations of other technologies to the Internet.

Most of the technologies that are unique to the Internet require communication to be done in text—letters with some symbols and punctuation. Communicating effectively involves taking the time, except in informal communications, to use correct grammar, spelling, and punctuation and writing an appropriate message. When replying to a message include the pertinent parts of the message and use an appropriate and interesting subject header in any case.

When you're communicating on the Internet take special care not to give out personal information to strangers and to treat others with respect. Be aware of the risks involved in communicating with people you cannot see and may never meet in person. Take time to consider what you write to others, and be careful to avoid humor and sarcasm except with the best of friends. You can't assume that your messages are private, so be careful about what you write.

Several issues related to ethical and legal considerations arise from using the Internet for communication. The manner in which communication is implemented on the Internet makes it susceptible to monitoring. You can't assume that communications are private. Some believe that sending email is like sending a message on a postcard. Some laws have been enacted to help protect privacy during electronic communications. These, however, have been difficult to enforce and are rarely applied. One way to protect privacy is to encrypt or code a message. A common way of encrypting messages is through the use of public and private keys. Although software for encryption is readily available, current policies and laws prohibit its export.

Another area of concern is dealing with abusive or offensive communications. Laws that apply to libel, harassment, and abuse have been applied to cases where the offending behavior has occurred on the Internet. Unsolicited email or other forms of communication is called spam. It definitely is an annoyance, but also quite costly to the people who receive the junk email or other communications. It's relatively inexpensive to produce, because most of the cost of transporting the email is shifted to the receiver and all people that use the networks supporting the Internet.

Selected Terms Discussed in This Chapter

asynchronous

avatar

chat room

conferencing

cookie

Electronic Communications
   Privacy Act (ECPA)

email discussion group

emoticon

encryption

interest group

Internet Relay Chat (IRC)

IP telephony

listserv

mailing list   smiley
MOO   spam
MUD   synchronous communication
PGP   virtual community
public key encryption

Exercises and Projects

1. We've mentioned that email and Usenet news are forms of asynchronous communication. Explain whether voicemail is another example of asynchronous communication. Do the same for ordinary paper mail.

2. Do you know what an autoresponder is? Read the Web page "Auto Responder Comparison," **http://www.makura.com/auto/ autocomp.html**, and write answers to the following questions:
   a. What is an autoresponder?
   b. What are the different types of autoresponders?
   c. How should you prepare your information for an autoresponder?
   d. Explain how a business or organization of your choice could use and benefit from an autoresponder.

3. Retrieve the Web page "The IRC Prelude," **http://www.irchelp.org/ irchelp/new2irc.html**, and answer these questions: What is a channel operator? What is the /dcc chat command? What is Automatic dcc and why is it a bad idea?

4. Want to try chatting? Excite People & Chat is a collection of chat rooms and forums. It is similar to Yahoo! Chat, but you can enter a chat room as a guest without registering for the service. The home page for this service has the URL **http://www.excite.com/ communities**.
   a. Before you start chatting click on the hyperlink Community Standards and read the page about chat rooms, **http:// www.excite.com/communities/resources/standards/chat**. Write a synopsis of the chat guidelines.
   b. Go back to Excite People & Chat. Click on the hyperlink, **Chat Now,** that takes you to the chat rooms. Select the hyperlink **Chat as a guest**. Select a category and list the three chat rooms that have the most people online.
   c. Visit one of the chat rooms you selected in part b. Give the handles of five of the people in the room.
   d. Enter the chat room. Keep track of what people are saying for the first 15 minutes or so and then write a synopsis of the discussion.

e. Now enter a chat room whose topic is important to your academic or professional work. Which one did you choose? Why? Give a description of your experiences in that chat room.

5. Take a look at the home page for the Electronic Privacy Information Center (EPIC), **http://www.epic.org**.

a. Select two items from the section "Latest News." Give a synopsis and a URL to use for more details about each item.

b. Follow the hyperlink to the EPIC Online Guide to Privacy Resources. List the names of five international privacy sites. Follow a hyperlink to one of the sites and describe what's available at that site.

6. Compare two resources for privacy: "EPIC Online Guide to Privacy Resources," **http://www.epic.org/privacy/privacy_resources_faq.html**, and "The Privacy Pages," **http://www.2020tech.com/maildrop/privacy.html**. Give a summary of what's at each site. Which of the two is more appropriate to your interests? Explain.

7. Take some time to explore the Web sites mentioned in the text that deal with effective email, "A Beginner's Guide to Effective Email" by Kaitlin Duck Sherwood, **http://www.webfoot.com/advice/estyle.html**, and "BUSINESS NETIQUETTE INTERNATIONAL" by Frederick Pearce, **http://www.bspage.com/1netiq/Netiq.html**.

a. Each site lists several tips about writing effective email. Pick the three most important tips. Why did you choose those three?

b. Write a two- to three-page report that summarizes the type of information each site has available and then compares one site to the other. Conclude the report by explaining which of the two sites gives tips that are more appropriate to your professional or academic tasks.

8. Visit the home page for CAUCE, **http://www.cauce.org**.

a. Describe the membership, history, and purpose of CAUCE. (*Hint:* Follow the hyperlink "Who Is CAUCE?")

b. Follow the hyperlink "About the Problem" and read the resulting Web page. It lists at least six major points about the problem with spam. What are those points? Give a brief summary of each.

c. The Web site also lists several things you should not do when dealing with spam or spammers. What are they? List the items and give a brief summary of each.

d. How do you feel about spam? Suppose you were selling a product that you knew would be a great success if enough people knew about it. Would you send email to several thousand people describing the product? Explain your answer. Now suppose you had some information that you felt anyone could benefit from and you were willing to share the information at no cost. Would you send email to several thousand people to spread the information? Explain. (Let's assume that there was no problem for you to send the email to several thousand addresses.)

9. Visit the Web site "Anti-Spam Resource Center," **http://www.earthlink.org/internet/security/spam/index.html**.
   a. Follow the link **Spam Prevention Tips**. This Web page contains links to sites that give tips to help you prevent spam. Select one of the links and give its URL, its title, and a synopsis of the tips at that site.
   b. Go back to "Anti-Spam Resource Center" and follow the link **Anti-Spam Legislation and Lawsuits**, **http://www.earthlink.org/internet/security/spam/index.html**. List three of the items that deal with laws passed by states. Describe the status of U.S. legislation dealing with spam, using one or more of the items on that page as a reference.

We've discussed a variety of means of using the Internet for communication including email, discussion groups, Usenet newsgroups, chat rooms, MUDs or MOOs, and Internet conferencing. These next three exercises deal with ways of using the forms of communication.

10. Consider the communication that takes places between all participants in a class—student to student, student to teacher, and teacher to student. For each of the forms of communication we mentioned, describe how it may be used in a meaningful way to support activities and communication in a class or say why it isn't appropriate.

11. Suppose you're in the real estate business. Describe ways to use these different modes of communication in a meaningful way. For each type of activity note its advantages, disadvantages, and significance.

12. Pick another business or organization and describe which of the communication technologies would be well suited for use by people directly involved in the business or organization who happen to all be in one building. Describe which of the technologies would be well suited to support the activities of the business or organization, but to be used by a diverse group of customers or members.

Chapter 4

ELECTRONIC MAIL

Electronic mail, or email, was one of the first Internet services available. People enjoy, value, and appreciate being able to communicate with others. Email has special features that make it different and more useful in some cases than other ways of communicating such as writing letters on paper and mailing them, talking on a telephone, or sending a fax. When you send an email, the receiver doesn't have to be connected to the Internet at the same time. It's just as easy to send a message to many people as it is to send it to one person. You can reply to email at your convenience—receiving it doesn't necessarily interrupt your work or recreation. With most modern email programs, you can include text, images, and sound within a single message. Because email is quickly becoming a preferred method of communication, you'll want to learn about how it works and how you can use it effectively.

Goals/Objectives

~ Understand the concepts associated with electronic mail

~ Gain a working knowledge of an email system to read, send, and otherwise manipulate electronic mail folders

~ Be aware of common features of modern email systems

~ Learn how to work with email in text and nontext formats

~ Learn the basic features of an email system

Topics

~ How Email Works

~ Advantages and Limitations of Email

~ Email Programs and Their Features

~ Email Addresses

~ Dissecting a Piece of Email—Headers, Message Body, and Signature

~ Attachments and Nontext Email

~ Using Outlook Express for Email

How Email Works

Electronic mail, or email, lets you communicate with other people on the Internet. It's used for all types of communications: personal, business, and professional. You can send messages to anyone with an Internet address, and likewise, you can receive email from anywhere on the Internet. With more than 200 million people having some sort of connection to the Internet and the increasing use of the Internet in all aspects of our society, email gives you an opportunity to communicate with people nearby and around the world in a relatively quick and efficient manner.

Email programs are called *mail user agents* because they act on the user's behalf. The email program acts as a go-between for you and computer systems, and the computer systems handle the details of delivering and receiving mail.

When you compose your message, it's all in one piece, but when it's sent out to the Internet, it's divided into several pieces called *packets.* The number of packets depends on the size of the message.

The packets can travel and arrive at their destination in any order, and they don't all have to take the same path. When you communicate with a remote site, you may think you have a direct connection, but that's usually not the case. At the destination, the packets are collected and put in order so the email is back in its original form. If a packet contains an error or is missing, the destination sends a request back to the source asking for the message to be re-sent. All of this takes place according to *SMTP*, *Simple Mail Transfer Protocol*, the standard protocol used on the Internet to transport email between computer systems.

Advantages and Limitations of Email

Advantages

Email has a number of advantages over some other forms of communication. It's quick, convenient, and nonintrusive.

∾ Email usually reaches its destination in a matter of minutes or seconds.

∾ You can send letters, notes, files, data, or reports all using the same techniques.

∾ You don't have to worry about interrupting someone when you send email. The email is sent and delivered by one computer system communicating with another across the Internet. Although it is put into someone's mailbox, the recipient isn't interrupted by the arrival of email.

- You can deal with your email at your convenience, reading it and working with it when you have the time.

- You don't have to be shy about using email to communicate with anyone. You can write to anyone with an Internet email address. But remember that email isn't anonymous—each message carries the return address of the sender.

- The cost to you for email has nothing to do with distance, and in many cases, the cost doesn't depend on the size of the message. Most Internet access charges either are based on the number of hours per month you access the Internet or are a flat monthly fee.

Limitations

Although email is an effective and popular way to communicate, there are some drawbacks to its use.

- Email isn't necessarily private. Since messages are passed from one system to another, and sometimes through several systems or networks, there are many opportunities for someone to intercept or read email.

- Some email systems can send or receive text files only. Even though you can send and receive images, programs, files produced by word-processing programs, or multimedia messages, some folks may not be able to view them.

- It's possible to forge email. This is not common, but it is possible to forge the address of the sender. You may want to take steps to confirm the source of some email you receive.

THE ESSENTIAL INFORMATION IS: You use an email program on your computer to compose, send, read, and manage email. Once you compose (write) a message you can send it on the Internet in electronic form, where it usually passes through several other sites before reaching its destination. Once there, it is held until the person to whom it's addressed reads it, saves it in a file, or deletes it. The recipient does not have to be logged in or using a computer for the email to be delivered. When she does use her computer and checks for email, it will be delivered to her.

Email messages can arrive at any time. They're added to a file, your mailbox or inbox, which is part of a directory that holds all the email for the system. The mailbox holds the messages on the server addressed to you, and only you (or the system administrator) can read your mail. On many systems, the maximum size of the mailbox is limited and the amount of time email is held is limited as well. It's important that you delete old email so new mail won't be rejected because your mailbox is full.

Review the sections in Chapter 3 that deal with effective Internet communication and proper behavior and etiquette.

Email Programs and Their Features

Email Programs

If you read your email using a micro-computer then you probably contact a computer system that acts as a mail server. That computer system is the one that receives the email for you from others on the Internet. The mail is held for you until you check it. The program you use to work with your email, the mail user agent, is also called an *email client*. It works directly with the email server.

There are several different types of email programs or systems.

- **Mail systems designed for proprietary networks.** These email systems were originally designed for use on private or proprietary networks that used protocols different from the Internet protocols. They have been extended to work with Internet mail. Examples of these are GroupWise, cc:Mail, and AOL Mail.

- **Mail clients designed for text-based mainframe or minicomputer systems.** These are designed for use on a computer terminal. The terminal can be physically connected to a computer or a network, or it can be a virtual terminal that's accessed through Telnet (an Internet protocol for setting up a terminal session). Until the mid 1990s these email systems were the prevalent Internet email clients, and they are common on Unix, VAX, and IBM mainframe systems. Elm, Pine, and Mailx are examples of this type of email program.

- **Mail clients designed for microcomputer systems.** Your computer acts as a client and sends a request to the mail server to see if there is mail and to bring it to your computer. This exchange between the two computer systems is usually done using *POP*, *Post Office Protocol*, or *IMAP*, *Internet Message Address Protocol*. You or someone else has to set the Internet addresses on your computer for the outgoing and incoming mail servers. This is also explained in Chapter 2 in the section on getting set for email. With these common types of clients the email is delivered to the microcomputer you're using from the mail server. That way you can work in an offline mode if you'd like, connecting to the Internet only to retrieve and send email.

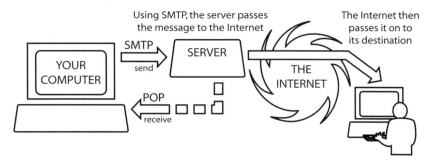

These clients are designed to work on a microcomputer so they have features that take advantage of the available graphical interface, text formatting, and file management facilities. Many of these email clients allow for including multimedia elements and Web page elements using HTML as part of a message. Some popular email clients are Eudora, Netscape Messenger, and Microsoft Outlook Express. We will go over details of using Outlook Express later in this chapter.

∾ **Web-based email services.** You use these mail systems, sometimes called free email systems, through a Web page. Some examples are:

∾ Anglefire, **http://email.angelfire.com**

∾ Hotmail, **http://www.hotmail.com**

∾ Yahoo! Mail, **http://mail.yahoo.com**

These Web-based email services allow you to retrieve your email using a Web browser. They offer several advantages:

∾ Using one of these services you can check your email from any location that has access to the Web—your office, your home, a public computer lab, or a public library.

∾ These services let you check email from one or more POP email servers. This is useful if you have more than one email account or if you change your ISP.

Fy COMPARING EMAIL CLIENTS

If you've got a choice of email clients then you'll want to know what features each client supports and how it would fit your needs. These two Web pages compare features of popular email clients. Note that the first one is published by Qualcomm, the company that supports and markets Eudora.

∾ "Eudora Mail Client—Feature Comparison"
http://eudora.qualcomm.com/pro_email/comparison.html

∾ "It's in the mail: CNET compares the top email clients"
http://www.cnet.com/Content/Reviews/Compare/Emailclients/index.html

∾ If your employer provides you with email you may be able to access these systems without having your email monitored.

You register at one of these sites to get a login name and password. In exchange you give up some information about yourself and advertisements are displayed when you use these services for email.

∾ Take a look at the Web site "Free Web-based Email Services," **http://www.emailaddresses.com/email_web.htm**, for more information and links to several of these services.

Common Features of Email Systems

No matter which email system or program you happen to be using, there are certain features that are common to all modern email systems. Here's a list:

Feature	Comments
Read	Naturally you expect to use the email program to check your mailbox and read messages. Usually you'll be able to choose which message to read from a list of messages. Some email programs can be set to notify you when new mail arrives.
Delete	To delete a message from a list of messages you make a specific request to do so, such as pressing the Delete key. Some email systems keep these deleted messages in a folder named Trash so you can change your mind and recall them. In those cases you'll have to be sure to occasionally delete messages from your Trash—and then they're gone for good!
File	With this feature you can save email in different folders or mailboxes. This helps manage your email.
Print	Sometimes you'll want a hard copy of a message. This lets you send the current message to the printer.
Save	This feature lets you save a message from the mailbox to a file on your computer. This way you can keep messages around without clogging your mailbox.
Compose	Composing a message means writing a message or putting a message together by copying text from other programs. You can expect the email program to include a way to check spelling in the message. Some email programs allow you to use HTML to compose messages.

Attachments	You can include nontext items such as images, data, programs, documents, or spreadsheets with a message.
Signature	This feature automatically adds some information—usually your name, address, phone number and so on—to all outgoing email.
Reply	You use this feature to reply to the current message. Usually the original message is included as part of the reply. Recall the tip for effective email communication that said to only include portions that are pertinent to your reply. You'll be able to choose whether to reply to the sender of the message or to everyone who was on the address list of the message.
Forward	The current message is passed on to another email address. The forwarded mail is email that you send, so at that point your address is used for the return address.
Mark	You'll be able to mark a group of messages so you can apply most of the features above to the group all at once.
Sort	You can sort a list of messages by subject, sender, date sent, and so on.
Address Book	This lets you keep a list of addresses so you don't have to remember them all. You'll also be able to use nicknames or aliases with the addresses, for example **karen** for **khartman@mwc.edu**.
Online Help	This can answer your questions or let you know how to use the features of the email system.

Some mail programs also allow you to encrypt a message and include a digital signature to help protect your privacy, as discussed in Chapter 3.

Email Addresses

The Format of an Internet Email Address

An email address on the Internet usually has the form:

local-address@domain-name

local-address *is often the user's login name, the name given to get in touch with the Internet server*

The character @, called the at sign

The Internet domain name of the computer system that handles the email for the user

Sometimes the domain-name portion is the name of a specific computer, such as **oregano.mwc.edu**. It could be more general, such as **earthlink.net**. In this case the systems at the site **earthlink.net** handle delivering mail to the computer that acts as the incoming mail server for the addressee. The portions or fields making up the domain name are separated by periods (the periods are called dots).

Here's an example:

ernie@paprika.mwc.edu

If you were going to tell someone the address, you would say "ernie at paprika dot mwc dot edu." *Ernie* and *paprika* are pronounced as words, but *mwc* (em double-u see) and *edu* (e dee you) are pronounced as individual letters.

Finding Someone's Email Address

Once you get the bug of communicating by email, you'll probably start to want the email addresses of your friends, and there may be other times you'll want to know someone's email address. There are some methods and services to help find email addresses, but none of them are guaranteed to always give satisfactory results.

The problem with finding someone's email address is that there is no central directory or any central agency that registers each user. Users are added and deleted by individual Internet sites; the decisions are made locally. It might be helpful to have a directory of all Internet users and their email addresses, but such a directory just doesn't exist.

Here are a few ways to find someone's email address:

∾ Call or write (using paper mail) to ask for an email address.

∾ Check for an email address on a resume, a business card, stationery, or a Web page.

∾ Look at the return address in the From:, Return-Path:, or Reply-To: email header.

∾ If you know the school the person attends or an organization with which he or she is affiliated, check the Web page for the school or organization for ways to find the email addresses of students, faculty, or employees.

∾ Try a Web-based "white pages" service to search for an address. Some examples are
  ∾ InfoSpace, **http://www.infospace.com**
  ∾ Switchboard, **http://www.switchboard.com**

∾ Consult some directories for collections or lists of email addresses. One site is "Finding Email Addresses," **http://www.emailaddresses .com/email_find.htm**.

∾ Read and use "FAQ: How to Find People's Email Addresses," **http://www.qucis.queensu.ca/FAQs/email/finding.html**, maintained by David Alex Lamb (**dalamb@cs.queensu.ca**). It contains many resources and tips for finding email addresses.

We cover this topic in more detail in Chapter 10.

Dissecting a Piece of Email—Headers, Message Body, and Signature

A piece of email has three main parts:

1. Headers
2. Message body
3. Signature

Some messages also include other files called attachments. We'll deal with those in a later section.

Headers

Headers are pieces of information that tell you and the email system several important things about a piece of email. Each header has a specific name and a specific purpose. They're all generated and put in the proper form by the email program used to compose the message. Some headers are typed in, and others, such as the date, are entered automatically.

When you read an email message, you're likely to see these common headers:

Subject: The subject of the email

Date: When the email was sent

From: The email address of the sender

To: The email address of the recipient

Message Body

The message body is the content of the email—what you send

WORKING ONLINE AND OFFLINE
Most email systems let you choose whether to work online or offline. That way you can do your work but not have to be connected to the Internet. You go online to get and send messages, and work offline when you're replying to messages or composing new ones.

Initially you connect to the Internet and go online. You contact your mail server and retrieve any messages. Then you disconnect from the Internet. That takes you to offline mode. You can reply to any messages or create new ones in offline mode. The email program will save the messages you'll want to send in a list. When you're ready to send the messages to addresses on the Internet, go to online mode. Give the command to send off the messages you've written and to download any new ones that have arrived.

and what you receive. Most of the time you'll probably be writing email for another human to read, and in that case there aren't any special rules for the format of the message body. Sometimes, though, you may be sending email to a computer system where your message will be interpreted by a computer program. In that case you'll be given instructions to use specific words or phrases in the message body.

Signature

The *signature* isn't a signed name but a sequence of lines, usually giving some information about the person who sent the email. It is made up of anything the user wants to include. Typically, a signature has the full name of the sender and some information about how to contact the sender by email, phone, or fax. A signature is optional, but you'll want to be sure that one is included with professional or business communications. Some signatures also contain a favorite quotation or some graphics created by typing characters from the keyboard. Try to keep yours brief. The longer it is, the more bytes or characters that have to be sent, and so the more traffic to be carried on the Internet. It's fun to be creative and come up with a clever signature, but try to limit it to five lines.

Here's an example:

```
--
Ernest Ackermann            http://www.mwc.edu/ernie
Department of Computer Science   Mary Washington College
Fredericksburg, VA 22401-5358    VOICE 540 - 654 - 1320
ernie@paprika.mwc.edu            FAX   540 - 654 - 1068
```

You don't have to type in the signature each time. The email program automatically appends it to each outgoing message. The way you create a signature may differ from one email program to another. We'll go over the details for setting up a signature with Outlook Express in the section "Setting Mail Options."

Figure 4.1 shows an email message with several of its parts labeled.

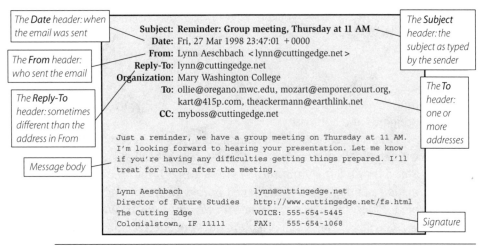

Figure 4.1   An Email Message Dissected

CAN MY COMPUTER GET A VIRUS FROM READING AN EMAIL MESSAGE?
It's not possible to get a computer virus from ordinary text email messages. But it is possible for a virus to be part of an attachment. To protect your computer system don't open any attachment without scanning it first for a virus, and don't use a word-processing or spreadsheet program to read your email, unless you can check it for macro-type viruses.

A computer virus needs to be attached to or part of an executing or running program. This is similar to a biological virus that needs to be part of a living host. We'll see that it's possible to include a program as an attachment to an email message. The program that's been encoded and attached may have a virus that could infect your computer system, but only if you open the attachment or decode the program. The sensible thing to do is to scan any attachment for a virus.

Word-processing programs and spreadsheet programs sometimes allow a document to contain macros, a way of combining several commands, instructions, or steps into one command. The macros are like programs in that they contain a set of instructions that are executed by the computer. Some mischievous and (perhaps) malicious people have found ways to include a virus in a macro. When you open an email using a word-processing program or a spreadsheet program, you run the risk of your computer getting a virus.

Every once in a while a new hoax pops up about a virus being spread by opening or reading an email message. Take a look at the Web site "Computer Virus Myths," **http://kumite.com/myths**, by Rob Rosenberger for more information about these hoaxes. You'll also want to check that page before repeating a message you've received about a virus.

Attachments and Nontext Email

An **attachment** is a file that's sent along with email and is usually viewed separately from the message body. Oftentimes people use attachments to send along other types of files such as ones that contain an image, multimedia, a program, a document written using a word-processing program, or a spreadsheet.

The protocols used to exchange mail between computer systems were originally written to handle only text, so-called **ASCII (American Standard Code for Information Interchange)**, files. Files containing information in other formats are called **binary files**. To send information in binary files, the files have to be **encoded** into ASCII. When the message is received, the attachment holding the encoded file has to be **decoded** from ASCII back to binary.

Many email systems take care of the encoding or decoding, but there are different schemes used. **BinHex** has been used on Macintosh systems; uuencode and uudecode have been typically used on Unix computer systems. Many email programs now handle the encoding and decoding using **MIME (multipurpose Internet mail extensions)** types. MIME is the standard way to work with nontext files as part of email or Usenet articles.

If you're dealing with an email program that doesn't automatically decode attachments then a message containing attachments might look like the following. We show only the first two lines of the encoded image.

```
MIME-Version: 1.0
To: ernie@mwc.edu, lynn@parika.mwc.edu
Subject: Possible cover art

This is a multi-part message in MIME format.
--------------D4B77BA884126A233B3C35E7
Content-Type: text/plain; charset=us-ascii
Content-Transfer-Encoding: 7bit

Hi -
Tom sent me a sample of some of the art FBA is thinking of
using for the cover. It's in the attachment. Let me know your
opinion of it.

Thanks
--------------D4B77BA884126A233B3C35E7
Content-Type: image/jpeg; name="smcover.jpg"
Content-Transfer-Encoding: base64
Content-Disposition: inline; filename="smcover.jpg"

/9j/4AAQSkZJRgABAQAAAQABAAD/2wBDAAMCAgMCAgMEAwMEBQgFBQQEBHBw
DAsKCwsNDhIQDQ4RDgsLEBYQERMUFRUVDA8XGBYUGBIUFRT/2wBDAQBQkFBQ
```

The body of the message is plain text or ASCII

The attachment is an encoded JPEG (Joint Photographic Experts Group) image file

Figure 4.2   An Email with an Encoded Attachment

Adding and Viewing Attachments

When you work with an email program that automatically encodes and decodes binary files, you can sometimes view the attachment when you're viewing the message. If the image can't be viewed or the attachment is a file of another type (a word-processing document, a spreadsheet, a database, or a program), then you'll likely be able to save the file or open an application to work with it. Here's how we sent the image mentioned in Figure 4.2, using Outlook Express.

1. **Compose the message.**

   ∾ If Outlook Express is already started then click on **File** in the menu bar, select **New**, and then select **Mail Message**. You can send email from Internet Explorer too; click on **File** in the menu bar, select **New**, and then select **Message**. In any case a window like the one in Figure 4.3 appears. In Figure 4.3 we've filled in the addresses, the subject, and the body of the message. We've left out the signature to save space here.

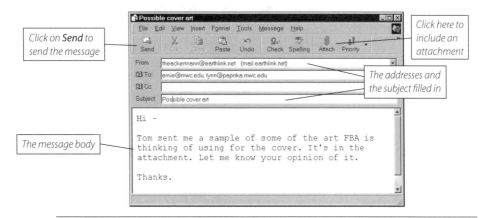

Figure 4.3   Composing a Message

2. **Include the attachment.**

   ∾ Click on **Attach** as shown in Figure 4.3. A menu appears from which we can choose to attach a file.

   ∾ Select the file to attach from the Insert Attachment dialog box shown in Figure 4.4.

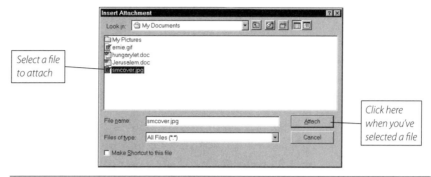

Figure 4.4   The Dialog Box for Selecting an Attachment

3. Send the message.

∾   Click on **Send** as shown in Figure 4.3.

When the message arrives, we can view it by clicking on the entry in Inbox (the folder that holds incoming messages). Figure 4.5 shows a portion of the email when viewed using Outlook Express.

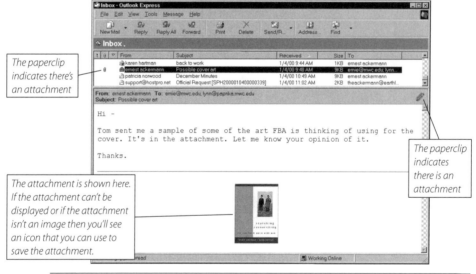

Figure 4.5   An Email Message with a Decoded Attachment

Email with HTML

Some email programs such as Eudora, Outlook Express, and Netscape Messenger can work with messages that contain HTML. They can display a message that's written the same way as a Web page. The service In-Box Direct, **http://form.netscape.com/ibd**, provides ways to get news stories and other types of messages delivered in HTML format.

Outlook Express and other email clients make it relatively easy to compose email that includes HTML. You can choose fonts, colors, and images for your email. We go over some of the details of HTML in Chapter 14. If you choose to send email in that form you need to be sure the person you're sending it to can read email in HTML format. If they can't then they may not be able to read it at all. We only use plain text and attachments for the examples in this book so the messages can be read by anyone.

Using Outlook Express for Email

In this section we'll look at using the email program Outlook Express. It's included with all computer systems that use Microsoft Windows 95/98 or NT as the operating system, and it's included with Microsoft Internet Explorer. You'll find that the commands and procedures are similar to those used with other email programs. Even if you use a different email system, reading through this section lets you learn about some of the features available in an email system. First we'll show the windows used to read and compose email and then cover these topics:

~ Starting Outlook Express

~ Setting Mail Options

~ The Outlook Express Mail Window

~ Reading Email

~ Saving Messages

~ Printing Messages

~ Deleting Messages

~ Composing and Sending Email

~ Replying to a Message

~ Forwarding Email

~ Working with the Address Book

> **Fyi** GETTING HELP
>
> For the first few times you use Outlook Express, you'll want to have the Help window on the screen so you can refer to it quickly. When Outlook Express is started, press the function key **F1** or use the keyboard shortcut **Alt** + **H** and then select **Contents and Index**.

Starting Outlook Express

Outlook Express is software, a program that runs or executes on your computer. It is an email client, or a mail user agent. Its purpose is to make it possible for you to send, receive, and manage Internet email. Outlook Express comes with versions of Microsoft's popular operating systems—Windows 95/98 and NT—that are installed on most microcomputers. It also is included with Microsoft Internet Explorer. There probably is an icon on your desktop for Outlook Express. If so, then double-click on it to start the program. Otherwise click on **Mail** in the toolbar of Internet Explorer and select **Read Mail**.

Setting Mail Options

We discussed setting the crucial email options in Chapter 2. They're crucial in the sense that you won't be able to send or receive mail unless these are set properly. They are:

○ Identity—your name and email address

○ Mail Server—the Internet names or addresses of the incoming and outgoing email servers

You may find that these are set when your computer is set up or when your system is configured by the software provided by your Internet service. If you need a refresher on these options, start Outlook Express, click on **Help** in the menu bar, and select the topic "Getting Started with Outlook Express."

○ If you're using Netscape as your browser and email client then take a look at the excellent tutorial by Key Point Software, "e-mail tutorial," **http://www.keypoint.com/tutorials/email/index.htm**.

○ If you're using Eudora then take a look at the tutorials at the Web page "Eudora Pro Online Tutorials," **http://www.eudora.com/techsupport/tutorials**.

○ If you're using some other email client then check its documentation and help information.

We'll go over setting a few options here that relate to sending and receiving messages, composing messages, and including a signature file. These and other options are set by selecting options from a collection of panels. Here's how to do it:

○ Click on **Tools** in the Outlook Express menu bar and select **Options**.

This brings up the collection of panels shown in Figure 4.6. We'll first cover the general options, then go to the ones for composing email, and then go to the one that deals with signatures. You can see there are others. Use the online help to work through them if you'd like to try changing options.

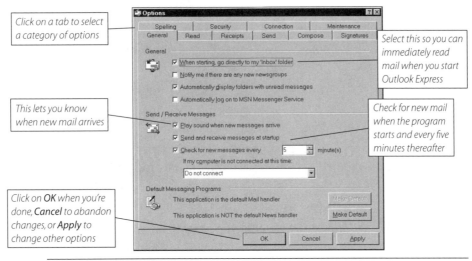

Click on a tab to select a category of options

Select this so you can immediately read mail when you start Outlook Express

This lets you know when new mail arrives

Check for new mail when the program starts and every five minutes thereafter

*Click on **OK** when you're done, **Cancel** to abandon changes, or **Apply** to change other options*

Figure 4.6   General Options

If options are set as shown in Figure 4.6 then:

∿ we'll be ready to read email when Outlook Express starts,

∿ a sound is played (a short beep) when new mail arrives,

∿ the POP or IMAP server is checked for new messages when Outlook Express starts and will be checked for new messages every five minutes, and

∿ we won't be automatically connected to the Internet when we start this email client.

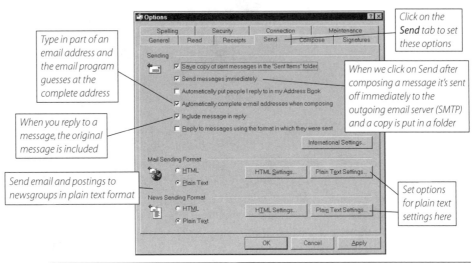

*Click on the **Send** tab to set these options*

Type in part of an email address and the email program guesses at the complete address

When we click on Send after composing a message it's sent off immediately to the outgoing email server (SMTP) and a copy is put in a folder

When you reply to a message, the original message is included

Send email and postings to newsgroups in plain text format

Set options for plain text settings here

Figure 4.7   Send Options

Setting the send options as we have in Figure 4.7 has the following effects:

∿ Email is automatically sent to the outgoing (SMTP) mail server to be delivered through the Internet.

∿ A copy of each message is saved in the folder named Sent Items.

∿ This program will try to automatically complete email addresses based on addresses in the address book.

∿ A copy of the original message is automatically included when you reply, though you'll only want to include the parts that are pertinent to your reply.

∿ Email messages and newsgroups postings are composed as plain text.

We set the format for outgoing messages to plain text. This doesn't allow us anything fancy, but it does guarantee that our messages will be readable by anyone and compatible with other email systems. When we need to send fancier email, we can change these settings.

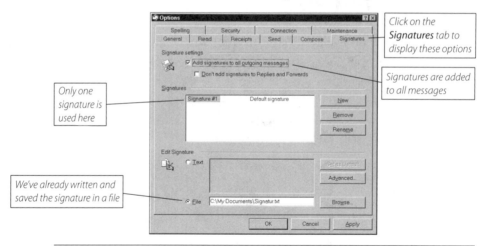

Figure 4.8   Signature Options

We set the signature option to add a signature to all outgoing email. Signatures were discussed earlier in this chapter. One signature is specified here. Some folks have more than one, for example, one for informal email and another for professional communications. The signature is in the file we've specified. The signature is kept in a text file and can be created using the simple text editor Notepad that's included with computers that use Microsoft Windows. Here's how:

∿ Click on **Start**, then **Run**.

∿ Type **Notepad** in the dialog box that pops up and press [**Enter**].

∿ A Notepad window opens. Type what you'd like for your email signature.

∿ Save to a file named **Signatur.txt** in the folder **My Documents** or in some other folder where you will remember where it is.

The Outlook Express Mail Window

Figure 4.9 shows an example of an Outlook Express mail window. We'll go over its major features.

Essential Points About the Mail Window

∿ As in other windows, there is a menu bar with pulldown menus and a toolbar.

∿ The top portion (called a frame) of the window contains information about your messages. It holds a list of the messages in the current folder.

∿ The bottom frame holds the current message, the one highlighted in the upper frame.

∿ Click on any message to read it.

∿ In the drop-down folder list, click on a folder to select it and get another list of messages.

∿ Once a message is open for reading you can print it, delete it, or save it to a different folder.

∿ You send a reply by clicking on the button labeled **Reply**, or forward the message to another Internet address by clicking on the button **Forward**.

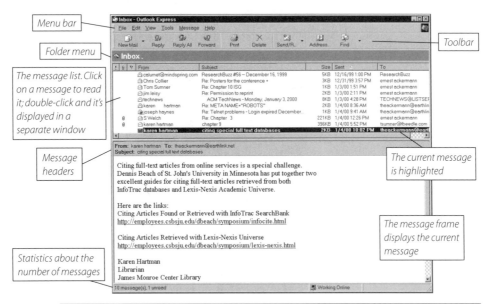

Figure 4.9   The Outlook Express Mail Window

Notice the window is divided into two frames—one for the list of messages and one to display a message. Each of these can have its own scroll bar, and you can move through one independent of the others. This display arrangement or layout can be changed—click on **View** in the menu bar and select **Layout** to put the messages and the message list side by side, for example. It may be different on the computer you use, but don't be confused. We discuss some of the common elements here.

Menu Bar

Each entry in the menu bar represents a pulldown menu with access to the email program's features. We'll describe what you can find on the menus here.

File
- Create a new message.
- Save the current message or attachment.
- Work with your mail folders—open, create, rename, delete, or compact a folder. Compacting means permanently removing any messages that have been deleted from a folder.
- Print the current message.
- View the properties of the current message.
- Go to offline mode from online mode or vice versa.
- Close the mail window and end the mail session.

Edit
- Copy a selection from the message frame to the clipboard so it can be pasted into another application.
- Delete a message.
- Move or copy the selected message(s) to another folder.
- Search for specific text within the current message, all messages, or address directories.
- Mark a message as read or unread.

View
- Set options for which messages are displayed, for example, only unread messages, and for the layout of the message list and the message view. These options deal with how the list of messages in a folder and individual messages are displayed.
- Sort messages in ascending or descending order by a variety of criteria including date, subject, or sender.
- Set the size of the display text.
- Go to the next or previous message, or go to the next folder. You can also specify to go to the next unread message.

Tools	∾	Send and receive messages in case you've been working offline.
	∾	Synchronize folders on your PC and those on the mail server. Do this before going to offline mode.
	∾	Access the address book.
	∾	Set message rules or filters. These rules can help process email automatically. For example, all incoming mail from a specified address or with a certain Subject header can be put into a folder.
	∾	Set up and manage accounts for different incoming or outgoing servers.
	∾	Go to the Options panels to set other options.
Message	∾	Compose a new message.
	∾	Reply to or forward the current message.
	∾	Create a rule from the current message. Create a specific rule for the sender of the current message. This creates a rule that automatically moves any incoming mail from the sender to the deleted mail list.
	∾	Mark or flag the current message.
Help	∾	Access online help.

Toolbar

The toolbar is a sequence of items that you click on to perform an indicated action. We'll discuss them by listing the labels.

New Mail	Compose a new message as plain text or using HTML. You can also use this to send a Web page.
Reply	Compose a reply to the sender of the current message.
Reply All	Compose a reply to the sender. The reply is also sent to everyone else to whom the original message was addressed.
Forward	Forward the selected message(s) to another Internet address. A new message window opens with the Subject header filled in. You supply the address and anything else you'd like to say, and the original message is sent along.
Print	Print the current message.

Delete	Move the selected message(s) to the deleted messages folder.
Send/Receive	Send or receive messages. Use this if you've been working offline.
Address	Access the address book to find, change, add, or delete an entry.
Find	Search for specific text within the current message, all messages, or address directories.

Folders, the List of Messages, and the Message Display

Folders	◦ The drop-down list of folders in the upper-left portion of the email window holds a list of folders or mailboxes. Select one by clicking on its name. You can create folders for saved messages by clicking on **File** in the menu bar and selecting **Folder**.
	◦ Folders help you organize the messages you've received if, for example, you get a number of messages on a topic or from the same person. You can go through a folder replying to, deleting, printing, or forwarding the messages.
	◦ Three folders will usually be present: **Inbox**, messages you've received but haven't put into any other folder; **Sent Items**, copies of the messages you've sent; and **Deleted Items**, copies of messages you've deleted.
Message List	◦ The Messages frame shows a list of the email messages in the current folder. The list is arranged either by date, subject, or sender.
	◦ The headings along the top of the panel are Subject, Sender, and Date. Others may be added. Messages that haven't been read appear in bold with a closed envelope icon. Ones that have been read appear in plain font. The icon for a message that's been replied to is marked with a red arrow. A paperclip icon appears in front of messages that have attachments. When a message is sent it can be marked with a priority, such as

urgent, and any priority markings are listed here. You may mark a message with a flag, perhaps as a reminder to go back and read it. Clicking on a message in the list displays it in the message display area.

~ Using the vertical scroll bar in this pane lets you scroll through the list. If all the headers don't show, or the listing seems cramped, change the size of the mail window.

Message Display Area

~ Email messages are displayed in the bottom pane of the mail window in the message display area.

~ To see a message, click on it in the message list or use **Next** in the toolbar.

~ A message is displayed with headers followed by the body of the message. Click in the message frame to use the scroll bars and arrow keys to go through the message.

~ Attachments are displayed if they are a file type that can be dealt with. If an attachment can't be viewed this way, it's displayed as an icon. Clicking on the icon lets you save the attachment or open it with an application. Remember to scan attachments for viruses!

Reading Email

Reading email is relatively easy. In most cases you just start the mail program and select which messages to read. We'll go over how you can read your email in Example 4.1.

A note about examples. Many of the chapters in this book include activities and examples. Both are meant to help you learn concepts and to demonstrate techniques. Activities show you a sequence of steps you can follow exactly and get the same or similar results as those shown in the text. Examples, such as the ones in this chapter, use situations that can't easily be duplicated. They show the steps you need to follow, but you will not be able to get the same results. You need to use examples as guides and apply the concepts to your situation.

OPENING THE MAIL WINDOW, READING A MESSAGE, AND CLOSING MAIL

Overview

You open the mail window by either starting Outlook Express on its own or starting it through the browser. If necessary, give your email password; type it in the dialog box that appears on the screen. If there's email waiting for you on your mail server, it will be delivered to you and listed in the message list. If there is no new mail, you can select a message from the message list. We'll follow these steps:

1. Open the mail window.
2. Read the email.
3. Close the mail window.

Details

1. Open the mail window.

 If there is an Outlook Express icon on your desktop, Outlook Express, then double-click on it to start the program. Otherwise click on **Mail** in the toolbar of Internet Explorer and select **Read Mail**.

Opening the mail window checks for new mail, lists your messages, and displays a new message. The current message is highlighted as shown in Figure 4.9.

Inbox is the folder that's currently open. To see the messages in another folder, click on the drop-down folder list and select a folder from the list. (You'll see later how to save messages in folders.) The current message is displayed in the message display area.

2. Read the email.

Try these steps with your email system or think about following these steps with a mail window like the one shown in Figure 4.9.

 To read any message, click on its entry in the message list.

 To read the next message in the list, press the down-arrow key. To read the previous message in the list, press the up-arrow key.

Viewing or reading a message shows it in the bottom pane. As you're reading your messages, new messages might arrive for you. You check the incoming server for them by clicking on **Send and Receive All** in the toolbar. If there is any new email, it's delivered and added to the message list.

When you're done working with your mail, you may want to close the mail window.

3. Close the mail window.

   Click on **File** in the menu bar and select **Exit** to close the mail window.

END OF EXAMPLE 4.1

In Example 4.1 we went through the basic steps to follow to read your email. Now we'll discuss saving email messages.

Saving Messages

Saving a Message in a File

To save an email message in a file, go to the message list and

〰 highlight the entry for the message you want to save by clicking on it.

〰 click on **File** on the menu bar and select **Save As**, or press **Ctrl** + **S**.

〰 in the Save As dialog box, type in the name of the file to hold the message. If you pick a name that already exists, you'll be asked if you really want to replace it with the message you're going to save.

Saving a message to a file is useful if you're going to use the body of the message with some other program. Suppose, for example, your partner sends you a copy of a project she's working on that you'd like to include in a presentation. You might want to save it in a file and then import or copy it into the presentation.

Saving a Message in a Folder

Saving email in folders is a convenient way to organize your email. Since you create the folders, you may want to have some that deal with a specific topic or project and others that hold the email you've received from one person. You can go through a folder to reply to, delete, print, and forward messages.

〰 To create a folder, click on **File** on the menu bar and select the item **New Folder**. A dialog box pops up and you type in the name of the folder. You can create the folder as a folder inside the current one, or at or above the same level of the current folder.

〰 To save a message into a folder, go to the message list and highlight the message you want to save by clicking on it. More than one message can be saved into a folder by highlighting a group of messages. Now click on **Edit** on the menu bar, and then choose either **Move to Folder** or **Copy to Folder**. Choosing either one brings up a menu from which you choose the folder you want to hold the message(s).

Printing Messages

∾ To print a message, select it by clicking on its entry in the message list and then click on **Print** in the toolbar.

Printing is allowed only if an entry is highlighted. A window pops up, the same one you see when printing from any Windows application. You can select a printer, set options (if necessary), and finally click on the button **OK** or **Cancel**.

Deleting Messages

Deleting messages is easy and necessary to keep the amount of email in the Inbox and other folders under control. Highlight the entries in the message list of one or several messages and press the icon labeled **Delete** or press the ⌨Delete key on the keyboard. Deleting a message sends it to the folder **Deleted Items**. You can go into that folder to reclaim a message, in case you delete one by mistake. Deleting a message from the folder **Deleted Items** removes it permanently.

∾ You can delete messages from the **Inbox** or any other folder. You probably face some limit on the amount of space you're allowed so think about deleting messages regularly. Do a little more than think about it—delete some messages.

The next example goes through the steps to create a folder, save messages to a folder, and delete some messages.

> **HIGHLIGHTING OR SELECTING SEVERAL MESSAGES**
>
> To select more than one message from the message list:
>
> ∾ First select one message by clicking on it.
> ∾ Move the mouse pointer to another message, but don't click yet.
> ∾ To select all the messages including the first one marked up to and including the message at the mouse pointer, press Shift and click.
> ∾ To select the message at the pointer and the first message highlighted press Ctrl and click. If others are highlighted, the one at the mouse pointer will be added to the group.

Example 4.2

CREATING A FOLDER AND SAVING AND DELETING EMAIL

Overview

In this example we'll save email into a new folder and then delete some messages. We'll follow these steps after starting Internet Explorer:

1. Open the mail window.

2. Create a new folder.
3. Move several messages to the new folder.
4. Delete several messages.

Details

1. Open the mail window.

(*Do it!*)   Click on **Mail** in the toolbar and choose **Read Mail**.

Suppose that after we open the mail window and check for new email we see the mail window as shown in Figure 4.10.

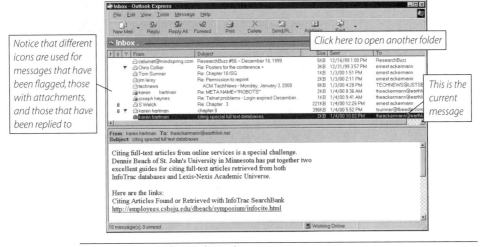

Notice that different icons are used for messages that have been flagged, those with attachments, and those that have been replied to

Click here to open another folder

This is the current message

Figure 4.10   The Mail Window

2. Create a new folder.

We've got several messages from Karen Hartman and we're going to save them into a folder named **Karen Hartman**.

(*Do it!*)   Click on **File** in the menu bar, choose **Folder**, and then select **New**.

A dialog box pops up in which you type the name of the folder.

(*Do it!*)   Type **Karen Hartman** and click on the **OK** button.

A folder named **Karen Hartman** is created. If after we put messages in the folder we want to read the messages we can click on the drop-down menu of folders to read what's there.

3. Move several messages to the new folder.

Now that the folder is created we can mark several messages from Karen Hartman and move them into the folder.

(*Do it!*)   Click on the entry for the first message from Karen Hartman in the message list.

(Do it!) Move the mouse pointer to the second entry from Karen Hartman in the message list, press **Ctrl**, and press the (left) mouse button.

Continue this process until all the messages from Karen Hartman are highlighted. Figure 4.11 shows the messages highlighted.

Messages from Karen Hartman are highlighted

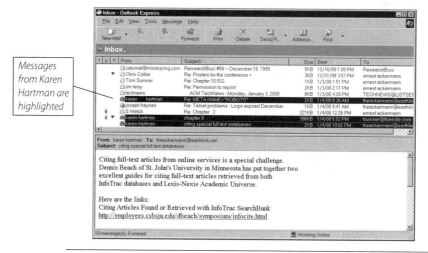

Figure 4.11   The Mail Window After Highlighting Messages

Now we're ready to move the messages to the **Karen Hartman** folder. This will take them out of **Inbox**. We can save other messages from Karen, if she ever writes to us again, in the same folder.

(Do it!) Click on **Edit** on the menu bar and then choose **Move to Folder**.

Another menu appears listing the names of the folders.

(Do it!) Click on **Karen Hartman**.

The messages will be copied to the folder named **Karen Hartman** and then removed from the folder named **Inbox**.

4. Delete several messages.

To demonstrate how to mark a range of messages and delete them, we'll delete three messages from **Inbox**. We show the messages marked in Figure 4.12.

(Do it!) Click on the message from Tom Sumner.

(Do it!) Move the mouse pointer down two messages, but don't click.

(Do it!) Press **Shift** on the keyboard and click the left mouse button.

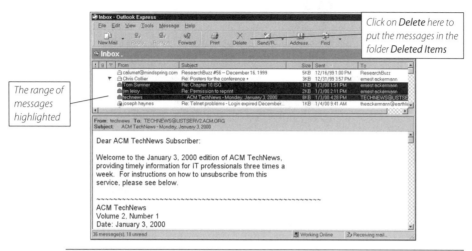

Click on **Delete** here to put the messages in the folder **Deleted Items**

The range of messages highlighted

Figure 4.12   A Range of Messages Highlighted

To delete the messages we need to click on **Delete**.

Click on **Delete** in the toolbar.

This moves them to the folder **Deleted Items**. At some point you'll want to delete them from **Deleted Items** as well. You do that by clicking on **Edit** in the menu bar and selecting **Empty 'Deleted Items' Folder**.

Items deleted from a folder still occupy some space in a folder. This is so it's easier to restore them if necessary. To free up the space and really remove them from a folder, you need to compress or compact the folder. This is common in email programs. To do that, click on **File** in the menu bar, select **Folder**, and then select **Compact** (to compact the current folder) or **Compact all folders**.

END OF EXAMPLE 4.2

Composing and Sending Email

Clicking on **New Mail** in the toolbar of Outlook Express opens a window called the mail composition window, as shown in Figure 4.13 below. It too has a menu bar and a toolbar. You can also open this while you're using Internet Explorer by clicking on **File** in the menu bar, selecting **New**, and then selecting **Message**. You do the same if you're using Netscape Navigator.

Essential Points About the Message Composition Window

○ Once the window (called the Mail Composition Window) is active, you can compose or write a message.

      Ω Position the cursor in the bottom frame with the mouse and start typing.

      Ω Fill in the address (**Send To**) and subject, and send off when you're ready.

      Ω Commands to fill in and modify the panes in the window are available through the pull-down menus in the menu bar items in the toolbar.

Figure 4.13 shows a message that is ready to send. It's addressed to several people. The header **Cc** is used to send a copy of the message to an Internet address. The text in the message body was typed directly into the message using the keyboard. We discussed attaching files in the section "Attachments and Nontext Email" of this chapter.

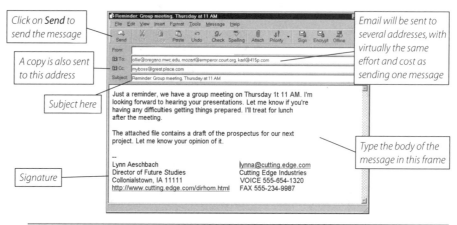

Figure 4.13   Composing Email—A Complete Message

Composing the Message Body

      Ω Type your message into the message body or compose the message using tools or programs with which you're comfortable.

      Ω You can copy text from another Windows application or a Web page. Any text on the clipboard can be pasted into the mail message. To copy and paste between applications click on **Edit** on the menu bar and select the appropriate action.

      Ω Whether you type your message, include something from another application, or a combination of these, the email program will take care of formatting the text. Type or copy the message and press ⌷**Enter**⌷ at the end of a paragraph.

      Ω Click on **Spell** to check the spelling in the message before sending it out!

Including HTML

∾ To use HTML to compose a message click on **Format** in the menu bar and select **Rich Text (HTML)**.

Replying to a Message

You reply to the current message by clicking on **Reply**. You do this while you're reading a message or by clicking on its entry in the message list.

∾ Click on **Reply** to bring up a mail composition window just like the one for a new message. In this case the **To** address is automatically filled with the Internet address taken from the original message.

∾ The **Subject** will be set to **Re:** followed by the subject of the original message. If the address list in the original message includes several people you can send a reply to everyone on the **To** or **Cc** list by pressing the icon labeled **Reply All**. *Be sure you don't send something to a group that you'd like to send to an individual.*

∾ The options are set to include the original message. It's a good idea to include the original message so your reply can be read in context. You'll have to edit the message to include only the important portions.

Figure 4.14 shows what a user would see if he started a reply to everyone who received the email in Figure 4.13.

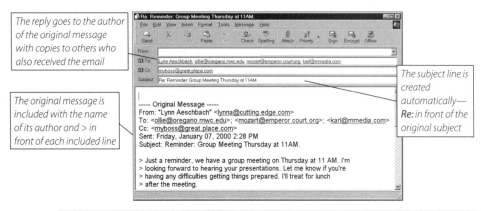

The reply goes to the author of the original message with copies to others who also received the email

The original message is included with the name of its author and > in front of each included line

The subject line is created automatically—Re: in front of the original subject

Figure 4.14   Replying to All Recipients and Including the Original Message

∾ Type/compose your reply, deleting lines from the original and including your own as you see fit.

∾ Use the arrow keys or the mouse to move the cursor to wherever you want to type.

∾ Use the mouse to highlight a portion of the text and then the items in the Edit menu to copy, cut, or paste a portion of the message.

∿ When the message is complete, you can send it off by clicking on the icon labeled **Send**.

Forwarding Email

Forwarding email means passing the email you've received on to another address. Do this by highlighting one or more entries in the message list and then clicking on the icon labeled **Forward**.

∿ When you select a message to be forwarded, a message composition window pops up.

∿ The Subject header is filled in with **Fw:** ***Subject of the original message*** and the message being forwarded is included as an attachment. Any attachments to the original message are also included with the forwarded message.

∿ You can include anything you'd like in the body of the forwarded email.

Working with the Address Book

Outlook Express includes an integrated address book. It's a good place to keep frequently used addresses. That way you won't have to remember people's addresses or save messages just because you need someone's address.

∿ You give each address a nickname or shortened form that you can use when you're composing or replying to a message.

∿ Several addresses can be grouped together so you can send email to all members of a group or organization simultaneously.

∿ When you're using the mail composition window, clicking on the icon next to the header **To** or **Cc** opens a copy of the address book so you can select an address for the **To**, **Cc**, or **Bcc** header. (**Bcc** is like **Cc**. A copy of the message is sent, but none of the recipients—except for the ones listed under **Bcc**—know a copy is being sent.)

Adding Addresses

You can add addresses by typing them in or having the program take them directly from a message.

∿ To take an address from the current message, click on **Tools** on the menu bar and then choose **Add Sender to Address Book**. Outlook Express fills in the name and email address by taking them from the appropriate headers in the message.

∿ To add a nickname or other information to the entry in the address book click on **Address** in the menu bar of the mail window, right-click on the name in the address book, and select **Properties**. A window with several panels pops up. Figure 4.15 shows this window with the **Name** panel selected. Edit the entries to suit your needs.

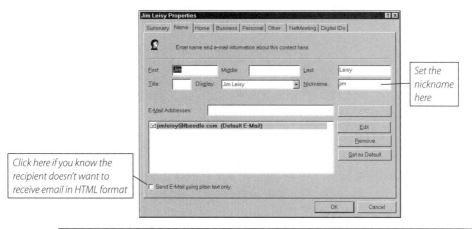

Set the nickname here

Click here if you know the recipient doesn't want to receive email in HTML format

Figure 4.15   Properties for an Entry in the Address Book

∾ To add an address manually, click on **Address** in the menu bar of the mail window. Once the address book is open, click on **New** on its toolbar. A window similar to the one shown in Figure 4.15 will pop up. You can then add the appropriate information.

After you've added information in the panels of the properties window, click on the button labeled **OK** to save it in the address book. You can change the information for an entry at any time by opening the address book, right-clicking on the entry, and then choosing **Properties**. Figure 4.16 shows an address book.

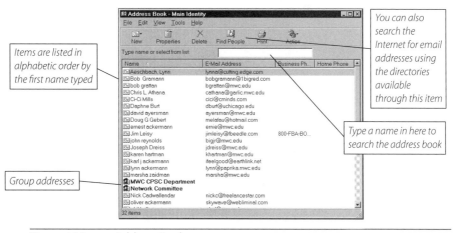

Items are listed in alphabetic order by the first name typed

Group addresses

You can also search the Internet for email addresses using the directories available through this item

Type a name in here to search the address book

Figure 4.16   Address Book

Working with a Mailing List or Group Address

You can create a mailing list, a list of addresses associated with a single name, that lets you send one email message to a group. This is particularly useful if you regularly need to send or share email with several people.

∿ To create a new group, first open the address book, click on **New** in the address book toolbar, and choose **New Group**. A window appears similar to the one shown in Figure 4.17. Type in the name of the group.

∿ To add items to the group either type them in or select them from the list of current addresses.

Figure 4.17 shows a completed entry for a group address. After you fill in the information, an icon—with the name you typed for it—will appear in the address book.

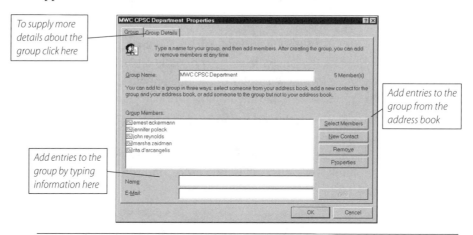

Figure 4.17   A Completed Entry for a Group Address

∿ To add names, open the address book and double-click on the group name.

Deleting Addresses

Addresses can be deleted from the address book by first opening the address book, then highlighting an address (clicking on it once), and finally pressing the **Delete** key. Addresses used in mailing lists are aliases or copies of addresses from the list of individuals. Deleting one that's part of a list removes only that copy of it. Deleting a name from the list of individuals removes the name completely from the book, including from all lists in which it appears.

Using Addresses

You use the nickname you've assigned to an address when you want to send, reply to, or forward email to it. The address will be looked up in the address book. Nicknames are useful with names you'll be using frequently. But you don't have to remember them. Whenever you're composing a message, click on the icon labeled **Address** to get the address book displayed on the screen. Then double-click on the name you want to use and you're set.

Summary

Electronic mail allows users on the Internet to communicate with each other electronically. Using the email program with Netscape Communicator, you can compose messages and then send them to any other Internet address. You can read the messages you've received, save them to a file, print them, or delete them. You can also reply to a message or forward one to another Internet address. There are several other email clients available and other ways to work with email on the Internet.

An email message consists of three main parts: the headers, which contain information about the address of the sender, the address of the recipient, when the message was sent, and other items; the message body, which holds the text portion of the email; and an optional signature, which holds information about the sender such as full name, mailing address, phone number, etc. The signature, which should be limited to four or five lines, is put into a file that can be automatically included with each message.

In order to send email, you give the Internet address of the recipient, compose or write the message, and then give a command to send it on its way. The message is broken up into packets, each containing the address of the sender and the address of the recipient, and the packets are routed through several sites on the Internet to the destination. The computer systems on the Internet handle the transmission and delivery of the email. Once email arrives at a site, it's put into a system mailbox for an individual user. The user can read the email on the system by using an email program like the one available with Microsoft Outlook Express.

Email is a convenient and efficient means of communication. However, most communication is done by the text of messages, so you have to be considerate and careful to communicate effectively, without misunderstandings. Since you probably have a limited amount of space for your email, be sure to get rid of unwanted or unnecessary email and also be sure to send concise, appropriate messages to others. Email isn't necessarily private. Because it's transmitted electronically, there are several opportunities for someone to read your messages. It's relatively easy to forward copies of email so a message sent to one person can be easily transmitted to others.

Email or Internet addresses usually have the form of **local-name@domain-name**. *Local-name* is often the login or user name of the person receiving the email, and *domain-name* is the Internet name of the site or computer system receiving the messages. It's possible to send email to addresses on networks not on the Internet. You need to know the proper form of an address to communicate with users on these networks.

Finding someone's email address isn't always easy. There is no central directory keeping a list of the email address for everyone on the Internet. If you want to find someone's address, one of the best things to do is to call or write that person and ask for the email address. There are a number of automated services to use to search for an email address.

The email program Outlook Express was discussed in this chapter. It's a full-featured email program. You need to set some preferences before using it. Messages can be saved into folders, and can include text and other types (images, sounds, programs, spreadsheets, word-processing documents, Web pages, etc.) of items as part of the message or as attachments. The program includes an address book. Reading and managing email is done in the mail window, and you compose email in a message composition window. Online help is available.

Selected Terms Used in This Chapter

American Standard Code for
   Information Interchange
   (ASCII)
attachment
binary file
BinHex
decoded
email client
encoded

Internet Message Address
   Protocol (IMAP)
mail user agent
multipurpose Internet mail
   extensions (MIME)
Post Office Protocol (POP)
signature
Simple Mail Transfer Protocol
   (SMTP)

Exercises and Projects
Your Email

1. What is your email address? What is the email address of someone at your site to contact if you have questions or problems?

2. What is the name of the SMTP server for your email? Do you use a POP server? What's its Internet address or name?

3. Is there a quota or limit on your email? What is it?

Using Email

4. Send email to yourself with a reminder about something you need to do in the next few days.

5. Read your email. Reply to at least one message. Delete two messages and forward one message.

6. Send a message, using multiple addresses, to at least three other people.

7. Using your email program, save a message to a folder and print the same message.

8. Create a signature for yourself and test it by sending yourself a short message.

9. Do the following:
   a. Find a picture of Salvador Dali on the Internet and send it as an attachment to an email message.
   b. Find an image of a piece of work by Salvador Dali on the Internet and send it as an attachment to an email message.

10. Learn how to create a filter or rule for your email system. For each of the parts below, send yourself a message with the subject "testing filters" to demonstrate that you've completed the exercise.
    a. Create a filter or rule that automatically puts all email with the subject "testing filters" in the **Deleted Items** or **Trash** folder.
    b. Create a folder named **testing** and create a filter or rule that automatically puts all incoming messages with the subject "testing filters" in the folder named **testing**.

Free Email

11. Consider the policies of free email systems.
    a. Go to the home page for Hotmail, **http://www.hotmail.com**, and click on "Who Should Sign up?" What does that page tell you?
    b. You'll find a link to Hotmail's privacy policy on the Hotmail home page. What does the privacy policy tell you about what Hotmail may do with the profile information you supply?
    c. Take a look at Anglefire's terms of service, **http://email.anglefire .com/freemail/Agreement.html**. Under what conditions may it disclose registration information and what is its policy on promotional messages?

12. The Web page "Different Types of Free Email," **http://www .emailaddresses.com/guide_types2.htm**, gives pros and cons of POP email systems and Web-based email systems. Considering your needs, decide whether POP or Web-based email is better for you. Write a paragraph supporting your choice using some of the points made in the Web page.

Finding Email Addresses

13. Use Switchboard, **http://www.switchboard.com**, or InfoSpace, **http://www.infospace.com**, to
   a. search for an email address for an author of this book
   b. search for your own email address or email addresses of people with the same last name as yours
   c. search for the email address of a friend

Spam Myths

14. Suppose you receive an email message that says that you shouldn't open a message with the subject "Happy Times." Go to "Computer Virus Myths," **http://kumite.com/myths**, to determine whether this is a myth. Write down the steps you followed once you accessed that Web site. Write a paragraph or two describing the virus or myth and its history.

Chapter 5

EMAIL

DISCUSSION

GROUPS

*F*an-out: the sending of *one* message to a group and having it *automatically* distributed or made available to *every member* of the group. That's one of the important features of email discussion groups and Usenet newsgroups. They are a great way to share information. There are thousands of these groups, on all sorts of topics. Some groups have just a few participants while others have thousands. Some of the people who participate in the discussions are beginners and others are experts. One person posts a message and others read it and respond to it at a convenient time. Another characteristic of this sort of communication is called "fan-in." That means that an individual in the group receives all the messages sent to the group. One person asks a question, and replies can come from anywhere in the world. We'll discuss email discussion groups in this chapter and Usenet newsgroups in the next.

Email discussion groups are an important resource for finding information, getting answers to questions, and supporting virtual communities. There are just a few things to know about joining and using the services of a group. To take full advantage of the available resources you'll also want to know how to find groups, how to search their archives, and how to behave (rules of etiquette) for these types of group discussion.

Goals/Objectives
- Understand the nature of email discussion groups
- Know what resources are available through these groups
- Learn how to work with email discussion groups
- Understand netiquette issues related to participating in email discussion groups

Topics

- ∾ An Overview
- ∾ Essential Information
- ∾ Details of Working with a Discussion Group
- ∾ Finding the Discussion Groups You'd Like to Join
- ∾ Proper Etiquette and Behavior Within a Group

An Overview

People have been using email since the beginning of the Internet, and those with common interests have formed *email discussion groups*—also called *interest groups, mailing lists,* or *listservs*—based on specific topics. We'll use the terms *discussion group* and *list* to refer to any of these types of groups. These groups foster discussions as individuals compose and post messages, answer questions, and respond to other people's statements.

The groups operate and discuss topics in a truly asynchronous, "any place, any time" manner. When an individual posts or sends a message, it's distributed or made available to the group. The message is delivered through email. Individuals participate at their convenience. They don't have to participate at a fixed time or in the same real or virtual space.

All the advantages, disadvantages, and tips for effective communication that we listed in the previous chapter on email and Internet communication apply here. Take a moment to review them while you're reading and working with this chapter.

Email discussion groups give you valuable resources when you're searching for information on specific topics or seeking answers to questions. Here are a few reasons that these resources are so helpful:

- ∾ The group itself. Replying to messages, giving help, and supplying accurate information when possible are part of Internet culture. Although it's unreasonable to expect group members to do your research for you, the group can be very helpful.

- ∾ The discussions—the messages or articles—are often archived and can be searched and retrieved.

> **BE PREPARED FOR MORE EMAIL**
> If you join a group that has lots of members, you might be flooded with email, so be prepared if you join a popular group or one with lots of messages per day. In some groups or lists you can request that messages arrive in digest format. A digest is one email message that contains several other messages (to cut down on the clutter in your mailbox).

Essential
Information

Email discussion groups are made up of people anywhere on the Internet who agree to communicate, using email, as a group sharing messages related to a certain topic. The group named Gardens, for example, is a group where people use email to discuss aspects of home gardening. Anyone can join or **subscribe** to the group. Usually, discussions are on the main topic, but messages on other topics are tolerated or redirected to other groups.

The communication in these groups is two-way, but each member chooses his or her level of participation. The groups also serve as a means of fostering virtual communities since they are collections of people with an interest in communicating with each other.

When someone types a message and sends it to a group, the message is routed, virtually immediately, through email, to all members of the group. This is what we mean by the term **fan-out**. Anyone on the group can respond to the message, either by replying to the group or sending email to the individual who sent the original message. This is **fan-in**. Responses can come from around the world or next door. Members of the group don't all have to be using their computers at the same time to participate in the discussion.

Table 5.1 lists the essential features and concepts connected with using an email discussion group.

Feature/Concept	Explanation
It's all done by email.	All communication in a discussion group is carried on by email. A user joins or subscribes to a group (the request to join is made by email) and then shares in the discussions of the group. A message sent to the group is broadcast via email to all members of the group, so these discussions are public.
You decide how much you want to participate.	You don't have to respond to every message; you can use your email system just to read or even ignore some of the discussions. It's usually a good idea to only read messages when you first join a group so you can get an idea of the general tone and level of the discussion. Some folks use the term **lurking** to describe the behavior of observing the

discussions. Lurking is just fine; it may be exactly what you want.

A group or list is managed (when everything goes well) by software.

Most of the management of a list, tasks like adding new members or subscribers and removing members who choose to leave (or **unsubscribe** from) a list, is handled automatically by software running on the computer that serves as the host system for the list. Requests for service are handled by commands sent to an email address, called the **administrative address**, which passes the commands on to the software managing the list. Messages to the administrative address are processed by a computer program, so they have to be in a format that follows very strict and specific rules.

There are two addresses associated with a discussion group, the administrative address and the *group address*.

When you're a member of a list you need to know two addresses and you need to know when to use them.

1. **The administrative address.** That's the address you use to join or subscribe to the group. It's used for administrative requests, such as subscribing to the group or getting a list of members.

2. **The group address.** That's the address you use to communicate with the group. Once you've joined the group you send email to the group address and it gets sent to all the other members of the group.

Each group has a name.

The name of a discussion group is usually part of the group address. Here are some examples:

- ∾ **Travel** is the name of a discussion group for open, unmoderated discussion about international travel (the *list address* is **travel@cuy.net**).
- ∾ **C-opera** is the name of a list about contemporary opera and music

theater (the list address is **c-opera@listserv.unb.ca**).

~ **Net-happenings** is a list used for announcing new or changed Web sites and other Internet resources (the list address is **net-happenings@cs.wisc.edu**).

~ **Net-Essentials-L** is the name of one of several lists set up for practicing using a discussion group (the list address is **Net-Essentials-L@listproc.mwc.edu**).

Your messages are public.	Your original message or reply to a message from a group is sent to all members of the group, so think twice about what you write and check your message for spelling and grammar. ~ If you mean to write to an individual in the group then be sure to address your message to that person.
The membership list may be available to everyone in the group.	Some discussion groups make their membership list (names and email addresses) available to any member of the group. Any member can retrieve the list by sending a command to the administrative address.
It's easy to get help.	Send a simple message (HELP) to the administrative address and you'll receive by email a list of all the commands you can use with the list. This works for any type of software managing a list.

Table 5.1   Essential Features and Concepts of Email Discussion Groups

Details of Working with a Discussion Group

How do you join and participate in a group? To put things in context we'll give an overview of working with a discussion group we've set up named **Net-Essentials-L**. We'll use it for examples here and elsewhere in the chapter. Don't worry if some of the terms we use here are unfamiliar. Read on and you'll see they're explained later.

Table 5.2 shows a list of steps you'll likely go through in working with a discussion group.

1. Identify or choose a group.	You'll find out about groups by reading about them on the Internet, getting recommendations from friends, or searching a collection of lists. We'll point out some ways of finding the name and administrative address for a list below.
2. Join the group by sending email to the **administrative address**.	You'll send email to the administrative address with the body of the message having the form subscribe *list-name your-name* The address used to join the group **Net-Essentials-L** is **listproc@listproc.mwc.edu**. Check the section in this chapter that gives the proper form to use for the type of list or group you're working with.
3. Communicate with members of the group by receiving email from and sending email to the **group address**.	The group address for **Net-Essentials-L** is **Net-Essentials-L@listproc.mwc.edu**. If you want to post a question, make a statement, or help someone out, you send email to **Net-Essentials-L@listproc.mwc.edu**.
4. Use services available from the list.	The services available and the ways to access these services will most likely be contained in the reply you get from the administrative address when you join the list. Save that reply since you may need it later. Services include access to a list of members, archives of previous discussions, and so forth.
5. Unsubscribe or leave a group.	To unsubscribe, send email to the administrative address, not to the group address. In most cases, the body of the email message is unsubscribe *list-name your-name* Check the section in this chapter that gives the proper form to use for the type of list or group you're working with.

Table 5.2   Steps in Working with a Discussion Group

The commands you use to join and request some services are often cryptic and have to be stated precisely in a specific format. A computer program, not a human, usually interprets them. Email sent to an administrative address is passed on to a computer program. The program acts as an intelligent agent or helper.

When you join the group you'll get an email message about the commands you'll need to use. For example, it will tell you how to get help and information about other commands.

ti Remember never to send a message to join (subscribe) or leave (sign off) to a group or list address. You use the administrative address for that.

It's easy to make a mistake. If you send a request to the wrong address, a member of the list will usually remind you of the correct address. If you send a message that's passed on to the managing software but was meant for the members of the list, you'll usually get a reply indicating an error.

Be sure to save that email, since it contains important information.

How to Join, Contribute to, and Leave a Discussion Group

In this section we'll go over the commands you use to join and access other services of a discussion group. We already know that you send email to the administrative address for group services. The specific commands depend on the type of software that's used to manage the group. Here we'll concentrate on the most common ones: Listserv, Listproc, and Majordomo.

You can usually tell which software manages the list by looking at the administrative address. For example, if the address is **listproc@coco.great.edu** (a fictitious address), Listproc is being used.

The type of software maintaining the group is chosen when the group is created; it isn't a decision each member can make. When you join the group you'll get information about the commands to use, and you can usually get help from other members of the list.

How to Join a List

To join a list you need to send email to the administrative address for the list. The email should contain the word SUBSCRIBE (usually SUB will do) and the name of the list. For most lists you also need to include your full name (first name and last name). Some versions of Majordomo software don't allow you to include your full name as part of the request to join the list. Be sure to follow the instructions.

Regardless of the type of list, the command to subscribe to the list has to be in a specific format. You're not writing something for another person to read, you're giving a command to some software. Also, you don't have to supply your email address; it's passed along automatically to the administrative address. The software that manages the list takes your name and address and adds them to the list of members.

What Happens Next?

You'll receive a response from the software managing the list within a few minutes or hours. That is, of course, provided you've used the proper address and the list still exists.

In some cases you'll be asked to confirm your request to subscribe, but in many cases you'll receive an immediate email message welcoming you to the list. **Save the welcome message!** It usually contains important information about communicating with the group and how to get help and more information. You might need to know about commands to leave the group and to request other services from the software that manages the list. Once again, **save that message!** You'll probably need it in the future.

Figure 5.1 is an excerpt from a sample welcome message. The message is from Listproc and is for **Net-Essentials-L**.

A DESCRIPTION OF THE LIST NET-ESSENTIALS-L

List name:
Net-Essentials-L
Administrative address:
listproc@listproc.mwc.edu
Group address:
Net-Essentials-L@listproc.mwc.edu
Brief description:
Discussions related to the topics, activities, exercises, and projects in the book *Internet and Web Essentials* by Ackermann & Hartman
To join:
Send email to Listproc@Listproc. mwc.edu with the message subscribe Net-Essentials-L *your-full-name*
For example:
subscribe Net-Essentials-L Chris Athana

---

tip BE PERSISTENT!

It's easy to make a mistake when you're beginning to work with email discussion groups. Sometimes you'll send a message to the wrong address or in an improper form. It seems that these things happen to everyone. If a message doesn't go through or you get email that your message wasn't in the proper form, try again.

```
Subject: SUBSCRIBE NET-ESSENTIALS-L KAREN HARTMAN
Date: Tue, 4 May 1998 08:25:56 -0400
From: listproc@listproc.mwc.edu
To: khartman@mwc.edu

You have been added to list net-essentials-
l@listproc.mwc.edu. The system has recorded your address
as
                        khartman@mwc.edu
and in order for your messages to get posted (if the list
accepts postings), you will have to send them from this
address, unless the list does not require subscription
for posting.
If a message is ever rejected, please contact the list's
owner:

    ernie@paprika.mwc.edu

To post messages, simply send normal email to
net-essentials-l@listproc.mwc.edu. Your message will
automatically be forwarded to other members of the list.

For information on this service and how to use it, send
the following request in the body of a mail message to
listproc@listproc.mwc.edu:
                        HELP

All requests should be addressed to
listproc@listproc.mwc.edu.
```

The address of the list owner, the person responsible for the group

The group address. Send email here to communicate with other members.

Administrative address

Figure 5.1   A Welcome Message from Listproc—Very Important!

How to Communicate with and Contribute to an Email Discussion Group

∾ Any message that you want to go to all the members of the group should be sent to the group address. Email that's sent to the group address is either sent to all members of the group or sent to a moderator who decides whether to distribute the message to the rest of the group.

∾ Remember, don't send email meant for the members of the group to the administrative address.

∾ Write to the owner or moderator when you have questions about the nature of the group, if you think something is wrong with the list's operation, or to volunteer to help the moderator. If you're having technical problems first try to solve them yourself. You'll probably get the moderator's address with your "welcome to the group" email. We've marked it in Figure 5.1.

~ If you have problems sending or posting a message to a group, try posting a message from the address you used to subscribe to the group. Many groups allow you to send a message to the group only from the same address you used to join or subscribe to the group.

Communicate with a Member or the Whole Group?

You can send email either to everyone in the group or to only the one who originated a message. Usually if you use the reply feature of your email program, a message will be sent to the group. You shouldn't respond to the group when you mean to respond to the individual. If you see a message on the group that was obviously meant for an individual, you might want to send a gentle reminder to the person who made the mistake.

How Can You Tell If a Message Came from a Group or from an Individual?

Using reply in the email program would send a message to the group. Look at the email headers Reply-To, From, and To. Each email message carries with it a collection of headers that include information about who would receive a reply (Reply-To), who sent the message (From), and to whom the message was sent (To). If an email message has the header Reply-To, the address after Reply-To is the address your email program uses when you choose the reply option or operation. You find the address of the person who sent the original message by looking at the header From. You can also look at the header To to see if the email was sent to all members of the group or especially to you. Figure 5.2 shows the pertinent information.

```
                                              Using reply in the email
                                              program would send a
    Reply-To: Net-Essentials-L@listproc.mwc.edu    message to the group
Use this    From: cathana@right.here.edu
address     To: Multiple recipients of the list <Net-Essentials-L>
for a
personal    A friend told me about CyberTimes, an online journal or
reply       publication about Internet and Web news. I'd appreciate it
            if someone could tell me the URL or address.

            Thanks in advance,
            Chris Athana
            cathana@right.here.edu
```

Figure 5.2   An Example Message to an Email Group

Here are two responses to this message. The first is the type of response that could properly go to just the individual sending the original message (**cathana@right.here.edu**) or to the entire group. Since the response might benefit everyone on the list, it's appropriate to reply to the group.

```
The URL for CyberTimes is http://www.nytimes.com/yr/mo/
day/cyber/. It's published by the NY Times. Another
source for a similar type of news is Wired News,
http://www.wired.com/news/.
```

The next response should be sent only to the person who sent the original message (**cathana@right.here.edu**), definitely not to the entire group. Chris may appreciate the message, but other members won't.

```
Chris,
How are you? I haven't heard from you in a while. Send
me some email and I'll give you the answers to all
your questions.

J. Richmond - richster@far.away.com
```

Figure 5.3 can help you decide which email address to use for the different types of communication with an email discussion group.

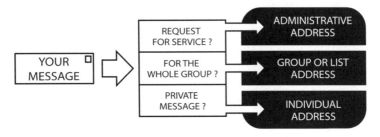

Figure 5.3   Which Address to Use for Discussion Group Messages

Leaving or Unsubscribing from a Group

∾ To leave or unsubscribe from a group, send email to the administrative address. The message needs to have the name of the group you want to leave since several groups may be managed by the same software at a site.

The name of the group is represented by *GROUP-NAME* below. In most cases, you need to send the email message to leave or unsubscribe from the same Internet address you used to join the group. If you have difficulty leaving a group, write to the group owner or moderator.

In the cases of Listserv and Listproc, you send the message:

```
unsubscribe GROUP-NAME
```

You may have to include your email address if Majordomo is being used to manage a list, if you gave it when you joined the group, or if you're leaving from a different address. Send either the message above or

```
unsubscribe LIST-NAME YOUR-CURRENT-EMAIL-ADDRESS
```

For example, the administrative address for the group Net-Essentials-L is **LISTPROC@listproc.mwc.edu**, so to leave you would send the following message to that address:

```
unsubscribe net-essentials-l
```

☙ *Remember:* Send email to the administrative address to unsubscribe from or leave an email group.

Getting Services and Archives from a Discussion Group

All the commands for services are sent by email to the administrative address. That way the software that manages the list may detect the commands. Sending a command to the group generally does nothing except prompt several members of the group to reply with reminders that the commands were sent to the wrong address.

Table 5.3 lists many of the common services available through discussion groups. We name and describe each service and give the corresponding command for each of the major types of software—Listserv, Listproc, and Majordomo—used to manage groups. Remember to send the command in the body of an email message addressed to the administrative address for the group.

Service	Listserv Command	Listproc Command	Majordomo Command
Get a list of all commands	HELP	HELP	HELP
Get a list of group members	REVIEW *Group-Name*	REVIEW *Group-Name*	WHO *Group-Name*
Temporarily suspend messages	SET *Group-Name* NOMAIL	SET *Group-Name* MAIL POSTPONE	Not possible
Resume getting messages	SET *Group-Name* MAIL	SET *Group-Name* MAIL	Not possible
Switch to digest mode; get one message from the group that holds a digest of all other messages. A	SET *Group-Name* MAIL DIGEST	SET *Group-Name* MAIL DIGEST	SUBSCRIBE *Group-Name* DIGEST UNSUBSCRIBE *Group-Name*

digest is sent at specified times, depending on the number of messages sent to the group.			Majordomo requires two commands, both included in the same message.
Find out what's in a group's archives	INDEX *Group-Name*	INDEX *Group-Name*	INDEX *Group-Name*
Retrieve a file from a group's archives	GET *File-Name File-Type Group-Name* For example: GET AOU91 TXT BIRDCHAT	GET *Group-Name File-Name* For example: GET PHOTO-L PHOTO-L.Sep-25	GET *Group-Name File-Name* For example: GET F-COSTUME TOPICS

Table 5.3   Services Available Through Discussion Groups

You'll use the entries in Table 5.3 to help you use the services available from a discussion group. If you want more information about working with these or other types of groups take a look at "Discussion Lists: Mailing List Manager Commands," **http://lawwww.cwru.edu/cwrulaw/faculty/milles/mailser.html**, by James Milles.

Before we leave this section we want to note that access to discussion groups and their archives is becoming available through forms interfaces that are part of Web pages.

∾ Some discussion groups let you join, leave, and use the services of the group through a forms-based Web page. One example is "SF-Lovers Digest," **http://sflovers.rutgers.edu/Digest**.

∾ Archives of discussion groups are usually categorized only by date, so it may be difficult to search the archives for messages related to a specific subject. There is some progress being made in this area. The University of Buffalo, for example, provides a forms-based interface for searching the archives of the groups hosted there. Use the URL **http://listserv.acsu.buffalo.edu/archives** to try this service.

Finding the Discussion Groups You'd Like to Join

There are over 90,000 email discussion groups with more added each day. Because of this large number it is virtually impossible to keep current with the available groups. It's probably more important (and certainly more practical) for you to know how to find the names of groups that focus on a topic you'd like to find out about.

Finding a Group Dealing with a Specific Topic

There are a number of different ways that you can find out about discussion groups you may want to join. You're likely to hear about some groups from the folks you correspond with on the Internet; you'll also see groups mentioned if you read Usenet news; you'll see some mentioned in other things you read; or you can use one of the services available on the Web that are listed in Table 5.4.

When you use these services you type in a keyword or key phrase, and the software searches a database of group names, descriptions, and associated addresses. You'll get the information you need (group name, address for joining the group, address of the group, address of the group owner or moderator, etc.) for the appropriate groups.

Fy MAILING LIST OF THE DAY

TipWorld, **http://www.tipworld .com**, is a service that will send you email once a day about one or several topics. To get email about its mailing list of the day, use the URL to access the site on the Web and select **Email Mailing List of the Day**. Once you fill in your email address and select the email program you use, you'll get a message each day with information about a discussion group. Note that this is a commercial service and the mail you get will contain advertisements.

Name	Brief Description	URL
CataList, the official catalog of LISTSERV lists	Ability to search or browse the database of over 17,000 public groups that use LISTSERV.	**http://www.lsoft.com/ lists/listref.html**
Liszt, the mailing list directory	One of the most extensive resources for finding discussion groups. In addition to searching for a group, you can also browse the directory.	**http://www.liszt.com**
Publicly Accessible Mailing Lists	This Web site, maintained by Stephanie and Peter da Silva, is an authoritative resource for information about email discussion groups. You can search or browse the database.	**http://paml.alastra.com**

Table 5.4   Web Sites for Finding Discussion Groups

Now we'll go through an activity to show how to search for a discussion group and to take a look at the type of information you may find. We'll use Liszt. It's one of the best directories to use.

Remember that the Web is always changing, and there is a possibility that the results you get may differ from those shown here. Don't let this confuse you. These activities demonstrate fundamental skills that don't change, even though the number of results obtained or the actual screens may look very different.

Activity 5.1

FINDING A DISCUSSION GROUP

Overview

One of the most comprehensive collections of discussion groups that has been designed for searching the Web is Liszt, the mailing list directory. The site is relatively easy to use and gives useful information about the discussion groups in its database. We can search by typing one or more keywords into a form. Instructions are readily available through hyperlinks on the home page. A subject guide to selected discussion groups is also on the home page.

We'll follow these steps:

1. Access the home page for Liszt.
2. Search for discussion groups dealing with science fiction.
3. Browse the results to learn about the discussion groups found and how to subscribe.

Details

We assume that the Web browser is already started and is available on the screen.

1. Access the home page for Liszt.

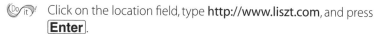 Click on the location field, type **http://www.liszt.com**, and press **Enter**.

Using this URL, we go to the home page for Liszt. A portion of it appears in Figure 5.4. Like other Web or Internet services, Liszt regularly improves or expands its service. The Web pages you see may be different from these, but they will be similar.

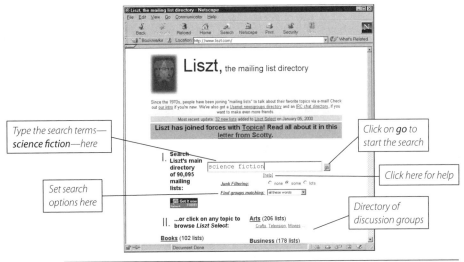

Figure 5.4   The Liszt Home Page

2. Search for discussion groups dealing with science fiction.

Liszt's home page has a place next to the button labeled **go** for you to type keywords. You can also use an asterisk (*) in a word as a wildcard. Click on the hyperlink **help** for complete information about search expressions. Here, we'll type **science fiction**, as shown in Figure 5.4, and click on **go**.

Type **science fiction** in the form and click on the **go** button.

By default, Liszt searches its database for descriptions of discussion groups that contain *all* the terms. A portion of the Web page showing the search results appears in Figure 5.5. Your results may not be exactly the same as these.

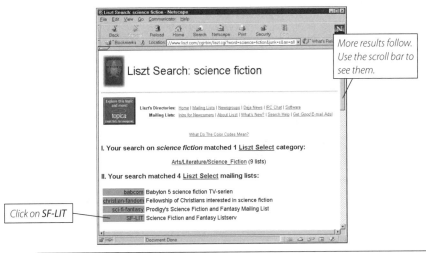

Figure 5.5   Search Results Using "science fiction"

3. Browse the results to learn about the discussion groups found and how to subscribe.

Figure 5.5 shows a portion of the Web page that holds the search results. The results are color-coded, indicating how much information is available. (The system is explained on the Web page.) Clicking on any of the results brings up an intermediate page with links for more information. We will click on **SF-LIT**.

 Click on **SF-LIT**.

Figure 5.6 shows a portion of the page that appears.

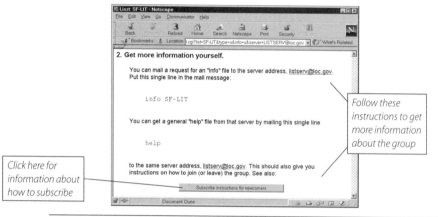

Figure 5.6   A Web Page About the Discussion Group SF-LIT

To get information about the discussion group follow the instructions under the heading "Get more information yourself." You'll have to send a request for information by email to the administrative address. The information you receive usually includes a statement of the list's purpose and the name and email address of the person in charge of the list.

Clicking on the button labeled **Subscribe instructions for newcomers** yields information about subscribing, including the administrative and group addresses for the discussion group.

 Click on **Subscribe instructions for newcomers**.

Figure 5.7 shows a portion of the Web page that tells how to subscribe to the group. Read through the information on the Web page before subscribing to any group. It contains lots of good advice. There's more useful information further down the Web page.

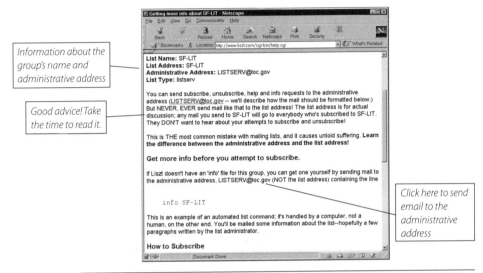

Information about the group's name and administrative address

Good advice! Take the time to read it.

Click here to send email to the administrative address

Figure 5.7   Information About Subscribing to the Discussion Group

You can join the group at this point by clicking on the hyperlink that represents the administrative address. When you have finished with this page, click the **Back** icon in the toolbar to return to the list of discussion groups in Figure 5.5. Look at these lists, or search for more.

END OF ACTIVITY 5.1

Activity 5.1 showed how to use Liszt to search for discussion groups based on a topic. For each group found, we could have retrieved information about the group and ways of subscribing. Liszt has discussion groups or mailing lists arranged into a subject directory. In addition, you can use Liszt to search for Usenet newsgroups. You use the other search services mentioned in this chapter in a similar manner.

Now that we've explained how to use and find discussion groups, it's time to move on to the important issues related to etiquette and behavior in these types of Internet discussions.

INFORMATION ABOUT DISCUSSION GROUPS ON THE WEB

∾ "Email Discussion Groups/Lists and Resources" by Bob and Varda Novick and Impulse Research Corp.
http://www.webcom.com/ impulse/list.html

∾ "Internet Mailing Lists Guides and Resources"
http://www.ifla.org/I/ training/listserv/lists.htm

Proper Etiquette and Behavior Within a Group

Discussion groups and newsgroups are great ways to communicate with people throughout the world or maybe even nearby. Members have discussions, post information, and ask questions. All of this is carried on within a community (the members of the group) sharing a common interest. Most communities have some rules of etiquette or behavior. Table 5.5 lists some tips and guidelines for proper etiquette and behavior. We'll refer to these again in Chapter 6, and add these to the guidelines for etiquette and behavior that we gave in Chapter 3.

Tip/Guideline	Explanation
Spend some time getting to know the group.	When you first join a discussion group, take a little time to see the types of items discussed and the tone of the discussion. Read the articles in a newsgroup before posting. You may also find that the questions you have are currently being answered.
Posting or sending a message to the group is a public act.	Everything you write to the group may be distributed to all group members or posted worldwide through Usenet. If you're working with a group that isn't moderated (most aren't), your messages go directly to the group. Don't embarrass yourself. A friend, relative, or supervisor may also be a member of the group.
Think before you respond to a message.	If someone writes something that upsets you, take a little time to formulate an appropriate, considered response that deals with the issue. Think about the source of the message and take a few minutes or hours before you respond. Don't respond too quickly to something that upsets you, and don't criticize others too hastily or without good reason.
Write easy-to-read messages.	The material you write to the group should be grammatically correct, concise, and thoughtful. If the message must go on for several screens, it's a good idea to summarize it and to invite others to ask you for more information.

Group members are people like you and need to be treated with respect and courtesy.	Respond to messages as if you were talking face to face. A member may be from a different culture, may not be familiar with your language, and may have different views and values from your own. It's better to think before you write than to be sorry afterward.
When responding, include only the pertinent portions of the original message.	Let's say that a group member starts a discussion and writes something about 40 lines long. You want to respond, but only to one portion of it. In your follow-up message, include just the portion that's relevant to your response.
When you ask group members any questions, post a summary of the responses.	With a summary, everyone in the group benefits from the responses to your question. Naturally, this applies only if you get several responses and if the answers to the question are of general interest.
Think about whether a response to a message should go to the group or to an individual.	Messages to the group should be of general interest. They may be requests on your part for advice or for help in solving a problem. You'll know the email address of the person who made the original request, and you can send a response to that person if it's appropriate.
Post test messages to groups designed for testing.	Post messages that test whether you're following proper procedures and if your computer system is properly configured to discussion groups and newsgroups designed for that purpose. To test your hand at email discussion groups use Net-Essentials-L, described earlier in this chapter.

Table 5.5   Tips and Guidelines for Working with a Discussion Group or Newsgroup

Another excellent source for rules of etiquette for discussion groups is the section "LISTSERVS/MAILING LISTS/ DISCUSSION GROUPS" of Arlene Rinaldi's "The Net: User Guidelines and Netiquette," **http://www.fau.edu/rinaldi/net/dis.html**.

Summary

Email discussion groups are examples of asynchronous group communication on the Internet. Group members communicate via email, with messages broadcast to all group members.

Several thousand discussion groups are available and active on the Internet. The email groups may be called mailing lists, discussion groups, Listserv lists, or interest groups. Regardless of the name, each consists of a group of members on the Internet. This way, communities or collections of people can discuss items related to a common topic, find information about the topic, make announcements to the group, and ask questions and receive help from other group members. The large number of groups or lists guarantees a wide range of topics. The groups are particularly useful to people who want to discuss issues with a large or diverse group. The groups extend any resources beyond a local site.

When you communicate with an email discussion group you send messages to the list by using the list address. Commands and requests for service are usually sent to the administrative address. For example, the group SF-LIT, which deals with a variety of topics related to science fiction literature, has **SF-LIT@loc.gov** as the list address and **listserv@loc.gov** as the administrative address. You use this second address to join the group, leave or unsubscribe from the group, request archived files from the group, and get a list of the members of the group. Be sure you use the correct address when you communicate with the group or list. Most lists also have a person designated as the list owner, list administrator, or moderator. That person is in charge of the list, and you send him or her email if you have problems using the list or questions about the operation of the list. Some lists are moderated. Messages sent to the list first go to the moderator, who decides whether to pass the messages on to all group members.

Several "lists of lists" and other documents related to using discussion groups are available as part of the World Wide Web. There are also services on the Web to find discussion groups and to search or retrieve groups' archives.

The email discussion groups can be thought of as communities of people sharing common interests. There are generally accepted rules of behavior or etiquette for list members. These include providing appropriate, thoughtful, and concise messages to a group, providing a summary of the responses received in answer to a question, and communicating with other group members in a civil and respectful manner.

Selected Terms Used in This Chapter

administrative address

email discussion group

fan-in

fan-out

group address

interest group

list address

listserv

lurking

mailing list

subscribe

unsubscribe

Exercises and Projects

1. Practice subscribing to or joining an email discussion group. One you can use for practice is Net-Essentials-L with the administrative address **Listproc@listproc.mwc.edu**. Send an email message to the administrative address with this in the message body:

   `subscribe Net-Essentials-L` *your-full-name*

2. Search for email discussion groups. Several sites on the World Wide Web let you search for and find the names of discussion groups. Using the sites below come up with a list of three discussion groups along with the administrative address and list address for each.

   ~ CataList, the official catalog of LISTSERV lists
     http://www.lsoft.com/lists/listref.html

   ~ Liszt, the mailing list directory
     http://www.liszt.com

   ~ Publicly Accessible Mailing Lists
     http://www.neosoft.com/internet/paml

3. Do the following:

   a. Subscribe to the three discussion groups you found in the previous exercise. Did any require a reply or other authorization?

   b. Compare the welcome messages you get from the groups. Which was most helpful? Why?

4. Use the three groups you subscribed to above.

   a. Send the command to the administrative address to get a list of the members.

   b. Send the command to the administrative address to get a list of archives or files.

5. Now unsubscribe from each of the lists you've just joined.

6. Using one of the discussion groups you found in exercise 2, use each of the services listed above to search for that list. For each service write a brief description of the type of information it had available. Is there one service you prefer over the others? Why is that the case?

7. Search the archives of a discussion group using the Web-based services at LISTSERV.ACSU.BUFFALO.EDU. Open the Web page "LISTSERV archives at LISTSERV.ACSU.BUFFALO.EDU," **http://listserv.acsu.buffalo.edu/archives**. You can search the list archives of any of the discussion groups listed. Here, when you search, the results are displayed in the browser's window. Select a list based on your interests and get familiar with searching the archives. What list did you select? What search phrase and options did you use for the search? What were the results?

8. Subscribe to an email discussion group of your choice.
   a. Explain why you chose that group.
   b. For about a week, keep track of the email from two of the groups you've joined.
   c. Write a few sentences describing the type of mail that came from the group.
   d. Is the mail from these groups the type of mail you expected? Explain.

9. Send or post a question to one of the lists you've joined. Think about the question before you post it and check your spelling and typing before you send it.
   a. What responses did you receive by the end of one week?
   b. Summarize the responses and post the summary to the list.

10. Go to the Web site "List-Etiquette.com," **http://List-Etiquette.com/**, and look over the rules of etiquette for discussion list members. (It's also a good site to visit if you're thinking about moderating or forming an email discussion group.)
    a. State the rules that deal with spam, copyright, and HTML.
    b. Do you think the rules are reasonable? Explain your answer.

Chapter 6

USENET NEWS

*R*eading and writing the news; that's what Usenet is about. Started in 1979 so that people on one computer system could share news (announcements, information, comments, and discussions) with people at another site, Usenet news was developed using technology different from the Internet. Now it is available to everyone and is an important part of the way people communicate with each other on the Internet.

The messages that make up the news are called articles, each article is part of one or more newsgroups, and the newsgroups are passed from one computer system to another through Usenet servers; email isn't involved. Posted articles can be on a new topic or can be a reply to an existing article. The articles are read using software called a newsreader. Millions of people around the world read and post messages to newsgroups. There's the same sort of fan-out and fan-in as with email discussion groups.

To use Usenet effectively you'll want to know how to use a newsreader, how to find one or more groups whose articles might be pertinent to a specific topic or question, and how to access archives of past articles. You'll also want to know the proper etiquette for working in its sometimes free-wheeling environment. There's little control or censorship in Usenet. This gives Usenet its vitality and helps make the Internet as a whole an important outlet for unfettered free speech.

Goals/Objectives

~ Understand the nature of Usenet news

~ Know the resources available through Usenet

~ Learn how to work with Usenet news through a specific newsreader

~ Understand issues related to participating in Usenet newsgroups

Topics

Overview and Essential Information

Usenet news, sometimes called just news, is a popular means of communication on the Internet. The news is a collection of ***articles*** arranged into categories called ***newsgroups***. Anyone with access to a ***news server*** can post an article to a newsgroup and thus to Usenet. The articles are very much like email messages and they have many of the same headers. The big difference is that the articles are addressed to a newsgroup and anyone with access to a ***newsreader*** can read any of the articles. Before we get too far ahead of ourselves we ought to say a little more about the servers. A news server is a computer that's used to hold the collections of articles that make up newsgroups and to run the programs that pass any new articles posted to its newsgroups on to any other server that carries the same newsgroups. An individual uses another type of program called a newsreader that acts as a client with the server. The newsreader also acts as an agent for the individual so she can read, post, or otherwise manipulate articles and newsgroups.

You use Usenet news for the same reasons you use a discussion group—to exchange or read information dealing with specific topics. These are some ways that Usenet news differs from discussion groups:

∾   With Usenet you have access to many groups. Some sites carry thousands of groups; others carry fewer or different ones depending on the policies and procedures of that site.

∾   Messages to a group aren't exchanged between individuals using email; instead, messages are passed from one computer system to another.

∾   There's no formal process for subscribing to or joining newsgroups. Anyone can read and post to any newsgroups carried by his or her news server.

∾   An individual uses software called a newsreader to read and deal with the news (articles) available through Usenet, instead of using an email program or sending commands to a remote site.

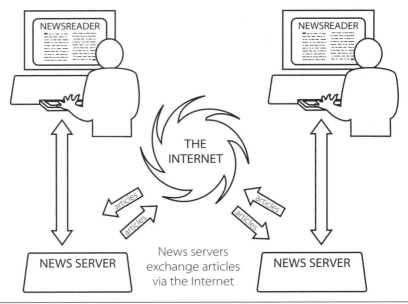

Figure 6.1   The Relationship of Users, Newsreaders, and News Servers

Web-based services for reading and posting news are also popular. One such service is Deja.com, **http://www.deja.com/usenet**. It gives a very easy-to-use interface to Usenet, and it has some excellent searching features so you can search recent and archived articles for information. Deja.com, formerly known as Deja News, started archiving Usenet articles in 1995.

Once you get comfortable using Usenet news, you'll find it a valuable resource with which you can find answers to different types of questions, get help on a variety of topics, and keep up with what's happening in the world and on the Internet.

With what we've said above as an introduction, we list some of the essential information about Usenet in Table 6.1 below.

Fyi WHAT IS USENET?
SOME CLASSIC PAPERS
∾ "What is Usenet?"
http://www.faqs.org/faqs/ usenet/what-is/part1
∾ "What is Usenet? A second opinion."
http://www.faqs.org/faqs/ usenet/what-is/part2

Feature/Concept	Explanation
Usenet news is a collection of articles arranged into newsgroups.	Usenet was originated so people at one computer site could exchange information or communicate with a group of users at another site. The number of articles (messages) and computer sites involved with Usenet has grown so that now people

An individual uses a program called a *newsreader* to select newsgroups and then to read and post articles.

throughout the world add thousands of new articles daily. Having the articles arranged in categories makes it possible for a user to focus on an area or topic of interest.

In order to read or post articles you need to either use a program called a newsreader that runs as a client on your computer or use a Web-based service to read and post messages.

People at each site can read the articles, ignore the articles, save or print the articles, respond to an article's author through e-mail, or **post** their own articles. Posting means composing either an original article or a response to someone else's article and then passing it on to Usenet.

Microsoft Outlook Express, distributed with Internet Explorer, includes a newsreader. Netscape Communicator also includes a newsreader. (You can access it by selecting **Newsgroups** from the pull-down menu **Communicator** in the menu bar.) There are several other free newsreaders. One that's highly recommended is Free Agent, available through the Free Agent home page, **http://www.forteinc.com/agent/freagent.htm**. You can read a comparison of different newsreaders in "Making News: 6 Usenet newsreaders compared," **http://coverage.cnet.com/Content/Reviews/Compare/Newsreader**.

A news server makes the news—newsgroups and articles—available. News servers exchange articles and newsgroups.

To access Usenet news you have to connect to a news server. Many ISPs make Usenet news available. Ask your ISP or network support group for the Internet domain name of the news server you may use. The newsreader program contacts the server so you can access newsgroups and articles. News servers exchange newsgroups and articles. That way when you post an article it's made available to other servers participating in Usenet.

Each newsgroup has a name that gives the main topic for the articles in the group. The groups are arranged or named according to a hierarchy.

When you look at the name of a newsgroup, you'll see it usually consists of several words or names separated by periods. The first part of the newsgroup name is the name of the top level of the hierarchy. Moving to the right, the names become more specific.

Consider the newsgroup name **rec.music.makers.guitar.acoustic**.

- Starting on the left, **rec** is the name of a top-level category that includes groups that deal with artistic activities, hobbies, or recreational activities.
- The next name, **music**, indicates the group deals with topics related to music.
- The next, **makers**, tells you this group is about performing or playing music rather than another activity such as reviewing music or collecting recordings.
- The next name, **guitar**, identifies the group as one that deals with performing guitar music. What type of guitar? That's next.
- The final name **acoustic** identifies this group as one that deals with discussions or other matters related to playing or performing acoustic guitar.

Here are a few other groups in the **rec.music** hierarchy to give you a feeling for this naming scheme:

> **rec.music.makers.piano**
> **rec.music.makers.percussion**
> **rec.music.marketplace**
> **rec.music.reggae**
> **rec.music.reviews**

There are over 30,000 newsgroups and several major, top-level categories. We won't list the categories here. A complete list, "Master List of Newsgroup Hierarchies," **http://www.magma.ca/~leisen/mlnh/index.html**, is maintained by Lewis S. Eisen.

All articles belong to one or more newsgroups.	Many newsgroups have charters that state the purpose of the newsgroup and the topics discussed within the group. An article is either a follow-up to another article or a post on a different topic. The term for posting an article to more than one newsgroup is ***cross-posting***.
Articles on the same topic are sometimes arranged into threads.	There may be several articles on the same topic in a single newsgroup. If each of the articles was posted as a follow-up to some original article, then the collection of these articles is called a ***thread***. You'll probably want to have articles arranged into threads. It really helps to have this sort of organization of a collection of articles in a particular group. You follow a thread by reading the articles in the thread one after the other.
Posting to Usenet is a public act.	When you post an article or reply to one in Usenet, you're creating an article that will be available to the thousands of computer systems and millions of people who make up the infrastructure of Usenet. The information you give in the identity preferences for your newsreader or Web-based Usenet service—your email address, name, and organization—are part of the article. So think twice about what you write and check your message for spelling and grammar.

∾ If you mean to write to an individual in the group, then be sure to address your message to that person.

You may find some articles or discussions in some groups offensive.	There is no central control over what's posted to Usenet. What offends you may not offend others, and a topic that bothers you may be important to others to be able to discuss. Some of the information on Usenet is illegal, such as pirated software. Some newsgroups contain pornographic or "X-rated" material. Whether a newsgroup is available on a news server depends on the policies of the organization that provides the

news server. But it's always your choice as to which articles to read and which newsgroups to look through. Sometimes you can tell the nature of a group by its title. The articles in the newsgroup titled **alt.sadistic.dentists** may or may not be offensive, but you can tell from the title whether reading the articles may be worth your time. Individual users take the responsibility for the types of information they will consider.

There is no single person, group, or computer system in charge. There is virtually no censorship on Usenet.

All the computers and people who are part of Usenet support it and manage it. It's similar to a bulletin board system (bbs), except that most bulletin boards are managed by one person and are run on one computer. Anyone with a connection to a news server may post an article, so free speech is encouraged and tolerated even when the postings are offensive.

Usenet is a community with its own generally agreed upon code of etiquette. Several articles that deal with Usenet etiquette are listed in the section "Usenet News Etiquette."

Control over which newsgroups are available is all at the local level since each news server is configured to accept or reject certain newsgroups. If you think some newsgroups ought to be available to you or some should be unavailable to anyone using a news server, then write or call the person or group that administers or sets policy for the news server.

Using Usenet can be so appealing that you spend too much time doing it.

Remember that you have a life outside of Usenet and you ought to pay attention to it. Get your other work done, take a walk, and spend some time with other human beings (assuming they're not all on Usenet).

Table 6.1   Essential Information About Usenet

Now we're ready to go to the section that gives some of the details of working with Usenet.

Details of Working with Usenet News

We'll go over some of the steps to follow to work with Usenet news. We're going to use the newsreader that is included with Outlook Express to demonstrate the concepts involved here. Other newsreaders are similar. If you don't have access to a newsreader or a system that acts as a news server then you can read and post messages through a Web-based service such as Deja.com, **http://www.deja.com/usenet**. Deja.com requires you to register—give your name and some demographic information about yourself—before you use its service for posting articles.

A QUICK VIEW OF HOW USENET WORKS

A person starts his newsreader and selects a newsgroup from a list of ones he regularly reads. He decides to post an article to a newsgroup, composes an article on his computer (in much the same way he composes an email message), and sends it on to the newsgroup. The article is sent to his news server and then on to another news server, possibly with other articles. From there it is distributed to other sites, and so on. People at other Usenet sites read the article on their systems. Someone decides she would like to respond to his article. She either sends email to him or posts a follow-up article. The follow-up article is distributed around Usenet with the same subject heading as the original article. Sometimes, several people at different places on Usenet respond with follow-up articles. Discussions start this way. Sometimes they stay on the same topic, but sometimes not. It's informative, it's creative, it's dynamic, and it's exciting!

Once you get your newsreader configured and set up, you'll be able to choose newsgroups to read and then one or more articles in a newsgroup. The newsreader will let you select a group from all the newsgroups available on the news server. Selecting a newsgroup is called *subscribing* to a newsgroup in Usenet terminology. You'll be able to subscribe to newsgroups at any time. Subscribing means nothing more than that the newsgroup is put on a list of newsgroups you'll see when you start your newsreader; you don't send anyone your name and email address as when you subscribe to an email discussion group. After selecting a newsgroup you're ready to read, reply to, print, save, or file articles in the newsgroup. You can also post an article to the newsgroup.

You'll find that working with articles is a lot like working with email. The major differences are that the articles or messages are arranged into groups, and instead of sending a message to an address you post an article to a group.

Now for the Details

The very first step is to set the address of the news server. We know that news servers exchange articles, and you use a newsreader to access articles and newsgroups. This means that when the newsreader is configured, or set up, you need to supply the Internet domain name or IP address of a news server so you can read or post news. The section "Getting Set for Email and Usenet" in Chapter 2 covers the details of setting the address and filling in the other information to get the newsreader set.

Once the newsreader is set, we're ready to subscribe to some newsgroups. We'll go over subscribing to newsgroups and take a look at reading some articles in Activity 6.1 below.

> Remember that Usenet is always changing and that your results will differ from those shown here. Don't let this confuse you. The activities demonstrate fundamental skills. These skills don't change, even though what you see will be different.

SUBSCRIBING TO NEWSGROUPS AND READING ARTICLES

Overview

We'll be using Outlook Express for this activity. If you're using another newsreader you'll find the concepts are similar but the details may be different. We're assuming the Internet domain name or IP address of the Usenet news server has already been entered and the newsreader is properly configured. Check the online help for your newsreader when you have questions.

The first time you use your newsreader you may have to subscribe to (select) some newsgroups. We'll go through the steps to follow in this activity. We're going to subscribe to the groups **news.newusers.questions** and **news.answers**. They're good places to start. **news.newusers.questions** is dedicated to questions from new Usenet users. There is no such thing as a "dumb question" here, but it's not a place for conversational or frivolous postings, or postings to test whether you're able to post articles to Usenet. Before posting to the newsgroup, check to see if someone else has asked a similar question. The group **news.answers** is where periodic Usenet postings and FAQs (frequently asked questions) are put.

We'll follow these steps:

1. Start the newsreader.
2. Choose and subscribe to newsgroups from the list of available news-groups.
3. Select a newsgroup from the list of subscribed newsgroups.
4. Read articles in the newsgroup.

Details

1. Start the newsreader.

 If there is an Outlook Express icon on your desktop, , then double-click on it to start the program. Once it's started click on **Read News**. Otherwise click on **Mail** in the toolbar of Internet Explorer and select **Read News**.

We'll assume you're not subscribed to any newsgroups. When the newsreader starts, it will display a message similar to the one in Figure 6.2.

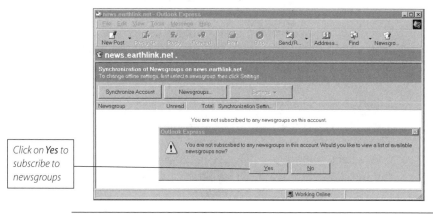

*Click on **Yes** to subscribe to newsgroups*

Figure 6.2   The "Not Subscribed to Any Newsgroups" Message from Outlook Express

2. Choose and subscribe to newsgroups from the list of available newsgroups.

Now we're ready to select or subscribe to some newsgroups.

Click on **Yes** in the dialog box.

If the newsreader is set so some newsgroups have already been subscribed to, click on **Newsgroups** in the toolbar to subscribe to newsgroups. You can do this any time you want to subscribe to a newsgroup.

Another window appears that you can use to subscribe to news-groups. It is shown in Figure 6.3.

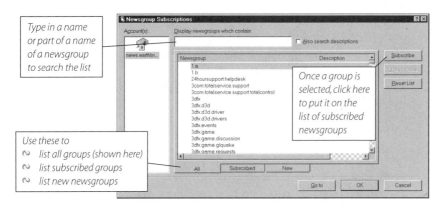

Type in a name
or part of a name
of a newsgroup
to search the list

Once a group is
selected, click here
to put it on the
list of subscribed
newsgroups

Use these to
~   list all groups (shown here)
~   list subscribed groups
~   list new newsgroups

Figure 6.3   A List of Available Newsgroups

You'll select newsgroups from the list in the window. You can also
search for newsgroups by title. Click on **Reset List** to send a request
to the news server to update the list of newsgroups. The list of
newsgroups that you're working with now is on *your* computer and
it could be different than the list of newsgroups on the server. It
may take one or several minutes for the list of newsgroups to appear
after you click on **Reset List**. The amount of time it takes depends
on the size of the list and the speed of the Internet connection. The
list, which may have several thousand entries, has to be downloaded
from the news server.

We'll be subscribing to **news.answers** and **news.newusers.questions**.
The most direct way to do that here is to type the name of each and
then select the group. There are other ways though: we could browse
through the entire list or we could type **news** in the search box and
browse the resulting list.

Type **news.answers** in the search form as shown in Figure 6.4.

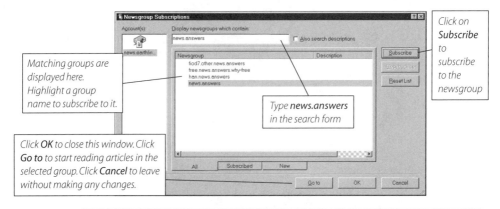

Click on
Subscribe
to
subscribe
to the
newsgroup

Matching groups are
displayed here.
Highlight a group
name to subscribe to it.

Type *news.answers*
in the search form

Click **OK** to close this window. Click
Go to to start reading articles in the
selected group. Click **Cancel** to leave
without making any changes.

Figure 6.4   Newsgroup Subscriptions; Subscribing to **news.answers**

Once the name of a newsgroup is highlighted, you subscribe to the group by clicking on **Subscribe** as shown in Figure 6.4.

(Do it)! Highlight the name **news.answers** and click on **Subscribe**.

You can also subscribe to a newsgroup by double-clicking on its name. Figure 6.4 doesn't show it too well, but there's also a button you can use to **_unsubscribe_** from a group. Clicking on **Unsubscribe** removes the name of the group from the list of subscribed groups.

You follow similar steps to subscribe to **news.newusers.questions**.

(Do it)! Type **news.newusers.questions** in the search form as shown in Figure 6.4.

(Do it)! Highlight the name **news.newusers.questions** and click on **Subscribe**.

We'll now go on to reading some articles in the newsgroup **news.answers**.

(Do it)! Click on **OK** to end subscribing.

Clicking on **OK** closes the window shown in Figure 6.4 and opens another, like the one shown in Figure 6.5, that lists the names of the newsgroups that have been subscribed to.

3. **Select a newsgroup from the list of subscribed newsgroups.**

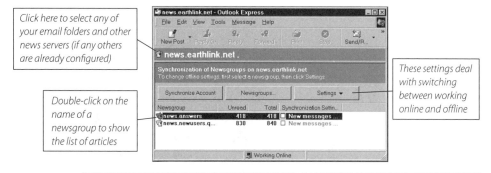

Click here to select any of your email folders and other news servers (if any others are already configured)

Double-click on the name of a newsgroup to show the list of articles

These settings deal with switching between working online and offline

Figure 6.5   A List of Subscribed Newsgroups

(Do it)! Double-click on **news.answers**.

When you double-click on the name of a newsgroup, a window similar to the email window opens with a list of the articles in the group and a display of the current article, as shown in Figure 6.6.

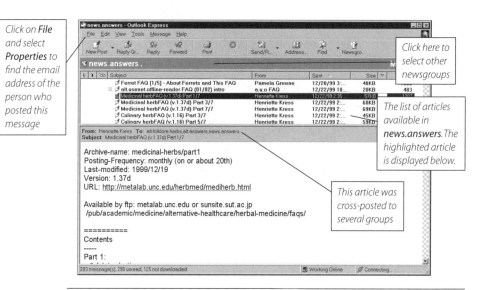

Figure 6.6   Reading an Article in a Newsgroup

Note the following:

∾   The window is divided into two frames: one for the list of messages and the other to display the current message.

∾   Click on the name of an article to have it displayed in the article frame.

∾   Unread messages are displayed in bold in the message list.

∾   Threads are marked by an icon in the left column.

∾   Note the menu bar and toolbar are the same as those in the mail window.

∾   With news you can choose to mark an article, a thread, or a range of articles as read or unread. You cannot delete an article.

∾   When you select a newsgroup, the newsreader first checks with the server to see if there are any new articles in the newsgroup. If so they, along with others, are listed. (The articles stay on the server until you read them.)

∾   All newsreaders allow you to set a preference so that only unread articles are listed, although you can choose to have all articles on the list. You'll want to be sure that articles are listed in threads as well.

4. Read articles in the newsgroup.

You can browse through the subject lines of each article.

Do it   Click on a subject in the list of articles to read an article.

You can also search for articles based on the subject or author. Articles are generally not downloaded or brought to your computer until you read them. That's why you generally won't be able to search through the body of articles on the server.

END OF ACTIVITY 6.1

In Activity 6.1 we showed how to start the newsreader, subscribe to newsgroups, and read articles in a newsgroup. You follow the same steps to subscribe to any newsgroup and to read articles in a subscribed newsgroup. To remove a newsgroup from the subscription list, display the subscription list, highlight the name of the group, and click on **Unsubscribe**.

You saw in Figure 6.6 of Activity 6.1 that the window that's used to display the articles in a newsgroup is similar to the window used to display email messages. Indeed, working with Usenet articles is similar to working with email. Here are some of the ways of working with newsgroup articles.

Another way to see the articles in a newsgroup is to type the URL for the newsgroup in the location field of the browser window. A newsgroup URL has the form **news:*newsgroup-name***. For example, the URL for the group **rec.music.makers.guitar.acoustic** is **news:rec.music.makers. guitar.acoustic**.

Type that in the location field of the browser and press **Enter**, and if your news server carries that group you'll be able to read articles in the group and the group will be automatically added to your list of subscribed newsgroups.

Saving, Mailing, or Printing an Article

A Usenet article can be saved to a file, mailed to someone else, or printed in much the same way you would work with an email message.

Let's suppose you're reading an article, as shown in Figure 6.6.

If you want to ...	then ...
Save the article in a file	Click on **File** in the menu bar and select **Save As**. A Save As dialog box pops up. Select or create a folder to hold the article.
File the article in a folder	Click on **Edit** in the menu bar and select **Copy to Folder**. Select a pre-existing folder or create a new one to hold the message.
Mail the article to another Internet address	Click on the item labeled **Forward** in the toolbar.

| | ~ When you select messages to be forwarded, a message composition window pops up.
~ The Subject header is filled in with **Fwd: *Title of the article*** and the article being forwarded is included. |
| Print the article | Click on the item **Print** in the toolbar.
~ A window pops up, the familiar one you see for printing from most types of programs. You can select a printer, set options (if necessary), and finally click on the button **OK** or **Cancel**. |

Table 6.2   Saving, Mailing, or Printing an Article

Replying to an Article

You have the choice of posting a ***follow-up*** article (which is passed to all other Usenet sites), writing directly through email to the author, or doing a combination of the two—posting a follow-up and sending it to the author by email.

There are two items on the toolbar for you to use.

~ Click on **Reply Group** to post a follow-up.

~ Click on **Reply** to post a message only to the author.

In each case a message composition window pops up. If the reply is a follow-up then the message is addressed to the newsgroup. If the reply is to the author then it's automatically addressed to the author. In either case, the subject is **Re:** followed by the subject of the original article. The text of the original article is also included. Remember to only keep pertinent parts of the original article when posting a reply or follow-up.

> **FOLLOW-UP OR EMAIL?**
>
> Suppose an article is posted in **rec.music.bluenote.blues** discussing the impact of Muddy Waters' music on English rock bands, and you think something important was left out. You might want to post a follow-up responding to the original article. Your follow-up article would be sent to any site that carries **rec.music.bluenote.blues**. You ought to post a follow-up for the same reasons you would send a reply via email to an author, except your reply should be interesting to enough people to be distributed to all of Usenet.

Posting an Article

Posting an article means composing an original message or article and having it distributed throughout all of Usenet.

To post an article:

~ Select a group by clicking on the name of the newsgroup from the newsgroup list. If you're reading or selecting articles, your post will go to the group you're reading.

~ Click on the item **New Post** in the toolbar.

~ A window will pop up—the same one you use to post a follow-up article or write an email message. The name of the newsgroup will be filled automatically into the frame labeled Newsgroups. Type the subject of your article in the frame labeled Subject. Choose a subject that isn't too long and clearly states the purpose of your article. Read several articles in the group to see the form that others use.

> **tip** BEFORE YOU POST
>
> ~ Read "A Primer on How to Work with the Usenet Community." You'll find it posted in **news.announce.newusers** and available through the URL **http://www.faqs.org/faqs/usenet/primer/part1**.
>
> ~ Be sure to select the right newsgroup for the article. Once you select a newsgroup check the FAQ for the newsgroup to see if your question is answered there.

~ Compose your article. Type it into the large frame of the window. If you have a signature file, its contents will be put automatically into the message. You can send attachments with the article by clicking on the button labeled Attachments. Don't include large text or binary files (usually images) unless that sort of information is normally posted to the newsgroup. Click on **Spelling** to have your spelling checked.

~ Click on the icon labeled **Send** to post your article. If you don't want to post it—you've made too many typing mistakes or you change your mind—click on **File** in the menu bar and select **Close** or press **Ctrl** + **W** from the keyboard. You'll have one more chance to post the article, but if you don't want to send it, click the button labeled **No**.

~ Use the newsgroup **alt.test** for posting an article that's meant to test your connection to Usenet. Figure 6.7 shows a test posting to **alt.test**.

Click here to post the message

The name of newsgroup goes here

Use these to check spelling, include an attachment, and perform other tasks

Subject

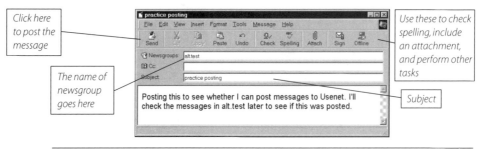

Figure 6.7   A Posting to alt.test

Using FAQs, Finding Newsgroups, and Searching Archives

FAQs

FAQ stands for *frequently asked questions*, a collection of common questions with answers. (Some people also use the term to refer to a single question.) Many of these are written and maintained by volunteers who put together and maintain a collection of questions and answers. Most newsgroups have an informative and useful FAQ. You can find it posted either in the newsgroup the FAQ was created for or in **news.answers**. Several newsgroups hold these FAQs; you'll see them referred to as the *.answers newsgroups. Some of these are **alt.answers**, **comp.answers**, and **sci.answers**. Here is a short list of FAQs to give you an idea of the variety of topics:

    Comp.Object FAQ
    comp.graphics.animation FAQ
    rec.games.netrek FAQ List
    FAQ: Old Time Radio (OTR)
    rec.sport.hockey FAQ
    FAQ: Sci.Polymers
    FAQ: rec.music.dylan
    rec.martial-arts FAQ

Be sure to consult the FAQ for information before you post a question to a newsgroup. It's annoying to other people reading the newsgroup to see questions that they know are in the FAQ. It may be embarrassing for you if you post a question to a newsgroup and you get several replies (or follow-ups) let-

Fyi MORE INFORMATION ABOUT USENET

~ "news.newusers.questions Links Page"
  http://www.geocities.com/ResearchTriangle/8211/nnqlinks.html

~ "Usenet: Reading and Writing the News"
  http://www.webliminal.com/Lrn-web05.html

~ "Usenet References"
  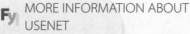
  http://www.faqs.org/usenet

ting you (and everyone else reading the newsgroup) know that you should read the FAQ before asking other questions.

The FAQ for a group will be posted regularly to the group and also to one of the *.answers groups, such as **news.answers**. If you can't find the FAQ you're looking for there, try looking at "Internet FAQ Archives," **http://www.faqs.org/faqs**.

Recommended Newsgroups for Information About Usenet

There are several newsgroups that a beginning or infrequent user should browse. These newsgroups include information about Usenet, lists of FAQs for Usenet and several newsgroups, and articles that will help you use Usenet. The newsgroups are:

news.announce.newgroups	Articles dealing with forming and announcing new newsgroups. It's a place to get lists of all newsgroups.
news.announce.newusers	Explanatory and important articles for new or infrequent Usenet users.
news.answers	This is where periodic Usenet postings are put. The periodic postings are primarily FAQs. This is often the first place you should look when you have a question.
news.newusers.questions	This newsgroup is dedicated to questions from new Usenet users. There is no such thing as a "dumb question" here. You ought to browse this group to see if others have asked the same question that's been bothering you. Once you get some expertise in using Usenet, you'll want to check this group to see if you can help someone.

Finding Newsgroups

There are thousands of newsgroups. How can you decide which to read or even find out which ones exist?

There are several lists of newsgroups available through Usenet. Keep your eye on the newsgroup **news.answers**, **news.lists**, or **news.groups** so you can read or save these listings when they appear (usually monthly).

Some sites on the WWW provide the facilities for searching for newsgroups. For the sites we'll mention, use the URL to bring up a Web page. On that page you enter a keyword or phrase, click on a button labeled **Search**, and then work with the results.

Site Name	URL	Description
Deja.com Interest Finder	**http://www.deja.com/ home_if.shtml**	Here you do a keyword search for newsgroups that contain discussions matching your request.
Liszt's Usenet Newsgroups Directory	**http://www.liszt.com/news**	You can search by keywords for a newsgroup or browse its directory.
Tile.Net/News	**http://tile.net/news**	Use keyword searching or browsing to find newsgroups.

Searching Archives of Usenet Articles

There's lots of useful information posted to Usenet. A search of the archives of posted articles is a good place to start when you want information about recent events, a particular product or brand, a company, or leads for jobs. Very little of this information is edited or reviewed, so you have to take time to verify information and not take it at face value.

Several of the major search engines include options for searching Usenet news:

Name	URL	Way to Search Usenet Archives
AltaVista	**http://www.altavista.com**	Use the search form and click on the button **Discussion Groups** just below the search form.
HotBot	**http://hotbot.lycos.com/usenet**	Use the search form.
Infoseek	**http://infoseek.go.com**	Click on **Search Options** on the main page and then select **Usenet**.

The primary search service dedicated to Usenet archives is Deja.com, **http://www.deja.com/usenet**. Both HotBot and Infoseek, mentioned above, use the services of Deja.com. It was the first search engine devoted to Usenet. In addition to searching, it allows you to post articles, browse, and find newsgroups. The archives go back to 1995.

We've mentioned Deja.com so frequently in this chapter it's appropriate that we include a figure showing its Usenet page and noting several of its features.

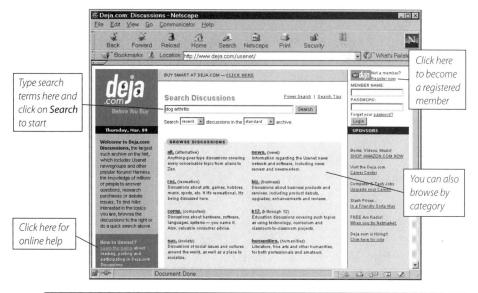

*Type search terms here and click on **Search** to start*

Click here to become a registered member

Click here for online help

You can also browse by category

Figure 6.8   The Deja.com Usenet Page

Usenet News Etiquette

Table 5.5 on page 158 lists tips and guidelines for working with Usenet newsgroups and email discussion groups. We'll list them here and refer you to Table 5.5 for a more detailed explanation of each one.

- Spend some time getting to know the group.
- Posting or sending a message to the group is a public act.
- Think before you respond to a message.
- Write easy-to-read messages.
- Group members are people like you and need to be treated with respect and courtesy.
- When responding, include only the pertinent portions of the original message.
- When you ask group members any questions, post a summary of the responses.

~ Think about whether a response to a message should go to the group or to an individual.

~ Post test messages to groups designed for testing.

Over the years, several documents have been developed about proper Usenet etiquette. These are regularly posted in **news.announce.newusers**, **news.answers**, or **news.newusers.questions**. Here is a list of some that you ought to read:

~ "A Primer on How to Work with the Usenet Community," **http://www.faqs.org/faqs/usenet/primer/part1**

~ "How to Make the Best Use of Usenet News," **http://www.netscape.com/eng/mozilla/1.1/news/news2.html**

~ "Emily Postnews Answers Your Questions on Netiquette," **http://www.faqs.org/faqs/usenet/emily-postnews/part1/**

~ "Rules for Posting to Usenet," **http://www.faqs.org/faqs/usenet/posting-rules/part1/**

~ "Hints on Writing Style for Usenet," **http://www.faqs.org/faqs/usenet/writing-style/part1/**

~ "FAQ on Making and Using a .signature File," **http://www.faqs.org/faqs/usenet/signature-faq/**

~ "How to Find the Right Place to Post (FAQ)," **http://www.faqs.org/faqs/finding-groups/general/**

Summary

The news is a collection of messages called articles. Each article is designated as belonging to one or more newsgroups. These articles are passed from one computer system to another. The newsgroups are arranged into categories in a hierarchical manner. Users at a site can usually select any of the groups that are available and can often reply to or post an article. Some estimates put the number of participants at more than 40 million worldwide.

Usenet is a community of users helping each other and exchanging opinions. A code of behavior has developed. The rules are, of course, voluntary, but users are expected to obtain a copy of some articles about working with Usenet and to follow the rules. Several newsgroups carry regular postings of articles meant to inform the Usenet community. These are often found in the groups **news.announce.newgroups**, **news.announce.newusers**, and **news.answers**.

You use software called a newsreader to work with the articles and newsgroups in Usenet news. Several different newsreaders are available.

The one you use will depend on your preferences and what's available on the system with which you access Usenet.

You'll probably find Usenet a valuable resource for information on a wide array of topics. It can be enjoyable to read and participate in the discussions. Services are available on the World Wide Web to search for newsgroups related to a specific topic and to search for articles that contain keywords or phrases.

The email discussion groups and Usenet newsgroups can be thought of as communities of people sharing common interests. There are generally accepted rules of behavior or etiquette for list members. These include providing appropriate, thoughtful, and concise messages to the group, providing a summary of the responses received in answer to a question, and communicating with other group members in a civil and respectful manner.

Selected Terms Used in This Chapter

article	newsreader
cross-posting	news server
follow-up	post
frequently asked questions	subscribe
(FAQ)	thread
newsgroup	unsubscribe

Exercises and Projects

1. Start your newsreader.
   a. What's the Internet domain name or IP address of your news server?
   b. What are the names of some of the newsgroups available?
   c. What's in the newsgroup **comp.internet.net-happenings**?

2. Take a look at the articles in the newsgroup **news.answers**.
   a. What are the titles of the five most recent articles?
   b. Find a FAQ in the list of articles in that newsgroup. Give its title, the name of the person who maintains it, and the date it was last modified.

3. Take a look at the articles posted to **news.newusers.questions** in the past 24 hours.
   a. How many were posted?
   b. Give a brief description of the topics of the articles.
   c. About how many were questions and about how many were answers to questions?

4. Take a look at the newsgroups **alt.answers**, **comp.answers**, **sci.answers**, and **soc.answers**. What's the difference between the four newsgroups?

5. Monitor the questions on **news.newusers.questions** for a few days. List at least one question you feel you could answer or find the answer to the question. If it's appropriate, post an answer to the question.

6. Go to "news.newusers.questions Links Page," **http://www.geocities.com/ResearchTriangle/8211/nnqlinks.html**.
   a. That page states that news.newusers.questions is a moderated newsgroup. What does that mean?
   b. Go to the section titled "What You Need to Know." What does it say about the topics Making Money Fast Schemes and Advertising and Selling?
   c. Go to the section "How Newsgroups Work." You can probably get to it by scrolling down the page. You'll see the topic "Disappearing Articles." What's it about?

7. Search for newsgroups.
   a. Use the search form for finding newsgroups at Liszt, **http://www.liszt.com/news**. Search for newsgroups dealing with mental health. What newsgroups did you find? What information does Liszt give about a newsgroup? Is it useful?
   b. Use the search form for Usenet newsgroups at Tile.Net, **http://tile.net/news**. Search for newsgroups that deal with mental health. What newsgroups did you find? What information does Tile.Net give about a newsgroup? Is it useful?
   c. Compare Liszt and Tile.Net in terms of using these services for keyword searching. Which do you prefer? Why?

8. Use either Liszt or Tile.Net for the following.
   a. Find newsgroups that deal with dining. You'll see that some focus on eating out in certain geographical areas. What is a dining newsgroup for an area near where you live?
   b. Find newsgroups that include recipes. Subscribe to one of the newsgroups and browse the articles until you find a recipe for something you'd like to eat. Print the recipe.
   c. Find newsgroups that deal with a sport that interests you. Select one group. Which is it? Select an article in the group and mail it to yourself and a friend.

9. Use Deja.com, **http://www.deja.com**, to search archives of news-groups.
   a. Search the archives for articles using the search phrase "alternative health care." Read the first five articles listed. What are they about? Which one do you find the most interesting? Explain.
   b. For the article you found most interesting in part a, click on the name of the author when the article is in the browser's window. What do you find out about the author?
   c. Now search the archives for articles on a subject you choose. Read some of the articles. If you think it's appropriate—according to the "Usenet News Etiquette" section in this chapter—post a follow-up message to the group or email a reply to the author for one of the articles you've found.

10. Use the URL **http://www.deja.com/help/faq.shtml** to read the Deja.com FAQ.
    a. How do you report abusive or invasive messages posted through Deja.com?
    b. How can you prevent articles you write from appearing in the archives?
    c. How can you remove articles you've posted to Usenet from the Deja.com archives?

11. Go to the Web site "Internet FAQ Archives," **http://www.faqs.org/faqs**.
    a. Find a FAQ that deals with health care for dogs. What is its title? When was it last updated?
    b. Is there a FAQ that deals with health care for cats? What is its title? When was it last updated?
    c. Give the title, date of the last update, author, and URL of three FAQs that deal with a topic you're studying, related to your business, or related to a hobby or recreational interest of yours.

Chapter 7

GETTING AROUND THE WORLD WIDE WEB—USING A WEB BROWSER

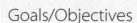

*T*he World Wide Web is a vast collection of information that is connected or linked together. You can access all this information through one program or tool, the Web browser. This is significant because it gives you essentially one way of doing things, one interface to many different types of information in a variety of media formats. We introduced the Web browser in the first chapter, and we've spent the past few chapters dealing with communication on the Internet. Here we'll go over some of the details, concepts, and techniques that will help you become proficient in the ways you use your browser to explore the World Wide Web. This also helps you understand new concepts and terms that will surely come up as the nature of the Web and the browsers themselves change. The browser is what you use to surf the Net, and you'll have a better time doing it when you're comfortable with the browser's features and capabilities. You'll also find that the Web browser is what we'll cover in the next few chapters as you learn about searching for and using information on the Web.

Goals/Objectives

- Learn the functions and capabilities of a Web browser
- Learn the ways to navigate around the Web
- Become aware of security issues and the trail you leave behind as you browse the Web

Topics

- ∾ Using the Browser's Window
- ∾ Similar Ways of Working with Netscape and Internet Explorer
- ∾ Navigating the Web
- ∾ Security and Privacy on the Web

Using the Browser's Window

When you start a Web browser the browser's window appears on the screen. It's the Web browser's job to retrieve and display a file inside the window.

Whenever you start a browser or access a hyperlink, the browser—which is a computer program—sends a request to have a file transferred to it. The browser then interprets the information in the file so that it can be viewed in the browser's window, or in some cases, viewed through another program. For example, if a hyperlink points to a text file, then the file is displayed in the window as ordinary text. If the hyperlink points to a document written in Hypertext Markup Language (HTML), then the browser displays it. If the file is a sound file or an animation, then a program different from the browser is started so the file can be heard or seen. Most of the facilities and capabilities are built into the browser, but in some cases, your computer needs to be equipped with special equipment or programs. A good example of this is when a hyperlink points to a sound file. Your computer needs to have a sound card, speakers, and the software to play the sounds.

What is in the window will change as you go from site to site, but each window has the same format. The items that help you work with the Web document in the window include the scroll bar, the menu bar, and the toolbar, which are the same every time you use the browser. The major components of a Web page displayed by Netscape and Internet Explorer are labeled in Figure 7.1.

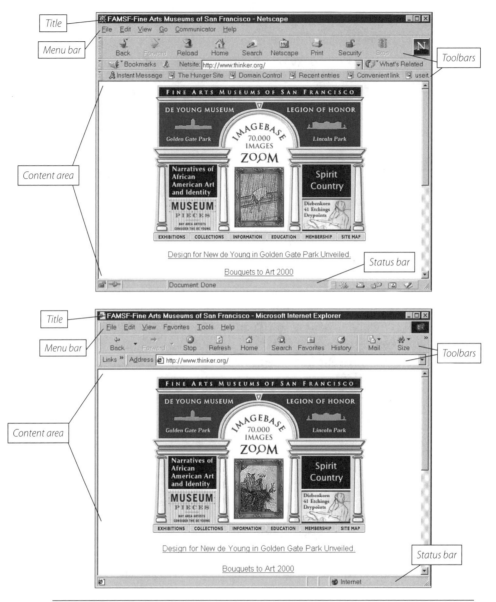

Figure 7.1   Netscape Window and Internet Explorer Window
with Common Components Labeled

The browser lets you access, retrieve, work with, and enjoy the information and resources that make up the World Wide Web. To coin a phrase, the browser is your window to the Web.

In this section, we'll look at the items and techniques the browsers Netscape Navigator and Microsoft Internet Explorer have in common. We'll also look at each in some detail.

Items Common to the Netscape and Internet Explorer Browser Windows

The windows for Netscape Navigator and Microsoft Internet Explorer are by and large the same. Here we'll list and discuss the elements common to both.

Title

The title of a Web page is created when the page is written. A page's title is not the same as its URL, just as a book's title is different from its library call number.

Menu Bar

The **menu bar** is a list of items, each representing a menu from which you can choose an action.

You choose any of these by moving the mouse pointer to the word and clicking on it. You can also activate one of these choices by using the **Alt** key along with the underlined letter. For example, to display the menu associated with File, use **Alt** + **F**.

Selecting an item from the menu bar brings up a pulldown menu with several options. For example, if you click on **File** (or use **Alt** + F), you see the menu shown to the right.

Select any highlighted item in that menu either by clicking on it with the mouse or by pressing the underlined character in its name. To print the current Web page, you can click on **Print** in this menu or you can press **P** (upper- or lowercase). Some items on the menu are followed by **Ctrl** + a letter, such as the following:

Save As...   **Ctrl** + S

This means that to select the command from the menu, you can either click on **Save As** or use a keyboard shortcut, **Ctrl** + **S**. With this particular command, you save a copy of the Web page in a file on your computer.

Toolbars

Like other Windows software, Web browsers have one or more rows of icons or items called **toolbars** just below the menu bar. Each item works like a button. When you press it with the mouse, some operation or action takes place.

The icons give you a visual clue to the operation or action they represent. The commands they represent are all available through the items on the menu bar, but the icons give a direct path—a shortcut—to the commands.

Content Area or Document View

The **content area** is the portion of the window that holds the document, page, or other resource as your browser presents it. It can contain text or images.

Sometimes the content area is divided into or consists of several independent portions called **frames**. Each frame has its own scroll bar, and you can move through one frame while staying in the same place in others.

The content area holds the Web page you're viewing, which likely contains hyperlinks in text or graphic format. Clicking on a hyperlink with the *left* mouse button allows you to follow the link. Clicking with the *right* mouse button (or holding down the mouse button without clicking if your mouse has only one button) brings up a menu that gives you options for working with a hyperlink.

Scroll Bar

If the document doesn't fit into the window it will be displayed with vertical and/or horizontal **scroll bars**. The horizontal one is at the bottom of the window, and the vertical one is at the right of the window. These scroll bars and their associated arrows help you move through the document. The scroll bars work the same way as those in common Microsoft Windows applications.

Status Bar

When you are retrieving a document, opening a location, or following a hyperlink, the bar along the bottom of the window (the **status bar**) holds the URL that's being used. It also lets you know whether a site is being contacted, if it's responding, and how the transmission is progressing.

Similarities Between Working with Netscape and Internet Explorer

Netscape Navigator and Microsoft Internet Explorer employ many of the same techniques for working with the browser. We'll discuss them here, noting that there are some differences.

Starting the Browser

The Web browser is a program, software that will run or execute on your computer. So you start it the way you start other programs. To start a Web browser session, double-click on the icon for the browser. Look for an icon that looks like one of the following:

To start Netscape: **To start Internet Explorer:**

Netscape   Netscape   Internet
Communicator   Communicator   Netscape   Explorer

Ending a Browser Session

You stop the Web browser program in the same way that you end almost any other Windows program or application. Here are some ways to do that:

∾   Press **Alt** + **F4**.

∾   Double-click on the upper-left corner.

∾   Click on the **X** in the upper-right corner.

∾   Click on **File** in the menu bar, and then click on **Close**, **Exit**, or **Quit**.

Getting Help

When you have a question about using the browser check the online help by pressing **F1** or clicking on **Help** in the menu bar.

Keyboard Shortcuts

You can access all the commands for using a Web browser by pointing and clicking on a word, icon, or portion of the window, but sometimes you may want to give a command using the keyboard. To do this, use the key labeled **Ctrl** or **Alt**, along with another key. For example, to print the current Web page, you can select **Print** from a menu or use **Ctrl** + P. Using **Ctrl** + P means holding down the key labeled **Ctrl**, pressing the key labeled P, and then releasing them both. As another example, giving the command **Alt** + H will display a menu of items to select for online help. You hold down the key labeled **Alt**, press H, and then release them both.

To see a complete list of keyboard shortcuts take a look at "Using Keyboard Shortcuts," **http://home.netscape.com/browsers/using/ieusers/browsing/shortcuts.html**. This table shows some of the keyboard shortcuts common to both browsers:

Ctrl + A	Select all	**Ctrl** + P	Print the current page
Ctrl + C	Copy	**Ctrl** + R	Reload the current page
Ctrl + V	Paste	**Alt** + H	Display the online help menu

Ctrl + X	Cut	**Alt** + ←	Go back one page
Ctrl + F	Find in the page	**Alt** + →	Go forward one page
Ctrl + B	Organize bookmarks or favorites	**Alt** + **F4**	Close the window
Ctrl + N	Open a new window	**F1**	Display
Ctrl + O	Open the address/ location box	**Esc**	Stop loading the current page

Table 7.1   Keyboard Shortcuts

Copying and Pasting

You can copy the text on a Web page to another Windows application, such as a word-processing or spreadsheet program, or to a form or the location field in the browser's window. Highlight the text by pressing the left mouse button and dragging it over the text. Click the right mouse button and select **Copy**. Put the mouse pointer into another Windows application, click the right mouse button, and select **Paste**.

You can copy a hyperlink by moving the mouse pointer over the hyperlink, pressing the right mouse button, and selecting **Copy Link Location**.

Details About the Netscape Navigator Window

We'll go over some of the details of the items available through the Netscape browser's window.

Menu Bar

The menu bar near the top of the window includes:

File   Edit   View   Go   Communicator   Help

Fy MORE ABOUT BROWSERS

~ "Browser News," the latest information about browsers
http://www.upsdell.com/ BrowserNews

~ "Browsers," lots of information and links from CNET
http://home.cnet.com/ category/0-3773.html

~ "Open Directory - Computers: Software: Internet: Clients: WWW: Browsers," links to a variety of information about browsers
http://dmoz.org/Computers/ Software/Internet/Clients/ WWW/Browsers

~ "Web Browsers," an introduction from webTeacher
http://www.webteacher.org/ winnet/browser/browser.html

Here are some details about each of the pulldown menus:

File

Using the commands in the File menu, you can open a new browser window, send an email message, or open a page in the Web editor (Composer) that's part of Netscape Communicator. You can also use this menu to open a page in the browser—either a Web page (which you would open by giving its URL) or a file on your computer. You can go in offline mode to work with files or messages on your computer without being connected to the Internet. The menu options also allow you to print, mail, or save the current document into a file. This menu has items that permit you to close the window, close all the Netscape windows, or both. There are also menu items that let you work with frames if they're present.

Edit

Use the Edit menu to copy items from the current document to other applications, such as a word–processing program. You can also use **Copy** and **Paste** to copy URLs or email addresses from one window into the location field or address field of a message. In addition, the menu contains the item **Find**, which presents a dialog box that lets you search the current document for a word or phrase. The item **Search Internet** is used to search for items on the Internet. **Preferences** brings up a screen through which you set preferences to customize the browser and how it works with your computer. There's a separate item for the preferences that you must set to use email and Usenet news. These include specifying the Internet address of the mail and news·servers.

View

The items on the View menu change what you see and how you view those items. You can use this menu to hide any of the toolbars (or to show them if they're not in view) or to change the font size (the size of the letters in the Web page). You also use the View menu to reload a copy of the current document; this is useful if there have been some changes to the source page since it was originally loaded or if the images in a document were not loaded automatically. The menu has items to stop the current page from loading or to stop animations. The item **Page Source** lets you view the source version of the current page so you can see which HTML commands were used to create it. Selecting **Page Info** shows information about the current document, such as when it was last modified and whether it's a secure document (used for commercial or private transactions).

Go

Items in the Go menu take you to different documents or pages that you have viewed during the current Netscape session. Netscape keeps a list of the pages (the history list) you've traveled through to reach the current document. You can choose **Back** to return to the previous page or **Forward** to move to a page from which you've just come back. You can also go to the home page for that session or to any of the recent pages on the history list.

Communicator

This menu gives access to the browser, email, newsgroups, the visual editor for Web pages (Composer), the bookmark list, and the history list through the item **Tools**. You also have access to the **Address Book** for email. Selecting **Security Info** gives information about the current Web page, including whether it was sent in a secure (encrypted) mode and the name of the Web server from which it was sent.

Help

Choose the Help menu to obtain information about using the Web browser. This menu includes a link to online help, product information and support (which itself has links to lots of helpful information), information about plug-ins or helpers, and other items.

Toolbars

There are several toolbars in Netscape Navigator: the navigation toolbar (also called the command toolbar), the location toolbar, and the personal toolbar. You can hide each toolbar by clicking on its left edge, making it disappear from the browser window. Click on the edge again to make it reappear.

Navigation Toolbar

Table 7.2 explains the items in the *navigation toolbar*—also called the command toolbar.

Name	Explanation
Back, Forward	These two items with directional arrows move between documents or Web pages that you've already seen.
Reload	This item reloads the current Web page from the source. If the page may have changed since you last viewed it, you may want to reload it.
Home	This takes you to your home page, the one you first saw when you started the browser.

Search	This item takes you to a Web page where you select a service to search the WWW. You type in one or more keywords and wait for results, or select items from a directory.
Images	This item appears only if Navigator has been set so that it will not automatically display images while loading a Web page. With that setting, Web pages load more quickly. To load the images, click on this button. To set a preference for automatically or not automatically loading images, select **Preferences** from **Edit** in the menu bar, then select **Advanced**, and finally click on the box next to **Automatically load images**.
My Netscape	This item takes you to a site where you can select information you'd like to see whenever you select this item. The types of information available include entertainment guides, weather forecasts, and news reports.
Print	This item allows you to print the current document.
Security	This item displays the page dealing with security information. You can use this option to check security, obtain encryption information about the current Web page, set a Netscape password for yourself, and perform other security-related tasks.
Stop	This item stops a current Web page from loading. This is useful if it's taking a long time to contact a site or load a page.

Table 7.2   Items in the Navigation Toolbar

Location Toolbar

The *location toolbar* includes the Bookmark Quickfile icon, which serves as a link to the bookmark list; the Page Proxy icon, which lets you add sites to the bookmark list, the personal toolbar, or the desktop; the *location field*, which holds the URL for the current Web page; and the What's Related button. We'll discuss the essential features of each.

Bookmark Quickfile Icon

The Bookmark Quickfile icon labeled Bookmarks is used to bring up a menu of items:

Add Bookmark

Use this to add the URL and title of the current Web page to the bookmark list. Once something is in the bookmark list, you can access the Web page in one or two clicks. The bookmark list is therefore very useful when you're doing research.

File Bookmark

Use this to view what's in the bookmark list.

Edit Bookmarks

Use this to arrange bookmarks into folders, rename items, delete items, and otherwise manage the list.

Page Proxy Icon

You use the Page Proxy icon, or Page icon for short, to copy the URL of the current Web page. Move the mouse pointer over the icon and hold down the left mouse button. Then drag it to the desktop to make a shortcut to the Web page. Click on the shortcut and you'll go directly to the Web page. Alternately, drag it to the personal toolbar where it will be added as an icon. As a third option, drag it to the Bookmarks icon and add it to the bookmark list or click on **File Bookmark** and select the folder to which it will be added.

Location Field

The location field holds the URL of the current Web page. We've seen how you can go directly to a Web page by clicking on the location field, typing in the URL, and pressing $\boxed{\text{Enter}}$. Clicking on the arrow displays a list of URLs for Web pages you've visited recently. Click on any one to go directly to it.

What's Related

Clicking on the button labeled **What's Related** brings up a menu of Web sites related to the current Web site and information about the site. This doesn't necessarily give information about a Web page. Clicking on **What's Related** brings up information on sites

related to the server's domain name only. If the URL were **http://www.library.mwc.edu/ compsci.html**, for example, then clicking on **What's Related** would bring up information on servers that host pages similar to those at mwc.edu. For more information about this check the Netscape site "About What's Related," **http://home.netscape.com/escapes/ related**.

Personal Toolbar

The personal toolbar contains icons that represent Web pages. Clicking on an item takes you directly to that Web page. What you see the first time you use Netscape varies depending on what version you're using or whether someone else has used the browser. Typically the personal toolbar contains links to services offered by Netscape.

There are two ways to put items in the personal toolbar. One way is to use the Page icon to place (drag and drop) an icon for the current Web page into the personal toolbar. In this way, the personal toolbar consists of hyperlinks to Web sites. Another way is to select a folder (a collection of bookmarks) in the bookmark list as the one that will be used for the personal toolbar entries. Check the online help for a way to do that. Personal toolbar entries give you quick access to a collection of bookmarks that might be useful when you're researching a topic.

Status Bar

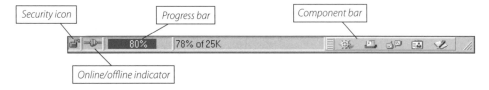

The icon on the left that looks like a lock is the Security icon. Clicking on it brings up the same window as clicking on the Security icon in the navigation toolbar. If it looks like the lock is open, then the document you're viewing has not passed through secure channels. If the lock is closed, then some security has been put in place during the transmission of the Web page or document.

Information available through the World Wide Web passes across the Internet. That means that any site on the path of the transmission can intercept the packets that make up the document or Web page. Thus, it's difficult to guarantee the security or privacy of information (such as a credit card number) exchanged on the WWW. We all face that same problem whenever we use a portable wireless telephone.

Netscape Communications Corporation and others provide the means to guarantee secure transmissions. If the document you're working with is secure, the lock will be closed. It's not a good idea to send sensitive or valuable information through the WWW if the lock isn't closed, but that's always up to you.

Component Bar

Netscape Communicator consists of several software tools for working on the Web and the Internet. The component bar gives quick access to some of these: Navigator for browsing the Web, Messenger for working with email and Usenet news, Address Book for managing email addresses, and Composer for writing Web pages. Clicking on any of these takes you to them. If mail arrives while you're using Netscape, a green arrow appears as part of the mail icon.

Fy TUTORIALS AND GUIDES FOR NETSCAPE NAVIGATOR

~ Grenville CAP – Netscape Tutorial
http://www.recorder.ca/grenvillecap/tutorial/tutorial/tut-004a1.htm

~ Internet Navigator – MODULE 1 – Browser Tutorial and Internet Overview
http://www.lib.utah.edu/navigator/Module1/index.html

~ Navigating the World Wide Web with Netscape Communicator
http://www.albany.edu/library/internet/communicator95.html

~ Netscape Navigator Tutorial
http://www.eiu.edu/~mediasrv/netscape/menu.html

Details About the Microsoft Internet Explorer Window

We'll go over some of the details of the items available through the Internet Explorer window.

Menu Bar

The menu bar near the top of the window includes:

File   Edit   View   Favorites   Tools   Help

Here are some details about each of the pulldown menus:

File

Using the commands in the File menu, you can open a new browser window, send an email message, or open a page in an HTML editor (you set this in Internet Options on the Tools menu). You can also use this menu to open a page in the browser—either a Web page (which you would open by giving its URL) or a file on your computer. You can go in offline mode to work with files or messages on your computer without being connected to the Internet. The menu options also allow you to print, mail, save the current document into a file, or create a desktop shortcut to the Web page.

Edit

Use the Edit menu to copy items from the current document to other applications, such as a word-processing program. You can also use **Copy** and **Paste** to copy URLs or email addresses from one window into the location field or address field of a message. In addition, the menu contains the item **Find**, which presents a dialog box that lets you search the current document for a word or phrase.

View

The items on the View menu change what you see and how you view those items. You can use this menu to hide any of the toolbars (or to show them if they're not in view) or to change the font size (the size of the letters in the Web page). By choosing an item in **Explorer Bar** you split the content area so that a frame is created on the left titled Search, Favorites, History, or Folders.

You also use the View menu to reload a copy of the current document; this is useful if there have been some changes to the source page since it was originally loaded or if the images in a document were not loaded automatically. The menu has items to stop the current page from loading. The item **Source** lets you view the source version of the current page so you can see which HTML elements were used to create it. The item **Go To** brings up another menu so you can travel **Back** or **Forward** through the list of most recently accessed Web pages.

Favorites

This gives quick access to the favorites list. It contains an item to add the current page to the favorites list and an item to organize or manage the list of folders in the favorites collection.

Tools

This menu gives access to the email and Usenet newsgroups. There's an item to use to check for updates of Microsoft software. Another item takes you to related Web sites. The last item, **Internet Options**, is what you use to set preferences and options to customize the browser and how its various components work with your computer system.

Help

Choose the Help menu to obtain information about using the Web browser. This menu includes a link to online help, an online tutorial to help you use Internet Explorer, and links to other information about this browser.

Toolbars

There are several toolbars in Microsoft Internet Explorer: the standard buttons toolbar, the links toolbar, and the address toolbar.

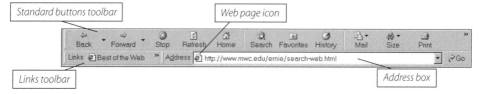

The Standard Buttons Toolbar

Table 7.3 explains the items in the standard buttons toolbar.

Name	Explanation
Back, Forward	These two items with directional arrows move between documents or Web pages that you've already seen. Back takes you to the previous page, and Forward can only be used if you've previously used Back. To obtain a list of sites to go back to or forward to, put the mouse pointer on either of these icons and click the right mouse button.
Stop	This item stops a current Web page from loading. This is useful if it's taking a long time to contact a site or load a page.
Refresh	This item reloads the current Web page from the source. If the page may have changed since you last viewed it, you may want to reload it.
Home	This item takes you to your home page, the one you first saw when you started the browser.
Search	This item takes you to a Web page where you select a service to search the WWW. You type in one or more keywords and wait for results, or select items from a directory. You'll get a Web page with hyperlinks to resources that match the keyword(s) you typed.
Favorites	This item takes you to your favorites list. A frame opens on the left of the content area showing the items and folders in the favorites list.
History	This item opens the history list in a frame to the left of the content area.

Mail	Use this to access email and Usenet newsgroups with your computer.
Size	Use this to change the size of the font in the content window.
Print	This item allows you to print the current document.

Table 7.3   Items in the Standard Buttons Toolbar

Address Box

The **address box** shows the URL for the current Web page. You can type a URL in this box, press **Enter**, and access a Web page. Once the Web page is displayed, a Web page icon appears to its left. You can click and drag this icon to add the Web page to the favorites list, to create a shortcut to the page on your desktop, or to add the page to the links toolbar. To do that move the mouse pointer to the Web page icon, press the (left) mouse button and hold it down. Now move the mouse pointer to a folder in the favorites folder or to the desktop, and release the mouse button.

You'll see that as you type in a URL the browser shows a list of URLs from the history list that start with the letters you've typed so far. You can save typing by selecting the URL you're intending to type.

The Links Toolbar

The links toolbar contains icons that represent other Web pages. Clicking on an item takes you directly to that Web page. What you see the first time you use Internet Explorer varies depending on what version you're using or whether someone else has used the browser. Typically the links toolbar contains links to services offered by Microsoft.

To add an item to the links toolbar, drag the Web page icon from the address bar to the links bar. The links bar is also a folder in the favorites list. You can add an item to the links bar the same way you add an item to any other favorites folder; drag and drop works here too. To delete

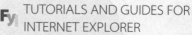

Fyi TUTORIALS AND GUIDES FOR INTERNET EXPLORER

~ Grenville CAP - Internet Explorer Tutorial
http://www.recorder.ca/ grenvillecap/tutorial/tutorial/ tut-004b1.htm

~ Complete Internet Guide and Web Tutorial: All about browsers, searching, building Web pages and more
http://www.microsoft.com/ insider/internet/default.htm

~ Internet Explorer 5 in the Classroom
http://www.actden.com/ ie5/begin

~ Internet Explorer Tutorial
http://www.eiu.edu/ ~mediasrv/ie/menu.html

an item, click on **Favorites** in the standard buttons bar, select the folder links, click on an item using the right mouse button, and select **Delete**.

Status Bar

The status bar shows information about the page as it is being retrieved and displayed, the progress of that retrieval (shown in the status bar), and what security zone is assigned to the current Web page. Internet Explorer has four predefined security zones: Internet, Local Intranet (pages from your own network or computer), Trusted, and Restricted. These zones are used for security purposes. For more information on using these zones, read the sections "Protecting Your Computer While You're Online" and "Sending Information over the Internet Safely" in the online help; press **F1** and click **Contents**.

Now we'll go on to looking at how to use the browser to navigate the Web.

Navigating the Web

Navigation and travel are the ways people describe accessing and using the Internet; it has been called the "Information Highway." Netscape Corporation calls its browser Navigator and uses nautical imagery, such as a pilot's wheel and a lighthouse, as icons. Microsoft Corporation has named its browser Internet Explorer and its ads ask the question "where do you want to go today?" While the navigational theme is just a metaphor (the truth is you don't travel anywhere when you access the Internet), it is commonly accepted and useful for describing a primary function of a Web browser.

Starting at Home

When you start a Web browser, the first page or document you see is called the *home page* for the browser. It's where you start on the WWW. The term is also used another way. Individuals, corporations, institutions, and organizations often have a page or document on the WWW that gives information about them. For example, the URL for the home page for the Smithsonian Institution is **http://www.si.edu**, the URL for the home page for MTV is **http://www.mtv.com**, and one of the authors' home page has the URL **http://www.library.mwc.edu/ ~ khartman**.

Moving Through a Page

Since most Web pages contain more information than can be displayed in one window, you need to know how to move through a page to view all the information. Here are some ways to do that.

- **Using the Scroll Bars.** You can move around or through a document by using the vertical and horizontal scroll bars on the right and bottom of the window. The scroll bars on a browser window are used the same way as in other Windows applications.

- **Using the Keyboard.** Pressing the up or down arrow will move you up or down one line. Pressing the **PgUp** key moves up one window length and pressing **PgDn** moves down one window length. Pressing **Ctrl** + **Home** takes you to the beginning of the document and pressing **Ctrl** + **End** takes you to its end.

- **Finding Text or Searching a Page.** You can search a Web page for a word, a portion of a word, a phrase, or, more generally, any string of characters. To find a string you first have to bring up the dialog box labeled "Find," as shown in Figure 7.2. Type **Ctrl** + **F** on the keyboard.

Figure 7.2   The Find Box

Once the Find dialog box is up, you type in a string (words or characters) and press **Enter** or click on the button **Find Next**. Click **Cancel** to cancel a search. You can select the direction of the search: **Down** from your current position to the end of the Web page or **Up** from the current position to the beginning. Click the box **Match case** if you want to match the string exactly.

Moving from Page to Page: Hyperlinks

You can always tell when the pointer is over a hyperlink because it will change to an image of a hand with a pointing index finger. When this happens, you click on the hyperlink and take a look at the document on the other end. Also the browser displays the URL of the target document in the status bar. Hyperlinks are often underlined or displayed in a distinctive color.

In some cases a small pop-up text box will appear next to the pointer when it's moved over an image. This is called *alternate text*, and it's a description of the hyperlink put in by the author or designer of the Web page.

Followings links from one document to another in a freewheeling way is what is meant by the phase "surfing the Web." When you "surf the Web," you go with the flow by surrendering to the serendipity of unstructured exploration and discovery.

Moving Back and Forward

You'll be able to move backwards and forward through the documents that you have viewed during a session. The easiest way is to click on the items **Back** or **Forward** in the toolbar just below the menu bar.

Back and Forward always take you in through all the Web pages that you have viewed in the same order or in the reverse order that you have viewed them.

You can go back or forward one site at a time or you can select from a list of sites. To go back one site at a time, repeatedly click on **Back**. To go forward one at a time, press **Forward**. To skip to a desired site, do the following:

- Move the mouse pointer so it's over Back on the navigation toolbar.

- Click the right mouse button.

- Click on any site from the list of sites that appears.

Returning to Visited Sites and the History List

The Web browser keeps a record of the path you've taken to get to the current location. To see the path and select a site from it:

 Click on **Go** in the menu bar.

 Click on **View** in the menu bar and select **Go To**.

The browser also keeps track of all the Web pages visited recently in the *history list*. You can use this list to go directly to a Web page without having to go through all the pages in between.

- To display the history list, press [Ctrl] + **H** on the keyboard.

Figure 7.3 illustrates a portion of a sample history list in Netscape Navigator. If you're using Internet Explorer then the history list is displayed as a list of folders in a frame to the left of the content area. You can select and highlight any item by using the up or down arrow on the keyboard or by using the mouse. Once you've highlighted the location you want, double-clicking will take you to the selected page. Click with the right mouse button to copy or delete entries or to add an entry to the bookmark list.

Figure 7.3   The Netscape Navigator History List

The number of days an item may be kept on the history list is set as follows:

 Click on **Edit** in the menu bar, select **Preferences**, and then select the panel titled **Navigator**.

 Click on **Tools** in the menu bar, select **Internet Options**, and then select the panel titled **General**.

Keeping Track—The Bookmark List (Netscape) and the Favorites List (Internet Explorer)

The *bookmark* or *favorites list* is a collection of hyperlinks to Web pages that you want to save from session to session. They could be Web pages or sites you especially like, ones you find useful, or ones you've looked at briefly but want to return to in the future. This is particularly good when you're starting to research a topic. Activity 11.2 (Chapter 11) shows how to use the bookmark list to construct a bibliography.

Each item on the bookmark or favorites list is fundamentally a hyperlink. The browser includes software to manage and arrange the list. You can add items, delete items, arrange them into folders, and so on.

To display the list:

 Use the keyboard shortcut **Ctrl** + **B**. The bookmark list is displayed in a separate window.

 Click on **Favorites** in the toolbar. The favorites list is displayed as a list of folders and hyperlinks in a frame to the left of the content area.

Figure 7.4 shows a sample Internet Explorer favorites list. The Netscape bookmark list is similar. The folder "Imported bookmarks" was created using a utility included with Internet Explorer to convert Netscape bookmarks to favorites. Click on a folder to display its contents, and double-click on an entry to follow the hyperlink.

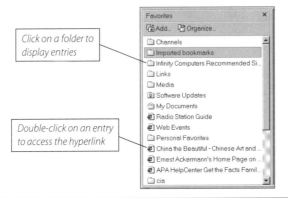

Click on a folder to display entries

Double-click on an entry to access the hyperlink

Figure 7.4   The Internet Explorer Favorites List

∾ Use the keyboard shortcut $\boxed{\text{Ctrl}}$ + **D** to add a hyperlink to the Web page you're currently viewing to either the bookmark or favorites list.

Now that we've covered the navigational basics of using a browser, how about we have some fun and practice? We're going to start at the World Wide Web Virtual Library, take a look at sites that deal with surfing and Hawaii, and then check out some Web resources related to golf.

Remember that the Web is always changing, and there is a possibility that the results you get may differ from those shown here. Don't let this confuse you. These activities are meant to help you learn fundamental skills that don't change, even though the results obtained or the actual screens may look very different.

Activity
7.1

BROWSING THE WWW VIRTUAL LIBRARY - SPORT

Overview

This activity takes us to the WWW Virtual Library. It's a good place to keep in your bookmark or favorites list and contains hyperlinks to information on lots of subjects from Aboriginal Studies to Zoos. Going from site to site is sometimes called browsing or surfing the Internet. Just to show how easy it is to visit a number of sites, regardless of where they are located, we will look in the subject area Sport. We'll find information about surfing (on the water), take a look at some sites in Hawaii, and then take a look at some information about golf—check out the links (Oops, a pun!).

Although this example focuses on the topic of sports, you will also see hyperlinks that could easily take you to different topics if or when you choose to follow them. It's this interconnection of sites and topics that makes the term World Wide Web appropriate. We'll be using Netscape Navigator for this activity. If you use Internet Explorer you'll see that the concepts and most of the details are the same.

We'll assume the computer has established a connection to the Internet and the browser is already started. Here are the steps we'll follow:

1. Display the home page for the World Wide Web Virtual Library (WWW Virtual Library).
2. Select the hyperlink to the Sport home page.
3. Find hyperlinks dealing with surfing in the Sport section.
4. Select the hyperlink for La Jolla surfing.
5. Browse the La Jolla Surfing site for pictures about surfing and weather information.
6. Visit a site with information about Hawaii.
7. Use the history list to go back to the Sport home page.
8. Get information about golf (explore the links!).

While you're going through the steps in this example, practice using Back and Forward in the navigation toolbar. As long as you click on **Forward** as many times as you click on **Back**, you won't lose your place.

Details

1. **Display the home page for the World Wide Web Virtual Library (WWW Virtual Library).**

   When you start your Web browser, your home page will appear on the screen. There just might be a hyperlink to the WWW Virtual Library on that page. Browse through your home page to look for it. If you don't find a hyperlink to the Virtual Library, then follow these instructions:

    Click on the location field, type **http://www.vlib.org**, and then press **Enter**.

   The home page for WWW Virtual Library is shown in Figure 7.5.

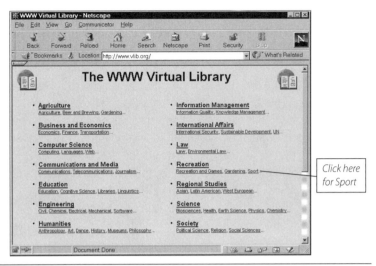

Figure 7.5   The Home Page for WWW Virtual Library

2. Select the hyperlink to the Sport home page.

The home page for the WWW Virtual Library lists major categories and subcategories. We see there is one labeled Sport, as shown in Figure 7.5.

Click on the hyperlink **Sport** on the home page for WWW Virtual Library.

In a few seconds you should see the Web page for the section Sport in the WWW Virtual Library, as shown in Figure 7.6.

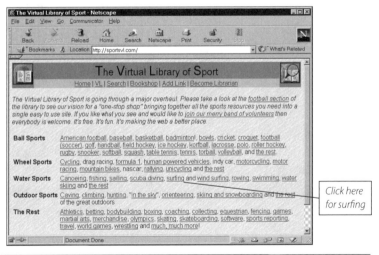

Figure 7.6   The Home Page for the Sport Section of WWW Virtual Library

3. Find hyperlinks dealing with surfing in the Sport section.

We'll follow a hyperlink to get to the water surfing section.

(Do it) Look for the heading Water Sports. Use the scroll bar, the **PgDn** key, or the **↓** key if necessary.

(Do it) Click on the hyperlink **surfing** as shown in Figure 7.6.

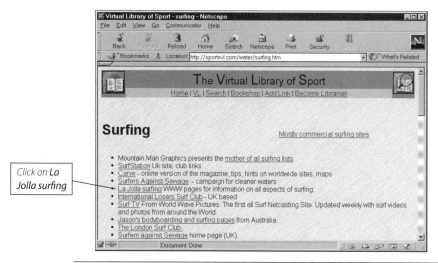

Figure 7.7   The Virtual Library of Sport - Surfing

The Virtual Library of Sport section for surfing as shown in Figure 7.7 appears in a few seconds. Using the scroll bar, you can see that this collection has lots of links to information about surfing. You may want to explore some on your own. We're going to follow the hyperlink "La Jolla surfing." La Jolla is in California, near San Diego. It's the home of the Scripps Research Oceanographic Institute and a great place for surfing. The Web site is also a great place for information about surfing.

4. Select the hyperlink for La Jolla surfing.

(Do it) Click on the hyperlink **La Jolla surfing**.

The Web page titled "La Jolla Surfing" appears. It's shown in Figure 7.8.

*Click on **Weather** for hyperlinks to satellite images, ocean temperature maps, and other interesting resources*

*Click on **Photos** for a gallery of photographs dealing with surfing*

Notice that this portion of the Web page is in a frame

Figure 7.8   The Web Page "La Jolla Surfing"

5. Browse the La Jolla Surfing site for pictures about surfing and weather information.

This is a very nice Web site and has won several awards. The links across the top go to other sections of this Web site. The large picture on the home page is inside of its own frame. You'll see when you follow hyperlinks from this Web site that the resulting information is displayed inside that frame. This keeps the main menus in the window, but it also cuts down on the amount of available space for the information that's in a frame. The frame has its own scroll bar and you'll have to use that to view information that is in the frame but not present on the screen.

> **tip** VIEWING A FRAME IN A NEW WINDOW
>
> You can open a frame in a new window. That way the contents of the frame can use all of the browser's content area. Move the mouse pointer to the frame, and click the right mouse button. A menu pops up. Select **Open Frame in New Window**. This is available to you if you're using Netscape Navigator version 4 or greater or Internet Explorer version 5.01 or greater.

Take a look at the surfing photographs available through this Web site.

(Do it) Click on the hyperlink **Photos**.

This brings up a collection of hyperlinks. Each link leads to a group of small images. (Just so you know, small images like these are sometimes called **thumbnails**.) Click on any of the small images and a larger one appears in the frame. This presents a virtual photographic gallery—real surfing "eye candy." As you move through the collection you may want to return to a previous frame or window. Use Back and Forward in the toolbar to navigate through frames or windows you've visited.

(Do it)! Click on the hyperlink **Weather** on the La Jolla Surfing home page as shown in Figure 7.8.

Clicking on **Weather** brings up a new image in the frame and also changes the menu on the left. Figure 7.9 shows what we see after clicking on **Weather**.

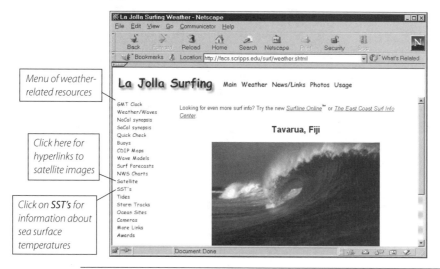

Menu of weather-related resources

Click here for hyperlinks to satellite images

*Click on **SST's** for information about sea surface temperatures*

Figure 7.9   The La Jolla Surfing Weather Web Page

Now we're going to look at some maps and images from satellite photos and imaging.

(Do it)! Click on the hyperlink **Satellite** on the La Jolla Surfing Weather page.

(Do it)! Click on the hyperlink **NOAA's Geostationary Satellite Server**.

This brings a Web page to your browser with links to a variety of images gathered by satellites. We show a portion of it in Figure 7.10.

Figure 7.10   NOAA Geostationary Satellite Server Images

(Do it)!   Click on any of the thumbnails to see a larger image.

Take your time looking around.

We're going to go back to the satellite page and select a link to the School of Ocean and Earth Science and Technology, part of the University of Hawaii. Why? Well, thinking about surfing and viewing this Web site, a site that deals with Hawaii seems appealing. As it turns out, this site has several links to other information about Hawaii.

6. Visit a site with information about Hawaii.

First we'll get back to the page that lists satellite Web sites.

(Do it)!   Return to the list of hyperlinks to satellite Web sites by clicking on **Satellite** in the menu, as shown in Figure 7.10.

(Do it)!   Click on the hyperlink **soest: School of Ocean & Earth Science & Technology**.

This takes you to the home page for the School of Ocean and Earth Science and Technology—the URL is **http://www.soest.hawaii.edu/** in case you want to visit and this path doesn't take you there. We see it's part of the University of Hawaii. There are several links on this page that lead to some great sites about Hawaii. Some of the links are shown in Figure 7.11.

(Do it)!   Use the scroll bar to view the list of links on the School of Ocean & Earth Science & Technology Web page.

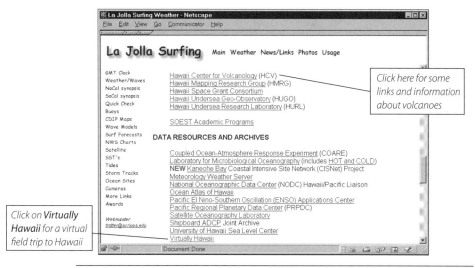

Figure 7.11   Links About Hawaii on the SOEST Web Page

There are several interesting sites listed. We've pointed out two of them that you may want to visit.

 Click on the hyperlink **Hawaii Center for Volcanology**.

This takes you to a site with information about volcanoes and volcanology and several links to other sites dealing with these topics. When you're ready, come back to the page shown in Figure 7.11.

 Click on **Back**, as many times as needed, to return to the page pictured in Figure 7.11.

Now for a virtual field trip.

 Click on the hyperlink **Virtually Hawaii**.

Take your time; look around for a while. You decide when to leave this section. When you're ready, we'll go through the steps of using the history list to get back to the WWW Virtual Library Sport section.

7. **Use the history list to go back to the Sport home page.**

   We've traveled through several pages and now would like to get back to the home page for Sport in the WWW Virtual Library. Certainly one way to do that is by clicking on **Back** in the navigation toolbar until the proper page appears. But we'd have to go through all the intervening pages! It's quicker to select the site from the history list. You can get to the list by pressing **Ctrl** + **H** on the keyboard.

    Press **Ctrl** + H on the keyboard.

   This displays the history list, as shown in Figure 7.12.

Click on the most
recent entry for the
Virtual Library of Sport

Figure 7.12   The History List

 Return to the Virtual Library of Sport by double-clicking on the most recent entry for that site in the history list.

Once the Sport page appears, you may want to close the history list. Do it the same way you'd close any window.

8. Get information about golf (explore the links!).

Now you are at the Virtual Library of Sport home page as shown in Figure 7.6. We'll follow some (hyper)links for information about golf. Look for the hyperlink to golf; it's in the list of links to the right of Ball Sports.

 Click on the hyperlink **golf**.

There's lots to see here, and the choice is yours. Two items with links to lots of other information about golf are GolfWeb and The Virtual Golfer.

 Explore the links!

Clicking on either of those hyperlinks opens a new window for the Web sites they reference. You probably have at least two windows open at this point. Feel free to close any or all of them, or spend some more time navigating the Web.

That's it!

END OF ACTIVITY 7.1

In Activity 7.1 we used some of the navigational features of the Web browser to view Web pages from a variety of sites around the world. Now on to discuss some issues related to security and privacy on the Web, a very important topic!

Security and Privacy on the Web

It's easy to get the impression that we're browsing the Web and using Internet services in an anonymous manner. But that's not the case. Every time you visit a Web site some information about your computer system is transmitted to the server. When you fill out a form the information you provide is passed to a server. Some Web sites track the activities of users through the use of **cookies**. That is information that a Web server passes to or retrieves from the client, the computer that is using a Web browser. You also need to be aware of the risks involved with giving out personal information through email, chat groups, and forms. Since it may be difficult to know with whom you are communicating, you especially need to be careful about disclosing personal information. Children especially need to know about and be informed of the risks and dangers involved with using the Internet.

Now we'll look at issues related to security or secure transmission of information and privacy when using a Web browser.

Computer and Network Security

When you use a computer system connected to the Internet, you're able to reach a rich variety of sites and information. By the same token, any system connected to the Internet can be reached in some manner by any of the other computer systems connected to the Internet. Partaking of the material on the Internet also means that you have to be concerned about the security of your computer system and other systems. The reason for the concern about your system is obvious—you don't want unauthorized persons accessing your information or information belonging to others who share your system. You want to protect your system from malicious or unintentional actions that could destroy stored information or halt your system. You also don't want others masquerading as you. You need to be concerned about the security of other systems so you can have some faith in the information you retrieve from those systems, and so you can conduct some business transactions. A lack of security can result in damage, theft, and what may be worse in some cases, a lack of confidence or trust.

Maintaining security becomes more important as we use the Internet for commercial transactions or transmitting sensitive data. There is always the chance that new services introduced to the Internet won't be completely tested for security flaws or that security problems will be discovered. While it's exciting to be at the cutting edge, there's some virtue in not adopting the latest service or the latest version of software until it has been around for a while. This gives the Internet community a chance to discover problems. Several agencies are dedicated to finding, publicizing, and dealing with security problems. The U.S. Department of Energy maintains "CIAC (Computer Incident Advisory Capability) Security Website," **http://www.ciac.org**.

When you access the Internet by using a login name, your primary defense against intrusion is your password. You need to choose a password that will be difficult to guess. This means choosing a password that's at least six characters long. You'll also want to use a password that contains upper- and lowercase letters and some nonalphabetic characters. Additionally, the password shouldn't represent a word, and it shouldn't be something that's easy to identify with you such as a phone number, room number, birthdate, or license number. Some bad choices are Skippy, 3451234a, or gloria4me. Better choices might be All452on, jmr!pmQ7, or sHo = 7otg. Naturally, you have to choose something you'll remember. Never write down your password; doing that makes it easy to find.

Persons who try to gain unauthorized access to a system are called crackers. A cracker will, by some means, get a copy of the password file for a system containing the names of all the users along with their passwords. (In some cases the permissions on a password file are set so anyone can read it. This is necessary for certain programs to run. Fortunately, the passwords are encrypted.) Once a cracker gets a copy of a password file, she will run a program that attempts to guess the encrypted passwords. If a password is an encrypted version of a word, a word in reverse order, or a word with one numeral or punctuation mark, it is not too difficult for the program to decipher it. If a cracker has one password on a system, she can gain access to that login name and from there possibly go to other portions of the system. So, in addition to creating a good password, you also need to change it regularly.

Because connecting a network to the Internet allows access to that network, system administrators and other persons concerned with network security are very concerned about making that connection. One device or part of a network that can help enhance security is called a *firewall*. A firewall can be a separate computer, a router, or some other network device that allows certain packets into a network. (Remember that all information is passed throughout the Internet as packets.) By using a firewall and configuring it correctly, only certain types of Internet services can be allowed through to the network. Organizations with firewalls often place their Web, FTP, and other servers on one part of their network and put a firewall system between those servers and the rest of the network. The firewall restricts access to the protected internal network by letting through only packets associated with certain protocols. Email can still be delivered, and sometimes Telnet to the internal network is allowed. If you are on the protected portion of the network, behind the firewall, then you can access Internet and Web sites on the Internet, but they may not be able to gain direct access to you. Firewalls also perform logging and auditing functions so that if security is breached, the source of the problem may be determined.

You don't need to be paranoid about security, but you do need to be aware of anything that seems suspicious. Report any suspicious activity or changes to your directory or files to your system or network administrator. He or she can take actions to track down a possible break in security. Be suspicious if you're asked for your password at unusual times. You should be asked for it only when you log in. Never give your password to anyone. If a program changes its behavior in terms of requiring more information from you than it did before, it could be an unauthorized user replaced the original program with another. This is called a Trojan horse, because of the similarity of the program to the classic Greek tale. What appears to be benign could hide some malicious actions or threats.

Fy SECURITY TIPS

~ "Computer Security Information"
http://www.alw.nih.gov/
Security/security.html
~ "Selecting Good Passwords"
http://www.alw.nih.gov/
Security/Docs/passwd.html
~ "Internet Firewalls Frequently
Asked Questions"
http://www.v-one.com/
documents/fw-faq.htm
~ "Virus Bulletin"
http://www.virusbtn.com

One type of program that causes problems for Internet users is called a *virus*. A virus doesn't necessarily copy your data or attempt to use your system. However, it can make it difficult or impossible to use your system. A virus is a piece of code or instructions that attaches itself to existing programs. Just like a biological virus, a computer virus can't run or exist on its own, but must be part of an executing program. When these programs are run, the added instructions are also executed. Sometimes the virus does nothing more than announce its presence; in other cases the virus erases files from your disk. A virus moves from system to system by being part of an executable program. Be careful where you get programs. You can obtain a program that scans your system for viruses and also checks programs you load onto your system for known viruses. Use these antivirus programs to check new programs you load on your system. Also be sure to have a backup copy of your files so they can be restored if they're inadvertently or maliciously erased.

Getting documents and images from other sites on the Internet won't bring a virus to your system. It comes only from running programs on your system. Viruses can exist in executable programs and also have been found in word-processing documents that contain portions of code called macros.

Security is your responsibility and being paranoid about it isn't a solution. You need to take appropriate steps to protect the security of your computer, your information, and your network.

Secure Transmission of Information with a Web Browser

To keep the transmission of information secure we need to guarantee that unauthorized persons cannot view the information and that the received information isn't forged. Both of these are crucial for reliable commercial transactions via a Web browser. A potential buyer may be reluctant to make a purchase using a Web page if he feels uncomfortable about transmitting his credit card number on the Internet. A seller or a buyer may be reluctant to conduct business on the Internet unless he can somehow be sure of the identity of the party he is dealing with.

Encryption

As packets travel from network to network there's really very little to prevent someone (with the proper expertise and equipment) from viewing the contents of the packets. Several encryption schemes or algorithms have been devised to convert messages or any other form of information (even a Web page) into a coded form. In order to read or decode the message, the recipient needs to supply a password. Another way to handle this is to set up a secure path through the Internet. Requiring a password to enter "secure-server mode" does this. The server and the browser encrypt and decrypt all the packets passed between the two sites.

Digital Certificates

A packet of information on the Internet contains the Internet address of the sender, but this can be forged. One method of protecting against this type of forgery is through the use of *digital certificates*. A digital certificate identifies the holder of the certificate. The certificates

Fy DIGITAL CERTIFICATES

∾ Digital Certificates
http://www.brokat.com/int/ netsecurity/authenticate/ certificate.html

∾ FAQ Digital Certificates
http://www.cyfi.com/ products/dcfaq.htm

∾ Security : Technologies : E-commerce - Public Key Infrastructure (PKI)
http://www.ibm.com/security/ technologies/techpki.html

are used to encrypt and decrypt information as well as to provide digital signatures to guarantee the identity of the sender and the authenticity of a certificate. The certificate is used as a public key to encrypt information through Web servers and browsers. Recall that public-key encryption was discussed in Chapter 3. A digital signature is a code that's used to guarantee the identity of the sender and the authenticity of a certificate. An individual or organization obtains a certificate from a company, called a ***certificate authority***, that guarantees the identity of the holder of the certificate. The certificate is attached to the message or Web page and can be used to guarantee the authenticity of information.

Web Page Security Information

The browser is capable of determining the security information about a page. We can examine whether a page is encrypted and whether there are digital certificates associated with it. If the page was encrypted or there is a certificate associated with it then you'll see a closed padlock in the status bar, whether you're using Netscape or Internet Explorer.

~ To view the security information about a page, click on the padlock icon in the status bar.

Figure 7.13 shows the security information displayed by Netscape Navigator for a Web page that permits secure transmission of information. This Web page is one used for making travel reservations.

You can get several types of information related to security and how the browser handles secure or insecure documents. The online help available from the Security Info page gives some useful information about security as it relates to the browser. You can also get information about security issues by clicking on **Help** in the menu bar and selecting **Security**.

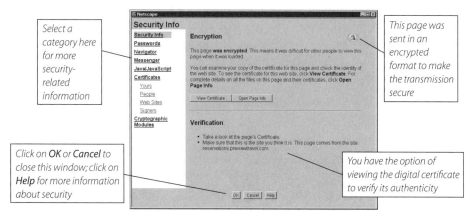

Figure 7.13   The Security Information Window for a Secure Web Page (in Netscape Navigator)

If the document you're working with is secure, the lock will be closed. It's not a good idea to send sensitive or valuable information through the WWW if the lock isn't closed.

Privacy on the Web

When you retrieve Web pages while visiting sites on the Web, you leave a trail of your activity behind. Much of the trail is generated automatically. Web servers record information about every request and your client also records information about the sites you visit. Sometimes we give out information about ourselves. That's fine as long as we're aware of who is collecting the information and how it will be used.

What Happens When You Go to a Web Site— What the Server Knows

When you go to a Web site, either by clicking on a hyperlink or by typing in a URL in the location field, your browser (the client program) sends a request to a Web server. This request includes the IP address of your computer system, the URL of the file or Web page you've requested, the time the request was made, and whether the request was successful. If you clicked on a hyperlink from a Web page, the URL of the Web page is also passed to the server. All of this information is kept in log files on the server. It's possible to have the log files analyzed and track all access to a Web server.

The Trail Left on Your Computer

We've seen that each server keeps log files to identify requests for Web pages. So in that sense you leave a trail of your activities on each of the Web servers that you contact. There's also a trail of your activities kept on the computer you use to access the Web. Recently accessed Web pages and a list of the URLs accessed are kept in the **cache**—a folder or directory that contains recently viewed Web pages, images, and other resources—and the history list. If you're using a computer to access the Web in a public place, such as a lab or a library, then it's possible for someone to check on your activities.

Cache

Most Web browsers keep copies of recently accessed Web pages, images, and other files. Netscape and other browsers call this the cache; Microsoft Internet Explorer calls these temporary Internet files. When you return to a Web page you've visited recently, the browser first checks to see if it's available in the cache and retrieves it from your computer rather than retrieving it from a remote site. It's much faster to retrieve a Web page from the cache rather than from a remote site. This is convenient, but it also leaves a record of your activities. It is possible to clear the cache or remove the temporary files.

 If you're using Netscape: Bring up the Preferences panel by clicking on **Edit** in the menu bar and selecting **Preferences**; next bring up the Cache panel by clicking on **Advanced** and then clicking on **Cache**; and finally clear the disk cache by clicking on **Clear Disk Cache**.

 If you're using Internet Explorer: Click on **Tools** in the menu bar, select **Internet Options**, then click on the tab **General** (if it's not already in the foreground). Now click on **Delete Files** in the section titled "Temporary Internet Files."

History List

The Web browser keeps a record of the path you've taken to get to the current location. To see the path and select a site from it,

 Click on **Go** in the menu bar.

 Click on **View** in the menu bar and select **Go To**.

The browser also keeps a list of all the Web pages visited recently in the history list. This list is kept around for a time period specified in days. You can set the number of days an item may be kept on the list. You can also delete the files from the history list.

 Click on **Edit** in the menu bar, select **Preferences**, and then click on **Navigator**. Set the number of days items are kept in the history list or delete the entire list (click on **Clear History**) here.

 Click on **Tools** in the menu bar, select **Internet Options**, then click on the tab **General** (if it's not already in the foreground). Set the number of days items are kept in the history list or delete the entire list (click on **Clear History**) here.

Cookies

A cookie is information that's passed to a Web server by the Web browser program. A Web server requests and/or writes a cookie to your computer only if you access a Web page that contains the commands to do that. Cookies are used to store information such as a login name and password or information about what portions of a Web site were visited on your computer. When you request a Web page a server can retrieve the information that it stored on your computer. Netscape developed the terms and methods for working with cookies.

Cookies are sometimes viewed as an invasion of privacy, but they are useful to you in some cases. Suppose you want to visit a site frequently that requires you to give a password or a site that you can customize to match your preferences. The protocol HTTP is used when you visit a Web site. When a Web page is requested,

 COOKIES

~ "cookie – Webopedia Definition and Links"
http://webopedia.internet.com/TERM/c/cookie.html

~ "The Truth About Cookies" by Christopher Barr
http://www.cnet.com/Content/Voices/Barr/042996

~ "An Introduction to Cookies"
http://www.hotwired.com/webmonkey/geektalk/96/45/index3a.html?tw=backend

a connection is made between the client and the server and the server delivers a Web page. Once the page has been transmitted the connection is terminated. If you visit a site again, the server, through HTTP, has no information about a previous visit. Cookies can be used to keep track of your password or keep track of some preferences you've set for every visit to that site. That way you don't have to enter the information each time you visit.

Web browsers allow you to control how you will deal with cookies:

 You have the option to not accept any cookies, to accept only cookies that get returned to the server that put them on your computer, or to be warned before accepting a cookie. To do that click on **Edit** in the menu bar, select **Preferences**, and then click on **Advanced**.

 You can set security zones for different types of Web sites. To set security zones, click on **Tools** in the menu bar, select **Internet Options**, then click on the tab **Security** (if it's not already in the foreground). To customize how cookies are dealt with, click on **Customize**.

Giving Out Information About Yourself and Your Family

There are a number of situations in which you may be asked or tempted to give out personal information. These can range from being asked to fill out a form to download some software or sign up for a service on the Web to being asked for your address or phone number through email or a chat group. Any information you put into a form will be passed to a Web server and find its way into a database. Disclosing your street address to a business sometimes results in your receiving junk mail, and disclosing your email address may result in your getting unsolicited junk email, or "spam" as it's called. You can't be sure how the information will be used or marketed unless the organization gathering the data makes some explicit guarantees. We hear about and come across situations of fraudulent practices and schemes that swindle money from unsuspecting individuals in our daily lives, and we're just as likely to come across those types of situations when were using the Internet. It's relatively easy to create an Internet or Web presence that makes an individual, a company, or an organization appear to be legitimate and trustworthy. Because of this we need to be all the more skeptical and cautious when conducting personal or commercial dealings on the Internet.

More dangerous situations can arise when we develop a relationship with someone through email or a chat group. These can arise because when we're communicating with someone on the Internet most of the communication is through text. We don't get to hear the person's voice or see them. We may see a picture or they may tell us about themselves, but we may never know with whom we are communicating. For example, I may be involved in a long series of email messages or have several conversations in a chat room with a person who claims to be my age and gender. The person may even send me a photograph. It could be that the person is totally misrepresenting their true self. So we need to be very careful about giving out any personal information, and we certainly wouldn't make arrangements to meet the person without having the meeting take place in a public location and without taking other precautions.

Children particularly need to discuss these issues with their parents, and they need to understand clearly stated rules about not giving out any personal information or telling someone where they go to school or play.

Fyi PRIVACY AND SNOOPING

~ "Privacy Analysis of Your Internet Connection" by The Anonymizer
http://privacy.net/anonymizer

~ "Privacy Initiatives" by Federal Trade Commission
http://www.ftc.gov/privacy/index.html

~ "Someone to Watch over You" by Andrew Leonard
http://www.salon.com/sept97/21st/article970918.html

Common sense tells us not to give out personal information, home phone numbers, or home addresses to people we don't know. We're likely not to do that in our daily lives when we don't know the person who is asking for the information, and it is just as important to apply the same rules when we're using the Internet or the World Wide Web. The Internet and the World Wide Web give us lots of opportunities for learning, recreation, and communication. We don't need to be rude or unfriendly, but we do need to be careful, safe, and secure.

tip The Web page "Staying Street Smart on the Web!," **http://www.yahooligans.com/docs/safety**, is a good place to find information about Internet safety issues for children and parents.

Summary

The Web browser is your access point to the information and resources that make up the World Wide Web. When you click on a hyperlink or type a URL in the location field or address box the browser requests information from a Web server. When the information is delivered it is the browser's job to display the information or start another program to deal with it.

The commands you use to work with the Web browser are available through the menu bar, the toolbars, the keyboard, and the menus that pop up when you use the right or secondary mouse button. These ways of accessing commands or features stay the same, regardless of what you're viewing or working with on the World Wide Web. The menu bar is a collection of pulldown menus that you can use for almost every operation or command. The toolbar has a number of items, often displayed as text and icons, that give quick access to some of the commands in the menu bar. Several commands are also available as keyboard shortcuts, meaning that you can type them directly on the keyboard instead of using a mouse.

Once a page is in the browser's window, you can move around the page using the keyboard, the scroll bars, or the mouse. You can search for words in the page.

To go to another page, move the mouse to a hyperlink (the pointer turns into a hand) and click on it. You can also type a URL in the location bar or address box and then press **Enter** to access it.

The browser keeps track of the sites you've visited during recent sessions. It does this so that you can backtrack and return to sites during a session. The history list holds links to all the sites that you have visited recently. You can collect a set of hyperlinks in the bookmark or favorites list. These will be available from one session to the next. The browser contains commands to let you maintain and manage your bookmark or favorites list.

Security and privacy on the World Wide Web are important topics for a variety of reasons, including an individual's desire for privacy, the increased use of the Internet for commercial transactions, and the need to maintain the integrity of information. If you access the Internet by logging into a computer system, you need to take care to choose a password that will be difficult to guess. Furthermore, you should notice and report any unusual circumstances or modifications.

Selected Terms Used in This Chapter

address box	history list
alternate text	home page
bookmark list	location field
cache	location toolbar
certificate authority	menu bar
content area	navigation toolbar
cookie	scroll bar
digital certificate	status bar
favorites list	thumbnail
firewall	toolbar
frame	virus

Exercises and Projects

As you work through these exercises and projects you'll get practice using your Web browser and have the opportunity to visit several different Web sites.

1. Use your browser to view the Web page "About the World Wide Web," **http://www.w3.org/WWW**. Follow the link **International World Wide Web Conferences**.
   a. Where and when did the first international WWW conference take place?
   b. Name the winner and honorable mention recipients in the cateegory Best Campus-Wide Information Service at that conference.
   c. Where and when did the eighth international WWW conference take place?
   d. What are the titles and the names of the people responsible for the poster that won the Best Poster award.
   e. Go back to "About the World Wide Web." Follow the link labeled **CERN**. What is CERN?

2. This exercise deals with the online help provided through your browser.

    a. Click on **Help** in the menu bar, and select the item that begins with the word **About**. What's displayed? What's the name and version of the browser you're using?

    b. Press **F1** on the keyboard. That should open the online Help window. Find a section on customizing the browser. Write down step-by-step instructions for changing fonts and background colors.

    c. With the Help window still open, click on **Index** and type the word **cookies** in the search form. Read the Help information about cookies. What did you learn that you didn't know before?

3. Use your browser to access the WWW Virtual Library, **http://www.vlib.org**, and find the section Broadcasters.

    a. What are the names of four broadcasters listed, each from a different continent? Also give the URLs of their Web sites.

    b. Visit each of the sites and write a brief description of each.

    c. Find at least one site in a foreign country that lets you listen to or view a broadcast. Give the URL and take advantage of the opportunity to hear or see a broadcast. Describe the broadcast.

4. Use your browser to access the Web site with the URL **http://www.excite.com/travel/regions/europe**. Follow links on this page (you can use the hyperlinks embedded in the map) to get information to answer the following.

    a. What's the weather like in Venice today?

    b. What's the best time to visit Venice?

    c. What's listed in the category Features and Events?

    d. What's the weather like in Bergamo?

    e. Now visit the online version of "Rough Guides," **http://travel.roughguides.com**, and look for information about Bergamo. What are some of the main sites to visit there?

5. Access the history list.

    a. What are the five sites most recently visited?

    b. What are the five sites that have been in the history list the longest?

    c. Empty the history list.

6. The Web page "E&P Media Links," **http://emedia1.mediainfo.com/emedia**, has lists of newspapers on the Web. Follow links to five different newspapers from five different continents.

    a. Add a link to each in your bookmark or favorites list.

b. Using the online help, create a folder in the bookmark or favorites list titled **Newspapers** and move the bookmarks for the individual newspapers into that folder.

7. Use your browser to access the American Memory Collection at the Library of Congress, **http://www.loc.gov**.
   a. Find the collection "Southern Mosaic: The John and Ruby Lomax 1939 Southern States Recording Trip." Give its URL.
   b. Move the mouse pointer so it's not on an image or a hyperlink. Press the right or secondary mouse button. What's displayed? How is it useful?
   c. Move the mouse pointer so it's over a hyperlink. What's displayed? How is it different than what was displayed in part b?
   d. Using the mouse and the right or secondary mouse button, open the section **Audio Subject** in a separate window. In that window follow the hyperlink **Blues songs**. Pick out one recording and listen to it. What's the title of the recording and who performs it?
   e. Now go back to the Web page you found in part a. Search the collection to find a photograph that contains both a fiddle and a banjo. What's the title of the photograph?
   f. The description of the photograph you fond in part e contains a link **Rights and Reproductions**. Follow that link. What does the text say about the use of this image?

8. Here are the names of three newsgroups on the topic of Web browsers.
   ~ **comp.infosystems.browsers.mac**
   ~ **comp.infosystems.browsers.misc**
   ~ **comp.infosystems.browsers.ms-windows**
   Subscribe to one of these groups and read some of the articles.
   a. What's the most popular topic?
   b. Find one question that was asked and answered in the newsgroup. State the question and give a summary of the answers.

9. Visit the Web site Webopedia, **http://www.webopedia.com**.
   a. Look up the term *digital certificate*. Give a brief definition.
   b. Explain what is meant by the term *certificate authority*.
   c. What's the difference between a digital certificate and a digital signature?

10. Visit the Web site "Privacy Analysis of Your Internet Connection," **http://privacy.net/anonymizer**. The information that's displayed is part of the trail you leave behind when you surf the Web.
    a. What is your IP address?
    b. Was a persistent cookie added to your computer? What is it?

     c. Are there any plug-ins installed on your computer? If so list five of them.

     d. What's the answer to the question, "Does your browser give out your email address?"

     e. How does this Web page determine whether your browser gives out your email address?

11. Visit the Web site "Anonymizer," **http://www.anonymizer.com**.

     a. What services does it offer?

     b. Do you think you would need to use any of its services? Explain.

     c. Try out Anonymizer surfing and describe how it works.

12. Visit the Web site "Privacy Initiatives," **http://www.ftc.gov/privacy/index.html**.

     a. List three initiatives that you think are most important and state why that is the case.

     b. Write a short paper (one to three pages) describing one of the initiatives in detail.

13. Visit the Web page "Staying Street Smart on the Web!" **http://www.yahooligans.com/docs/safety**.

     a. Follow the hyperlink **What you should know as a parent** and describe the risks mentioned on that Web page.

     b. Go back to the previous Web page and click on the link **Yahooligans! Privacy Policy**. What is the privacy policy and what does TRUSTe have to do with it?

14. Visit the Web page "Virus Bulletin," **http://www.virusbtn.com**.

     a. There are several hyperlinks on that page. Visit all or a few and list three that you think would be useful to you. Explain why you choose those three.

     b. Follow the hyperlink **Virus Analyses** and read about the Win32/SKA virus. What does it do to an infected computer?

     c. Go back to the previous page and follow the hyperlink **Virus Hoax Listing**. What do they recommend you do when you receive a virus warning message?

Chapter 8

FINDING INFORMATION

ON THE WORLD

WIDE WEB

All types of digital information are on the World Wide Web. You can find everything from government statistics, fast-breaking news stories, up-to-the-minute weather reports, sales catalogs, and business information to radio programs, movies, music, and virtual art galleries and museums. In addition to the educational institutions, corporations, associations, and government agencies that generate an immense collection of valuable information, hundreds of thousands of individuals contribute to this vast accumulation of resources by adding their personal pages to the Web all over the world.

Finding these resources can be a challenge. This is why you'll find that becoming proficient in evaluating your information needs effectively and learning database search techniques are some of the most important skills you can acquire. In this chapter, we'll focus on search tools that are evolving to meet the needs of many users and show you, with examples, how to use the major types. All of the resources covered have their advantages and disadvantages, and depending on what kind of information you're looking for and how experienced a user you are, each can be useful. Also, many social and ethical issues arise because of the diverse content on the Web. This chapter will provide a brief overview of free speech, censorship, and intellectual property issues.

Goals/Objectives

- Know the difference between a directory and a search engine
- Know when a particular type of tool should be used in the research process
- Know how a search engine is constructed
- Comprehend the advantages and disadvantages of the search tools discussed
- Gain a basic understanding of how intelligent agents work
- Become familiar with censorship and intellectual property issues

Topics

- ∾ The First Step: Evaluating Your Information Needs
- ∾ Choosing the Best Search Tool to Start With
- ∾ Directories
- ∾ Virtual Libraries
- ∾ Search Engines and Meta-Search Tools
- ∾ Intelligent Agents
- ∾ Content Issues: Pornography, Free Speech, Censorship, Filtering, and Copyright

The First Step: Evaluating Your Information Needs

Before you get online and start your search for information, think about what types of material you're looking for. Are you interested in finding facts to support an argument, authoritative opinions, statistics, research reports, descriptions of events, images, or movie reviews? Do you need current information or facts about an event that occurred 20 years ago? When is the Web a smart place to start? Sometimes the information you want is on the Web but is difficult to find. A reference book in your library may have the information you need and may be found more quickly. Don't think that just because you can't locate the material you need on the Web that it doesn't exist. It may seem that the Web would contain all the information that you'd need, but this is not always the case.

Types of Information Most Likely Found on the Internet and the World Wide Web

- ∾ **Current information.** Many newspapers and popular magazines have Web versions that provide news updates throughout the day. Current financial and weather information is also easily accessible.

- ∾ **U.S. government information.** Most federal, state, and local government agencies provide statistics and other information freely and in a timely manner.

- ∾ **Popular culture.** It's easy to find information on the latest movie or best-selling book.

- ∾ **Full-text versions of books and other materials that are not under copyright restriction.** For example, Shakespeare's plays, the Bible, *Canterbury Tales,* and hundreds of other full-text literary resources are available. Several of them have been made into searchable databases, which have enhanced scholarly research in the humanities.

- **Business and company information.** Not only do many companies provide their Web pages and annual reports, there are also several databases that provide in-depth financial and other information about companies.

- **Consumer information.** The Internet is a virtual gold mine of information for people who are interested in buying a particular item and want opinions from people about it. With access to everything from automobile reviews on the Web to Usenet newsgroups, consumers can find out about almost any item before they buy it.

- **Medical information.** In addition to the hospitals, pharmaceutical companies, and nonprofit organizations that provide excellent sources of medical information, the National Library of Medicine has freely provided the MEDLINE database to the public since late 1997.

- **Entertainment.** The Web is becoming the first place many go to find games, audio files, and video clips.

- **Software.** The Web hosts software archives in which you can search for and *download* software to your computer without cost.

- **Unique archival sites.** For example, the Library of Congress archives Americana in its American Memory collection.

Some Reasons Why the World Wide Web Won't Have Everything You Are Looking For

- Publishing companies and authors who make money by creating and providing information usually choose to use the traditional publishing marketplace and not make the information free via the Internet.

- Scholars most often choose to publish their research in reputable scholarly journals and university presses rather than on the Web. More academic journals are becoming Web-based, but a subscription to the online version often costs as much as the paper form.

- Several organizations and institutions would like to publish valuable information on the Web but don't because of a lack of staff or funding.

- The Web tends to include information that is in demand to a large portion of the public. The Web can't be relied upon consistently for historical information, which isn't in high demand. For example, if you needed today's weather data for Minneapolis, Minnesota, the Web will certainly have it. But if you wanted Minneapolis climatic data for November 1976, you perhaps would not find it on the Web.

Sometimes you'll find that by evaluating your needs before starting your research, you don't need to get online at all. You may find out that your library has an excellent CD-ROM database that provides historical meteorological data for the entire United States. Perhaps your library will have a better source in paper form. Don't be shy about asking a reference librarian to help you determine whether the Internet or some other resource will have the most appropriate material to choose from on the topic you are researching.

Choosing the Best Search Tool to Start With

Once you've decided that the Web is likely to have the information you're seeking, you'll need to choose an appropriate search tool. Table 8.1 shows the major types of search tools available on the World Wide Web and their major characteristics.

Type of Search Tool	Major Characteristics
Directories and virtual libraries	∾ Contain topical lists of selected resources, hierarchically arranged ∾ Many directories rate and review Web resources ∾ Meant to be browsed, but can also be searched by keyword ∾ Depend on people for selection and control of the included resources ∾ Usually best for broad topics ∾ Updated less frequently than search engine databases ∾ Tend to have small databases ∾ Contain links to subject guides and specialized databases
Search engines	∾ Attempt to index as much of the Web as possible ∾ Most are full-text databases ∾ Require knowledge of search techniques to guarantee good results ∾ Databases are created by computer programs called *spiders* or *robots* ∾ Most often used for multifaceted topics and obscure subjects ∾ Search very large databases that are updated frequently

Meta-search tools		Some allow you to search several search engines simultaneously
		Some supply lists of databases that can be searched directly from their pages
		Provide a good way to keep up with new search engines
		May not fully exploit the features of individual search engines, so you must keep your search simple
Intelligent agents		Software entities that perform tasks on your behalf
		Some can send the information requested on a schedule that you define
		Sometimes referred to as *bots* or *robots*
		Agents work with some degree of autonomy

Table 8.1   Major Search Tools and Their Characteristics

Selecting a Tool Wisely: Knowing the Difference Between a Directory and a Search Engine

As you can see from the list, there are several types of search tools. How do you choose the best one to start with? Knowing the difference between a search engine and a directory is crucial to your success. Browsing **directories** can be a very effective way to find the resources you need, especially if you're sure of the general information you're looking for. If you need specific information, however, a search engine is the tool you'll want to use. The reason for this is that directories cover a small portion of the Web, and they don't index all of the words that appear in the Web pages they catalog. Search engine databases, however, aim to cover as much of the Web as possible, and most index every word in every Web page. Directories depend on human beings to create and maintain their collections; virtual libraries are the most dependent on people.

Here's an example that illustrates the difference between search engines and directories. Let's say we wanted to find information on a multifaceted topic, such as the regulation of food safety. We maybe would find something about it by browsing in a directory, but we'd have to be sure of the category that included it. Would we look under science, health, or government? We could search the directory using the keywords **food**, **safety**, and **government**, but if these words didn't appear in the categories, Web page titles, or annotations, there would be no results. In a search engine database, by contrast, all we would need to do is type **"food safety" AND government** in a search form.

There Are Always Exceptions

Sometimes even specific information is more easily found in a directory than in a search engine. For instance, let's say you wanted to know who was the first prime minister of India. If you typed in the search expression **"prime minister" AND India**, you'd probably get thousands of hits and many of them would be about the current prime minister and not the one you were looking for. A directory maybe would be the best place to go for this. There may be a site that focuses on India's history and politics, which would give a detailed listing of past leadership in the country and other statistics.

Virtual Libraries: Directories with a Difference

Virtual libraries are similar to traditional libraries, in that the information specialists who manage them select and catalog the Web pages that are included in their directories, much as librarians select and catalog materials that are included in their libraries. Virtual libraries are the best directories to go to for subject guides, reference works, and specialized databases. For example, if you were looking for the state of Minnesota's climate statistics for November 1976, you would want to find a site that collects authoritative weather data. You maybe would want to start out by using a virtual library to help you find hyperlinks to a meteorological database.

A Checklist to Help You Choose the Right Tool

Directories and virtual libraries are most useful when you
- are at the beginning of your research
- are searching for an overview of a topic
- want evaluated resources
- are searching for facts (for example, population statistics or country information)
- need to find a specialized database for specific information

Search engines should be consulted when you
- are searching for a multifaceted topic
- are looking for a person's name
- want very recent information on a topic
- want to limit your search to a certain period of time
- are searching for obscure information

Meta-search tools should be used when you
- want to save time by getting an idea of what is available from several tools at once
- are searching for very obscure topics

Personal agents are useful when you

~ regularly search for the same type of information

~ want a program to repeat a search over and over again

~ want a program to perform a particular task with the information it finds, for example, compare prices of certain items

Now that you have an idea of what types of tools are available, the next sections will cover each in detail. For the most common types of tools (directories, virtual libraries, and search engines), we've supplied hands-on activities to give you practical experience in how to use them. The exercises at the end of the chapter will give you an opportunity to try meta-search tools and intelligent agents.

Directories

Directories, sometimes referred to as subject catalogs, are topical lists of selected Web resources arranged in a hierarchical way. By hierarchical we mean that the **subject categories** are arranged from broadest to most specific. For example, this is a **hierarchy:**

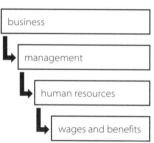

In this example, **management** is a subcategory of **business, human resources** is a subcategory of **management**, and **wages and benefits** is a subcategory of **human resources**. In a hypertext environment like the World Wide Web, browsing from one subject to a more detailed part of that subject is quite simple. If you clicked on **business**, which is the **top-level category** or heading, the computer screen would fill with a list of subject categories narrower than **business** including, in our example, **management**. Clicking on **management** would cause the screen to fill with even more subject categories. You would choose the subject you wanted, **human resources**. Then you would click on one of the items in the last subcategory, **wages and benefits**. After you chose each subcategory, the screen would fill with a list of Web pages that you could then choose by clicking on their titles.

The following are the most well known directories on the World Wide Web:

Directory	URL
Galaxy	**http://galaxy.einet.net**
Go Network	**http://www.go.com**

HotBot Directory	**http://www.hotbot.com**
LookSmart	**http://www.looksmart.com**
Magellan Web Guide	**http://magellan.excite.com**
Open Directory Project	**http://dmoz.org**
WebCrawler Channels	**http://webcrawler.com**
Yahoo!	**http://www.yahoo.com**

Table 8.2   Major Directories on the World Wide Web

Many of the major search tools contain a directory and a search engine. This way you can try both methods in one service. The directory part of the search engine is usually a subset of the entire database, and the sites listed in a directory are often evaluated, summarized, and given ratings. For example, Magellan is a search engine database that indexes a large part of the Web, but its directory, Magellan Web Guide, which includes rated and reviewed Web pages, covers a small portion of the resources available in the search engine database.

Characteristics of Directories

While all directories are reliant upon people to select, maintain, and update their resource lists, each one differs from the others mainly by the level of quality control involved in the management of the directory.

For example, some directories have very little control over their collections, relying on Web page submitters to provide annotations and decisions about where their resource should be placed in the directory's hierarchy. Other directories are much more selective about not only which resources are included, but also where in the subject hierarchy the pages will be located, and they write detailed annotations of them, which can be evaluative, descriptive, or both. Many annotated directories also rate Web resources using criteria that vary from one directory to another. Some of the inherent strengths of directories can also be weaknesses and vice versa. We'll examine some of these strengths and weaknesses here.

Fyi INFORMATION ON THE WEB ABOUT DIRECTORIES

~ "Searching by Means of Subject Directories"
http://www.monash.com/ spidap1.html#directories

~ "Comparing Internet Subject Directories"
http://www.notess.com /search/dir

~ "Using Subject Directories: A Tutorial"
http://home.sprintmail.com/ ~debflanagan/subject.html

Strengths of Directories

- ~ Directories contain fewer resources than search engine databases
- ~ Many directories rate, annotate, or categorize the chosen resources
- ~ Directories are more likely to retrieve relevant results

Because directories are maintained by people, they contain fewer resources than search engine databases. This can be a plus, especially when you are looking for information on a general topic. In addition, many directories rate, annotate, analyze, evaluate, and categorize the resources that are included, so you can quickly access useful resources. While we'll be discussing the evaluation of Internet resources in detail later in the book, now is a good time to bring up the issue of quality control and filtering of WWW sites. With thousands of resources appearing on the Web each day, it is important that there are people determining which sites and pages on the World Wide Web have the highest quality. For example, if we wanted to find some foreign language dictionaries and translation services on the Web, we could try Magellan's directory. Magellan's Web Guide is an annotated directory that also selects the best sites and gives them ratings and often reviews. Figure 8.1 shows the top-level categories of Magellan. We could click on **Reference** first.

Figure 8.1   The Magellan Web Guide Directory

After you chose **Reference**, your browser window would show subcategories that you would then choose from. A logical choice would be **Dictionaries & Thesauri**. Finally, you'd have more choices that would lead you to the results you wanted. After choosing **Foreign Language**, you would get a list of resources that you could then look through. If you scrolled down the list, you'd find a list of translation services and translating dictionaries, as shown in Figure 8.2.

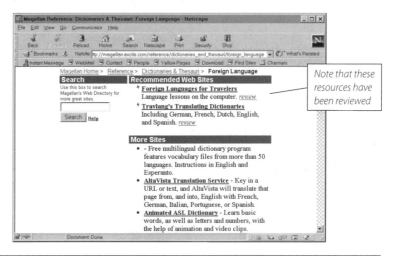

Figure 8.2   Foreign Language Dictionaries Found by Browsing Magellan

Weaknesses of Directories

∼ Arbitrary hierarchical arrangements

∼ Infrequently updated

∼ Subjectivity of rating and annotating of resources

It may be helpful to think of browsing a directory by subject like going through subjects in a card catalog. You may find exactly what you are looking for by browsing through many pages or cards filled with information, but then again, you may miss some related information because your subject may appear in many different cate-gories. For example, we found resources on translating foreign languages in the foreign lan-guage dictionaries category in Magellan, but there may be information on this in the Busi-ness category too, since busi-nesspeople often have a need for translation services. Browsing a

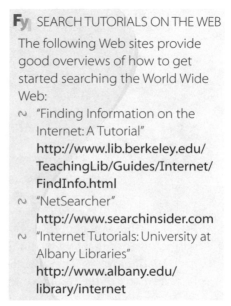

Fy SEARCH TUTORIALS ON THE WEB

The following Web sites provide good overviews of how to get started searching the World Wide Web:

∼ "Finding Information on the Internet: A Tutorial"
    http://www.lib.berkeley.edu/ TeachingLib/Guides/Internet/ FindInfo.html

∼ "NetSearcher"
    http://www.searchinsider.com

∼ "Internet Tutorials: University at Albany Libraries"
    http://www.albany.edu/ library/internet

directory requires that you think categorically about the subject you are looking for. Many directories have simple keyword searching ability for just this reason. Keyword searching was created to help you find information without having to know which category the information may be in. A well-designed directory with keyword searching ability can help alleviate the problem of arbitrary hierarchical arrangements.

Since directories are maintained by people, they are not updated as quickly as search engine databases, which rely on computer programs to add new Web pages automatically. Keep this in mind when you are looking for very recent information.

Another potential drawback, especially in those directories that rate and review resources, is the fact that someone else has selected, rated, and possibly reviewed a resource, and this subjectivity by its very nature restricts your choices. You may not agree with the selections or ratings that the directory administrators have made. What seems a good resource to one person may not seem that way to the next. This is why it's important that the directory management has well-stated criteria for its selection and rating of resources.

Now that we've discussed the major characteristics of directories, let's try an activity in the most popular directory on the Web today, Yahoo! Yahoo! is the most comprehensive directory on the Web. You can browse Yahoo! by subject category or you can search it by keyword. If you do a search and the keyword isn't found in the database, Yahoo! automatically sends your search request to a full-text search engine. In the following activity, we'll browse Yahoo! for our topic and then we'll search the database by typing in a keyword.

> Remember that the Web is always changing and there is a possibility that the results you get may differ from those shown here. Don't let this confuse you. These activities are meant to demonstrate fundamental skills that don't change, even though the number of results obtained or the actual screens may look very different.

USING A DIRECTORY TO FIND INFORMATION

Overview

In this activity, we'll go to the directory Yahoo! and browse its subject categories for information on international refugees. We're looking for authoritative information, including statistics. We'll find some information on this topic by browsing the subject categories and then find more resources by searching using a keyword. We'll compare the results from browsing by subject and searching by keyword and show you the differences between the two modes.

We'll follow these steps:

1. Open the location for Yahoo! (We'll assume the Web browser is started.)
2. Browse Yahoo! for information on refugees.
3. Search Yahoo! by typing in **refugees** in the search form.
4. Bookmark the most promising Web page.

Details

1. Open the location for Yahoo!

(Do it)! Point to the location field and click. The URL of the current Web page will change color. Now you can type in the URL for Yahoo!

(Do it)! Type **http://www.yahoo.com** and press **Enter**.

2. Browse Yahoo! for information on refugees.

Browsing a directory requires that you make guesses about what your topic's hierarchical placement might be. In this activity, we'll start with the top-level category **Society and Culture** since our topic has to do with the movement of people.

(Do it)! Click on **Society and Culture**, as shown in Figure 8.3.

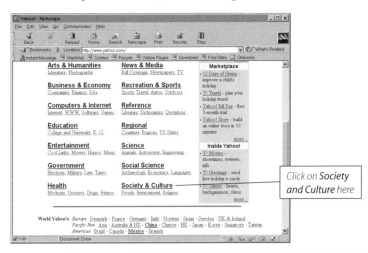

Figure 8.3   Yahoo!'s Top-Level Categories

Figure 8.4 shows the categories that are under **Society and Culture**. There are a few categories that may provide you with connections to information about refugees. **People** might provide some useful links, as might the category **Cultures and Groups**. The **Issues & Causes** category, however, seems to us the best category to choose.

(Do it)   Click on **Issues and Causes**.

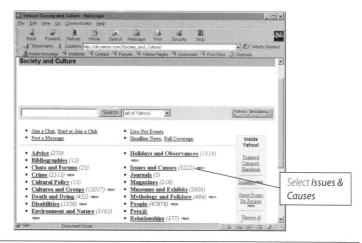

Figure 8.4   The Subcategories of Society and Culture:
                    Issues and Causes in Yahoo!

Scroll down the list of subcategories until you find a term related to the topic of refugees. **Human Rights** seems to be the best category to choose. We have read a lot about the international refugee situation in the context of human rights.

(Do it)   Click on **Human Rights**.

Figure 8.5 shows the results of selecting **Human Rights**. Note that there is subcategory entitled **Refugees**.

(Do it)   Click on **Refugees**, as shown in Figure 8.5.

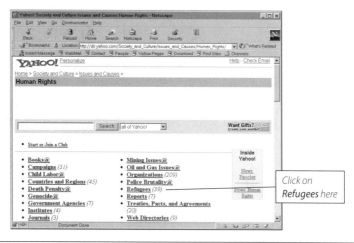

Figure 8.5   The Subcategories of Human Rights in Yahoo!

Any one of the Web pages retrieved, shown in Figure 8.6, may be useful.

3. Search Yahoo! by typing in **refugees** in the search form.

It's a good idea to also do a keyword search to check for items in other categories. To do that, type a keyword in the search form, select whether to search the whole database or just this category, and click on **Search**.

 Type **refugees** in the search form provided, as shown in Figure 8.6. Make sure **Search all of Yahoo** is selected, and click on **Search**.

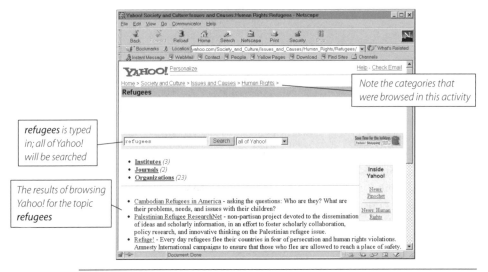

Figure 8.6   The Results of Browsing Yahoo! and the Initiation of a Keyword Search

Figure 8.7 shows the results of this keyword search. Note the second category match is from a category that we didn't find by browsing. It is a subcategory of Government: International Organizations: United Nations: Programs and is called United Nations High Commissioner for Refugees. This category looks extremely promising because it is information provided by the United Nations, which may have the authoritative data we need.

 Click on **Government: International Organizations: United Nations: Programs: United Nations High Commissioner for Refugees**, as shown in Figure 8.7.

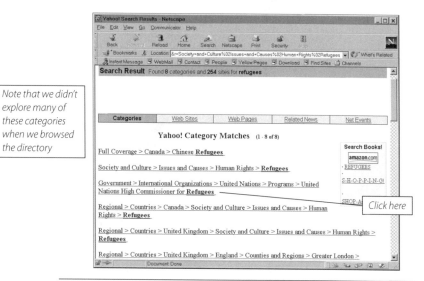

Note that we didn't explore many of these categories when we browsed the directory

Figure 8.7 The Results of Searching for the Keyword **refugees** in Yahoo!

You'll now have a few hyperlinks to choose from.

Click on **United Nations High Commissioner for Refugees (UNHCR)**.

4. Bookmark the most promising Web page.

This Web page is exactly what we are looking for. The United Nations is a reliable source, and it keeps annual worldwide demographic statistics. After exploring this site's links and discovering that it lists numbers and types of refugees in all the countries of the world, we decide to bookmark it so that we can come back to it later.

Click on **Bookmarks** in the location toolbar. Point your mouse to **Add Bookmark** and click.

The title of the Web page is automatically added to your bookmark list. You can access this Web page later by clicking on the title from your list. If you are using Internet Explorer for this activity, simply click on **Favorites** and select **Add to Favorites** from the pulldown menu.

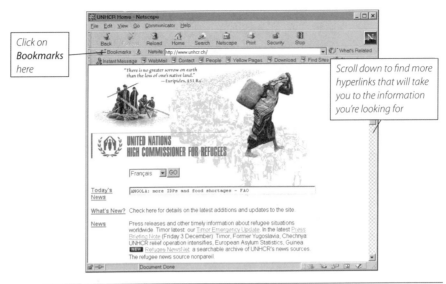

Click on **Bookmarks** here

Scroll down to find more hyperlinks that will take you to the information you're looking for

Figure 8.8   The United Nations High Commissioner for Refugees Web Page

END OF ACTIVITY 8.1

Keyword searching helps us find Web information faster in the same way that computerized library catalogs help us find books faster. If you don't want to take the time to browse categories in a directory, you may search the directory by keyword. Or you can do both. It is a good idea to use different tactics when looking for something on the Web.

Virtual Libraries

Virtual libraries are directories that contain collections of resources that librarians and information specialists have carefully chosen and have organized in a logical way. The Web pages included are usually evaluated by someone knowledgeable in that particular field. Virtual libraries typically provide an organizational hierarchy with subject categories to facilitate browsing. Most include query interfaces in order to perform simple searches. Virtual libraries are great places to begin your research. The following is a list of a few of the most well known virtual libraries on the Web:

Virtual Library	URL
The Argus Clearinghouse	**http://www.clearinghouse.net**
Britannica	**http://www.britannica.com**

INFOMINE	**http://infomine.ucr.edu**
The Internet Public Library	**http://www.ipl.org**
Librarians' Index to the Internet	**http://lii.org**
WWW Virtual Library	**http://www.vlib.org**

Table 8.3   Virtual Libraries

The main difference between virtual libraries and the directories we talked about earlier in the chapter is that virtual libraries are much smaller since the resources included are very carefully selected. The people who organize virtual libraries are usually on the lookout for three major types of information: *subject guides, reference works,* and *specialized databases.*

Subject Guides

A subject guide is a World Wide Web resource that is devoted to including the hyperlinks of most, if not all, Web pages on a particular subject. For example, the resource devoted to listing Web pages on environmental ethics pictured in Figure 8.9 is a subject guide. Some people refer to subject guides as meta-pages.

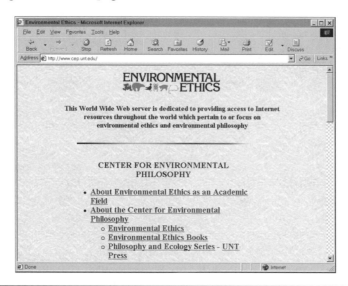

Figure 8.9   The Environmental Ethics Subject Guide, **http://www.cep.unt.edu**

Reference Works

The other common type of resource that is collected by virtual libraries is a reference work. A reference work is a full-text document with self-contained information. In other words, it doesn't necessarily contain hyperlinks to other resources. A reference work on the World Wide Web is very similar to its print counterpart. A dictionary on the Web would look very much like a dictionary on the reference shelf. The only difference would be that it would allow you to move around the document by clicking hyperlinks instead of turning pages and looking in the index for related topics. There are encyclopedias, handbooks, dictionaries, directories, and many other types of reference works on the World Wide Web. The work pictured in Figure 8.10, "The World Factbook 1999," is a reference work.

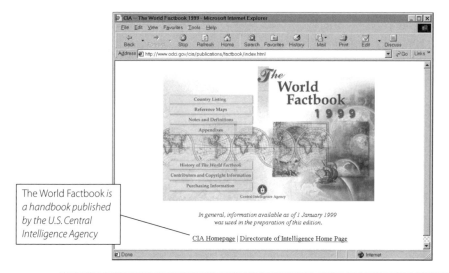

The World Factbook *is a handbook published by the U.S. Central Intelligence Agency*

Figure 8.10   The World Factbook 1999, **http://www.odci.gov/ cia/publications/factbook/index.html**

Specialized Databases

Virtual libraries are useful for finding specialized databases as well. A specialized database is an index that catalogs certain material like patent literature, journal article citations, company financial data, court decisions, and so forth. Specialized databases can usually be searched by keyword and often support a myriad of sophisticated search features and capabilities. Figure 8.11 shows the home page of PubMed, the National Library of Medicine's search service. PubMed includes MEDLINE, a database of the premier medical journal article citations and abstracts that covers more than 3,500 international journal titles.

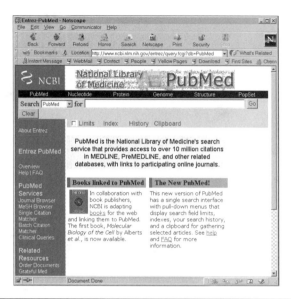

Figure 8.11   PubMed: The National Library of Medicine's Search Service for the MEDLINE Database, **http://www.ncbi.nlm.nih.gov/PubMed**

Let's do a brief activity to show you how useful a virtual library can be.

USING VIRTUAL LIBRARIES TO FIND INFORMATION

Overview

In this activity, we are going to look for information on the country Azerbaijan. We hope to find a reference work; for example, an encyclopedia-type publication that will give the history of the country, statistics, and other general information. A virtual library is an excellent place to start looking for information like this. We'll use the virtual library developed by librarians at the Berkeley, California, public library called the Librarians' Index to the Internet.

We'll follow these steps:
1. Go to the home page for the Librarians' Index to the Internet.
2. Browse the subject categories for country information.
3. Access the Country Studies/Area Handbooks Web page.
4. Choose **Azerbaijan**.
5. Explore the country study for Azerbaijan by searching it by keyword.

Details

1. Go to the home page for the Librarians' Index to the Internet.

(Do it) Point to the location field and click. Now you can type in the URL for the Librarians' Index to the Internet.

(Do it) Type **http://lii.org** and press **Enter**.

The home page is shown in Figure 8.12. Note that it looks very similar to Yahoo!, with the alphabetical list of top-level subject categories on the first page and the search form at the top.

2. Browse the subject categories for country information.

Again, we have to make an educated guess when browsing subject categories in a directory. In this case, it's pretty straightforward. We'll need to choose **Cultures (World)**.

(Do it) Click on **Cultures (World)** as shown in Figure 8.12.

Figure 8.12   The Librarians' Index to the Internet Home Page

3. Access the Country Studies/Area Handbooks Web page.

The first Web page in the list of results is **Country Studies/Area Handbooks**. The annotation indicates that this is a series of books that have been translated into HTML and put on the Web by the Library of Congress and the Department of the Army. Let's see if Azerbaijan has been included.

(Do it) Click on **Country Studies/Area Handbooks** as shown in Figure 8.13.

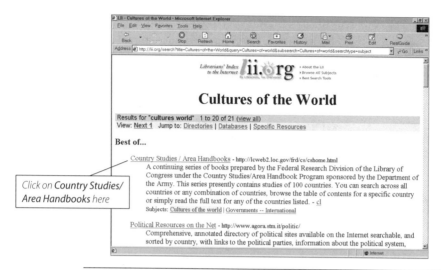

Figure 8.13   Web Pages in the Cultures of the World Category

4. Choose **Azerbaijan.**

 From the Library of Congress' Country Studies home page, click on **Browse.**

Figure 8.14 shows a list of the countries included in this series. Note that Azerbaijan is listed.

 Click on **Azerbaijan.**

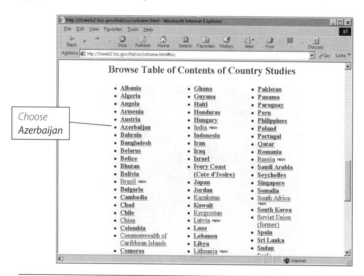

Figure 8.14   A List of the Country Studies Available

5. **Explore the country study for Azerbaijan by searching it by keyword.**

If you want to search for a specific topic within the country study, you can search by keyword. Keeping with our topic in the last activity, let's try seeing if there is any information on refugees.

(Do it)   In the search form, type in **refugees** and click on **SEARCH**, as shown in Figure 8.15.

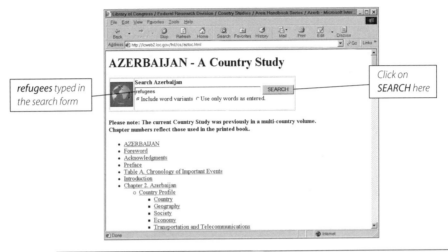

Figure 8.15   **refugees** Typed in the Search Form

Figure 8.16 shows the results of the search. You can click on any of the 13 resulting hyperlinks to be taken to the parts of the country study that had the word *refugees* in the text.

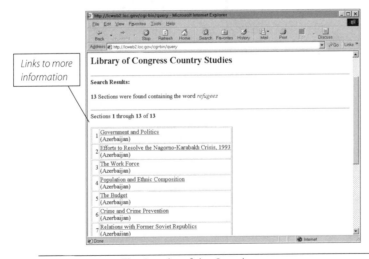

Figure 8.16   The Results of the Search

END OF ACTIVITY 8.2

Directories and virtual libraries can be useful if you have a broad subject and aren't sure how to narrow it down. They are also helpful if you want to get a general idea about what resources are out there to help you focus your topic. Virtual libraries are especially useful as a starting point for research on a particular topic or as a place to find subject guides, reference works, and specialized databases. But if you want to zero in quickly on Web pages that are very specifically related to your topic, or if your topic is either multifaceted or extremely detailed and you are sure about the keywords you are going to use, a search engine is what you need. In the following sections, we'll explore search engines and give a brief overview of the most common keyword search features.

Search Engines and Meta-Search Tools

Search engines are tools that use computer programs called *spiders* or *robots* to automatically gather information on the Internet to create databases. These computer programs go out on the Internet and locate hyperlinks that are available to the public. These resources are retrieved and put into a database that you can search by using the search engine. These robot programs were created because the number of Internet documents increases so rapidly that people can't keep up with indexing them manually. Each of the major search engines attempts to do the same thing, index as much of the Web as possible, so they handle a huge amount of data.

There are advantages to computer-generated databases. They are frequently updated, give access to very large collections, and are useful for providing the most comprehensive search results. If you are looking for a specific concept or phrase or if your topic is multifaceted, a search engine is the best place to start. And you would be smart to look in more than one, because each engine gives different results.

The major search engines are:

Fyi SEARCH ENGINE INFORMATION ON THE WORLD WIDE WEB

~ "Search Engine Watch"
http://searchenginewatch.com

~ "Understanding and Comparing Search Engines"
http://web.hamline.edu/ Administration/Libraries/ search/comparisons.html

~ "Lost in Cyberspace"
http://www.newscientist.com/ keysites/networld/lost.html

Search Engine	URL
AltaVista	**http://www.altavista.com**
Excite	**http://www.excite.com**
Google	**http://www.google.com**
HotBot	**http://hotbot.lycos.com**
Infoseek	**http:// infoseek.go.com**
Lycos	**http://www.lycos.com**
Northern Light	**http://www.northernlight.com**
WebCrawler	**http://www.webcrawler.com**

Table 8.4   The Major Search Engines

Search Engine Similarities

All of the major engines are similar in that you enter keywords, phrases, or proper names in a ***search form***. After clicking on **Search**, **Submit**, **Find**, or some other command button, the database returns a collection of hyperlinks to your screen, which are usually listed according to their ***relevance*** to the keyword(s) you typed in, from most relevant to least relevant. Search engines determine relevancy in different ways. Generally, it's determined by how many times the search terms appear in the document. All search engines have online help to get you acquainted with their search features. Two common search features that most search engines support are ***Boolean searching*** and ***phrase searching***. These and other search features available on many search engines, including relevancy ranking, field searching, truncation searching, and proximity searching, will be discussed in Chapter 9.

Boolean Operators

Boolean Operator	Function
AND	Placing **AND** between keywords in your search expression narrows the search results. For example, **CANOES AND KAYAKS** would narrow your search so that you would retrieve only those sites that had *both* the words canoes and kayaks in them.
OR	Placing **OR** between keywords broadens your search results.

For example, **CANOES OR KAYAKS** would retrieve only those sites that had *either* the word canoes *or* the word kayaks in them.

NOT

The **NOT** operator narrows a search.

For example, **CANOES NOT KAYAKS** would retrieve those pages that had the word canoes in them but *not* kayaks.

Table 8.5	Boolean Operators

In some search engines, if nothing is typed between two words, the engine assumes an OR is between them. This is what we'd refer to as a ***default setting***. In order to override this feature, you'd either have to type AND between the words or put a + before both words, depending on the search features supported by the search engine.

Phrase Searching

Let's say you are searching for information on chaos theory. If you typed in the two words **chaos theory** separated by a space, the system you're using may assume that you are in effect saying **chaos AND theory** or that you are saying **chaos OR theory**, depending on the search engine. Even if the search engine defaulted to AND, your search results would not be very precise, because the words chaos and theory could appear separately from each other throughout the document.

∿ Most search engines support phrase searching, which requires the use of double quotation marks around the phrase. In our example, we would type **"chaos theory"**.

∿ Searching by phrase guarantees that the words you type in will appear adjacent to each other, in the order you typed them.

∿ Some search tools default to phrase searching when words are typed with no Boolean operator between them.

∿ To determine how a search tool handles phrases, always check its help section.

Search Engine Differences

The major search engines differ in several ways:

∿ the size of the index

∿ the search features (many search engines support the same features but require you to use different *syntax* in order to initiate them)

∿ how frequently the database is updated

∿ their relevancy algorithms

∿ their overall ease of use

It is important to know these differences, because in order to do an exhaustive search of the World Wide Web, you must be familiar with a few different search tools. No single search engine can be relied upon to satisfy every query.

At this point it would be helpful to give you an example of how search features work. This activity will focus on how to create a **search expression** using features discussed above: phrase searching and Boolean searching.

USING A SEARCH ENGINE TO FIND INFORMATION

Overview

In this activity, we're going to continue searching for information about Azerbaijan. This time we'd like to focus on refugees from a human rights perspective. For a multifaceted search like this, a search engine is the best tool to use. We'll use the search engine database called HotBot. HotBot indexes every word in the Web pages that are included in its database. In order to retrieve the most relevant results, we'll use Boolean operators and phrase searching, two of the most useful search features.

We'll follow these steps:

1. Go to the home page for HotBot.
2. Read the help section to determine which search features are supported.
3. Type a search expression in the form provided.
4. Examine the results and click on a hyperlink that appears to be relevant.

Details

1. Go to the home page for HotBot.

Point to the location field and click. The URL of the current Web page will change color. Now you can type in the URL for HotBot.

Type **http://hotbot.lycos.com** in the location field and press **Enter**.

Your screen should look like the one pictured in Figure 8.17.

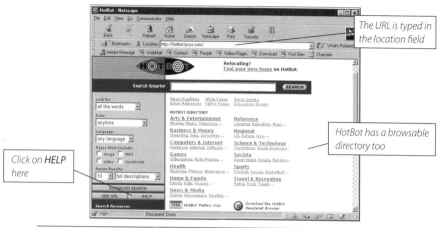

Figure 8.17   HotBot's Home Page

2. Read the help section to determine which search features are supported.

Before we type a search expression in the search form, we need to think a bit about how we're going to construct the search request. First of all, we want to search for *human rights* as a phrase. We also need to find both the words *refugees* and *Azerbaijan* in the Web pages. Therefore, we need to find out if HotBot supports Boolean searching and phrase searching. The best place to find out is the help section.

(Do it) Click on **HELP,** as shown in Figure 8.17.

Your screen will fill with several hyperlinks that provide different types of information about HotBot. The most useful hyperlink for searching help is the Basic Search link.

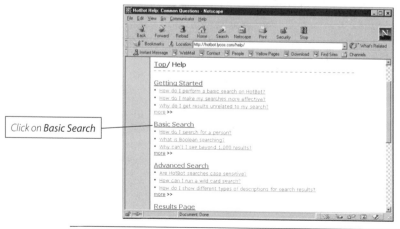

Figure 8.18   Categories in HotBot's Help Section

(Do it)!   Click on **Basic Search**, as shown in Figure 8.18.

After reading about which search features HotBot supports, we can conclude that HotBot

∾   requires quotation marks around words that must appear next to each other, in the order specified. This means that you would place quotation marks around a phrase.

∾   supports Boolean searching, using AND, OR, and NOT. In order to perform a Boolean search, you need to select **Boolean phrase** from the pulldown menu on the home page that is located next to the words **Look for**.

∾   is mostly case insensitive. This means that you don't need to capitalize proper nouns.

As you become more adept at searching and more familiar with the particular search tool you're using, you may not need to check the help section.

After you're finished looking at the help pages, scroll up to the top.

(Do it)!   Click on the HotBot icon. This should bring you back to HotBot's home page.

3. **Type a search expression in the form provided.**

(Do it)!   Type the following search expression in the search form provided on HotBot's home page: **"human rights" and azerbaijan and refugees**

(Do it)!   Click on the arrow next to the search form titled **Look for**. Choose **Boolean phrase** from the list of choices.

(Do it)!   Click on **SEARCH** and wait for HotBot to deliver links to Web pages that match your query.

This search will result in links to Web pages that have the phrase *human rights,* the word *Azerbaijan,* and the word *refugees* in them. You can see the search keywords typed in the search form in Figure 8.19.

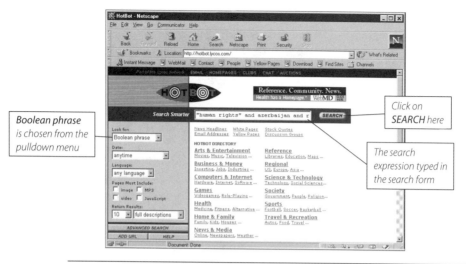

Boolean phrase is chosen from the pulldown menu

Click on SEARCH here

The search expression typed in the search form

Figure 8.19   The Search Expression Typed in HotBot's Search Form

4. Examine the results and click on a hyperlink that appears to be relevant.

Figure 8.20 shows the first few pages that appear in the results. Most search engines list the results according to relevancy. Note that the first one on the list is 99% relevant to the search expression.

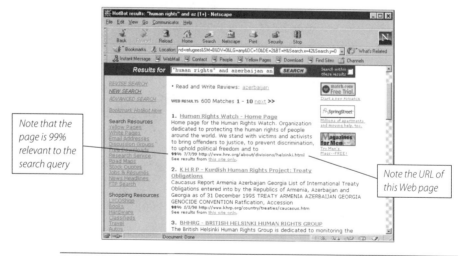

Note that the page is 99% relevant to the search query

Note the URL of this Web page

Figure 8.20   The Results of the HotBot Search

Note the first hyperlink that appears on the list of results in Figure 8.20. Your results may be different. This Web page, according to HotBot, is the most relevant. "Human Rights Watch - Home Page" consists of information provided by a group that reports on human rights issues in all countries of the world. By looking at the first part of the URL, **http://www.hrw.org**, you can determine that an organization has published this information. Before you bookmark the site and use it to further your research, you might want to look up **www.hrw.org** and find out what this organization is, what it does, and what it has to report about Azerbaijan's human rights and refugee situation.

END OF ACTIVITY 8.3

In the previous activity we searched HotBot for relevant Web pages focusing on the human rights situation for Azerbaijani refugees. Since we wanted to search for *human rights* as a phrase, we needed to use a search engine that supported phrase searching. We found out by looking in HotBot's help section that it does support phrase searching with quotation marks. HotBot also supports Boolean searching, which we also needed in our search expression. The Boolean operator used in this search expression was the operator AND. AND narrows results, while OR expands them.

Meta-Search Tools

It can be confusing and time-consuming to do your search in several databases, especially if you have to keep track of all of their differences. To try to solve some of these problems, database providers have come up with **meta-search tools**. Meta-search tools that allow you to search several search engines simultaneously are often called **parallel-search tools** or **unified search interfaces**. These tools allow you to use several search engines simultaneously. The parallel-search tool collects the most relevant sites in each database and sends them to your screen. Instead of building their own databases, meta-search tools use the major search engines and directories that already exist on the Internet and provide the user with search forms or interfaces for submitting queries to these search tools. Table 8.6 shows the most popular meta-search tools and their URLs.

Parallel-Search Tool	URL
All-in-One Search Page	**http://www.allonesearch.com**
Dogpile	**http://www.dogpile.com**
Fossick.com	**http://www.fossick.com**
MetaCrawler	**http://www.metacrawler.com**
ProFusion	**http://www.profusion.com**
SavvySearch	**http://www.savvysearch.com**
SEARCH.COM	**http://www.search.com**

Table 8.6   The Most Popular Meta-Search Tools

Some sites merely list World Wide Web search tools with their search forms so you can search them one at a time. These are called ***all-in-one search tools***. These resources can be helpful for keeping up-to-date with new databases on the Web.

A keyword search will consult several search tools at once

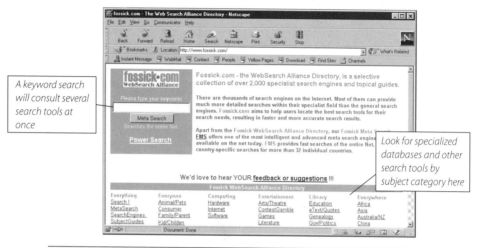

Look for specialized databases and other search tools by subject category here

Figure 8.21   Fossick.com: A Meta-Search Tool

Intelligent Agents

Overwhelmed with the task of searching the Web? Are your work life and personal life becoming too complex for you to perform repetitive search tasks efficiently and promptly? If so, you may want to use agents to help you. ***Agents*** are software entities that gather information or accomplish tasks without your immediate presence. You tell an agent what actions you want performed and the agent then executes them on your behalf. Agents can perform the repetitive tasks of searching databases, retrieving and filtering information, and delivering information back to you. For example, an agent might compare airfare prices for a particular destination that you request and send the lowest fare to your desktop. These agents are sometimes referred to as ***intelligent agents***, ***personal agents***, or ***bots***

Fy WANT TO READ MORE ABOUT AGENTS? CHECK OUT THESE SITES:

~ "BotSpot"
  http://botspot.com

~ "Competing for the Future with Intelligent Agents"
  http://home1.gte.net/ pfingar/agents_doc_rev4.htm

~ "Is It an Agent, or Just a Program?: A Taxonomy for Autonomous Agents"
  http://www.msci.memphis.edu/ ~franklin/AgentProg.html

(short for robots). An example of an agent, or bot, is The Go Network's My Page, **http://mypage.go.com**, shown in Figure 8.22. My Page searches for news stories, weather, health updates, and practically anything that you request it to. First, you register for this free service, personalize it, and then access it with a login and password that you have created.

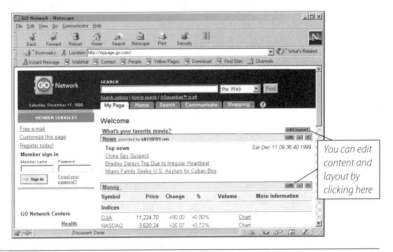

Figure 8.22   The Go Network's My Page

My Page acts like a meta-search engine in that it searches several sites simultaneously. You can also set up a personal agent that will search continuously for information on your topic and alert you when it finds something.

Content Issues: Pornography, Free Speech, Censorship, Filtering, and Copyright

Because any individual or organization can publish information on the Internet easily and without editorial and other content control, you can expect to come across material that mirrors the wide range of preferences and interests of people throughout the world. A small proportion of the material found may be offensive to some people or inappropriate for children. Sexually explicit or pornographic material may exist as text, pictures, or chat and can be accessed deliberately or unintentionally. Several pornographic sites require a fee for access. Seldom does one encounter explicit material in a casual way—usually there is an introductory page that warns the user that the material linked to it is for adult viewing only; there may be a fee incurred to view the site as well. The focus of the debate about this so-called "cyberporn" has been whether it's appropriate for the material to be readily available to children and whether it's appropriate to pass laws that restrict the content of the Internet.

Free Speech vs. Censorship

The debate regarding civil liberties, free speech, and sexually explicit material led to the United States Congress approving and the President of the United States signing legislation called the **Communications Decency Act of 1996**. On June 27, 1997, in Reno vs. American Civil Liberties Union, the U.S. Supreme Court ruled that this act abridged the freedom of speech that is protected by the First Amendment. The court stated, "The interest in encouraging freedom of expression in a democratic society outweighs any theoretical but unproven benefit of censorship." You can read this opinion by going to **http://supct.law.cornell.edu/supct/html/ 96-511.ZO.html**. This opinion held that the Internet should not be viewed as a broadcast medium like television or radio, but as a medium in which individuals are guaranteed free speech.

Filtering and Blocking Devices

Parents and others concerned about what children may be viewing on the Web can install computer programs that restrict the material that can be accessed. These programs are referred to as *filters* or *blocking devices*. The programs control access to information in a number of possible ways:

- by providing a list of sources that have been selected and identified as being appropriate for children,
- by blocking inappropriate sites that the user chooses, or
- by filtering messages or Web sites that contain objectionable words that either the user or the software developer chooses.

Fyi INFORMATION ON FILTERING AND BLOCKING DEVICES

- "TIFAP: The Internet Filter Assessment Project" **http://www.bluehighways. com/tifap**
- "Statement on Internet Filtering" **http://www.ala.org/ alaorg/oif/filt_stm.html**

While filters may be helpful, keep in mind that they may screen some sites with useful material. For example, Web pages for gay teens, safe sex information, or information about drug legalization or other controversial issues may not appear in the results list because certain words have been filtered out and therefore made inaccessible. Certain medical topics like breast cancer may also be avoided because the words that describe these medical conditions and body parts may be on the filter list. It is for this reason that the American Library Association has stated in "Access to Electronic Information, Services, and Networks: An Interpretation of the Library Bill of Rights," **http://www.ala.org/alaorg/oif/electacc.html**, that by using filters, a library would be restricting access to information when it's a library's role to provide access to information and let users choose what they want to read, hear, or see. Opponents of this view say that libraries don't generally collect pornography in book or magazine form, so why should libraries allow this material to be accessed on the Internet? In the future, filtering or blocking software may be developed that could be turned on or off, so that individuals could choose to have restrictions placed on their searches or not.

Intellectual Property and Copyright

You know there is a wealth of files, documents, images, and other types of items available on the Internet. They can be viewed, copied, printed, downloaded, saved in a file, or passed on to others. Just because we can copy or duplicate information we find on the Internet, is it legal or ethical to do so? Many, if not most, of these items don't exist in a physical form, so ownership rights that depend on something having a physical form perhaps don't make sense. The notion of ownership of these items, whether they have a physical form, does make sense in terms of intellectual property. There are a number of laws and agreements throughout the world to protect intellectual property rights.

Only the owners of information can grant the right to copy or duplicate it. This is called the copyright. Many documents on the Internet contain a statement asserting that the document is copyrighted and giving permission to distribute the document in an electronic form, provided it isn't sold or made part of some commercial venture. The copyright laws of the United States, the Universal Copyright Convention, or the Berne Union generally protect items that don't contain these statements. Most copyright conventions or statutes include a provision so that individuals may make copies of portions of a document for short-term use. If information is obtainable on the Internet and there is no charge to access the information, it often can be shared in an electronic form. That certainly doesn't mean you can copy images or documents and make them available on the Internet, or make copies and share them in a printed form with others. Quite naturally, many people who create or provide material on the Internet expect to get credit and be paid for their work.

One issue that may need to be resolved in the future is the physical nature of information on the Internet. In most cases, an item exists on one disk and is viewed in an electronic form. It has no tangible, physical form when it's transmitted. United States copyright law states that copyright protection begins once the work is in "fixed form," so the original portion of these works is protected by copyright. The notion of fixed form is much easier to determine with more traditional works, such as books, poems,

> **Fyi** INFORMATION ABOUT COPYRIGHT AND INTELLECTUAL PROPERTY RIGHTS
>
> ~ "Copyright Basics"
> http://lcweb.loc.gov/copyright/circs/circ1.html
> ~ "Information Policy: Copyright and Intellectual Property"
> http://www.ifla.org/II/cpyright.htm

stories, sound recordings, and motion pictures. Naturally, it seems reasonable to say a work is in fixed form when stored on a disk, but can we say the same about material being transmitted through several networks? Another issue is how an information provider can know if the information is being copied and stored. Current laws and conventions were written for works that exist in some definite physical form, and the nature of that form may make it difficult or time-consuming to make unauthorized copies. But information transmitted on the Internet or other networks is very easy to copy. When you copy something in digital form, you make an exact duplicate. Each copy is as good as the original. The ease with which works can be copied and distributed may require a law different from current copyright statutes.

Not all cultures have the same attitudes about ownership of information. Some cultures have a long tradition of sharing information and works created by individuals. Other groups feel all information should be free, and so they think it's appropriate to make works available only if there is no charge for use of the works. The worldwide nature of the Internet and other networks requires addressing these cultural differences. When the United States deals with some countries, it may withhold a certain level of trading status if they don't abide by international copyright conventions.

Summary

This chapter introduced several types of search tools available on the World Wide Web. These tools—directories and virtual libraries, search engines and meta-search tools, specialized databases, and intelligent agents—are all useful ways to find information. Directories, sometimes referred to as subject catalogs, are topical lists of selected Web resources, arranged in a hierarchical way. Directories differ from search engines in one major way: the human element involved in collecting the information and maintaining it. While search engine databases are created by computer programs, directories are created and maintained by people. Directories don't cover the entire Web. In fact, directories are quite small collections of resources, compared to the huge databases that search engines search. Browsing directories can be a very effective way to find the resources you need, especially if you're sure where the information you're searching for would appear on the Web.

Virtual libraries are directories that contain collections of resources that librarians or information specialists have carefully chosen and have organized in a logical way. Virtual libraries typically provide an organizational hierarchy with subject categories to facilitate browsing. The main difference between virtual libraries and directories is that virtual libraries are much smaller since the resources included are very carefully selected. The people who organize virtual libraries are usually on the lookout for three major types of information: subject guides, reference works, and specialized databases.

Search engines are tools that use computer programs called spiders or robots to automatically gather information on the Internet and create full-text databases. Spiders go out on the Internet and locate hyperlinks that are available to the public. The spiders then load these resources in a database, which you can then search with the search engine. The major search engines all attempt to do the same thing—index the entire Web—so they handle a huge amount of data. Meta-search tools allow you to search several search engines simultaneously or provide a list of search forms to allow you to search one tool at a time.

Intelligent agents can perform repetitive tasks like searching databases and retrieving and filtering information.

The information found on the World Wide Web is diverse and some of it may be offensive to some people or inappropriate for children. There are software programs that have been designed to block or filter Web sites that have certain words in them. There was a movement to force the government to control the content on the Web and the Internet. The U.S. Supreme Court ruled in 1997 that the Communications Decency Act of 1996 was unconstitutional in that it abridged the freedom of speech upheld by the First Amendment.

Selected Terms Used in This Chapter

agent
all-in-one search tool
blocking device
Boolean searching
bot
Communications Decency Act of
　1996
default setting
directory
download
filter
hierarchy
intelligent agent
meta-search tool
parallel-search tool
personal agent

phrase searching
reference work
relevance
robot
search engine
search expression
search form
specialized database
spider
subject category
subject guide
syntax
top-level category
unified search interface
virtual library

Exercises and Projects

1. Using the Librarians' Index to the Internet, **http://lii.org**, find a Web site devoted to the writings and teachings of philosopher George Gurdjieff. Find it by searching with keywords and browsing the subject categories. Provide the strategies that you used for each method.

2. Browse Yahoo!, **http://www.yahoo.com**, for a list of zip code directories. Write down the top-level category and all the subcategories you clicked on to reach the list.

3. Using WebCrawler, **http://www.webcrawler.com**, look for the home page of Mary Washington College. First search for it by typing in **Mary Washington College**. Note how many results were returned. Try it again with quotation marks around the phrase. How were the results affected? Why?

4. Using the Argus Clearinghouse, **http://www.clearinghouse.net**, find a subject guide on social and ethical reporting. What is the title and URL of the subject guide? When was the subject guide updated? What is the rating of the guide?

5. Using Northern Light, **http://www.northernlight.com**, find out when Anne Morrow Lindbergh's classic book *Gift from the Sea* was published. Write down the search expression that you used.

6. Using MetaCrawler, **http://www.metacrawler.com**, find information on the Witch of Yazoo. Write down the search expression you used. Please explain what you found out about the Witch of Yazoo.

7. Using AltaVista's directory, **http://www.altavista.com**, find a list of personal stories related to Alzheimer's disease by browsing. Describe the steps you took to find them. What are their titles and URLs?

8. Using HotBot, **http://www.hotbot.com**, search for information on Thomas Merton. Use the pulldown menu to help you search for a person's name. Write down the URLs for the three most relevant Web pages you found.

9. Starting with the meta-search tool Fossick.com, **http://www.fossick.com**, find the theatre database On Broadway. Using this resource, find out which play won the Tony Award for best play of 1999. Describe the steps you took to find this information.

10. Go to Go Network's My Page, **http://mypage.go.com**, register as a member, and customize the page so that you receive items that interest you. Monitor the page for week or so. Explain how the service retrieved the items you requested.

Chapter 9

SUCCESSFUL

SEARCH

STRATEGIES

Searching online databases for the information you need can be a demanding task. Several major search tools are available: which one do you start with? And once you have accessed a search tool, especially a search engine, how do you formulate a search request that will provide the best results? The databases on the Web, especially those that are full-text and searchable by keyword, have different rules and features that you need to be aware of before you are able to get the most out of them. Some of these databases have features that make it easier for you to find certain types of information, for example, pictures, people, or companies. Others allow you to narrow results by field or by date.

Databases not only have different search features, they also have different output features that you need to familiarize yourself with. For example, each database determines the relevancy of search results differently. There may be ways for you to manipulate a database to make sure the most relevant documents are displayed toward the beginning of your search results list instead of toward the end. Some databases make it easy for you to modify your results without having to type in an entirely new search expression. This chapter focuses on the features common to most databases and will help you determine when it may be advantageous for you to use a more obscure one and how to find out if a search tool supports a particular feature. The chapter also introduces the 10-step basic search strategy. This strategy requires thinking about the type of information you need to find, determining which search features are needed to guarantee the best results, and then modifying your search if needed.

Goals/Objectives

~ Become familiar with the search features common to search engines

~ Learn how to develop a search strategy before typing a search expression

~ Learn how to translate a topic into a useful search expression using the search features appropriate to the search tool

Topics

- ∾ Search Engine Databases
- ∾ Search Features Common to Most Search Engine Databases
- ∾ Output Features Common to Most Search Engines
- ∾ A Basic Search Strategy: The 10 Steps
- ∾ Formulating Search Expressions: Some Examples

Search Engine Databases

Search engines are the most powerful searching tools on the World Wide Web; the most popular are those that access the largest databases. Many also index Usenet groups and FTP archives as well. None of the search engines are exactly alike. Some are better for certain kinds of information than others. Maybe you've tried a few search engines and sometimes have found that the engines retrieved too many documents that weren't at all what you were looking for, and perhaps other times they didn't retrieve enough information. This chapter should clear up some ambiguities about why some searches work well and others don't.

As you learned in Chapter 8, search engines are tools that use computer programs to automatically gather information on the Internet to create databases. Even though most of the major search engine databases attempt to index the entire Web, none of them actually do. One search engine may not pick up the same documents another one does. Search engines are the best tools to use when you are looking for very specific information or when your research topic has many facets. We also learned in Chapter 8 that directories are helpful when you are looking for general and single-faceted topics. Usually when you need information on a very detailed or multifaceted subject, however, a search engine will give you not only more information, but also the most precise and up-to-date information possible. In addition to this, each engine has a different way of determining which pages are most relevant to your search request. In one database, a relevant document may be first on the list; in another database, the document may be the fiftieth, if it appears at all. In order to retrieve the most comprehensive results, you should understand how information in search engines is indexed, the common search and output features engines support, and how to formulate a search strategy.

Let's review the major search engines on the World Wide Web:

Search Engine	URL
AltaVista	http://www.altavista.com
Excite	http://www.excite.com
Google	http://www.google.com
HotBot	http://hotbot.lycos.com
Infoseek	http://infoseek.go.com
Lycos	http://www.lycos.com
Northern Light	http://www.northernlight.com
WebCrawler	http://www.webcrawler.com

Table 9.1   Major Search Engines

Indexing

Knowing how search engine databases are indexed can help you select the most appropriate tool for your research needs, retrieve the most relevant information, and understand why results vary from one database to another. In Chapter 8, we discussed directories and how human beings control their contents. In some directories and virtual libraries, site managers, librarians, or information specialists assign subject headings or descriptors to Web pages. They describe a Web page with a few words. This enables you to find that page if any of the words you type match the words used to describe the page. This is helpful, especially if you're not sure in which subject category the information you're looking for is located.

In search engines, a computer program called a *spider* or *robot* gathers new documents from the World Wide Web. The program retrieves hyperlinks that are attached to these documents, loads them into a database, and indexes them using a formula that differs

 MORE ABOUT SPIDERS, ROBOTS, AND INDEXING

~ "Robot-Driven Search Engines: A Bibliography"
http://www.curtin.edu.au/curtin/library/staffpages/gwpersonal/senginestudy/sengbib.htm

~ "The Web Robots Pages"
http://info.webcrawler.com/mak/projects/robots/robots.html

~ "AskScott: Web Searching Tutorial: Methods of Indexing"
http://www.askscott.com/sec1.html#methods

~ "Search Engines: How Software Agents and Search Engines Work"
http://webreference.com/content/search/how.html

from database to database. The search engine then searches the database looking for the documents that contain the **keywords** you used in the **search expression**. Although robots have many different ways of collecting information from Web pages, the major search engines all claim to index the entire text of each Web document in their databases. This is called **full-text indexing**. All of the major search engines are full-text databases.

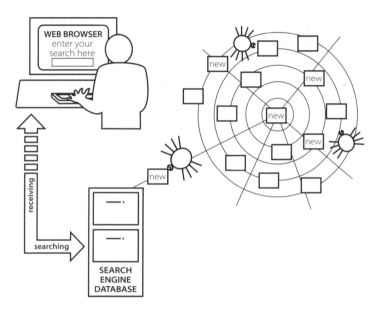

Some robot programs are intuitive; they know which words are important to the meaning of the entire Web page, and some of them can find synonyms to the words and add them to the index. Some full-text databases, such as Excite, use a robot that enables them to search on concepts, as well as on the search query words. In some search engines, the robot skips over words that appear often, such as prepositions and articles. These common words are called **stop words**.

Some search engines allow Web page submitters to attach meta-tags to their pages. **Meta-tags** are keywords that describe the page but don't appear on the page. They appear only in the HTML source document. You can view the HTML source code by looking at the page source. In Netscape, click on **View**, and then **Page Source**; in Internet Explorer, you also click on **View**, and then select **Source**. Meta-tags allow Web pages that don't have a lot of text in them to come up in a keyword search.

Becoming proficient in search techniques is crucial in a full-text indexing environment. The chance of retrieving irrelevant material is high when you can type in a word and conceivably retrieve every document that has that word in it. The following two sections define search features and can be referred to when formulating search expressions.

Search Features Common to Most Search Engine Databases

It's important to understand the different search features before you begin using a search engine for research. The reason for this is that each search engine has its own way of interpreting and manipulating search expressions. In addition, many search engines have *default settings* that you may need to override if you want to obtain the most precise results. Because a search can bring up so many pages, it is very easy to have a lot of hits with few that are relevant to your query. This is called *low precision/high recall*. You may be satisfied with having very precise search results with a small set returned. This is defined as *high precision/low recall*. Ideally, using the search expression you entered, the search engine would retrieve all of the relevant documents you need. This would be described as *high precision/high recall*.

Search engines support many search features, though not all engines support each one. Even if they do support a feature, they may use different syntax in expressing the feature. Before you use any of these search features, you need to check the search engines' help pages to see how the feature is expressed, if it is supported at all. We will now list the most common search features and explain how each feature is used.

Boolean Operators

We discussed Boolean operators briefly in Chapter 8. Knowing how to apply Boolean operators in search expressions is extremely important. The diagrams show the different operators and how they are used.

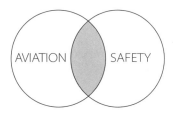

Figure 9.1   aviation AND safety

Use an AND between search terms when you need to narrow your search. The AND indicates that only those Web pages having both words in them will be retrieved. Some search engines automatically assume an AND relationship between two words if you don't type anything between them. This would be a default setting of the search engine.

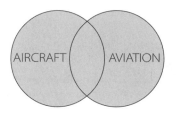

Figure 9.2   aircraft OR aviation

An OR between search terms will make your resulting set larger. When you use OR, Web pages that have either term will be retrieved. Many search engines automatically place an OR between two words if there is nothing typed between them. This would be a default setting of the search engine.

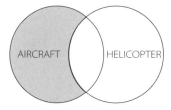

Figure 9.3   aircraft NOT helicopters

The NOT operator is used when a term needs to be excluded. In this example, Web pages with *aircraft* will be retrieved, but those that have the word *helicopters* in them will not be retrieved. Some search engines require an AND in front of NOT. In that case, the expression would be written like this: **aircraft AND NOT helicopters**

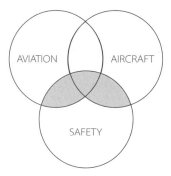

Figure 9.4   safety AND (aviation OR aircraft)

This example shows **nested Boolean logic**. Use this logic when you need to include ANDs and ORs in the same search statement. For example, say that there is a term that must appear in your results. You want to search for this term along with a concept that you can describe with synonyms. To do this, you would need to tell the search engine to find records with two or more of the synonyms and then to combine this result with the search for the first term. In the example above, the parentheses indicate that *aviation* OR *aircraft* will be processed first, and that this result will be combined with *safety*. If the parentheses were not there, the search engine would perform the search from left to right. All pages with both of the words *safety* AND

> **SHOULD BOOLEAN OPERATORS BE CAPITALIZED IN SEARCH EXPRESSIONS?**
> When describing Boolean operators, we have capitalized them to distinguish them from the words that appear around them in the paragraph. Most search engines, however, recognize Boolean operators typed either way, as capital letters, or lowercase. Of all the search engines listed on page 269, Excite is the only one that requires that Boolean operators be typed in uppercase letters.

aviation would be found first, and then all pages with the word *aircraft* would be included. This would give you an unacceptable result, so you must be careful when using nested Boolean logic.

Implied Boolean Operators

Implied Boolean operators, or pseudo-Boolean operators, are shortcuts to typing AND and NOT. In most search engines that support this feature, you would type + before a word or phrase that must appear in the document and - before a word or phrase that must not appear in a document. For example, if you were looking for documents that must have the word *aircraft* but not the word *helicopters* in them, you could state the search using implied Boolean operators like this:

+ aircraft -helicopters

Natural Language Searching

Natural language searching is the capability of entering a search expression in the form of a question or a statement. For example, the following is a natural language search expression: "In what year was Martin Luther King's birthday made a national holiday?" And the following: "I need a recipe for peanut butter fudge." In natural language searching, the search tool will disregard stop words and pick out the significant terms and connect them with whatever the default feature of the search engine is, for example, OR. In the examples above, stop words in most search engines would be the following: in, what, was, a, I, for.

Phrase Searching

A phrase is a string of words that must appear next to each other. *Global warming* is a phrase, as is *chronic fatigue syndrome*. Use phrase-searching capability when the words you are searching for must appear next to each other and must appear in the order in which you typed them. Most search engines require double quotation marks to differentiate a phrase from words searched by themselves. The two phrases mentioned above would be expressed like this: "global warming" and "chronic fatigue syndrome". *Phrase searching* is one of the most helpful search features, as it increases the chance that your search will have relevant results.

Proximity Searching

Proximity operators are words such as NEAR or WITHIN. What if, for example, you were trying to find information on the effects of chlorofluorocarbons on global warming. Maybe you would want to retrieve results that have the word *chlorofluorocarbons* very close to the phrase *global warming*. By placing the word NEAR between the two segments of the search expression, you would achieve more relevant results than if the words appeared in the same document but were perhaps pages apart. This is called *proximity searching*.

Truncation

Truncation looks for multiple forms of a word. Some search engines refer to truncation as *stemming*. For example, if you were researching postmodern art, you might want to retrieve all the records that had the root word *postmodern,* as well as *postmodernist* or *postmodernism.* Most search engines support truncation by allowing you to place an asterisk (*) at the end of the root word. You would need to see the help screen in the search engine you are using to find out which symbol is used. For example, in this case we would type **postmodern***. Some search engines automatically truncate words. In those databases, you could type **postmodern** and be assured that all the endings would also be retrieved. In these cases, truncation is a default setting of the search engine. If you didn't want your search expression to be truncated, you would need to override the default feature. You would find out how to do this by reading the search engine's help pages.

Wildcards

Using **wildcards** allows you to search for words that have most of the word in common, except for maybe a letter or two. For example, we might want to search for both *woman* and *women*. Instead of typing **woman OR**

women, we could place a wildcard character (most often an asterisk) to replace the fourth letter. It would look like this: **wom*n**

Field Searching

Web pages can be broken down into many parts. These parts, or *fields*, include titles, URLs, text, summaries or annotations (if present), and so forth. (See Figure 9.5.) *Field searching* limits your search to certain fields. This ability to search by field can increase the relevance of the retrieved records. In AltaVista, for example, you could search for a picture of the Statue of Liberty by typing **image:"Statue of Liberty"** in the search form.

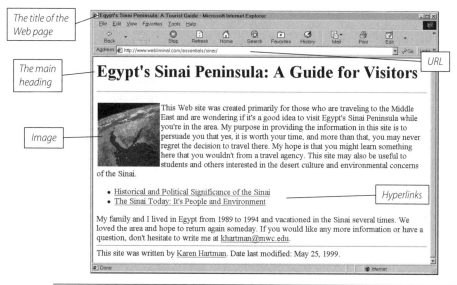

Figure 9.5   The Parts of a Web Page

Case Sensitivity

Case sensitivity is an important feature, especially if you are looking for proper names. Some search engines recognize capitalization, but some do not. If a search engine does recognize capital letters, it can lead to a much more precise search, especially if you're looking for proper names such as Sting, the Who, or Brad Pitt. If the search engine you were using didn't recognize capitals, just think of the results you'd get by entering **sting** in the search query box.

Concept Searching

Concept searching occurs when a search engine automatically searches for Web pages that have similar terms to the ones you entered in the search query box. Excite supports this feature.

Limiting by Date

Some search engines allow you to search the Web for pages that were created or modified between certain dates. In *limiting by date*, you can find only the pages that were entered in the past month, in the past year, or in a particular year. AltaVista and HotBot support this feature.

Language

The ability to limit results to a specific language can be useful. AltaVista supports this feature. AltaVista will also translate documents into many languages for you.

Output Features Common to Most Search Engines

The way a search engine displays results can help you decide which search engine to use. The following features are common to many engines, but as we saw earlier with the search features, the engines all have different ways of determining and showing these features.

Relevancy Ranking

Most search engines measure each Web page's relevance to your search query and arrange the search results from the most relevant to the least relevant. This is called *relevancy ranking*. Each search engine has its own algorithm for determining relevance, but it usually involves counting how many times the words in your query appear in the Web pages. In some search engines, a document is considered more relevant if the words appear in certain fields, for example, the title or summary field. In other search engines, relevance is determined by the number of times the keyword appears in a Web page divided by the total number of words in the page. This gives a percentage, and the page with the largest percentage appears first on the list.

Fyi MORE INFORMATION ABOUT SEARCH FEATURES AND SEARCH STRATEGIES

~ "Using a Search Engine"
http://www.askscott.com/sec2.html

~ "Boolean Searching"
http://exlibris.colgate.edu/web/finding/finding8.html

~ "Searcher: The Magazine for Database Professionals"
http://www.infotoday.com/searcher

~ "How to Do Field Searching in Web Search Engines"
http://www.onlineinc.com/onlinemag/OL1998/hock5.html

Annotations or Summaries

Some search engines include short descriptive paragraphs of each Web page they return to you. These annotations, or summaries, can help you decide whether or not to open a Web page, especially if the page has no title or if the title doesn't describe the page in detail.

Results Per Page

In some search engines, the **results per page** option allows you to choose how many results you want listed per page. This can be a time saver, because it sometimes takes a while to go from page to page as you look through results. There are also some search engines that limit the number of results that are listed, regardless of how many actual Web pages resulted from the search performed.

Sorting and Grouping Results

Some services allow you to choose how you want your results sorted—by relevance, URL, location, organization, and so forth. This feature is known as sorting. Some others place results in categories, such as Northern Light's Custom Search Folders.

Duplicate Detection

It is not unusual to retrieve several instances of the same Web page in your results. Some search engines detect these duplicates and remove them. In meta-search engines or unified search interfaces, **duplicate detection** is a common feature.

Modification of Search Results

Some search engines will insert a copy of your search request on the first page of your results to make it easier for you to modify the query if you so desire. With others, you may be required to return to the original search form before making this modification of search results. Some search engines allow you to search only the results of an earlier search, which can be extremely helpful.

A Basic Search Strategy: The 10 Steps

The following list provides a guideline for you to follow in formulating search requests, viewing and evaluating search results, and modifying search results. These procedures can be followed for virtually any search request, from the simplest to the most complicated. For some search requests, you may not want or need to go through a formal search strategy. If you want to save time in the long run, however, it's a good idea to follow a strategy, especially when you're new to a particular search engine. A basic search strategy can help you get used to each search engine's features and how they are expressed in a search query. Following the 10 steps is also recommended if your search is multifaceted and you want to get the most relevant results.

The 10 steps are as follows:

1. Identify the important concepts of your search.
2. Choose the keywords that describe these concepts.
3. Determine whether there are synonyms, related terms, or other variations of the keywords that should be included.
4. Determine which search features may apply, including truncation, phrase searching, Boolean operators, and so forth.
5. Choose a search engine.
6. Read the search instructions on the search engine's home page. Look for sections entitled "Help," "Advanced Search," "Frequently Asked Questions," and so forth.
7. Create a search expression using syntax that is appropriate for the search engine.
8. Evaluate the results. How many hits were returned? Were the results relevant to your query?
9. Modify your search if needed. Go back to Steps 2 through 4 and revise your query accordingly.
10. Try the same search in a different search engine, following Steps 5 through 9.

In order to show how the basic search strategy can help you formulate search expressions, we'll take the following topic and apply it to the 10 steps.

Topic

We are looking for Web documents that would support an argument for raising the legal driving age. We are interested in studies that show teenagers are involved in more accidents, due to inexperience, than older drivers.

1. **Identify the important concepts of your search.**
   Teenagers are involved in more accidents, due to inexperience. The legal driving age should be raised.

2. **Choose the keywords that describe these concepts.**
   Teenage, driving age, accidents

3. Determine whether there are synonyms, related terms, or other variations of the keywords that should be included.

For teenage: teen, teens, teenagers, adolescent, adolescence
For driving age: none
For accidents: safety

4. Determine which search features may apply, including truncation, phrase searching, Boolean operators, and so forth.

The following chart shows the three concepts and lists the synonyms for each term used, plus which ones will be truncated and when phrase searching will be utilized.

Concept 1	Concept 2	Concept 3
AND	AND	
teen*	driving age	accident*
OR		OR
adolescen*		safety
(* denotes the word will be truncated)	(phrase)	

5. Choose a search engine.

Because we have used truncation as a desired search feature, we need to use a search engine that supports it. Northern Light and AltaVista are two search engines that support truncation. These two also support Boolean searching, which is necessary since we need to use the OR operator. All of the search engines support phrase searching. If you choose to do the search in a database that doesn't support truncation, you could use the Boolean OR between the complete words.

6. Read the search instructions on the search engine's home page. Look for sections entitled "Help," "Advanced Search," "Frequently Asked Questions," and so forth.

After choosing the search engine we're going to use, it's a good idea to look at the help section so we can determine how to construct our search expression.

7. Create a search expression using syntax that is appropriate for the search engine.

After reading the search help, we're ready to formulate the search expression. If we chose a search engine that supported Boolean searching and truncation, this would be a possible way to express it:

(teen* OR adolescen*) AND "driving age" AND (accident* OR safety)

We must remember that if we have ORs and ANDs in a search expression we must put parentheses around the ORs to make sure that these operations are performed first. This is an example of nested Boolean logic.

If we chose a database that didn't support Boolean searching, like Infoseek or AltaVista's main search mode, the implied Boolean features could be applied as follows:

+teen* adolescen* +"driving age" +accidents safety

Notice that we didn't put a + in front of adolescen* or safety. In AltaVista's main search, and in several other search engines that support implied Boolean searching, if there is no + before a word or phrase, the default connector is the Boolean OR.

8. **Evaluate the results. How many hits were returned? Were the results relevant to your query?**
We'll need to look at the documents in the first page or two of the results to determine how relevant they are to our query. It's a good idea to click on a few titles and scan the documents, looking for how our keywords are expressed in the text. We can use the Find feature located under Edit in the browser's menu bar to help locate the keywords.

9. **Modify your search if needed. Go back to Steps 2 through 4 and revise your query accordingly.**
We may decide to limit the results to educational sites, for example, all URLs that end in **.edu**. Or we may want to narrow the results to the last six months.

The following guidelines may help you modify your search requests:
If you feel that your search has yielded too few Web pages (low recall), there are several things to consider:
- Perhaps the search expression was too specific; go back and remove some terms that are connected by ANDs.
- Perhaps there are more terms to use. Think of more synonyms to OR together. Try truncating more words if possible.
- Check spelling and syntax (a forgotten quotation mark or missing parentheses).
- Read the instructions on the help pages again.

If your search has given you too many results and many are unrelated to your topic (low precision/high recall), consider the following:
- Narrow your search to specific fields, if possible.

     ↷   Use more specific terms; for example, instead of cancer, use the specific type of cancer in which you're interested.

     ↷   Add additional terms with AND or NOT.

     ↷   Remove some synonyms if possible.

10. **Try the same search in a different search engine, following Steps 5 through 9.**

    We may drastically modify our search in another database, or perhaps we'll simply remove the truncation feature and try the same basic search in a database that doesn't support it, like HotBot. It's always a good idea to try a search in another database. Not every search engine indexes the same documents, nor does each search engine use the same relevancy algorithm. The way a search engine determines relevancy affects the order that results are listed in.

    > Remember that the Web is always changing and that your results may differ from those shown here. Don't let this confuse you. The activities are meant to demonstrate fundamental skills. These skills don't change, even though the number of results obtained or the actual screens may look very different.

    Now we'll do a hands-on activity to explain these concepts in a more practical way.

USING THE BASIC SEARCH STRATEGY TO FIND INFORMATION IN SEARCH ENGINES

Overview

In this activity, we're going to search for resources on a multifaceted topic. We want to find World Wide Web documents that focus on how global warming and climate change can promote the spread of infectious diseases. We think that some of the research published on this topic is available on the Web.

Following the steps of the basic search strategy, we need to examine the facts of our search, choosing the appropriate keywords and determining which search features apply. Then we'll go to the search engine we've chosen, Northern Light, and read the search instructions. We'll formulate the search expression using Northern Light's full Boolean search capability. We'll then open a document and show you how to find the keywords in the text of the document. After performing this search in Northern Light, we'll go to another search engine, AltaVista, and look for the same topic there. We'll use AltaVista's main search capability, which supports implied Boolean operators (the + and -).

Details

1. **Identify the important concepts of your search.**

   The most important concepts of this search are the effects of global warming and climate change on the spread of infectious diseases.

2. **Choose the keywords that describe these concepts.**

   The main terms or keywords include the following: global warming, climate change, and infectious diseases.

3. **Determine whether there are synonyms, related terms, or other variations of the keywords that should be included.**

   For global warming: ozone depletion, greenhouse effect

   For climate change: none

   For infectious diseases: none

4. **Determine which search features may apply, including truncation, phrase searching, Boolean operators, and so forth.**

   When developing a search expression, keep in mind that you place OR between synonyms and AND between the different concepts, or facets, of the search topic. Writing down all the synonyms may help with the construction of the final search phraseology. Table 9.2 shows the three major concepts, or facets, of the search topic with their synonyms (if any) connected with the appropriate Boolean operators. Note that if we truncated the word *disease,* we would retrieve the words *disease* and *diseases.* Before you get online, take a few minutes to determine if you have used all the search features that you possibly can. It may save you a lot of time in the long run.

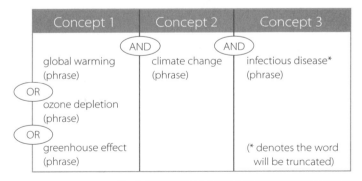

Table 9.2   Formulation of the Search Strategy

5. **Choose a search engine.**

We've decided to use Northern Light for this part of the activity. Let's discover a bit about this search engine. Northern Light, **http:// www.northernlight.com**, is a full-text database that not only indexes World Wide Web documents, but also includes a fee-based database containing about a million articles from about 5,000 sources. These sources include journals, newspapers, books, and other types of publications. If you want to view a document from this special collection, you will be charged a fee. Northern Light has another unique feature: the way it organizes results. In addition to listing the results of your search by relevancy, Northern Light organizes the results for you in what it calls Custom Search Folders. These folders provide a way for you to screen, or filter, your results and can help prevent information overload. These folders are created anew with each search you perform, so the headings vary depending on the subject matter. There are four major kinds of folders: type, subject, source, and language. A type folder might be "press releases" or "job advertisements." A subject folder may be "global warming" or "epidemics." Source folders would be something like "www.globalchange.org" or "commercial sites." A language folder would group non-English-language sites together, which can be help-ful.

First we need to open Northern Light.

(Do it)! Click on the location field, type **http://www.northernlight.com**, and press **Enter**.

6. **Read the search instructions on the search engine's home page. Look for sections entitled "Help," "Advanced Search," "Frequently Asked Questions," and so forth.**

(Do it)! Click on **Tips** on Northern Light's home page.

Scroll down and read the search help. Your screen should look similar to the one pictured in Figure 9.6. Note that Northern Light supports full Boolean searching.

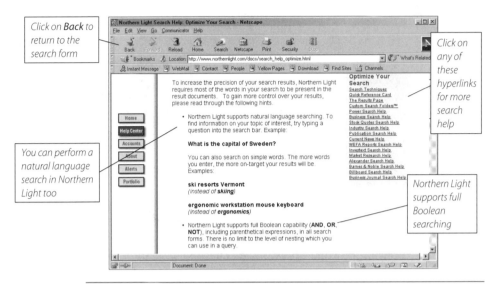

*Click on **Back** to return to the search form*

Click on any of these hyperlinks for more search help

You can perform a natural language search in Northern Light too

Northern Light supports full Boolean searching

Figure 9.6   Search Help in Northern Light

7. Create a search expression using syntax that is appropriate for the search engine.

After reading the help section, we have determined that Northern Light, in addition to supporting full Boolean searching,

~ automatically searches for the singular and plural forms of words so there is no need to truncate "infectious disease" and

~ supports phrase searching.

Let's see what results the search expression brings us in Northern Light.

(Do it) Click on the **Back** icon to return to Northern Light's search form.

(Do it) Type the following in the search form:
("global warming" or "ozone depletion" or "greenhouse effect") and "climate change" and "infectious disease"

(Do it) Click on **Search**.

Figure 9.7 shows the results of this search query. Note how Northern Light provides the list of results in order of relevancy on the right, and has placed these same documents in folders along the left. Because of our interest in infectious disease, we might want to click on the folder entitled Infectious & communicable diseases.

(Do it) Click on the folder **Infectious & communicable diseases**, as shown in Figure 9.7.

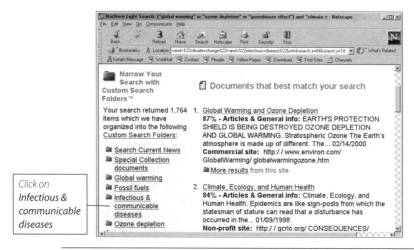

Figure 9.7   Northern Light's Search Results

8. Evaluate the results. How many hits were returned? Were the results relevant to your query?

Figure 9.8 shows some of the contents of the Infectious & communicable diseases folder. There are 134 Web pages in this folder. (Your results may show a different number.) These Web pages are further subdivided by the subjects listed along the left side of the window. Note that these documents are primarily about health problems caused by the effects of global warming and climate change and they appear to be relevant. To begin to evaluate selected Web resources, open a few Web pages and do a Find command to locate the keywords that were included in your search expression.

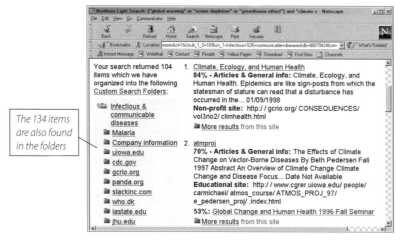

Figure 9.8   The Results in the Infectious & Communicable Diseases Folder

(Do it!) Click on a title that appears to be relevant.

Examine the page. A good way to determine the usefulness of a document is to find out where in the document your keywords appear and how they are used. Let's try it!

(Do it!) Click on **Edit** in the menu bar at the top of the screen. Choose **Find in Page**.

(Do it!) Type **infectious disease** in the form next to Find what.

(Do it!) Click on **Find Next**.

You'll be taken to that part of the page where the word or phrase you typed is found. The word or phrase will be highlighted. See Figure 9.9.

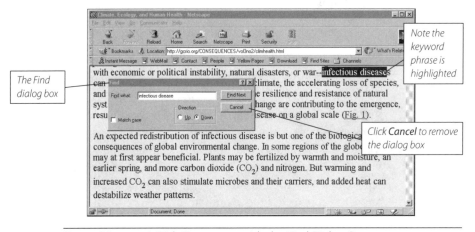

Figure 9.9   A Web Document with the Find Dialog Box

9. **Modify your search if needed. Go back to Steps 2 through 4 and revise your query accordingly.**

We could go back and remove *"infectious disease"* and try searching for *epidemics* instead. We could also try searching for a specific disease, for example, malaria or dengue fever. For the purposes of this activity, and because we're quite satisfied with our search results, we'll stop here.

10. **Try the same search in a different search engine, following Steps 5 through 9.**

Let's see how a different search engine handles this topic. We're going to try AltaVista's main search mode.

Performing the Search in AltaVista's Main Search Using Implied Boolean Operators

Overview

In the next part of this activity, we will use AltaVista's main search mode. It supports implied Boolean searching, so we'll have to work around the lack of the Boolean OR.

We'll follow these steps, which correspond to Steps 6 through 9 of the basic search strategy:

1. Read the search instructions on the search engine's home page. Look for sections entitled "Help," "Advanced Search," "Frequently Asked Questions," and so forth.
2. Create a search expression using syntax that is appropriate for the search engine.
3. Evaluate the results. How many hits were returned? Were the results relevant to your query?
4. Modify your search if needed. Go back and revise your query accordingly.

Details

First, we need to access AltaVista.

 Click on the location field, type **http://www.altavista.com**, and press **Enter**.

1. Read the search instructions on the search engine's home page. Look for sections entitled "Help," "Advanced Search," "Frequently Asked Questions," and so forth.

AltaVista has two search modes: main and advanced. The main search mode only supports implied Boolean, or pseudo-Boolean, searching. This means that you could perform an AND and NOT search by typing a + before a word that has to appear in each of the resulting pages and a - before words that you don't want in the results.

When you open AltaVista, you'll see the main search form, as shown in Figure 9.10. Then you'll want to look at the search instructions.

 Click on the **Help** hyperlink, as shown in Figure 9.10.

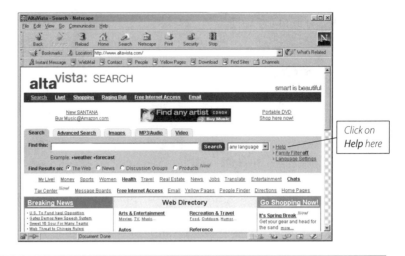

Figure 9.10   AltaVista's Home Page

Your screen will fill with information about searching AltaVista more effectively.

See Figure 9.11 for some parts of the search help information.

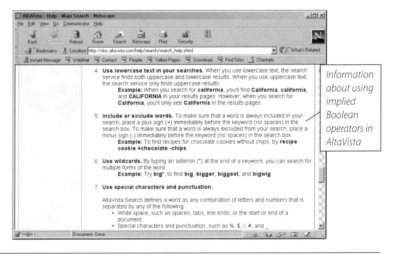

Figure 9.11   Search Help in AltaVista

After reading the extensive help screens in AltaVista, you can start determining how to construct your search expression. In addition to reviewing how to combine Boolean operators with phrases and parentheses, you'll need to find out how AltaVista truncates words. When you're finished with the help section, return to the main search form.

Click on **Back** to return to the main search form.

2. Create a search expression using syntax that is appropriate for the search engine.

Now that you've read the search help, it's time to formulate the search expression. We've learned that AltaVista uses double quotation marks around words that should be searched as a phrase and that we can truncate a word by simply putting an asterisk after the root of the word. It will help to write the search expression out before typing it in the search form. Here is a possible way to express this search:

+ "global warming" "ozone depletion" "greenhouse effect"
+ "climate change" + "infectious disease*"

Note that those phrases that do not have a + in front of them need not appear in the results. They *may* appear in the results. This is the best way to get around the fact that AltaVista's main search doesn't support full Boolean searching with nesting capability.

Keep in mind that you can always modify your search later. Let's try entering it in AltaVista's main search form.

(Do it!) Enter the search expression in the form provided, as shown in Figure 9.12.

(Do it!) Click on **Search**.

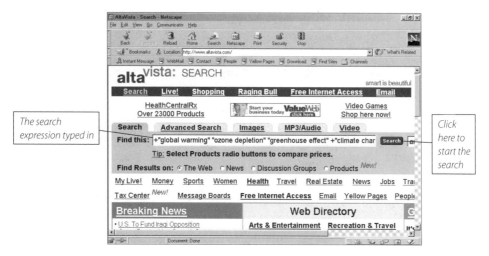

Figure 9.12   Using Implied Boolean Operators in AltaVista

3. Evaluate the results. How many hits were returned? Were the results relevant to your query?

Note the number of hits this search has returned to your screen. Look at a few of the titles. Do they appear to be relevant?

4. Modify your search if needed. Go back to Steps 2 through 4 and revise your query accordingly.

The results seem relevant, and the number of hits is an adequate set with which to work. If we wanted, we could at this point go to AltaVista's advanced search and search by date, or we could do a full Boolean search, modifying it with keywords that we found in the Web pages that were in the resulting list. But for now, we are satisfied with the results we have, and will go on to other examples.

END OF ACTIVITY 9.1

In this activity we searched for information on the same multifaceted topic in two different search engines, AltaVista's main search and Northern Light. The two services had quite different search and output features. We saw the importance of reading each search engine's documentation before searching. Both of the search engines provided relevant results but neither gave the same results.

Formulating Search Expressions: Some Examples

In this section, we'll give brief overviews of topics and search expressions that could be used in various search engines. These aren't meant to be the only correct expressions; they are just possible ways to formulate the queries.

Topic

You're looking for recent information (within the last six months) on the Shining Path, a revolutionary group in Peru. You don't want information on Tupac Amaru, which is another active group there. Keep in mind that Shining Path is Sendero Luminoso in Spanish (and Spanish is the official language of Peru).

Check the search engine's help pages; you may need to insert AND NOT

Poss** Search Expressions

(("shining path" or "sendero luminoso") not "tupac amaru") and peru
OR
+ "shining path" "sendero luminoso" + peru -"tupac amaru"

Note: We didn't put a + in front of "sendero luminoso" because we weren't requiring that the phrase be present in the resulting documents. This is the best way to mimic the Boolean OR when using implied Boolean operators.

Topic

You're looking for Web documents on teenage girls and how their likelihood to develop eating disorders is related to their levels of self-esteem.

Possible Search Expressions
(teenage or adolescen*) and girls and ("eating disorders" or "anorexia nervosa" or bulimia) and ("self-esteem" or "self-respect")
OR
teenage adolescen* +girls + "eating disorders" "anorexia nervosa" bulimia + "self-esteem"

Topic

You want to find a list of the writings of Saki, also know as Hector Munro.

Possible Search Expressions
(saki or munro) and (writings or bibliography)
OR
+saki munro +writings bibliography

> Note there is no + before munro or bibliography. This means the words aren't required to be in the Web pages.

OR
Go to HotBot and choose **this person** from the pulldown menu and type in **Hector Munro** or **Saki**.

Topic

You want to find documents on recycling plastic products.

Possible Search Expressions
recycling and products and (plastic or plastics)
OR
recycling and products and plastic*

> Use this for a database that doesn't support truncation

OR
+recycling +plastic* +products

Topic

You are searching for information that supports your thesis that gender bias has affected career choices for women, starting when they were schoolgirls.

Possible Search Expressions
(girls or women or female) and gender and bias and ("computer science" or comput* or engineering) and stereotyp*
OR
+girls women female +gender bias + "computer science" comput* engineering* +sterotyp*

Topic

You are looking for an image of a bird common in the Middle East and Africa called the hoopoe.

In AltaVista, **http://www.altavista.com**

There are two ways to search for images in AltaVista. Click on **images, audio & video** from the main search page. Click on the radio button next to the format you want; in this situation, you'd choose **image**. In the search form, type in **hoopoe**, and click on **search**. You can also search for an image from AltaVista's main search page. Simply type in the field name **image**, then a colon (:), followed by a name describing the image you're looking for. It would look like this: **image:hoopoe**

In Lycos, **http://www.lycos.com**

Choose **Lycos Rich Media** from the main search page. Select the radio button next to **pictures**. Type **hoopoe** in the search form and click on **Go Get It!** From the results listed, you can link directly to the Web page in which the image appears by clicking on **link to page**.

In HotBot, **http://www. hotbot.lycos.com**

Choose **image** from the menu and type in the word **hoopoe** in the search form. This would retrieve Web pages that have the word *hoopoe* in the pages and contain images. You would find that most pages would have an image of a hoopoe, but some may mention hoopoes in the text yet have images totally unrelated to the bird.

Topic

You want to find out what poem contains the line "Till human voices wake us, and we drown."

Search Expression
"till human voices wake us and we drown"

There is no need to type in the comma.

Summary

Search engines are tools that search databases created by computer programs commonly referred to as spiders or robots. These spiders comb the World Wide Web, select every single word of every Web page they find, and put all of these words in a database that the search engine then searches for us, with the help of our search request. Each of these full-text databases accesses its database differently. Even though many search engine databases attempt to cover the entire Web, none of them actually do. The Web is getting too large for any one database to index all of it. In addition to this, the same search performed in more than one database never returns the same exact results. If you want to do a thorough search, it is wise to become familiar with a few of the different search engines. To understand search engines, it is important to become familiar with the major search features, such as Boolean logic, phrase searching, truncation, and others, before you get online. It is also necessary to read each individual search engine's documentation before typing the search request in the query box. It is also a good idea to get in the habit of checking the documentation often, since search engines are constantly changing their search and output features.

In this chapter, we introduced the basic search strategy, a 10-step procedure that can help you formulate search requests, submit them to search engines, and modify the results retrieved. We have focused on the major search engines on the World Wide Web, but there are several hundred smaller search engines on the Web that search smaller databases. We'll discuss these in some detail in Chapter 10, "Specialized Databases." In addition, there are other search engines that are not free to the public, but require passwords or paid subscriptions. Our intent in this chapter is to give you a foundation for searching any database, no matter if it is fee-based or not, large or small. All of the steps in the basic search strategy apply to any online database.

Selected Terms Used in This Chapter

case sensitivity	natural language searching
concept searching	nested Boolean logic
default setting	phrase searching
duplicate detection	proximity searching
field	relevancy ranking
field searching	results per page
full-text indexing	robot
high precision/high recall	search expression
high precision/low recall	spider
implied Boolean operators	stemming
keywords	stop words
limiting by date	truncation
low precision/high recall	wildcard
meta-tags	

Exercises and Projects

1. Using the advanced search mode in AltaVista, **http://www.altavista .com**, and Infoseek, **http:// infoseek.go.com**, look for relevant resources on the following topics. Write down the first three relevant Web pages retrieved by both search engines. Were any the same? Write down the search expression you used for each topic in each database used. For each topic, list any problems you had and list how many times you needed to modify the search request in each search engine.
    - the writings of Iris Murdoch
    - symptoms of schistosomiasis
    - chronic fatigue syndrome
    - the history of surfboarding

2. Using AltaVista, **http://www.altavista.com**, find the length of the Golden Gate Bridge by using natural language searching and by using implied Boolean operators. How were your results different? Did either way result in more relevant results?

3. Find information on the history of the Eiffel Tower. Perform the search in Northern Light, **http://www.northernlight.com**, and MetaCrawler, **http://www.metacrawler.com**. Write down the search expressions you used in each database to get the results.

4. Using Northern Light, **http://northernlight.com**, find the periodic table of elements. How many hyperlinks did you find? Compare two of the periodic tables that you found. Which one was easier to use? Why?

5. Perform a search in HotBot, **http://hotbot.lycos.com**, using all of steps in the basic search strategy on the following topic: the problems encountered in scuba diving. Give special consideration to finding possible synonyms and using truncation. Write down the steps you went through. What problems, if any, did you encounter? Did you need to modify your search strategy? If so, how did you do this?

6. Use MetaCrawler, **http://www.metacrawler.com**, to find information on baby boomers and social security. How many results did you get? Write down the first three Web page titles and their URLs that appear in the results list. Write down the search expression that you used.

7. Using AltaVista, **http://www.altavista.com**, and HotBot, **http:// www.hotbot.com**, find images of the Shroud of Turin. Describe the steps you took to find these images in each search engine.

8. Using AltaVista's advanced search mode, **http://www.altavista.com**, look for information on how mad cow disease causes Creutzfeldt-Jakob disease in humans. Keep in mind that mad cow disease is also known as Bovine Spongiform Encephalopathy, and incorporate this into your search in the correct way. Write down the search expression that you used and the total number of hits you retrieved. Did the results appear to be relevant to your search request? Write down three of the most relevant titles with their URLs.

9. Go to Northern Light, **http://www.northernlight.com**, and select the power search mode. Search for government documents that have dealt with the subject of school violence. Limit your search to resources that have been added to the database in the past six months. Describe in detail which categories you chose and how you limited your search by date.

10. You are looking for clinical trials designed for sufferers of Gulf War Syndrome. Try to find hyperlinks to this information by *browsing* Yahoo!, **http://www.yahoo.com**, and *searching* HotBot, **http://www.hotbot.com**. Describe the search strategies you used in both services. Which tool provided the most relevant information?

Chapter 10

SPECIALIZED

DATABASES

∿

The amount of information on the World Wide Web is growing so fast that it is difficult for the major search engines to index all of it. Much of what is available on the World Wide Web that is not accessible from the major search engines is to be found in **specialized databases**. Some folks describe this group of specialized databases as the *invisible Web* or the *hidden Internet*. Specialized databases are indexes that can be searched, much like the search engines explored in Chapters 8 and 9. The main difference is that specialized databases are collections on particular subjects, such as government data files, census information, news and magazine archives, email address directories, company financial information, medical information, and so forth. You can find information in these special databases that you would not locate by using a global Web search engine. When you know of a specialized database on the subject you are researching, using that database may save you time and give you reliable and relevant information.

There are also databases on the Web that require a subscription fee. These are commonly referred to as *commercial* or *proprietary databases*. You can sometimes access these databases at libraries that subscribe to them or you can subscribe to them yourself. In this chapter, we'll show you how to find information about people and companies by using some of the special databases freely available on the Web. As you go through the chapter, you may want to review the search features and the 10-step basic search strategy introduced in Chapter 9.

Goals/Objectives

∿   Know the reasons why some Web information is not indexed in the major search engines

∿   Know how to find specialized databases and become familiar with several types

∿   Learn how to find information about people and businesses

∿   Develop a practical methodology for using several types of search tools to find specific types of information

Topics

Why Information in Specialized Databases Is Not Accessible via Search Engines

The major search engines discussed in Chapters 8 and 9 build their databases by collecting URLs that exist on the World Wide Web. The Web pages that are attached to the URLs are then indexed. When you type a word or words in a search engine's search form, you retrieve a list of URLs that already exist in the search engine's database. To put it simply, a search engine typically cannot search a specialized database because of the following reasons:

∾ A database usually cannot search another database without some very special programming. Think about it. The search engine you are using may come across a specialized database but then may be stopped from going any further because the special database has a search form that requests information from the user. For example, you wouldn't look in AltaVista to see what books are in your library, you'd look at your library's Web-based catalog.

∾ Many specialized databases contain information that is retrieved dynamically every time a request is made, and the URLs that are generated are different each time. A search engine can't build its database with URLs that may work today and not tomorrow. (Although we have seen that occasionally a search engine picks up information from a dynamic Web site and indexes the unstable URL. If you retrieved that page from your results list, your keywords wouldn't appear.)

> **READ MORE ABOUT IT**
>
> Researchers Steve Lawrence and Lee Giles have shown that search engines are not indexing even half of the information available on the Web. Their research is published in **Nature**, Vol. 400, July 1999, p. 107–109. You can read about the results of this recent study at **http://www.wwwmetrics.com**.

~ Search engines can't index content from specially formatted files. For example, the content in Adobe PDF (portable document format) files is inaccessible to search engines because the text is formatted in such a way as to be nonindexable.

How to Find Specialized Databases

By some accounts, there are more than 7,000 specialized databases on the World Wide Web. How do you find them? Sometimes you'll stumble across specialized databases while doing a keyword search in a search engine. Occasionally, a Web page will have a hyperlink to a database, or a friend or colleague will tell you about a particular site. There is a more precise way to find them, but even this is not always foolproof. Virtual libraries, meta-search tools that include lists of databases, and directories are often the best sources to use when looking for specialized databases. It's important to keep in mind that if you don't find what you're looking for in one resource, that doesn't mean it doesn't exist. You may find it in another resource.

The following tools are the most helpful in listing specialized databases and *subject guides*:

Tool	URL and Description
Beaucoup	**http://www.beaucoup.com** Beaucoup lists more than 2,500 specialized databases and directories and also serves as a meta-search tool.
Internet Public Library (IPL) Reference Center	**http://www.ipl.org/ref** The IPL is a virtual library that provides a good starting point for finding reference works, subject guides, and specialized databases.
Fossick.com	**http://www.fossick.com** This meta-search tool contains links to hundreds of specialized databases.
The InvisibleWeb	**http://www.invisibleweb.com** Produced by IntelliSeek, Inc., the InvisibleWeb is a well-organized, comprehensive directory of thousands of specialized databases.
LibrarySpot	**http://www.libraryspot.com/** LibrarySpot collects links to quality reference resources and provides links to more than 2,500 libraries around the world.

Librarians' Index to the Internet	**http://www.lii.org/internetindex** A virtual library that is both searchable and browsable, this is an excellent source for specialized databases.
The Scout Report	**http://www.scout.cs.wisc.edu/report/ sr/current/index.html** The Scout Report is a good way to keep up with new search tools, especially specialized databases. You can view its weekly report and its archive of previous Scout Reports on the Web. You can also have the report delivered to you via email by subscribing through a listserv. Send an email message to **scout-report-request@cs.wisc.edu**. Type **subscribe to scout-report** in the body of the message.

Table 10.1   Some Tools That List Specialized Databases

Proprietary and Free Databases

There are hundreds of **proprietary** or **commercial databases** on the World Wide Web, but these are available only if you or your organization has purchased access to them. For example, FirstSearch, **http://www. ref.oclc.org**; DialogWeb, **http://www.dialogweb.com**; STN, **http:// www.cas.org/stn.html**; and Lexis-Nexis, **http://www.lexisnexis.com**, all provide proprietary databases.

Proprietary databases have certain value-added features that databases in the public domain do not have. Here are some examples of that enhanced content:

∿ Proprietary databases are likely to include extra information that helps researchers. For example, most of the databases in FirstSearch (the Online Computer Library Center's (OCLC) proprietary database system) have links to library holdings. This means that if you find an article or book in a database provided by FirstSearch, such as MEDLINE, you can immediately find out which libraries own the material. Even though MEDLINE is available free to the public from the National Library of Medicine, you might prefer to use the First-Search version if you want to know who has the listed journal articles.

∿ Proprietary databases also allow you to download information easily. For instance, some of these databases include financial information that is commonly free to the public, but they charge for the use of their databases because they have made it much easier for the user to download the information to a spreadsheet program.

∾ Proprietary databases often index material that others do not. The information is distinguished by its uniqueness, its historical value, or its competitive value (for example, private company financial information).

∾ Proprietary database systems are more responsible to their users. Because they cost money, they are more apt to provide training and other user support, such as newsletters that update their services.

∾ There are also databases on the Web that are free to the public but charge for the full text of the articles. The Electric Library, **http://www.elibrary.com**, and Northern Light, **http://www.northernlight.com**, are examples of this type of database. Many newspaper archives work the same way. You can search the archive, but if you want a copy of the newspaper article, there is a fee involved. For all of these fee-based databases, the fees can be paid with a credit card on an article-by-article basis, through an account, or through a monthly charge.

Accessing Fee-based Databases

If you would like to have a list of the proprietary databases on the market, you might access "FACSNET: Computer Assisted Research," **http://www.facsnet.org/report_tools/CAR/cardirec.htm**, a Web page published by the Poynter Institute for Media Studies.

Remember, you can always ask a reference librarian at your local library about accessing proprietary databases. The library may have several databases on CD-ROM or may have purchased access to databases via the Internet. The specialized databases covered in this chapter are free and open to anyone.

Using Specialized Databases to Find Information About People

Some say that connecting with people is the greatest thing about the Internet and the World Wide Web. Finding people that you have lost touch with can be fun. You can find an old high school friend's email or street address or maybe even her telephone number by using special Web databases that compile this information. There are ways to find people who have similar interests as you, including ways to contact them to share information. The Web is also a great place to find experts or people who are well-versed in subjects that you know little or nothing about. The Web can also help you find biographical information about famous and not-so-famous people.

Email and Telephone Directories

There are several email and telephone directories on the World Wide Web. They are often referred to as **people-finders** or **white page services**. These services give you fast access to very large databases of email addresses, phone numbers, street addresses, and other information. Some services also provide maps, driving directions, and information about businesses in a specific area. Here are some good occasions for using these services:

- You met people at a conference, business meeting, or class reunion, and you want to get in touch with them again.

- You wonder which of your old or current friends have email and what their addresses might be.

- You're visiting a friend and want a map to his house.

The following are some of the most popular email and telephone directories on the Web.

Title	URL
411 Locate	http://www.411locate.com
AnyWho	http://www.anywho.com
Bigfoot	http://bigfoot.com
Switchboard	http://www.switchboard.com
Telephone Directories on the Web	http://www.teldir.com/eng/name/us/pn
Yahoo! People Search	http://people.yahoo.com
InfoSpace	http://www.infospace.com

It may be helpful to go to a directory, virtual library, or meta-search tool that lists several services. Figure 10.1 shows part of such a list in the meta-search tool All-in-One Search Page, **http://www.allonesearch.com/all1user.html**.

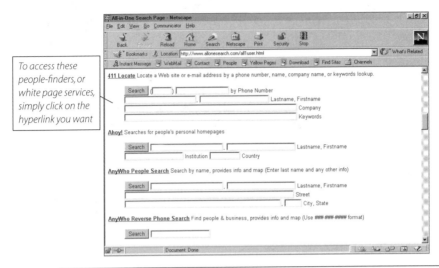

To access these people-finders, or white page services, simply click on the hyperlink you want

Figure 10.1   All-in-One Search Page's Listing of People-Finders

If you try more than one service, you'll notice that they are similar. They all search their databases using the information you enter into fields. Each field holds a specific type of information that matches entries in the database. For example, typing **San Francisco** in the field labeled Last Name isn't likely to help you find information about an address in San Francisco. The database will instead be searched for people whose last name is San Francisco. This type of searching, which is based on the entries or values of specific predefined categories, is called *field searching*.

Disadvantages of White Page Services

The major disadvantage of using these services is that often you won't be able to find the information you'd like for a particular individual. Listings appear when people register their names and addresses in these services. Individual listings also come from addresses people use when they post an article on Usenet or from membership or mailing lists that are often related to computers. It is impossible to find a directory of everyone with access to the Internet—there's no central registry service for Internet users, and no single agency could keep pace with the increasing number of people using the Internet and World Wide Web. Sometimes you can only find information

Remember that the Web is always changing and that your results may differ from those shown here. Don't let this confuse you. The activities demonstrate fundamental skills. These skills don't change, even though the number of results obtained or the actual screens may look very different.

for folks who use computers and the Internet or information that may be out-of-date or inaccurate. On the other hand, these services may be the only means of finding someone's email address quickly. The surest way, if you can do it, is to ask people directly for their email addresses!

Now we'll show you how to use one of the white page services to find an email address. We'll also look for a street address and a telephone number.

FINDING AN INDIVIDUAL'S EMAIL ADDRESS, PHONE NUMBER, AND MAILING ADDRESS

Overview

In this activity, we'll use the Web service Yahoo! People Search to search for an individual's email address, specifically that of Ernest Ackermann. You could follow the steps we go through here to search for anyone's email address, phone number, or mailing address. The details may be different if you're using something other than Yahoo! People Search, but the steps will be almost the same. Here are the steps we'll take:

1. Go to the home page for Yahoo! People Search.
2. Fill in the form.
3. Activate the search and note the results.
4. Search for a phone number and note the results.

Details

We assume you've started your browser.

1. Go to the home page for Yahoo! People Search.

 Click on the location field, type **http://people.yahoo.com**, and press **Enter**.

The home page for Yahoo! People Search, with the information necessary for our search, appears in Figure 10.2. We've noted a number of features and options. Take a few moments to see what's available at this Web site. Click on the hyperlink **Help** at the bottom of the page to learn more about using the service, and don't be shy about trying interesting links. There is also a link that allows you to register or

 tip Remember that anyone on the Web can access this information, so don't include information that you wouldn't feel comfortable and safe sharing with any stranger browsing through this database.

add information about yourself. Once you've registered yourself with People Search, there are several services that are available to you, located on the left side of the page in Figure 10.2.

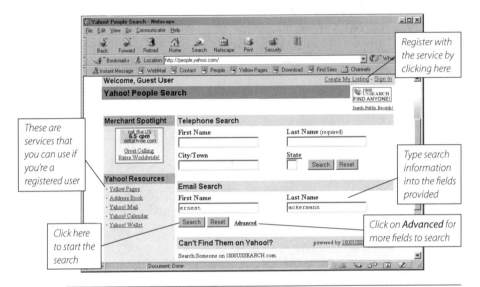

Figure 10.2   The Home Page for Yahoo! People Search

2. **Fill in the form.**

   Figure 10.2 shows information entered into the Email Search section. If you'd like to have more fields to choose from, you could click on the **Advanced** hyperlink.

    In the Email Search section of the Yahoo! People Search home page, type **ernest** into the First Name field and **ackermann** into the Last Name field. Note that Ackermann ends with *two* n's.

3. **Activate the search and note the results.**

    Click on the button labeled **Search**.

   Clicking on the **Search** button sends the search request to Yahoo! People Search for processing. Figure 10.3 shows the results of our search.

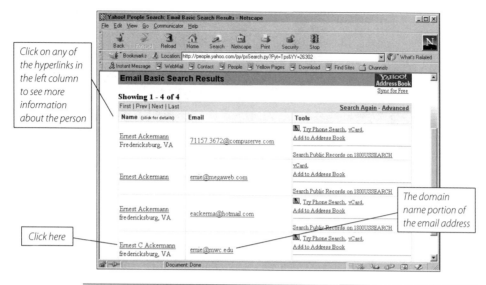

Click on any of the hyperlinks in the left column to see more information about the person

The domain name portion of the email address

Click here

Figure 10.3   The Results of Our Search for an Email Address

Figure 10.3 shows four entries with the first name Ernest and the last name Ackermann. We can't tell from here which entry is the one we want, but we can use the domain name or email location information to help us choose. Since the Ackermann we're looking for works at Mary Washington College, we might try the **@mwc.edu** listing first. (Except for the possible waste of time, there's no harm in trying all of them.)

t|p Sometimes the search criteria may not yield any results or may give too many results. If we don't get any results, we might want to make the search more general by typing in just the first initial of the person's first name. You might also like to do an advanced search, which includes more fields to choose from. Figure 10.6 shows the Advanced Email Search page.

Click on the link **ernest c ackermann**.

Clicking on the link **ernest c ackermann** brings up a Web page, shown in Figure 10.4. Relatively speaking, it gives a lot of information about Ackermann, including his email address, a link to his home page, and alternate email addresses.

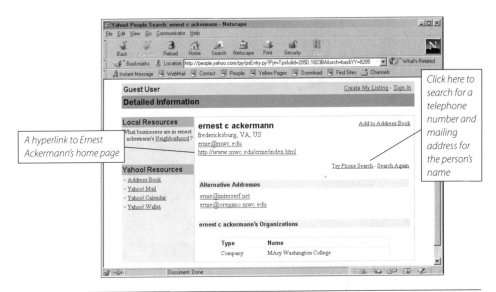

Figure 10.4   Yahoo! People Search Results for **ernest c ackermann**

4. Search for a phone number and note the results.

(Do it!)   Click on the hyperlink **Try Phone Search**.

Figure 10.5 shows that Ernest Ackermann's telephone number is not listed in Yahoo! People Search.

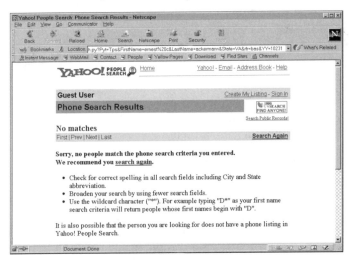

Figure 10.5   Result of Searching for Ernest Ackermann's Telephone Number in Yahoo! People Search

Now would be a good time to try another service if you want to find Ernest Ackermann's telephone number and address. A couple of services you might want to try are Bigfoot, **http://bigfoot.com**, and Switchboard, **http://www.switchboard.com**. We won't try them here; we'll trust you to try them on your own.

Figure 10.6 shows the advanced email search page in Yahoo! People Search that we mentioned earlier in the activity. Note the number of possible fields to search. You can access this advanced form by clicking on **Advanced** in the email search section on Yahoo! People Search's home page, as shown in Figure 10.2.

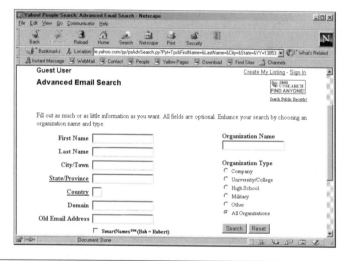

Figure 10.6   The Advanced Email Search Form in Yahoo! People Search

END OF ACTIVITY 10.1

In Activity 10.1, we looked for an individual's email and street address using Yahoo! People Search, one of many search services. Other services may be somewhat different, but they will be similar enough that you'll be able to use them without any trouble.

Privacy and Ethical Issues

In Activity 10.1, you saw how easy it is to find an individual's email address, phone number, and mailing address. Services such as the one you used make it possible to search a centralized collection of millions of records in seconds. This capability raises a number of questions related to privacy and the ethical use of the information in such records. An example of such a question is this: Where does the information in these databases originate? Most of the services obtain their information from public sources, such as published phone books and registration lists for online services. All services encourage individuals to register with them.

If you register, you must provide information about yourself. In return, you gain access to some features not available to the general public. Some services only list information provided by registered users or by those who have supplied data on another voluntary basis.

What control does an individual have over the information in these databases? Much of it comes from public sources, such as phone books, so accuracy and issues of whether a listing appears at all sometimes need to be addressed at the source of the information. You can request that you not be listed in such services. Most of the online white page services make it relatively easy for you to do that. The problem is that you have to send an email request or fill out a form for *each* service. There's no way to ask that information about yourself be hidden or removed from every service at once.

Can users perform so-called reverse searches? For example, can they type in a phone number and find the name and address of the person with that number? This feature isn't available in most services, but it is available in some. Using this capability would help someone identify a person based on the phone number. Services in which the user pays a fee for searching often permit these reverse searches. These include CD-ROM databases that give full access to phone book information.

Almost all questions related to ethical use of the information deal with use of the information for online junk mail—mass mailings related to commercial activity. Such unsolicited email (usually advertising something or soliciting money) is called **spam**. Phone listings in online databases could also be used to generate lists for commercial telemarketing calls.

Most of the services on the Web include a policy statement saying that the information they provide isn't to be used for commercial purposes, but the services don't police the people searching their databases. In their statements, they promise only to respond to complaints from others. It's really up to individuals to protect their privacy and to demand ethical behavior on the Internet and the Web.

Before registering for one of these services, you need to read the policies about how your personal information will be used. You can usually find such policies by clicking on a hyperlink labeled **Help**, **About**, **Acceptable Use Policy**, or **FAQ** from the services' Web pages.

The questions raised by the use of this technology are typical of what we need to be aware of and concerned about as more information becomes readily available through the use of computers, networks, and other technologies. There are lots of advantages to using these tools, but we need to think about, and act on, the ramifications of making this type of information so easily accessible.

Searching for Experts and People Who Share Your Interests

The Internet has made it much easier to find people that share your interests or people who may know something that you'd like to know about. The quickest way is to search the Usenet section of Deja.com, **http:// www.deja.com/usenet**, for the subject you're interested in and read some of the articles posted. You can note the names of the newsgroups that hold the articles in case you want to read other articles in that group. By clicking on the hyperlink for an article's author, you can obtain a summary of the information from the Deja.com database about articles posted by this author, including the number of articles posted and the names of the newsgroups in which you can find the author's articles. You could send email to authors if you had questions or comments about what they wrote, thereby taking advantage of their expertise.

Fy SEARCH ENGINES THAT INDEX USENET NEWSGROUP ARTICLES

AltaVista **http://www.altavista.com**
Select **Discussion Groups**

HotBot **http://www.hotbot. lycos.com**
Select **Discussion Groups**

Infoseek **http://www.infoseek. com**
Select **Newsgroups**

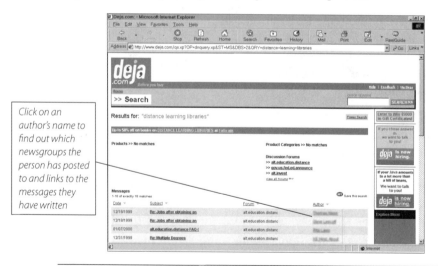

Click on an author's name to find out which newsgroups the person has posted to and links to the messages they have written

Figure 10.7   The Results of a Subject Search in Deja.com

You can also find people that share your interests by searching discussion group archives. Some discussion groups or listservs have their own archives that you can search. You can search discussion group archives that are hosted by the University of Buffalo by accessing **http://listserv.**

acsu.buffalo.edu/archives. Some search engines index discussion group postings too. See Chapter 6 for more information.

Searching for Biographical Information

Searching for information about people that includes more than a cursory address or telephone number can be a challenge. There are several types of resources you can use.

Searching Newsgroup and Discussion Group Archives by Name

You can search Usenet news archives or discussion group archives using a person's name instead of a subject. For example, if you were looking for a bit of information about Ernest Ackermann's interests, you could try typing his name in Deja.com's search form and accessing messages that he submitted to newsgroups or discussion groups.

Using Search Engines to Find Information About People

Some search engines make it easy for you to search for a person's name. In HotBot, **http://www.hotbot.lycos.com**, for example, you can select **the person** from the Look for pulldown menu. In any search engine you can also search for a person's name by enclosing the name in quotation marks.

Fy SELECTED BIOGRAPHICAL DATABASES ON THE WEB
- ~ "Biographical Dictionary" http://www.s9.com/biography
- ~ "Biography.com" http://www.biography.com
- ~ "Distinguished Women of Past and Present" http://www. DistinguishedWomen.com

Searching for People in Association or Organization Directories

If you know a person's profession, you can try to find more information about him by searching a professional association directory, if one exists for the profession you need. There are a few databases that list organizations and associations. You can find these databases by accessing a virtual library. You could follow these steps, for example:

- ~ Open the Librarians' Index to the Internet at **http://lii.org**.

- ~ Click on **Organizations**, as shown in Figure 10.8. You retrieve a list of more than 50 sites. Many of the sites listed are databases or guides that contain hyperlinks to individual organizations' Web sites.

- ~ One of the sites on this list is called ASAE Member Associations Online and is a product of the American Society of Association Executives. The database contains 1,900 associations and organizations.

∾ Let's say the person you are looking for is a physician. You can search the database by typing in a word or words that may be in the title of the association you're looking for. For a doctor, you may want to type in medical. A list of several associations are returned to the browser window.

∾ If you chose the American Medical Association, you'd find that this association has a "doctor finder" that you can search. This database indexes the names of virtually all the licensed physicians in the United States. If you enter in the doctor's name you are looking for, the database will return to your screen a profile of the doctor, including her address, her telephone number, the medical school she attended, where she did her residency training, the year she graduated from medical school, the medical specialty she practices, and if she is board-certified.

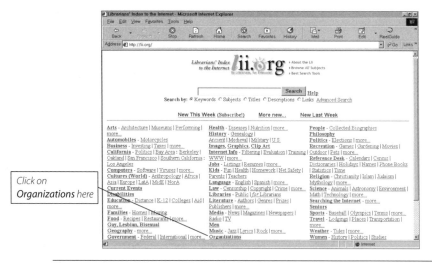

Figure 10.8   Librarians' Index to the Internet

Searching for People in Newspaper Archives

Newspapers can provide a wealth of information about people. Many newspapers have made their archives available for free on the World Wide Web. Again, a virtual library like the Librarians' Index to the Internet can help you find a list of newspaper archives. Figure 10.9 shows Newspaper Archives on the Web, a site that was found by clicking on **Newspapers** in the Media category. This site sorts newspaper archive links by state. The dates that the newspaper archive covers are included and, if there is a fee for searching or retrieving articles, this information is given as well. We'll show how to search a newspaper archive in the next section of this chapter.

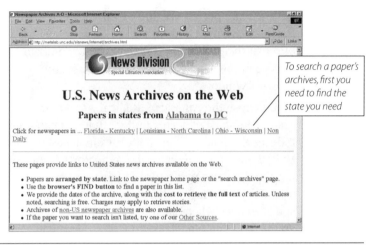

To search a paper's archives, first you need to find the state you need

Figure 10.9   Newspaper Archives on the Web

Finding Biography Databases

There are several databases on the Web that focus on biographical information. The people included in these databases are usually famous people. If you clicked on **Collected Biographies** in the People category in the Librarians' Index to the Internet, you'd find several sites that include biographical databases.

Searching for Company and Industry Information

The World Wide Web has become a useful place to conduct business research. Most companies use their home pages as marketing or communications tools. These home pages may include annual reports, press releases, and biographies of the people in top-level management. The home pages may also include information about companies' products and services, including catalogs.

tip If you want to find a company's home page but don't know the URL, you can often guess it by typing the company's name with **http:///www.** at the beginning and **.com** at the end. For example, if you were looking for the home page for Sears, Roebuck, and Company, you could try typing **http://www.sears.com**. This is the correct URL for Sears, Roebuck, and Company. You could also use a search engine to look for the company's name, limiting the results to URLs that include **sears.com**.

If you want to do industry research, you can use business-related subject guides. These contain hyperlinks to businesses within the particular industry that interests you. You can easily find subject guides in virtual libraries and major directories.

You can also find business directories on the Web by using one of the virtual libraries or meta-search tools listed at the beginning of this chapter. Keep in mind that companies that provide the most financial information on the Web are usually publicly traded. Public companies are required to provide very detailed information about themselves to the U.S. government, whereas privately held companies are not. If a private company is listed in a nonproprietary (open to the public) database, some financial information will be available, but not nearly as much as if it were a public company.

 Activity 10.2

FINDING COMPANY INFORMATION

Overview

In this activity, we'll find information about a specific company. The company we'll be searching for is Apple Computer. Suppose you need to find a home page, an address, an annual report, a 10-K report, and recent newspaper articles about this company. There are several company directories on the Web that would provide a starting place for this type of research. Virtual libraries and meta-search tools list databases by subject. You'll need to go to one to find company databases. In this activity, we'll go to the InvisibleWeb, **http://www.invisibleweb.com**, which is a directory that provides hyperlinks to specialized databases. After we find a company directory that gives general information, we'll search it. We'll find basic information about Apple Computer, and then use the InvisibleWeb again to help us find a link to Disclosure's Securities and Exchange Commission (SEC) EDGAR database. This database contains the full text of 10-K and other reports that public companies are required by law to submit to the SEC. Next, we'll go to the Newspaper Archives on the Web, **http://sunsite.unc.edu/slanews/internet/archives.html**, which was covered earlier in the chapter (see Figure 10.9), and search the *San Francisco Chronicle* and *Examiner* for articles on Apple Computer. Apple's headquarters is near San Francisco, so it makes sense for us to search that city's newspapers.

Let's get started!

We're assuming that you have a browser program set up on your computer, you have a way of connecting to the Internet, and the browser is started.

We'll follow these steps:

1. Go to the InvisibleWeb and find a company directory.
2. Search Companies Online to find the company's address, home page, and other basic information.
3. Find a 10-K report for the company.
4. Find newspaper articles about the company.

Details

1. **Go to the InvisibleWeb and find a company directory.**

    (Do it) Click on the location field, type **http://www.invisibleweb.com**, and press **Enter**.

    Note the directory structure of the InvisibleWeb in Figure 10.10. Under the main heading of Business is the subcategory Company Research. It makes sense that this subcategory would have databases listed that would help us locate information about a company.

    (Do it) Click on **Company Research**.

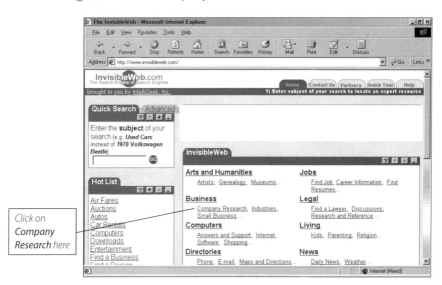

Click on Company Research here

Figure 10.10   The InvisibleWeb

Figure 10.11 shows the list of resources in this category. Because we are looking for general information about a company, the link **Company Profiles** may be the best category to choose.

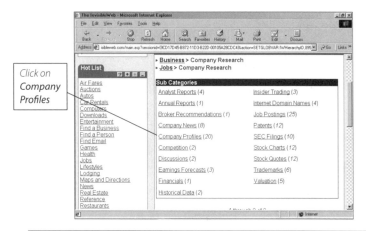

Figure 10.11   Categories in the Company Research
                Section of the InvisibleWeb

A list of databases will appear in the window. One of them is entitled
Companies Online. This is the database we want to access.

(Do it)! Click on **Companies Online**.

**2. Search Companies Online to find the company's address, home
page, and other basic information.**

(Do it)! Type **apple computer** in the Company Name field.

(Do it)! Click on **Go Get It!**, as shown in Figure 10.12.

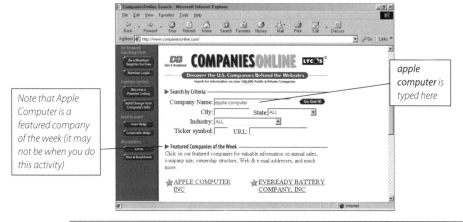

Figure 10.12   Companies Online with **apple computer** Typed In

Your window will fill with different links to choose from.

(Do it)! Click on **APPLE COMPUTER INC.**

Figure 10.13 shows a portion of the entry for Apple Computer Inc.

Figure 10.13   A Portion of the Entry for Apple Computer

Note the information provided by Companies Online. If you scrolled down the page, you would find a lot more information about Apple, including hyperlinks to its Web pages and some primary financial information.

3. Find a 10-K report for the company.

The Securities and Exchange Commission requires public companies to make an annual financial disclosure, called a 10-K report. The 10-K not only gives recent financial information about the company, it also lists the top people in the company, their salaries, and stock ownership information. To obtain Apple's 10-K, you need to find the database that contains this information. We'll need to go back to the InvisibleWeb and see if we can find it.

There are three ways to return to the InvisibleWeb.

- Click on **Back** several times until you are at the InvisibleWeb.
- Type **http://www.invisibleweb.com** in the location field and press **Enter**.
- Click on the arrow next to the address box or location field, locate **www.invisibleweb.com** on the list of recently visited Web pages, highlight it with your mouse, and click.

Once back in the InvisibleWeb, click on the subcategory **Company Research**, as we did in Step 1.

Find the subcategory **SEC Filings** and click on it. Figure 10.11 shows the page that you will choose SEC Filings from.

There are several databases that provide SEC filings. A portion of the list is shown in Figure 10.14.

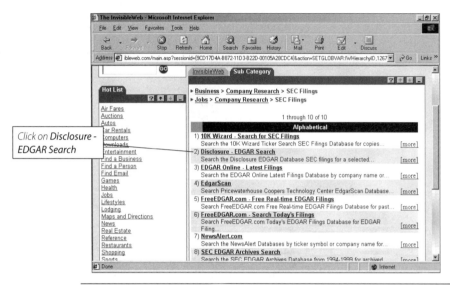

Figure 10.14   Accessing Disclosure SEC Filings
                 from the InvisibleWeb Directory

While any of these databases would probably give us the information
we are looking for, let's choose the Disclosure - EDGAR Search
database.

(Do it)!   Click on **Disclosure - EDGAR Search,** as shown in Figure 10.14.

Figure 10.15 shows the Disclosure search form. We are looking for
an annual report, which is the 10-K. Notice that in Figure 10.15, we
have chosen **Annual Reports** from the Filing Type pulldown menu in
addition to choosing **10-K** from the Detailed pulldown menu. There
is no need to choose both, but we did just to illustrate how they are
both the same type of report.

(Do it)!   Type **apple computer** in the search form provided.

(Do it)!   Choose the filing type you request, in this case, the **10-K**, or annual
           report.

(Do it)!   Click on **search** to activate the request.

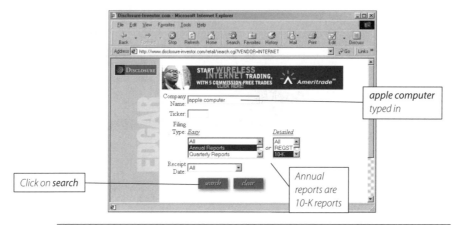

Figure 10.15   Searching Disclosure EDGAR for Apple
                Computer's Annual (10-K) Reports

The window should look like the one pictured in Figure 10.16. There are
several filings listed. To access the most recent annual report, click on the
first 10-K hyperlink, as shown in Figure 10.16.

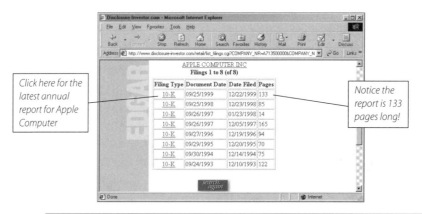

Figure 10.16   Apple Computer 10-K Reports

4. Find newspaper articles about the company.

In the section on searching for people earlier in the chapter, we
introduced a Web site called Newspaper Archives on the Web. To
refresh your memory, look at Figure 10.9. We need to access this
site now.

 Click on the location field and type this URL:

http://sunsite.unc.edu/slanews/ internet/archives.html

Your window should look similar to the one in Figure 10.17. Since
the headquarters for Apple Computer is located near San Francisco,
California, it may be a good idea to search one of that city's newspa-

pers. The *San Francisco Chronicle* and *Examiner* are listed, so let's try one of them.

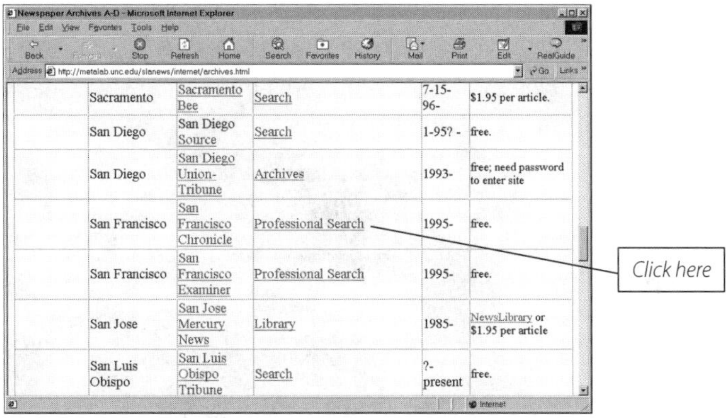

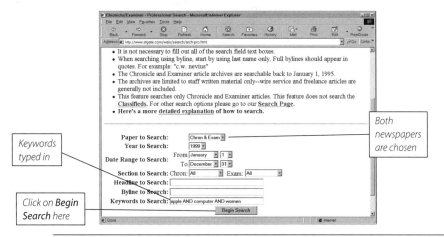

Figure 10.17   Newspaper Archives on the Web

(Do it)!   Click on **Professional Search** next to San Francisco Chronicle.

Note in Figure 10.18 that you can search the *Chronicle* and the *Examiner* at the same time from this Web site. Note also that there are search tips for searching this database. You must capitalize AND, OR, and NOT when using them in a search expression.

Figure 10.18   Searching the *San Francisco Chronicle* and *Examiner*

(Do it)!   Use the pulldown menu next to Paper to Search and choose **Chron & Exam**.

(Do it)!   From the pulldown menu next to Year to Search, choose **1999**.

Note that we can search headlines and bylines or the entire text of the articles using keywords. Let's do a keyword search on how Apple computer products appeal to women.

(Do it) In the field next to Keywords to Search, type **apple AND computer AND women**.

(Do it) Click on **Begin Search**.

Figure 10.19 shows the results of this search. Since we are looking for articles that discuss Apple's marketing strategies to women, let's look for an article that pertains to this.

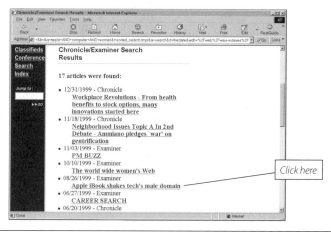

Figure 10.19   The Results of Searching the Archive

(Do it) Click on **Apple iBook shakes tech's male domain**, as shown in Figure 10.19.

Figure 10.20 shows the article we chose. Note that you can get a copy of the article without the graphics and advertising by clicking on **printer-friendly version** in the right side of the window.

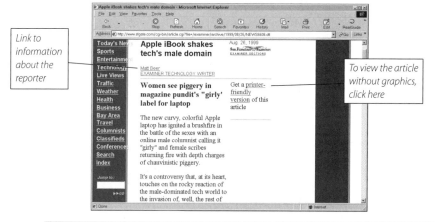

Figure 10.20   A Newspaper Article from the *San Francisco Examiner*

END OF ACTIVITY 10.2

Although this activity skimmed the surface of the types of business information available on the Web, we hope that it gave you an overview of what's involved with searching about a company from scratch. Using special databases for information like this is much more effective than using global search engines because they allow researchers to focus on specific types of information.

Summary

Specialized databases are searchable collections on particular subjects. The U.S. government and nonprofit organizations maintain many of the free, nonproprietary databases on the Web, but commercial databases are also starting to appear with greater frequency.

You can easily find specialized databases by accessing virtual libraries, meta-search tools, or directories such as the InvisibleWeb. Specialized databases are also found in subject guides. These databases are like search engines, in that they support different search features. Most databases have search instruction pages that you should read before you start searching.

Selected Terms Used in This Chapter

commercial database

field searching

people-finder

proprietary database

spam

specialized database

subject guide

white page service

Exercises and Projects

1. You are starting a running program and want to find out about how to train for a 10K run that is scheduled in your town. Go to Deja.com, **http://www.deja.com/usenet**, and perform a keyword search for items on this topic. Once you have the results, click on a few articles and see if they are relevant. If not, modify the search. Provide the search expressions you used. Once you are satisfied with the relevancy of the articles retrieved, write down three of the discussion groups or newsgroups that were accessed.

2. Go to Fossick.com, **http://www.fossick.com**, and locate the Human Rights Internet database. Describe the steps you took to find it. Using this database, search for reports on the death penalty. How many results did you retrieve? List the titles of three that appear interesting or provocative.

3. Using the InvisibleWeb, **http://www.invisibleweb.com**, find Martindale-Hubbell's Lawyers.Com, a directory of lawyers and law firms in the United States. Describes the steps you took to find this

database. Access the database and search for attorneys or law firms in your state that specialize in environmental law. How many firms or attorneys did you find? List at least two, including their addresses.

4. Go to the Librarians' Index to the Internet, **http://lii.org**. Find the IBM Intellectual Property Network. Explain the steps you took to locate it. Look for patents granted since 1995 on the subject of graphical user interfaces. How many patents did you find? Write down the numbers and titles of three patents you found.

5. Use Yahoo!, **http://www.yahoo.com**, to find the Internet Movie Database. Explain the procedure you followed to locate this database. Once you have accessed it, find out who played Boo Radley in the 1962 film *To Kill a Mockingbird*. What are three other movies he or she had a role in?

6. Using the Internet Public Library, **http://www.ipl.org**, find the food database Epicurious. Describe how you found it. Search the database for recipes that might interest you. Describe the search you did and the recipes you found.

7. Go to the Internet Public Library, **http://www.ipl.org**, and find the Web site entitled "Foreign Languages for Travelers." Describe the steps you took to find this database. While you are here, find Arabic words for numbers. Describe the steps you took to find these words. What happens when you click on one of the Arabic words?

8. Go to the home page for the InfoSpace Web site, **http://www. infospace.com**.
   a. Find the address and phone number for Radio City Music Hall in New York City.
   b. Using the facilities at InfoSpace, print a map that shows where to find Radio City Music Hall and obtain driving directions from your location to Radio City Music Hall.
   c. Repeat a. and b. for the Wells Fargo Bank in San Francisco.

9. You are looking for information about the drug astemizole. You'd like to know about its effects and what it is used for. Go to the Scout Report, **http://www.scout.cs.wisc.edu/report/sr/current/ index.html**, and search for the database entitled PharmInfoNet DrugDB. Describe how you found this database. Then search DrugDB for information about the drug. What is this drug's trade name? What is it used for? Why was the drug removed from the U.S. market?

10. Go to LibrarySpot, **http://www.libraryspot.com**, and locate a genealogy database by clicking on the hyperlink entitled **Genealogy**. Do a search on your family name. Did you find any historical information on your family? Which databases did you try?

Chapter 11

SELECTING, EVALUATING, AND CITING INFORMATION FROM THE INTERNET

Critical thinking skills have always been important to the process of searching for and using information from media such as books, journal articles, radio broadcasts, television reports, and so forth. With the advent of the Internet and the World Wide Web, these skills have become even more crucial. Traditional books and journal articles need to pass some kind of editorial scrutiny before being published. Web pages, however, can appear without a single person ever reading them through to check for accuracy. Libraries have collection development policies that govern what material they will and will not buy; the Internet and the Web, having no such policies, collect anything. This isn't to say that there isn't quality information on the Internet. There are thousands of high-caliber Web pages and well-regarded databases. It is your responsibility to quickly decide whether a page is worth selecting and then determine, using well-established guidelines, whether the Web page or Internet resource is worth using in your research paper, project, or presentation.

After you determine that a resource is worthy of inclusion as support for a research paper, it is important that you cite it properly so that others who read your work can refer to it. Citing information is as important for Internet resources as it is for any traditional resource. Readers can view or read the original sources to check for accuracy, to see excerpts or ideas in the context of the original piece, or to obtain more information about the subject being covered. You'll also want to cite resources to let people know where they can find information on the Internet, whether you're preparing a formal research paper or including identifying information about the resource in an email message to a friend. And finally, a major reason to properly acknowledge the source of information is to give credit to others whose ideas or expressions you have used in your writing. This chapter will provide guidelines for citing Web and Internet resources properly.

Goals/Objectives

- Develop a process of using critical thinking skills to help select and evaluate Web documents so that you can decide if the information is appropriate and reliable

- Obtain knowledge of URL formats

- Learn the basic elements required in an Internet and Web citation and how to cite different types of resources

- Learn how to manage bookmarked Web sites and use the bookmarks to create citations for a bibliography

Topics

- Reasons to Evaluate

- Guidelines for Evaluation

- Citing Internet and Web Information: URL Formats

- Guidelines for Citing Internet and Web Resources

Reasons to Evaluate

We use the information we find on the Internet or Web for a variety of purposes. Sometimes we use it for entertainment, recreation, or casual conversation. When we use it for research, to bolster a belief, or to choose a particular course of action, we have to be sure the information is reliable and authoritative. That puts us in the position of having to verify the information and make judgments about its appropriateness. Reliable information is one of the most important things in life. In order to make decisions and understand our world, we need the most truthful information that we can find.

The nature of the Internet and the World Wide Web makes it easy for almost anyone to create and disperse information. People also have the freedom to design their pages to advertise products or disseminate propaganda unnoticeable within the context of a research report. Thinking critically about information and its sources means being able to separate facts from opinions. We have to be able to verify information and know its source, we have to determine whether the facts are current, and we need to know why someone offered the information at all. In some situations, we don't have to do all the work ourselves. Some librarians and other information specialists have established virtual libraries on the Web in which the listed sources have been reviewed and evaluated. The following are the major virtual libraries:

Virtual Library	URL
Argus Clearinghouse	**http://www.clearinghouse.net**
Britannica	**http://www.britannica.com**
Internet Public Library	**http://www.ipl.org**
Librarians' Index to the Internet	**http://lii.org**
WWW Virtual Library	**http://vlib.org**

Table 11.1   Virtual Libraries

Although these sites can be very useful in helping you find authoritative and reliable information, you still need to decide if the information is appropriate for your purposes. For example, if you wanted information before buying a CD player, product announcements from manufacturers would give you some data, but they would probably not be the right type of source for impartial brand comparisons. If, however, you were researching techniques for advertising electronic consumer products, the advertisements would probably be good resource material.

Once you find some information, regardless of whether the resource is a book, journal article, Web page, or data from a CD-ROM, a librarian can help you evaluate its usefulness and quality. Librarians, particularly reference librarians, are trained professionals who have lots of experience with evaluating resources. They can tell you within seconds if information is relevant, authoritative, and appropriate for your research needs.

> **Fyi** WEB PAGES THAT FOCUS ON EVALUATING WEB RESOURCES
> ~ "Evaluating Information Found on the Internet"
> http://milton.mse.jhu.edu:/research/education/net.html
> ~ "Evaluating the Documents You Have Found on the World Wide Web"
> http://www.curtin.edu.au/curtin/library/staffpages/gwpersonal/senginestudy/zeval.htm
> ~ "Bibliography on Evaluating Internet Resources"
> http://www.lib.vt.edu/research/libinst/evalbiblio.html
> ~ "Evaluating Quality on the Net"
> http://www.tiac.net/users/hope/findqual.html

Guidelines for Evaluation

After typing an appropriate search expression in a search tool, scan the results. Open a document, and if it isn't readily apparent why that resource has come up in your hit list, activate the Find operation by clicking on **Edit**, choosing **Find in Page** or **Find in Frame**, and typing one of your keywords in the search form. Find will take you to the part of the Web page where the word or phrase appears. Sometimes the Find option won't locate the keyword or phrase in the page. This may mean that an earlier version of the page contained the keyword. You'll often find that the keyword is used in a context that is irrelevant to your research needs. Once you've found a page that appears to be fairly applicable to your topic, you can begin to use the guidelines for evaluation. The determination of information quality is not a cut-and-dried process. You can infer quality by clues that will either support or negate your research. Sometimes you need to rely on your intuition or your own previous knowledge about a particular piece of information. Noting this, the following guidelines are just that, guidelines. They are not meant to be absolute rules for evaluating documents found on the Internet and the Web. They are questions that you should ask yourself when looking at Web pages and other Internet sources.

Who Is the Author or Institution?

∿ If the resource was written by an individual, does it offer or give links to biographical information about the author? For example, does it mention educational or other credentials, an occupation, or an institutional affiliation?

∿ If an institution produced the resource, does it provide links to information about itself, including its purpose, history, and street address?

∿ Have you seen the author's or institution's name cited in other sources or bibliographies?

∿ If the page is part of a larger institution's Web site, does the institution appear to filter the information that appears at its site? Was the information screened before it was put on the Web?

∿ What clues does the URL give you about the source's authority? A tilde (~) in the Web page's URL usually indicates that it is a personal page, rather than part of an institutional Web site. Also, make a mental note of the domain section of the URL, as follows:

.edu   educational (can be anything from serious university research to a student's or faculty member's home page, which vary in reliability)

.gov   governmental (usually contains reliable data)

.com   commercial (may be trying to sell a product)

.net   network (may provide services to commercial or individual customers)

.org   organization (usually created by a nonprofit institution; may be trying to persuade the reader; may be biased)

.mil   United States military sites, agencies, and some academies

Countries other than the United States use two-letter codes as the final part of their domain names. The United States uses **us** in the domain name when designating state and local government hosts, as well as public schools (**k12** is often used).

Fy DOMAIN NAME INFORMATION
- ∿ "Web Naming and Addressing Overview"
  http://www.w3.org/Addressing
- ∿ "Domain Name Tutorial"
  http://www.lmcs.com/ domain.html
- ∿ "HotBot Help: Top Level Domains"
  http://hotbot.lycos.com/ help/domains.asp

Who Is the Audience?

- ∿ Is the Web page intended for the general public, or is it meant for scholars, practitioners, children, and so forth? Is the audience clearly stated?
- ∿ Does the Web page meet the needs of its stated audience?

Is the Content Accurate, Objective, and Supported by Other Sources?

- ∿ Are there political, ideological, cultural, religious, or institutional biases?
- ∿ Is the content intended to be a brief overview of the topic or an in-depth analysis?
- ∿ If the information is opinion, is this clearly stated?
- ∿ If there are facts and statistics included, are they properly cited?
- ∿ Is it clear how the data was collected, and is it presented in a logical, organized way?
- ∿ Is there a bibliography at the end of the document?

What Is the Purpose of the Information?

- ∿ Is the purpose of the information to inform, explain, persuade, market a product, or advocate a cause?
- ∿ Is the purpose clearly stated?
- ∿ Does the resource fulfill the stated purpose?

How Current Is the Information?

- ∿ Does the Web page have a date that indicates when it was placed on the Web?
- ∿ Is it clear when the page was last updated?

- Is some of the information obviously out-of-date?

- Does the page creator mention how frequently the material is updated?

Discussion and Tips

Who Is the Author or Institution?

If you're not familiar with the author or institution responsible for producing the information, you'll need to do some checking to determine if the source is reliable and authoritative. You can't consider the resource reliable if you don't know who wrote it or what institution published it. A well-designed Web page makes it easy for you to find information about the author, company, institution, or organization that published the page. Usually there is a hyperlink to this information from each major page you access. For example, consider the document "CDT Children's Privacy Issues Page," **http://www.cdt.org/privacy/children/index.html**. Looking at this Web page, we can see that the Center for Democracy and Telecommunications (CDT) has made it available. There are hyperlinks from that Web page to the home page for CDT. You can follow the hyperlinks to find out more about the CDT, or you can go to the home page by typing the URL **http://www.cdt.org** in the location field and pressing **Enter**. When you can't find your way to a home page or other information, try using a search engine, directory, or some other service to search the Web or Usenet for the information.

To find information about individual authors, you can use many of the strategies covered in Chapter 10: search Usenet and discussion group archives, perform a search for the author's name in search engines, search newspaper archives, or access association directories.

Who Is the Audience?

Web pages are sometimes written to give information to a specific group: the general public, researchers and scholars, professionals in a specific field, children, potential customers, or others. By determining the intended audience, you will be better able to decide if the information is relevant and appropriate for your purpose. Suppose you are preparing a report on sustainable forest management. An appropriate information resource, whether in print or on the Web, is one that is written for your level of expertise and for the expertise of your audience. The Web page "Forest Service Mission, Vision, and Guiding Principles," by the United States Department of Agriculture, Forest Service, **http://www.fs.fed.us/intro/mvgp.html**, might be useful for a general overview of the issues and principles involved in forest management. On the other hand, the Web page "Alternatives to Methyl Bromide: Research Needs for California," **http://www.cdpr.ca.gov/docs/dprdocs/methbrom/mb4chg.htm**, is more appropriate for a specialized audience.

Knowing what the intended audience is can also alert you to possible bias. For example, let's say you were looking for information on the anti-acne drug Accutane. You found an in-depth article called "Should Your Teenager Use Accutane?" and were informed of both the negatives and positives of this drug, complete with explanations of the possible side effects. By examining the URL and accessing hyperlinks within the document, you found out that the page was published by a well-known pharmaceutical company. Immediately you would realize that the likely intended audience was potential customers. This wouldn't mean that you couldn't use the information. Just being aware of bias and hidden persuasion in Web pages makes you more information savvy and aware.

tip SHORTENING URLS

If a Web page doesn't contain the name of its author or institution and there are no hyperlinks to Web pages that give that information, you can manipulate the URL to try to find it. For example, if you found material at the URL **http://www.ncrel.org/sdrs/ areas/ ma0bibp.htm**, and you wanted to quickly find out the name of the publishing body, you could delete the parts of the URL back to the domain section (everything after **org/**) and press **Enter**. This would give you **http://www.ncrel.org**, the home page for this institution, which happens to be the North Central Regional Educational Laboratory. To find out more about this organization, you could do a search in a search engine, typing in its name as a phrase. You could also go to a proprietary source or print source like *The Encyclopedia of Associations* to get more information. There are also some sites that list association Web pages that may include the organization you are looking for.

Is the Content Accurate, Objective, and Supported by Other Sources?

One of the first things to look for in a Web page is spelling errors. Spelling and grammatical errors not only indicate a lack of editorial control, but also undermine the accuracy of the information. It is also extremely important that statistics, research findings, and other claims are documented and cited very carefully. Otherwise, the author could be distorting information or using unreliable data. In the best situations, claims or statistics on Web pages are supported by original research or by hyperlinks or footnotes to the primary sources of the information.

Sometimes, however, you'll have to verify the accuracy and objectivity of published information on your own. A good way to do this is by checking to see if the information can be corroborated by other sources. Some researchers promote the triangulation process: finding at least three sources that agree with the opinion or findings that the author expounds as fact. If the sources don't agree, you'll need to do more work before you conclude your research. Remember that traditional resources like books, journal articles, and other material available in libraries may contain more comprehensive information than what is on the Web. You can use those resources as part of the triangulation process as well.

What Is the Purpose of the Information?

When you're evaluating information that you've found on the World Wide Web, on the Internet, or in print, you need to consider its purpose. You need to ask yourself, is this page on the Web to persuade, inform, teach, or entertain? Information on the Web can be produced in a variety of formats and styles, and the appearance sometimes gives a clue to its intent. Web pages aimed to market something are often designed in a clever way to catch our attention and emphasize a product. Some Web pages that are primarily oriented toward marketing a product do not clearly distinguish between the informational content of the page and the advertising. It may appear to be an informational page but actually is an advertisement.

How Current Is the Information?

You must note when the material you find was created and then decide if it is still useful for your purposes. If you are doing research in an area that is constantly changing, such as business, technology, political science, or medicine, the date is very important. For example, a Web page dated 1995 on the latest techniques in biotechnology should not be relied upon to give state-of-the-art information, because the field is changing so quickly. In other fields, the date may not be so important; for example, a site created in 1995 that covers the U.S. Civil War may be as relevant and useful as one published in 1998. In any case, a Web page should include the date it was created and/or modified. Usually, this information can be found at the top or bottom of a Web page. If it isn't displayed, you may be able to find the date the Web page was last modified on the server. If you're using Netscape Navigator, click on **View** in the menu bar and select **Page Info**. That will sometimes tell you the date of the last modification to the file. While Microsoft Internet Explorer has no similar feature, there are ways to enable the browser to create page modified information. We will discuss this in detail later in the chapter. Email messages and Usenet news articles usually have the date the message was posted. This information is part of the message or is in the header information.

The following activity will illustrate how these guidelines can help in the evaluation of a Web page.

Remember that the Web is always changing and there is a possibility that the results you get may differ from those shown here. Don't let this confuse you. These activities are meant to demonstrate fundamental skills that don't change, even though the number of results obtained or the actual screens may look very different.

USING THE GUIDELINES TO EVALUATE A RESOURCE

Overview

In this activity, we'll apply the guidelines for evaluating a Web page. If we were researching a topic related to searching the Web and evaluating Web documents, we would possibly come across a Web page called "Meeting the Challenge of Critically Evaluating Information on the Internet and the World Wide Web," **http://www.library.mwc.edu/ ~ khartman/educom98.html**. This is the Web page we'll evaluate in this activity. We'll go through the guidelines by answering the questions discussed earlier:

1. Who is the author or institution?
2. Who is the audience?
3. Is the content accurate, objective, and supported by other sources?
4. What is the purpose of the information?
5. How current is the information?

We will be using Netscape Navigator for this activity primarily because of its Page Info feature. You could use Internet Explorer if you prefer, but keep in mind that you would not be able to view the date the page was modified on the server using this browser.

Details

1. Who is the author or institution?

We'll assume your Web browser is already started.

 Type **http://www.library.mwc.edu/~khartman/educom98.html** in the location field and press **Enter**.

This page has two authors, and they appear at both the beginning and the end of the page, as shown in Figures 11.1 and 11.2. We can see that the authors are affiliated with Mary Washington College. Both authors have home pages, which can be accessed by clicking on their names. If we viewed the home pages, we'd find out that Ernest Ackermann is a professor of computer science at the college and Karen Hartman is a librarian there. This information helps establish the authors' credentials, which influences our assessment of the resource we're considering.

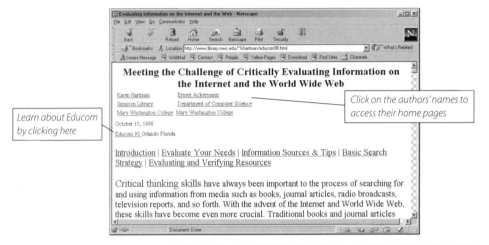

Figure 11.1   The Beginning of "Meeting the Challenge of Critically Evaluating Information on the Internet and the World Wide Web"

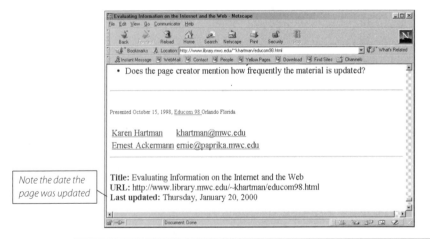

Figure 11.2   The End of "Meeting the Challenge of Critically Evaluating Information Found on the Internet and the World Wide Web"

We can search the Web for other information about the authors or for hyperlinks to resources that cite their work. One way is to use

AltaVista, **http://www.altavista.com,** or some other search engine and enclose the names in quotation marks. When we tried this in AltaVista for Ernest Ackermann, more than 250 Web pages were returned. Many referred to pages he had written, several were related to courses he teaches, and several were from other sources citing his work.

Another way is to use Deja.com to see if either of the authors has posted any articles or messages in Usenet or other discussion groups.

(Do it)! Go to the Deja.com Usenet page by typing **http://deja.com/usenet** in the location field and pressing **Enter**.

When we tried typing **karen hartman** in the search form we did not retrieve any articles written by Karen Hartman at Mary Washington College. Let's try the power search mode and see if that helps.

(Do it)! Click on the hyperlink **Power Search**.

(Do it)! Type **"mary washington college"** in the search form.

We include quotes around the words because we want the words to be searched as a phrase. We know Deja.com supports this feature because we have read Deja.com's help pages.

(Do it)! Type **karen hartman** in the author field.

Figure 11.4 shows Deja.com's power search mode with **mary washington college** and **karen hartman** typed in. The reason we typed the search this way is because we want articles written by the Karen Hartman who is affiliated with Mary Washington College.

(Do it)! Click **Search**, as shown in Figure 11.3.

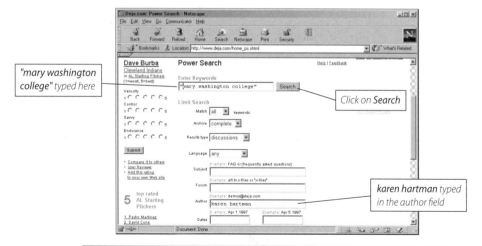

Figure 11.3   The Deja.com Power Search Form

Figure 11.4 shows that this search resulted in one message.

Click on **Re: References: Student Ques**.

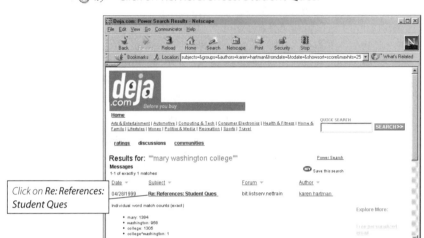

Click on Re: References: Student Ques

Figure 11.4   Results of Searching for Articles
by Karen Hartman in Deja.com

Figure 11.5 shows the message written by Karen Hartman in response to an individual's request for information about citing electronic resources. The forum for this discussion is NETTRAIN. NETTRAIN addresses issues related to teaching others to use the Internet and the World Wide Web. It's a moderated group, so the postings go through initial screenings to make sure they are appropriate for the list. By reading the message and clicking on the hyperlink for the author's name, you may find links to other messages the author has written.

The name of the forum: Nettrain

Click on the author's name to find other articles, if any

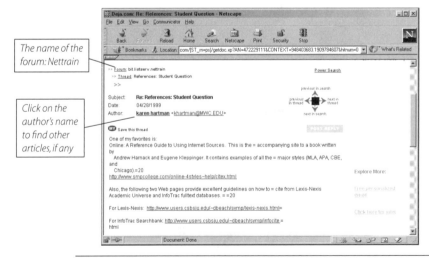

Figure 11.5   A Message in Deja.com Written by Karen Hartman

Another way to determine a source's authority uses the URL as a clue. In this case, the URL is **http://www.library.mwc.edu/ ~ khartman/ educom98.html**. The domain name **www.library. mwc.edu** ends with **.edu**, so the site hosting the page is an educational institution in the United States. If this were an educational institution in another country, the domain name would end with a two-letter abbreviation for the country and probably wouldn't have **edu** in its name. The next part of the URL, **~ khartman**, suggests that this page was most likely posted by the author, rather than by the institution. Therefore, the URL alone tells us that an individual at an educational institution in the United States published this resource on the Web. The best bet to find out more is to visit the Web site. Visiting the site with URL **http://www.library.mwc.edu** and following appropriate hyperlinks would tell us that the institution is a library at a liberal arts, state-supported college in Virginia. Since the Web resource deals with teaching, it seems appropriate for it to be available at such a site.

2. **Who is the audience?**

In Figure 11.1 we see the hyperlink **Educom 98**. Following that link takes us to a document holding the proceedings of Educom 98, which was held in Orlando, Florida. By clicking on **Educom 98**, we retrieve a page that appears like the one pictured in Figure 11.6. This conference focuses on using technology in an instructional program at an educational institution. From this information and from reading the resource we're considering, we see that the audience consists of educators who want to use technology, specifically the World Wide Web, to support instruction.

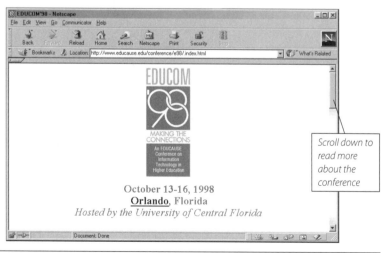

Figure 11.6   Information about the Educom 98 Conference

3. Is the content accurate, objective, and supported by other sources?

As we read the Web page we're considering, we determine that the page is accurate and objective by noting several clues: the words are spelled correctly, the ideas are expressed in objective terms, and the page lists several references, in the form of Web hyperlinks, which may be checked to corroborate the information.

4. What is the purpose of the information?

The main purpose of the page is to help educators formulate search expressions appropriately and to provide guidelines about how to evaluate information found on the World Wide Web. We can infer the purpose by reading the page and noting who the audience is.

5. How current is the information?

In Figure 11.1, we see that the material was presented on October 15, 1998. It was last updated, as shown in Figure 11.2, on January 20, 2000, as well. If, however, we clicked on **View** in the menu bar and chose **Page Info**, we would see that the page was indeed modified on that date. It's always a good idea to check the Page Info screen because people often forget to add to their Web pages the date a page was updated.

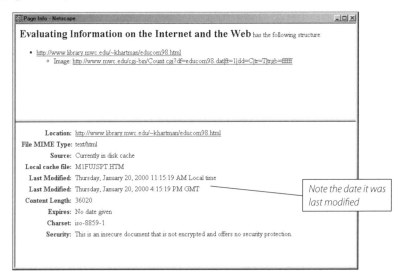

Figure 11.7   Netscape's Page Info Screen

In general, any information about a specific technology may be relevant for about two years after the last update. Information related to the contents of Web pages or the teaching practices and methods applicable to teaching with the Web will probably be relevant for more than two years after the date of publication.

END OF ACTIVITY 11.1

Activity 11.1 took us through the process of evaluating a Web page. The page chosen was well-designed and proved to be a model for what information a Web page should include to provide useful, reliable information for the audience for which it was intended.

Citing Internet and Web Information: URL Formats

Unlike a citation for a printed work, a citation for a Web or Internet resource must have information about how to access it. This is often indicated through the work's URL (Uniform Resource Locator). In addition to telling you where to access a work, a URL serves to retrieve the work. For that reason, we have to be precise about all the symbols in the URL and about capitalization.

There are other differences as well. Works that appear in print—such as books, essays, articles, or songs—have a definite publication date associated with them. Documents on the Web sometimes include information about when they were first created or last revised, but not always. Add to that the fact that authors can revise work on the Web at any time. It may therefore be more important to cite the date on which a work was viewed or retrieved.

Everything on the Web has a URL, indicating where the resource is located and how to access it. We've seen lots of URLs throughout this text. Here are some examples:

http://www.loc.gov	The home page for the Library of Congress
http://vlib.org/Overview.html	The WWW Virtual Library arranged by subject
http://www.library.mwc.edu/ ~ khartman/educom98.html	A presentation given at Educom 98 by Ernest Ackermann and Karen Hartman
http://webopedia.internet.com/ TERM/v/virus.html	The entry for the term *virus* in PC Webopedia
ftp://ftp.jpl.nasa.gov/pub/ images/browse	The NASA Jet Propulsion Laboratory's directory of image files

You'll find it helpful to think of a URL as having the following form:

how-to-get-there://where-to-go/what-to-get

or, in more technical language:

**transfer protocol://domain name/directory/subdirectory/
file name.file type**

For example, take the URL **http://www.library.mwc.edu/ ~ khartman/
educom98.html**.

~   **http** is the transfer protocol

~   **www** is the host computer name (also called the third-level domain
    name)

    library.mwc is the second-level domain name

    edu is the top-level domain name

~   **~ khartman** is the directory name

~   **educom98** is the file name and **html** is its file type

You probably already know some ways in which URLs are used. For
example, all hyperlinks on Web pages are represented as URLs. Entries in
bookmark and history files are stored as URLs. You type in a URL when
you want to direct your browser to go to a specific Web page. When you
cite a resource on the World Wide Web, you need to include its URL.
You'll also want to include the URL when you're telling someone else
about a resource, such as in an email message. Here's an example:

```
If you haven't already seen this fabulous page, you
must look at it. It's called "A Business Researcher's
Interests" and is hosted by @BRINT. The URL is:
http://www.brint.com/interest.html
It's one of the best subject guides I've ever used.
```

That way, a friend reading the message could use her browser to go
directly to the items you mention.

By providing the name of a Web server and the name of a file or
directory holding certain information, a URL tells you how to retrieve
the information; from the URL alone, you know which Internet protocol
to use when retrieving the information and where it's located. If only a
domain or server name is present, as in **http://www.loc.gov**, then a file
will still be retrieved. Web servers are configured to pass along a certain
file (usually named **index.html** or **index.htm**) when the URL contains
only the name of the server or only the name of a directory. Table 11.2
lists the two types of URLs that you're likely to use when citing resources
from the World Wide Web. The URLs are arranged by Internet protocol.

Resource or Service	Beginning of URL	Example	Description
Web pages	**http://**	**http://nmaa-ryder. si.edu/artdir/ treasures.html**	Selections from the Permanent Collection of the National Museum of American Art
FTP	**ftp://**	**ftp://ftp.jpl.nasa. gov/pub/images/ browse**	A directory of images from NASA Jet Propulsion Laboratory's public information FTP archive

Table 11.2   Types of URLs Arranged by Protocol

It's important to be precise when you write URLs, because a Web browser uses the URL to access the file and bring it to your computer. More specifically, the browser sends a request extracted from the information in the URL to a Web server. Remember, we're talking about having one computer communicate with another; as amazing as some computer systems are, they generally need very precise instructions. Therefore, you have to be careful about spaces (generally there aren't blank spaces in URLs), symbols (interchanging a slash and a period won't retrieve appropriate results), and capitalization.

Here's an example. Let's say we wanted to access the Web page that we discussed earlier in the chapter:

http://www.library.mwc.edu/ ~ khartman/educom98.html
Forgetting to include the tilde before **khartman** and writing the URL as **http://www.library.mwc.edu/khartman/educom98.html** would cause the browser to give the following response:

```
404 Not Found

The requested URL /khartman/educom98.html was not found
on this server.
```

That would tell us that the name of the Web server, **www.library.mwc.edu**, was correct but that there was something wrong with the rest of the URL.

Guidelines for Citing Internet and Web Resources

When you're looking for the proper way to cite resources in a report or research paper, you must first see if there is a required or accepted citation style. If you're writing a paper for a class, check with your instructor. If you're writing for a periodical or some other publication (either in print or electronic form), see if the editor or publisher has guidelines.

Proper formats for citations from printed sources are very well established. Three commonly used formats are APA (American Psychological Association) style, MLA (Modern Language Association) style, and the Chicago Manual of Style (University of Chicago). Each of these institutions publishes a handbook or publication guide that explains how to cite information. These organizations are beginning to have accepted guidelines for citing information from the Internet and the Web, but not all have complete instructions.

Fy WEB RESOURCES ABOUT CITING INFORMATION FOUND ON THE INTERNET AND THE WORLD WIDE WEB

- "MLA Style: Documenting Sources from the World Wide Web"
  http://www.mla.org/style/sources.htm
- "Electronic Reference Formats Recommended by the American Psychological Association"
  http://www.apa.org/journals/webref.html
- "IPL FARQ: Citing Electronic Resources"
  http://www.ipl.org/ref/QUE/FARQ/netciteFARQ.html
- "ONLINE! Citation Styles"
  http://www.bedfordstmartins.com/online/citex.html

Difficulties in Citing Web or Internet Resources

- Web and Internet resources may be updated or modified at any time.
- These resources may not have titles or major headings.
- Web pages don't have page numbers.
- While thoughtful people have been working to expand existing standards, there are some differences of opinion about the format of citations for Web and Internet items.

Differences Between Styles

Some formats include a URL in angle brackets (< >), and others do not. Some advise including the place of publication if the Web resource is a copy of a printed work. Several say to put the date of last revision and to place in parentheses the date on which you accessed the document, whereas others do not make this recommendation. There is, however, considerable agreement on the basic information to be included in a citation of a Web resource.

> **tip** When you have specific questions about citing Internet and Web sources, check some of the Web resources listed in this chapter, and be sure to check with whoever is going to be evaluating or editing your work.

The Dates Are Important

You'll see that the guidelines for citations or references to Web or Internet resources all contain two dates: the date of publication or revision and the date of last access. The reason we need both dates has to do with the nature of digital media as it's made available or published on the Web. Works in print form are different from digital works; printed documents have a tangible, physical form. We all know we can pick up and feel a magazine or journal in our hands, or we can use a book or periodical as a pillow. It's pretty hard to do that with a Web page! This tangible nature of a printed work also gives an edition or revision a permanent nature. It's usually possible to assign a date of publication to a work, and if there are revisions or different editions of a work, it's possible to date and look at the revisions. If a new edition of a printed work exists, that doesn't mean that older editions or versions were destroyed.

The situation is different for Web documents and other items in digital form on the Internet, for several reasons. They don't have a tangible form. It's relatively easy for an author to publish a work (the work usually only needs to be in a certain directory on a computer that functions as a Web server). It's easy to modify or revise a work. Furthermore, when a work is revised, the previous version is often replaced by or overwritten with the new version. Because of this last point, the most recent version may be the only one that exists. The version you cited might not exist anymore. It is therefore necessary to include the date you accessed or read a work listed in a citation or reference. You may also want to keep a copy of the document in a file (save it while browsing) or print a copy of it to provide as documentation if someone questions your sources.

Ways to Find Out When a Page Was Modified

෬   To find the date a work was last revised, see if the date is mentioned as part of the work. You'll often see a line like **Last modified: Wednesday, January 15, 1997** in a Web document.

If you don't find this information on the Web page or you want to verify this date, you can do the following:

෬   If you're using Netscape Navigator, click on **View** in the menu bar and select **Page Info**. That will tell you the date on which the file was last modified, as well as the document's title. If the page you're citing is a frame, first right-click on the frame, choose **View**, and then select **Frame Info**.

෬   If you're using Microsoft Internet Explorer version 5, there's nothing that gives the date last modified as Page Info does in Navigator. Selecting **Properties** from the menu you see when you click on **File** in the menu bar only tells you the current date or the date you saved a shortcut to the Web page. There is a tool named Page Freshness available at a Web site names "Bookmarklets," **http://www.bookmarklets.com**. The items at the Web site are small programs written in JavaScript. You can add any of them to your favorites list. Once they're in the favorites list you can use them by clicking on **Favorites** in the navigation toolbar, and then clicking on the bookmarklet in the favorites list. (You can also add these to the bookmark list if you're using Navigator and use them in a similar manner.)

Follow these steps to obtain and use the Page Freshness bookmarklet.

1. Type the URL **http://www.bookmarklets.com/tools/ frames.phtml#pgfrshfrm** in the address box and press [Enter].
2. Move the mouse pointer over the hyperlink **Page Freshness**, read its description, and click the right mouse button.
3. Select **Add to Favorites** to add the bookmarklet to the favorites list.

Citation Examples

In this section, we will provide citation examples using established citation formats. The styles that we will be using are Modern Language Association (MLA), American Psychological Association (APA), and Chicago Manual of Style. The types of resources that we will cite are Web pages, email messages, discussion group messages, Usenet newsgroup messages, and FTP resources. The common elements in citations for different types of resources will be listed, and a citation example for each type of included Internet resource will be given in one of the styles. The information provided is general in nature, and it is not meant to cover every situation. We suggest that if you have a specific citation question that is not covered here, you go to one of the citation guides listed in the FYI on page 340 or visit your library. Librarians are usually willing to assist you in locating and using citation style guides as long as you indicate which style you have been instructed to use.

Web Pages

The major citation styles agree that the following elements should be included in a citation for a Web page:

~ Author's name

~ Document title

~ Title of larger or complete work, if relevant

~ Date of publication or last revision

~ Date page was accessed

~ URL

A Citation Example Using MLA Style

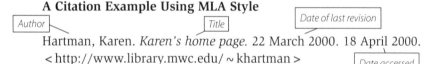

| Author | | Title | | Date of last revision |

Hartman, Karen. *Karen's home page.* 22 March 2000. 18 April 2000.
< http://www.library.mwc.edu/ ~ khartman >

| URL | | Date accessed |

In the citation, note that the URL is placed in angle brackets. This is a feature of MLA and Chicago Manual of Style. APA doesn't require brackets around the URL.

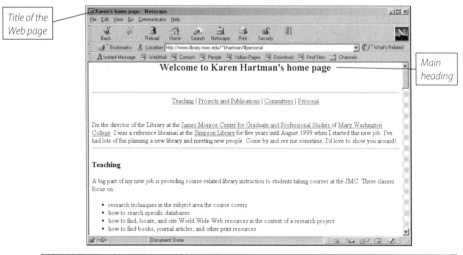

Figure 11.8   Determining the Title of a Web Page

~ The author is evident in the main heading of the Web page, as shown in Figure 11.8. The author's name is also found at the end of the Web page.

∾   We found the date of the last revision at the end of the document. You could also determine that date by looking at Page Info in Netscape, as we mentioned earlier.

∾   We determined the Web page title by using the title found at the top of the browser window. This is the same title that showed up as a hyperlink in the search results if you used a search engine. You could also find the title by viewing Netscape's Page Info window. The title is specified in the HTML source for the page and doesn't necessarily show up in the text of the document as you view it with a browser. There are cases when the title is uninformative or not descriptive. In these situations, the first main heading can be used. Some documents have no title. (If a document doesn't have a title, you can construct one by using the major heading or the first line of text. You should enclose this title in square brackets to show that you created it.)

The following is a portion of the HTML code for the Web page cited above. The exact text of the title of a Web page is surrounded by the tags < TITLE > and < /TITLE > in the HTML source for the page. The source for this page begins with:

```
<HTML>                          The title of the Web page
<HEAD>
<TITLE>Karen's home page</TITLE>
</HEAD>
<BODY bgcolor="White" text="Black" background="grnsand.jpg"
link="Navy" vlink="Maroon">
<h2><center>Welcome to Karen Hartman's home page</center></h2>
```

Citing a Web Page That Is Part of a Larger or Complete Work

Many Web pages are parts of larger works or projects. In each of these cases, you need to not only provide the author and title of the individual document, but also the title of the larger work, its editor, and the institution that sponsors the site (if applicable). In many instances, you'll want to include information about the complete work in order to put the document in its proper context and to credit the editor and/or institution that has helped to make the work available. This additional information may help the reader find the Web page again if the URL changes. The following shows how you would cite a page that was part of a larger work.

A Citation Example Using MLA Style

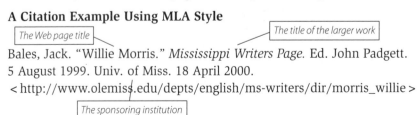

The Web page title   The title of the larger work

Bales, Jack. "Willie Morris." *Mississippi Writers Page*. Ed. John Padgett. 5 August 1999. Univ. of Miss. 18 April 2000. < http://www.olemiss.edu/depts/english/ms-writers/dir/morris_willie >

The sponsoring institution

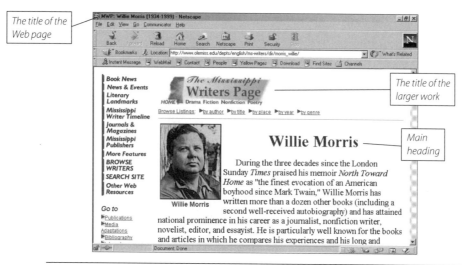

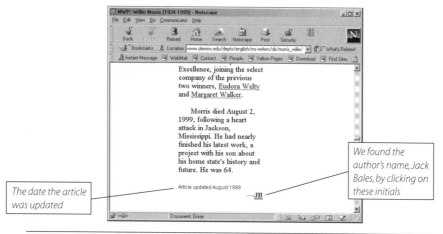

Figure 11.9   A Web Page That Is Part of a Larger Work

In this citation, we determined:

~ The title of the Web page should simply be "Willie Morris" because the title at the top of the browser window uses the initials *MWP* (Mississippi Writers Page), which is uninformative. *Willie Morris* is part of the title and it is also the main heading, so we use it as the Web page title. See Figure 11.9.

~ The writer of this page was found by clicking on the initials at the end of the article, as shown in Figure 11.10.

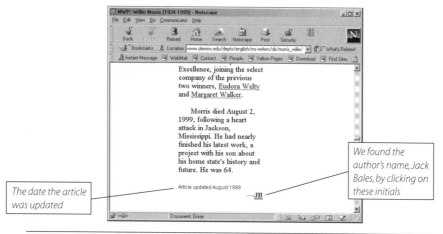

Figure 11.10   Finding the Author of the Willie Morris Page

~ The editor of the larger work is John Padgett. We found that out by looking at the very end of the Web page, as shown in Figure 11.11.

∾   The date of the publication was located at the end of the article and at the end of the Web page.

∾   We found, also at the end of the page, that the University of Mississippi is responsible for sponsoring this site.

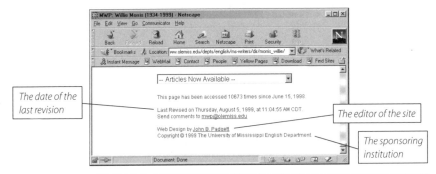

Figure 11.11   Important Information Located at the End of the Web Page

Email Messages

The elements required to cite an email message are:

∾   Author's name

∾   Subject of message

∾   Date message was sent

∾   Type of communication: personal, distribution list, office communication

∾   Date accessed

All of these are usually displayed by the software you use to read email and are available as standard headers in a message.

Citation Examples Using Chicago Manual of Style

Mills, C. "Getting gigs in Nashville." 13 May 1996, personal email (13 December 1996).

Ackermann, E. "Working on post-tenure review." 2 Feb. 1997, distribution list (4 Feb. 1997).

Discussion Group or Listserv Messages

A citation for an email message that was generated in a discussion group or listserv needs to include the discussion group's address. If the message can be retrieved through an archive, the citation needs to include the URL of the Web page that allows access to the archive. The elements required to cite discussion group or listserv messages are:

∾   Author's name

∾   Subject of message or title of posting

∾   Date of posting

∾   URL of listserv or discussion group

∾   URL of archive, if applicable

∾   Date accessed

A Citation Example Using APA Style

Ackermann, E. (1999, March 7) Re: Bookmark files with Netscape 4.0
Retrieved February 14, 2000 from the listserv: http://acsu.buffalo.edu/
cgi-bin/wa?S1 = nettrain

Usenet Newsgroup Articles

Usenet news consists of a collection of articles, each part of a specific
newsgroup. The articles, like email messages, have headers that give us
the information we need for the citation. These are the items to include in
the citation of a Usenet article:

∾   Author's name

∾   Subject of message

∾   Name of newsgroup

∾   Date message was posted

∾   Date of access

A Citation Example Using MLA Style

Ackermann, E. "Question about keeping Bay plant indoors." Online posting. 3 Dec. 1995. 13 Feb. 1997 < news:rec.gardens > .

Electronic Journal Articles

An article in an electronic journal can be cited very much like any other
Web resource. If you were citing an article in a journal, it would be
reasonable to include the journal name, volume, issue, and date. If you
were citing a resource from a printed journal, you would also include
page numbers, but that doesn't apply in this case. Some citation styles
require a paragraph count instead. The URL gives the location of the
article. The citation should contain the following elements:

∾   Author's name

∾   Title of article

∾   Title of journal, volume and issue numbers, date of publication

∾   Date of last revision, if known and if different from date of publica-
    tion

∾   Date accessed

∾   URL

A Citation Example Using MLA Style

Harnack, A., and Kleppinger, G. "Beyond the MLA Handbook: Documenting Electronic Sources on the Internet." *Kairos: 1.2. Summer 1996.* June 11, 1996. 10 Feb. 1999.
< http://english.ttu.edu/kairos/1.2/inbox/mla.html >

A Citation Example Using APA Style

Agre, P. (1995, November). Designing Genres for New Media: Social, Economic, and Political Contexts. *The Network Observer 2, 11.* Retrieved April 18, 2000 from the World Wide Web: http://communication.ucsd.edu/pagre/tno/ november-1995.html#designing

FTP Resources

FTP stands for File Transfer Protocol. Before Web browsers came into popular use, FTP was the most popular way to retrieve and send files from one computer to another on the Internet. We will be discussing FTP in detail in Chapter 13, "Transferring Files Using FTP." A citation for a file available by FTP usually contains the following elements:

- Name of author or institution
- Title of document
- Size of document, if relevant
- Date of last revision
- URL
- Date accessed

Citation Examples Using Chicago Manual of Style

American Civil Liberties Union, "Briefing Paper Number 5, Drug Testing in the Work Place." 19 Nov. 1992.
< ftp://ftp.eff.org/pub/Privacy/Medical/ aclu_drug_testing_workplace.faq >
(13 Feb. 2000)

If there's no obvious title for a file, as in the case of a file that holds an image, then use the file name as the title of the work. An example is the file that holds an image of Mars, cited in the following way:

Mars1.gif [535K], 16 Jan 1995, < ftp://ftp.jpl.nasa.gov/pub/images/ browse/mars1.gif > (13 May 1999).

Note that we have included the size of the file as well.

Recording Citation Information

When doing research on the Internet, it's smart to record the document information by either printing the resource or making a browser bookmark so that you can return to the resource easily. Bookmarking resources is a good habit to get into. The bookmark saves the Web page title and URL accurately so you don't have to write it down and risk losing it. Even if you share a computer with others, you can save your bookmarks to a file on a disk and import them to your computer later. Netscape Navigator's Bookmark Properties option allows you to describe the bookmark, which is an efficient way to create a bibliography entry. The following hands-on activity will demonstrate how to use a bookmark list to help create a bibliography of cited Internet resources. Before you get started with the activity, you might like to read the tip about how to create bookmarks.

tip HOW TO CREATE BROWSER BOOKMARKS OR FAVORITES

~ **Web pages**
In Netscape: Click **Bookmarks** and select **Add Bookmark** from the Bookmarks menu while the selected Web page is in the browser window. To review how to bookmark a Web page using Netscape, see Activity 8.1.

In Internet Explorer: Click on **Favorites** and select **Add to Favorites** while the selected Web page is in the browser window.

~ **Frames**
In Netscape: Right-click inside the frame you want to bookmark. Select **Add Bookmark** from the resulting menu.

In Internet Explorer: Right-click in the frame and select **Add to Favorites**.

CITING RESOURCES AND CREATING A BIBLIOGRAPHY USING BOOKMARKS

Overview

This activity begins with a list of hyperlinks that have been selected from a list of search results. Netscape is the browser used for this activity because Netscape provides the ability to annotate bookmarks so that a record can be kept for the later purpose of creating a bibliography. The topic of the research was global warming and climate change and how the third world is being affected by these environmental concerns. The search engine used was Northern Light, **http://www.northernlight.com**, and the search expression was **"global warming" AND "climate change" AND "third world"**. Each resource has already been evaluated using the guidelines laid out earlier in the chapter. While the primary focus of the activity is to show you how to use bookmarks to help keep track of citation information, you should learn some bookmark management skills as well. The resource file we'll be working with is on the activities and exercises disk that accompanies this book. We'll access each one of the resources and create bookmarks for them. We will go through the steps of citing one of the resources. This information will be inserted on the Bookmark Properties window attached to the resource's bookmark. We'll also show how to save a bookmark list to a floppy disk. We'll show how the bookmark file appears if each resource was cited and the file was saved to a disk. This finished product is a bibliography that could then be inserted into a word-processing document or Web page that contains your research report.

Details

We'll follow these steps:

1. Access the list of resources on the activities and exercises disk.
2. Create bookmarks for all the resources.
3. Cite a bookmarked resource.
4. Use Bookmark Properties to store the citation information for the cited resource.
5. Create a bibliography using the bookmark list.

Let's get started!

1. Access the list of resources on the activities and exercises disk.

We are assuming that Netscape Navigator is open and you are ready to go.

(Do it)   Insert the activities and exercises disk into Drive A:.

(Do it)   Click on **Start**, and choose **Run**.

(Do it)   Type **a:** in the dialog box.

(Do it)   Double-click on the folder **chap11**.

(Do it)   Double-click on the folder **Activity 11-2**.

(Do it)   Highlight **Activity 11-2** and click on **Open**.

Now the hyperlinks will appear in your window. It should look like Figure 11.12.

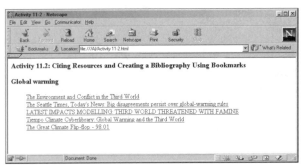

Figure 11.12   The List of Resources to be Cited

2. Create bookmarks for all the resources.

 Click on the first hyper-link, **The Environment and Conflict in the Third World**.

Wait for the Web page to be retrieved.

 Click on **Bookmarks** in the location toolbar, and highlight **Add Bookmark**.

Follow this procedure for every resource on the list.

3. Cite a bookmarked resource.

 From the list of book-marks, highlight the bookmark with the title **The Environment and Conflict in the Third World** and double-click on it.

Figure 11.14 shows the beginning of this Web page. We determine that this is a research paper. Using the citation guideline discussed earlier, we can fill in the following pieces of information:

~ *Author:* Geoffrey Dabelko

~ *Title of the work:* "The Environment and Conflict in the Third World: Examining Linkage, Context and Policy"

~ *Name of program:* Occasional Paper No. 12, Harrison Program on the Future Global Agenda. University of Maryland, College Park, January 1996. (Note that we added this category to illustrate that sometimes a work is not exactly a journal article, but may be a paper that is part of a collection, a larger work, or in this case, a special program.)

tip PLACING BOOKMARKS IN A FOLDER

~ First, create a folder by clicking on **File**, then select **New Folder**

~ A Bookmark Properties window will appear, as shown in Figure 11.13.

~ You fill in the name and the description, clicking on **OK** when finished.

You can move resources into a folder by

~ clicking on bookmarks one by one and dragging them to the appropriate folder, or

~ highlighting the item, selecting **Cut** from the **Edit** menu, highlighting the folder, and selecting **Paste** from the **Edit** menu.

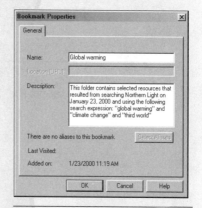

Figure 11.13   Bookmark Properties for a Folder

∾ ***Date of last revision:***

∾ **URL:** http://www.bsos.umd.edu/harrison/papers/paper12.htm

∾ **Date accessed:** 23 January 2000

It is clear that we still need to know when the page was revised or modified. To do this, we'll look at the document's information.

(Do it)!   Click on **View** and choose **Page Info** from the pulldown menu, as shown in Figure 11.14.

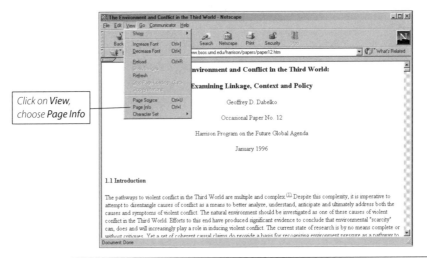

Figure 11.14   Finding Document Information for a Web Page

Figure 11.15 shows the date the page was last modified, which was October 1, 1997.

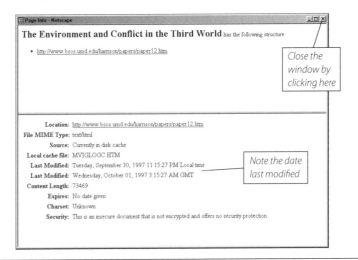

Figure 11.15   The Page Info Window for "The Environment and Conflict in the Third World"

Now that we have this information, we can cite our resource. First, we need to close the Page Info window.

(Do it)! Close the window by clicking the **X** in the upper-right corner, as shown in Figure 11.15.

4. Use Bookmark Properties to store the citation information for the cited resource.

(Do it)! Return to the bookmark list by clicking **Bookmarks** in the location toolbar.

(Do it)! Choose **Edit Bookmarks**.

(Do it)! Highlight the **The Environment and Conflict in the Third World** bookmark but do not open the file.

(Do it)! Right-click on the hyperlink, and choose **Bookmark Properties** from the pulldown menu, as shown in Figure 11.16.

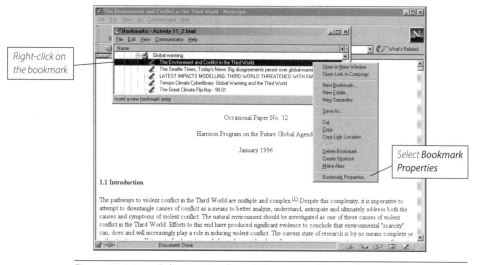

Figure 11.16   Selecting Bookmark Properties for a Web Page

The Bookmark Properties window appears. Note in Figure 11.17 that the Web page title and the URL are inserted in the **Name** and **Location (URL)** fields. You can fill in the appropriate citation information in the window next to **Description**.

To insert the URL in the description window,

~ Highlight the URL and right-click

~ Choose **Copy**

~ Move the cursor to the description window in the appropriate place and right-click

    ◌ Choose **Paste**

The URL is now copied exactly as it appears in the bookmark file. (You aren't able to see it here, because the information will not fit into the window provided). This is important because it is difficult to type URLs accurately. Note that Bookmark Properties records the date and the time this page was added to the bookmark list and when it was last viewed.

 Type the citation information in the **Description** field.

 Click on **OK**.

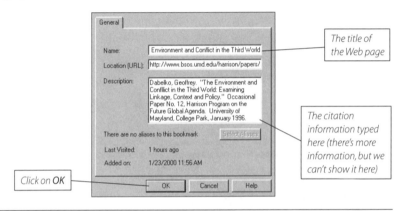

Figure 11.17   Using the Bookmark Properties Window
to Document Citation Information

5. Create a bibliography using the bookmark list.

If this were an actual research project, you would want to cite every resource on the bookmark list exactly as we cited the research paper, following the appropriate citation guidelines for each. For this activity, we won't cite any more resources, but we will show you how to create a bibliography with the citations attached to the resources. First, you'll need to save the bookmark list. We'll save this list to the disk in the A: drive.

 Click on **Bookmarks** in the Location toolbar.

 Click on **Edit Bookmarks**.

 Choose **Save As** from the File menu.

 Choose Drive A:.

 Name the file **globalwarming**.

To view the bibliography, click on **Start** and then **Run**. Type **A:** into the search form. Open the file named **globalwarming.htm**.

Figure 11.18 shows how the bibliography would look if each resource was described in the Bookmark Properties for each bookmark. The resources were cited using APA style. While the entire list isn't shown here, note that the items are in alphabetical order. This was accomplished by opening the file using Netscape Composer or some other Web page editor and rearranging the citations. This file could be transferred to a word-processing file, attached to your research paper, and integrated with other citations gathered from print resources. These items could also be cut and pasted into alphabetical order. Note that the Bookmark Properties window doesn't allow for the use of italics. You would need to use your word–processing program or Web page editor to make the appropriate changes.

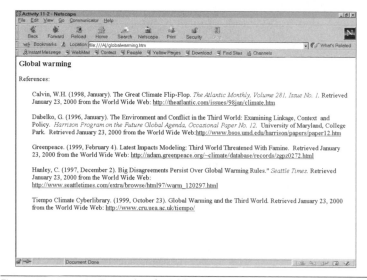

Figure 11.18   An Example of a Bibliography Using the Bookmark File

END OF ACTIVITY 11.2

This activity focused primarily on how to use bookmarks to manage your citation information for resources found on the World Wide Web. The citation model examined was for a research paper published by an American university. You would follow a similar process for any type of Web resource.

Summary

The World Wide Web gives us access to a great variety of information on many different topics. When we want to use the information or resources we find on the Web for information or research purposes, we need to exercise some care to make sure they are authentic, reliable, and authoritative. We need to be equally cautious when we use information from other sources.

Print sources that are available to us through a research or academic library have often been put through a screening process by professional librarians. There are several virtual libraries on the Web, and it's useful to consult some of these when doing research. Information in such libraries is selected and evaluated before it's listed.

It pays to be skeptical or critical of the information we want to use. It's relatively easy to publish information on the Web, and information can be presented in such a way as to hide its intent or purpose. Generally, as we evaluate documents, we also learn more about the topic we're considering.

The general guidelines to follow when evaluating resources are:

~ Who is the author or institution?

~ Who is the audience?

~ Is the content accurate, objective, and supported by other sources?

~ What is the purpose of the information?

~ How current is the information?

Citing references or writing a bibliography is usually part of creating a research report. You provide citations so others may check or examine the resources used in the report. There are several agreed-upon styles for citing documents in print format. When using resources from the Web or the Internet, it is necessary to have a uniform citation format. This chapter presents a set of formats for documenting or citing information obtained from the Web or the Internet.

Citations to documents and other information found on the Web or Internet always include the URL, or Uniform Resource Locator. A URL includes the names of the Web server and the file or directory holding the information. The URL therefore tells you which Internet protocol to use to retrieve the information and where it's located. You need to be precise in terms of spelling and capitalization when writing a URL, as a computer will be interpreting it. We listed URL formats for common Web or Internet services.

There is no uniform agreement on how to cite information from the Web or Internet. Most styles suggest that a citation include the author's name, the work's title, the date the information was last revised, the date the information was accessed, and the URL. The date of access is included because it's relatively easy to modify information on the Web and the information may not always be the same as when it was accessed for research. We discussed methods for determining the date of access and the title of a Web document. Using bookmarks in Netscape Navigator is an excellent way to organize resources you've found on the Internet. They can be used to help manage citations.

Exercises and Projects

1. Here's a collection of Web pages dealing with the issue of sustainable forest management. Write a short evaluation of each, focusing on whether the information is presented with a bias or with the intent to advocate a cause.

   ∿ "Guaranteeing the future of our forests through sustainable forest management"
   http://www.nafi.com.au/faq/management/sustainable.html

   ∿ "Forest Management Policy"
   http://www.sierraclub.org/policy/conservation/forest.asp

   ∿ "The Sustainable Forestry Initiative (SFI)ᴿᴹ Program"
   http://www.afandpa.org/forestry/sfi/sfi_report.cfm

   ∿ "Owens Forest Products: Forest Facts"
   http://www.hdwds.com/forest_facts.htm

2. One virtual library with a clear statement of how items are selected and rated is the Argus Clearinghouse, **http://www.clearinghouse.net**. Go there and find information about how sites are rated or selected. Compare the criteria it uses to those we've discussed in this chapter. How do those sets of criteria compare?

3. In this exercise, we'll use some of the guides for evaluating Web resources to assess documents. As a sample document, use either "CDT Children's Privacy Issues Page," **http://www.cdt.org/privacy/children/index.html**, or "Tools for Teaching: The World Wide Web and a Web Browser," **http://www1.mwc.edu/~ernie/facacad/WWW-Teaching.html**.

   a. Evaluate the document using the checklist developed by the Colorado State University Libraries on the Web page entitled "How to Evaluate a Web Page," **http://manta.library.colostate.edu/howto/evalweb2.html**.

   b. Evaluate the document using an appropriate checklist. You can find one on the Web page "Evaluating Web Resources," Jan Alexander and Marsha Tate, Wolfgram Memorial Library, Widener University, **http://www2.widener.edu/Wolfgram-Memorial-Library/webeval.htm**.

4. Go to the home page for the organization entitled Global Warming, at **http://www.globalwarming.org**. Evaluate this site by answering these questions: Who is responsible for this site? What is its purpose?

Is there a bias presented in the information provided? Does the group cite research studies it reports on?

5. In Activity 11.1 we evaluated a work entitled "Meeting the Challenge of Critically Evaluating Information on the Internet and the World Wide Web." How would you cite this resource in a bibliography?

6. Write a citation for the document on the Web with the URL **http:// www1.mwc.edu/~ernie/ curpres/cur1.html**.

7. In this chapter, we showed you how to use Deja.com, **http://www. deja.com**, to search archives of Usenet articles. Search for articles about waffle irons. Select two of the articles and write citations for them using MLA style.

8. There's an article titled "Information Literacy as a Liberal Art" in a 1996 issue of *Educom Review.* Use a search engine to find the article, and then write a citation for it using APA style.

9. Some search services allow the use of Boolean expressions and provide online help or tips. For each of the following services, find the portion of online help that tells how to use Boolean expressions, and write a citation to that resource:
   a. Northern Light, **http://www.northernlight.com**
   b. Google, **http://www.google.com**
   c. Deja.com, **http://www.deja.com**
   d. Argus Clearinghouse, **http://www.clearinghouse.net**

10. Retrieve and read through the resource below, and then cite the Web pages in Exercise 1 using the MLA style formats given.
   ∾   "MLA-Style Models for Citing Internet Sources," Harnack and Kleppinger, **http://www.bedfordstmartins.com/online/ cite5.html**

Chapter 12

MANAGING AND USING INFORMATION FROM THE INTERNET AND THE WORLD WIDE WEB

Once you become adept at searching for and finding relevant information on the Internet, you may find yourself wanting to know more about how to manage and use the information you find. Some examples of ways to use Internet information are saving and printing Web pages and frames, emailing Web pages to other people, capturing images and using them in other documents, downloading data into spreadsheets, and many others. Many of the procedures and tips shown in this chapter concern browser functions, while others require an understanding of the different types of files (for example, text, image, and data files) that are on the Internet and how to manipulate them using other software. Chapter 13 will continue this discussion, focusing on how to transfer files from one computer to another on the Internet using FTP (File Transfer Protocol). Because this chapter focuses on taking information from the Internet and either sharing it with or distributing it to others, copyright and intellectual property issues will also be discussed.

Goals/Objectives

∾ Become familiar with the major file types that can be found on the Internet and the World Wide Web

∾ Gain a basic understanding of the copyright issues related to using digital information

∾ Learn how to download images and other files from the Web

Topics

- ∾ Common Types of Files on the Internet and the Web
- ∾ Considering Copyright Guidelines Before Sharing and Copying Information
- ∾ Capturing and Using Text, Images, and Data from the Web and the Internet
- ∾ Procedures and Steps for Managing Internet and Web Information

Common Types of Files on the Internet and the Web

Web pages can contain text, images, video, audio, and other types of information. These will be part of the Web page, or the Web page will have hyperlinks to the information. Although information can appear as text, it is sometimes stored in a compressed format (to save space) or in some other format. In many cases, your browser can display the information, if it's an image or a video for example, or it can convert the information to sound, if it's an audio file (and if your computer is equipped with a sound card and speakers or earphones). In other cases, you need to get the appropriate software so that your computer can deal with the file.

Sometimes you can tell a file's type by its name. The letters following the dot (.) at the end of a file name are called the file extension portion of the file name. Files whose names end with **.txt** or **.text**, for example, usually contain only plain, printable characters.

Table 12.1 covers some of the more common file formats. For more information about working with different file formats, check the help in the menu bars of your browser.

Fyi INFORMATION ABOUT FILE FORMATS

- ∾ "Every File Format in the World" **http://www.whatis.com/ff.htm**
- ∾ "File Extensions, Formats, and Utilities" **http://www.stack.com**

File Type	File Extension	Specific Format	Description
Text files	.txt .asc	Plain text files	Plain text files contain printable characters, like the ones you see on this page, but without special fonts or typefaces, such as italic or bold. They're

(Table 12.1—Continued on next page)

File Type	File Extension	Specific Format	Description
			also called ASCII (rhymes with "pass key") files. ASCII stands for American Standard Code for Information Interchange, and it is the standard code used to represent characters in digital format in a computer. All browsers can display these files. The files often appear as if they were typed on a typewriter or computer terminal.
	.ps	PostScript files	The PostScript file format was invented by Adobe Systems. The files contain text but usually not in a readable format. The files also contain commands that a printer or display device interprets; the commands pertain to the formatting of different fonts, font sizes, and images in the file.
	.pdf	Portable Document Format	Adobe Systems also invented PDF. These files contain instructions that allow them to be displayed with different fonts, typefaces, colors, and images. You can view these files on your computer if you have Acrobat Reader, which is free from the Adobe Acrobat Web site, **http://adobe.com/ prodindex/acrobat**.
	.doc .wpd .rtf	Word-processing files	Files produced by word-processing software contain text along with commands that format the text. Most of these files are in a format that other word-processing software can deal with, usually after being converted from one form to another. They can't be displayed as plain text files, however. Files produced by Microsoft Word usually have names ending with .doc, and files produced by WordPerfect have names ending with .wpd. RTF stands for Rich Text Format, a format that can be interpreted by several different word-processing programs.
Data files	.xls .wks .wk1	Spread-sheet files	Files produced by spreadsheet programs are in a special nontext format that's interpreted and used by

(Table 12.1—Continued on next page)

File Type	File Extension	Specific Format	Description
			the software. Two major types of files are the ones produced by Microsoft Excel and Lotus 1-2-3. Excel spreadsheet file names end with .xls, and Lotus 1-2-3 file names end with .wks or .wk1. If you see file extensions like this on files you want to use, you'll need a spreadsheet program to display them. The newer versions of Excel and Lotus 1-2-3 can deal with data with any of the file extensions listed.
Image files	.gif	Graphic Interchange Format	Graphic images are stored in files in a variety of formats. As a part of a Web page or on their own, most browsers can display images stored in GIF or
	.jpg .jpeg	Joint Photographic Expert Group	JPEG format. Another format, TIFF, can store high-quality images. If your browser cannot display files in TIFF, you'll have to get some other software to display them. These two shareware
	.tif .tiff	Tagged Image File Format	programs can display images in various formats and can convert them from one format to another:

    ~ Lview Pro
        http://www.lview.com
    ~ Paint Shop Pro
        http://www.jasc.com/psp.html

File Type	File Extension	Specific Format	Description
Audio files	.au	Next/Sun format	These files contain information in an audio or sound format. With a sound card and speakers, you can play such
	.wav	A standard format for computers using MS Windows	files on your computer. If you're using Netscape Navigator or Microsoft Internet Explorer, the browser contains the software to deal with all these types. Next/Sun and WAV files tend to be very large and thus may take a long
	.ra .ram	RealAudio format	time to retrieve. The RealAudio format uses a different technology, called streaming technology, by which sound
	.mp3	MP3 or MPEG-1 Audio Layer3	becomes available as it is being transferred to your computer through the Internet. RealPlayer, a free player for RealAudio files, is available using the

(Table 12.1—Continued on next page)

File Type	File Extension	Specific Format	Description
			URL **http://www.real.com/player/index.html**. MP3 is a format and a method for compressing audio files. The compression scheme results in files that are less than a tenth of the original size with virtually no loss of sound quality.
Multi-media files	.mpg .mpeg	Moving Picture Expert Group	With these types of files, you can view video and hear accompanying sound. It's similar to viewing a movie or television show. There are several popular
	.mov .qt	QuickTime	formats, including MPEG, QuickTime (created by Apple Computer), RealVideo (created by RealNetworks,
	.rm .ram	RealVideo	Inc.), and Shockwave (created by Macromedia, Inc.). Netscape Navigator version 3.0 or later can display files in
	.dcr .dir .dxr	Shockwave	the MPEG format. A QuickTime player is available at no cost at **http://quicktime.apple.com/sw**. RealPlayer, a free player for RealVideo files, is available at **http://www.real.com /products/playerdl.html**. A free player for Macromedia Shockwave files is available at **http://www.macromedia.com/shockwave/download/**.
Com-pressed files	.zip .gz	Most common types of compressed format files	A file is compressed to save space on a server or to be transferred over the Internet more quickly. There are many types of compressed files, but the most common are those ending with .zip. If you retrieve a file in compressed format, you'll need software to uncompress the file. Two popular shareware programs work with these types of files: ～ PKZIP, **http://www.pkware.com** ～ WinZip, **http://www.winzip.com** See "A Note About Compressed Files" in the section that follows this table.

Table 12.1   File Types and Their Extensions

A Note About Compressed Files

You'll likely find yourself in a situation where you'll have to deal with *compressed files*. Many sites on the Web make compressed files available to the public. You may want to retrieve, copy, or *download* a copy of one of these compressed files to your computer. Often the files are packages or collections of related files. The files, or packages, are processed by a compression program, which reduces the total number of bytes necessary to represent the information that is in the package. Reducing the size of the file means it takes less time to download the file. Before you can use a compressed file, you must uncompress it, using PKZIP or WinZip, as listed in Table 12.1.

Any single file or collection of files can be compressed and transmitted. In the course of writing this book, we used this technology to transfer chapters back and forth between the publisher, editors, and ourselves. Since each chapter has so many images, the files were quite large. To solve this size problem, we put each chapter and the images into a single package and then compressed it using either PKZIP or WinZip. We then attached the files to email messages or sent them using FTP. The people on either end uncompressed the files using PKZIP or WinZip.

To get your own copy of either utility, follow these directions:

∾ To get a copy of PKZIP:

Go to the home page for PKWARE, **http://www.pkware.com**. Spend a little time reading about PKZIP, the way it works, and file compression in general. Click on the hyperlink that takes you through the steps of downloading the software. Store the software in a new folder. Once it has finished downloading, there will be a new application (program) in the folder. Click on it and follow the instructions. It will install itself in a directory or folder. Once it's installed, go to that directory, using Windows Explorer. Read the file named **Readme**, which contains information about the files you've installed. The program's name is PKZIP; click on it when you need to use it.

∾ To get a copy of WinZip:

Go to the home page for WinZip with the URL **http://www.winzip. com**. Spend a little time reading about WinZip, how it works, and about the topic of file compression. Click on the hyperlink that takes you through the steps of downloading the software. Store the software in a new folder. Once it's finished downloading there will be a new application (program) in the folder. Click on it and it will lead you through the steps of installing the program in a folder on your computer. The name of the program is WinZip; click on it when you need it.

Considering Copyright Guidelines Before Sharing and Copying Information

Much of what you find on the Web and Internet can be saved in a file on your computer, which makes it easy to share and distribute information to others. Exchanging information was one of the main reasons the Internet began, and it is a desirable activity, but there is a drawback. Free access to information makes it difficult to control unauthorized distribution of anything that's available. Anyone with a Web browser can make an exact digital copy of information. This sometimes is illegal.

Only the owners of the information can grant the right to copy or duplicate materials. This is called the ***copyright***. Some documents on the Internet contain a statement asserting the copyright and giving permission for distributing the document in an electronic form, provided it isn't sold or made part of some commercial product. For example, here's a quote from **http://metalab.unc.edu/expo/vatican.exhibit/exhibit/About.html** describing limitations on the use of the materials in the exhibit "Rome Reborn" offered by the Library of Congress:

> The text and images in the Online Exhibit ROME REBORN:
> THE VATICAN LIBRARY AND RENAISSANCE CULTURE are for
> the personal use of students, scholars, and the public. Any com-
> mercial use or publication of them is strictly prohibited.

Regardless of whether a Web page is accompanied by a statement asserting copyright, it is still protected by the copyright laws of the United States, the Universal Copyright Convention, or the Berne Union. Most copyright conventions or statutes include a provision that makes it possible for individuals to copy portions of a document for short-term use. This is known as ***fair use***. If information is obtainable on the Internet and there is no charge to access the information, it often can be shared in an electronic form. That certainly doesn't mean you can copy images or documents and make them available on the Internet, make copies and share them in a printed form, or distribute them to several people using email attachments. Quite naturally, many people who create or provide material available on the Internet expect to get credit and/or be paid for their work.

Remember that anything available in electronic form on the Internet or World Wide Web is a copyrighted work, and you need to treat it in the same way as a book, a journal article, artwork, a play, or a piece of recorded music.

Speaking of recorded music, many of you may have heard of the MP3 controversy in the news. People have copied music from CDs, created files in MP3 format, and made these files available on the Web for other people to download without charge. MP3 is a standard technology and a format for compressing sound into a relatively small file. The neat thing about MP3 technology is that the sound quality is not reduced. MP3 files sound as good as the originals, so people are tempted to download the music they like without buying CDs. The songs that are copied illegally are called "pirated copies." Almost all of the songs recorded by musicians are copyrighted. This means that

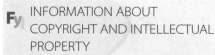

Fyi INFORMATION ABOUT COPYRIGHT AND INTELLECTUAL PROPERTY

∾ "The Copyright Website" by Benedict O'Mahoney **http://www.benedict.com**
∾ "The Intellectual Property Law Server" by George A. Wowk **http://www.intelproplaw.com**

the musician or the recording company that published the music has the right to determine how the music is distributed, and how much will be charged for it. Copyright laws apply to MP3 just as they do to other formats. It is perfectly legal for you to make MP3s from your own CD collection and keep them on your computer. But the minute you distribute the MP3s on the Internet, you are breaking the law. There are MP3 files on the Web that are legal to download. Some artists place their songs on the Web and make them freely available. This way people get a preview of their music so that maybe they will buy tickets to a concert, or buy the artists' latest CDs. We will show you how to download legal MP3 music and play it on an MP3 player in Chapter 13.

To put it simply, just because something is available on the Web doesn't mean that you may copy it. You are allowed to copy the material for personal use, but in almost every case, you cannot use it for commercial purposes or distribute it freely without written permission from the copyright holder.

Capturing and Using Text, Images, and Data from the Web and the Internet

There are several browser options for retrieving material from the Web. The following section will provide brief step-by-step instructions on how to work with information that you find. If the procedures differ between Netscape and Internet Explorer, then the details will be shown for both.

After this section is a hands-on activity covering how to save and insert images into a word-processing document.

The following are the examples that will be shown:

~ Printing an Entire Web Page

~ Saving the Text of a Web Page

~ Printing Part of a Web Page

~ Saving Part of a Web Page

~ Capturing and Downloading Statistical Tables into a Spreadsheet or Word-processing Document

Printing an Entire Web Page

You've found a Web page that has information you need. You can print it out if you wish. Before you print a Web page in its entirety, you might want to make sure how many pages it consists of. You can do this by accessing Print Preview, which is located in the File menu, as shown in Figure 12.1. Without finding this out, you may print out more pages than you actually need.

1. After determining that you want the entire Web page printed, simply click on **File** in the menu bar and select **Print**.
2. When the Print menu pops up, click on **OK**.

Click on Print Preview to find out how many pages the document has

To print the entire Web page, click on Print

You could also click on the Print button if you didn't care about how many pages were in the Web page

Figure 12.1   How to Print an Entire Web Page

Internet Explorer doesn't have the Print Preview option, so it is impossible to find out how many printed pages the Web page will produce.

1. Click on **File** and select **Print**.
2. When the print menu pops up, click on **OK**.

Saving the Text of a Web Page

You have found a valuable resource on the Web, and you'd like to read the information later, but you're not connected to a printer. You can download the page to a diskette in the A: drive or to a drive on your computer. Remember that when you download a Web page you'll be obtaining the text only, and not any images that may be in the page. Images must be captured separately.

1. While viewing the desired Web page, click on **File**.
2. Choose **Save As** from the pulldown menu.
3. Click on the down arrow next to the Save in field and choose the appropriate drive and/or folder to place the Web page in. In Figure 12.2, we chose the A: drive.
4. If saving to the A: drive, put a diskette in the drive before saving.
5. You can rename the file if you want by typing in a name in the File name field.
6. Choose **Plain Text (*.txt)** from the Save as type pulldown menu.
7. Click on **Save**.

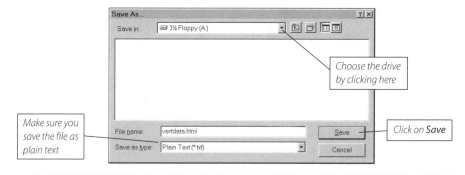

Figure 12.2   Saving a Web Page to the A: Drive

1. Click on **File** and select **Save As**.
2. Choose which drive you want the file to be saved in.
3. Choose **Text file (*.txt)** from the pulldown menu next to Save as type.
4. Click on **Save**.

Printing Part of a Web Page

You have found useful information that exists on a couple of pages of a much larger Web page. You can print one section of a Web page if you'd like.

1. While you are viewing the Web page, click on **File**.
2. Select **Print Preview**.
3. Note the page numbers in the bottom left corner of each page.
4. Click on **Next Page** until you come to the page(s) you want to print.
5. When you come to the page(s) you want to print, click on **Print**, as shown in Figure 12.3.
6. After the print menu appears, click on the radio button next to **Pages** and type the page number(s) you need to print.
7. Click on **OK**.
8. When you're finished with Print Preview, click on **Close**.

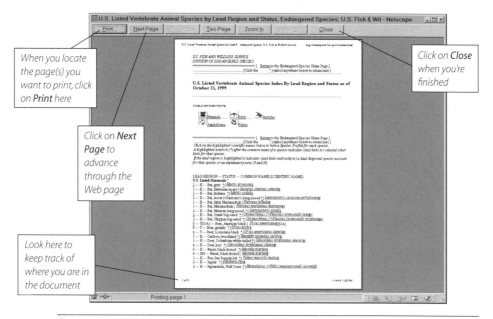

Figure 12.3   Using Print Preview to Print Part of a Web Page

1. Use the left mouse button to highlight the section of text that you want to print.
2. Click on **File** and then select **Print**.
3. On the Print menu, click on the radio button next to **Selection**, as shown in Figure 12.4.
4. Click on **OK**.

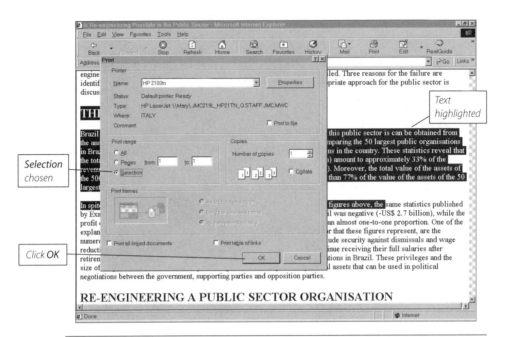

Figure 12.4   Printing Part of a Web Page in Internet Explorer

Saving Part of a Web Page

Here are a few examples of when you would save part of a Web page instead of printing part of a Web page:

↬ You aren't attached to a printer and you want to have the information you found accessible at a later time, but you don't want the entire page saved.

↬ You want to save less than one page, for example, a paragraph or a table.

↬ You want to have the information in electronic form.

Remember, if you download the text from a Web page and plan to use the information you located in a paper or presentation, you must cite the information properly.

The following are the simple steps to save parts of Web pages:

1. Highlight the part of the Web page you want to save by holding down the left mouse button and dragging the cursor across the text you want. When you have reached the last line, release the mouse button.

2. Click on **Edit** in the menu bar and select **Copy**.

3. Open the word-processing program you intend to use and create a new document.

4. Click on **Edit** in the menu bar and select **Paste**.

Note: If you are using a computer that doesn't have word-processing software installed, you can use Notepad, which is available in Windows. Notepad is located in the Accessories folder under Programs. You could copy the part of the Web page you wanted to Notepad and then save the file (click on **File** and select **Save As**) to a diskette in the A: drive or to your computer.

Capturing and Downloading Statistical Tables into a Spreadsheet or Word-processing Document

Statistical tables abound on the Internet, especially in government Web sites. Since government data is in the public domain and free to use as you want, you won't have to ask permission to use it, but you will need to cite it properly so that people know where you got the data. In this example, we'll show how to download a statistical table that is in worksheet format (**.wk1**) into a spreadsheet program. Using a spreadsheet allows you to perform calculations with the numbers that are in the columns and rows. We'll be using Microsoft Excel, but using another spreadsheet program would follow a similar procedure.

Some statistical tables are not in a worksheet format, but may be in *delimited format*. This means that the data fields are separated by commas, tabs, semicolons, or some other delimiter. Excel makes it easy for you to download a file that is delimited. Many other statistical tables are in text format. If the data is in text format, you can still download it in a spreadsheet program, but you'll need to change the column sizes to accommodate the data.

Figure 12.5 shows a list of statistical information you can download from the *Economic Report of the President.* The URL is **http://w3.access.gpo.gov/usbudget/fy1998/erp_wk1.html**.

1. To download an individual file from the list, hold down the [Shift] key and click with the left mouse button on the file you want. In this example, we'll click on the first one listed, as shown in Figure 12.5.

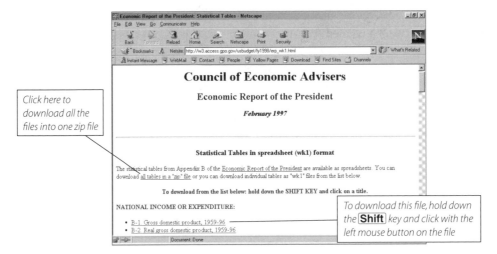

Figure 12.5   Economic Report of the President Statistical Tables

2. A dialog box will pop up on the screen, as shown in Figure 12.6. You'll need to decide where to save the file. You can choose a folder from the pulldown menu next to Save in. In this example, we will choose to put the file directly into the **Excel** folder, which is on the **C:** drive in the **Msoffice** folder. Note that the file is named **b001**. Click on **Save**.

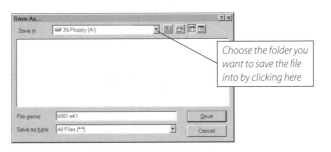

Figure 12.6   Saving a Spreadsheet File

Now you need to open the Microsoft Excel spreadsheet program. Click on **Start** and then choose **Programs**. Choose **Microsoft Excel** from the menu. When Excel is open, click on **File** and choose **Open** from the menu. You'll want to look in the **Excel** folder for the file we downloaded. You'll need to choose **All Files** from the pulldown menu next to Files of type.

3. You should see the file named **b001.wk1** on the list of files. Click on it, as shown in Figure 12.7.

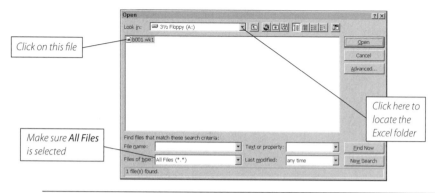

Click on this file

Click here to locate the Excel folder

Make sure **All Files** is selected

Figure 12.7   Opening a File in Excel

The file is automatically placed into a spreadsheet. Since this file was already in worksheet format (**.wk1**), it downloaded directly into the Excel program, as shown in Figure 12.8.

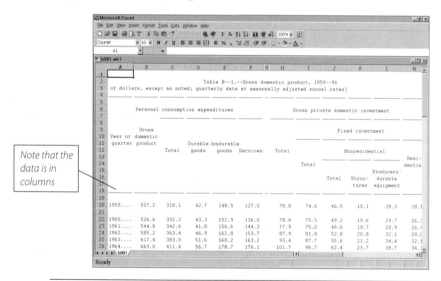

Note that the data is in columns

Figure 12.8   The File **b001.wk1** as an Excel Spreadsheet

Sometimes you want to capture statistical data to insert in a word-processing document. To do this, follow these steps:

1. Copy and paste the statistical table like you would copy a portion of any Web page. If the tabular configuration is distorted, you might want to try changing the font to Courier or some other nonproportional font so that the columns don't appear crooked.

2. Save the file as a text file, just as you would save a Web page.

Another useful skill to learn is how to save images and insert them into documents; for example, word-processing documents or PowerPoint presentations. Activity 12.1 will take you through the simple steps of this process.

CAPTURING AND DOWNLOADING IMAGES INTO A WORD-PROCESSING DOCUMENT

Overview

This activity will take you step-by-step through the process of saving an image and inserting it into a word-processing document. First we'll go to Karen Hartman's home page and save an image that is on the page. After the image is saved, you'll insert the image into a word-processing document. We'll follow these steps:

1. Go to Karen Hartman's home page.
2. Find the image of Nuweiba and save it.
3. Create a word-processing document.
4. Insert the image into the document.

Details

Before we begin, make sure your browser is opened and ready to go. We are using Netscape for this activity, but you can accomplish the same tasks using Internet Explorer.

1. Go to Karen Hartman's home page.

 Type **http://www.library.mwc.edu/~khartman** in the location field and press **Enter**.

 Click on the **Personal** hyperlink at the top of the page.

2. Find the image of Nuweiba and save it.

 Scroll down until you see the image of a resort with mountains in the background.

The image that we will be saving appears in Figure 12.9. Whenever you want to save an image and use it for your own purposes, you should try to notify the person responsible for putting the image on the Web to ask permission to use the image. Sometimes this is impossible, and if you aren't using the image for commercial purposes, it probably falls within the realm of "fair use" to use the image, especially for educational reasons. In any case, it's still a courtesy to try to obtain permission. On this Web page, there is a place to email the author and ask if it's okay to use her image. Let's go ahead and save the image.

 Place your mouse on the image and right-click.

A menu will appear, as shown in Figure 12.9.

(Do it)! Choose **Save Image As** (if you're using Internet Explorer, the choice will be **Save Picture As**).

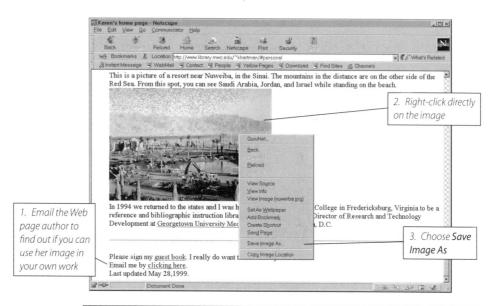

Figure 12.9   Saving an Image You Find on the World Wide Web

Now you'll need to decide where you want to put the image. You should save it to the drive that's most convenient for you. For the purposes of this activity, we will save to a diskette in the A: drive. Figure 12.10 shows the Save As window.

(Do it)! Click on the arrow next to the field labeled **Save in**. Choose **3½ Floppy (A:)**, as shown in Figure 12.10.

(Do it)! Click on **Save**, as shown in Figure 12.10.

Note that the image is a JPEG file.

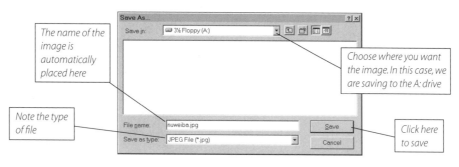

Figure 12.10   Saving an Image to the A: Drive

3. Create a word-processing document.

    (Do it)!   Open Microsoft Word.

    (Do it)!   Click on **File** and then select **New**.

    (Do it)!   Click on the **Blank Document** icon.

4. Insert the image into the document.

Note that the document pictured in Figure 12.11 has text typed in it. You don't need to type any text. Just place the cursor at the spot you'd like the picture to be inserted. Click on **Insert** in the menu bar, as shown in Figure 12.11.

    (Do it)!   After selecting **Picture** from the pulldown menu that appears, click on **From File**, also shown in Figure 12.11.

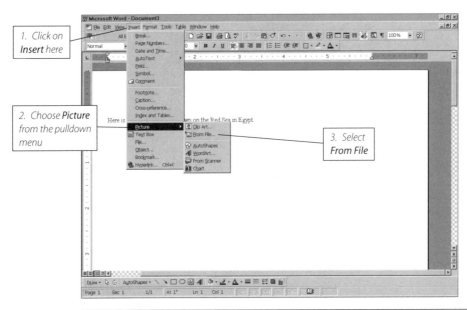

1. Click on Insert here

2. Choose Picture from the pulldown menu

3. Select From File

Figure 12.11   Using Word to Insert a Picture in a Document

From the Insert Picture dialog box that pops up, you'll need to choose the drive and folder that holds the image you want to insert. In this example, we saved the image to the diskette in the A: drive. To make it easier to find an image, choose **All Pictures** from the pulldown menu next to the Files of type field, as shown in Figure 12.12.

    (Do it)!   Highlight the name of the image, **nuweiba**, and click on **Insert**.

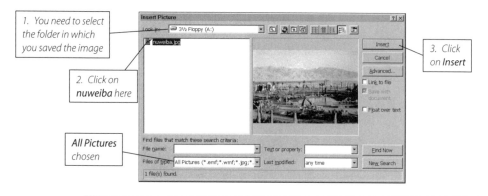

Figure 12.12   Steps for Inserting a Picture into a Word Document

Figure 12.13 shows the picture inserted into the Word document. You can resize the image by clicking on it and dragging a border arrow in any direction you want.

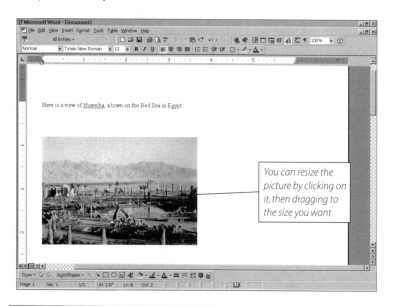

Figure 12.13   The Picture Inserted into the Word Document

If this were an actual research project, you would cite the title of the image, the author of the Web page, and the Web page's URL.

END OF ACTIVITY 12.1

Activity 12.1 illustrated how easy it is to copy an image and use it for your own purposes. The way the Web works makes it simple to take material and use it as your own. You should always be mindful of being courteous when using others' work and citing it properly.

Procedures and Steps for Managing Internet and Web Information

The following chart is a helpful reference to procedures outlined previously and to others that weren't discussed. (If steps differ in the two browsers, individual instructions are given.)

Procedure	Steps
Saving the text of a Web page (remember to cite the Web page properly if you're incorporating it into your own work)	1. Click on **File**. 2. Choose **Save As**. 3. Choose the drive and folder in which to place the Web page. 4. Select **Plain Text (*.txt)** from the pulldown menu. 5. Click on **Save**.
	1. Click on **File**. 2. Choose **Save As**. 3. Choose the drive and folder in which to place the Web page. 4. Select **Text File (*.txt)** from the pulldown menu. 5. Click on **Save**.
Saving a portion of a Web page (remember to cite the page properly)	1. Highlight the portion of the Web page you want by holding down the left mouse button and dragging the cursor down the screen. 2. Choose **Edit**, then **Copy**. 3. Open a word-processing file or Notepad, which is located under Accessories in Windows 95/98. 4. Choose **Edit**, then **Paste**. 5. The portion of the Web page you highlighted will be placed in the document.
Saving items on a Web page into a file (without viewing them first)	1. Move the mouse pointer to the hyperlink and click the right mouse button. 2. Select **Save Link As** from the menu that appears. 3. A Save As dialog box will pop up where you can select the drive to save to. 4. Click on **Save**.
	1. Move the mouse pointer to the hyperlink and click the right mouse button. 2. Select **Save Target As** from the menu that appears.

(Table 12.2—Continued on next page)

Procedure	Steps
	3. A Save As dialog box will pop up. You'll need to select the drive where you want the link to be copied to. 4. Click on **Save**. Whenever you save a file from the Internet, there's a possibility that the file will contain a computer virus or other software that may damage or erase files. A good source for information about computer viruses is "virus - PC Webopaedia," **http://www.pcwebopedia.com/ virus.htm**.
Printing a Web page	1. Click on **File** in the menu bar. 2. Choose **Print**. 3. Click **OK**.
Printing parts of a Web page	N 1. Click on **File** in the menu bar. 2. Select **Print Preview**. 3. Click on **Next Page** until you find the page you want to print. 4. Click on **Print**. 5. Select the page number(s) you want printed. 6. Click **OK**.
	e 1. Highlight the portion of the Web page you want to print by holding down the left mouse button and dragging the cursor down the screen. 2. Click on **File** in the menu bar. 3. Select **Print**. 4. In the box labeled **Print range**, choose the **Selection** option. 5. Click **OK**.
Emailing a Web page (emailing a Web page means sending only the text on the page or sending the source)	N 1. Click on **File** in the menu bar. 2. Select **Send Page**. (If the page you're trying to send is a frame, you'll select **Send Frame**.) 3. Type the email address of the person you are sending the message to in the line next to To. 4. To send the Web page text in the body of the email message, click **Quote**. The Web page is automatically made an attachment. 5. Click on **Send**.
	e 1. Click on **File** in the menu bar. 2. Select **Send**. 3. You can choose **Page by email** or **Link by email**. 4. Type the email address of the person you are sending the message to in the line next to To. 5. Click on **Send**.

(Table 12.2—Continued on next page)

Procedure	Steps
Printing a page that is wider than 8½ inches	1. Click on **File** in the menu bar. 2. Select **Print**. 3. Click on **Properties** in the Print menu. 4. Choose **Landscape**. 5. Click **OK**.
Printing pages with dark backgrounds	1. Click on **Edit** in the menu bar. 2. Select **Preferences** from the menu. 3. Click on **Colors** in the menu of categories. (It's a subcategory of Appearance.) 4. Select a background color. Since you want to be able to print, white would be a good choice. 5. Select a text color. You might want to choose black. 6. Check the box next to **Always use my colors, overriding document**. 7. Click **OK**. 8. Proceed with printing the Web page.
	1. Click on **Tools** in the menu bar. 2. Select **Internet Options** from the menu. 3. Click on **Colors**. 4. Deselect **Use Windows Colors** by clicking the radio button next to it. 5. Select the background color you want; usually white is a good choice. 6. Click **OK**.
Saving a frame	1. Click on the frame you want to save. 2. Click on **File**. 3. Choose **Save Frame As**. 4. Select **Plain Text (*.txt)** from the pulldown menu next to **Save as type**. 5. Create a new file name if you want. 6. Click on **Save**.
	1. Click on the frame you want to save. 2. Click on **File**. 3. Choose **Save As**. 4. Select **Text File (*txt)** from pulldown menu. 5. Create a new file name if you want. 6. Click on **Save**.
Printing a frame	1. Click on the frame you want to print. 2. Click on **File** in the menu bar. 3. Choose **Print Frame**. 4. Click **OK** on the print menu.

(Table 12.2—Continued on next page)

Procedure	Steps
	1. Click on the frame you want to print. 2. Click on **File** in the menu bar. 3. Choose **Print**. 4. Click **OK** on the print menu.
Using your browser to view local files	1. Choose **File** from the menu bar. 2. Select **Open Page**. 3. You can type in the file name or click on **Choose File** and search until you find the one you want to view. 4. Click on **Open**.
	1. Choose **File** from the menu bar. 2. Select **Open**. 3. You can type the file name or click on **Browse** and search until you find the one you want to view. 4. Click **OK**.
Capturing images (it's a good idea to ask permission before you use an image. And remember to cite it properly.)	1. Right-click on the image. 2. Choose **Save As** from the pop-up menu. 3. Click on **Save** to save the image in the drive and folder listed, or use the other buttons next to the folder names to select another drive and folder.
	1. Right-click on the image. 2. Choose **Save Picture As** from the pop-up menu. 3. Click on **Save** to save the image in the drive and folder listed, or use the other buttons next to the older names to select another drive and folder.
Inserting images into documents (Word documents, Web pages, or PowerPoint presentations)	1. Open the document in which you want the have the image inserted. 2. Make sure your cursor is located where you want the image to be located. 3. Click on **Insert** in the menu bar. 4. Choose **Picture**. 5. Choose **From File**. 6. Locate the drive and folder name that holds the image. (If the image is on a diskette, insert the diskette in the A drive.) 7. After locating the image file, highlight it and click on **Insert**.
Downloading statistical tables into a spreadsheet	1. If the table is already in a worksheet format, either follow the directions from the Web page or click on **File** and select **Save As**.

(Table 12.2—Continued on next page)

Procedure	Steps
	2. Choose a folder in which to place the file. You can choose the Excel folder if you like.
	3. Open the Microsoft Excel program by clicking on **Start** and then **Programs**. Choose **Microsoft Excel** from the menu.
	4. When Excel is open, click on **File** and choose **Open** from the menu.
	5. Choose **All Files** from the pulldown menu next to **Files of type**.
	6. Click on the file you downloaded. If the file is delimited or in fixed-width format, you'll have to indicate which format. If it is delimited, you'll need to determine which delimiter the file uses: commas, tabs, semicolons, or some other delimiter. Click on **Next** until the spreadsheet is ready to load. If the file is already in a spreadsheet format, it will automatically load into the spreadsheet.
Downloading statistical tables into word-processing documents	1. Highlight the table by holding down the left mouse button and dragging the cursor down the screen until the table is highlighted.
	2. Choose **Edit,** then **Copy**.
	3. Open a word-processing document or Notepad, which is located under Accessories in Windows 95/98.
	4. Choose **Edit,** then **Paste**.
	5. If the tabular configuration is distorted, change the font to Courier or some other nonproportional font.
	OR
	1. If the table is an entire Web page, click on **File**, choose **Save As**, and place the file in a folder.
	2. Select **Plain Text (*.txt)** from the pulldown menu and name it something new.
	3. Click on **Save**.
	4. Open a word-processing program or Notepad, open the saved text file, and save it using the menu provided.
	5. If the tabular configuration is distorted, change the font to Courier or some other nonproportional font.

Table 12.2   Procedures and Steps in Netscape and Internet Explorer

Summary

Web pages may contain text, images, video, audio, and other types of information. These will be part of the Web page, or they will be accessed with hyperlinks. Information available on the Web is in a myriad of file formats. This chapter covered the common types of files that are found on the Internet and how to work with them. You can usually tell a file's type by its name. The letters following the dot (.) at the end of a file name are called the file extension portion of the file name. You may find yourself in a situation where you'll have to deal with compressed files. Before you can use a compressed file, you must uncompress it, using PKZIP or WinZip.

Using information from the Internet requires a familiarity with intellectual property issues. Much of what you find on the Internet and World Wide Web can be downloaded and distributed to others easily. Only the owners of the information can grant the right to copy or duplicate materials. This is called the copyright. In almost every case, you are required to obtain written permission from the copyright holder before distributing information on the Internet. Most copyright laws include a provision that makes it possible for individuals to copy portions of a document for short-term use. This is known as fair use.

There are many browser capabilities that allow you to download, capture, copy, email, and print information from the Internet. These basic skills were outlined in this chapter. If differences exist between the two major browsers, Netscape and Internet Explorer, then each procedure was explained.

Selected Terms Used in This Chapter

compressed file	download
copyright	fair use
delimited format	

Exercises and Projects

1. Perform a search in your favorite search engine. From the list of results, choose one Web page to download to a diskette in your A: drive. Write down the URL of the page you chose and the steps you took to save this page. How many pages does the Web page have? If there is an image in the Web page, save it separately and describe the steps you took to accomplish this. Provide the image file name with the correct file type. Is it a **.jpeg**, **.gif**, or **.tiff** image?

2. You may have seen the motion picture *Amistad* and want to read the full-text of the U.S. Supreme Court opinion that ruled in that famous case. The full-text of the opinion is included in the Findlaw Web site at **http://caselaw.findlaw.com/amistad_case.html**. Go to this URL and look it over. It is a lengthy opinion, and you decide that you only need to print out page 10. Your assignment is to print out this page only. What steps did you go through to accomplish this? Please be specific.

3. Go to Whatis.com, **http://www.whatis.com**, and either search for or browse the directory to find the section on file formats. What is ASO? How about DEM? Go to Wotsit's Formats, **http://www.wotsit.org**, and find more information about DEM. Write a sentence describing DEM files.

4. Access the U.S. Census Bureau's National Population Projection's page at **http://www.census.gov/population/www/projections/natproj.html**. You will see that the "Assumptions and Methodology" section is offered in both an HTML version and a PDF version. Look at both versions of this document and give two reasons why using the HTML version might be preferable to using the PDF version.

5. Go to the Library of Congress' American Memory online collections, **http://memory.loc.gov/ammem/collections/finder.html**. Find sound recordings by the Omaha Indians. The sound recordings are available in two formats, real audio and wav. What are the advantages of having more than one audio format available?

6. The Copyright Website, by Benedict O'Mahoney, at **http://www.benedict.com**, is an excellent site for copyright information. Go to the World Wide Web section, read it, and answer the following questions:
   ∾ Why does the author say that a URL is not copyrightable?
   ∾ When would a list of facts (for example, a telephone book listing), be copyrightable?
   ∾ What did the case Feist v. Rural Telephone decide?
   Give two examples of when it is legal to copy links from other peoples' pages for your own Web page. Give one example of when it is not legal to copy information from others for your Web page.

7. Are titles of books and other creations copyrightable? How about ideas and discoveries? How long after an author's death is his or her work under copyright protection? The Library of Congress' Copyright Basics page, at **http://www.loc.gov/circ/circ1.html**, can help you answer these questions.

8. You want to use a graphical image file (**.gif**) that you found in a federal government Web (**.gov**) site. You want to know if you can use this image in your Web page without asking permission and without infringing copyright. Read the section "Public Domain" in The Copyright Website at **http://www.benedict.com/basic/public/public.htm** to help you make a decision. What is the public domain? Can you use the image without infringing copyright?

9. After reading the Web page discussed in Exercise 8, you want to email the text of the page to a friend. Describe the steps, using both Netscape and Internet Explorer to perform this task.

10. Go to the following Web pages that deal with fair use:
    - "Fair Use of Copyrighted Works: A Crucial Element in Educating America," **http://www.cetus.org/fairindex.html**
    - "10 Big Myths About Copyright Explained," **http://www.templetons.com/brad/copymyths.html**

    After reading the information provided, write a short paragraph that defines "fair use" in your own words.

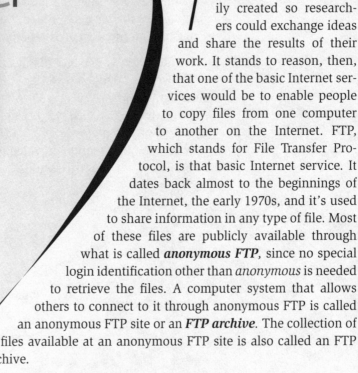

Chapter 13

TRANSFERRING FILES USING FTP

~

The Internet was primarily created so researchers could exchange ideas and share the results of their work. It stands to reason, then, that one of the basic Internet services would be to enable people to copy files from one computer to another on the Internet. FTP, which stands for File Transfer Protocol, is that basic Internet service. It dates back almost to the beginnings of the Internet, the early 1970s, and it's used to share information in any type of file. Most of these files are publicly available through what is called *anonymous FTP*, since no special login identification other than *anonymous* is needed to retrieve the files. A computer system that allows others to connect to it through anonymous FTP is called an anonymous FTP site or an *FTP archive*. The collection of files available at an anonymous FTP site is also called an FTP archive.

Goals/Objectives
~ Learn how to download a file by using anonymous FTP
~ Know how to locate and download software
~ Know how to uncompress compressed programs and files
~ Learn how to use an FTP client program

Topics
~ FTP Overview
~ Downloading a File by Anonymous FTP
~ Locating FTP Archives and Other Sites for Finding Software
~ Downloading and Working with Files from Software Archives
~ Using an FTP Client Program

FTP Overview

What is now the World Wide Web wouldn't have been possible without the notions associated with FTP and its use. FTP can be used to transfer any type of file. It's commonly used nowadays to distribute software throughout the Internet. Most of these software programs are available as ***shareware***, which means that you retrieve (***download***) the program from an archive, use it, and purchase it if you find the program useful. Software programs known as ***freeware*** are those that don't require a fee to download. FTP is an efficient way to transfer files when you know the exact name and location of the file—and that's all included in its URL. Using FTP, you can also transfer a file from your computer to another. This is called ***uploading*** a file. When you upload, you usually have to give a login name and password to the other computer system; it's not the same as anonymous FTP. This turns out to be a good way to work on one computer and transfer your work to another. Some people use this technique to update or create Web pages. They do their work on one computer and then transfer the files to a computer that acts as a Web server.

These days, much of the access to files by FTP is through a Web browser. As you know, that means you need to be familiar with the URL format for FTP. Here is the general form of a URL for anonymous FTP:

ftp://*name-of-ftp-site*/*directory-name*/*file-name*

Suppose a friend tells you, "I found this picture of Mars with great detail and colors. You can get it by anonymous FTP at the FTP site for the Jet Propulsion Laboratory, **ftp.jpl.nasa.gov**. You'll want to get the file **marglobe.gif**. It's in the directory **pub/images/browse**. There are also some animations at the same site in **pub/images/anim**." You'd like to view the image, and she's told you everything you need to retrieve it. The URL for that file is **ftp://ftp.jpl.nasa.gov/pub/images/browse/marglobe.gif**.

Matching this to the general form, we have the following:

Domain name of FTP site   Directory name   File name

ftp://ftp.jpl.nasa.gov/pub/images/browse/marglobe.gif

You can also use a URL to refer to a directory. For example, if you use the URL **ftp://ftp.jpl.nasa.gov/pub/images/browse**, the Web browser displays a list of all the files or subdirectories in the directory **/pub/images/browse**, as displayed in Figure 13.1. Each file or subdirectory is represented as a hyperlink, and you can view it by clicking on its name.

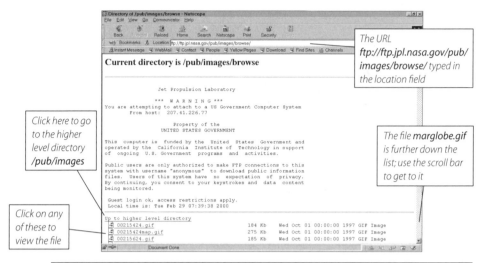

Figure 13.1   An FTP Archive Displaying Directory Files

Downloading a File by Anonymous FTP

There are two ways to retrieve a file—that is, copy it from a remote site to the computer you're using. The browser makes it possible for you to download files using anonymous FTP without having to type **anonymous** as a user ID or giving a password.

Method 1: View the File First, and Then Save It Using the File Menu

If you type a file's URL or if you click on a hyperlink, the file will be transferred to the Web browser. This is useful if you want to view the file before you save it, but the file will be transferred to your computer first. If the browser is configured to display or play a file of that type, you'll see (and hear, if possible) the file's contents in the Web browser window. Some examples of these types of files are text files, Web pages that are text files with HTML commands, and GIF or JPEG image files.

The file may also be displayed in a window created by another program called a *helper application*. If there is no helper application installed to display the file, a message box pops up saying "No Viewer Configured for File Type." If the file is displayed in the browser window, select **Save As** from the **File** pulldown menu in the menu bar. This opens a Save As dialog box on the screen. Set the directory or folder name, and then click on the button labeled **Save**. If the file comes up in the window for another application, such as Microsoft Word, save it through the commands for that application. See the tip below to handle a file type that doesn't match any type that your browser can work with.

Method 2: Save the Hyperlink in a File Without Viewing It by Using the Right Mouse Button or Shift and Click

If a hyperlink to a file is present in the Web browser's window, you can save the hyperlink. To retrieve the file without viewing it, put the mouse pointer on the hyperlink and press the right mouse button. When a menu pops up, choose **Save Link As** (in Netscape) or **Save Target As** (in Internet Explorer). This opens a Save As dialog box on the screen. Set the directory or folder name, and then click on the **Save** button.

Another way to do this is to place the pointer on a hyperlink. Then hold down the **Shift** key, click on the hyperlink, and release the **Shift** key. This immediately opens a Save As dialog box. You can save it to the file you've specified on your computer.

tip   WHAT TO DO WHEN "NO VIEWER CONFIGURED FOR FILE TYPE" POPS UP

The message "No Viewer Configured for File Type" means you've come across a file type that your browser doesn't know how to handle at the present time. Select the option that lets you Save to Disk. A Save As dialog box pops up, asking you to specify the folder in which you want to store the file. If you want to see or hear the file, then be sure you have any hardware and software you need to uncompress, display, or play the file after it has been transmitted. There are lots of variations and possibilities for the necessary equipment and programs, so we can't cover all of them here. But if you do have everything you need, you may want to configure the browser so that it knows what to do with files of that type in the future. In your browser's Help, you can find instructions about informing the browser about a particular helper application. Click on **Preferences** on the **Edit** pulldown menu in the menu bar, select the **Applications** panel, and click on the **Help** button if you're using Netscape Navigator.

Locating FTP Archives and Other Sites for Finding Software

One of the first search services available on the Internet was designed to find files stored in FTP archives. Peter Deutsch, Alan Emtage, and Bill Heelan at McGill University created a service named Archie (short for *archive*) in 1990 and released it for public use. It worked by indexing the names of files from entries in many FTP archives. This index, in turn, took the form of a database.

When a user supplied a search term, Archie displayed the locations of matching files. It worked very much like many of the search engines we've discussed in earlier chapters. Archie was available with an interface specially designed for use with a Web browser. You entered the name or a portion of the name of the file that you were looking for. Archie returned a collection of hyperlinks to files or directories that matched the name used in the search box.

FTP archives are a collection of directories arranged according to some scheme. A common arrangement is for the top level to be arranged by the type of computer system (such as Mac, PC, and Unix) and for the levels below that to be ordered according to the type of software (such as games, utilities, and Internet). You start at the home or root directory and, by clicking on hyperlinks that represent folders or directories, you move to or browse through the archive. Once you've located the file you want, you can download it using one of the methods described above. Because millions of files are available through FTP, you can appreciate how difficult it is to find the name of a file and its archive without some automated search tool.

Fy HERE'S A LIST OF GENERAL-PURPOSE FTP ARCHIVES ON THE WEB

~ "UIArchive, University of Illinois at Urbana-Champaign"
http://uiarchive.cso.uiuc.edu

~ "Wuarchive, Washington University in St. Louis"
http://ftp.wustl.edu

~ "Garbo, University of Vassa, Finland"
http://garbo.uwasa.fi

Using Archie was all well and good, provided you knew the name or a portion of the name of the file you were seeking. Sometimes you needed to guess what the name might be, which proved to be difficult. A better approach is to arrange files in categories according to their function—such as sound files, desktop utilities, games, HTML editors, and so forth—and description. If there is a way to search the collection by file names and descriptions, then the service is more useful. Several of these are available on the Web. We'll look at some in the next activity and in the exercises. Many of the files accessible through these sites are software, programs, or collections of programs and other files, which are distributed as shareware. The files are in either executable form (their names end with **.exe**) or compressed form (their names end with **.zip** or **.gz**).

Here are a few sources on the Web that list FTP and software or shareware archives:

Source That Lists Software or Shareware Archives	URL
Librarians' Index to the Internet	**http://lii.org**, then select **Computers**, then **Software**
Nerd's Heaven: The Software Directory Directory	**http://boole.stanford.edu/ nerdsheaven.html**
Yahoo!: Computers and Internet: Software: Shareware	**http://www.yahoo.com/ computers_and_internet/ software/shareware**

Downloading and Working with Files from Software Archives

Several services on the Web act as archives and distributors of software in the form of shareware or freeware. Each service supplies links to the programs; when you click on the link, the software is transferred to your computer, essentially by FTP. In other words, you select the software you'd like, and you then use a Web browser to download it to your computer.

Shareware Often Comes in Packages

Most of the files in the archives are packages, or collections of related files. These are in packages because to install, run, and use a single program usually requires several files, such as program libraries, instructions for installing and registering the program, and online help files. When you retrieve these, you get all the files you need combined in one file, the package.

The files or packages are processed by a compression program, which reduces the total number of bytes necessary to represent the information in the package. Reducing the size of a file means it takes less time to download the file. Because of this compression, you must do two things to the package after you receive it: uncompress it and extract the individual files from the package.

Compressed files or packages have names that usually end in **.zip**. Two popular compression programs are PKZIP and WinZip (which are both shareware). You will definitely want a copy of either of those utilities. We discussed these compression programs and how to download them in Chapter 12.

How can we extract the files necessary for those compression programs or similar packages? These and many other packages are in what is called a self-extracting archive. The package's file name ends in **.exe**.

When you click on the name, it starts extracting its own components. For example, the software for the Netscape and Microsoft browsers is in that format.

This compressed format isn't used only with programs. Any single file or collection of files can be compressed and transmitted in that compressed format. In the course of writing this book, we used this technology. Because each chapter has so many images, the files were quite large. We put each chapter and the images into a single package and then compressed it using either PKZIP or WinZip. We used FTP or email to send the compressed packages to the publisher.

Downloading and Installing Software

Here are the steps involved in downloading and installing shareware or freeware programs and associated files:

~ Find the program you want to retrieve in a software archive.

~ Create a folder or directory to hold the program from the archive on your computer.

~ Click on the hyperlink in the software archive to the program. As soon as you indicate where it should go using a Save As dialog box, it will be transferred to your computer.

~ If the file name ends in **.exe**, then it's likely a self-extracting archive. Locate it using Windows Explorer and double-click on it. It will either install itself—follow the instructions—or it will extract its parts into the current directory.

~ If the file name ends in **.zip**, then you have to use a program such as PKZIP or WinZip to extract the components. You usually select the folder or directory in which they will go. To obtain a copy of PKZIP or WinZip, see Chapter 12.

~ In either case, look for a file with a name similar to **Readme** or **Instructions** to see what steps you need to take to install the program or to work with the files in the package. In many cases, the extracted files need to go through some other processing by a program named **Setup** before they are ready to use.

~ Be sure to check the program and associated files for computer viruses. Many of the archives check files for viruses before making them available to the public, but you ought to check them yourself.

Acquiring Antivirus Software

You will also want a program that checks files for computer viruses. Several are available, and you can get shareware versions to evaluate and determine which you like best. One, F-PROT, makes its software free to individuals; commercial customers or organizations must pay for using it. Here are three sites that offer shareware versions of their antivirus and virus protection software:

Antivirus Shareware	URL
F-PROT, Data Fellows	**http://www.datafellows.com/ download-purchase/tools.html**
Norton AntiVirus, Symantec	**http://www.symantec.com/avcenter**
VirusScan, McAfee	**http://www.mcafee.com/ centers/anti-virus**

If you don't have an antivirus program on your computer, visit one of the sites, download the most recent version, and install it. Any of the antivirus programs from the sites listed above come as compressed packages. After you download one of these, you'll need to use the software to uncompress and extract the files into a folder. Once you have done that, look for a file with a name such as **Readme** to get instructions on how to install the software. In many cases, you can install the programs on your system by clicking on an application or program in the folder named **Setup**. You follow the same steps for installing these programs as for almost any other software that you download.

Using Software Archives and FTP Search Services

In an earlier section of this chapter, we listed the URLs of some lists of software archives or sites in which you find software to download through FTP.

What You'll Find in the Archives

Software archives maintain their own collections of files, and FTP archives have hyperlinks to the files, which are usually stored at the Web site for the person or organization that markets the software. Both types include a search form so you can search the collection for files, and several also have reviews, descriptions, and links to the software arranged into categories so you can browse the items accessible through the archive.

The files are usually arranged in categories according to the type of software, such as games, Internet, utilities, and personal use. Sometimes they are also arranged according to the type of operating system they're designed for, such as MS-DOS, Windows 3.x, Windows 95/98/NT, or Macintosh.

Some archives are dedicated to programs for a particular operating system, and some only to Internet software. Two examples are

WinFiles.com, which specializes in software for Windows systems, and TUCOWS, which has software to be used for working with the Internet. ZDNet Software Library is a good example of a full-featured software archive with extensive reviews of many of the items it lists.

General Archive	URL
DOWNLOAD.COM	http://www.download.com
File Mine	http://www.filemine.com
Shareware.com	http://www.shareware.com
ZDNet Software Library	http://www.zdnet.com/downloads

Specialized Archive	URL
Stroud's Consummate Winsock Applications	http://cws.internet.com
TUCOWS	http://tucows.com
WinFiles.com	http://www.winfiles.com

Before You Download

We're going to demonstrate downloading and installing some software in Activity 13.1. Before you download software, you need to answer a few questions for yourself.

Is the program appropriate for my computer system?
Most of the software archives include a description of the system requirements for the software you'll download. Check that you have enough memory (RAM) to run the program (some require 16 megabytes to run properly) and that you have the correct operating system. Software that's developed for a Windows 95/98 or Windows NT system won't work properly if it's installed on a system running Windows 3.1 or on a Macintosh system.

Do I have enough storage space on my disk to hold the software?
Again, look at the system requirements to see that you have enough disk space to hold the new program along with your other software.

Do I meet the licensing requirements?
Most software is available as shareware to anyone, but some software is available only to educational or nonprofit institutions. The software will likely come with a licensing agreement; you'll need to read this and decide whether to consent to it.

Do I have permission to install the software?

If you're working on your home computer, then there's probably no problem. However, if you're working on a computer that's owned by your school or company—and probably being shared by others—check local policies to see whether you may install new software on the computer.

Do I have the software I need to install the software I downloaded?

Check to see if you have the proper software, such as PKZIP or WinZip, to extract the parts of the package. Oftentimes, this will be stated in the description of the software. Also look at the name of the package. If it ends with **.zip**, then you'll need a program such as the one we've mentioned to install it. For information on obtaining PKZIP or WinZip, see Chapter 12.

Will the software have a detrimental impact on other software on my computer?

This isn't always easy to answer until the software is installed, in which case it may be too late. Read as much as you can about the software before installing it to see if it will have a detrimental impact on existing programs or system configuration. Be sure you can check it for viruses before installing it.

Will I be able to "uninstall" the program if things don't go well?

Most software nowadays comes with a program that makes it easy to remove the primary program and all associated files if and when you need to do this.

Now we'll go through some of the details involved in downloading and installing software from an archive.

> Remember that the Web is always changing and that your results may differ from those shown here. Don't let this confuse you. The activities demonstrate fundamental skills. These skills don't change, even though the number of results obtained or the actual screens may look very different.

LOCATING AND DOWNLOADING AN MP3 PLAYER AND MP3 FILES

Overview

In Chapter 12 we discussed the legal aspects of downloading and copying information from the Internet, using MP3 as an example of a file type that is frequently pirated and downloaded illegally. Not all MP3 files are illegally placed on the Web. There are many artists who regularly make their music available on the Web for public use. This is a convenient way for relatively new musicians to get noticed and listened to. We understand the allure of being able to play music on your computer and want to show you how to download a player that will allow you to play MP3 files. We will find an MP3 player in a software archive and download it from there. We will then locate a piece of music from an MP3 library that lists legal MP3s. We will show you how to download the file to your computer and play the music on your MP3 player. Here are the steps we'll follow:

1. Go to the home page for ZDNet Downloads.
2. Browse the directory for MP3 players.
3. Select an MP3 player to download and check its system requirements.
4. Download the MP3 player.
5. Search an MP3 library for an MP3 to download.
6. Download an MP3.
7. Open the MP3 player.
8. Play the music using the MP3 player.

Details

We'll assume that the Web browser is started and displayed on the screen. We are using Internet Explorer for this activity, but Netscape will work much the same.

1. Go to the home page for ZDNet Downloads.

> Click on the address bar, type **http://www.zdnet.com/downloads**, and press **Enter**.

The ZDNet Downloads directory is a large, well-organized, and well-maintained software archive. The home page appears in Figure 13.2.

Figure 13.2   The Home Page for ZDNet Downloads

We see from the home page that we can search or browse the archive either by type of software or by type of computer system. Several types of software and individual programs are listed. We also note there's a Help hyperlink and a hyperlink called the EZ Download Guide. We know from using other search services that it's a good idea to click on **Help** or any type of search guide available on the service's home page and do some reading before we continue.

(Do it)′ Click on the hyperlink **EZ Download Guide**.

We'll follow the steps listed there after we select the software to download. In the next step we'll browse the directory for MP3 players, but it's worth spending a little time looking at some of the other categories as well.

2. Browse the directory for MP3 players.

Note in Figure 13.2 that there is a category entitled MP3 Central. This appears to be the category where we'll find MP3 players. Note that we could also search for MP3 players by typing **mp3 players** in the search form.

(Do it)′ Click on **MP3 Central**.

(Do it)′ In the window that appears, find a hyperlink entitled **Top 50 MP3 Tools**, and click on it.

Your window will look similar to the one shown in Figure 13.3.

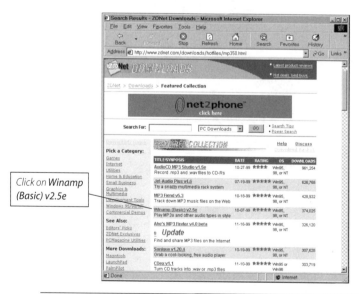

Figure 13.3   A List of the Most Popular MP3 Players According to ZDNet

3. Select an MP3 player to download and check its system require-ments.

As you can see from this list, there are several MP3 players to choose from. Winamp catches our eye, as we have heard about this player from friends and have read about it in other sources. Let's see what Winamp is all about.

(Do it) Click on **Winamp (Basic) v2.5e**, as shown in Figure 13.3.

Figure 13.4 shows the information that ZDNet provides about Winamp. Take some time to read the system requirements, downloads to date, compressed file size, and other facts. We see that Winamp is designed to run on a computer that uses a Windows operating system and that in compressed form it takes up 602,112 bytes. Once it is expanded, we can expect it to take up about twice as much space, so we'll need to decide if we have enough disk space to install it. If we feel the software will be useful to us, and it will run on our computer, we can start downloading it.

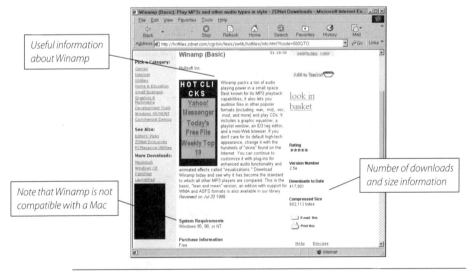

Figure 13.4   Information About Winamp

4. Download the MP3 player.

We're going to follow the steps in the ZDNet download guide.

(Do it) First we'll create a folder to hold the package. We're using Windows 98, so the first thing we'll do is activate Windows Explorer by clicking on the **Start** button, selecting **Programs**, and then choosing **Windows Explorer**.

(Do it) We'll use Windows Explorer to display the contents of Drive C:. Click on **File** in the menu bar, select **New**, and then click on **Folder**.

The window you'll see appears in Figure 13.5. If you are using other software to manage your files, read the instructions in the download guide.

*Click on **File**, choose **New**, and select **Folder***

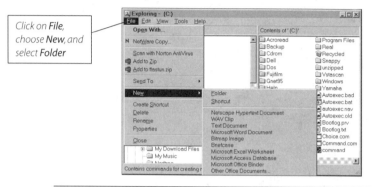

Figure 13.5   Creating a New Folder Using Windows Explorer

A new folder is created. We'll name it **WinAmp**.

Type **WinAmp** for the folder's name and press **Enter**.

Now we're ready for the second step in the download process. We can use the browser to transfer the file from ZDNet Downloads to our system. Be sure the Web page shown in Figure 13.4 is still available.

Return to the browser window and click on the hyperlink **Download Now**.

The browser will attempt to transfer the file to your computer using FTP. You'll likely get a dialog box message such as "unknown file type" or some other warning. In any case, you'll want to click on a button that lets you save the file to disk. Figure 13.6 shows the dialog box that appeared in the browser we are using (Internet Explorer).

Make sure you save to disk

Click OK

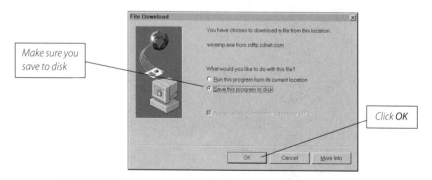

Figure 13.6   The File Download Dialog Box

You want to save the file to your disk. Click on a button that lets you do this. A Save As dialog box will appear.

Use the controls in the Save As dialog box to select the folder **WinAmp**, as shown in Figure 13.7. Then click on **Save**.

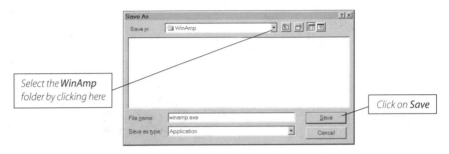

Select the **WinAmp** folder by clicking here

Click on **Save**

Figure 13.7   The Save As Dialog Box with WinAmp as the Selected Folder

A window entitled "Saving Location" pops up on the screen to show the estimated time it will take to download the file and the progress of the download. Depending on the speed of your modem, how busy the server is at ZDNet, and current Internet traffic, it could take a few minutes or longer (up to an hour in extreme cases) to download the file. Figure 13.8 shows the "Download complete" box. It shows that the program is now completed loaded on your computer.

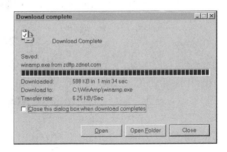

Figure 13.8   The "Download complete" Dialog Box

 Close the "Download complete" box by clicking on **Close**. It may close automatically.

Now we're ready to install the MP3 player. The downloaded file will be in the **WinAmp** folder we created on Drive C:. To see what it looks like, use Windows Explorer to open the folder **WinAmp**. If you minimized the Windows Explorer window, click on its icon in the taskbar (next to the Start button).

 Double-click on the **WinAmp** folder.

The contents indicate that the file is an executable file, as shown in Figure 13.9. All we need to do is double-click on the file name **winamp.exe**, and Winamp will begin its installation.

Double-click on the file **winamp.exe**.

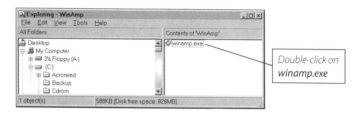

Figure 13.9   Using Explorer to Select **winamp.exe**

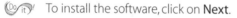

After double-clicking on **winamp.exe**, a program will start to lead us through the installation process. We will take all the usual options as the installation or setup program proceeds. The first thing you'll be asked to do is read a license agreement, as shown in Figure 13.10.

Click on the box next to "I have read and agree to the terms of this license agreement."

To install the software, click on **Next**.

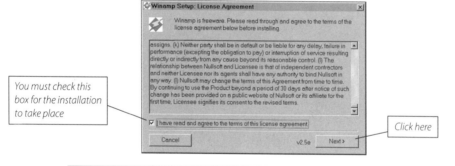

Figure 13.10   The License Agreement for Winamp

You will click on the **Next** button as you go through the setup process. You will also be shown the Winamp settings that you may accept or not. One of the settings is "Add icon to desktop." All of the settings are recommended, so we'll keep all of them. When the setup program finishes, Winamp will be installed in the folder **C:\Program Files\winamp**, and Winamp will be added as an icon to your desktop. At the end of the process, a **Run Winamp** button will be provided, which you will be instructed to select.

Click on **Run Winamp**.

The Winamp player will appear on your desktop. You can close the player by clicking the **X** in the upper-right corner.

One more thing: Now that we've installed Winamp, we don't need the files in the folder **C:\WinAmp** anymore. It's safe to delete this folder at this point.

Now let's locate some music to play on the player!

5. Search an MP3 library for an MP3 to download.

First we need to find an MP3 library to search. One good place to go for a listing of MP3 libraries is the Librarians' Index to the Internet, **http://lii.org**. We can find a collection of MP3 libraries by entering **mp3** in the search form. One of the libraries listed is MP3.com. This is what the reviewer had to say about MP3.com:

MP3.com—**http://www.mp3.com**

"This site is dedicated to the mp3 file format for high quality compressed sound files. It has explanations and tips for beginners, software reviews, hardware information, links to thousands of legitimate music downloads in many different categories of music, and more."

In the address bar, type the URL for MP3.com, **http://mp3.com**, and press **Enter**.

Figure 13.11 shows the home page. Note that MP3.com is arranged much like a regular directory that we are familiar with. You can search the database or browse the subject categories. We are interested in downloading a piece of music by our favorite classical composer, Wolfgang Mozart.

Type **mozart** in the search form and click on **Search**.

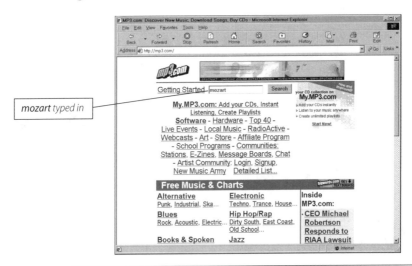

Figure 13.11   MP3.com, a Music Library

Figure 13.12 shows a portion of the results of this search. The third item interests us the most, so we'll click on its hyperlink to find out more about it.

 Click on **Spotlight Mozart**, as shown in Figure 13.12.

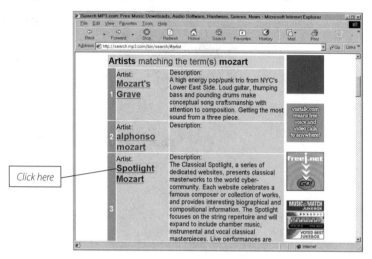

Figure 13.12   The Results of a Search for Mozart in MP3.com

6. **Download an MP3.**

Figure 13.13 shows the information about a Mozart piece that is part of Spotlight Mozart. Note that if you clicked on **Play**, you could hear the music in a few seconds. To download the music to your computer, you'll need to click on the **Download** hyperlink. A simple click will begin the download process.

 Click on **Download**, as shown in Figure 13.13.

 **MORE INFORMATION ABOUT MP3s**

MP3 libraries:
- ～ EMusic.com, **http://emusic.com**
- ～ Listen.com, **http://listen.com**
- ～ Lycos Music, **http://music. lycos.com**

Making your own MP3s:
- ～ Audiograbber, **http://www. audiograbber.com-us.net**
- ～ MusicMatch Jukebox, **http:// www.musicmatch.com**
- ～ MP3 - A CNET Topic Center, **http://home.cnet.com/ category/0-4004.html**
- ～ Easy CD-DA Extractor, **http:// www.poikosoft.com/cdda**

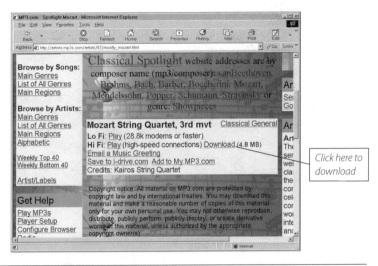

Figure 13.13   Mozart String Quartet, 3rd Movement

You may be asked to provide your email address or zip code information. You must do this in order for the download to proceed.

Do it! After you have filled in the required information, click on **continue
download**.

Just as when we downloaded the MP3 player, your browser will give
you a choice of whether you want to open the file in the current
location or if you want to save it to a disk. You want to save it
to a disk.

Do it! Make sure the radio button next to **Save this file to disk** is selected,
and click on **OK**, as shown in Figure 13.14.

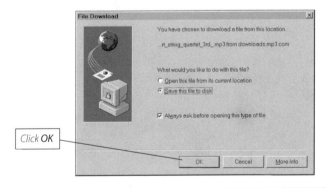

Figure 13.14   The Beginning of the MP3 Download

A Save As dialog box will pop up. Winamp should appear in the Save
in field, and the MP3 file name will appear in the File name field. This
will allow the MP3 file to be saved in the Winamp folder.

 Click on **Save**, as shown in Figure 13.15.

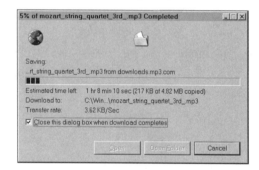

Figure 13.15   The MP3 File Will Be Saved in the Winamp Folder

Figure 13.16 shows the MP3 download in process. Depending on the speed of your modem and current Internet traffic, it could take a minute or 30 or more minutes.

Figure 13.16   Saving the MP3, with the Download Progress Indicated

7. **Open the MP3 player.**

You should notice a Winamp icon on your desktop.

If you have this icon, simply click on it. If you don't have the icon, go to **Start**, choose **Programs**, and find **Winamp**.

Your Winamp player will look like the one in Figure 13.17.

Don't like the look of your MP3 player? You can choose from thousands of "skins" to change your player's surface. Read about it at Winamp's home page, **http://www.winamp.com**.

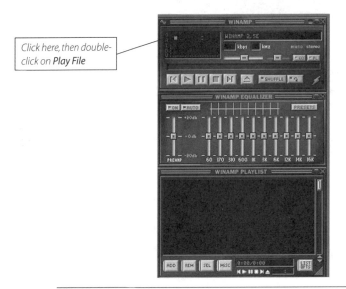

Click here, then double-click on Play File

Figure 13.17   The WinAmp Player: How It Looks on Your Desktop When Opened

8. Play the music using the MP3 player.

(Do it)!   Click on the icon in the upper-left corner of the Winamp player, choose **Play File**, and double-click.

An Open file(s) box will pop up, like the one shown in Figure 13.18.

(Do it)!   Click on **Open**.

The Mozart String Quartet 3rd Movement will open in the Winamp player.

(Do it)!   To play the music, you'll need to use the controls on the face of the player; for example, the right-facing arrow would be clicked on to play. The MP3 player is designed to resemble a tape or CD player, so it should be familiar to you.

Highlight the MP3 file

Click Open and the music will play

Figure 13.18   Playing an MP3 on Your MP3 Player

Wasn't that fun?

END OF ACTIVITY 13.1

In Activity 13.1, we downloaded and installed a program from a software archive. In this case, the software we downloaded was an MP3 player. We also downloaded a file from an MP3 music directory to our computer. The steps we followed were fairly typical, although the details can change, depending on the browser used, the program downloaded, and the software archive or library selected.

Using an FTP Client Program

In the examples and activities discussed so far in this chapter, we have used FTP through the Web browser. That may be all you need to search for and retrieve information from the Web or Internet using FTP. Sometimes, though, you may want to use an FTP program that's separate from the browser. To use an FTP program this way, you'll still need an Internet connection from your computer. The program you run will download files from a server or upload files from your computer to a server. The FTP program you use acts as a client.

When you work with an FTP client to contact another computer (called the *server* or *host*), you'll need to have certain pieces of information. The following list explains what you must know.

You'll need the Internet *domain name* or address of the server, or host.
The client uses the domain name to contact the server. Earlier in the chapter, in the section "FTP Overview," we pointed out the domain name portion of a URL that implies the use of FTP.

If you're going to be downloading software, you'll need a user name and a password on the host.
If you're using anonymous FTP, the user name is *anonymous* and the password is your email address. If you're going to download some files from your user account on the server system, you'll use your assigned user name and password.

If you're going to be uploading files to another computer, you'll need a user name and password on the host.
The user name and password enable you to upload files to a directory or folder that isn't necessarily available to the public.

Of course, you'll also need an FTP client for your computer. Several are available as shareware, but one in particular is highly recommended. It's WS_FTP, and it's free for personal use. To get a copy appropriate for your system, go to CNET's DOWNLOAD.COM, **http://download.cnet.com/downloads**, and search for WS_FTP. You can download the program from CNET.

We'll briefly go over how to use WS_FTP, but look at some of these guides for more help when you're ready. First download and install the appropriate version of the software from CNET. Use the same techniques discussed in Activity 13.1.

> **Fy** Several very good guides to using WS_FTP are available on the Web. Here's a short list:
>
> ~ "How to Use WS_FTP"
> **http://www.albany.edu/ library/internet/ws_ftp.html**
> ~ "Installing and Configuring WS_FTP"
> **http://usats.com/ learn/ftp.shtml**

Once the program is installed, start it by selecting it from the Start menu, clicking on an icon on your desktop, or clicking on an icon in a folder. Which one of these you choose depends on how it was installed. When it starts, a session profile pops onto the screen.

Figure 13.19 shows a session profile for connecting to a system with the host name (same as the domain name) **library.mwc.edu**. The user ID or login name for this user is **khartman**. A password isn't typed in here; it will be typed in when the host system is contacted. If a password were saved with this profile, then anyone using the computer could access the files belonging to user **khartman** on **library.mwc.edu**. If this were to be an anonymous FTP session, then the box labeled **Anonymous** would be checked. You can select other servers with different profiles by clicking on the button to the right of the profile name.

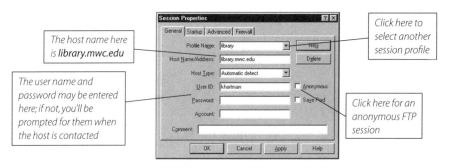

Figure 13.19   A Sample Session Profile for WS_FTP

To contact the host, click on the button labeled **OK**. Acting as a client, WS_FTP attempts to contact the host system. Another window pops up that shows whether the host has been contacted. The user then has control over the transfer of files.

Figure 13.20 shows the window that appears when WS_FTP starts an FTP session with **library.mwc.edu**. The left column lists the files in the current folder of your computer, the client. The right column lists the files in the directory with which you've connected on the host computer.

You can choose a file to transfer by selecting it from the appropriate column. You'll see that there are scroll bars to let you scroll through the list of files and directories on both the client and host computers. In each column, the subdirectories of the current directory are listed in the upper panel and the files are listed in the lower panel.

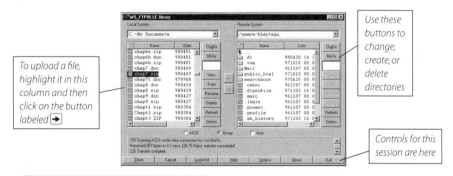

To upload a file, highlight it in this column and then click on the button labeled [→]

Use these buttons to change, create, or delete directories

Controls for this session are here

Figure 13.20   A Session Window for WS_FTP

Suppose we want to upload the file named **chap7.zip** from the client computer—that's the computer we're using—to the host. We highlight **chap7.zip** as shown in Figure 13.20 and click on the button labeled [→]. In doing so, we move the file from the client (listed on the left) to the host (listed on the right).

After we click on [→], another dialog box called Transfer Status pops up showing information about the transfer of the file from one computer to another over the Internet. The items shown include the total number of bytes to transfer, the number transferred so far, the rate of transfer, how much time has been spent so far, and the estimated remaining time. That window will stay on the screen until the transfer is complete. You can stop the transfer by clicking on the **Cancel** button.

To download a file, select the directory on the local system that will hold the file, highlight the name of the file in the list on the right, and click on [←].

WS_FTP is one example of an FTP client. It presents a graphical user interface for transferring files between a client and server. Other client programs have a strictly text-based interface. With those, you use a command **get**, as in **get etiquet.zip**, to download a file. You use the command **put**, as in **put chap1.zip**, to upload a file.

Summary

FTP stands for File Transfer Protocol. With FTP, you can share or copy files from one Internet site to another. Anonymous FTP is the term used for when you copy a file from one computer to another without giving a login name or a password. Collections of files available by anonymous FTP are called anonymous FTP archives.

Literally trillions of bytes of information, programs, and resources are available by anonymous FTP. Archie, one of the first Internet search programs, is a tool specifically designed for searching anonymous FTP archives. When you supply a keyword, the names of the files, directories, and sites in the database are searched. Several other search services and software libraries search a database that holds descriptions and reviews of software available through anonymous FTP. Some of the software archives also have entries arranged by the type of program (for example, antivirus programs) or by the operating system (for example, Windows 95 or Macintosh).

Transferring a file from another computer to the computer you're using is called downloading. That's what you do when you retrieve a program from an FTP archive or software library. Many of the programs depend on a number of auxiliary files to be run and used effectively, such as online help files. These files are put together into a package, and the contents are compressed to allow for easier and faster storage and transfer.

After you retrieve one of these packages of software, you need to process it to extract the components. If the package name ends with **.exe**, then it's a self-extracting archive. Click on the name of the package, and it will unpack itself. If the name ends with **.zip**, you'll need to use a program, such as PKZIP or WinZip.

Once the files are extracted, you will run a program (application) to install the program. To be safe, you'll also want to scan the software for computer viruses before you install it. Look for a file with a name such as **Readme**, and read it before you install the program. It may help you decide whether the program is appropriate for you and your computer system. Sometimes the **Readme** file is available after installing the program. Finally, look for a program—often named **Setup** or **Install**—that you'll run to install the program.

An FTP client program is one that you run on your computer to exchange files with another computer that acts as the host, or server. This program is not usually part of a Web browser. To access another computer through FTP, you need to give the client program the Internet domain name for the host computer. That's the part of the URL that immediately follows **ftp://**. For example, in the URL **ftp://ftp. jpl.nasa.gov/pub/images/browse/marglobe.gif**, the domain name is **ftp.jpl.nasa.gov**. Once connected, you can upload files from your computer to the host or download files from the host to your computer. You can do either one by using a graphical interface provided by the client or by using the commands **put** and **get**.

There are many ways to retrieve information you have found on the Internet. You can save images and insert them into word-processing documents on your computer or into PowerPoint presentations. You can also print or save portions of Web pages and download data into spreadsheets. This chapter provided step-by-step instructions for accomplishing many of these procedures.

Selected Terms Used in This Chapter

anonymous FTP	FTP archive
domain name	shareware
download	upload
freeware	

Exercises and Projects

This set of exercises or projects is designed to give you practice using different techniques of retrieving information that were covered in this chapter. In some exercises, you will be asked to find the location, or URL, of similar files or resources. To do that, feel free to use any of the search services with which you're familiar.

1. Use your Web browser to retrieve the document with the URL **ftp://ftp.coriolis.com/pub/VDM/ewriter.htm**.
   a. What is the document about?
   b. What is the domain name of the site being contacted?
   c. What protocol is used to transfer the file? Explain.
   d. What language is the document written in?

2. Retrieve a copy of "Anonymous FTP Frequently Asked Questions (FAQ) List," **ftp://rtfm.mit.edu/pub/usenet-by-group/news.answers/ftp-list/faq**. Put it in your bookmark list.
   a. The FAQ contains an answer to this question: "What types of FTP information are available?" Write a summary of the answer.
   b. Give a brief synopsis of the copyright notice you see when you connect by anonymous FTP to the directory **pub/usenet-by-group at rtfm.mit.edu**.

3. Go to the FTP site with the URL **ftp://ftp.happypuppy.com**. What kind of files does this site provide? What are cheats?

4. Retrieve a copy of the file with the URL **ftp://nic.merit.edu/introducing.the.internet/answers.to.new.user.questions**. Using that file, write a one- or two-sentence answer to each of the following questions.
   a. What is the difference between the *Internet* and an *internet*?

b. What is an advantage of the domain name system (DNS)?

c. What is the definition of *TCP/IP*?

5. Using the images available through the URL **ftp://ftp.jpl.nasa.gov/ pub/images/browse**, collect the URLs for images of all the planets in the solar system. Put them in one bookmark folder.

6. Go to the software archive ZDNet Downloads, **http://www.zdnet. com/downloads**, and search for a program that lets you experience Neko.

7. Do you need an alarm while you're using your computer? Again go to the software archive ZDNet Downloads, **http://www.zdnet.com/ downloads**. This time search for programs that act as alarm clocks. Choose one program to download, and explain why you made that choice. Download and install the program. Did it work as you anticipated it would? If you're not happy with it, remove it from your computer system.

8. Go to the software archive File Mine, **http://www.filemine.com**, and search for a program that deals with math games, specifically fractions. Choose one program to download, and explain why you made that choice. Download and install the program. Did it work as you anticipated it would? If you're not happy with it, remove it from your computer system.

9. In Exercises 7 and 8 we used two different archives. Write a few sentences comparing the features of the two. Which do you prefer? Why?

10. Go to CNET.com, **http://home.cnet.com**, and search for information using FTP as the keyword. Find out and list the FTP clients that CNET recommends. What are some of the special features that make these FTP clients so attractive? Locate an FTP message board from this location and see if anyone has offered an opinion on these recommended FTP clients. If so, include information from one of the opinions in your answer. From this same site, find the list of the top 10 FTP sites and list the top five.

11. Assuming you have downloaded an MP3 player to your computer, go to MP3.com and search for music by the rock group Skywave. Describe the steps you took to download the MP3 file and play the music successfully. Which song did you choose?

Chapter 14

PUTTING

INFORMATION ON

THE WEB

The growth of the Internet and the Web increases the opportunities to make information available to a wide audience. This is no accident—the structure of the Internet, the protocols (HTTP, for example), and HTML are all designed so they may be used by anyone. We can contribute to the Internet and the World Wide Web because the protocols that form the technical basis for the Internet treat all networks as equal. This is different from broadcast media such as radio and TV where there's a definite separation between systems that transmit information and those that receive it. Participation and involvement have always been important parts of the culture and social aspects of the Internet.

It's common nowadays to have a Web site. Organizations, businesses, and schools have Web sites; there are Web sites for individuals, clubs, products, movies, and political parties; there are a large number of sites that deal with scientific and other scholarly research, technical issues, and health issues; and there are some sites that are part of the Web just for fun!

In this and the next two chapters we'll spend some time dealing with the issues related to designing, writing, constructing, installing, and evaluating Web pages and Web sites. These are important topics because the Web is becoming one of the preferred means of distributing information and conducting business. Perhaps you've already written or designed Web pages. If not, it is very likely that you will write a Web page for a personal or business reason in the near future. In any case, your use of the Web—as both a consumer and a producer—will increase in the future. Knowing more about how Web pages are constructed, how their components affect the client and the server, and what most people consider appropriate and of high quality will help you be both a better producer and consumer of information on the Internet. This is the kind of stuff that you need to know! Here's the plan for the following two chapters:

∼ Chapter 15 will deal with HTML—what you need to know to write a Web page.

∼ Chapter 16 will deal with adding multimedia elements and some interactive elements to your Web pages.

Goals/Objectives

- Understand the concepts associated with putting information on the World Wide Web

- Know the primary issues related to designing a Web page and a Web site

- Know some of the prevalent technologies used for constructing Web pages and Web sites

- Be able to evaluate a Web page or a Web site

- Know the means and resources to announce and publicize a Web site

Topics

- An Overview of Concepts Related to Writing and Publishing a Web Page

- Designing a Web Page

- Designing a Web Site

- Technologies Used to Create a Web Page

- Evaluating the Quality of a Web Page or Web Site

- Putting Your Information on the Web

- Publicizing a Web Page—Getting It Noticed

An Overview of Concepts Related to Writing and Publishing a Web Page

The tremendous increase in the number of resources on the Internet and in the use of the Internet in recent years has been in part due to the use of graphical Web browsers and the ease with which one can make information available as a Web page or Web site. The release of the first popular Web browser with a graphical user interface, Mosaic, in 1993 marked the beginning of a period of astounding growth for the Internet. For example, the number of host systems went from approximately 2 million in 1993 to almost 60 million in the beginning of 2000. There were essentially only a handful of Web pages available in the early part of 1993 and estimates at the time of this writing put the number of Web pages at over 1 billion, with thousands being added each day.

Graphical Web browsers are available at little or no cost, they are relatively easy to use, and they can display information using different fonts, colors, and media. The protocol for exchanging information on the Web, HTTP, supports hypertext and hypermedia, which make for interesting, intuitive, and useful ways of arranging information. The language used to specify the content of Web pages (HTML) is not difficult to learn, and it makes it possible to construct attractive, well-designed documents (Web pages). The growth of the Internet and the way information can be displayed using a Web browser have caught the interest of the media and commercial interests, which further fuels the growth.

Before going further let's review some of what we've said about the technical aspects of Web pages in previous chapters. Having a good understanding of what a Web page is and how it's handled by the client and the server will help us when we construct, design, and discuss Web pages.

Fy INTERNET AND WEB STATISTICS

~ "CyberAtlas"
    http://cyberatlas.internet.com
~ "Internet Domain Survey"
    http://www.isc.org/ds
~ "Media Metrix"
    http://www.mediametrix.com
~ "Nua Internet Surveys"
    http://www.nua.ie/surveys

~ Web pages are files in which **HTML** (Hypertext Markup Language) is used to specify the format of the Web page, images to be displayed, hyperlinks, and possibly other elements.

~ A Web browser interprets the HTML in the file and then displays the Web page. The HTML gives the browser information about how to display or represent information in the file.

~ In order to make a file part of the Web and available to anyone on the Internet, the file has to be stored on a computer that acts as a Web server. That means it's connected to the Internet and running Web server software. The file is then available to anyone on the Internet through its URL, which contains the **Internet domain name** of the computer that hosts the Web server. In many cases the file is viewed as a Web page by using a Web browser. The Web page that lists Ernest Ackermann's office hours, for example, is in a file named **offhrs.html** in his home Web directory on the computer whose Internet domain name is **www1.mwc.edu**. This is reflected in its URL, **http://www1.mwc.edu/ ~ ernie/offhrs.html**.

~ The Web browser acts as a client and sends requests to the Web server for the files that are displayed as Web pages. There are several events that occur when a Web page is requested. Here are the four primary events:

1. You click on a hyperlink or type a URL in the location field.
2. The browser formulates a request to a Web server. The server is software that is running on a computer whose Internet domain name is the part of the URL after the first // and before

the first / (slash). For example, if you use the URL **http://www.webliminal.com/search/10steps.html**, then a request for a Web page is sent from your browser to the computer whose Internet domain name is **www.webliminal.com**.

3. The server processes the request. If it's possible, it sends the file that represents the Web page that you requested to the browser.

4. The browser interprets the contents of the file and displays the Web page.

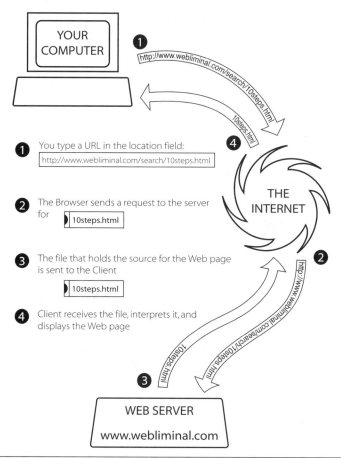

Figure 14.1   How Servers and Clients Work with Each Other

Now on to talking about design issues.

Designing a Web Page

A Web page is an electronic publication. It's a means for communicating ideas and providing services on the Internet. Creating an effective Web page—one that makes an impact on a reader and communicates your message—involves coming up with appropriate content, suitable two-dimensional design or layout, and appropriate use of multimedia. These components have to be put together in a way that takes into account the fact that someone will be viewing and using your information with a Web browser on the Internet. This means that an understanding of technical issues related to the Internet and the ways a browser displays information is also involved. Here are the major points you need to consider when designing a Web page.

Technical Issues Affecting Web Design: Color & Resolution

One difficulty with designing a Web page is that a number of technical conditions that affect the way a page looks can't be controlled—the size and type of font set by the user, the number of colors displayed on a monitor, and the screen resolution of a monitor. Users can set preferences on their Web browsers controlling the type and size of font used to display text. So text that you design to look "just right" in terms of size and placement may appear differently to different users.

When you design you have no control over the type of monitor or display used to view your Web page. Some monitors will be set to display 16 colors, some 256 colors, and some millions of colors. An image that looks great on a display capable of displaying lots of colors may not look very good when fewer colors are available. If you're designing for a general audience then stick with the 216 colors that both Netscape and Internet Explorer use. Those colors are also displayed by both Macs and PCs.

The screen resolution or number of pixels in the viewing window affects the way a Web

Fy BROWSER-SAFE COLORS

~ "The Browser-Safe Color Palette," http://www.lynda.com/hex.html, by Lynda Weinman, an expert on design. She covers the topic of color representation in more detail and her page has links to others that show the colors.

~ "In Design School, They Promised No Math: A Web color primer," http://webreview.com/pub/97/11/28/tools/index.html, by Bob Schmitt

~ "Color Tables," http://mrlxp2.mrl.uiuc.edu/~www/rgbtbl.html, by Gernot Metze

page appears. Images and text have their dimensions ultimately specified in terms of pixels regardless of what's being used to view them. The greater the number of pixels, the finer the resolution. An image on a screen with a resolution of 1,024 by 768 pixels will generally look better and be sharper than on a screen with a resolution of 800 by 600 pixels or 640 by 480 pixels. An image that's 300 by 400 pixels, say, will appear much smaller on a screen whose resolution is 1,024 by 768 pixels than it will appear on a screen with a resolution of 640 by 480 pixels. Furthermore, the size of the browser window can be changed by the user. So as you design a page you need to think about what it will look like on different types of monitors and with different user configurations.

A middle-of-the-road approach is to design a Web page that uses the browser-safe color palette and looks good on a monitor that has a resolution of 800 by 600 pixels. Compromises have to be made because it's impossible to predict the type of monitor used and the way the Web browser options are set.

Design Considerations

There's no substitute for planning and design. Take the time to think about what you want to do and how you can accomplish it. Virtually everyone who writes about Web page design stresses the importance of developing and including good content. Some people may be attracted by a flashy Web page, but they're not likely to come back unless the page has the content they need. We'll look at several design considerations here.

Develop a clear statement of the purpose of the Web page or Web site.
What do you want to accomplish through your Web page? Do you want to write a personal Web page, provide information about a topic, describe a concept or process, serve as a gateway to other information, sell a product, or advocate a cause? These aren't the only things you may want to accomplish. What's important is that you spend some time coming up with the purpose and objective of your Web page.

Identify your audience.
Identifying the audience helps you to develop the proper content and design. Do you expect the page or topic to appeal to people in a specific age group? Will the readers likely be experienced Internet or computer users? Can you make any assumptions about the type of network or computer equipment your readers will have? These are just some of the questions you'll need to consider. For example, suppose the topic is international trade agreements. If the target audience is people in the banking industry, then the Web page or Web site will probably be markedly different from one designed for high school students.

Take a look at other sites or pages that have a similar purpose.
See what others have done for Web pages that have a purpose similar to
yours. Make a note of appealing style elements and useful features. Here's
a list of some Web sites arranged by their purpose.

Purpose	Title	URL
Personal home page	"Welcome to Karen Hartman's home page"	http://www.library.mwc.edu/ ~ khartman
Explain a topic or concept	"The Trail You Leave On the Web"	http://www.webliminal.com/trail.html
Explain a process	"Basic Search Strategy: The Ten Steps"	http://www.webliminal.com/search/10steps.htm
Serve as a gateway to other information	"Guides to HTML"	http://www.hypernews.org/HyperNews/get/www/html/guides.html
Provide information about a topic	"Directories and Virtual Libraries"	http://www.webliminal.com/search/search-web04.html
Sell a product	"Amazon.com"	http://www.amazon.com
Advocate a cause	"Support Our Effort to Stop Spam!"	http://www.cauce.org/join.html
Act as a portal	"Excite"	http://www.excite.com

Identify the material you will use to accomplish your purpose.
Focus on the content you'll be providing in the Web page or Web site.
Develop an outline for the Web page. Think about the major topics,
images, or hyperlinks. Then develop each of these with enough detail so
that they can be completed after making final design decisions.

**Establish the layout or format of the Web page. Adopt a uniform and
appropriate style for a single Web page and for all the Web pages in
the Web site.**
Think about the structure of the Web page. If the page can't be displayed
in one window, you'll want to give important information a prominent
position at the top of the page, and you'll probably want to provide a table
of contents or links to other parts of the document or other pages in your
site. See, for example, the Web page "Internet Today! Finding Information," **http://www.webliminal.com/internet-today/it-chap04.html.**

Include an email address for comments, the name of the author/ designer/producer, the URL for the page, and the date the Web page was last modified. These items are usually placed at the bottom of the Web page. The email address is there in case someone reading the page has a question or suggestion about the Web page or its content. Web pages ought to contain the name(s) of the person(s) responsible for developing the Web page. This gives credit and responsibility where they are due. The URL for the page is included so that someone reading it will know how to reach it on the Web in case the page is printed or reproduced in some other manner. Knowing when something was changed last is helpful for readers to keep track of the most recent version of a document, and it also gives an indication of the timeliness of the content of the Web page.

Consider drawing a design or diagram that shows the layout of the pages. Figure 14.2 shows two possible layout schemes. In any case, keep the design simple. It will be easier for you to do well, and it will be easier for your readers to deal with.

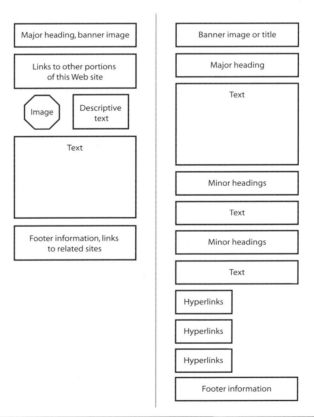

Figure 14.2   Page Layouts for Text and Images on a Web Page

Use relatively small images and limit the number of images in your Web page.

The issue here is the amount of time it will take to retrieve the Web page. Think about the type of equipment that your readers will be using to view your Web page.

It usually takes many more bytes to represent an image than text. That means it may take a relatively long time for someone to view a Web page that has a number of images or a large image. Let's calculate how long it would take to display an image whose size is 63 kilobytes being received on a computer that's using a 56.7K (bits per second) modem to connect to the Internet. The modem can receive information at a rate of roughly 56,700 bits per second. Since each byte consists of 8 bits, the modem can receive information at $56,700/8 = 7,087.5$ bytes per second. It doesn't seem to make sense to talk about a half byte here so let's say that information is received at a maximum speed of 7,000 bytes per second. Since the size of the file holding the image is approximately 63,000 bytes, it would take 63,000/7,000 or approximately 9 seconds to deliver the image to the browser. Notice we're also ignoring any delay due to Internet traffic. Some, but not all, folks might be willing to wait that long for the image along with anything else on the Web page. If several images that size are on the page, the wait becomes unreasonable. One thing to do is to represent the image on the page by a small version called a *thumbnail*. Another possibility is to reduce the number of colors in the image (this is also called reducing the color depth) so the image can be represented with fewer bytes. Either can be made into a hyperlink to the full image. This gives access to the image in all its glory, but doesn't necessarily delay viewing of the entire Web page. We talk more about this in Chapter 16.

Use proper spacing and emphasis.

Let the spacing reflect the organization of the text and content of the Web page. If the page has several distinct sections, separate them with a shaded bar (< HR >) or blank spaces. Use bold or italic font appropriately. Section headings ought to be

Fy GUIDES TO WEB DESIGN

~ "Guide to Web Style," **http://www.sun.com/styleguide**, by Rick Levine

~ "Web Style Guide," **http://info.med.yale.edu/caim/manual/index.html**, by Patrick Lynch and Sarah Horton

~ "Art and the Zen of Web Sites," **http://www.tlc-systems.com/webtips.shtml**, by Tony Karp

emphasized, as well as important subsections or words. On the other hand, you need not overdo the use of spacing, shaded bars, and emphasized text. Because something can be done doesn't mean it has to be done.

Use features that most browsers can deal with.

You'll find that some HTML or other features used in developing Web pages are treated differently by different browsers. Try to stick to the HTML and features that most browsers support. They support many of the same tags, but there are differences. There is no universal agreement on which version of HTML to support. The HTML you use in a Web page ought to be chosen to give the page the format you'd like and to be displayed that way by popular Web browsers. The Web site "The Compendium of HTML Elements," **http://www.htmlcompendium.org/ 0frame.htm**, includes a description of all HTML tags and a table for each tag that tells which versions of the popular browsers recognize the tags. Use the information in the compendium to help you choose appropriate HTML. Then view the Web page with several browsers on different types of computers to check the design.

Use proper grammar and spelling.

You want your page to be effective and well received. Grammatical or spelling errors don't give a good impression of you and can turn off a reader pretty quickly.

Go over all the previous items, think more about your purpose, and improve your design.

In some sense the design process goes on and on. The initial design will be implemented as a Web page that can be viewed as a file on one computer system, or perhaps a team on a local network will review it. Use the opportunities you have to revise and improve the design. Eventually a version is placed on the Web, but there is still chance for revision. Some people put icons or images on their pages that state the page is "under construction." The truth is that most pages are often modified and adopt a different design. Plan to revise and reevaluate your work.

Designing a Web Site

A Web site is a collection of Web pages that have a common theme or purpose. For example, most organizations have Web sites whose purpose is to provide information about the organization. The Web site for a college or university will usually consist of a collection of Web sites, one for the institution with links to the Web sites for individual departments and offices. In some cases it's best to take a long document and divide it into several smaller documents with ways to move between them.

Several of the design considerations for a Web page also apply when you're designing a Web site:

∾ Develop a clear statement of the purpose of the Web site.

∾ Identify the material you will use to accomplish your purpose.

~ Identify your audience.

~ Take a look at other sites that have a similar purpose.

When people visit your Web site you'll want them to be able to navigate through the site, get from one page to another, in an easy and logical manner. You'll also want the pages in the site to have a similar format or design so visitors feel that the design of the pages indicates a common theme or sense of place. A third

> **Fy** INFORMATION ARCHITECTURE
>
> The arrangement and accessibility of information in your Web site is very important to visitors.
>
> ~ "Web Architect"
> http://webreview.com/wr/pub/at/Web_Architect
>
> ~ "Information Architecture Tutorial"
> http://hotwired.lycos.com/webmonkey/design/tutorials/tutorial1.html

issue deals with a topic that's described as information architecture—the arrangement of information on your Web site. With this in mind, we can add these things to consider when you're putting together a Web site:

~ Adopt a uniform format or style for the pages that make up the Web site.

~ Make it easy for visitors to find or visit the information that you want them to access.

~ Provide each page with some navigational tools that help them go through the Web site.

There are several ways that the Web pages making up the Web site can be connected. You need to plan the arrangement of pages so that it best suits your needs in accomplishing the purpose you've set for the Web site, and so the arrangement meets your visitors' needs. Here are a few typical arrangements of Web sites:

~ **Hierarchical.** This is useful for information that's easily divided into categories or topic areas.

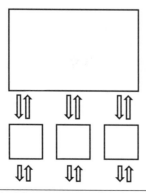

Figure 14.3   A Hierarchical Arrangement of Web Pages

~ **Sequential.** All pages are of equal status. You'd like users to go from one page to another, with each having a link to the first page, which serves as a starting point. The first page often has links to the individual pages; it fulfills the same function as a book's table of contents (except there's a hyperlink to each item listed).

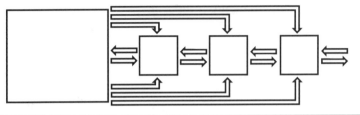

Figure 14.4   A Sequential Arrangement with a Header or First Page

~ **Equality**—All pages have equal status. The pages are connected in a circular arrangement, sometimes called a ring.

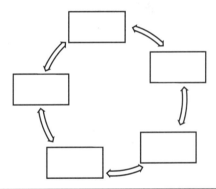

Figure 14.5   Equal Status of All Pages or a Web Ring

You'll find many variations on these themes, and it's your task to determine what is best for your Web site. Many sites use a combination of these. Whatever you choose, remember to keep in mind that you arrange the information in a way that meets the purpose of the Web site and keeps your visitors satisfied.

Technologies Used to Create a Web Page

From our earlier discussions we know that a Web browser uses the text and HTML tags that are in a source file to display a Web page. When we use the term "write a Web page" we mean take the content and design, incorporate the appropriate HTML tags, and put that into a source file. We'll be able to view the source file using a Web browser on our computer, and, when it's ready, make the file accessible to anyone on the Internet.

A source file for a Web page consists entirely of plain, printable characters. There are no special fonts or margins, as is the case in word-processing documents, and it doesn't contain any multimedia items such as images, audio, or video. It is a plain text file, sometimes called an *ASCII* (rhymes with pass-key) file. Because of this plain format you don't necessarily need any special tools or editors to create Web pages. You'll find it's easier to create more complicated Web pages using editors designed for that purpose, but you can get along with any word–processing program or editor that can create text files and can save files with an extension of **.htm** or **.html**. We'll discuss some of the different technologies or tools to use to write Web pages, including:

∾   General-purpose text editors

∾   HTML editors

∾   Tools to convert from other formats to HTML

∾   Create-a-page services

∾   Visual editors

Some of these provide lots of assistance to help you write the HTML for a Web page. That's very helpful sometimes, but as you use these tools you get further removed from the control you have when you write the HTML yourself. Naturally, it's a trade-off. Most experts say that an individual needs to know HTML and should choose a tool that allows her to modify the source HTML when necessary, and use more sophisticated tools for the assistance they may provide.

General-Purpose Text Editors

These are the most basic editors to use to write a Web page. They allow you to write plain text and save it in a file that will be the source for a Web page. An example of this type of editor is Notepad; it's a standard program that is included with Microsoft Windows. (To access it click on **Start**, then click on **Run**, type **notepad**, and press ⏎Enter⏎.) It's useful when you need to write a few Web pages without using some of the more complicated structures of HTML, and it's also useful to make changes to Web pages created with other technologies. We'll use it for the activities in the next chapter. It doesn't provide any HTML-specific help, but it's sufficient for many jobs. To view your Web page you'll have to save it in a file with the extension .htm or .html, and then open the file using the browser.

HTML Editors

These editors focus on the HTML that you use to write a Web page. In these *HTML editors* the toolbar contains icons and buttons that can be used to insert HTML tags. For example there are typically icons to insert the HTML tags necessary to represent text in bold, represent items as a numbered list, and add a hyperlink. There is also typically an item to allow you to preview the Web page that's being created by displaying it in a browser window. Some of these editors are basic (such as DiDa, **http:// home.netvigator.com/ ~ godfreyk/dida**) and good for beginners, while others (such as HomeSite, **http://www.allaire.com/products/homesite/ index.cfm**) are fully featured and useful to Web page writers and developers with more experience.

One editor worthy of note is Arachnophilia. It's good for a beginner and also has a number of features useful to someone with experience. It's available at "Arachnophilia Home Page," **http://www.arachnoid.com/ arachnophilia/index.html**. It's free. As Paul Lutus, the author of Arachnophilia, says, it's not about money. The software is distributed as "careware." Lutus asks only that you stop complaining or whining for whatever period you choose and make young people feel welcome on earth. What a concept!

Tools to Convert from Other Formats to HTML

Recent versions of popular word-processing, spreadsheet, and demonstration programs (such as PowerPoint) contain the tools to convert your work from those special formats to HTML. In Microsoft Word, for example, converting a Word document to HTML is as easy as clicking on **File** in the menu bar and selecting **Save as Html**. Once the document is saved, Word lets you edit it, not with HTML, but using the Web toolbar. In that state you're using Word as a visual Web page editor.

Create-a-Page Services

There are several services on the Web that will help you create a Web page. They are good places to get an idea of what is possible with HTML as well as create a Web page quickly. Netscape has a service "Netscape Page Wizard," **http://home.netscape.com/assist/ net_sites/starter/wizard/index.html**, that you may want to try. Some sites that provide free Web page space such as Tripod, **http://www .tripod.lycos.com**, or GeoCities, **http://geocities.yahoo.com/home**, give their registered members access to tools to create Web pages. Several Internet service providers also make tools available online. When you use these you create a Web page using a visual editor. When the page is complete you save it to your computer or on the server provided by the Web page service.

Visual Editors

These editors have icons, buttons, and menus like the more advanced text-based HTML editors, but they allow you to write a Web page without having to know any HTML or even see any HTML! Actions such as changing fonts, adding colors, inserting images or hyperlinks, or including tables or lists are all available from the menu bar or toolbars. The results of these actions immediately appear in the editor's window. It's similar to composing a document using a word-processing program. These tools are relatively easy to use, but when you use them you're giving up the control you have when you write a Web page using HTML. These editors usually make it possible for you to view and modify the HTML if necessary, but in some cases it may be difficult to do so. (Experts agree there is no perfect visual editor and at some point in the development of a Web site a Web page author will eventually have to modify or insert HTML.) These *visual editors*, like their text-based counterparts, relieve you from many of the details of HTML. This allows you to concentrate more on content and design, and to concentrate on HTML when it's necessary. Some of these visual editors also allow you to create and manage a Web site. Two examples are Microsoft FrontPage, **http://www.microsoft.com/frontpage**, and Macromedia Dreamweaver, **http://www.macromedia.com/software/dreamweaver**. Both Netscape Communicator and Microsoft Internet Explorer include a free visual editor. Netscape Composer is the visual editor that comes with Communicator, and FrontPage Express is included with Internet Explorer. Either is fine for many design and writing tasks, but neither includes some of the features available in other, sometimes costly, visual editors.

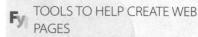

TOOLS TO HELP CREATE WEB PAGES

~ "Web Building"
http://www.snap.com/directory/category/0,16,-13092,00.html

~ "Web Developer's Virtual Library: VL-WWW: HTML_Editors"
http://www.stars.com/Vlib/Providers/HTML_Editors.html

~ "HTML Editors"
http://dir.yahoo.com/Computers_and_Internet/Software/Internet/World_Wide_Web/HTML_Editors

Evaluating the Quality of a Web Page or Web Site

You've seen and worked with quite a few Web pages and Web sites by now, and you probably have a good idea of what makes some sites more effective or more valuable than others. Here we'll consider some criteria for evaluating the quality of a Web page and a Web site. You'll notice that these correspond to the primary points discussed in the section "Design Considerations" above.

Content

Some points to consider are

Accuracy	Is the information correct? Is the information biased?
Focus	Is the purpose of the Web page apparent and does the content accomplish the intended purpose?
Appropriateness	Is the material on the page appropriate for the topic and the audience?
Coverage	Does the content address the main topic at an appropriate level of depth and breadth?
Value and interest	Does the content provide information that will be interesting and valuable to the intended reader?
Links to other material	Do the links on the page lead to other pages that pertain to the purpose, or support and further explain the content?
Grammar, spelling, and vocabulary	Is the text appropriate in terms of spelling, grammar, and vocabulary for the intended audience?

In Chapter 11 we dealt with evaluating the accuracy and purpose of the content of a Web page.

Design

The design of a Web page in this context deals with the appearance and presentation of the material.

Attractiveness	Is the design pleasing? Does it captivate the viewer's attention?
Layout	Is the layout appropriate and does it guide the viewer through the content?
Use of colors	Do the colors of background, text, and images enhance the viewer's experience?
Use of images	Are the images used pertinent to the topic? Are they necessary? Are the images of appropriate size and in appropriate locations in the page?

| Use of animation and other media | If animated images or other media such as video or audio are used, do they enhance the presentation? |

Accessibility

Accessibility refers to the availability of the Web page and its components. Does the page load quickly? Do prospective readers need any special hardware or software to experience or view the content?

| Download time | How long does it take to download the portion of the Web page that appears in one window on the screen? How long does it take to down-load the entire Web page? The answers to these depend on the speed of the reader's connection to the Internet. Most prospective readers won't wait more than 10 or 15 seconds before getting some meaningful or attractive information. |

| Plug-ins necessary | What, if any, plug-ins or other applications are required to view or otherwise experience the Web page? Are they readily available? Does the need for plug-ins put an unnecessary burden on the reader? Could the information be presented in an equally effective way that doesn't require the plug-ins? |

| Hyperlinks | Are all the hyperlinks valid, that is, do they all lead to existing and appropriate Web sites? Links to pages that are no longer available, so-called dead links, are sometimes unavoidable, but the links need to be tested regularly. |

| Browser compatibility | How does the Web page look with different browsers and different versions of the same browser? Features, plug-ins, and HTML that work with only one browser restrict the audience, and make the Web page less accessible. Check the Web page with different browsers. |

| Java and JavaScript | If the Web page includes Java applets, what effect do they have on the time it takes to load the Web page? Is the increased functionality worth the time it takes to load and start an applet? Using JavaScript doesn't increase loading time appreciably, but it does need to be written |

so that it's not misinterpreted by a browser that doesn't recognize it.

Navigation

Here we need to evaluate the capabilities for getting around a single page if it doesn't normally fit within a window and moving through the collection of pages that make up a Web site.

Within a page	What navigational aids are provided within a Web page, provided that it isn't displayed in one window? The reader will be able to use the browser's ways of navigating through a page such as scroll bars, `Ctrl` + `Home`, and so on. If they're necessary, then other navigational aids need to be present. If it's a long document, are there links to the sections of the document at the beginning and end?
From page to page	Is it clear how to navigate through the Web site? Is the logical organization of the information at the Web site evident and accessible? Is there a sense of place or location in the Web site so that it's easy to get to the information at the site?

Every visitor does a quick evaluation or assessment each time they visit a Web page or Web site. While each visitor will not do a full evaluation of a Web page, it's an exercise that you ought to go through. This will help you critique and improve your own work. By evaluating another's Web site, you can help them to improve, and it will also make you a more informed Web page or site designer or information architect. It's also useful to think about evaluation of a Web site throughout the design and implementation phases of Web projects.

Fyi EVALUATING WEB PAGES AND WEB SITES

~ "Evaluation of information sources," **http://www.vuw.ac. nz/~agsmith/evaln/evaln.htm**, by Alastair Smith

~ "Evaluating Quality on the Net," **http://www.tiac.net/users/ hope/findqual.html**, by Hope Tillman

~ "Commentary: Measuring quality and impact of the world wide web," **http://www.bmj. com/archive/7098ip2.htm**, by Jeremy C. Wyatt

Putting Your Information on the Web

To make your Web pages available to everyone else on the Internet, the Web page and all supporting files have to be placed on a computer that acts as a *Web server*. That computer runs the software and has the Internet connections so that information on it can be retrieved by using a URL that starts with **http://**. Most Internet service providers provide this service to their customers at no charge. If your organization, school, or company has a Web server, check to see what specific procedures and policies you need to follow to make your Web page available on the Web.

There are a number of "free" *Web presence providers*. These providers generally allow you to put files on their servers in exchange for an advertisement they display each time someone views one of your Web pages.

> **Fyi** SELECTING A WEB PRESENCE PROVIDER
>
> ∾ "How to Select a Web Presence Provider," **http://www.4w.com/wpp.html**, by Mark Dahmke, for tips about making a selection and questions to ask.
>
> ∾ "Web Hosting," **http://www.dmoz.org/Computers/Internet/Commercial_Services/Web_Hosting**, for lists of providers.

Most people who set up a commercial Web site arrange to have their pages hosted by a firm that specializes in providing a Web presence for companies and organizations. This is usually more economical than supplying and maintaining the network connections, computer systems, and associated staff. You'll need to select and register a domain name for your site, such as **mycompany.com**. Most Web presence providers will handle the registration process for you at no charge, but you may have to pay the registration fee. At the time of this writing the registration fee for a domain name in the U.S. is $35.00 per year. Fees for hosting a Web site range from about $20 per month to a few hundred dollars per month depending on the types of services you want to provide, the amount of disk space you'll need for your site, and other factors. Some providers base their fee on the amount of traffic measured in the amount of bytes transferred per month. You will want to choose a Web presence provider that has the services you need and at a price you can afford. Check to see the support it provides for developing Web pages. You'll also want to consider the provider's reputation, its past service record, and the type and speed of connection it has to the Internet.

When you have made arrangements and checked the policies for making information on the Web, you are ready to move the file or files from your computer to the computer that will be the Web server. You'll need to check with your Web presence provider to know the exact procedures to follow. One possibility is that your organization has a campus-wide or company-wide network and your files will have to be placed in a specific folder or directory that is directly accessible from your computer. In other cases you'll use FTP (File Transfer Protocol), which we discussed in Chapter 13. In either case it's important for you to know

∾   where the source files for the Web page(s) are on your computer.

∾   where you need to place the files on the Web server.

We'll go over an example that shows how to transfer a Web page from a computer to a Web server using FTP and Netscape Navigator. We're going to use Netscape Navigator because it includes the utilities and features that make it relatively easy to use to upload a file.

> Remember that this is an example and the details may vary when you try to follow the procedures in the example. Don't let this confuse you. The example demonstrates fundamental skills and shows the steps you need to follow, but you will not be able to get the same results. You need to use this example as a guide and apply the concepts to your situation.

TRANSFERRING THE SOURCE FILE FOR A WEB PAGE FROM A COMPUTER TO A WEB SERVER USING FTP AND NETSCAPE NAVIGATOR

Overview

In this example we show one way to transfer a file from your computer to a Web server using FTP and Netscape Navigator. This describes one way to copy a source file for a Web page and associated files, such as images, to a Web server. Sometimes the term **uploading** is used to describe this process because the files are copied from a computer to one that serves the Internet. The exact steps to follow and the methods used may be different in some cases. Here we'll use a URL that starts with **ftp://** to copy the file. We use a URL because we're using a Web browser, and the URL starts with **ftp://** because we're using FTP to copy the file.

Before we transfer the file we need to make note of some information that we'll need to copy a file to the correct location on the server:

∾   the Internet domain name of the computer that is the Web server

    ~   the user name or login name on the server
    ~   the password necessary to log in to the Web server
    ~   the path to the directory or folder that holds files for Web pages on the server
    ~   the name of the folder on your computer that holds the file to be copied
    ~   the name of the file to be copied
    ~   the URL of the Web page once the file is copied to the server—we'll want this so we can view the file after it's copied to the server

After we have that information noted we'll go through the steps to copy or upload a file to the server. We're assuming that the browser is started and visible.

1. Make note of the information necessary to copy a file to a Web server, and the file's URL once it's uploaded.
2. Type the FTP URL for the server, including your user name and the path to the directory or folder where the file should be placed.
3. Give the commands necessary to upload the file to the server.
4. Transfer the file.

Once that's done, the URL can be typed in the location field to view the Web page.

Details

1. Make note of the information necessary to copy a file to a Web server, and the file's URL once it's uploaded.

Let's suppose that the source for a Web page is in the file named **visons.html** and it's in a folder named **WebPages** on our computer. The server's name is **www.mwc.edu**, the user name is **webteam1**, the password is . . . (well, passwords are supposed to be secret so we won't write it down), and files that will be available on the Web are placed in the directory with the path name **/users/webteam1/ public_html**.

Here's the information we need:

Server's Internet domain name	**www.mwc.edu**
User name	Webteam1
Password	******** (it's a secret)
Path to the directory on the server that holds the files for Web pages	**/users/webteam1/ public_html/**
Folder on our computer containing the file	**WebPages**

Name of the file	visons.html
URL of the Web page once the file is copied to the server	http://www.mwc.edu/ ~ webteam1/visions.html

2. Type the FTP URL for the server, including your user name and the path to the directory or folder where the file should be placed.

With the information in Step 1 we can form the URL we need to contact the server as shown here:

Note the placement of @ between the user name and the server's name, and how the path to the directory holding the files for Web pages follows the server's name. Now we're ready to proceed.

Double-click on the location field, type in the URL shown in Figure 14.6, and press **Enter**.

Figure 14.6   The FTP URL Typed in the Location Field

A password entry dialog box will appear on the screen.

Type in the password as shown in Figure 14.7 and click on **OK**.

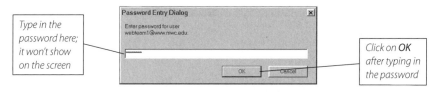

Figure 14.7   The Password Entry Dialog Box

The browser will send the password to the server, and if all goes well, a list of files in the directory will appear in the window.

3.   Give the commands necessary to upload the file to the server.

Now we're ready to upload the file to the Web server. It will be placed in the directory we've named.

Click on **File** in the menu bar and select **Upload File**, as shown in Figure 14.8.

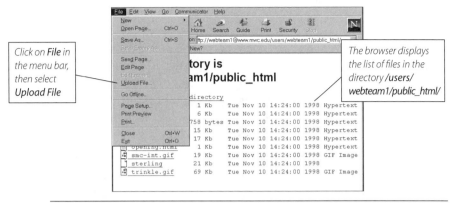

*Click on **File** in the menu bar, then select **Upload File***

The browser displays the list of files in the directory /users/webteam1/public_html/

Figure 14.8   Selecting Upload File

4. Transfer the file.

After you select **Upload File** a File Upload dialog box appears. It's similar to a Save As box, which we've used before. We'll probably have to select the folder **WebPages** from the folders on our computer. Then we're ready to select the file **visions.html**. Figure 14.9 shows that file selected.

(Do it)!   Select the file **visions.html** and click on **Open**.

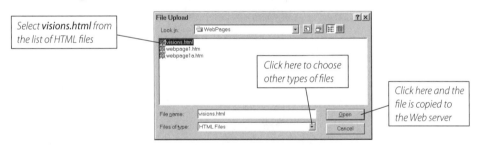

*Select **visions.html** from the list of HTML files*

Click here to choose other types of files

Click here and the file is copied to the Web server

Figure 14.9   Selecting visions.html to Upload to the Web Server

The file is transferred to the server, and the browser shows an updated list of files in the directory **/users/webteam1/public_html/**. Now you can view the Web page with the browser!

(Do it)!   Double-click on the location field, type **http://www.mwc.edu/ ~webteam1/visions.html**, and press **Enter**.

END OF EXAMPLE 14.1

In Example 14.1 we showed how an HTML file (the source for a Web page) may be transferred to a Web server using FTP and Netscape Navigator. Other files or even other types of files can be uploaded or copied to a Web server this way.

Publicizing a Web Page—Getting It Noticed

Once you put your page on a Web server, you're a (Web) published author! There are a number of ways to publicize your Web page. You can submit the URL to several search engines and directories, announce it on certain Usenet newsgroups, or submit the URL and a description to Web sites that announce new Web pages or sites. Other alternatives include:

~ paying for advertising on other Web sites.

~ joining a free banner exchange program. You make up an image with a hyperlink to your Web page and you agree to display banners from other sites on your page. For more information see "Link Trade: Free Banner Exchange," **http://www.linktrade.net**, and the associated FAQ with the URL **http://www.linktrade.net/faq.shtml**. Another site to visit is "LinkExchange Banner Network," **http://adnetwork.bcentral.com**.

~ joining a Web ring. That is a collection of Web sites on a specific topic, each with a link to another site that's a part of the ring. Of course, there are several Web rings that are set up to include Web pages on any topic. WebRing maintains a directory of Web rings. Give it a look at **http://www.webring.org**.

Before you submit the URL you will want to do what you can so that people will find your Web page by using a search tool. When a search tool searches its database, it returns a list of URLs to Web pages ranked according to some relevancy scheme. Search tools don't give out the details of the schemes or algorithms they use to rank results. However, they seem to follow some general rules, such as:

~ words or phrases in the title and headings carry more weight than those in the text

~ the number of times a word or phrase appears increases the relevancy ranking

As you might guess, commercial organizations have a relatively high stake in getting their sites to appear when someone searches for information on the topic of their Web site. There are

 GETTING YOUR WEB SITE NOTICED

~ "Search Engine Submission Tips," **http://www.searchenginewatch.com/webmasters/index.html**, by Danny Sullivan

~ "Search Engine Placement Tips, Techniques and Help in Ten Steps," **http://www.infoscavenger.com/engine.htm**

~ "Promotion 101: Web Site Marketing and Promotion Info Center," **http://www.Promotion101.com**

several sites that give detailed information about getting a Web site noticed by a search engine.

You can announce your page by submitting it to several special locations on the World Wide Web: What's New Web pages, Web directories, and search engines. These services give you forms to fill out telling the URL for your page, your name and email address, and some descriptive information about the Web page. Depending on the workload, it may take a service several days or weeks to list your Web page. There's generally no charge to have a Web page listed by these services. When you submit a request to be listed in a directory you'll also have to pick the category to contain the listing. To choose the appropriate category, find pages on the same or a similar topic within the directory and use their category. You can also submit an announcement of your page to a mailing list and to Usenet newsgroups. One newsgroup for announcing new noncommercial Web sites is **comp.infosystems.www. announce**. Take a look at the FAQ for the group, **http://www. sangfroid.com/charter.html**, before submitting your announcement.

In addition to the individual services and sites, there are Web pages that can be used to submit a URL to several services at once. One of these is "Information City: Promote Your Site," **http://www.FreeReports.net/ submit.html**. That site can be used to submit a Web page's URL to several search engines and directories. You can even use it to join a Web ring. There are a number of services advertised on the Web that will help market your Web site and submit it to several search engines and directories. These generally are not free. You can submit your URLs to sites just as well as they can.

Fy PUBLICIZING A WEB SITE
Tips and Lists of Services:
- "FAQ: How to Announce Your New Web Site," **http://ep.com/ faq/webannounce.html**
- "How to Publicize Your Web Site over the Internet," **http://www. samizdat.com/public.html**
- "Web Site Announcing and Search Engine Placements," **http://tsworldofdesign .com/promotion/ website%20_announcing.htm**

Directories:
- "Computers: Internet: WWW: Website Promotion," **http://www.dmoz.org/ Computers/Internet/ WWW/Website_Promotion**
- "Computers and Internet: Internet: World Wide Web: Announcement Services," **http://www.yahoo.com/ Computers_and_Internet/ Internet/World_Wide_Web/ Announcement_Services**

Getting your Web page announced properly can take some work, but people are going to have to know about it in order to find it among the millions on the World Wide Web.

Summary

The Internet and the Web have been designed so that it's possible to be an information provider as well as a consumer. The protocols that support the Internet give all nodes equal status, Web browsers with graphical interfaces are commonly used, and the means for preparing Web pages are not difficult. This has led to a large amount of information available in the form of Web pages, and the expectation that virtually every organization or business has a Web presence. These factors make it important that you understand the technical and design issues involved in creating, providing, and evaluating Web pages and Web sites.

The source for a Web page is a plain text file that contains HTML tags. A browser, acting as a client, requests the source for a Web page from a computer that acts as a Web server. When the file is retrieved, the browser displays it in its window. In order to make information available on the Web, then, it is necessary to place the source on a Web server.

Designing a Web page involves several facets. Most importantly you need to identify the purpose of the page. Other items to consider include being aware of the technical considerations involved in displaying a Web page, identifying the audience, looking at other Web pages with a similar purpose, identifying the content, and coming up with an appropriate design. The Web page ought to be tested with more than one computer system and browser.

A Web site is a collection of Web pages with a common theme or purpose. In designing a Web site you need to come up with a scheme for presenting and arranging the information. The presentation ought to support the fact that the information is related, and the arrangement often should mirror the logical structure of the information.

A Web page can be written using a simple text editor, but there are other types of editors or ways to create a Web page. These include HTML editors—text editors that include easy ways to insert HTML tags into a file, conversion tools—tools that convert a file from one format such as a spreadsheet or word-processing document to HTML, services that create a Web page out of information you provide, and visual editors—editors that provide tools to produce a Web page without you having to insert HTML.

There are several issues to consider when evaluating a Web page. These include

~ content
~ design
~ accessibility
~ navigation

Putting information on the Web means taking your source files and placing them on a Web server. Some Internet service providers, Web-based services, and organizations provide space for Web pages. If these don't suit your needs, you can pay a monthly fee to a Web presence provider—a company that provides space for and tools to create and maintain a Web site. FTP is often used to transfer a source file to a Web server.

Once a Web page or site is on a Web server you'll want to make it possible for other people to find it easily. There are several services that will submit the URL to various search engines and directories. It's also possible to advertise your site on the Web either through paid advertisements or so-called link exchanges. Be sure to read tips available on the Web about ways to announce your Web site and to get it noticed.

Selected Terms Used in This Chapter

ASCII	uploading
HTML	visual editor
HTML editor	Web presence provider
Internet domain name	Web server
thumbnail	

Exercises and Projects

1. Congratulations! You've just been made president of Way-Cool Music! The company has released five new CDs and has 15 others that it markets. You want to have a Web site for the company.
   a. What's the purpose of the home page?
   b. What are the major elements that will be on the home page?
   c. Who is your audience?
   d. What's the purpose of the Web site?
   e. Draw a diagram that shows the structure of the Web site.

2. You've been hired by Stafford County Traffic Court to put together a Web presence for the court. Folks won't be able to make a virtual court appearance, but information that the general public needs to know about the court should be available through the Web site.
   a. Find two or three Web sites for traffic courts in other parts of the U.S. and give their URLs.

b. Using the designs for traffic courts that you've found, draw a diagram that shows the structure of the Web site you might suggest to Stafford County Traffic Court.

3. You've volunteered to serve as Webmaster for the Tierra Club. The Tierra Club is an environmental organization concerned with protecting the environment on the (fictitious) Caribbean island named Tierra. It gets its funding through grants, donations, and the sale of Tierra Gear™.
    a. Write a purpose for the Tierra Club Web site.
    b. What ought to be on the home page?
    c. Draw a diagram or top-level design for the Web page that people will use if they want to make a donation to the Tierra Club.

4. Think about designing a one-page Web site that tells something about you.
    a. What's the purpose of the page? (Be specific.)
    b. Who is the audience?
    c. Try the Netscape Page Wizard at **http://home.netscape.com/ assist/net_sites/starter/wizard/index.html** to create the Web page.
    d. Get a printed copy of the Web page.

5. Lou Rosenfeld often writes on the issue of information architecture. Read his article "Is Less Really More?" **http://webreview.com/wr/ pub/98/10/02/arch/index.html**.
    a. The paper describes a usability study. What was studied and what methods were used?
    b. What point or points is the author trying to make with the article?
    c. What is the conclusion? Do you agree? Explain.

6. Samantha Bailey also writes about information architecture. Read her article "Navigating the Information Architecture Maze," **http://webreview.com/pub/97/11/14/arch/index.html**.
    a. She mentions five shortcuts to use. What are they?
    b. What does she mean by a content inventory?
    c. Which of the shortcuts do you think would take the most time to accomplish? Explain.

7. The Argus Clearinghouse, **http://www.clearinghouse.net**, is a Web site and virtual library—it collects, reviews, and rates sources. The rating system it uses is described on the Web page "Ratings System," **http://www.clearinghouse.net/ratings.html**.
    a. Use the Clearinghouse rating system to evaluate each of the following Web sites:

       ∾ BUBL Link: 610 Medical sciences, medicine
          http://link.bubl.ac.uk/medicine
       ∾ OnHealth
          http://www.onhealth.com/ch1/0,1091,,00.htm
       ∾ Martindale's Health Science Guide
          http://www-sci.lib.uci.edu/ ~ martindale/
          MedicalResources.html

    b. Is the Clearinghouse's rating system useful in helping decide which of the Web sites would be more suitable for you? Why or why not?

8. Go to the Web page "Searching and Researching on the Internet and the World Wide Web," **http://www.webliminal.com/search/index.html**. Evaluate the page using the criteria given in the section "Evaluating the Quality of a Web Page or Web Site."

9. The Web page in the previous exercise is the home page for a Web site. Is the navigation at the site adequate according to the criteria discussed in the text? Explain.

10. Visit the home page for the InterNIC Web site, **http://rs.internic.net/index.html**. Using the information on links from that page answer the following.

    a. What does it mean to register a domain name?

    b. Suppose you wanted to register the domain name **redrock.com**. What are three places where that could be done?

    c. What is ICANN?

    d. Suppose I have a dispute with someone else about registering a domain name. How could that be resolved?

11. Suppose you're in charge of finding a home for a Web site for a local charitable, nonprofit organization. The Web site will need between 10 and 20 megabytes of space. The organization would like to be able to use forms to collect information from visitors and prefers that no ads be placed on the Web pages. They would like it very much if they didn't have to pay for the service. Fortunately you know about FreeWebspace.net, **http://www.freewebspace.net**. Use the facilities at that site to develop a recommendation of at most three servers that would be appropriate for the organization. Write the recommendation stating why you chose the servers in the form of a one-page report.

12. Suppose you've been selected to serve as Webmaster for the company mentioned in Exercise 1 above. It's up to you to recommend three Web presence providers to meet the information and e-commerce needs of the company. Some friends recommend that you use

the facilities at "HostSearch," **http://www.hostsearch.com**, or at "HostIndex," **http://www.hostindex.com**. Come up with at most three servers and appropriate Web hosting packages for the company. Write your recommendation as a two-page report.

13. It's your job to be sure the Web site that's designed for the company in Exercise 1 is submitted to several search engines.

   a. Visit the Web page "Search Engine Submission Tips," **http://www.searchenginewatch.com/webmasters/index.html**. Read the entire article and pay special attention to the section "Search Engine Design Tips," **http://www.searchenginewatch.com/webmasters/tips.html**. Using the tips in that section write some specific recommendations for the design of the Web site for the company in Exercise 1 above.

   b. You can use the information and form on the Web page "Add a Page, Remove a Page," **http://www.altavista.com/cgi-bin/query?pg = addurl**, to add the URL of your Web site to AltaVista. What happens when a page is added in this way?

   c. The Web site "Promotion 101: Web Site Marketing and Promotion Info Center," **http://www.Promotion101.com**, has a link to a Web page where you can register your site with up to 20 search engines. Is this the same as registering a domain name? Explain.

14. Use the facilities at **http://www.netmechanic.com** to determine how long it would take you to retrieve the home page for your school, company, or organization if you were using a 56K modem. Some experts say that most folks will wait eight seconds for a page to download before they move on. Does the page meet that criterion?

   a. If it's recommended, what can be done to speed the download time?

   b. What other recommendations does NetMechanic offer?

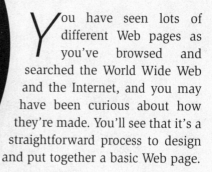

Chapter 15

WRITING

WEB

PAGES

∿

You have seen lots of different Web pages as you've browsed and searched the World Wide Web and the Internet, and you may have been curious about how they're made. You'll see that it's a straightforward process to design and put together a basic Web page.

In the previous chapter we discussed issues related to designing and evaluating Web sites and putting a Web page on the Web. Here we'll concentrate on learning and using basic HTML so you can bring your designs to the Web. Some more advanced topics that help enhance Web pages are discussed in Chapter 16.

Remember that Web pages are text or ASCII files in which HTML (Hypertext Markup Language) is used to specify the format of the Web page, images to be displayed, *hyperlinks,* and possibly other elements.

The browser interprets the HTML and displays the page. If the HTML says to display a word or phrase in the file in bold font, for example, the browser does it. If the HTML tags say to display an image, the browser takes care of that as well. If the tag says that what follows is a hyperlink to some other page, the browser displays the text as a hyperlink and associates it with the specified URL. Hyperlinks on a page can be to other pages or to other types of files, such as sound or video files, images, and some types of interactive programs. Regardless of where the source for a Web page is—on your computer or on a remote Web server—it has the same format and the browser interprets it in the same way.

Goals/Objectives

∿   Understand the relationship between a source file and a Web page

∿   Know basic HTML for producing a Web page

∿   Be capable of writing a Web page that contains one or more images, tables, or lists

Topics

- Description of a Web Page
- Viewing the Source Version of a Web Page
- Introduction to HTML
- Resources for More Information on Creating Web Pages

Description of a Web Page

A **Web page** is a text file that contains HTML codes or tags. A **text file** is a file that contains plain printable characters. The HTML tags give the browser instructions about how to display or represent information in the file. The text file is called the **source file** or just the *source* for the Web page.

The name of the source file has to end with the extension **.htm** or **.html**. Some examples are **resources.htm**, **mvtool12.htm**, **index.html**, and **weather.html**. If the name doesn't have that form, HTML tags may be ignored. It is possible for a Web page to contain no HTML tags; in that case, the text is displayed in plain form and there's no title on the Web page.

Figures 15.1 and 15.2 show the source for a Web page and the Web page as it's displayed by a browser. Several items have been labeled so you can see the relationship between the HTML tags and what's displayed by the browser. You can learn something about using HTML from looking at the source (Figure 15.1) and how it's displayed by the browser (Figure 15.2). Here are a few things to notice:

- The HTML tags are contained in angle brackets < >; for example, < TITLE > and < IMG SRC = "intcover.gif" > .

- Many HTML tags come in pairs. One tag in the pair uses a slash (/), such as < I > and < /I > or < H1 > and < /H1 > . The first tag tells the browser to start (< I >) and the second to stop (< /I >) displaying the text between them in italic font.

- To write comments or notes in a document that don't show up in the window, surround the comments with < !-- and -- > .

- Looking at the page displayed by the browser, you can see that hard returns and spaces are generally ignored by the browser. You can use the HTML tag < P > to indicate the start of a new paragraph.

- < A HREF = "*URL*" > ... *text* ... < /A > is an HTML tag for a hyperlink. Any URL may be used between the quotation marks.

~ < IMG SRC = "*file name*" > is an HTML tag for an image. Put the name of the file or a hyperlink to a file containing the image between the quotation marks.

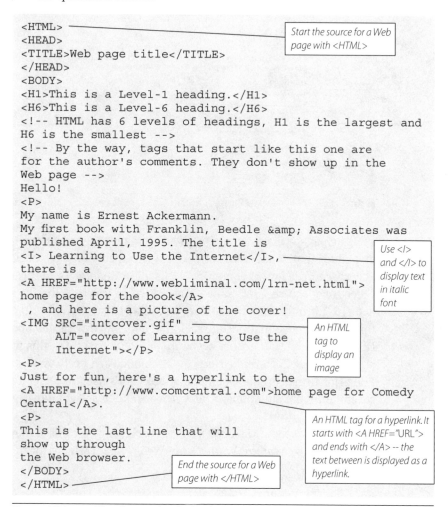

```
<HTML>
<HEAD>
<TITLE>Web page title</TITLE>
</HEAD>
<BODY>
<H1>This is a Level-1 heading.</H1>
<H6>This is a Level-6 heading.</H6>
<!-- HTML has 6 levels of headings, H1 is the largest and
H6 is the smallest -->
<!-- By the way, tags that start like this one are
for the author's comments. They don't show up in the
Web page -->
Hello!
<P>
My name is Ernest Ackermann.
My first book with Franklin, Beedle &amp; Associates was
published April, 1995. The title is
<I> Learning to Use the Internet</I>,
there is a
<A HREF="http://www.webliminal.com/lrn-net.html">
home page for the book</A>
, and here is a picture of the cover!
<IMG SRC="intcover.gif"
    ALT="cover of Learning to Use the
    Internet"></P>
<P>
Just for fun, here's a hyperlink to the
<A HREF="http://www.comcentral.com">home page for Comedy
Central</A>.
<P>
This is the last line that will
show up through
the Web browser.
</BODY>
</HTML>
```

Start the source for a Web page with <HTML>

Use <I> and </I> to display text in italic font

An HTML tag to display an image

An HTML tag for a hyperlink. It starts with <A HREF="URL"> and ends with </A> -- the text between is displayed as a hyperlink.

End the source for a Web page with </HTML>

Figure 15.1   The Source for the Web Page in Figure 15.2

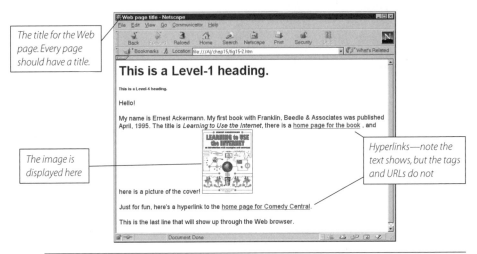

Figure 15.2   The Web Page, with the Source Shown in Figure 15.1,
                as Displayed by the Web Browser

The page was written using the simple text editor Notepad, although any editor that could create and save a text file could have been used. Several sources for other editors are listed in Chapter 14 in the section "Technologies Used to Create a Web Page." In this case the file's name is **fig15-2.htm** and it's in the directory **chap15** on Drive A:. To display this Web page we first put the disk that's included with this book in Drive A:. Then we used the keyboard shortcut **Ctrl** + **O**—this works with either Internet Explorer or Navigator—and clicked on **Browse** or **Choose File**. This brings up the Open dialog box that's used to select a file in several different situations. Select Drive A:, then select **chap15**, and then select **fig15-2.html**.

Looking at the URLs used in the hyperlinks, you can see they reference other Web pages on the World Wide Web. The HTML tag for the image

```
<IMG SRC="intcover.gif"
     ALT="cover of Learning to Use the Internet">
```

uses SRC to specify the source for the image. In this case the URL used for the image, **intcover.gif**, is rather plain. There's no domain name or leading directories. The Web browser interprets this to mean that the file is in the same directory and on the same server as the source for the Web page. This means that if we copy the source file to a folder on a Web server, then we have to copy the image file to the same folder in order to use this simple form of a URL.

The URL in the < IMG SRC = "*URL*" > tag could have linked to any image on the Internet. That same image could have been displayed using the tag

```
<IMG SRC="http://www.webliminal.com/essentials/
intcover.gif"
  ALT="cover of Learning to Use the Internet">
```

since that file is also stored on the Web server at **www.webliminal.com**. The browser retrieves the file from the server through the Internet using the URL **http://www.webliminal.com/essentials/intcover.gif** and then displays it. The person viewing the page wouldn't necessarily know where the file holding the image is located.

One more comment about the IMG tag. ALT is used to specify what is called *alternate text*. The text is displayed when someone selects or moves the mouse over the image. The text is used to provide some information about the image—it's important to include alternate text in this way to further describe a Web site and to make a Web site accessible to persons who may be vision impaired.

Figures 15.1 and 15.2 give you a basic idea of what a Web page contains, what HTML tags look like, and how HTML tags can be used. Regardless of how advanced or complex a Web page can be, remember that it contains the text you see on a page, HTML tags, and other items called *elements*. The elements can be images, hyperlinks to audio files, hyperlinks to other parts of the document, hyperlinks to other portions of the Web, interactive programs, scripts, and inline plug-ins.

Viewing the Source Version of a Web Page

You can view the source version of any Web page. This lets you see the HTML used to create the page. Here's how:

 Click on **View** from the menu bar and then choose **Page Source**.

 Click on **View** from the menu bar and then choose **Source**.

Try it out. Take a look at the view you get of the source file for the Web page shown in Figure 15.2. It will be similar to what we've shown in Figure 15.1.

Viewing the document source with Netscape shows the HTML tags and URLs in a different font and color, making them easy to pick out.

Viewing the source is a good way to see how a Web page is constructed and to learn from the work of others. It's not intended to be used for copying someone else's work. A Web page belongs to the author just like anything else, such as a book or tape, that someone has created and developed. If you see something you like, view the source, study how it was done, and then adapt the techniques you see to your own work.

Introduction to HTML

Web pages are written using **HTML** **(Hypertext Markup Language)**. HTML consists of a collection of instructions, called **tags**, that the Web browser interprets to display a Web page. The commands or instructions are written in HTML, but the effects of the tags aren't seen until a Web browser or some program interprets the HTML. For example, the tags <B> and </B> placed around text indicate that the enclosed text is to be displayed in bold format. So if

```
Be sure to follow the <B>Yellow Brick Road</B> to get
to Oz.
```

were part of a Web page, it would be displayed as

Be sure to follow the **Yellow Brick Road** to get to Oz.

The commands and the way browsers interpret HTML have more to do with the organization of a document than with its format. A number of commands can control the way text is displayed, but HTML emphasizes the hypermedia aspects of the World Wide Web. Extra spaces, tabs, and line lengths, for example, are generally ignored by the browser; the text is made to fit within the browser's window.

HTML includes the commands or tags to create hyperlinks from one part of a Web page to another part of the same page and to create hyperlinks to other Web pages or resources on the Internet. In other words, these hyperlinks are embedded into or become part of the Web page. **URLs** are used to create the hyperlinks. The same process of embedding hyperlinks in a document is used to embed images. The text, images, and hyperlinks are called elements of a Web page.

When we work with HTML in this chapter we'll write the HTML using a simple text editor, save the file as a text file, and then view it with a browser. This way we'll be able to concentrate on the basics. You'll find HTML is not difficult. Organizing a body of material and developing an effective design are the harder tasks. We'll give some pointers about style and list some resources to style guides on the Web in a following section.

In this section we'll concentrate on the HTML tags that do basic formatting, create lists, include hyperlinks to other Web pages and resources, and include images in Web pages. We'll also talk about using background colors, background images, and tables.

Some more advanced aspects of HTML are covered in Chapter 16. There are lots of resources dealing with creating, designing, and implementing Web pages. Two places that offer lots of help are CNET's site "Web Building," **http://www.builder.com**, and "Developer's Corner," **http://www.webreference.com/dev**. A good background in the basics—what we cover in this chapter—is what you need to know to go further. After you understand the basics and have some confidence, you'll be ready to go forward on your own.

The General Form of HTML Tags

All HTML tags begin with the character < (left angle bracket) and end with the character > (right angle bracket). The exceptions are the tags that represent special individual characters, such as the right or left angle bracket. Some of the tags come in pairs; they surround or enclose text. The second tag is like the first except that there's a slash (/) after <. The text between the tags is treated some special way. For example, the text between the tags <I> and </I> is displayed in italic font. You can see this in Figures 15.1 and 15.2. Some tags may occur singly and cause an action. We've written the tags in uppercase, but the browser ignores the case of the letters in a tag. Remember, though, that in a URL, it's very important to use the proper case for names of files.

The Structure of a Web Page—Head and Body

Each Web page ought to start with the tag <HTML> and end with </HTML>. Between those tags, a Web page has two distinct parts: the head or heading, which gives some information about the Web page, and the body, which contains the elements or content of the Web page. The title of the Web page, for example, goes in the heading section. The other information that may be put in the heading section concerns issues that are more advanced than we're dealing with here. Use the tags <HEAD> and </HEAD> to denote the heading of the Web page, and use <BODY> and </BODY> to mark off the body of the page. The items in the heading section aren't normally displayed as part of the Web page. Figure 15.1 shows the proper use of the tags to declare the document as being written in HTML and to denote the heading and body sections. Figure 15.3 gives a brief outline.

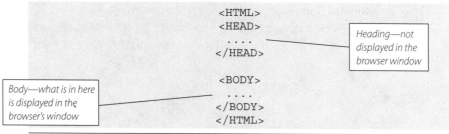

Figure 15.3   An Outline of the Head and Body Sections of a Web Page

Title

Every Web page needs a title. The title doesn't appear as part of the Web page, but it is visible at the very top of the browser window, as shown in Figure 15.2. The title is put between the tags < TITLE > and < /TITLE >, in the heading section of a Web page, as shown in Figure 15.1. The title is important—it's the name that appears in a bookmark list, it's used for writing a citation, it's the name that appears when someone uses a search engine to find the page, and what's in the title can play a significant role in how a search engine ranks the Web page.

Author's Comments

The author of a Web page can include comments that are part of the source for the page but aren't displayed when the browser displays the page. Comments are useful as notes about how the page was constructed or what might need to be changed in the future. Comments serve as reminders not only to the person writing the page but also to anyone who might have to modify the page. Professional computer programmers learn early in their training that they need to include comments as part of a computer program so the next person who has to perform some maintenance on the program can understand the purpose and methods of the program. The same holds true for Web pages. Comments need to be surrounded by < !-- and -- >, as shown in Figure 15.1.

Headings

Web pages can be given a structure. You can start with a top-level heading and then have several levels of subheadings. One method used for constructing a Web page is to restate the title at the top of the body section as a level-1 heading using the tags < H1 > and < /H1 >, then give a level-2 heading using < H2 > and < /H2 >, then a third-level heading, and so on. There are six levels of headings using the tags < H1 >, < H2 >, < H3 >, and on through < H6 >. The different levels of headings control the size of the characters displayed. In Figure 15.2 we used < H1 > and < H6 >, and you can see the difference in Figure 15.2. Figure 15.4 shows a portion of the source for the Web page shown in Figure 15.5. Here the title was restated as a level-3 heading, < H4 > was used for the subheadings, and < H6 > was for the small lettering for the illustrator's name.

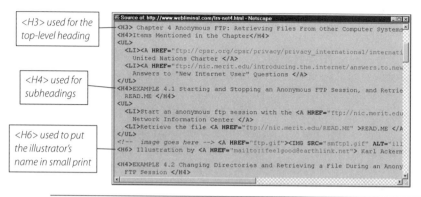

<H3> used for the top-level heading

<H4> used for subheadings

<H6> used to put the illustrator's name in small print

Figure 15.4   The Source for the Web Page in Figure 15.5

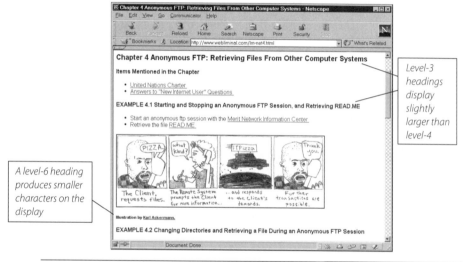

Level-3 headings display slightly larger than level-4

A level-6 heading produces smaller characters on the display

Figure 15.5   The Web Page with the Source in Figure 15.4

Paragraphs, Line Breaks, and Horizontal Lines

Blank spaces on a line and blank lines in a source document don't show up when an HTML document is displayed by a Web browser; they're ignored. The source documents in Figures 15.1 and 15.4 contain blank spaces and lines that don't appear in the Web pages, as shown in Figures 15.2 and 15.5. The advantage to this is that lines are adjusted or formatted by the browser so they fit nicely within the window. There's also a disadvantage: You need to use an HTML tag to specifically mark the beginning of a paragraph or the end of a line.

∾ Use < P > to mark the beginning of a paragraph. When the browser interprets this tag, a blank line is displayed, and the text following the < P > starts on a new line. Another way to think about this is that < P > is used to separate paragraphs.

∾ Use < BR > to separate lines. The text following the tag < BR > is placed at the beginning of the next line in the browser's window.

∾ The tag < HR > puts a horizontal or shadow line on the Web page. Like < BR >, it can be used to separate lines. Often it's used to separate sections of a Web page. The length of the shadow line is automatically adjusted so it's always the width of the window.

Figures 15.6 and 15.7 show the document source and the browser view of a page that uses < BR >, < P >, and < HR >. These tags can be placed anywhere on a line or between lines. We don't use a matching tag with these tags.

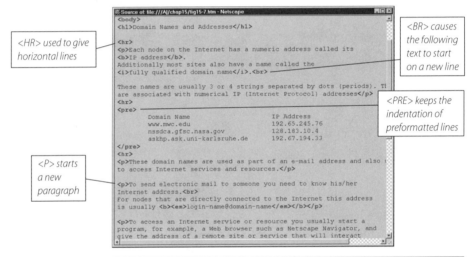

Figure 15.6   The Source for a Web Page Using <B>, <P>, and <HR>

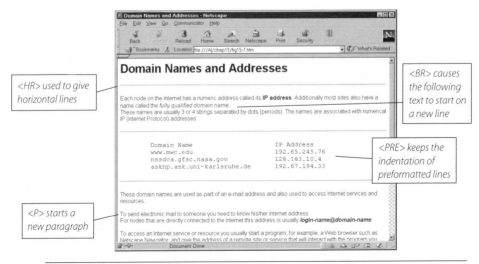

Figure 15.7   The Web Page with the Source in Figure 15.6

Character Formatting—Italic, Bold, and Emphasized

HTML tags can be used to display parts of the text in bold or italic font. To display text in bold font, surround it with the tags < B > and < /B > . To display text in italic font use the tags < I > and < /I > . Both of these are used in the source document shown in Figure 15.6. The tags < EM > and < /EM > are also used to display text in italic font. The portion of the source in Figure 15.6 that reads < B > < EM > login-name @domain-name < /EM > < /B > displays the enclosed text in bold and italic font.

Why use < EM > and not < I > for italic font? Some browsers don't display text in italic font, and some people think it's better to use the tag < EM > to let the browser determine how the text will be displayed. < EM > means *emphasize* to a browser and many browsers will display the text in italics. If a browser can't display text in italic font, it will use some other font to emphasize the text. There are other tags that behave this way; < STRONG > and < B > can usually be used in place of each other.

Preformatted Text

We've seen that blank spaces on a line (except for the ones necessary for proper punctuation) and blank lines are ignored when an HTML source document is displayed as a Web page. Sometimes, though, you want to have certain spacing or indenting. Use the HTML tag < PRE > to tell the browser not to automatically rearrange or format the text. Putting < PRE > and < /PRE > around text indicates that it's preformatted, and the browser shouldn't change the way it's to be displayed. Text within the tags is displayed in fixed-width font, usually Courier, and looks different from other text displayed by the browser. Figure 15.6 shows the use of the tags < PRE > and < /PRE > , and Figure 15.7 shows how the browser displays the text.

Quoted Text

To display quoted text in a Web browser, use the HTML tags < BLOCKQUOTE > and < /BLOCKQUOTE > . As an example, Figure 15.8 shows a portion of the source document for the Web page displayed in Figure 15.9.

```
Civil disobedience is certainly not a new notion, and
there's a long tradition of times when history has shown
it to be necessary and reasonable. The authors of the
<I>Declaration of Independence</I> stated conditions
under which they felt civil disobedience is justified.
```

```
<BLOCKQUOTE>"Prudence, indeed, will dictate that
Governments long established should not be changed for
light and transient causes; and accordingly all experience
hath shown that mankind are more disposed to suffer,
while evils are sufferable than to right themselves by
abolishing the forms to which they are accustomed. But
when a long train of abuses and usurpations, pursuing
invariably the same object, evinces a design to reduce
them under absolute Despotism, it is their right, it is
their duty, to throw off such Government, and to provide
new Guards for their future security." — Declaration of
Independence
</BLOCKQUOTE>

References to other sources justifying civil disobedience
are given at the end of this chapter.
```

Figure 15.8   Source Code Showing Use of <BLOCKQUOTE> and </BLOCKQUOTE>

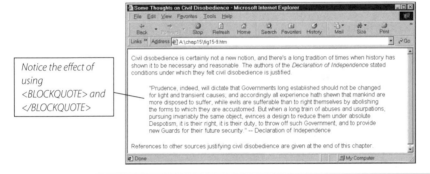

Notice the effect of using <BLOCKQUOTE> and </BLOCKQUOTE>

Figure 15.9   A Web Page Showing the Effect of <BLOCKQUOTE> and </BLOCKQUOTE>

Special Characters

Here's a question for you. If a Web browser interprets the character < as the beginning of an HTML tag, then how can we display < on a Web page? HTML has ways of representing that and other special characters. The format is an ampersand followed by some letters and a semi-colon. Here are some examples:

<   to represent   <

>   to represent   >

&   to represent   &

"   to represent   "

       to represent   a space

Lists

HTML has tags for several different types of lists. Additionally, the lists can be nested so one type of list is inside another. The types of lists supported by HTML are as follows:

- Ordered (numbered) lists
- Unordered lists
- Descriptive lists

Hey! We just used an unordered list to show the types of lists you can represent with HTML.

Ordered or Numbered Lists

Ordered lists are lists in which each item is numbered. You don't need to do the numbering; the Web browser does this automatically. The first item on the list is numbered 1. If you change the list and add items, the browser takes care of renumbering them correctly. It's no surprise that ordered lists are also referred to as numbered lists.

Fy SPECIAL CHARACTERS

The special characters that can be represented with HTML are part of the standards for sets of codes defined by the International Organization for Standardization (ISO).

- "Martin Ramsch - iso8859-1 table"
  http://www.uni-passau.de/ ~ramsch/iso8859-1.html
- "ISO8859-1/HTML Stuff"
  http://ppewww.ph.gla.ac.uk/ ~flavell/iso8859
- "ISO Lating-1 Character Set"
  http://www.obliquity.com/ computer/html/symbols.html

The rules for using HTML to construct ordered lists are as follows:

1. An ordered list starts with the tag < OL > and ends with the tag < /OL > .
2. Each item in the list starts with < LI > .

Figure 15.10 shows a simple example of using these rules, and Figure 15.11 shows how it would be displayed.

```
This is an example of an <B>unordered list</B>.
<P>
What is the Internet?
We'll look at it from these points of view.
<OL>
<LI> From a social point of view.
<LI> From a practical point of view emphasizing resources.
<LI> From a technical point of view.
</OL>
```

Figure 15.10   An Example of Using HTML to Produce an Ordered List

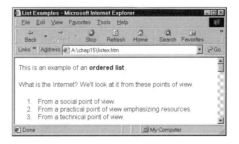

Figure 15.11   An Ordered List on a Web Page

Unordered Lists (Bulleted Lists)

Each item in an unordered list is marked with a dot called a bullet. The term *unordered* means the items aren't numbered, but they do appear in the order given in the source document. These lists also go by the names *unnumbered lists* or *bulleted lists*.

The rules for using HTML to construct unordered lists are as follows:

1. An unordered list starts with the tag < UL > and ends with the tag < /UL >.
2. Each item in the list starts with < LI >.

Figure 15.12 shows a simple example of using these rules, and Figure 15.13 shows how it would be displayed.

```
This is an example of an <B>unordered list</B>.
<P>
What is the Internet?
We'll look at it from these points of view.
<UL>
<LI>From a social point of view.
<LI>From a practical point of view emphasizing resources.
<LI>From a technical point of view.
</UL>
```

Figure 15.12   An Example of Using HTML to Produce an Unordered List

Figure 15.13   An Unordered List on a Web Page

Descriptive Lists (Indenting)

Each item in a descriptive list has a title and then an indented description of the title. The items aren't marked with numbers or dots (bullets) as are ordered or unordered lists.

The rules for using HTML to construct descriptive lists are:

1. A descriptive list starts and ends with the tags < DL > and < /DL > respectively.
2. The descriptive title for each item starts with the tag < DT > .
3. The indented description for a title is marked with < DD > .

Figures 15.14 and 15.15 are examples of descriptive lists.

```
This is an example of a <B>descriptive list</B>.
<P>
What is the Internet?
We'll look at it from these points of view.
<DL>
<DT>From a social point of view.
<DD>Consider the Internet in terms of individuals and
groups of users. We'll focus on using the Internet for
communication and the virtual communities that have arisen
in recent times.
<DT>From a practical point of view emphasizing resources.
<DD>Consider the Internet as a vast storehouse of
information. We'll also stress the fact that the
information isn't only "on the shelf", but that there are
lots of people to answer questions and give support.
<DT>From a technical point of view.
<DD>Here's where we give an introduction to some of the
technical details and issues. We'll look at the Internet
as a network of networks, explain how the networks can
communicate, and cover some details about connecting to
the Internet.
</DL>
```

Figure 15.14   An Example of Using HTML to Produce a Descriptive List

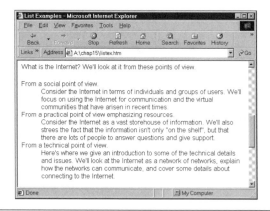

Figure 15.15   A Web Page Using a Descriptive List

You can also use descriptive lists to write bibliographies in HTML. Figure 15.16 shows the source code for the bibliography shown in Figure 15.17.

```
<H3>Bibliography</H3>
<DL>
<DT>Ackermann, Ernest C. (1995).
<DD><I>Learning to Use the Internet</I>,
Wilsonville, OR: Franklin, Beedle &amp; Associates.

<DT>Comer, Douglas.
<DD><I>The Internet Book: Everything You Need to Know
about Computer Networking and How the Internet Works</I>,
Englewood Cliffs, NJ: Prentice-Hall.

<DT>Groves, Dawn (1995).
<DD><I>The Web Page Workbook</I>,
Wilsonville, OR: Franklin, Beedle &amp; Associates.

<DT>Liu, C., Peek, J., Jones, R., Buus, B, and Nye,
A. (1994).
<DD><I> Managing Internet Information Services: World Wide
Web, Gopher, FTP, and More</I>,
Sebastopol, CA: O'Reilly &amp; Associates.
```

Figure 15.16   Source HTML for a Bibliography

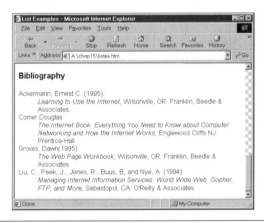

Figure 15.17   A Web Page Bibliography

Nested Lists

Any of the types of lists can be nested; that is, one put inside another. You'll notice that the symbol used to mark items in unordered lists changes shape when these lists are nested. Here's an example showing nested lists. Figure 15.18 shows the source and Figure 15.19 the portion of the Web page shown in the source. Here we have one ordered (numbered) list with several unordered lists nested inside. We've marked the first nested list in Figure 15.18.

```
<H2>Topic 2: Understanding the Internet: How it Works</H2>

<OL>                              The ordered (numbered) list starts here
  <LI>IP Addresses
                                        The first item in the ordered list
    <UL>
      <LI><A HREF="http://www.sandybay.com/pc-web/
      IP_address.htm">
          IP address - PC Webopedia Definition and Links</A>
      <LI><A HREF="http://www.chami.com/tips/internet/
      011097I.html">
          What class should my TCP/IP network be?</A>
      <LI><A HREF="http://www.slac.stanford.edu/cgi-
      bin/traceroute.pl">
          Traceroute from www.slac.stanford.edu</A>
    </UL>
                                The first nested unordered list ends here
  <LI>Domain names and DNS
    <UL>
      <LI><A HREF="http://webopedia.internet.com/TERM/d/
      domain_name.html">
          domain name - Webopedia Definition and Links</A>
      <LI><A HREF="http://www.dns.net/dnsrd/">
          DNS Resources Directory</A>
      <LI> <A HREF="http://hotwired.lycos.com/webmonkey/
      geektalk/97/03/index4a.html">
          Exploring the Domain Name Space</A>
    </UL>
  <LI>HTTP
    <UL>
      <LI> <A HREF="http://www.FreeSoft.org/CIE/Topics/
      102.htm">
          HTTP Protocol Overview</A>
      <LI> <A HREF="http://www.w3.org/Protocols/HTTP/
      HTTP2.html">
          HTTP: A protocol for networked information</A>
    </UL>
</OL>
```

The first nested unordered list starts here

The second item in the ordered list starts here

Figure 15.18   The Source for the Web Page in Figure 15.19

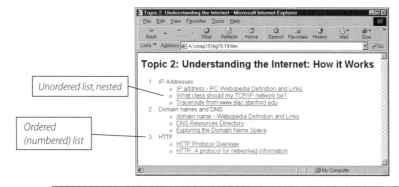

Unordered list, nested

Ordered (numbered) list

Figure 15.19   A Web Page Using Nested Lists

Hyperlinks

HTML was designed to allow for the construction of hypertext, hypermedia documents, or Web pages. One of the advantages of HTML is that
with it we can create hyperlinks from a resource on the World Wide
Web to another Web page or from one part of a Web page to another
part of the same page. We'll cover both of these types of hyperlinks in
this section.

Hyperlinks to Other Resources on the Web

To use HTML to represent a hyperlink to a resource on the WWW, you
use two tags, with text or an image between them. The first tag starts
with < A HREF = " and includes the URL or link for the resource. The
matching tag is < /A > . As you've already seen, many HTML tags appear
in pairs. We'll look at an example before giving the rules for these types
of tags.

Here's an example of the HTML tags used for creating a hyperlink:

```
The home page for <A HREF="http://www1.mwc.edu/~ernie/
index.html">Ernest Ackermann</A> has a link to materials
for workshops and tutorials.
```

A Web browser would display that HTML as:

The home page for <u>Ernest Ackermann</u> has a link to materials for
workshops and tutorials.

If someone clicked on <u>Ernest Ackermann</u> in the browser's window, the
browser would open the location and go to the resource given by the
URL.

The HTML rules for creating hyperlinks are generalizations of the
example above.

∾ The first tag has the form < A HREF = "*URL*" > . A URL for an actual
  Web page is substituted for *URL* between the pair of quotation marks
  (").

∾ The closing tag is < /A > .

∾ The tags aren't visible on the Web page.

∾ The text between the two tags appears on the Web page as underlined
  or highlighted text.

∾ If there's an image between the two tags, its border is highlighted.

∾ Clicking on the text or image opens the location or takes the user to
  the Web resource given by the URL.

Figures 15.20 and 15.21 show the use of HTML tags for hyperlinks
from a Web page to other resources on the Web. Figure 15.20 shows the

HTML source, and Figure 15.21 shows the Web page. There are hyperlinks to sites at more than one location—a Web page can contain hyperlinks to many different locations and resources. Near the bottom of the page an image is used within the tags for a hyperlink; otherwise the hyperlinks all appear as text. We'll discuss displaying images in the next section. You'll notice that this uses some HTML tags we've discussed before. Try to predict what the page will look like before looking at Figure 15.21.

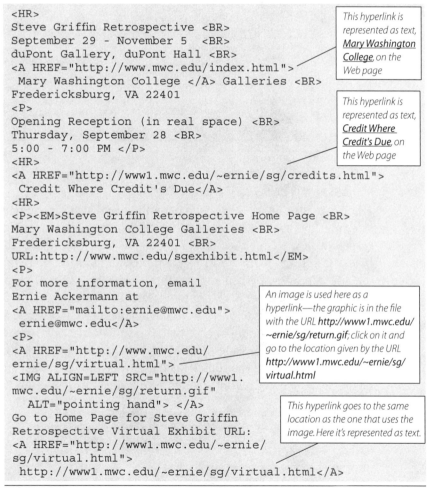

```
<HR>
Steve Griffin Retrospective <BR>
September 29 - November 5  <BR>
duPont Gallery, duPont Hall <BR>
<A HREF="http://www.mwc.edu/index.html">
 Mary Washington College </A> Galleries <BR>
Fredericksburg, VA 22401
<P>
Opening Reception (in real space) <BR>
Thursday, September 28 <BR>
5:00 - 7:00 PM </P>
<HR>
<A HREF="http://www1.mwc.edu/~ernie/sg/credits.html">
 Credit Where Credit's Due</A>
<HR>
<P><EM>Steve Griffin Retrospective Home Page <BR>
Mary Washington College Galleries <BR>
Fredericksburg, VA 22401 <BR>
URL:http://www.mwc.edu/sgexhibit.html</EM>
<P>
For more information, email
Ernie Ackermann at
<A HREF="mailto:ernie@mwc.edu">
 ernie@mwc.edu</A>
<P>
<A HREF="http://www.mwc.edu/
ernie/sg/virtual.html">
<IMG ALIGN=LEFT SRC="http://www1.
mwc.edu/~ernie/sg/return.gif"
  ALT="pointing hand"> </A>
Go to Home Page for Steve Griffin
Retrospective Virtual Exhibit URL:
<A HREF="http://www1.mwc.edu/~ernie/
sg/virtual.html">
 http://www1.mwc.edu/~ernie/sg/virtual.html</A>
```

This hyperlink is represented as text, <u>Mary Washington College</u>, on the Web page

This hyperlink is represented as text, <u>Credit Where Credit's Due</u>, on the Web page

*An image is used here as a hyperlink—the graphic is in the file with the URL **http://www1.mwc.edu/~ernie/sg/return.gif**; click on it and go to the location given by the URL **http://www1.mwc.edu/~ernie/sg/virtual.html***

This hyperlink goes to the same location as the one that uses the image. Here it's represented as text.

Figure 15.20   The Source for the Hyperlinks Example

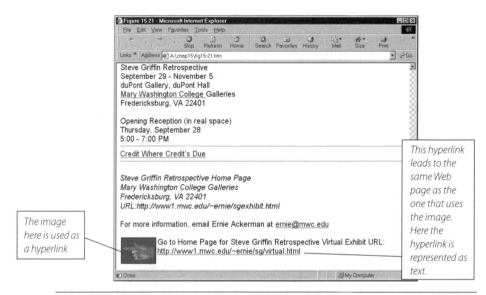

Figure 15.21   The Web Page Produced by the Source in Figure 15.20

Hyperlinks to Other Parts of a Web Page

HTML can also be used to create hyperlinks between several parts of the same document. This is useful when dealing with a long document. Hyperlinks for a table of contents or a list of sections can take the reader to specific parts of the document. Hyperlinks within a document are also appropriate when constructing a glossary—a list of terms and definitions—to allow the reader to consider some items in context.

Making a link from one part of the document to another section involves link tags and an anchor tag. The anchor marks a spot within the document, and the link tags are ties to that specific anchor. Figure 15.22 shows an example of the source for these types of hyperlinks, and Figure 15.23 shows how they would be displayed by a Web browser.

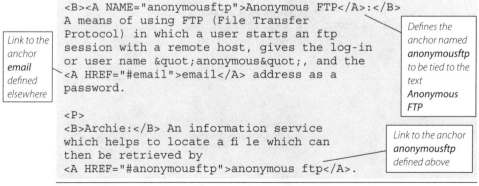

Figure 15.22   The Source for Hyperlinks Within a Document

Anonymous FTP: A means of using FTP (File Transfer Protocol) in which a user starts an ftp session with a remote host, gives the log-in or user name "anonymous", and the <u>email</u> address as a password.

Archie: An information service which helps to locate a file that can then be retrieved by <u>anonymous ftp</u>.

Figure 15.23   The Web Browser Display of the Source in Figure 15.23

Clicking on a hyperlink in Figure 15.23 takes the user to a portion of the document marked by anchor tags. Looking at the example in Figure 15.22 you see:

ℵ Anchor tags have the form < A NAME = "*word*" > *portion-of-document* < /A > where *word* is some term that's used in the link tags. When the link is selected, the page is displayed starting here.

ℵ Hyperlinks to portions of a document have the form < A HREF = "*#word*" > *text or image* < /A > . Clicking on the hyperlink takes the user to the portion of the document where the anchor word's definition appears.

The # character identifies the link as going to a portion of a document. The hyperlinks we've shown here are within one document or Web page. You can use the same idea to set up hyperlinks to portions of other documents, provided the document has anchors defined in it. The material in Figure 15.23 was taken from the Web page whose URL is **http://www1.mwc.edu/ ~ ernie/glossary.html**. If we wanted to make a hyperlink from another Web page to the portion of the glossary that gives the definition of anonymous FTP we'd use the URL **http://www1.mwc.edu/ ~ ernie/glossary.html#anonymousftp** in a link, as shown below.

```
Before 1990, you needed to learn how to use
<A HREF="http://www.mwc.edu/ernie/
glossary.html#anonymousftp">
anonymous ftp</A> to access most of the material on the
Internet
```

Images

A Web browser is capable of displaying images as part of a Web page. The basic HTML tag to use for an image has the form < IMG SRC = "*URL*" > where *URL* is the URL of a file that contains a digital representation of the image. Browsers can display images that are in GIF or JPEG format. The browser determines the format only by the name of the file. If the image is in GIF format, store it in a file whose name ends with **.gif**. For an image in JPEG format, store it in a file whose name ends with **.jpg**.

We've used HTML tags for images that appear in Web pages for some of the previous figures:

～ Figure 15.1

< IMG SRC = "intcover.gif" ALT = "cover of Learning to Use the Internet" >

～ Figure 15.20

< IMG ALIGN = LEFT SRC = "http://www1.mwc.edu/ ~ ernie/sg/ return.gif" ALT = "pointing hand" >

The second URL uses a complete fully qualified domain name. The first uses a relative name for the URL. A relative URL is easier to type in, but remember that using a relative URL implies the image is in the same directory or folder as the Web page source. That restricts the location of pages and images. In some cases it may be too restricting. To read more about using relative names versus fully qualified names, look at the section of "Composing Good HTML," **http://www.ology.org/ tilt/cgh**, by Eric Tilton dealing with this subject.

You can also give directions to the browser as to where the accompanying text will be displayed in relation to the image. Text can be displayed aligned at the top, middle, or bottom of an image. It's usually displayed to the left of the image. Use ALIGN = BOTTOM, ALIGN = MIDDLE, or ALIGN = TOP within the IMG tag; for example,

< IMG ALIGN = TOP SRC = "http://www.mwc.edu/ ernie/InternetToday/intcover.gif" ALT = "cover of Internet

tip MAKE SURE OTHERS CAN FIND YOUR IMAGES AND HYPERLINKS Avoid using a URL or file name that references a local file in terms of its location on your computer without giving the Internet address of the computer. An example of this would be the HTML tag <IMG SRC= "file:///C|nicestuff/greatpic.gif">.

That tag instructs the browser to display a file that's on the computer that's being used to run the Web browser. That means if someone viewing the page isn't using that same computer, then he won't be able to see it! Hyperlinks to resources that start with **file://** and don't give the Internet domain name will have the same problem. If you want the image or the hyperlink to be accessible from other computers on the Internet you need to use a URL that includes the domain name of the system that's running the Web server. If the image were to be displayed as part of a Web page whose URL is **http://www.circlea.com/ nicestuf/coolpage.html**, for example, you would put the image in the same directory or folder as the Web page and make its tag <IMG SRC="greatpic.gif">.

Today!" > . With these types of alignments only one line is displayed in the specified position and the remaining text (if there is any) is displayed beginning under the image. It's also possible to align text with the entire image, starting at the top, using ALIGN = LEFT or ALIGN = RIGHT. This puts the image to the left or to the right of the text.

The method of alignment is easier to think about when you see some examples, and we'll look at a Web page that contains some images that are aligned differently. The source for the Web page we'll look at is named **showalin.htm**. It is on the disk included with this book, in the folder named **chap15**—the same place as the other examples from this chapter.

Figure 15.24 shows the effect of using these three tags along with some accompanying text:

```
<IMG ALIGN=TOP SRC="http://www.webliminal.com/essentials/
fleethum.gif">
<IMG ALIGN=MIDDLE SRC="http://www.webliminal.com/
essentials/fleethum.gif">
<IMG ALIGN=BOTTOM SRC="http://www.webliminal.com/
essentials/fleethum.gif">
```

Figure 15.24   Alignment at the Top, Middle, and Bottom of an Image

Note that if the size of the font or the window were changed, the results would be different. What we see here depends on those items as well as the screen resolution (the number of pixels).

Figure 15.25 demonstrates the use of left and right alignment using the following tags:

```
<IMG ALIGN=LEFT SRC="http://www.webliminal.com/essentials/
fleethum.gif">
<IMG ALIGN=RIGHT SRC="http://www.webliminal.com/essentials/
fleethum.gif">
```

Figure 15.25   Demonstrating ALIGN=LEFT and ALIGN=RIGHT

The examples above show how to align text with images. We've used the attribute ALIGN to do that. The attribute is part of the HTML tag and it gives an attribute to the image that's displayed. There are other attributes that you can use. The list below describes some of them.

ALT = "*text*"

The text is displayed when the mouse pointer is moved over the image. This is useful to describe the image. For example, moving the mouse pointer over the image of Ernest Ackermann on his home page, **http:/ /www.webliminal.com/ernie**, displays **"picture of ernie"** because the IMG tag contains ALT = "picture of ernie".

ALIGN = "*alignment*"

This aligns the image with the border of the Web page. ALIGN = "LEFT" puts it on the left of a page and ALIGN = "RIGHT" puts it on the right.

HSPACE = "*width*"

This specifies the number of pixels between the left and right sides of the image and other elements of the Web page. For example, using HSPACE = "5" places 5 pixels between the left

	and right sides of the image and other items on a Web page.
VSPACE = "*width*"	This specifies the number of pixels between the top and bottom of the image and other elements of the Web page. For example, using VSPACE = "8" places 8 pixels between the top and bottom of the image and other items on a Web page.
BORDER = "*width*"	This specifies the border around an image. Using BORDER = "0" gives no border. To get a thick border use BORDER = "5".
HEIGHT = "*size*" WIDTH = "*size*"	Use these to specify the height and width of an image in pixels. If you position the mouse pointer over an image, right-click, and select **View Image**, the image is displayed in its own window with the size specified. Setting these makes a page load faster because the browser knows how many pixels to allocate for the image. For example, HEIGHT = "181" WIDTH = "163" specifies that an image will be 181 pixels high and 163 pixels wide.

Table 15.1   IMG Tag attributes

Background Colors and Images

Using HTML, you can set the background for a Web page so that it is a solid color or an image. You do this by setting an attribute in the < BODY > HTML tag. For example, to have a white background on a Web page use < BODY BGCOLOR = "WHITE" > . To set the background of a Web page to an image, say one that's in the file **mwc.gif**, use < BODY BACKGROUND = "mwc.gif" > . Only one of these, BGCOLOR or BACKGROUND, may be set in the < BODY > tag since the background will be either a color or an image, but not both. Setting a color or an image as the background on the Web page displays all the other text or images on top of the background.

The rules for the file name that's used with BACKGROUND are the same as for any image used in HTML. The file name can be a fully qualified URL with the domain name and the path, or it can be relative to the location of the file that holds the source for the Web page. Take a look at the Web page with the source named **bground.html** in the folder named **chap15** on the disk that's included with this book to see an example.

Colors may be designated by name—such as white, blue, or palegoldenrod—or they can be designated by a six-digit hexadecimal (base sixteen) numeral. Most folks are more comfortable with the names for colors. Netscape has a guide that lists the names of colors in the Web page "Color Values," **http://developer.netscape.com/docs/manuals/communicator/jsguide4/colors.htm**. (That's how we know the name palegoldenrod can be used for a color!) The six-digit numeral indicates the amount of red, green, and blue in the color. The colors are formed in a similar way to how light is mixed. By that we mean that giving the highest value to all three colors (designated by #FFFFFF) results in white, and giving the least value to each (designated by #000000) results in black. The first two characters after the # represent the amount of red, the next two the amount of green, and the last two the amount of blue. Using hexadecimal digits allows for 16 * 16 possibilities for each of the three colors and thus 16^6 (over 16 million) possible colors. Before you get too carried away with color possibilities remember that for best results you ought to stick with the 216 browser-safe colors as mentioned in Chapter 14. These colors are also discussed in the resources listed in the FYI above.

> **Fy** WEB PAGE COLORS
>
> Two places to refer to for advice and more information about using color in Web pages are:
>
> ~ "Annabella's HTML Help - Colors" by A. Ramsden **http://www.geocities.com/Heartland/Plains/6446/color.html**
> ~ "The Browser-Safe Color Palette" by Lynda Weinman **http://www.lynda.com/hex.html**

Tables

HTML deals with the structure of a document, but provides only a little help in terms of controlling the layout of a Web page. In the previous section we showed how using the attribute ALIGN with an IMG tag gives some help for aligning text with images. This is helpful, but it is not the best way to get a block of text to line up with an image. In some cases you'll want to put text or images into blocks, or into several rows and columns. The HTML tag to use for those tasks is < TABLE > .

The tags < TABLE > and < /TABLE > allow for the arrangement of items between them into rows and columns. For an example take a look at the Web pages "Tables example 1" and "Tables example 2." The source for each is in the files **tables1.html** and **tables2.html** in the folder **chap15** of the disk that's included with this book. Also take a look at the source for the Web pages to see how the HTML tags are used to create a table.

We'll give the basic structure of a table here. Think of a table as a collection of cells or items arranged in rows and columns. For example, the table here has three rows and two columns. Each item is called a cell.

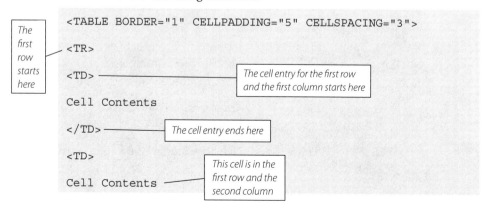

A table is started with the HTML tag < TABLE >. You may supply several attributes. Some of the common ones are

BORDER = "*width*"   This specifies the width in pixels of the borders in the table. For no border use 0, as in "Tables example 1." For a thick border try BORDER = "5".

CELLPADDING = "*width*"   This specifies the number of pixels that surround the text or image within a cell entry.

CELLSPACING = "*width*"   This specifies the number of pixels between cells.

Using these attributes we could specify a table with a border of one pixel, cell padding of five pixels, and space between cells of three pixels by specifying

```
<TABLE BORDER="1" CELLPADDING="5" CELLSPACING="3">
```

The tags < TR > and < /TR > are used to contain a row in a table. The tags < TD > and < /TD > are used to contain a cell in a table.

A table as specified above with three rows and two columns, then, would have the following structure:

```
<TABLE BORDER="1" CELLPADDING="5" CELLSPACING="3">

<TR>

<TD>

Cell Contents

</TD>

<TD>

Cell Contents
```

The first row starts here

The cell entry for the first row and the first column starts here

The cell entry ends here

This cell is in the first row and the second column

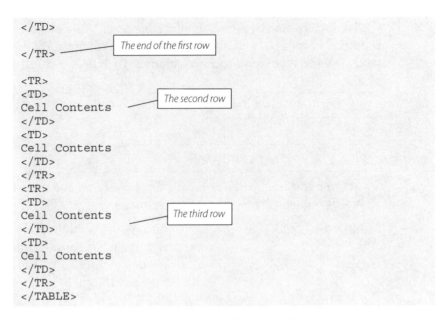

```
</TD>

</TR>                    The end of the first row

<TR>
<TD>
Cell Contents            The second row
</TD>
<TD>
Cell Contents
</TD>
</TR>
<TR>
<TD>
Cell Contents            The third row
</TD>
<TD>
Cell Contents
</TD>
</TR>
</TABLE>
```

You put the necessary text and HTML for the cell contents.

∾ **Try this!** Take a look at the source files **tables1.html** and **tables2.html** and determine how many rows and columns are in each.

We've given you the basics for the HTML needed for tables. Take a look at some of these other references for more information about using tables:

∾ The section on Tables in Part 3 of the NCSA's "A Beginner's Guide to HTML," **http://www.ncsa.uiuc.edu/General/Internet/WWW/ HTMLPrimerP3.html#TA**

∾ "Table Tutor" by Joe Barta, **http://junior.apk.net/ ~ jbarta/tutor/ tables/index.html**

Table 15.2 lists the tags we've mentioned in this chapter.

Tag	Purpose
< BODY > , < /BODY >	Marks the body of the document; what is displayed.
< HEAD > , < /HEAD >	Marks the heading section; contains a description of the document.
< HTML > , < /HTML >	Marks the HTML portion; the first and last tags in the file.
< TITLE > , < /TITLE >	The document title is put between these tags.

`< ! -- .. -- >`	Contains comments about the document; nothing is displayed.
`< H1 >`, `< /H1 >`	Level-1 headings in the body section; the largest font for a heading. There are six levels of headings: `< H1 > . . . < H6 >`, each one displayed smaller than the previous one with H6 being the smallest.
`< P >`	Starts a new paragraph.
`< BR >`	Starts a new line.
`< HR >`	A horizontal rule or shadow line; it looks like a divider between sections or items on the page.
`< I >`, `< /I >`	Italic text.
`< EM >`, `< /EM >`	Emphasized text, often displayed as italic.
`< B >`, `< /B >`	Bold text.
`< BLOCKQUOTE >`, `< /BLOCKQUOTE >`	Extended quotation.
`< PRE >`, `< /PRE >`	Preformatted text.
`&lt;, &gt;, &amp;`	Represent the special characters $<$, $>$, and &.
`< OL >`, `< /OL >`	An ordered or numbered list.
`< UL >`, `< /UL >`	An unordered or bulleted list.
`< LI >`	Marks a list element in an ordered or unordered list.
`< DL >`, `< /DL >`	A descriptive or indented list.
`< DT >`	Marks an item in a descriptive list.
`< DD >`	Describes an element in a descriptive list.
`< A HREF = "URL" >`, `< /A >`	Used to create a hyperlink. The text or image between the tags is represented as a hyperlink on the Web page.

	When it's selected, the actual URL given in place of *URL* is used to access a resource on the Web.
< IMG SRC = "*URL*" >	Used to display an image as part of a Web page. The actual URL given in place of *URL* represents an image file.
< TABLE > , < /TABLE >	Used to construct a table.

Table 15.2   HTML Tags

URL Formats

When you're writing Web pages you'll probably want to include hyper-links to other resources on the World Wide Web. You saw in the section above on hyperlinks that you do that by using a tag in the form of < A HREF = "*URL*" > where a specific URL is substituted for *URL*. We'll give the formats for URLs for different services or protocols on the Web later in this section.

Before going into the different formats for URLs, here's a quick review of the concept and general format of a URL. The purpose of a URL is to give the location and the means to get to a resource on the Internet. The Web browser uses it to access items, and it's becoming common to see it used as a way to let people know about a resource, a source of information, or an advertisement.

Recall the general form:

**transfer protocol://domain name/directory/subdirectory/
file name.file type**

Essentially this is like a sign pointing to something on the Internet. Starting at the far left, the portion of the URL up to the colon (:) tells what type of Internet service to use. The Internet domain name or address of the site supplying the information comes just after the characters ://. After the first single slash, you have the full path name of the item. One of the key items of a URL is the type of service or protocol it represents.

Here's a list of different URL types.

Resource	URL Begins	Example
Web pages	**http://**	**http://nmaa-ryder.si.edu/artdir/ treasures.html** Selections from the permanent collection of the National Museum of American Art
FTP	**ftp://**	**ftp://ftp.jpl.nasa.gov/ pub/images/browse/**

A directory of images from NASA Jet Propulsion Laboratory's public information FTP archive

telnet://   **telnet://locis.loc.gov**
Search holdings of Library of Congress
telnet://world@psupen.psu.edu
Pen pages (use the login name *world* once you're connected)

Two other services—email and Usenet news—have URLs, but their URLs are in a slightly different format. They do not include the ://.

Email   **mailto:**   **mailto:ernie@mwc.edu**
Send an email message to the address **ernie@mwc.edu**

Usenet news   **news:**   **news:rec.food.cooking**
The URL to access the articles in the newsgroup **rec.food.cooking**

WRITING A WEB PAGE

Overview

Now that we know something about HTML, HTML tags, and URLs, we'll put together a Web page. This Web page could be called a ***personal home page*** because it will give information about an individual. Thousands of folks have personal home pages. It's a way of letting others on the Internet know about you. An example of an excellent personal home page is "Jan's Home Page," **http://jan.redmood.com**, created by Jan Hanford.

In this activity we'll create two Web pages. One gives some work-related information and the other gives information about hobbies and interests. We'll put an image on each and eventually use tables on the second page. The pages will be linked. This activity shows some of the beginning stages of designing a personal Web site. It's not complete, but we don't have the space for a complete project.

At the end of each page we'll include an email address to use if readers have any questions about the Web page, and the date the Web page was last modified or changed.

You create the Web page by typing the HTML tags and text into a file on your computer using an editor or word-processing program. No matter what software you use to create the page, your work will be saved in a text or ASCII file. The image file with a picture of Ernest Ackermann was created by using a scanner to scan a photograph. The source files for the Web pages and images are all in the folder **chap15** on the disk that's included with this book.

We're going to write the pages in stages; first we'll write the HTML statements, then save them to a file, and finally use the Web browser to view what we've done so far. We'll use the editor Notepad, which is part of the basic accessories for a Microsoft Windows system. You can use whatever editor or word-processing program you'd like.

The steps we'll follow for this activity are:

1. Start Notepad.
2. Type the HTML and text for the first Web page.
3. Save the work into a file named **act151p1.html**.
4. Use the Web browser to view the page.
5. Add the image near the top of the page and other information at the end of the page.
6. Create another Web page in the same manner. Save it as **act151p2.html**. Include a hyperlink on both pages so viewers can go from one to the other.
7. Redo the HTML for the second page so some of the information is presented as a table. Save it as **act151p3.html**.
8. Modify the hyperlink on the first page so it takes the reader to the page whose source is **act151p3.html**.

Fy PERSONAL WEB PAGES

There are several collections of personal Web pages on the Web. Most allow you to list or register your personal Web page.

~ "One Nation Worldwide" **http://www.onww.com**

~ "Personal Pages Worldwide" **http://www.utexas.edu/ world/personal/index.html**

~ "WhoWhere? Personal Home Pages Directory" **http://homepages. whowhere.com**

Two interesting articles on the reasons people create personal Web pages are

~ "The World Wide Web as Social Hypertext," **http://www.pliant.org/ personal/Tom_Erickson/ SocialHypertext.html**, by Tom Erickson.

~ "Personal Home Pages and the Construction of Identities on the Web," **http://www.aber.ac. uk/media/Documents/short/ webident.html**, by Daniel Chandler.

Details

1. Start Notepad.

You start Notepad by selecting or clicking on its icon in the Accessories section of Microsoft Windows.

 Click on the **Start** button, move the pointer to **Programs**, then move the pointer to **Accessories**, and click on **Notepad**.

Once Notepad starts you'll see a window similar to the one in Figure 15.26, except there won't be any text in the window.

2. Type the HTML and text for the first Web page.

 Start typing the HTML and tags necessary for the items on the first Web page.

Figure 15.26 shows the HTML tags and text necessary to have the items we mentioned in section A displayed by a viewer.

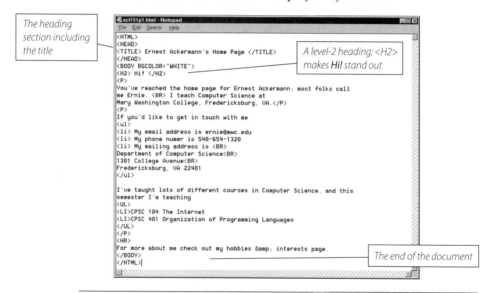

Figure 15.26   The Initial Text and HTML Tags for the Web Page

3. Save the work into a file named **act151p1.html**.

To look at what's been done so far with a Web browser, you need to save the work to a file.

 To save a file while using Notepad, click on **File** in the menu bar, choose **Save As**, and then give a file name.

You'll want to be sure of two things:

1. The name of the file ends with **.htm** or **.html**, such as **act151p1.html**.

2. You know the name of the directory or folder that holds the file so you can find it later.

If you have the opportunity, be sure to select an appropriate folder to hold the file. You might want to create a folder named **WebPages** to hold your work. Just to be specific for this example, the work will be saved in a file named **act151p1.html** in a folder (directory) named **chap15** on the disk in Drive A:.

Just suppose we were going to save the file in a different folder or directory named **WebPages**. You would first create the folder or directory using My Computer or Windows Explorer. After you selected **Save As** a dialog box would appear on the screen. You would type **C:\WebPages\act15p1.html** in the portion of the dialog box labeled **File name**.

4. **Use the Web browser to view the page.**

First be sure the Web browser is started. You don't necessarily have to connect to the Internet to view the file holding the Web page, because it's a local file. We'll use Internet Explorer to view the file. We wouldn't see much difference or change the steps much if we used Navigator. Choose whichever browser you'd like. We'll give the instructions for Internet Explorer.

Do it!   Click on **File** in the menu bar and then select **Open**.

This opens a dialog box labeled Open.

Do it!   Click on the button labeled **Browse**.

A dialog box will appear on the screen.

Do it!   Use the controls to get to the folder named **chap15** on the disk in Drive A:.

Do it!   Double-click on **act151p1.html** to view the Web page in the browser.

Only one more step to get the file displayed in the browser.

Do it!   Click on **OK** in the Open dialog box.

These steps cause the browser to display the Web page written above. It's shown in Figure 15.27.

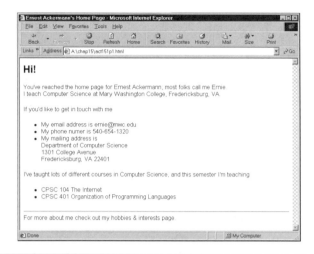

Figure 15.27   The Web Browser View of act151p1.html

How do you like it? It's not bad, but we're going to change it by adding some hyperlinks. Since the College has a home page, we'll add a hyperlink to that through the College's name. We'll also add a hyperlink so folks can send email by clicking on the email address on the screen, we'll make hyperlinks to the Web pages for the courses listed, and we'll make a hyperlink to the Web page that's going to list hobbies and interests. It may be that that Web page doesn't exist yet, but we can still make the hyperlink. We just have to be sure about the name of the file. To do that we have to:

1. Use the editor or word-processing program to edit or change the file holding the Web page.
2. Save the changes.
3. View the Web page with the browser again.

If both the editor and the browser are still on the screen, you have to click on the appropriate windows to use them. Otherwise, you need to start them.

As you make changes to **act151p1.html**, it's a good idea to keep viewing it with the browser. Make changes, save the changes, and then click on the icon labeled **Refresh** from the browser's toolbar. It's really useful to be able to make changes and see what they look like almost immediately, particularly when trying new things.

Figure 15.28 shows the portion of **act151p1.html** with the hyperlinks added. We've pointed out the tags to add. Note that we've used a relative URL—just the name of the file **act151p2.html**—for the hyperlink to the next Web page we're going to write.

HTML tags for a hyperlink to the MWC home page added here

The HTML tag for the email hyperlink added here

A hyperlink to another Web page here

Hyperlinks to Web pages for the courses here

```
act151p1.html - Notepad
File  Edit  Search  Help
<P>
You've reached the home page for Ernest Ackermann; most folks call
me Ernie. <BR> I teach Computer Science at
<a href="http://www.mwc.edu">Mary Washington College</a>, Fredericksburg, VA.</P>
<P>
If you'd like to get in touch with me
<ul>
<li> My email address is <a href="mailto:ernie@mwc.edu">ernie@mwc.edu</a>
<li> My phone numer is 540-654-1320
<li> My mailing address is <BR>
Department of Computer Science<BR>
1301 College Avenue<BR>
Fredericksburg, VA 22401
</ul>

I've taught lots of different courses in Computer Science, and this
semester I'm teaching
<UL>
<LI><a href="http://www1.mwc.edu/~ernie/cpsc104">CPSC 104 The Internet</a>
<LI><a href="http://www1.mwc.edu/~ernie/cpsc401">CPSC 401 Organization of Programmir
</UL>
</P>
<HR>
For more about me <a href="act151p2.html">check out my
hobbies &amp; interests page</a>.
</BODY>
</HTML>
```

Figure 15.28   act151p1.html Modified with Added Hyperlinks

 Click on **File** and select **Save** to save the modified source in the file act151p1.html.

 View the Web page with your browser.

How do you like it now? Make any changes you'd like. We're going to add an image near the top and put some information at the bottom of the page.

5. **Add the image near the top of the page and other information at the end of the page.**

We're going to add a picture at the top of the page and some information at the end. The picture is in a file in the GIF format and we'll use an IMG SRC tag to display it. The information at the end includes an email address to use if readers have questions about the Web page, and the date the Web page was last modified or changed.

To add the image, we'll include the HTML tag for the image between the lines

```
<P>
You've reached the home page for Ernest Ackermann;
most folks call me Ernie. <BR>
```

in the source.

 Add the line <IMG ALIGN=RIGHT SRC="erniebw.gif" alt="picture of Ernie">.

With this addition the source now contains

```
<P>
<IMG ALIGN=RIGHT SRC="erniebw.gif" alt="picture of
Ernie">
You've reached the home page for Ernest Ackermann;
most folks call me Ernie. <BR>
```

Using SRC = "erniebw.gif" implies the image is in the same directory as the Web page. We've made sure that's the case, so the Web page now looks like the one shown in Figure 15.29.

(Do it)/ Add the following information near the end of the file just before the tag </BODY>.

<hr>

Contact Ernest Ackermann,

<a href="mailto:ernie@mwc.edu">ernie@mwc.edu</a>,

for any questions/rants/raves about this Web page.

Last modified Feb 10, 2000.

(Do it)/ Click on **File** and select **Save** to save the modified source in the file act151p1.html.

(Do it)/ View the Web page with your browser.

The Web page now looks like the one we show in Figure 15.29.

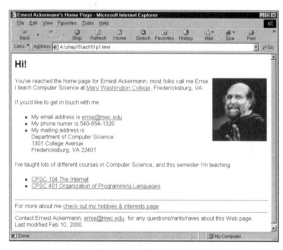

Figure 15.29   act151p1.html with an Image and Footer Information Added

Now on to writing another Web page to list hobbies and interests.

6. **Create another Web page in the same manner. Save it as act151p2.html. Include a hyperlink on both pages so viewers can go from one to the other.**

We're going to write a Web page that lists hobbies and interests. Before we get to this point we have to spend some time deciding on and finding the content. We want to list some hyperlinks to Web sites that we like that are related to these topics. Let's assume the hobbies and interests are gardening and photography, and we've collected some hyperlinks to sites we want to list. We also need to decide on the design of the page. There are several possibilities. We'll look at one in this section and another in the next. Here's a sketch of one design.

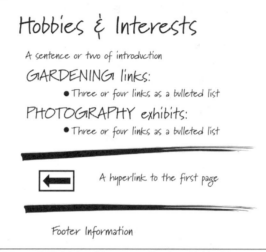

Figure 15.30   A Hobbies & Interests Design Using Lists

We'll use an image of an arrow that we've retrieved from MediaBuilder Icon Library, **http://www.mediabuilder.com/ graphicsicon.html**. That's a good resource for free images. The file holding the digital representation of the arrow is in the folder **chap15** on the disk included with this book.

Now we need to write the HTML for this page. This involves a main heading, some text, and two lists of hyperlinks. We also need to insert an image, a hyperlink to get us back to **act15l1p1.html**, and the footer information. Previous sections explain the HTML necessary for all these items.

Do it! Start Notepad and type the HTML necessary for this page.

Figure 15.31 shows some of the HTML for the page. To see all the HTML use Notepad to view the file **act15l1p2.html** on the disk that's included with this book.

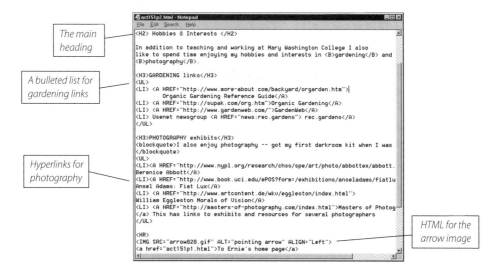

The main heading

A bulleted list for gardening links

Hyperlinks for photography

HTML for the arrow image

Figure 15.31   HTML for **act151p2.html**, Hobbies & Interests, Using Lists

(Do it!) Save the HTML in the file **act151p2.html**.

(Do it!) View the Web page.

The Web page is shown in Figure 15.32.

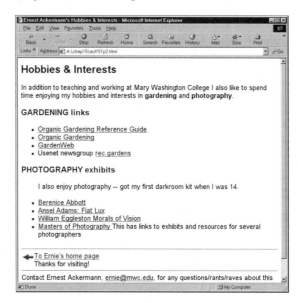

Figure 15.32   The Web Page View of the file **act151p2.html**,
Hobbies & Interests, Using Lists

7. **Redo the HTML for the second page so some of the information is presented as a table. Save it as act151p3.html.**

Now we're going to try the same information in a different design using tables. Here's a sketch of the design we'll use.

Figure 15.33   A Hobbies & Interests Design Using a Table

The HTML for a table is given in the previous section "Tables." Using Notepad we'll redo the HTML using tables as shown in Figure 15.33. We've constructed one table with two rows and two columns. One row is for gardening and the other is for photography. The source is in the file **act15l p3.html**.

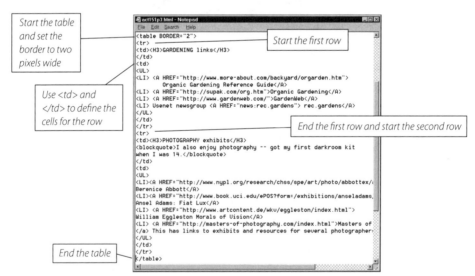

Figure 15.34   The HTML for Hobbies & Interests Using a Table

Now take a look at the Web page.

View the Web page with the source **act15l p3.html** in the folder **chap15**.

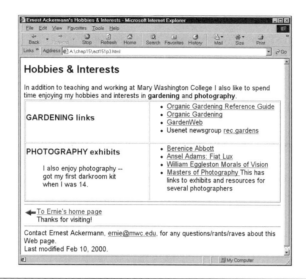

Figure 15.35   The Web Page View of the File **act151p3.html**,
                 Hobbies & Interests, Using a Table

Using a table gives us a more compact design. We like this better than using only lists, so we'll change the link in **act151p1.html** to go to this page.

8. Modify the hyperlink on the first page so it takes the reader to the page whose source is act151p3.html.

  (Do it) Open the file **act151p1.html** with Notepad and change the link at the bottom.

We need to change the HTML in **act151p1.html** from

```
For more about me <a href="act151p2.html">check out my
hobbies &amp; interests page</a>.
```

to

```
For more about me <a href="act151p3.html">check out my
hobbies &amp; interests page</a>.
```

Just so we have both versions available we'll save this modified version of the HTML in **act151p1T.html**.

  (Do it) Save the modified HTML in the file **act151p1T.html**.

Now we've got both versions available.

It's taken some work to develop two versions of the Web page, but we've got a good start on writing Web pages.

END OF ACTIVITY 15.1

Activity 15.1 showed just one possibility for design and linking of Web pages. A page to represent a business or organization needs to concentrate more on presenting an image of the organization, the services offered, and a means to get the reader involved in requesting information, services, or products. A page that focuses on a theme (such as guitars) or an event (such as an art exhibit) needs to present information, provide a means for folks to participate, and include hyperlinks to related resources or Web pages. Some pages are pure whimsy, entertainment, or playfulness. No matter what type of Web page you're constructing, think carefully about its purpose and design before writing, and search for Web pages with a similar topic or purpose. We can learn a lot from looking at each other's work.

Resources for More Information on Creating Web Pages

There's lots of help on the World Wide Web for creating Web pages and using HTML. Most of the major directories (such as Yahoo! and Excite) have sections on the topic, several discussion groups and newsgroups deal with HTML and authoring at basic and advanced levels, and there are several tutorials you can use with a Web browser to help you learn. We'll give some more detail about each of those areas below. In addition to what follows, you'll want to check your favorite library or bookstore—either in person or via the Internet—for books that deal with designing and constructing Web pages and Web sites.

Listings in Directories

Look at these sections of directories for information about HTML:

∾ Excite directory section HTML
  http://www.excite.com/computers_and_internet/internet/web_design/html

∾ Yahoo! directory section HTML
  http://dir.yahoo.com/Computers_and_Internet/Information_and_Documentation/Data_Formats/HTML

∾ The Virtual Library of WWW Development
  http://www.stars.com/Vlib/

Discussion Groups

Discussion groups are a way to share information and get questions answered. All the communication is carried on through email. Refer to these discussion groups for information about HTML:

∾ "HTML-L, HTML Assistance Mailing List"
To subscribe send email to **listserv@vm3090.ege.edu.tr** with the body of the message being **SUBSCRIBE HTML-L** *your-full-name*.

∾ "ADV-HTML, Advanced HTML Discussion List"
To subscribe send email to **listserv@ua1vm.ua.edu** with the body of the message being **SUBSCRIBE ADV-HTML** *your-full-name*.

Take a look at the document "World Wide Web Mailing Lists," **http://www.w3.org/Mail/Lists.html**, for a list of other discussion groups.

Newsgroups

Usenet newsgroups are another way to share information and get questions answered through group discussion. There are several newsgroups that deal with the issues of authoring Web pages:

∾ **comp.infosystems.www.authoring.html**
Discussion of issues related to HTML in terms of usage, standards, etc.

∾ **comp.infosystems.www.authoring.images**
Discussion of issues related to the use of images within Web pages

∾ **comp.infosystems.www.authoring.misc**
Discussion on any topics related to writing Web pages

Tutorials and Guides

There are several very good guides and tutorials for creating Web pages:

∾ "Ben's Planet: Complete HTML Reference Guide," **http://www.bensplanet.com/index.html**. Includes an HTML dictionary, a collection of articles about HTML, and an HTML forum

∾ "Web Design," **http://www.glassdog.com/design-o-rama**. An interesting and lively set of lessons and commentary about Web site design and construction.

∾ "Know the Code: HTML for Beginners," **http://builder.cnet.com/Authoring/Basics**. A straightforward introduction from CNET's builder.com.

∾ "NCSA—A Beginner's Guide to HTML," **http://www.ncsa.uiuc.edu/General/Internet/WWW/HTMLPrimer.html**. An excellent tutorial to take you through the basics of using HTML.

Summary

Web pages are text or ASCII files in which HTML, Hypertext Markup Language, is used to specify the format of the Web page, images to be displayed, hyperlinks, and possibly other elements. A Web browser interprets the HTML in the file, called the source file, and then displays the Web page. So one part of the task of writing Web pages is learning how to use HTML to design and implement appropriate and effective pages.

The source file for a Web page consists of text, URLs, and other elements along with tags or directives written according to the rules of HTML. HTML tags are enclosed between < and > . Some tags occur in pairs with the second being like the first, except a slash is used after < to indicate it's the matching tag; for example, < I > and < /I > . Other tags occur as single entities, such as < HR > . Tags can be written using upper- or lowercase letters; HTML ignores the case of letters in a tag. In URLs you have to pay strict attention to the case of the letters. An HTML document ought to have two parts, a heading and a body. The heading contains the title for the Web page, and the body holds the content—what will be displayed on the Web page. HTML tags can be used for some control over vertical spacing, such as ending lines and starting paragraphs, but otherwise most horizontal and vertical spacing within a source file is ignored. The browser takes care of fitting the page within its window. HTML tags are also used to specify up to six levels of headings in a document and control whether text is displayed in bold, italic, or plain font. Lists—numbered, bulleted, or descriptive—can be specified with HTML tags. HTML is also used to create and specify hyperlinks and place images within a Web page. The hyperlinks start with a tag of the form < A HREF = "*URL*" > (where you substitute an actual URL for *URL*), followed by text or a tag for an image, and then terminated with < /A > . The following:

```
It appears that <A HREF="http://www.mwc.edu/ernie/
index.html"> Ernest Ackermann</A> is the culprit!
```

would appear on a Web page as

It appears that <u>Ernest Ackermann</u> is the culprit!

Clicking, in the Web page, on <u>Ernest Ackermann</u> would cause the browser to open the location associated with **http://www.mwc.edu/ernie/index.html**. Images are put into Web pages using a tag of the form < IMG SRC = "*URL*" > where the URL of an image is put in for *URL*. The image needs to be either in GIF or JPEG format to be displayed by the Web browser. Text can be aligned with an image, either at the top, middle, or bottom. Images can be placed to the left or right of text. HTML does have lots of other tags; we've covered the basic ones in this chapter.

Since a source file is in text format, it can be created with any editor or word-processing program that allows you to save a file in text or ASCII form. No special program to create a Web page is necessary, but when there's lots to do or you have to convert from another format to a Web document, it's useful to have a program designed to create Web pages. Some are available as shareware, some as freeware, and some must be purchased before using them.

Learning HTML is one part of being able to create interesting and effective Web pages. You also need to be concerned with the content and the layout of the content.

Designing, creating, or writing a Web page is generally very satisfying. You create something and then let people around the world see it. Before making the page available to the world, you can develop it on your computer and view it with your Web browser. When you need help or want to pursue the topic further there are a number of resources, guides, newsgroups, and mailing lists on the Web to give help in creating or authoring Web pages. What fun!

Selected Terms Used in This Chapter

alternate text	source file
hyperlink	tag
Hypertext Markup Language (HTML)	text file
	URL
personal home page	Web page

Exercises and Projects

1. Find out if your organization, school, company, or Internet service provider has a home page.
   a. What's the URL?
   b. Take a look at the source view for the Web page in part a. What's in the heading section?
   c. To whom do you send email for suggestions or comments?
   d. When was the page last modified?

2. Make some modifications to the Web page in Activity 15.1.
   a. Replace the items in the first page so it describes what you do professionally or the classes you're taking.
   b. Replace the items in the second page to reflect your interests.
   c. Replace the image on the first page with a picture of yourself or an image that you find at MediaBuilder, **http://www.mediabuilder.com**, or Absolute Web Graphics Archive, **http://www.grsites.com/webgraphics**.

3. Suppose the file named **bobo.gif** holds an image in the GIF format, and it's in the same folder as a file that's the source for a Web

page. To answer the following questions, supply the HTML tags to accomplish the task described.

a. Write the HTML necessary and sufficient to display the image as part of a Web page.

b. Write the HTML necessary and sufficient so the image appears on the page as a hyperlink without any attached text. When someone clicks on it, the current Web page is replaced by a page consisting only of the image.

c. Write the HTML necessary and sufficient so the image appears as part of a Web page. Next to the image are the words "enter at your own risk." The words function as a hyperlink to **http://www.mwc.edu/ ~ ernie/funhouse.html**, but clicking on the picture does nothing.

4. Write the HTML necessary to display the list   Jennifer   as
                                                      Marsha
                                                      John
                                                      Rita
                                                      Ernie

a.   b.   c.
1. Jennifer   • Jennifer   1. Jennifer
2. Marsha   • Marsha   2. Marsha
3. John   • John   • John
4. Rita   • Rita   • Rita
5. Ernie   • Ernie   3. Ernie

5. The HTML tag < BODY BACKGROUND = "*URL*" > , where *URL* is the URL of an image file, makes that file the background for a Web page. That's the way some folks put a colorful background on their Web pages. Modify the Web page **act15lp 1.html** in the folder **chap15** on the disk included with this book

a. so that you use the file **purp.gif** (also included on the disk) as the background for the page.

b. so that you use a background you've obtained from MediaBuilder Background Library, **http://www.mediabuilder.com/ graphicsback.html**.

6. Read some of the articles in the newsgroup **comp.infosystems.www.authoring.html**. What are people talking about? Pick out two popular or interesting questions with answers. For each, give a statement, in your own words, of the question, and then give a summary of the answers.

7. Write the HTML necessary to produce a Web page with the same layout and content as Table 15.1 of this chapter.

8. Using the images available at "Welcome to the Planets," **http://pds.jpl.nasa.gov/planets**, create a Web page that has information about the planets in a table format. Each row will have the image of the planet in one cell, the name of the planet in the next, and its distance from the sun and its diameter in the third cell.

9. Create a Web page for a small business. Be sure the top of the Web page has the name of the business in large letters, with any email, telephone, and street address information on at most two lines under the name of the business. All of this should be centered. Next include any appropriate images and information about the business. Use a white or neutral background. Be sure to include footer information with a name and email address people can use to contact the business.

10. Create a Web site of two or three linked Web pages that tell about an interest or a hobby of yours. Make it interesting and informative. Include hyperlinks to some of the most important Web pages and WWW resources related to the subject or hobby.

11. Suppose you're in the business of creating Web pages for others. Design and build a Web page that describes your services and shows your work.

Chapter

16

ENHANCING

WEB

PAGES

You want to give the people who visit your Web pages a rich, full experience. You know the topic you want to address with a Web site and you know who your audience is. In the previous chapter we covered ways to develop and write Web pages using basic HTML. You can make fine Web pages this way. The methods we discussed covered including graphic (still) images on a Web page. The pages developed in the previous chapter are static; they provide information but don't act on any information from viewers except when they click on a hyperlink.

You've probably seen other Web pages that include animations, sound, and video, and you've worked with lots of Web pages that contain interactive or dynamic elements. Web-based search tools, for example, are typically designed to accept some information you've typed into a form and pass that information to a server. That produces a new Web page—the results page generated by the server and displayed in the browser. Web-based email and shopping also work that way. A user provides information or makes a selection that's sent to a server where the information is processed and some action is taken, an email is generated or an order for an item is processed. In some cases Web pages contain interactive elements—a running clock, a marquee displaying a message, or a guest book. We'll talk about including these types of elements in Web pages and some of the concepts involved in setting up Web services.

We'll look at using different types of media, adding interactive elements to our Web pages, and taking advantage of other ways to enhance your Web pages. By the phrase *enhance your Web pages* we mean make your pages more valuable and useful to the people who view and use them. The quality of the Web pages and sites you create depends on your design and technical skills, and on bringing interesting and useful content to the Web. Also, you need to consider the viewer's experience with a Web page.

Goals/Objectives

∾   Know the ways an image can be optimized to minimize downloading time

∾   Know some of the tools to use to optimize images

∾   Know the concepts involved in making audio and video files available through the Web

∾   Know the concepts associated with providing and adding interactive and dynamic elements to Web pages

∾   Gain a basic understanding of using Java applets, JavaScript, and CGI programs on Web pages

Topics

∾   Review of Client/Server Concepts

∾   Optimizing Images

∾   Animations

∾   Adding Audio

∾   Adding Video

∾   Adding Interactive and Dynamic Elements to Web Pages

∾   Using the Server to Provide Services and Process Data

Review of Client/ Server Concepts

Before we go forward with ways to enhance Web pages, recall how a server and a client interact to provide a Web page.

∾   The Web browser acts as a client and sends a request to a Web server for the file that is then displayed as a Web page. There are several events that occur when a Web page is requested. Here are the four primary events:

1. You click on a hyperlink or type a URL in the location field.

2. The browser formulates a request to a Web server. The server is software that is running on a computer whose Internet domain name is the part of the URL after the first // and before the first / (slash). For example, if we use the URL **http:// www.webliminal.com/essentials/getbooks.html**, then a request for a Web page is sent from your browser to the computer whose Internet domain name is **www.webliminal.com**.

3. The server, if it's possible, sends the file that represents the Web page that you requested to the browser.

4. The browser interprets the contents of the file and displays the Web page.

Whatever type of enhancement you use you'll want to be sure that a client can process it properly. The server sends the information, but it's up to the browser and the computer it's running on to make the information accessible to a person viewing the Web page. After the third step, the server is essentially removed from the process of displaying the Web page. For someone to view or hear something from the Web, then, it's necessary that the browser be able to display or play it. Sometimes a *plug-in*—other software that works with a Web browser—is used to view or display certain types of files as part of a Web page. For example, Shockwave from Macromedia is a plug-in that allows a browser to display interactive multimedia. You'll want to use common file types for representing images, audio, or video. Using common file types means that either the browser will be able to display the file or a plug-in will be readily available.

Remember that it takes more bytes to represent images, animations, video, and sound than it does for text. You'll need to keep this in mind so that it doesn't take an unreasonable amount of time to display your Web pages. Images, sound, and other multimedia displayed on a Web page aren't part of the source file sent to the client by the server; they are represented by HTML tags, such as the tag < IMG SRC = . . . > for an image. When the browser gets the source file, it sends requests for other Web page elements. Including multimedia elements therefore increases the time it takes to download a Web page. You want to provide a rich experience for people visiting your Web pages, but doing that increases the wait to get to your material. Seem like an impossible situation? It's not always easy, but we'll be discussing this in more detail later in the chapter.

Fy INFORMATION ABOUT USABILITY

~ "All Things Web: The Usable Web"
   http://www.pantos.org/
   atw/usable.html
~ "Usability"
   http://www.slais.ubc.ca/
   courses/libr559a/winter2000/
   resources/usability.htm
~ "Usability and Human Factors
   for the Internet"
   http://WebWord.com
~ "Usability Checklist for Site
   Developers"
   http://webreview.com/pub/1999/
   10/15/usability/index.html

For now, here is a short list of a few things you can do to help people visiting your Web page:

~ Include items that require a large number of bytes near the bottom of a Web page since a browser will start to display the first portion of a Web page as other elements are being retrieved.

~ Choose a way of representing an image, audio, or video that gives an adequate, but not necessarily the best, representation of the information.

~ List large files as hyperlinks; don't include them as an integral part of a Web page.

We've stressed two points that help to determine whether the elements you add to a Web page enhance or detract from the content:
1. The elements of a Web page have to be available in a reasonable amount of time
2. The elements in a Web page have to be in a digital format the client can deal with.

Now we're going to delve into some of the details of enhancing Web pages using different types of media and adding some interactive and dynamic elements to a Web page. You can think of this as being divided into three sections.

~ First we'll deal with images, animations, video, and audio. In Chapter 12 we discussed the common file formats used for images, audio, and multimedia on Web pages. We dealt with some issues related to viewing or hearing Web page elements of these types. In this chapter we'll cover some of the issues related to using these types of files when constructing Web pages.

~ Secondly we'll go over some of the concepts associated with adding interactive and dynamic elements to Web pages. We'll start with talking about using **Java applets** and **JavaScript** in Web pages. These work primarily with the client's computer system.

~ Lastly we'll take a look at the concept of the Common Gateway Interface (CGI) and the basics of using programs on a Web server to process information supplied via the Internet.

Optimizing Images

In this section we'll discuss some topics that relate to how you can use images in a way that enhances your Web pages. Recall that you display an image on a Web page using the HTML tag < IMG SRC = "*URL*" > . Here *URL* represents the URL of the file holding the image. Before going into the details of optimizing images we'll go over some basics about how images are represented and displayed on a computer.

The images and text on a computer screen are directly represented in the computer's memory unit. We can think of a computer display as divided up into a rectangular arrangement of pixels (short for *picture elements*), where each pixel corresponds to a location in the memory. Think of an image as a collection of pixels or memory locations. If one image is larger than another, then it stands to reason that the larger one will take up a larger portion of memory than the smaller image when they are displayed. Reducing the size of an image thus reduces the amount of memory needed to display it, and likewise reduces the size of the file holding the information. The number of colors or shades of gray in an image also affects the size of the file. More colors or shades of a color means more information. For example, if an image used 256 colors, we could represent the 256 colors using one byte or eight bits. (This is because with eight bits we can represent $2^8 = 256$ different things.) The pixels in memory are also represented by a collection of bits or bytes, and if our computer monitor were set to display 256 colors, then one byte of memory per pixel would be dedicated to the display. Some monitors are set to display more colors using 16 bits (2 bytes) or 24 bits (3 bytes) per pixel. Later we'll discuss how to reduce the size of a file holding an image by reducing the number of colors in the image.

Regardless of the number of colors available on our monitor, the person viewing our Web page may not see the colors we used in the same way. We may use more than 256 colors, but someone may view our Web page with a monitor set for only 256 colors. Furthermore, PC and Mac displays handle some of these colors differently. There are only 216 colors that we can count on for a true representation; others are approximated or *dithered*. Increasing the number of colors or shades of colors used gives a more natural appearance to an image, but we may be unnecessarily increasing the size of the file holding the image.

Here we'll concentrate on ways to use images while minimizing the time it takes before they can be viewed. With both of these formats, the image is stored in a compressed format to save space on the computer that's storing the image and also to cut down on the time it takes to send the file from a server.

Image File Formats

Two of the predominate formats used for storing images in files (for use on the Internet) are

| GIF, Graphic Interchange Format | This format was developed by a company named CompuServe and it holds the copyright. However, individuals and businesses may use GIF images on their pages without paying a royalty or license fee. The most recent version of GIF, GIF89a, allows for interlaced images and animated GIFs. Saying that a file is a GIF file is the same as saying that it contains an image stored in the GIF format. The name of a GIF file ends with the extension **.gif**, as in **essentials.gif**. |

JPEG, Joint Photographic Expert Group

The JPEG committee developed this method of compressing images, and there are no copyright restrictions on its use. It works best for images of natural scenes with lots of variety of color and brightness, like those we might capture using a camera. The quality of the compressed image can be controlled—usually increasing the amount of compression decreases the quality. A JPEG file is one that contains an image compressed according to the JPEG standard. The name of a JPEG file usually ends with **.jpg** but sometimes **.jpeg** is used.

Other formats are sometimes used for images on Web pages. Some of the formats are displayed directly by recent versions of the popular browsers while others require a plug-in for viewing. For example, the PNG, or Portable Network Graphics, format has been developed to use compression algorithms similar to GIF. PNG is license and royalty free and may be viewed directly with recent versions of Netscape and Internet Explorer. On the other hand, TIFF, Tagged Image File Format, can be viewed by a browser only if a plug-in is installed. Different formats are used because people have come up with different compression schemes (ways of reducing the size of the file that holds the image), and some are more appropriate for a specific medium. The size in bytes of an image file is an important consideration for Web designers. Reducing the number of bytes decreases the time it takes to download and hence view a file.

GIF uses what's called a ***lossless*** data compression scheme. Lossless means that no information is lost or left out. GIF works best when there are repeated patterns in an image. At most 256 colors may be used in a GIF image, so it's good for images with relatively large swaths of color. For example, we would expect good compression of an image that was a cartoon, a hand-drawn figure, a sign, or a poster with block letters on a simple background. When you save images in GIF you often can specify the number of colors to use for the image.

The JPEG standard uses a different scheme for compression. It falls in the category of ***lossy*** compression—it merely removes or throws away a portion of an image! The algorithms used to do this are designed to try to maintain the quality of the image so that it's acceptable for viewing by humans. JPEG works well with images that have lots of variation and colors—such as photographs or captured video images—but doesn't work well with the types of images that GIF compression handles well. JPEG allows for 24-bit color—that means 2^{24} or over 16 million colors.

We can conclude then that

~ we ought to use GIF when there are few colors in repeated patterns or relative large blocks of color in an image.

~ we should use JPEG when we're dealing with natural scenes or images with lots of variation of colors.

Once we've chosen the format for an image we can do other things to make it so the image can be viewed in a relatively short amount of time.

Ways to Reduce Download Time

One way to reduce the download time for people viewing our Web pages is to reduce the size of the file holding an image. Here are some ways to do that:

Reduce the size of the image

Reducing the size of the image essentially means reducing the number of pixels needed to display the image. The number of pixels translates directly into how many bytes it takes to represent the image. A smaller image is often a better design choice. Some people will be viewing your Web page on a monitor with 640-by-480 (pixels) resolution. An image that's 160 by 120 would take up more than a fourth of the window. Making the image smaller would make it easier to see it completely without having to use the scroll bars.

Some sites maintain two versions of each image, a smaller version that's part of the Web page and a larger, higher quality version that can be viewed by clicking on the smaller image. A small version of the complete image is called a *thumbnail*. Another way to get small representational images is to crop the full image so only a portion of it is displayed. Let's say we have a larger version of an image in a file named **image_large.gif** and a smaller version for a Web page named **image_small.gif** (suppose this smaller one is 80 by 100 pixels). We'd use the HTML `<a href="image_large.gif" border =0><IMG SRC="image_small.gif" WIDTH=80 HEIGHT=100> </a>`. The smaller image would be

Fyi SHAREWARE TO MANIPULATE IMAGES
For Windows systems try
~ Paint Shop Pro
http://www.jasc.com/
product.asp?pf_id=001
~ LView Pro
http://www.lview2.com
For Macs try GIFConverter, http://
www.kamit.com/gifconverter.

on the Web page and clicking on it would display the larger, higher quality image.

Reduce the number of colors

Reducing the number of colors in an image means that it will take fewer bytes to represent the image in GIF. (JPEG compression doesn't depend on the number of colors.) This is sometimes also called reducing the color depth.

For example, instead of using 256 different colors, using eight bits for the colors, try using 64 colors or six bits to represent the colors. Cutting back on the number of colors reduces the quality of the image, but in some cases it's acceptable or not very noticeable. Try different color depths and compare the images.

Once you've picked a good size and an appropriate color depth (number of colors) for an image, there are other things you can do to make it so the Web page loads more quickly or to hold the viewers' attention while they're waiting for a Web page with one or more images to load.

Use images more than once on related pages

When a browser retrieves a Web page it saves the source and images in its cache on a local disk. Most people will have the browser set so that files in the cache are accessed first instead of retrieving them from the Internet, during one session. That means that recurring files will be retrieved from the local disk, thus reducing the time it takes to load them.

Set the size of the image in HTML

You can set attributes for the horizontal and vertical dimensions of an image in the HTML tag for the image. For example, the tag < IMG SRC = "http://www1.mwc.edu/ ~ ernie/sg/ fleethum.gif" WIDTH = "123" HEIGHT = "106" > says to display the image whose URL is **http://www1.mwc.edu/ ~ ernie/sg/fleethum.gif** in a region 123 by 106 pixels. The browser uses the size information to determine the Web page layout before the image is retrieved. With this information the browser can display other portions of the page while the image is downloading. It doesn't help to get the image displayed sooner, but the people viewing the page have something else to look at while the image is downloading.

Save the image as interlaced or progressively encoded (JPEG)

A file that's saved as interlaced GIF or progressively encoded JPEG is displayed in a piecemeal fashion. A blurry or choppy image appears first, and it clears as the entire image is loaded. A person looking at a Web page with the image gets an impression of what it might look like before it is completely loaded. You can usually set whether an image is saved interlaced (for GIF files) or progressively encoded (for JPEG files) as an option with the software you use to work with images.

Here is a list of some examples you can view to see the effect of interlacing and encoding:

∾   Image as a GIF, no interlacing
    http://www.webliminal.com/ essentials/fleeing.html

∾   Image as an interlaced GIF
    http://www.webliminal.com /essentials/fleeing_interlaced.html

∾   Image as a progressively encoded JPEG
    http://www.webliminal.com/essentials/ fleeing_prog_encoded.html

Fy   REDUCING COLORS ON THE WEB
The Web site "Media Builder GIF Optimizer," **http://www. gifoptimizer.com**, offers a free service that lets you upload an image and then view it at various color depths. It also lets you view the image at different sizes. You select the version of least size with acceptable quality and then save it to your disk. This is a very useful site and definitely worth a visit.

Display a version of the image with only two colors while the full-color or grayscale image is loading

Netscape and Internet Explorer, but not all Web browsers, allow you to display one image and then have it replaced by another. That way you can show an image in two colors and while that's on the page, replace it with the full-color version of the image. The two-color version can generally be represented with much fewer bytes so it shows up in a relatively short time. This is done by using the attribute LOWSRC as part of an IMG tag. Here is an example: `<IMG SRC="fleeing.gif" LOWSRC="fleeing_lowsrc.gif">`. Take a look at the Web page **http://www.webliminal.com/ essentials/fleeing_lowsrc.html**. The way it loads is pretty neat, since the black-and-white image appears quickly and the full-color image slowly replaces it from the top to the bottom.

Animations

An animation is a collection of images that are displayed in sequence, one after another, so that it appears that there is some motion. You are probably familiar with flip books where you flip through pages, each containing a variation of an image, and it appears that the image is moving. We get the impression of movement because of the way our mind and eyes process the images, with some memory of the previous image as the new one is displayed. That same principle comes into play when we watch a cartoon or a motion picture. It's a sequence of one still image after another.

Several different technologies are used to produce animations. Some of them, such as Java, QuickTime, and Shockwave, use techniques and methods that require you to learn a fair amount about image manipulation and programming. One technology that's more accessible is animated GIF. An animation is put together by using several GIF files and storing them in one GIF file. You need to use GIF89a, the same type of GIF file that's used for interlaced images, mentioned in the previous section. The file contains all the images and some header information that sets the time delay between displaying images and whether to play the animation once or continuously loop through the images. Remember that one animated GIF is a collection of images, and it's the total of the sizes of the images that affects the download time of the animation. That's why it's common to see animations that are either small (reduced size) or don't include many images. On the other hand, once an animated GIF is downloaded the images are in the cache for the browser. That means that

Fyi POINTERS ABOUT ANIMATED GIFS

Shareware:
~ GIF Construction Set Professional
  http://www.mindworkshop.com/alchemy/gifcon.html
~ GIFmation
  http://www.boxtopsoft.com

Web pages and sites:
~ "Make Your GIFs Dance"
  http://builder.cnet.com/Graphics/Webanim
~ "GIF Animation on the WWW"
  http://members.aol.com/royalef/gifanim.htm
~ "Animated GIF's and Protein Chemistry"
  http://www2.ucsc.edu/~straycat/cpa.html

Collections of animated GIFs:
~ "The Expo"
  http://members.aol.com/royalef1/expo.htm
~ "Animation Factory"
  http://www.animfactory.com

a continuously playing or looping animation is downloaded only once. A browser can display animated GIFs without any plug-ins. Animated GIFs are a way to include animation in a Web page that's accessible to everyone using the common browsers. And you don't need to learn too many new techniques or concepts to create an animated GIF.

Adding Audio

Adding sound or audio to a Web page gives a person another way to experience the topic of the page. It's done by using HTML tags, and, as with images, having the audio information in a file in a specific digital format. Audio files tend to be large. It can take several hundred thousand or several million bytes to represent anything more than a 15-second clip of music or speech. Because of their large size it's best to have links to audio files on a Web page, so that someone viewing the page has the option of taking the time to download the audio file. A different technology called streaming audio (more generally known as **streaming media**) plays the audio as it's being downloaded. This makes receiving audio more appealing, but requires a plug-in. Several audio file formats require a plug-in, and while they are freely and readily available they do take time to load whenever they're needed. Still, audio is a very good way to provide information or entertainment on the Internet. In this section we'll only discuss some different file formats for audio and ways to make audio files accessible through HTML. Creating and storing audio information in a digital format won't be discussed here.

Fyi CREATING AUDIO FILES FOR YOUR WEB PAGE
- "Adam's Multimedia Tutorial" http://hotwired.lycos.com/ webmonkey/multimedia/ tutorials/tutorial3.html
- "Audio for the World Wide Web" http://wdvl.internet.com/ Multimedia/Sound/Audio
- "Make Some Noise! How to Add Audio to Your Site" http://builder.com/ Authoring/Audio

Audio File Types

There are several popular types of compression or encoding schemes used to store audio information. Each produces a particular type of file. The extension identifies the type of encoding used to create the file. People coming to your Web page can listen to these files provided they have a sound card and speakers on their computer. We list some of the common formats in two tables. Table 16.1 lists file types that have to be downloaded or retrieved from a server before they can be played. Except as noted below, both Netscape's and Microsoft's browsers include the necessary applications to play files of these types.

Name	Extension	Description and Comments
Audio Interchange File Format	aif	The Audio Interchange File Format (AIFF) is commonly used on Macintosh systems. This allows for monaural and stereo sound samples.
MIDI	mid midi	MIDI stands for musical instrument digital interface. It is a standard that's been adopted to control synthesizers and similar devices. A MIDI file contains the commands that are interpreted by a sound card or another MIDI device. The instructions then produce the audio or music.
MPEG-3	mp3	MPEG (Moving Picture Expert Group) offers high quality sound with a high degree of compression, but an MP3 player or plug-in is needed. There's lots of information about the MP3 format at Lycos' "MP3 Search," **http://mp3.lycos.com**.
Next/Sun	au	This is referred to as the Next/Sun format. It is also the standard audio file format for Java applications. It doesn't give results of high quality but it's adequate for many sound applications on the Internet.
Wave	wav	Waveform audio format (WAV) is a standard format for computers using Microsoft Windows. These files, like AIFF files, can be monaural or stereo.

Table 16.1   Audio File Types

Table 16.2 lists two popular audio file types that use streaming audio. The audio can be played as the file is downloaded or retrieved from the server. A certain amount of data is retrieved and then a portion of it is played. While it's playing, more is retrieved to keep the data going in a more or less steady stream to the program or device that's playing the audio.

Name	Extension	Description and Comments
Advanced Streaming Format	asf	This is Microsoft's version of a streaming format. It may be used for monaural or stereo audio and video. More information about using this format is available at the Microsoft Web page "Adding Streaming Media to Your Web Site with Windows Media Technologies," **http://msdn. microsoft.com/training/roadmaps/ roadmap2.asp**. Information and tools for producing files of this type, as well as the most recent version of the plug-in or application program needed to play files of this type, are available at the Web page "Windows Media," **http://www.microsoft.com/ windows/windowsmedia/default.asp**.
RealAudio	ra ram	RealAudio was the first format and is the current de facto standard for streaming audio files. RealAudio files can contain information in monaural or stereo format. A related file type, RealVideo, is used for multimedia presentations. Information about using and producing files in these formats is available from the Web page "RealNetworks.com Products," **http://www.realnetworks.com/ products/index.html**, from RealNetworks.com. The most recent version of the plug-in needed for these types of files is available from RealNetworks.

Table 16.2   Streaming Audio File Types

HTML for Audio

You essentially have two choices for using HTML for audio:

1. Include a hyperlink to an audio file so that the person accessing the Web page doesn't have to wait for the audio file to download or wait

for a plug-in to load. This is the most considerate thing to do unless the audio file is small.

2. Embed or make the audio file part of the Web page in the sense that the file loads and it is played as the page is loading.

The audio serves as a background sound. You'll want a really good reason for doing this since audio files are usually large and it takes a long time for one to load. A good recommendation to follow is to include the HTML that does this at the bottom of a Web page so that the text and images will download first. In other words, give the visitor to your Web site something to look at and think about while the audio file is being loaded.

> **Fyi** ABOUT AUDIO FILES
>
> More information about audio file formats:
> ~ "Audio File Format FAQ"
>   **http://home.sprynet.com/ ~cbagwell/audio.html**
> ~ "PC Webopaedia - Audio category page"
>   **http://webopedia.internet. com/Multimedia/Audio**
>
> Collections of audio files that you can use in Web pages:
> ~ "The MIDI Farm Internet"
>   **http://files.midifarm.com**
> ~ "MSDN Online Downloads Sounds TOC"
>   **http://msdn.microsoft.com/ downloads/sounds/toc.htm**
> ~ The Audio section of the World Wide Web Virtual Library
>   **http://archive.comlab.ox.ac. uk/audio.html**

A Hyperlink to an Audio File

You write the HTML for a hyperlink to a sound file the same way as other hyperlinks. Use the standard < A HREF . . . > tag. When you have a link to an audio resource, it's a good idea to say that's what it is and to give information about the type of file and its size. That helps visitors decide whether they want to spend the time required to hear the audio file. Here's an example:

```
<IMG SRC="sound.xbm">
<A HREF="http://www1.mwc.edu/~ernie/sg/flam.wav">
Griffin discussing Fleeing From Flamingos </A>, Audio WAV
format, 785K
```

The HTML looks like this on a Web page. We've included an icon to mark that the link points to an audio file and text that states the type of file and its size.

🔊 <u>Griffin discussing Fleeing From Flamingos</u>, Audio WAV format, 785K

Embedding the Audio—Background Sound

You can include sound as an integral part of a Web page so that the audio is played when the Web page is loaded or viewed. Using sound this way is similar to having an image on a page or having a background color or background image. There are two HTML tags that are currently used for this purpose. The EMBED tag was introduced by Netscape, it's recognized by the Netscape, Microsoft, and other browsers, and through the use of attributes you can give the person viewing the Web page some control over the sound. The other is the BGSOUND tag introduced by Microsoft. It's rather limited because Netscape Navigator and some other browsers don't interpret it, and it can only be used for background sound.

When you use embedded sound be sure to consider its effect on people visiting a Web page. There are situations where adding sound can help others understand the topic of the Web page and can provide a richer experience for visitors to the Web page. But including embed-ded or background sound means it will take longer to download

Fy DETAILS ABOUT THE EMBED TAG

~ The EMBED tag in the HTML Compendium
http://www.htmlcompendium .org/Aembed.htm

~ "Description of the EMBED Tag"
http://users.knoware.nl/users/ schluter/doc/tags/ TAG_EMBED.html

the page. The sound file has to be downloaded as the page is being retrieved. If a plug-in is required, it has to be loaded. The sound file will be played once, and you can use HTML to play the sound over and over again. The person visiting your Web page may be distracted or annoyed by the sound, or they may be viewing the page in an environment where sound isn't appropriate. With that said, here is the HTML you can used to embed an audio file in a Web page.

The tag < embed . . . > is used to embed sound (and other media such as video) in a Web page. The tag is an extension to standard HTML, but most popular browsers interpret the tag correctly. We'll show a couple of examples here that also show the use of some of the attributes for the tag. This tag automatically starts to play the file named **eeurope.mid**.

The audio starts playing as soon as it's retrieved and when the plug-in loads

Nothing appears on the Web page

```
<EMBED   SRC="eeurope.mid" autostart="true" hidden="true">
```

*The audio file **eeurope.mid** is specified by the SRC attribute*

In this example we'll show how to include a control console. The console is similar to a console on a tape player. It gives someone viewing the page control over the playing of the audio file. They can, for example, control the volume, stop the sound, replay the sound from the beginning, or play a section of it.

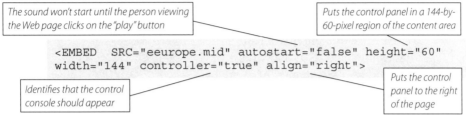

The sound won't start until the person viewing the Web page clicks on the "play" button

Puts the control panel in a 144-by-60-pixel region of the content area

```
<EMBED  SRC="eeurope.mid" autostart="false" height="60"
width="144" controller="true" align="right">
```

Identifies that the control console should appear

Puts the control panel to the right of the page

Some of the attributes we've used are new:

CONTROLLER   This is set to "true," which means the controller or console will appear with the video file. The console can be used to play the video and to control the volume of the accompanying audio.

AUTOSTART   Setting this to "true" starts playing the audio file as soon as it and its plug-in are loaded. Setting this to "false" gives the person downloading the Web page the option of when they want to start the audio.

HIDDEN   The default condition is "false" so that some sort of console or icon appears to represent the audio. Setting it to "true" hides the controls for the audio and sets the audio as background sound (or noise, depending on how you feel about it!).

Microsoft's tag < BGSOUND > can also be used to play sound when a Web page loads. It's simpler than the EMBED tag. Here's an example that will load the audio file **eeurope.mid** and loop through it four times. Nothing appears on the screen; only the sound is played.

```
<BGSOUND  SRC="eeurope.mid" loop="4">
```

For more details take a look at the section on the BGSOUND tag in the HTML Compendium at **http://www.htmlcompendium.org/ Abgsound.htm**.

We've taken a look at adding audio resources to Web pages. Now we'll consider some of the issues involved in using video on the Web. You'll see that many of the same issues, and even the same HTML, apply to video.

Adding Video

Adding video to a Web page is similar to adding audio. Video files tend to be even larger than audio files as they include visual information and often accompanying sound. Because the files are large you'll want to include links to video files so someone visiting your Web page can choose whether to take the time to download the video file. There are some popular streaming technologies that allow the video to be viewed and heard as it's downloading. In every case someone viewing the video file will have to have the proper plug-in installed. Video files are very large, and the video is sometimes encoded so it is displayed at a rate of 15 frames per second (fps) as a compromise to keep the file size reasonable. This gives a choppy effect since our eyes and minds process video information at a rate that requires 30 or 60 fps for smooth or full-motion video. Some formats, notably MPEG, offer very high compression rates so that the video information may be displayed at that rate. We'll mention some of the common video file formats and ways to include video in Web pages. Creating and storing video information in a digital format won't be discussed here.

Fy CREATING VIDEO FILES

~ "Adam's Multimedia Tutorial: Lesson 4"
http://www.hotwired.com/webmonkey/98/17/index3a.html
~ "How to Add Video to Your Site"
http://builder.com/Graphics/Video

Video File Types

There are several popular types of compression and encoding schemes used to store video information. Each produces a particular type of file. They can be identified by the extension to the file name. People coming to your Web page can view and listen to the accompanying audio (if it's part of the video) provided they have the necessary multimedia players or plug-ins and a sound card and speakers on their computer.

We list some of the common formats in two tables. Table 16.3 lists file types that have to be downloaded or retrieved from a server before they can be played.

Name	Extension	Description and Comments
AVI	avi	AVI stands for Audio Video Interleave. It is defined by Microsoft and is the de facto standard for multimedia data on a PC using the Windows operating system. A great resource for all sorts of information about AVI is "AVI Overview," **http://www.jmcgowan.com/avi.html**, by John McGowan.

MPEG	mpg mpeg	This standard format, developed by the Moving Picture Expert Group, gives good quality video (30 or 60 fps) and video with a high degree of compression. Take a look at "MPEG Pointers and Resources," **http://www.mpeg.org/MPEG**, for more information about MPEG.
QuickTime	mov qt	This format was developed by Apple Computer. It's built into the Macintosh operating system, and PCs with the Windows operating system can play video of this type by downloading the QuickTime player through a link from the QuickTime home page at **http://www.apple.com/quicktime**. The QuickTime player is capable of working with many different audio and video types. The QuickTime format also includes ways of presenting streaming video and other methods of dealing with video.

Table 16.3   Video File Types

Table 16.4 lists three popular video and multimedia file types that use a technology called streaming video. The video and audio (if it's present) can be played as the file is downloaded or retrieved from the server. A certain amount of data is retrieved, and then a portion of it is played. While it's playing more is retrieved to keep the data going in a more or less steady stream to the program or device that's playing the video. Some of these formats give video and multimedia presentations that appear choppy, while Shockwave generally displays video at 30 or 60 fps.

Name	Extension	Description and Comments
Advanced Streaming Format	asf	This is Microsoft's version of a streaming format, and Microsoft expects that this format will replace AVI. It may be used for monaural or stereo audio and video. See the entry for ASF in the audio section above for links to more information about ASF.

RealVideo	rm ram	The RealVideo format is used for multimedia presentations. It's related to the RealAudio format. The player for these types of files and information about using and producing files of this format are available from the RealNetworks home page at **http://www.real.com**.
Shockwave	dcr dir dxr	This was developed by and continues to be improved by Macromedia. Multimedia presentations developed using Macromedia's product Director are converted to Shockwave format. It allows for interactive multimedia presentations. Take a look at the Shockwave home page, **http://www.macromedia.com/shockwave**, for more information about and examples of the use of Shockwave. Shockwave files are almost always integrated into Web pages.

Table 16.4   Streaming Video File Types

HTML for Video or Multimedia

The HTML for adding video or multimedia elements is straightforward and similar to the HTML used for audio. You may include a hyperlink to the video or multimedia resource or embed the video within the Web page. Since video files are generally very large it's a good idea to tell people the size of the file they'll be downloading when they select a hyperlink to video. When video is embedded in a Web page you'll see that you can specify the size, in pixels, of the portion of the browser window used by the video, and you can provide a control console for someone viewing it. Most video formats require a plug-in, and some people viewing the page may not have the plug-in installed. You'll see how to include the URL of a Web page that has instructions about how to obtain the necessary plug-in in case it isn't installed. Now for some details about the HTML.

A Hyperlink to a Video File

You write the HTML for a hyperlink to a video file the same way as other hyperlinks. Use the tags < A HREF = "*URL of video file*" > *Text or image* < /A > .

Here's an example. When you have links to a video resource it's a good idea to identify it and to give information about the type of file and its size. That helps visitors decide whether they want to spend the time required to view it.

```
<img src="movie.gif">
<a href="4out5.mov"> Griffin discussing 4 Out Of 5</a>
QuickTime Movie (2,045,965 bytes)
```

Here's the way it looks on a Web page. Notice we've included an icon to mark that the link points to an audio file, and we've included the type of sound file and its size.

<u>Griffin discussing 4 Out Of 5</u> Quicktime Movie (2,045,965 bytes)

Embedding the Video

Using the HTML tag EMBED, you can include video as an integral part of a Web page so that the video is loaded along with the appropriate plug-in when the Web page is viewed. When you use video in this manner, be sure to consider its effect on people visiting your Web pages. The plug-in necessary for the video will have to be present on the computer used for viewing and it will have to be loaded before the video is displayed. Unless the video is in a streaming format, the entire file has to be downloaded. On a modem connection this could take 30 minutes or more for even a short video. With that said, here is the HTML you can use to embed a video file in a Web page.

Netscape defined the tag < embed . . . > to embed sound (and other media such as video) in a Web page. The tag is an extension to standard HTML, but Microsoft Internet Explorer and several other popular browsers interpret the tag correctly. The example below includes some of the attributes for the tag. For more details take a look at the section on the EMBED tag in the HTML Compendium at **http://www .htmlcompendium.org/Aembed.htm**.

```
<EMBED SRC="4out5.mov"
```
The video file 4out5.mov is specified by the SRC attribute

```
PLUGINSPAGE="http://quicktime.apple.com"
```
The URL of the Web page with information about the plug-in

```
CONTROLLER="true" AUTOSTART="false"
```
A controller panel or console is put on the Web page to give some control to the playback of the video, and the video won't start until the "play" button is clicked

Puts the control panel and the video in the content area in a space 240 by 193 pixels

```
WIDTH="240" HEIGHT="193">
```

We've introduced a new attribute here:

PLUGINSPAGE   This is the URL of a Web page that explains how to retrieve the plug-in required (QuickTime, in this example) in case the plug-in isn't installed on the computer requesting the Web page.

Now that we've discussed enhancing a Web page with images, animations, audio, and video we'll talk about adding interactive and dynamic elements to Web pages.

Adding Interactive and Dynamic Elements to Web Pages

There are several ways that Web pages can contain interactive or dynamic items or elements. Remember that when we request a Web page, the client sends a request to a server. The server passes along the source for the Web page, and if more elements are needed (such as images or embedded audio or video) they are retrieved separately from a server. When we use the term "interactive" we mean a person interacting with either the client or the server. It's useful to make the distinction as different techniques and concepts are involved in the two cases. For example, if someone viewing a Web page can make choices that change the content or appearance of a Web page, then they're interacting with the client. On the other hand, if they fill in a form for searching or placing an order, then it's a server that eventually processes the form. By dynamic we mean a Web page where the display changes based on content (such as video or animation), environment (a clock), or interaction from the user (the user makes choices that change content). The client most effectively handles all of these changes.

We've already discussed some ways to add animation and multimedia to Web pages. Here we'll discuss some other ways to provide animation, some ways to allow for interaction using the client, and some ways to work with a server to provide interactive services. We'll approach these issues by taking a look at three of the methods or technologies used to provide interactive and dynamic elements to Web pages. The first two are Java and JavaScript. They work with the client and are transported as part of a Web page. The last method, CGI, involves interacting with a server.

Java and JavaScript

Java is a programming language that's been used successfully in recent years to write programs called Java applets that come from a Web server and execute as part of a Web page. JavaScript is also a programming language, but the instructions are a part of a Web page and are interpreted and carried out by the browser. Applets written using Java are used to provide dynamic elements such as animations, sounds, and interactive programs. The browser interprets JavaScript programs or instructions. They often deal with the properties of a Web page—such as its background color and the values and contents of forms. JavaScript can also be used to open up or close browser windows, to implement a pulldown menu, and more generally to cause actions to occur in response to the movement and behavior of the mouse. Most importantly, the instructions for programs (the applets and scripts) can be passed over the Internet as part of a Web page. This means that programs can be used without having to have the source code or the instructions previously existing on a computer. The programs become part of the World Wide Web.

Java is an object-oriented language, considerably less complex than C++. If you're familiar with computer programming and C++, you'll be able to get comfortable with Java in a relatively short amount of time. (There are several excellent tutorials available on the World Wide Web.) If you haven't done much computer programming, you'll need to devote a good deal of effort and time to get to the point where you can create programs in Java or scripts in JavaScript. We don't go through the details—it would take several chapters—of the basics of programming in either of these languages. We'll include some examples of Java applets and examples of using JavaScript. Whether you're a programmer or not, it's a good idea to take some time to learn a little about Java and why it's important. You'll also want to get an understanding of using Java applets and JavaScript in a Web page.

An Overview of Java, Java Applets, and JavaScript

Java was developed by Sun Microsystems. Some of the terms used to describe the programming language Java are object-oriented, multithreaded, architecture-neutral, robust, secure, and high-performance. (Don't worry if those aren't familiar terms.) Since it's object-oriented, it has classes of objects with certain properties. Tool kits or packages can be constructed and used in a variety of environments. It's those capabilities combined with the fact that Java was designed to be used in a networked environment that make it work so well as part of Web browsers. Using a class called applet and a tool kit called the abstract windows tool kit takes care of many of the details of making a Java program part of a Web page.

A Java applet is a Java program that's constructed using the class named "applet" and the abstract windows tool kit. An applet is included

in a Web page using the HTML tags < APPLET *attributes for the applet >*
. . .   < /APPLET > . The programs are first written in Java and then
compiled or translated to **byte codes** using a Java compiler. When a Web
browser retrieves a page with the APPLET tag, the byte codes are sent to
the computer viewing the Web page to be executed there.

Browsers include an interpreter (a part of the browser
software) that will interpret and
execute instructions written in
a language called JavaScript.
These instructions are part of the
Web page and are translated or
interpreted by the browser on
the client system. They aren't
compiled first, as is the case
with Java programs. JavaScript
includes ways, for example, to
write instructions that respond
to events that occur while a

> **Fy** GOING TO THE SOURCE FOR
> INFORMATION ABOUT JAVA
> Sun Microsystems, who devel-
> oped Java, has some of the most
> complete online information
> about it too.
> ~ The Java home page
>   **http://java.sun.com**
> ~ Sun's Web page for applets
>   **http://java.sun.com/applets/
>   index.html**

person is viewing a Web page. These events include opening or closing
a browser window, moving the mouse over a region of a form, clicking
on a button on a Web page, or selecting an item from a menu. A script
can collect and verify input from a user before passing it back to a server
or an applet.

Most browsers can work with Java applets or JavaScript. Netscape
and Internet Explorer include the software necessary to interpret the byte
codes from applets and to interpret JavaScript.

In the next two sections we'll show how Java applets and JavaScript
are used in Web pages. We'll give a few examples and some resources for
collections of applets and scripts to examine. We won't go through any
detailed analysis of Java programs.

Using Applets

We'll show an example of using an applet on a Web page by taking
a look at "Java Applet Demo," **http://www.webliminal.com/essentials/
java/appletdemo.html**, shown in Figure 16.1. Take a look at the Web
page using your browser to see the scrolling marquee.

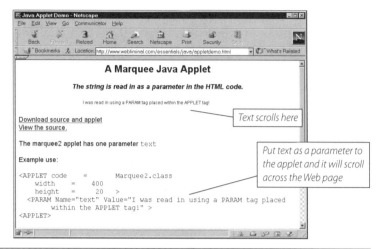

Figure 16.1   A Java Applet Demo—**http://www.webliminal.com/essentials/java/appletdemo.html**

There is one applet on the Web page. It produces a scrolling marquee with text that continuously scrolls from right to left. That sort of movement is possible only because the applet is executing instructions; it is a Java program. The applet allows the person putting the applet on a Web page to specify the text. The Web page shows how to include the applet on a Web page. If that wasn't there, you could look at the source for the page (click on **View** in the menu bar, then **Page Source**) to see how to use the applet.

To add an applet to a Web page you use the HTML tags < APPLET > and < /APPLET > . Remember that an applet is a Java program translated or compiled to byte-code format. We need to specify, at a minimum, two items:

∾ The name of the file that holds the applet	Using the attribute **code**
∾ The size, in pixels, of the portion of the window that will display the output of the applet	Using the attributes **width** and **height**

We may also specify the location of the applet using **codebase**—the URL of the folder or directory that holds the applet on the server. This is all specified as

```
<APPLET codebase = "http://www.webliminal.com/essentials/java/"
        code     = Marquee2.class
        width    = 400
        height   = 20 >
```

Specifying **codebase** allows us to use this applet regardless of where we put the source for the Web page. If we didn't specify **codebase**, the applet would have to reside in the same folder as the source for the Web page.

This applet displays a string of characters in the marquee and the string to be displayed is specified as input from the source of the Web page. It's common for applets to be written to take input from the Web page source. That way they can be customized to fit a specific situation or some aspects of their appearance can be modified. The input to an applet is specified in the HTML tag < PARAM . . . >.

```
<PARAM Name="text" Value="I was read in using a PARAM tag
placed within the APPLET tag!" >
```

In that tag we specify the name and value of one or more parameters (variables) passed to the applet as input. The name of the parameter here is "text" and its value is shown above in quotes on the right of the equal sign (=) after the word Value. The possible parameters are often specified as part of the documentation accompanying an applet. For example, Sun Microsystems has a collection of applets available to anyone on the Web page "Freebie Applets You Can Use," **http://java.sun.com/openstudio/index.html**, and each is accompanied by a Web page that lists, explains, and shows an example of using the parameters.

Finally we end the HTML for the applet with the tag

```
</APPLET>
```

The applet in Figure 16.1 came from the Java program **Marquee2.java**. The program was translated to byte codes using a Java compiler to produce the file **Marquee2.class**. When a Web browser retrieves the page, the byte codes are copied to the client and executed on the computer that's being used to view the page. (By the way, the code is checked to make sure it doesn't do anything unseemly like erase files from the client's disks.)

You could use the marquee applet on a Web page. (The author hereby gives permission. Be sure you have permission before using someone else's applet without modification.)

Fy WHERE TO FIND JAVA APPLETS

∼ "Gamelan: The Official Directory for Java"
http://www.gamelan.com

∼ EarthWeb's "JARS.COM: The #1 Java Review Service"
http://www.jars.com

∼ "The Java Boutique"
http://javaboutique.internet.com

The applet is included on the disk that comes with this book. It's in the file named **Marquee2.class** in the folder named **Java** in the folder **chap16**. If you wanted a Web page that had a scrolling marquee with the text "I feel Good!" in a space 450 by 50 pixels you'd use the following. Notice that since the attribute codebase isn't mentioned, the applet has to be in the same folder as the source for the Web page.

```
APPLET
        code    = Marquee2.class
        width   = 450
        height  = 50 >
        <PARAM Name="text" Value="I feel Good!">
</APPLET>
```

Try it! You'll see the space the marquee applet takes up is a little larger than on **http://www.webliminal.com/essentials/java/appletdemo.html**, but the scrolling letters aren't any bigger. That's because the size of the letters is specified in the program and not taken as input from the use of the applet.

To know about the possible input to the applet you can read instructions about the applet, read the Java source of the program, or look at the way the applet is already being used on a Web page to see what input variables appear in the HTML tags < PARAM Name = ". . ." Value = ". . ." >.

Using JavaScript

JavaScript is a language designed to make it possible to include some interactive or dynamic elements in Web pages. The language allows you to examine and modify portions of a Web document or page. You can similarly examine or modify some of its properties. For example, we can refer to the background color property of a document as **document.bgcolor**.

We show some relation between the elements in a Web page in Figure 16.2. We assume the diagram represents a document containing a form named

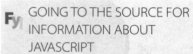
GOING TO THE SOURCE FOR INFORMATION ABOUT JAVASCRIPT
JavaScript was initially developed by Netscape. Netscape provides a good introduction to and complete details about JavaScript in these two documents:

~ "JavaScript Guide"
http://developer.netscape.com/docs/manuals/communicator/jsguide4/index.htm
~ "JavaScript Reference"
http://developer.netscape.com/docs/manuals/communicator/jsref/index.htm

"OrderForm" with two fields in it named "CustomerName" and "Access-Code."

ᔈ The expression **document.OrderForm.CustomerName** refers to the object **CustomerName** that's part of the object **OrderForm**, which in turn is part of the object **document**.

ᔈ In the same way **document.OrderForm.AccessCode** refers to the field named **AccessCode**.

ᔈ We can examine the value of a field with the expression **document.OrderForm.CustomerName.value**. In this way we think of value as a property of the object **document.OrderForm.CustomerName**.

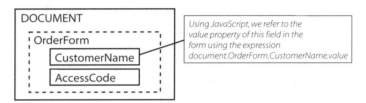

Figure 16.2   The JavaScript View of a Field in a Form

In this way JavaScript is an object-oriented language—when we use it we can think a Web page consists of some predefined objects, and these objects have properties. The objects and properties may be manipulated by using the language.

A form is set up on a Web page through HTML. Here are the tags and the text that define the form in Figure 16.2.

```
<FORM NAME="OrderForm">
Your Name:
<INPUT TYPE="text" NAME="CustomerName" SIZE="40" MAXLENGTH="80">
<p>
AccessCode:
<INPUT TYPE="text" NAME="AccessCode" SIZE="40" MAXLENGTH="80">
</FORM>
```

The statements or instructions of JavaScript are included as part of the source for a Web page, and they're interpreted by the browser. You can write functions or use built-in functions that are called upon when the page is displayed or when a user selects an item from a menu, clicks on a button, or changes the value in a field within a form. The functions (called *methods* in object-oriented parlance) can be used to perform calculations, verify input data, display images, or modify properties of the objects that are part of a Web page. JavaScript is also designed to make it relatively easy to handle certain events such as a mouse click on an object, a change in the value of an object, or movement of the mouse over an object. JavaScript is *not* derived from or related to Java. We can do more with Java since it can be used to support animation, sound, and several simultaneous processes. On the other hand, it's easier to write simple interactive or dynamic applications using JavaScript.

We won't go into many details of the language, but we'll give you enough to get started. We'll look at three examples using JavaScript.

∾ The first shows how to use JavaScript to display the current URL and the time of modification of the source of a Web page.

∾ In the second we modify a property of a document (the background color) based on a mouse click on a button.

∾ In the third we show how to implement a pulldown menu in a Web page.

Example 16.1 USING JAVASCRIPT TO DISPLAY THE URL OF A WEB PAGE AND WHEN THE PAGE WAS LAST MODIFIED

In this example we'll include some JavaScript statements in the body of a Web page. The statements give instructions to write some HTML code. That's done when the browser interprets the source for the Web page, so these statements affect what is displayed. They include instructions to write the URL, title, and date last modified for the Web page. Since they are in the body of the Web page, it's reasonable that there be some way to identify them as JavaScript to the browser.

A copy of the source for this example is on the disk that's included with this book. This and other JavaScript examples are in the directory named **javascript** in the directory named **chap16**. The name of the file is **jsexample1.html**.

The statements will be contained between the HTML tags

```
<script type="text/javascript" language="JavaScript">
<!--
```

and

```
// -- >
</script>
```

The first indicates that what follows is JavaScript and the browser needs to interpret it. Some older browsers don't interpret JavaScript and some people have their browser set so JavaScript isn't enabled. We include `< !--` and `// -- >` so a browser that doesn't interpret JavaScript will treat the lines between as comments. A browser that does interpret JavaScript will, in effect, ignore this.

Here are the complete JavaScript statements:

```
<script type="text/javascript" language="JavaScript">
<!--
var
  theTitle = document.title
  thePlace = document.location
  theDate = document.lastModified

document.write("<hr>");
document.write("The title of this page is: ",theTitle, "<br>");
document.write("Its URL is: ", thePlace, "<br>");
document.write("It was last updated: ", theDate,"<p>");
document.write("Please send comments/questions to ");
document.write("<a href=\"mailto:ernie@mwc.edu\">ernie@mwc.edu");
document.write();

//-->
</script>
```

> Set up variables whose values are the properties of the document we want to display

> We use **document.write** to write HTML code to the Web page

Figure 16.3   A JavaScript Excerpt from **jsexample1.html**, with the Results Shown in Figure 16.4

The program starts with the tag < script LANGUAGE = "Java Script" > , notifying the browser to interpret the statements as part of a JavaScript program.

One JavaScript object, **document.title**, is used. It represents the title of the Web page taken from what's between the tags < TITLE > and < /TITLE > . Its value is assigned to the variable **the Title**. Two properties of the document object are also used. The property **document.location** represents the URL of the Web page. It is assigned to the variable **theLocation**. The property **document.lastModified** represents the date and time the source file was modified on the server. Its value is assigned to the variable **the Date**. You will see a date different than the one shown in Figure 16.4.

After the variables are assigned values, we use the method **document.write** to create HTML statements that become part of the Web page.

We use the symbols \" (a backslash before a quotation mark) in the statement

```
document.write("<a href=\"mailto:ernie@mwc.edu\">ernie@mwc.edu");
```

because a quotation mark, ", is used to mark the start or end of a string in **document.write**, and we need to be sure that < **a href = "mailto: ernie@mwc.edu"** > is part of the Web page. The two occurrences of \" let " be written to the Web page.

These useful statements display information about a Web page that we normally place at the end of a Web page. Viewing **jsexample1.html** in the browser gives a display similar to the following:

The title of this page is: JavaScript Example. Demonstrates modifying HTML with document.write
Its URL is: file:///A|/chap16/javascript/jsexample1.html
It was last updated: Wednesday, February 09, 2000 20:35:38

Please send comments/questions to ernie@mwc.edu

Figure 16.4   The Results of the JavaScript in **jsexample1.html**, with a Portion of the Source Shown in Figure 16.3

END OF EXAMPLE 16.1

Now we present an example that shows how we can use JavaScript to deal with an event such as clicking on a button on a Web page.

USING JAVASCRIPT AND BUTTONS TO MODIFY A DOCUMENT'S PROPERTIES

In this example we'll show how to use buttons that incorporate the use of JavaScript. When someone who is viewing the Web page clicks on a button, we'll use JavaScript to handle that event, as it's called, and change the property **bgcolor** of the document. We also include a button and an associated action so that when it's clicked we go to another Web page.

A copy of the source for this example is on the disk that's included with this book. It is in the directory named **javascript** in the directory named **chap16**. The name of the file is **jsexample2.html**.

Take a look at this page with your browser. You'll see something similar to what's shown in Figure 16.5.

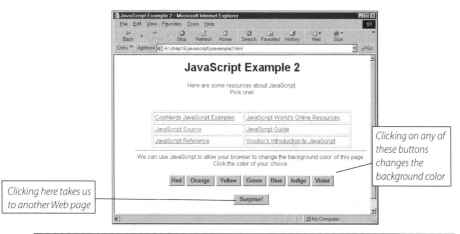

Figure 16.5   **jsexample2.html** Viewed with a Web Browser

It's the buttons on the page labeled **Red**, **Orange**, **Yellow**, **Green**, **Blue**, **Indigo**, **Violet**, and **Surprise!** that incorporate the use of JavaScript. Here's the pertinent portion of the source for that Web page:

```
<HR>We can use JavaScript to allow your browser to change the
background color of this page.</CENTER>
<CENTER>Click the color of your choice.</CENTER>
<!-- For JavaScript, we use HTML's FORM tag to 'surround' areas
of the document that will accept user input.  Here, we define
three buttons using the TYPE attribute; the VALUE field is used to
specify the text that will appear on the button. 'onClick' is a
JavaScript 'event handler' that will perform the action in quotes
when the button is clicked. When a button is clicked an onClick
event occurs, and with JavaScript we can set a property of the Web
page. We set the background color of the document to the specified
value. For the button labeled Surprise!, we set the location of
the document to a URL that takes us to another Web site. Just
imagine the fun you could have with this!! -->
<CENTER>
<FORM>
<INPUT TYPE="button" VALUE="Red" onClick="document.bgColor='RED'">
<INPUT TYPE="button" VALUE="Orange"
onClick="document.bgColor='ORANGE'">
<INPUT TYPE="button" VALUE="Yellow"
onClick="document.bgColor='YELLOW'">
<INPUT TYPE="button" VALUE="Green"
onClick="document.bgColor='GREEN'">
<INPUT TYPE="button" VALUE="Blue"
onClick="document.bgColor='BLUE'">
<INPUT TYPE="button" VALUE="Indigo"
onClick="document.bgColor='INDIGO'">
<INPUT TYPE="button" VALUE="Violet"
onClick="document.bgColor='VIOLET'">
<p>
<INPUT TYPE="button" VALUE="Surprise!" onClick="document.location=
'http://www.amused.com'">
</FORM>
</CENTER>
```

When someone clicks on the corresponding button JavaScript "handles" that event by modifying the background color property of the document

Figure 16.6   An Excerpt of the JavaScript Source from **jsexample2.html**

Most of the details are given in the HTML source. JavaScript includes event handlers, code that senses the motion or click of the mouse. We use the event handler **onClick** here to change the background color of the Web page. The **document.bgcolor** property within JavaScript specifies the background color of the Web page being viewed by the browser. (Take a look at "Using Navigator Objects," **http://developer.netscape.com/docs/manuals/communicator/jsguide4/navobj.htm**, for more information about objects and properties in JavaScript.) The HTML tag < FORM > is used to set up the buttons. When one is clicked on with the mouse, the event handler portion of JavaScript senses or "catches" the action or event, and the background color of the page is changed. On the last

Example 16.3—Using JavaScript to Build a Pulldown Menu of Hyperlinks 521

button, the one labeled Surprise!, **document.location** is changed when **onClick** occurs for that button. When someone clicks on it we retrieve the Web page whose URL is given.

END OF EXAMPLE 16.2

For our last example using JavaScript we'll build a pulldown menu of hyperlinks.

USING JAVASCRIPT TO BUILD A PULLDOWN MENU OF HYPERLINKS

In this last example we'll show how to set up a pulldown menu that contains hyperlinks. We'll construct a pulldown selection box or menu using an HTML form element. In order to make it so that when someone selects an item from the menu the appropriate action is taken, we need to use a few functions or methods written in JavaScript. Functions (methods) are written in the < HEAD > section of the Web page.

A copy of the source for this example is on the disk that's included with this book. This and other JavaScript examples are in the directory named **javascript** in the directory named **chap16**. The name of the file is **jsexample3.html**.

The pulldown menu works because of the way we use HTML and JavaScript. Using HTML we create a pulldown list from which we can select one item. We use JavaScript's event handling capabilities so that when someone selects an item from the menu a function is called that takes us to another Web page.

View the Web page with your browser. You'll see something similar to what's shown in Figure 16.7.

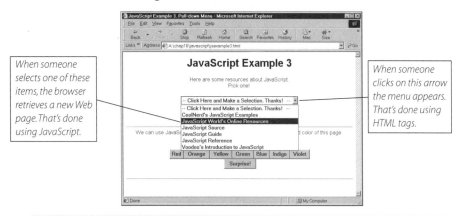

Figure 16.7   The Web Page **jsexample3.html**, Demonstrating Use of a Pulldown Menu

The HTML that provides the list of items is as follows:

```
<FORM>
  <SELECT name="choices" onChange="go(this.form)">
  <OPTION>-- Click Here and Make a Selection. Thanks! --
  <OPTION>CoolNerd's JavaScript Examples
  <OPTION>JavaScript World's Online Resources
  <OPTION>JavaScript Source
  <OPTION>JavaScript Guide
  <OPTION>JavaScript Reference
  <OPTION>Voodoo's Introduction to JavaScript
  </SELECT>
</FORM>
```

The tag

```
<SELECT name="choices" onChange="go(this.form)">
```

sets up a pulldown form, gives it the name **choices**, and specifies the use of the event handler **onChange**. That means that when someone selects an item from the list—when the selection changes—the function named **go** is applied to the current form.

Each item in the menu is listed with an < OPTION > tag. A method (function) named **buildArray** is used to create an array—a list of items in a specified order—of URLs that correspond to each of the items in the menu. The function **go** essentially takes the number of the item selected from the menu, then selects the corresponding URL from the array, and then uses that URL to change **document.location**.

Here are the JavaScript functions used for the pulldown menu of URLs.

```
function buildArray() {
  var a = buildArray.arguments;
  for (i=0; i<a.length; i++) {
    this[i] = a[i];
  }
  this.length = a.length;
}
```

> We will store the URLs in an array. This function creates the array from the list of URLs.

> Here we call the function **buildArray** to create the array. The URLs are added in the order they're listed here. The first one is empty—two quotes next to each other. That corresponds to the first form element that invites someone to make a choice. Also the first one has the index or number 0, the next 1, and so on.

```
var urls = new buildArray(
"",
"http://www.coolnerds.com/jscript/Default.htm",
"http://www.jsworld.com/help/resources/index.html",
"http://javascript.internet.com",
"http://developer.netscape.com/library/documentation/
communicator/jsguide4/index.htm",
"http://developer.netscape.com/library/documentation/
communicator/jsref/index.htm,
```

Example 16.3—Using JavaScript to Build a Pulldown Menu of Hyperlinks   523

```
"http://rummelplatz.uni-mannheim.de/~skoch/js/script.htm"
);

function go(form) {
  n = form.choices.selectedIndex;
  if (n != 0) {
    document.location = urls[n];
  }
}
```

> *This function takes a form as an argument. Another way to say this is that this is a method that is applied to a form object. We set n to the position of the selected item in the pulldown menu. Then we take the corresponding URL from the array and modify the value of document.location. Note that if the first item is selected then n = 0 and nothing is changed because we use if (n != 0), which means "if n is not equal to zero."*

Figure 16.8   The Source Code for the Functions Used in **jsexample3.html**

END OF EXAMPLE 16.3

This section presented a few examples of ways to use JavaScript to enhance Web pages with actions that take place on the client system. There's lots more that can be done, as JavaScript has more features than we've mentioned here. You'll want to look at some of the JavaScript resources listed in this chapter.

We've looked at enhancing Web pages or providing services through programs and features that are dealt with by the client system. It makes a lot of sense to put as much burden on the client, rather than the server, for Internet services. That way the people who are using the services have to do the most to support them. There are times, though, when the server or some other computer system needs to get involved. We'll look at using the server to provide services and process data in the next section.

Fyi JAVASCRIPT INFORMATION, TUTORIALS, AND GUIDES

~ "Coolnerds JavaScript Home Page"
http://www.coolnerds.com/jscript/Default.htm

~ "Voodoo's Introduction to JavaScript"
http://rummelplatz.uni-mannheim.de/~skoch/js/script.htm

~ "JavaScript Guide"
http://developer.netscape.com/docs/manuals/communicator/jsguide4/index.htm

~ JavaScript World's "Online Resources"
http://www.jsworld.com/help/resources/index.html

Using the Server to Provide Services and Process Data

You know that when we want to retrieve a Web page we need to supply a URL to a Web browser (the client) and that software deals with using the URL to contact a Web server. If it's possible to satisfy the request, the server sends a Web page to the client.

You also know that when you use a search engine, for example, the situation isn't as simple. You type some information or select options in a form and submit it to a server. The information is passed along to the server and a Web page is created and returned based on the submitted information or data. The results page that's returned was created by another program on the server that passed your data to a database, retrieved information, and created a Web page that the server returned to the client. This scenario is typical of the way a program can interact or interface with a Web server. The diagram in Figure 16.8 shows this interface between a Web server and another program. The portion marked with a circle represents the interface. That interface is called **Common Gateway Interface** or **CGI**.

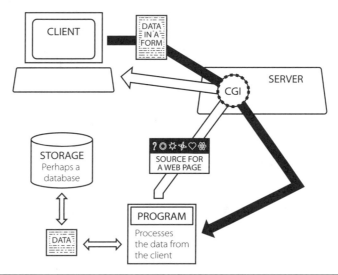

Figure 16.8   Interaction Between a Web Page Program and a Web Server

CGI isn't a program but a method for communication between the Web server software and another program on the same computer. The Web server, a program, and a Web page working together may use it to retrieve information from a database, as in the case of a search engine. This scenario is the basis for electronic commerce on the Internet. An order is posted using a Web interface and the information is handed off to a program that processes the order. There are other possibilities. You've no doubt seen a number of forms that are used to post a message to a discussion group, send a comment to a Webmaster, or post a message to a guest book. All of these require that a program different from the Web server program process the data, storing it into another file or database if necessary. It doesn't matter what language is used to write the program as long as the program can execute or be run on the Web server.

Here are the steps followed in CGI:

1. The server receives data and passes it to a program.
2. The program processes the incoming data.
3. The program generates or creates a Web page and the Web server passes it to back to the client.

Most Web page counters, programs that track or list the number of times a Web page is accessed, are also this type of CGI program. In this case, the number of times a Web page has been accessed is kept in a file. When the page is requested a program adds one to the value in the file and puts the new total back in the file.

When Common Gateway Interface is used, information is passed from a Web page to a program that processes the information. The information could be as simple as a single datum to signify that a Web page was accessed. It could also be the large amount of text necessary for an online purchase, registration, or a survey. In many cases we want these programs, and hence services, available to anyone on the Internet. This means that CGI programs need to be situated in a place (folder or directory) and have access privileges set so that they may be executed without any special privileges. Exactly where they are placed depends on how the Web server is configured. When this concept was first introduced they were typically placed in a directory named "cgi-bin." Still today, some people refer to these types of services or programs as cgi-bin programs. Because the access privileges must be set on these programs so they may be executed by anyone, special care has to be taken when they are programmed and tested. Before installing a CGI program, a Webmaster needs to be sure that the program doesn't pose a threat to the security of the system that hosts the server, and that the program operates properly.

Figure 16.9 shows how a Web server and a program on the server could be used to process an order and create a custom-made Web page confirming the order.

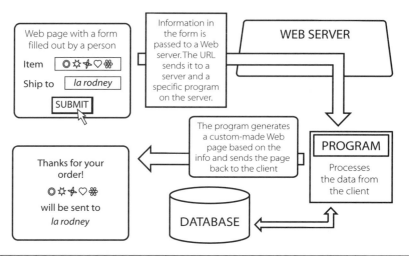

Figure 16.9   Demonstration of Using a Web Server
and a CGI Program for Order Processing

CGI programs can be written in any programming language as long as it can execute on a Web server. One programming language that's particularly popular for these types of applications is Perl. That's because:

≈ Perl contains elements that are particularly good for dealing with strings of characters.

≈ Perl makes it relatively easy to work with files on the server.

≈ programs written in Perl can be run on a number of different types of computer systems.

≈ Perl syntax is similar to C and C++.

We'll look at using some of these types of programs, but we'll skip the details of writing them. Most folks are more interested in using these programs in their Web pages than in writing them, and many Web presence providers provide CGI programs for their customers to use, but don't allow them to write or install their own programs. Topics such as programming or setting up a Web server ought to be covered in more depth than we can do well in this one section.

CGI programs are accessed through a Web page, and often times as part of a form. You'll need to know the proper HTML to use, the URL of the CGI program, and any variables that need be set as part of the form. We'll look at two examples of doing this below. Web page counters are often done slightly differently. They too are activated by HTML, but usually not as part of a form. The HTML for a page counter includes a link to a program that adds 1 to the total number of times the page is accessed. Take a look at some of the references we have for free Web page counters to see how this is done.

Example 16.4—Including Search Forms   527

If your Web presence provider gives access to CGI programs or if you use some of the free CGI services on the Web, you'll get a copy of the HTML to use. You then customize it as necessary to fit your application. Here are two examples of using CGI programs. The first demonstrates including a search form in a Web page, and the second involves using a response form. There are likely to be differences when you work with other CGI programs but the principles are the same:

~ know the appropriate HTML to use

~ know the URL of the CGI program

~ know what variables and values you have to supply or change

In addition to these you'll also need permission to use the CGI program. If you're going to use one of the services on the Web that provide these at no charge you may have to register for the service and show an advertisement each time the program or Web page counter is used. Otherwise check with your Web presence provider, organization, or school for the proper procedures for using CGI programs.

INCLUDING SEARCH FORMS

Some of the major search engines supply the HTML for forms that let you search their databases from your Web page. A copy of the source for this example is on the disk that's included with this book. This and other CGI examples are in the directory named **cgi** in the directory named **chap16**. The name of the file is **cgiexample1.html**.

(Do it!) View the Web page **cgiexample1.html** with your browser.

Figure 16.10 shows part of the Web page "CGI Example 1," whose source is in the file **cgiexample1.html**. The Web page contains two forms, one to search using HotBot and the other using Northern Light. We're using both to show some of the ways to use HTML to access a CGI program, not to show off the features of each form. The first form is available through the Web page "HotBot Tools," **http://hotbot.lycos.com/help/tools/Default.asp**, and the second at "Linking to Northern Light," **http://www.northernlight.com/docs/allies_company_addnl.html**.

The first form may be used to search the HotBot database of Web pages by entering keywords and then choosing how they'll be used—all the terms, any of the words, a phrase, and so on. The second may be used to search in all or any one of the types of resources available through Northern Light.

∾ Try the forms, look at the source, and see how they can be changed to search the domain that hosts your Web pages.

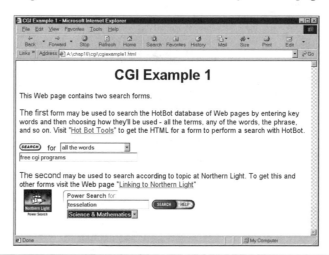

Figure 16.10   Search Forms that Access a CGI Program

We'll go over the HTML for the forms because it demonstrates some of the concepts of using CGI programs. For the first we have the following:

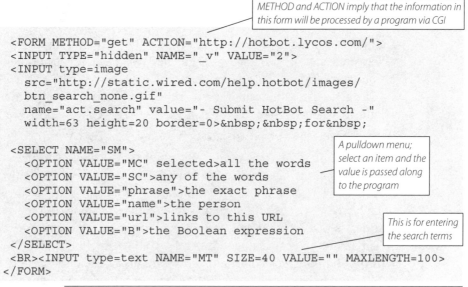

Figure 16.11   The Source for a HotBot Search Form,
as Shown in Figure 16.10

Notice that the FORM tag includes the keywords ACTION and METHOD. This is what connects the values of this form to a CGI program.

Example 16.4—Including Search Forms   529

~ ACTION is used to indicate the URL of the program that will process the data. The URL associated with ACTION is the same that's used for the home page for HotBot. When we use it here you'll see there are some values associated with it, and that causes the search program to perform the search and come back with a page of results.

~ METHOD indicates how the information is transferred. There are two methods for sending information to a CGI program, either as part of a URL or separately. These two are called GET—names and values of variables are passed as part of the URL—and POST—names and values of variables are passed by the client to the CGI program but they don't appear as part of the URL. When you use a form like this, you don't get to choose between the two methods. Usually the CGI program that will process the data is written to accept information by GET or POST. Since some browsers and servers limit the length of a URL to 128 or 256 characters, the POST method is used when more than just a few words are involved.

(Do it) Try the search form selecting **"all the words"** with the keywords **free cgi programs** as shown in Figure 16.10.

Once you click on **Search** the browser will send the URL **http://hotbot.lycos.com/?SM = MC&MT = free + cgi + programs&act.search.x = 37&act.search.y = 8**.

The values are appended to the URL for HotBot with a question mark (?) followed by pairs of names and values. There is an equal sign connecting names and values and an ampersand between each pair. Corresponding to the names of elements of the form, we see in the URL above:

~ the variable SM from the SELECT tag has the value MC

~ the variable MT holds the search terms

~ the last two, act.search.x and act.search.y, are the coordinates where the image was clicked

Going back to the page and selecting **"the exact phrase"** as a search option would give a URL that was very much the same except that the pair SM = MC would be replaced with SM = "phrase".

Now let's look at the HTML for the second form:

```
<table border="0" bgcolor="#FFFFFF">
<tr>
 <td valign=top><a href="http://www.northernlight.com/">
```

> Tables are used to keep images on both sides of the search form

```
<img src="http://www.northernlight.com/docs/gif/
nlogo_searchbar_power.gif"
 width=80 height=74 hspace=10 border=0 alt="Northern Light
 Search"></a></td>
<td><img border=0
    src="http://www.northernlight.com/docs/gif/
    transparent.gif" width=12 height=1></td>
<td valign="TOP">
<table border=0 cellspacing=0 cellpadding=0>
```

> The image is a hyperlink to the Northern Light home page

> METHOD and ACTION imply that the information in this form will be processed by a CGI program with the URL http://www.northernlight.com/nlquery.fcg

```
<FORM ACTION="http://www.northernlight.com/nlquery.fcg"
METHOD=get>
 <input type=hidden name=dx value=1004>
 <input type=hidden name=cb value=5>
 <tr> <td valign=top rowspan=4 nowrap align=right>
 <img src="http://www.northernlight.com/docs/gif/sr4_sdline.gif"
     border=0 width=14 height=49 alt="line"></td>
 <td align="LEFT" valign="TOP">
 <img src="http://www.northernlight.com/docs/gif/
 sr4_topline_2.gif"
     border=0  width=142 height=7 alt="line"><br>
 <font face="Arial, Helvetica" size="-1" color="#0000ff">
 <b>Power Search</b> for:</font></td>
 </tr> <tr> <td valign=middle>
 <input type=text size=27 name=qr maxsize=100 value="">
 </td><td> </td><td>
 <input name=sb type=image
 src="http://www.northernlight.com/docs/gif/btn_search.gif"
 width="73" height="28" border=0 alt="Search"><nobr>
 <a href="http://www.northernlight.com/docs/
 search_help_optimize.html">
 <img src="http://www.northernlight.com/docs/gif/
 btn_search_help.gif"
 border=0 width=51 height=28 alt="Help"></a></td>
 </tr>
<!-- These items are required to process the search correctly...
-->
        <tr><td>
        <select name="jtl" size=1>
        <option value="" selected>All subjects
        <option value="0:141">Arts
        <option value="0:88">Business &amp; Investing
        <option value="0:5">Computing &amp; Internet
        <option value="0:149">Contemporary life
        <option value="0:267">Education
        <option value="0:98">Entertainment
        <option value="0:153">Gov't, Law
        &amp; Politics
        <option value="0:100">Health &amp; Medicine
        <option value="0:183">Humanities
        <option value="0:27012">Products &amp; Services
        <option value="0:268">Reference
```

> Text box for the search terms

> Search button

> SELECT gives a pulldown menu. The OPTION that's selected will result in the variable jtl getting a value that is used to focus the search to a category.

Example 16.4—Including Search Forms   *531*

```
            <option value="0:70">Science &amp;
             Mathematics
            <option value="0:271">Social sciences
            <option value="0:113">Sports &amp; Recreation
            <option value="0:272">Technology
            <option value="0:187">Travel
      </select>
      </td> </tr>
   </form>
 </table>
</td>
</tr>
</table>
```

Figure 16.12   The Source for a Northern Light Search Form,
                 as Shown in Figure 16.10

When we select a subject area to search from Northern Light's database, type in keywords, and click on the button labeled **Search**, the Web server passes our search request to a program at **www.northernlight.com**. The program gets the names and values of variables from the URL, processes the information, and creates the Web page that the server returns to the client.

(Do it) Try the Northern Light search form, selecting **Science & Mathematics** with the search term **tessellation**.

Once you click on **Search** the browser will send the URL **http://www.northernlight.com/nlquery.fcg?dx = 1004&cb = 5&qr = tesselation&jtl = 0%3A70&sb.x = 51&sb.y = 12**.

The values are appended to the URL for Northern Light with a question mark (?) followed by pairs of names and values. There is an equal sign connecting names and values and an ampersand between each pair. Corresponding to the names of elements of the form, we see in the URL above:

∿   The variables **dx** and **cb** are "hidden" variables. Their values are set in the HTML and sent to the CGI-type program.

∿   The variable **qr** is set to the search term, tessellation.

∿   The variable **jtl** from the SELECT tag has the value **0%3A70**. That represents **0:70**, shown in the source. The program that processes the data will uses these values to focus the search.

∿   The last two, **sb.x** and **sb.y**, are the coordinates where the image was clicked.

END OF EXAMPLE 16.4

Now we'll take a look at an example that uses CGI to work with an email form. This is the kind of form someone might use to post comments to a Webmaster.

AN EMAIL FORM WITH CGI

In this example we'll look at using a CGI program that takes information from a form and sends it by email to a specified address. The address the information is sent to is a "hidden" variable in the form. The program has been written so any person who may access the Web server can use it. This is a typical situation. A Web presence provider will have several CGI programs or scripts available to its customers. Then through some customization, customers may use the CGI programs on their own Web sites. To use this email form a person would have to know:

∾ the URL of the CGI program

∾ that to customize the form they need to supply an email address as the value of the "hidden" variable **send_to**

A copy of the source for this example is on the disk that's included with this book. This and other CGI examples are in the directory named **cgi** in the directory named **chap16**. The name of the file is **cgiexample2.html**.

View the Web page **cgiexample2.html** with your browser. Figure 16.13 shows part of the Web page "CGI Example 2," whose source is in the file **cgiexample2.html**.

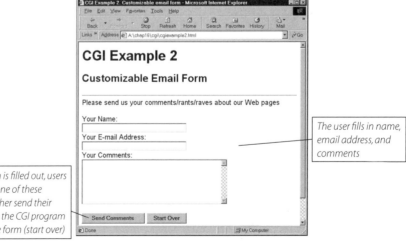

Figure 16.13   A Customizable Email Feedback Form

Example 16.5—An Email Form with CGI   *533*

Now let's take a look at the portion of the source that deals with the form.

```
<FORM METHOD="POST" ACTION="http://webliminal.com/cgi-bin/
comments1.pl">
```

> The FORM tag ties the values in this form to the CGI program with the URL *http://webliminal.com/cgi-bin/comments1.pl*. The method is POST so the values don't appear as part of the URL when someone clicks on **Send Comments**.

```
<!-- To customize this form. Enter your e-mail address in-->
<!-- place of justforfun@mwc.edu in the line below -->
```

> This is a place to customize the form so comments are sent to the address given here

```
<INPUT TYPE="hidden" NAME="send_to" VALUE="justforfun@mwc.edu">

<!--Note that you MUST have an input box with            -->
<!--NAME="feed_name" and one with NAME="feed_email" as   -->
<!--shown below                                          -->
<!--Someone using the form MUST supply a valid email address-->
Your Name:<br>
<INPUT TEXT NAME="feed_name" size=36><BR>
Your E-mail Address:<br>
<INPUT TEXT NAME="feed_email" size=36><BR>
Your Comments: <br>
<TEXTAREA WRAP=Virtual NAME="feed_comments" ROWS=6
COLS=40 ></TEXTAREA>
<P>
<INPUT TYPE="submit" VALUE="Send Comments">
<INPUT TYPE="reset" VALUE="Start Over">
</FORM>
```

> This is a requirement of the CGI program, not this form

> The user chooses one of these two buttons to send the comments or start over

Figure 16.14   The Source for the Web Page Shown in Figure 16.13

This type of form is often used to request feedback from people visiting a Web site. Here are a few things to note:

∿ The email address **justforfun@mwc.edu** has to be replaced in the HTML by the address to which the comments will be sent.

∿ The name of the CGI program used in this case, **comments1.pl**, has the extension **pl**, indicating that the program is written in Perl. This doesn't have any effect on using the program; however, we infer from the instructions on the form that when this is filled in, the user has to supply an email address; that's the way the program **comments1.pl** is written and it isn't controlled by the HTML.

END OF EXAMPLE 16.5

These two examples showed some of the ways to use CGI programs on Web pages. There are a number of different types of enhancements you can add to your Web pages including not only search forms and comment forms as shown above but also access counters, guest books, and more.

Check with your Web presence provider or organization to see what's available on the server you use. There are a number of sites on the Web that provide free access to CGI programs, provided that you register for the service. Other sites provide access for a fee. For these you'll need to copy the necessary HTML to access the CGI

Fyi SOME RESOURCES FOR YOUR WEB SITE
∾ "The CGI Resource Index"
http://www.cgi-resources.com
∾ "Website Resources"
http://www.websiteresources .com
∾ "Zuberlinks"
http://www.zuberlinks.com

programs, make necessary modifications, and paste it into your Web pages. There also are a number of sites on the Web that provide programs that can be used as CGI programs. To use these you'll have to install them in the appropriate directory or folder on the Web server. You'll need permission from the person or organization that manages your Web server. Then you'll need to come up with appropriate HTML or modify some sample HTML to access them.

Summary

There are a variety of ways to enhance a Web page with images, audio, video, and interactive or dynamic elements. By enhance we mean make a Web page more valuable and useful to our prospective readers. It is important to remember that adding elements to a Web page may in fact detract from the overall experience. Two issues to consider are the amount of time it will take to download and view a Web page, and whether the person viewing a Web page has the proper software and hardware installed to take advantage of the content you provide.

Images, animations, audio, and video can enhance a Web site if they're used appropriately. Think about the person who will be viewing or accessing the Web page, and use these elements with the goal of providing a richer experience. There are several considerations and techniques that can help with this.

Some ways to minimize the time it takes to view Web pages with images are to

∾ reduce the size and number of colors in an image

∾ use images more than once on related pages

∾ set the size of the image as an attribute of the < IMG . . . > HTML tag

∾ save an image as an interlaced GIF or a progressively encoded JPEG

∾ display a two-color version of an image while the full-color image is loading

Animated GIFs, a common way to provide animations, are collections of images. Take special care to minimize the size of each.

Audio information is stored in one of several different file types. Each represents a different compression or playback scheme. Some file types need to be downloaded completely before they can be played. Another technology called streaming—it's also used with video—downloads a portion of the file and starts playing the audio (or video) as portions of it are downloaded. Streaming file types and some others require that a plug-in be loaded first, before the file may be played. Plug-ins for popular file types are readily available, but needing one increases the amount of time before the file is played. There are two choices for giving access to audio on a Web site. One is to give a hyperlink to the audio file so that a person visiting the site may choose whether to access the file, and the other is to embed the audio file on a Web page. Audio files tend to be large, so the first option is often better for the visitor.

The considerations related to using video are similar to audio. There are different encoding and compression schemes including streaming video, the files are very large, and there are the same two ways to give access to video files.

There are some other ways to provide dynamic elements in Web pages. These are also used to produce interactive elements in a page or create Web pages as the result of user input. In this chapter we discuss Java, JavaScript, and CGI programs.

Programs written using Java can be distributed on the Internet and executed on several different types of computers. The programs are translated, using a Java compiler, into a format called byte codes. The byte codes can be executed on any computer with a Java interpreter, and the same byte codes are produced regardless of the type of computer used to develop the program. Java programs used on the Web are called applets. A Java applet is included in a Web page using the HTML tags < APPLET *specifics about an individual applet* > and < /APPLET > . The programs are first written in Java and then compiled or translated to byte codes using a Java compiler. When a Web browser retrieves a page with the APPLET tag, the byte codes are sent to the computer viewing the Web page to be executed there.

Most Web browsers include an interpreter (part of the browser software) that will interpret and execute instructions written in a language called JavaScript. These instructions are part of the Web page. They aren't compiled first, as is the case with Java programs. JavaScript includes ways, for example, to write instructions that respond to events that occur while a person is viewing a Web page. These events include opening or closing a Web page, moving the mouse over a region of a form, clicking on a button on a Web page, or selecting an item from a menu. A script could collect and verify input from a user before passing it back to a server or an applet.

CGI programs are programs that run or execute on a server, not the client, as is the case with Java and JavaScript. In a nutshell, a Web page (on a client system) through a form or an image tag references a CGI program. The input data for the program is taken from the Web page, the program processes the data, and the program may produce output as a Web page that is sent back to the client system.

If your Web presence provider gives access to CGI programs or if you use some of the free CGI services on the Web, you'll get a copy of the HTML to use. Then you customize it as necessary to fit your application. In either case you need to know:

∾ the appropriate HTML to use

∾ the URL of the CGI program

∾ what variables and values you have to supply or change

There are several sites on the Web that provide images, animations, sounds, video, Java applets, JavaScript programs, and CGI programs without charge. There are also many sites that can be helpful in working with different file types and learning how to use these elements in Web pages. It's great to have all these resources available, and great to have so much to learn! Just remember that a person viewing your Web page is a visitor and you need to make sure their visit is pleasant and enriching for them.

Selected Terms Used in This Chapter

byte code	JavaScript
Common Gateway Interface (CGI)	lossless
	lossy
dithered	plug-in
Java	streaming media
Java applet	thumbnail

Exercises and Projects

1. Visit the Web site "All Things Web: The Usable Web," **http://www. pantos.org/atw/usable.html**. Read the article "As Simple As Possible," **http://www.pantos.org/atw/35504.html**. List the main points made in that article. Does the design of the Web site "All Things Web," **http://www.pantos.org/atw**, indicate that those points were followed? Explain.

2. Visit the Web site "Bandwidth Conservation Society," **http://www.infohiway.com/way/faster**. Just what is the Bandwidth Conservation Society? What is its purpose? Describe what is available at that site.

3. Compare the two Web sites in Exercises 1 and 2. Which do you think is more useful? Under what conditions would you recommend one over the other? If you had to choose to recommend only one of these which would it be?

4. Visit the Web page "Usability Checklist for Site Developers," **http://webreview.com/pub/1999/10/15/usability/index.html**. What are the three primary usability principles stated on that Web page? The site lists 10 items for a checklist. Select five items and apply them to a popular Web site such as Yahoo!, **http://www.yahoo.com**, or CNN.com, **http://www.cnn.com**.

5. Go to the Web site "Media Builder GIF Optimizer," **http://www.gifoptimizer.com**. Using either an image of your own or one that's mentioned in the text (for example **http://www.webliminal.com/essentials/fleeing.gif**) try decreasing the color depth in the image so that the number of bytes necessary to represent the image is reduced by more than 30%. Describe your experience, including how much you could reduce the color depth and still maintain acceptable quality. Be sure to mention what was unacceptable about reducing the color depth further than you did. Save the reduced image on your computer.

6. Starting with the image you saved in the previous exercise, use the services at GIF Optimizer to reduce its size in pixels. Suppose you resize it so it's 50% of the original size. How does that decrease the number of bytes needed to represent the image? Save the image on your computer and create a Web page that has the original image, the image with the number of colors reduced, and the image with reduced size.

7. Go to the Web site "Sounds," **http://msdn.microsoft.com/downloads/sounds/toc.htm**, and experiment using some of the sounds as embedded audio. Take a piece that plays for several seconds and try it with autostart = "true" and autostart = "false". Which seems a better choice to you? Have a few other people try the page and get their opinions on which they prefer.

8. Go to the Library of Congress Web site "American Memory," **http://memory.loc.gov**. Find some examples of using video (excerpts from films in this case) and audio. If you need help in finding some of

these start at "Collection Finder," **http://memory.loc.gov/ammem/ collections/finder.html**, and click on **Motion Pictures** or **Sound Recordings**. Is access to specific audio or video resources provided as hyperlinks, or are they embedded? In most cases an individual item is available in several formats. Why do you think that's the case?

9. Take a look at the site "American Memory Viewer Information," **http://memory.loc.gov/ammem/amviewer.html**. Describe the Web site. How does this serve the needs of visitors? Explain whether you think it would be advisable or necessary to have a similar Web page for most multimedia-centered Web sites.

10. Visit the Web site "Freebie Applets You Can Use," **http://java.sun. com/openstudio/index.html**. Select an applet to add to one of your Web pages. Describe the steps you had to go through to make it work, and describe how well it works. Is your page with the applet available on the WWW? What's the URL?

11. Visit the Web site "Coolnerds JavaScript Examples," **http://www. coolnerds.com/jscript/jsexampl.htm**. Find an example of JavaScript that you'd like to use in one of your Web pages. Describe the steps you had to go through to make it work and how well it works. Is your page with the JavaScript available on the WWW? What's the URL? (If the Coolnerds site doesn't fit your needs try one of the other JavaScript resource sites mentioned in the text.)

12. View the Web page **cgiexample1.html**, shown in Figure 16.10. Try a search at HotBot for free cgi programs where you've selected **the exact phrase**. How does the URL generated indicate that a search for a phrase will be done?

13. Modify the source for the Web page **cgiexample1.html** (the file is on the disk included with this book in the **cgi** folder in the directory named **chap16**) to include a search form for another search engine. Here are some URLs to try for the source to add a search form:

    ~ Excite

    http://www.excite.com/info/linking_to_excite/ add_excite_search

    ~ SavvySearch

    http://www.savvysearch.com/addsavvy.html

    ~ Snap

    http://www.snap.com/main/help/item/ 0,11,home-8707,00.html?st.sn.ft.0.tlbx

14. Visit both "Website Resources," **http://www.websiteresources.com**, or "Zuberlinks," **http://www.zuberlinks.com**. Using the resources at one of those sites puts an access counter on one of your Web pages. Describe the process you went through to obtain permission to use the counter and the HTML necessary to put it into place. Evaluate the performance of the counter. Is it accurate? Does it work quickly? Do you get any reports about it?

15. Visit both "Website Resources," **http://www.websiteresources.com**, or "Beseen," **http://www.beseen.com**, to find a guest book to add to one of your Web pages. Describe the process you went through to obtain permission to use the guest book and the HTML necessary to put it into place. Evaluate the performance of the guest book.

SELECTED SEARCH TOOLS,
DIRECTORIES, VIRTUAL
LIBRARIES, AND
SPECIALIZED DATABASES

In this appendix, we list several of the tools and resources you can use for finding information:

∿ Search Engines

∿ Meta-search Tools

∿ Directories

∿ Virtual Libraries

We've discussed these types of tools and resources throughout the book. Here we give the name; the URLs of the home, help, and FAQ pages; and the features of each. You'll find this to be a handy reference when you need to use one of these and you want a quick synopsis of its characteristics.

Search Engines

Search engines build full-text databases of the words on Web pages. For each search engine we'll identify the types of searches available, the sources that can be searched, and output features. Here we'll list some of the major search engines.

AltaVista

Home page	**http://www.altavista.com**
Help	**http://doc.altavista.com/help/search/search_help.shtml**
FAQ	**http://doc.altavista.com/help/search/faq.shtml**
Types of searches	Keyword or phrase. Implied Boolean expressions in simple search, and full Boolean expressions in advanced search. Proximity, truncation, wildcards, case sensitivity, and field searching supported.
Sources to search	Web, Discussion Groups, News, and Shopping. Specialized search areas are Careers, Entertainment, Finance, Health,

News, and Travel. Search tools for finding audio, image, and multimedia resources.

Output features	Hyperlink, URL, and text from the Web page. Link to translation service. Ranked only by relevancy in simple search. User can supply ranking criteria in advanced search.

Excite

Home page	**http://www.excite.com**
Help	**http://www.excite.com/info/search_help**
FAQ	**http://www.excite.com/info**
Types of searches	Keyword (concept search) and phrase. Implied and full Boolean expressions allowed; note that AND, OR, and NOT must appear in uppercase.
Sources to search	Web pages (full text), Excite Web Guide, Usenet articles, and selected news sources.
Output features	Title (hyperlink), URL, summary, and link to similar sites. Ranked by relevancy or site. Links to sites in Excite Channels and Directory and news stories also displayed.

GO Network—Infoseek

Home page	**http://infoseek.go.com**
Help	**http://infoseek.go.com/ Help?pg = HelpIndex.html**
FAQ	None available.
Types of searches	Keyword or phrase. Implied Boolean expressions allowed.
Sources to search	Web, Usenet, news services, email addresses, and company profiles.
Output features	Title (hyperlink), summary, URL, and size. Can hide summary.

Google

Home page	**http://www.google.com**
Help	**http://www.google.com/help.html**
FAQ	**http://www.google.com/faq.html**
Types of searches	Keyword or phrase. Implied Boolean expressions only.

Sources to search	Web, U.S. government information, Apple Macintosh, and Linux resources.
Output features	Title, hyperlink, brief excerpt, and URL. Also contains a link to a cached copy of the Web page and a link to similar pages in the Google database.

HotBot

Home page	**http://hotbot.lycos.com**
Help	**http://hotbot.lycos.com/help**
FAQ	**http://hotbot.lycos.com/help**
Types of searches	Keyword or phrase. Implied and full Boolean expressions allowed.
Sources to search	Web, Usenet, news sites, classifieds, domain names, stocks, discussion groups, and shareware.
Output features	Full description: title (hyperlink), excerpt, URL, size, and date indexed. Brief: title (hyperlink) and one-line excerpt.

Lycos

Home page	**http://www.lycos.com**
Help	**http://www.lycos.com/help**
FAQ	**http://www.lycos.com/info**
Types of searches	Keyword. Implied Boolean expressions allowed. Can match all words (AND) or any words (OR). Boolean expressions allowed only with advanced search options. See the "Lycos Help" page for details.
Sources to search	Web, pictures, sounds, personal home pages, stocks, MP3, and Usenet news articles.
Output features	Title (hyperlink), excerpt, URL, and link to the site hosting the Web page.

Northern Light

Home page	**http://www.northernlight.com**
Help	**http://www.northernlight.com/docs/ search_help_optimize.html**
FAQ	**http://www.northernlight.com/docs/ about_company_mission.html**

Types of searches	Keyword, phrase, implied and full Boolean expressions, and fields.
Sources to search	Web and Special Collection.
Output features	Title (hyperlink), excerpt, and URL. Items arranged in folders determined for each search.

Snap.com

Home page	**http://www.snap.com**
Help	**http://home.snap.com/main/help/ item/0,11,home-8055,00.html**
FAQ	**http://www.snap.com/LMOID/ resource/0,566,home-650,00.html**
Types of searches	Keyword, Boolean expressions, phrase, and fields.
Sources to search	Web and Snap directory.
Output features	Items within a category include subcategories, links to featured sites, and links to specific sites.

WebCrawler

Home page	**http://www.webcrawler.com**
Help	**http://www.webcrawler.com/Help/Help.html**
FAQ	**http://www.webcrawler.com/ Help/AboutWC/AboutWC.html**
Types of searches	Keyword, phrase, and implied and full Boolean expressions.
Sources to search	Web.
Output features	Title (hyperlink), excerpt, and URL. Can hide excerpt.

Meta-search Tools

Meta-search tools allow you to use several search engines. Some sites merely list World Wide Web search tools with their search forms so you can search one at a time. These are called all-in-one search tools. If a meta-search tool allows you to search several search engines or directories simultaneously, it's called a parallel search tool. Some meta-search tools are good places to find lists of specialized databases. In addition to the URLs, we list the output and special features.

All-in-One Search Page

Home page	**http://www.allonesearch.com**
Help	None available.
FAQ	None available.
Output features	Either displays search results or search page for selected service.
Special features	Forms-based search services arranged by categories.

Dogpile

Home page	**http://www.dogpile.com**
Help	**http://www.dogpile.com/notes.html**
FAQ	None available.
Output features	Results arranged by relevance according to each search engine or resource contacted.
Special features	Keywords connected by AND is the default. Searching by phrase, Boolean expressions, and proximity operators.

Fossick.com—WebSearch Alliance Directory

Home page	**http://www.fossick.com**
Help	None available.
FAQ	**http://www.fossick.com/About.htm**
Output features	Results of parallel search are listed as title (hyperlink), excerpt, and hyperlink to the search tool that returned the result.
Special features	Specialized databases and search tools are each represented by an icon.

InvisibleWeb

Home page	**http://www.invisibleweb.com**
Help	Click on **Help** from the home page. The URLs for this page and the FAQ are generated at each mouse-click from a long string of characters so we don't list them here.
FAQ	Click on **FAQ** on the Help page.
Output features	A list of hyperlinks to special resources or specialized databases.

Special features	This site is a collection of links to specialized databases that often hold their information in some format different from HTML. Search engines don't index these sites.

MetaCrawler

Home page	**http://www.metacrawler.com**
Help	**http://www.metacrawler.com/help/faq**
FAQ	**http://www.metacrawler.com/help/faq**
Output features	Results arranged by location (domain name) or relevance. Duplicates eliminated.
Special features	Searching by phrase, as well as with AND and OR. Implied Boolean operators may be used. User may select Power Search. Metaspy, **http://www.metaspy.com**, lets you see what search terms other people are using.

SavvySearch

Home page	**http://www.savvysearch.com**
Help	**http://www.savvysearch.com/help.html**
FAQ	**http://www.savvysearch.com/faq.html**
Output features	Title as a hyperlink and search engine name always displayed. More information also available, including author, location, and brief description. Results may be displayed by the search engine used or integrated.
Special features	User may specify sources, such as search engines, Usenet, news, shareware, or directories. There is also a subject-oriented guide to collections of search tools.

SEARCH.COM

Home page	**http://www.search.com**
Help	**http://www.search.com/Help**
FAQ	**http://www.search.com/About**
Output features	Search form, description of search tool, tips for searching, and hyperlink to resource.
Special features	Search services and databases arranged by category and in alphabetical order. Individual services selected with a search form.

Directories

A directory, or subject catalog, is a collection of Internet and Web resources arranged in categories. There are many general-purpose directories on the Web, as well as lots of specialized ones. Here, we'll discuss some of the more popular and useful ones.

For each tool, we'll also indicate whether the items in the directory are rated, if entries are reviewed before being included, and if it's possible to search the directory. In addition, we'll present the directory's output features and any special features.

Excite

Home page	**http://www.excite.com**
Help	**http://www.excite.com/Info**
FAQ	None available.
Ratings	Top sites marked by an Excite logo.
Reviews	Items annotated, reviewed, and rated.
Searching	Search the directory or the Web.
Output features	Items are listed with title (as a hyperlink), rating, and review of the content.
Special features	Other specialized guides available include guides to weather, financial information, news, travel resources, yellow pages, maps and directions, and others. Also includes services for general Web searching. The information in this directory is similar to that in Magellan Internet Guide, **http://magellan.excite.com**, and in the directory section of WebCrawler Channels, **http://www.webcrawler.com**.

Galaxy

Home page	**http://galaxy.einet.net**
Help	**http://galaxy.einet.net/howto.html**
FAQ	None available.
Ratings	None available.
Reviews	Items reviewed. Excerpts available through the search tool.
Searching	Search the directory or the Web.
Output features	Items are listed with title (as a hyperlink),

| Special features | Resources in a subject area arranged by major subcategories (if any), academic organizations, collections, directories, discussion groups, government organizations, guides, nonprofit organizations, organizations, and periodicals. |

GO Network—Infoseek

Home page	Channels: **http://infoseek.go.com** Topics: **http://www.go.com/WebDir**
Help	**http://infoseek.go.com/** **Help?pg = HelpIndex.html**
FAQ	**http://info.go.com/doc/aboutGO.html**
Ratings	Entries in Topics are rated with one to three stars.
Reviews	Items reviewed and annotated.
Searching	Search form on each page lists directory entries and allows users to search current subject area or topic, the Web, Usenet news, news services, and companies.
Output features	Items listed with rating, title (hyperlink), summary, URL, and date added.
Special features	Each page of the directory provides access to specialized directories for news, business information, maps, and email and street addresses.

LookSmart

Home page	**http://www.looksmart.com**
Help	**http://www.looksmart.com/help/main.html**
FAQ	None available.
Ratings	None available.
Reviews	One-sentence description with each listing.
Searching	User can search the directory and the Web using search technology licensed from AltaVista.
Output features	Title (hyperlink) and brief description.
Special features	Up to three levels of the guide are present on the screen as the user moves through a subject area. LookSmart Live!, **http://www.looksmart.com/ live**, allows you to submit a question to a LookSmart editor.

Lycos

Home page	**http://www.lycos.com**
Help	**http://www.lycos.com/help**
FAQ	None available.
Ratings	Some, but unevenly applied.
Reviews	A one- or two-sentence annotation for each site.
Searching	User can do a forms-based search of the directory or of the current category within the directory.
Output features	Title (hyperlink) and a brief annotation for each site.

Magellan Internet Guide

Home page	**http://magellan.excite.com**
Help	**http://magellan.excite.com/ magellan/Info/advancedtips.html**
FAQ	None available.
Ratings	Top sites are marked with a star.
Reviews	Items annotated, reviewed, and rated.
Searching	Search tool with several options for searching rated and reviewed sites or entire Web.
Output features	Items are listed with title (as a hyperlink), rating, and review of the content.
Special features	Specialized guides, including guide to cities, email and street addresses, horoscopes, maps, sports scores, stocks, and weather.

NetGuide: Your Guide to the Net

Home page	**http://www.netguide.com**
Help	**http://www.netguide.com/AboutUs**
FAQ	None available.
Ratings	No ratings except on those listed in the categories available through **http://www.netguide.com/ Browse**.
Reviews	Brief review with each listing.
Searching	Search form available on each page, giving the option to search this subject guide.
Output features	Items within a category include subcategories, links to a featured site, and links to articles

	written for NetGuide on the subject within a category.
Special features	Stories or articles written for NetGuide that provide an in-depth discussion of a topic.

Open Directory Project

Home page	**http://dmoz.org**
Help	None available.
FAQ	**http://dmoz.org/about.html**
Ratings	Some sites are marked with a star. Sites are selected by volunteers and there is no uniform rating applied.
Reviews	An annotation or brief review accompanies each site.
Searching	Search form available on each page, giving the option to search within a category or the entire directory.
Output features	Items within a category include subcategories and links to individual sites.
Special features	This directory continues to be built and maintained by volunteer editors in each subject category. The contents are used by AltaVista, HotBot, Lycos, Netscape, and others. See "Sites Using ODP Data," **http://dmoz.org/Computers/ Internet/WWW/Searching_the_Web/ Directories/Open_Directory_Project/ Sites_Using_ODP_Data**.

Snap.com Web Directory

Home page	**http://www.snap.com**
Help	**http://home.snap.com/main/help/ item/0,11,home-8055,00.html**
FAQ	None available.
Ratings	Top sites within a category are marked with checkmark.
Reviews	Brief summary with each listing.
Searching	Search form available on each page, giving the option to search the category or the entire subject guide.

| Output features | Items within a category include subcategories, links to featured sites, and links to specific sites. |
| Special features | Can browse a category by letter. The home page has links to allow for personalization; links to several different types of resources such as news, maps, and weather; and links to channels or what Snap.com calls guides. |

WebCrawler

Home page	**http://www.webcrawler.com**
Help	**http://www.webcrawler.com/Help/Guide.html**
FAQ	None available.
Ratings	Top sites within a category are marked with checkmark.
Reviews	Some items are reviewed.
Searching	Search the directory or the Web.
Output features	Items are listed with title (as a hyperlink), rating, and review of the content.
Special features	Guides to weather, financial information, news, travel resources, yellow pages, maps and directions, and others. Also includes services for general Web searching. The information in this directory is the same as in Magellan Internet Guide, **http://magellan.excite.com**.

Yahoo!

Home page	**http://www.yahoo.com**
Help (general)	**http://howto.yahoo.com**
Help (searching)	**http://howto.yahoo.com/chapters/7/1.html**
FAQ	**http://www.yahoo.com/docs/info/faq.html**
Ratings	None available.
Reviews	No written reviews. Items included only after approval by Yahoo!
Searching	Search form available on each page, giving the option to search within current category, all categories, or Web.
Output features	Title (hyperlink) and brief annotation.
Special features	There are several regional or national editions of the guide and other special subject guides,

including Shopping, Yellow Pages, People Search, Maps, Classifieds, Personals, Message Boards, Chat, Email, Pager, My Yahoo!, Today's News, Sports, Weather, TV, and Stock Quotes.

Virtual Libraries

Virtual libraries are directories that contain collections of Internet or Web resources that have been reviewed and evaluated before they're included. For this reason, the resources tend to be useful, accurate, and authentic. Most of the resources are subject guides, specialized databases, and reference works such as encyclopedias and dictionaries. In many cases, you'll find that professional librarians staff and manage these virtual libraries.

For each item, we'll also state the output features and any special features.

The Argus Clearinghouse

Home page	**http://www.clearinghouse.net**
Help	**http://www.clearinghouse.net/searchtips.html**
FAQ	**http://www.clearinghouse.net/faq.html**
Output features	Topics arranged by category, each with a list of resources. Each item represented by title, hyperlink to resource, keywords, author's name and affiliation, date the Argus Clearinghouse last checked resource, overall rating, and rating in each category.
Special features	Searches full text of information pages, including titles, names of authors, institutions, and keywords.

Infomine: Scholarly Internet Resource Collections

Home page	**http://infomine.ucr.edu**
Help	**http://infomine.ucr.edu/help**
FAQ	**http://infomine.ucr.edu/welcome/about.html**
Output features	List of items in the collection, each as a hyperlink.
Special features	Thousands of items in the collection of reviewed resources. Each area of the collection is called an infomine. Areas can be browsed or searched. Multiple databases may be searched simultaneously. Easy-to-use interface.

Internet Public Library

Home page	**http://www.ipl.org**
Help	**http://www.ipl.org/about**
FAQ	**http://www.ipl.org/about/iplfaq.html**
Output features	Image-based and text-based interfaces to the main sections of the library.
Special features	Thousands of items in the collection of reviewed resources. The IPL is presented as Divisions: Reference (annotated subject guides), Youth, and Teen; Rooms: Exhibit Hall and Reading Room (a collection of online texts, serial publications, and newspapers); and Services: For Librarians, Directory & Tour, and Web Searching. All collections may be browsed, and most provide searching of titles and descriptions of resources.

Librarians' Index to the Internet

Home page	**http://lii.org**
Help	**http://lii.org/search/file/tips**
FAQ	**http://lii.org/search/file/about**
Output features	Subject guide arranged by category. Items reviewed, annotated, and represented as hyperlinks.
Special features	Can search by title, subject, annotation, or field.

World Wide Web Virtual Library

Home page	**http://www.vlib.org**
Help	**http://vl.bwh.harvard.edu/htdig/search.html**
FAQ	**http://www.vlib.org/AboutVL.html**
Output features	Items arranged as a subject catalog or alphabetically, depending on which URL is used to access the Library. No uniformity, because each category or topic is maintained by a volunteer, but each is meant to be a guide to all the major resources related to a specific topic.
Special features	Alphabetical arrangement and category subtree (subject guide).

Appendix B

FYIs

Chapter 1—Introduction to the Internet and the World Wide Web

To Learn More About the Internet and the World Wide Web

"Beginners Central"
http://www.northernwebs.com/bc

"Chapter 1: What is the Internet?"
http://members.unlimited.net/ ~ kumbach/internet/ whatsnet.html

"Getting Started on the Internet"
http://www.imagescape.com/ helpweb/welcome.html

Comparing Web Browsers

"Browsers: A CNET Topic Center"
http://home.cnet.com/category/ 0-3773.html

"BrowserWatch-Browser Blvd."
http://browserwatch.internet.com/ browsers.html

"Web Browser"
http://www.zdnet.com/products/ filter/guide/0,7267,1500102,00.html

Computer-Mediated Communication

"CMC Magazine Archive"
http://www.december.com/ cmc/mag/archive

"Journal of Computer-Mediated Communication"
http://www.ascusc.org/jcmc

Help for Web Page Authors and Web Site Designers

"Web Page Design and Layout"
http://dir.yahoo.com/Arts/ Design_Arts/Graphic_Design/ Web_Page_Design_and_Layout

"The Web Design Group's Links"
http://www.htmlhelp.com/links

Want to See How Business Can Be Done on the Internet?

Amazon.com
http://www.amazon.com

CDNOW
http://www.cdnow.com

Shopping.com
http://www.shopping.com/store

Guides to Netiquette

"The Net: User Guidelines and Netiquette"
http://www.fau.edu/rinaldi/ net/index.html

"Netiquette Home Page"
http://www.albion.com/ netiquette/index.html

"RFC 1855: Netiquette Guidelines"
http://marketing.tenagra.com/ rfc1855.html

History of the Internet and the World Wide Web

"A Brief History of the Internet"
http://www.isoc.org/internet/ history/brief.html

"Hobbes' Internet Timeline"
http://info.isoc.org/guest/zakon/ Internet/History/HIT.html

"Net Timeline"
http://www.pbs.org/internet/ timeline

Chapter 2—How the Internet Works and Getting Connected

Getting More Information About How the Internet Works

"Chapter 1: What is the Internet?"
http://members.unlimited.net/ ~kumbach/internet/whatsnet.html

"Connected: An Internet Encyclopedia"
http://www.FreeSoft.org/CIE/ index.htm

"20 questions: how the Net works"
http://www.cnet.com/Content/ Features/Techno/Networks

"Zen and the Art of the Internet"
http://www.cs.indiana.edu/ docproject/zen/zen-1.0_toc.html

Selecting an ISP and Getting Connected

"Dawn McGatney's Overview Guide to Finding an ISP"
http://dogwolf.seagull.net/ first.html

"Finding an Internet Service Provider"
http://hotwired.lycos.com/ webmonkey/guides/web/isp.html

"ISP Finder"
http://www.ispfinder.com

"Learn the Net: Getting Connected"
http://www.learnthenet.com/ english/html/04connec.htm

Chapter 3—Communication on the Internet

The History of IRC, MUDs, and MOOs

"Early IRC History"
http://www.the-project.org/ history.html

"The MUDex"
http://www.apocalypse.org/pub/ u/lpb/muddex

"MOO-Cows FAQ"
http://www.moo.mud.org/ moo-faq

Where Are the Chat Sites?

"The Free Chat Rooms"
http://www.free-chat-rooms.to

"The Webarrow Chat Directory"
**http://www.webarrow.net/
chatindex/list.html**

"Ultimate Chat"
http://www.ewsonline.com/chat

More Information About MUDs

"The MUD Resource Collection"
http://www.godlike.com/muds

"The MUDdex"
**http://www.apocalypse.org/pub/
u/lpb/muddex**

"The MUD FAQ"
**http://www.mudconnect.com/
mudfaq/index.html**

Further Resources About MOOs

"MOOs, Not Just Cows"
**http://www.cas.usf.edu/lis/
lis5937/moo.html**

The MOO at Diversity University
http://moo.du.org:8888

"The Purpose of MOOs"
**http://cinemaspace.berkeley.edu/
~ rachel/moo.html**

Comparing Instant Messaging Software

"Fast Talkers: CNET Reviews the
Top Instant Messengers"
**http://www.cnet.com/internet/
0-4023-7-1591649.html**

"Chat Goes to Work"
**http://www.zdnet.com/
products/stories/reviews/
0,4161,2411029,00.html**

More Information About Telephony, Video, and Internet Conferencing

Internet telephony:
"Sorting Out Internet Telephony"
**http://www.zdnet.com/
anchordesk/story/
story_2113.html**

"internetTelephony"
**http://www
.internettelephony.com**

CU-SeeMe:
"Video Conferencing with
CU-SeeMe"
**http://www.webmec.com/
cuseeme**

"CU-SeeMe Frequently Asked
Questions"
**http://support.wpine.com/
cuseeme**

Internet conferencing:
"Meeting of the Minds: 4 Net
conferencing programs"
**http://www.cnet.com/
Content/Reviews/Compare/
Netconference**

"Virtual Meeting Solutions"
**http://www.infoworld.com/
cgi-bin/displayTC.pl?/
970602comp.htm**

Tips on Writing Effective Email

"A Beginner's Guide to Effective
Email"
**http://www.webfoot.com/advice/
estyle.html**

"BUSINESS NETIQUETTE
INTERNATIONAL"
**http://www.bspage.com/
1netiq/Netiq.html**

More Information About PGP

"Introduction to PGP"
**http://web.bham.ac.uk/
N.M.Queen/pgp/pgp.html**

"The comp.security.pgp FAQ"
**http://www.cam.ac.uk.pgp.net/
pgpnet/pgp-faq**

"Where to Get the Pretty Good
Privacy Program (PGP) FAQ"
**http://www.cryptography.org/
getpgp.htm**

More Information About Electronic Privacy

"6.805/STS085: Readings on
Privacy Implications of Computer
Networks"
**http://www-swiss.ai.mit.edu/
6095/readings-privacy.html**

"EPIC Online Guide to Privacy
Resources"
**http://www.epic.org/privacy/
privacy_resources_faq.html**

"The Privacy Pages"
**http://www.2020tech.com/
maildrop/privacy.html**

Chapter 4—Electronic Mail

Comparing Email Clients

"Eudora Mail Client—Feature
Comparison"
**http://eudora.qualcomm.com/
pro_email/comparison.html**

"It's in the mail: CNET compares
the top email clients"
**http://www.cnet.com/Content/
Reviews/Compare/Emailclients/
index.html**

Chapter 5—Email Discussion Groups

Information About Discussion Groups on the Web

"Email Discussion Groups/Lists
and Resources"
**http://www.webcom.com/
impulse/list.html**

"Internet Mailing Lists Guides and
Resources"
**http://www.ifla.org/I/training/
listserv/lists.htm**

Chapter 6—Usenet News

What Is Usenet? Some Classic Papers

"What is Usenet?"
**http://www.faqs.org/faqs/usenet/
what-is/part1**

"What is Usenet? A second
opinion."
**http://www.faqs.org/faqs/usenet/
what-is/part2**

More Information About Usenet

"news.newusers.questions Links Page"
http://www.geocities.com/ ResearchTriangle/8211/ nnqlinks.html

"Usenet: Reading and Writing the News"
http://www.webliminal.com/ Lrn-web05.html

"Usenet References"
http://www.faqs.org/usenet

Chapter 7—Getting Around the World Wide Web—Using a Web Browser

More About Browsers

"Browser News"
http://www.upsdell.com/ BrowserNews

"Browsers"
http://home.cnet.com/category/ 0-3773.html

"Open Directory - Computers: Software: Internet: Clients: WWW: Browsers"
http://dmoz.org/Computers/ Software/Internet/Clients/ WWW/Browsers

"Web Browsers"
http://www.webteacher.org/ winnet/browser/browser.html

Tutorials and Guides for Netscape Navigator

"Grenville CAP – Netscape Tutorial"
http://www.recorder.ca/ grenvillecap/tutorial/tutorial/ tut-004a1.htm

"Internet Navigator – MODULE 1 – Browser Tutorial and Internet Overview"
http://www.lib.utah.edu/ navigator/Module1/index.html

"Navigating the World Wide Web with Netscape Communicator"
http://www.albany.edu/library/ internet/communicator95.html

"Netscape Navigator Tutorial"
http://www.eiu.edu/ ~ mediasrv/ netscape/menu.html

Tutorials and Guides for Internet Explorer

"Grenville CAP - Internet Explorer Tutorial"
http://www.recorder.ca/ grenvillecap/tutorial/tutorial/ tut-004b1.htm

"Complete Internet Guide and Web Tutorial: All about browsers, searching, building Web pages and more"
http://www.microsoft.com/ insider/internet/default.htm

"Internet Explorer 5 in the Classroom"
http://www.actden.com/ie5/begin

"Internet Explorer Tutorial"
http://www.eiu.edu/ ~ mediasrv/ ie/menu.html

Security Tips

"Computer Security Information"
**http://www.alw.nih.gov/Security/
security.html**

"Selecting Good Passwords"
**http://www.alw.nih.gov/Security/
Docs/passwd.html**

"Internet Firewalls Frequently
Asked Questions"
**http://www.v-one.com/
documents/fw-faq.htm**

"Virus Bulletin"
http://www.virusbtn.com

Digital Certificates

"Digital Certificates"
**http://www.brokat.com/int/
netsecurity/authenticate/
certificate.html**

"FAQ Digital Certificates"
**http://www.cyfi.com/products/
dcfaq.htm**

"Security : Technologies :
E-commerce - Public Key
Infrastructure (PKI)"
**http://www.ibm.com/security/
technologies/techpki.html**

Cookies

"cookie – Webopedia Definition
and Links"
**http://webopedia.internet.com/
TERM/c/cookie.html**

"The Truth About Cookies"
**http://www.cnet.com/Content/
Voices/Barr/042996**

"An Introduction to Cookies"
**http://www.hotwired.com/
webmonkey/geektalk/
96/45/index3a.html?tw = backend**

Privacy and Snooping

"Privacy Analysis of Your Internet
Connection"
http://privacy.net/anonymizer

"Privacy Initiatives"
**http://www.ftc.gov/privacy/
index.html**

"Someone to Watch over You"
**http://www.salon.com/sept97/
21st/article970918.html**

Chapter 8—Finding Information on the World Wide Web

Information on the Web About Directories

"Searching by Means of Subject
Directories"
**http://www.monash.com/
spidap1.html#directories**

"Comparing Internet Subject
Directories"
**http://www.notess.com/
search/dir**

"Using Subject Directories: A
Tutorial"
**http://home.sprintmail.com/
~ debflanagan/subject.html**

Search Tutorials on the Web

"Finding Information on the
Internet: A Tutorial"
**http://www.lib.berkeley.edu/
TeachingLib/Guides/Internet/
FindInfo.html**

"NetSearcher"
http://www.searchinsider.com

"Internet Tutorials: University at Albany Libraries"
http://www.albany.edu/ library/internet

Search Engine Information on the World Wide Web

"Search Engine Watch"
http://searchenginewatch.com

"Understanding and Comparing Search Engines"
http://web.hamline.edu/ Administration/Libraries/ search/comparisons.html

"Lost in Cyberspace"
http://www.newscientist.com/ keysites/networld/lost.html

Want to Read More About Agents? Check Out These Sites:

"BotSpot"
http://botspot.com

"Competing for the Future with Intelligent Agents"
http://home1.gte.net/pfingar/ agents_doc_rev4.htm

"Is It an Agent, or Just a Program?: A Taxonomy for Autonomous Agents"
http://www.msci.memphis.edu/ ~ franklin/AgentProg.html

Information on Filtering and Blocking Devices

"TIFAP: The Internet Filter Assessment Project"
http://www.bluehighways.com/ tifap

"Statement on Internet Filtering"
http://www.ala.org/alaorg/oif/ filt_stm.html

Information About Copyright and Intellectual Property Rights

"Copyright Basics"
http://lcweb.loc.gov/copyright/ circs/circ1.html

"Information Policy: Copyright and Intellectual Property"
http://www.ifla.org/II/ cpyright.htm

Chapter 9—Successful Search Strategies

More About Spiders, Robots, and Indexing

"Robot-Driven Search Engines: A Bibliography"
http://www.curtin.edu.au/curtin/ library/staffpages/gwpersonal/ senginestudy/sengbib.htm

"The Web Robots Pages"
http://info.webcrawler.com/mak/ projects/robots/robots.html

"AskScott: Web Searching Tutorial: Methods of Indexing"
http://www.askscott.com/ sec1.html#methods

"Search Engines: How Software Agents and Search Engines Work"
http://webreference.com/content/ search/how.html

More Information About Search Features and Search Strategies

"Using a Search Engine"
http://www.askscott.com/ sec2.html

"Boolean Searching"
http://exlibris.colgate.edu/ web/finding/finding8.html

"Searcher: The Magazine for Database Professionals"
http://www.infotoday.com/ searcher

"How to Do Field Searching in Web Search Engines"
http://www.onlineinc.com/ onlinemag/OL1998/hock5.html

Chapter 10—Specialized Databases

Search Engines That Index Usenet Newsgroup Articles

AltaVista
http://www.altavista.com
Select **Discussion Groups**

HotBot
http://www.hotbot.lycos.com
Select **Discussion Groups**

Infoseek
http://www.infoseek.com
Select Newsgroups

Selected Biographical Databases on the Web

"Biographical Dictionary"
http://www.s9.com/biography

"Biography.com"
http://www.biography.com

"Distinguished Women of Past and Present"
http://www .DistinguishedWomen.com

Chapter 11—Selecting, Evaluating, and Citing Information from the Internet

Web Pages That Focus on Evaluating Web Resources

"Evaluating Information Found on the Internet"
http://milton.mse.jhu.edu:/ research/education/net.html

"Evaluating the Documents You Have Found on the World Wide Web"
http://www.curtin.edu.au/curtin/ library/staffpages/gwpersonal/ senginestudy/zeval.htm

"Bibliography on Evaluating Internet Resources"
http://www.lib.vt.edu/ research/libinst/evalbiblio.html

"Evaluating Quality on the Net"
http://www.tiac.net/users/ hope/findqual.html

Domain Name Information

"Web Naming and Addressing Overview"
http://www.w3.org/Addressing

"Domain Name Tutorial"
http://www.lmcs.com/
domain.html

"HotBot Help: Top Level Domains"
http://hotbot.lycos.com/help/
domains.asp

Web Resources About Citing Information Found on the Internet and the World Wide Web

"MLA Style: Documenting Sources from the World Wide Web"
http://www.mla.org/style/
sources.htm

"Electronic Reference Formats Recommended by the American Psychological Association"
http://www.apa.org/journals/
webref.html

"IPL FARQ: Citing Electronic Resources"
http://www.ipl.org/ref/QUE/
FARQ/netciteFARQ.html

"ONLINE! Citation Styles"
http://www.bedfordstmartins
.com/online/citex.html

Chapter 12—Managing and Using Information from the Internet and the World Wide Web

Information About File Formats

"Every File Format in the World"
http://www.whatis.com/ff.htm

"File Extensions, Formats, and Utilities"
http://www.stack.com

Information About Copyright and Intellectual Property

"The Copyright Website"
http://www.benedict.com

"The Intellectual Property Law Server"
http://www.intelproplaw.com

Chapter 13—Transferring Files Using FTP

General-Purpose FTP Archives on the Web

"UIArchive, University of Illinois at Urbana-Champaign"
http://uiarchive.cso.uiuc.edu

"Wuarchive, Washington University in St. Louis"
http://ftp.wustl.edu

"Garbo, University of Vassa, Finland"
http://garbo.uwasa.fi

More Information About MP3s

MP3 libraries:
EMusic.com
http://emusic.com

Listen.com
http://listen.com

Lycos Music
http://music.lycos.com

Making your own MP3s:
Audiograbber
http://www.audiograbber
.com-us.net

"MusicMatch Jukebox"
http://www.musicmatch.com

"MP3 - A CNET Topic Center"
**http://home.cnet.com/
category/0-4004.html**

"Easy CD-DA Extractor"
**http://www.poikosoft.com/
cdda**

Guides to Using WS_FTP
"How to Use WS_FTP"
**http://www.albany.edu/
library/internet/ws_ftp.html**

"Installing and Configuring
WS_FTP"
http://usats.com/learn/ftp.shtml

Chapter 14—Putting Information on the Web

Internet and Web Statistics
"CyberAtlas"
http://cyberatlas.internet.com

"Internet Domain Survey"
http://www.isc.org/ds

"Media Metrix"
http://www.mediametrix.com

"Nua Internet Surveys"
http://www.nua.ie/surveys

Browser-Safe Colors
"The Browser-Safe Color Palette"
http://www.lynda.com/hex.html

"In Design School, They Promised
No Math: A Web color primer"
**http://webreview.com/pub/97/11/
28/tools/index.html**

"Color Tables"
**http://mrlxp2.mrl.uiuc.edu/
~ www/rgbtbl.html**

Guides to Web Design
"Guide to Web Style"
http://www.sun.com/styleguide

"Web Style Guide"
**http://info.med.yale.edu/caim/
manual/index.html**

"Art and the Zen of Web Sites"
**http://www.tlc-systems.com/
webtips.shtml**

Information Architecture
"Web Architect"
**http://webreview.com/wr/pub/
at/Web_Architect**

"Information Architecture Tutorial"
**http://hotwired.lycos.com/
webmonkey/design/tutorials/
tutorial1.html**

Tools to Help Create Web Pages
"Web Building"
**http://www.snap.com/directory/
category/0,16,-13092,00.html**

"Web Developer's Virtual Library:
VL-WWW: HTML_Editors"
**http://www.stars.com/Vlib/
Providers/HTML_Editors.html**

"HTML Editors"
**http://dir.yahoo.com/
Computers_and_Internet/Software/
Internet/World_Wide_Web/
HTML_Editors**

Evaluating Web Pages and Web Sites
"Evaluation of information
sources"
**http://www.vuw.ac.nz/ ~ agsmith/
evaln/evaln.htm**

"Evaluating Quality on the Net"
**http://www.tiac.net/users/
hope/findqual.html**

"Commentary: Measuring quality
and impact of the world wide web"
**http://www.bmj.com/archive/
7098ip2.htm**

Selecting a Web Presence Provider

"How to Select a Web Presence
Provider"
http://www.4w.com/wpp.html

"Web Hosting"
**http://www.dmoz.org/Computers/
Internet/Commercial_Services/
Web_Hosting**

Getting Your Web Site Noticed

"Search Engine Submission Tips"
**http://www.searchenginewatch
.com/webmasters/index.html**

"Search Engine Placement Tips,
Techniques and Help in Ten Steps"
**http://www.infoscavenger.com/
engine.htm**

"Promotion 101: Web Site
Marketing and Promotion Info
Center"
http://www.Promotion101.com

Publicizing a Web Site

Tips and Lists of Services:
"FAQ: How to Announce Your
New Web Site"
**http://ep.com/faq/
webannounce.html**

"How to Publicize Your Web Site
over the Internet"
**http://www.samizdat.com/
public.html**

"Web Site Announcing and
Search Engine Placements"
**http://tsworldofdesign
.com/promotion/
website%20_announcing.htm**

Directories:
"Computers: Internet: WWW:
Website Promotion"
**http://www.dmoz.org/
Computers/Internet/WWW/
Website_Promotion**

"Computers and Internet :
Internet : World Wide Web :
Announcement Services"
**http://www.yahoo.com/
Computers_and_Internet/
Internet/World_Wide_Web/
Announcement_Services**

Chapter 15—Writing Web Pages

Special Characters

"Martin Ramsch - iso8859-1 table"
**http://www.uni-passau.de/
~ ramsch/iso8859-1.html**

"ISO8859-1/HTML Stuff"
**http://ppewww.ph.gla.ac.uk/
~ flavell/iso8859**

"ISO Lating-1 Character Set"
**http://www.obliquity.com/
computer/html/symbols.html**

Web Page Colors

"Annabella's HTML Help - Colors"
**http://www.geocities.com/
Heartland/Plains/6446/color.html**

"The Browser-Safe Color Palette"
http://www.lynda.com/hex.html

Personal Web Pages

"One Nation Worldwide"
http://www.onww.com

"Personal Pages Worldwide"
**http://www.utexas.edu/world/
personal/index.html**

"WhoWhere? Personal Home Pages
Directory"
http://homepages.whowhere.com

"The World Wide Web as Social
Hypertext"
**http://www.pliant.org/personal/
Tom_Erickson/SocialHypertext.html**

"Personal Home Pages and the
Construction of Identities on the
Web"
**http://www.aber.ac.uk/media/
Documents/short/webident.html**

Chapter 16—Enhancing Web Pages

Information About Usability

"All Things Web: The Usable Web"
**http://www.pantos.org/atw/
usable.html**

"Usability"
**http://www.slais.ubc.ca/
courses/libr559a/winter2000/
resources/usability.htm**

"Usability and Human Factors for
the Internet"
http://WebWord.com

"Usability Checklist for Site
Developers"
**http://webreview.com/pub/1999/
10/15/usability/index.html**

Shareware to Manipulate Images

For Windows systems:
Paint Shop Pro
**http://www.jasc.com/
product.asp?pf_id = 001**

LView Pro
http://www.lview2.com

For Macs:
GIFConverter
**http://www.kamit.com/
gifconverter**

Reducing Colors on the Web

"Media Builder GIF Optimizer"
http://www.gifoptimizer.com

Pointers About Animated GIFs

Shareware:
GIF Construction Set
Professional
**http://www.mindworkshop
.com/alchemy/gifcon.html**

GIFmation
http://www.boxtopsoft.com

Web pages and sites:
"Make Your GIFs Dance"
**http://builder.cnet.com/
Graphics/Webanim**

"GIF Animation on the WWW"
**http://members.aol.com/
royalef/gifanim.htm**

"Animated GIFs and Protein Chemistry"
http://www2.ucsc.edu/ ~ straycat/cpa.html

Collections of animated GIFs:
"The Expo"
http://members.aol.com/ royalef1/expo.htm

"Animation Factory"
http://www.animfactory.com

Creating Audio Files for Your Web Page

"Adam's Multimedia Tutorial"
http://hotwired.lycos.com/ webmonkey/multimedia/ tutorials/tutorial3.html

"Audio for the World Wide Web"
http://wdvl.internet.com/ Multimedia/Sound/Audio

"Make Some Noise! How to Add Audio to Your Site"
http://builder.com/Authoring/ Audio

About Audio Files

More information about audio file formats:
"Audio File Format FAQ"
http://home.sprynet.com/ ~ cbagwell/audio.html

"PC Webopaedia - Audio category page"
http://webopedia.internet .com/Multimedia/Audio

Collections of audio files that you can use in Web pages:
"The MIDI Farm Internet"
http://files.midifarm.com

"MSDN Online Downloads Sounds TOC"
http://msdn.microsoft.com/ downloads/sounds/toc.htm

The Audio section of the World Wide Web Virtual Library
http://archive.comlab.ox.ac .uk/audio.html

Details About the EMBED Tag

The EMBED tag in the HTML Compendium
http://www.htmlcompendium .org/Aembed.htm

"Description of the EMBED Tag"
http://users.knoware.nl/users/ schluter/doc/tags/ TAG_EMBED.html

Creating Video Files

"Adam's Multimedia Tutorial: Lesson 4"
http://www.hotwired.com/ webmonkey/98/17/index3a.html

"How to Add Video to Your Site"
http://builder.com/Graphics/ Video

Going to the Source for Information About Java

"The Java home page"
http://java.sun.com

"Sun's Web page for applets"
http://java.sun.com/applets/ index.html

Where to Find Java Applets

"Gamelan: The Official Directory for Java"
http://www.gamelan.com

EarthWeb's "JARS.COM: The #1 Java Review Service"
http://www.jars.com

"The Java Boutique"
http://javaboutique.internet.com

Going to the Source for Information About JavaScript

"JavaScript Guide"
http://developer.netscape.com/ docs/manuals/communicator/ jsguide4/index.htm

"JavaScript Reference"
http://developer.netscape.com/ docs/manuals/communicator/ jsref/index.htm

JavaScript Information, Tutorials, and Guides

"Coolnerds JavaScript Home Page"
http://www.coolnerds.com/ jscript/Default.htm

"Voodoo's Introduction to JavaScript"
http://rummelplatz.uni-mannheim .de/ ~ skoch/js/script.htm

"JavaScript Guide"
http://developer.netscape.com/ docs/manuals/communicator/ jsguide4/index.htm

JavaScript World's "Online Resources"
http://www.jsworld.com/help/ resources/index.html

Some Resources for Your Web Site

"The CGI Resource Index"
http://www.cgi-resources.com

"Website Resources"
http://www.websiteresources.com

"Zuberlinks"
http://www.zuberlinks.com

GLOSSARY

24-bit color   A color system used in monitor display. 24-bit color provides 8 bits of information for each of the colors of the RGB system, allowing a total of 16,777,216 possible colors.

404 error   A response code or error transmitted by a Web server to a client when a requested Web page or file is not present on the server.

absolute URL   A URL (Uniform Resource Locator) that contains the Internet domain name of the server hosting the item to which the URL refers. For example, an absolute URL would be of the same form as **http://www.webliminal.com/search-web.html**. The Internet domain name of this server is **www.webliminal.com**.

acceptable use policy   Within the context of the Internet, a policy that states the proper or acceptable uses of a computer network.

address box   The pane in the browser window of Internet Explorer that holds the current document's URL. You can type a URL in this box and press Enter to access a Web page. See also *location field*.

administrative address   The address to use to join an email discussion group or interest group and to send requests for services.

agent   A program that gathers information or accomplishes tasks without your immediate presence. Agents are usually given very small and well-defined tasks. They are also called intelligent agents, personal agents, or bots.

all-in-one search tool   A tool that provides search forms for several search engines and directories all in one site. The tool also provides hyperlinks that allow you to go to the services directly.

alternate text   A description of a hyperlink or image, put in by the author of a Web page, that pops up when you move the mouse pointer over the hyperlink or image.

anchor element   An HTML element that declares content to be a hyperlink to a URL that is specified as the value of the HREF attribute.

anonymous FTP   A means of using FTP to make files readily available to the public. When you start an FTP session with a remote host, you give the login or user name "anonymous" and enter your email address as the password. When you use a URL that starts with **ftp://** and a domain name with a Web browser, an anonymous FTP session begins, and you don't have to enter a user name or password.

article   A message or file that is part of a Usenet newsgroup.

ASCII (American Standard Code for Information Interchange)   A code for representing characters in a numeric form. An ASCII file is one that contains characters that can be displayed on a screen or printed without formatting or using another program.

asynchronous communication   Communication where the sender and receiver don't participate at the same time, for example, email or voicemail.

attachment   A file that is sent as part of an email message but that is not in the body of the message. Images, programs, and word-processing files are usually sent as attachments because most email programs allow only plain text in the body of the message.

attribute   Specifies a property of an HTML element. Attributes are found in the start tag of an HTML element and often take values.

avatar   An icon, image, or figure that you can use to represent yourself in a chat room.

binary file   A file containing information such as a compressed archive, an image, a program, a spreadsheet, or a word-processing document. The items in the file usually cannot be displayed on a screen or printed without using some program.

BinHex   An encoding scheme that converts binary data into ASCII (American Standard Code for Information Interchange) characters.

blocking device   See *filter*.

body element   An HTML element that declares content to be the body of a document that can be displayed by a browser.

bookmark list   A list of links to items on the World Wide Web. Bookmark lists are usually created by individuals as they use Netscape. A good way to keep track of favorite or important sites, since they are saved and can be used at any time. See also *favorites list*.

Boolean searching   Searching that uses Boolean operators (AND, OR, and NOT) in the search expression. Especially helpful in multifaceted or specific topics, Boolean operators help expand or narrow the scope of your search. A search for rivers OR lakes returns documents with either word in them. A search for rivers AND lakes returns documents with both words in them. A search for rivers AND lakes NOT swamps returns documents that mention both rivers and lakes but omits those that also mention swamps.

bot   See *agent*.

bytecode   The compiled format for Java programs. Once a Java program has been converted to bytecode, it can be transferred across a network and executed by Java Virtual Machine. Bytecode files generally have the extension **.class**, as in **marquee.class**.

cache   A portion of memory (either in RAM or on a disk) set aside to hold the items retrieved most recently. For a Web browser, this refers to recent Web pages and images. The cache is used so that items may be retrieved more quickly without going back to the Internet. A browser can be set so that, in case an item hasn't changed, it will retrieve the item from the cache.

case sensitivity   The ability of a search tool to distinguish between uppercase and lowercase letters. Some search tools aren't case sensitive; no matter what you type, the tool picks up only lowercase matches. Search engines that are case sensitive strictly follow a search request; they'll return documents containing the words in the case in which they were entered in the search expression.

cellpadding   Space between the content of an HTML table cell and its border, specified in pixels.

cellspacing   Space between cells in an HTML table, specified in pixels.

certificate authority   A company that guarantees the identity of the holder of a digital certificate. A certificate is attached to a message or Web page and can be used to guarantee the authenticity of information.

CGI (Common Gateway Interface)   A specification for transferring information between programs that execute on a Web server and the server software itself. A typical situation is for a so-called CGI program to take input from the server software, process it, and write the output in the form of a Web page that is then passed to a client by the server.

chat room   A conference or forum that allows two or more people to converse with each other at the same time by taking turns typing messages.

client/server   A program or Internet service that sends commands to and receives information from a corresponding program, often at a remote site, called a server. Most Internet services run as client/server programs.

Telnet, for example, works this way. A user starts a client program on his computer that contacts a Telnet server.

commercial database   A database that requires you to pay a subscription cost before accessing it. It is also referred to as a proprietary database.

Communications Decency Act of 1996   Legislation approved by Congress that made it a criminal offense to include potentially indecent or offensive material on the Internet. The U.S. Supreme Court ruled in June of 1997 that this act abridged the freedom of speech that is protected by the First Amendment, and the act was ruled unconstitutional.

compiler   A program that translates a source file written in a programming language (that presumably a human can understand) into some form of machine language that can be dealt with by a computer.

compressed file   A file that has been processed by a program that applied an algorithm or scheme to compress or shrink it. A compressed file must first be uncompressed or transformed before it can be read, displayed, or used. Files available through anonymous FTP are often stored in compressed form.

concept searching   A feature enabling a search engine to find synonyms in its database. When you type in a word or phrase, the engine automatically searches for the word or phrase you want, plus words or phrases that may mean the same thing. For example, if the word *teenage* is in your search expression, the search engine also looks for the word *adolescent.*

conferencing   A conferencing system generally uses text, audio, and video for holding group meetings and uses protocols that allow for these means of synchronous communication on the Internet.

content area   The part of a Web browser window that contains the current Web page; it contains images, text, or hyperlinks.

cookie   A relatively small piece of information that is initially placed on a client's computer by a Web server. Once a cookie is present, the same Web server may read or rewrite the cookie. A Web server requests or writes a cookie to your computer only if you access a Web page that contains the commands to do that. Cookies are used to store information such as your login name and password or information about what portions of a Web site were visited on your computer. Sometimes viewed as an invasion of privacy, cookies are useful to you in some cases. Cookies can be used to keep track of your password or keep track of some preferences you've set for every visit to that site. You can set preferences in your browser to accept or reject cookies.

copyright   The right to copy or duplicate material such as images, music, and written works. Only the owners of the information can grant this right. Regardless of whether information on the Internet or a Web page is accompanied by a statement asserting copyright, it is still protected by the copyright laws of the United States, the Universal Copyright Convention, and the Berne Union.

cross-posting   Posting an article to more than one Usenet newsgroup.

data transfer rate   The speed at which a circuit or communications line can transfer information, usually measured in bits per second (bps).

decoded   Describes a file recreated in binary format that has been encoded or translated from binary to ASCII or text format. Binary files that are sent as attachments to email have to be encoded (translated from binary to ASCII) before they are sent and decoded (translated from ASCII to binary) when they are received before they can be used.

default setting   The configuration a search engine uses unless you override the setting by specifying another configuration. For example, in some search engines, the Boolean operator OR is the assumed relationship between two words unless you type AND between the words.

delimited format   A format often used to store tables of data. The data fields are separated by commas, tabs, semicolons, or some other delimiter. Spreadsheet programs usually include the facilities to import data that is in delimited format.

digital certificate   A device that is used to encrypt and decrypt information and to guarantee the identity of the sender and the authenticity of the information.

directory   A topical list of Internet resources, arranged hierarchically. Directories are meant to be browsed, but they can also be searched. Directories differ from search engines in one major way—the human element involved in collecting and updating the information.

discussion group   A group that discusses a single topic via email messages. An individual subscribes to or joins a discussion group electronically, and all messages sent to the group are distributed to the members by email.

dithered   An approximation of a requested color using two or more available colors. Dithering sometimes occurs when an image or background on a Web page requires a color that isn't available on the computer displaying the Web page. In that case the computer approximates the color by mixing two or more colors it can represent.

domain name   See *Internet domain name.*

domain name system   A system of computers and protocols on the Internet through which an Internet domain name is translated into an IP address.

download   To transfer or copy a file from another computer (the remote computer) to the computer you're using (the local computer). This term is often applied to the process of retrieving a file from a software library or FTP archive.

duplicate detection   An output feature of some search engines and meta-search tools that automatically filters out of your search results any URLs that are duplicated elsewhere in the results.

ECPA (Electronic Communications Privacy Act)   The U.S. law that prevents U.S. investigative agencies from intercepting or reading email messages without first obtaining a warrant.

electronic mail (email)   A basic Internet service that allows users to exchange messages electronically.

element   A distinctive part of an HTML document's structure, such as a title, heading, or list.

email client   The program you use to work with your email. Also called the mail user agent.

email discussion group   See *discussion group.*

emoticon   A symbol that can be typed using one or more characters to foster more expressive and efficient communication. For example, :-) and :) are used to represent a grin or smile. These are also used to denote that a sentence is to be interpreted as a joke.

encoded   Describes a file that's been translated from binary format to ASCII (American Standard Code for Information Interchange). This is done so the file can be sent using email.

encryption   A procedure to convert a file or message from its original form to one that can be read only by the intended recipient.

event handler   Java code that automatically responds to an event that occurs, such as the click of a mouse button.

fair use   A provision in most copyright conventions or statutes that makes it possible for individuals to copy portions of a document or other piece of work for short-term use.

fan-in   The receiving by an individual in a group of all the messages to the group. One person asks a question and replies can come from anywhere in the world.

fan-out   The sending of one message to a group and having it automatically distributed or made available to every member of the group.

FAQ (frequently asked questions)   A list, often associated with Usenet newsgroups, of commonly asked questions and answers on a specific topic. This is usually the first place users should look to find answers to questions or to get information on a topic.

favorites list   The name that Internet Explorer gives to an individual's collection of favorite URLs. The browser includes menu bar and toolbar links to the favorites list. This list is similar to the bookmark list kept by Netscape. See also *bookmark list*.

field   Part of a Web page or bibliographic record that is designated for a particular kind of data or text.

field searching   A strategy in which you limit a search to a particular field. In a search engine, you might search only the URL field. By narrowing the scope of searchable items, field searching helps to eliminate the chance of retrieving irrelevant information.

file name extension   The end of a file name in some operating systems where the name of a file ends with a period followed by (usually) two to four letters. The extension is used to associate an application program with the file. For example, the file containing this glossary is named **glossary.doc**. The file name extension is **.doc**. Clicking on the name of the file automatically opens the file with the Microsoft Word word-processing software.

filter   Software that filters out certain Web sites from the results of a search.

firewall   A security device or system, usually a combination of hardware and software meant to protect a local network from intruders from the Internet.

follow-up   An article posted in response to another article. The follow-up has the same subject as the original article.

frame   Some Web pages are divided into rectangular regions called frames. Each frame has its own scroll bar, and in fact, each frame represents an individual Web page.

freeware   Computer programs that have been made available to the public free of charge.

frequently asked questions (FAQ)   See *FAQ*.

FTP (File Transfer Protocol)   A means of transferring or sharing files across the Internet from one computer system to another.

FTP archive   A collection of files available through anonymous FTP.

full-text indexing   A search engine feature in which every word, significant or insignificant, is indexed and retrievable through a search. See also *stop word*.

group address   The address to use to send email to each member of a discussion group, interest group, listserv list, or mailing list.

hexadecimal   A numbering system that uses a base of 16. Computer programmers use hexadecimal numbers to represent binary numbers.

hierarchy   A list of subjects in a directory. The subjects are organized in successive ranks with the broadest listed first and with more specific aspects or subdivisions listed below.

high precision/high recall   A phenomenon that occurs during a search when you retrieve all the relevant documents in the database and retrieve no unwanted ones.

high precision/low recall   A phenomenon that occurs when a search yields a small set of hits. Although each one may be very relevant to the search topic, some relevant documents are missed.

history list   A list of Internet sites, services, and resources that have been accessed through a Web browser over a certain period of time.

home page   The first screen or page of a site accessible through a Web browser.

HTML (Hypertext Markup Language)   The format used for writing documents to be viewed with a Web browser. Items in the document can be text; images; sounds; or links to other HTML documents, sites, services, and resources on the Web.

HTML editor   An application program designed to facilitate the writing of HTML. For example, the toolbars often contain icons and buttons that can be used to enter HTML tags.

HTTP (Hypertext Transfer Protocol)   The standard protocol that World Wide Web servers and clients use to communicate.

hyperlink   A word, phrase, image, or region of an image that is often highlighted or colored differently and that can be selected as part of a Web page. Each hyperlink represents another Web page; a location in the current Web page; an image, audio, video, or multimedia file; or some other resource on the World Wide Web. When the hyperlink is selected, it activates the resource that it represents.

hypermedia   An extension to hypertext that includes graphics and audio.

hypertext   A way of viewing or working with a document in text format that allows you to follow cross-references to other Web resources. By clicking on an embedded hyperlink, the user can choose her own path through the hypertext material.

IMAP (Internet Message Address Protocol)   A protocol used to retrieve email from a mail server. It is similar to POP3 but has additional features.

implied Boolean operators   The characters + and -, which can be used to require or prohibit a word or phrase as part of a search expression. The + acts somewhat like AND, and the - acts as NOT would in a Boolean expression. For example, the Boolean expression rivers AND lakes NOT swamps may be expressed as +rivers +lakes -swamps.

intelligent agent   See *agent*.

interest group   A group that discusses and shares information about a single topic via email.

Internet   The collection of networks throughout the world that agree to communicate using specific telecommunication protocols, the most basic being Internet Protocol (IP) and Transmission Control Protocol (TCP), and the services supplied by those networks.

Internet domain name   The Internet name for a network or computer system. The name consists of a sequence of characters separated by periods, such as **www.mwc.edu**. The domain name is often the first part of the URL that follows ://. For example, the domain name in the URL **http://www.ckp.edu/technical/reference/swftp.html** is **www.ckp.edu**.

IP (Internet Protocol)   The basic protocol used for the Internet. Information is put into a single packet containing the addresses of the sender and the recipient, and then sent out. The receiving system removes the information from the packet.

IP address   An Internet address in numeric form. It consists of four numerals, each in the range of 0 through 255, separated by periods. An example is 192.65.245.76. Each computer connected to the Internet has an IP address assigned to it. The IP address is sometimes used for authentication.

IP telephony   Transmitting and receiving telephone messages via the Internet. Messages are broken into packets and exchanged using the Internet protocols.

IRC (Internet Relay Chat)   A synchronous communication system on the Internet. An individual uses an IRC client to contact one of the several IRC servers on the Internet. Once connected, the individual joins a channel or chat room and can communicate in realtime with others using the channel.

ISP (Internet service provider)   A usually commercial service that provides access to the Internet. Fees often depend on the amount of time and the maximum possible speed, in bits per second, of access to the Internet.

Java   An object-oriented programming language. The language was originally designed to be used to develop applications in networked devices. It has been used very successfully to make small applications available through Web pages in a platform-independent format as bytecodes.

Java applet A Java program that can be included as part of a Web page.

JavaScript A programming language used exclusively within Web pages. The statements in the language are made part of a source file to enable some interactive features such as mouse clicks and input to forms. JavaScript is not based on or part of Java.

JPEG (Joint Photographic Experts Group) A file format used to represent images. It supports more colors than GIF and offers greater compression. However, some detail is lost in the compression.

keyword A descriptive or significant word in a Web document.

limiting by date A search tool feature that allows you to limit search results to pages that were indexed after, before, or between certain dates.

list address See *group address.*

Listserv The type of software used to manage a listserv list.

listserv list A type of discussion group, interest group, or mailing list.

location field The pane on the browser window of Netscape that holds the current document's URL. You can type a URL in this box and press Enter to access a Web page. See also *address box.*

location toolbar The toolbar just above the content area in Netscape that includes the Bookmark Quickfile icon, which serves as a link to the bookmark list; the Page Proxy icon, which lets you add sites to the bookmark list, the personal toolbar, or the desktop; and the location field.

lossless A data compression scheme that doesn't throw away or otherwise leave out any information from the original, uncompressed file. Graphic Interchange Format, GIF, uses a lossless compression scheme.

lossy A data compression scheme that excludes or removes information it regards as unnecessary from the original, uncompressed file. The Joint Photographic Experts Group format, JPEG or JPG, uses a lossy compression scheme.

low precision/high recall A phenomenon that occurs during a search when you retrieve a large set of results, including many irrelevant documents.

lurking Reading the email or articles in a discussion group or newsgroup without contributing or posting messages.

mail user agent See *email client.*

mailing list   See *discussion group.*

menu bar   The sequence of pulldown menus located across the top of the Web browser window. All commands are accessible from the menu bar.

meta-search tool   A tool that provides either the ability to search more than one search engine or directory simultaneously or a list of search tools that can be accessed from its site. These two major types of meta-search tools are called parallel search tools and all-in-one search tools.

meta-tag   A keyword inserted in the meta-tag portion of an HTML source document by the Web page author. If Web pages don't have much text, meta-tags help them come up in a keyword search.

MIME (multipurpose Internet mail extensions)   Extensions to standard email programs making it easy to send, receive, and include nontext files.

MIME type   Code that specifies the content type of a multimedia file.

modem   The device used to allow a computer to communicate with another computer over a telephone line. It is needed because the computer's information is in digital form and information on many telephone lines is transmitted in analog form. A device to convert from one form to the other is a *mod*ulator and *dem*odulator, hence the term *modem.*

Moderator   A person who manages or administers a discussion group, interest group, listserv list, mailing list, or Usenet newsgroup. In most cases the moderator is a volunteer. Messages sent to the group are first read by the moderator, who then passes appropriate messages to the group.

MOO   Similar to a MUD, but the enabling software is written in an object-oriented manner. This allows persons unfamiliar with the intricacies of the software to be able to set up and manage a MOO.

MUD   Multiuser dimension or multiuser dungeon. Software that enables synchronous communication in a virtual world. It was originally designed to represent dungeons-and-dragons-type role-playing games.

natural language searching   The capability of entering a search expression in the form of a question or statement.

navigation toolbar   Often referred to as the command toolbar, this toolbar contains a sequence of icons or items that represent frequently used commands for navigation and other purposes, such as printing the current Web page.

nested Boolean logic   The use of parentheses in Boolean search expressions. For example, the nested expression **((rivers OR lakes) AND**

canoeing) NOT camping will find resources that contain first either the words *rivers* or *lakes* and then the term *canoeing,* but not resources that contain the term *camping.*

news server   A computer that is used to hold the collections of articles that make up newsgroups and to run the programs that pass any new articles posted to its newsgroups on to any other server that carries the same newsgroups.

newsgroup   A collection of Usenet articles arranged by topic. Some are specialized or technical groups (such as **comp.protocols.tcp-ip .domains**—topics related to Internet domain style names), some deal with recreational activities (such as **rec.outdoors.fishing.saltwater**—topics related to saltwater fishing), and one, **news.newusers.questions**, is dedicated to questions from new Usenet users.

newsreader   The software you use to read, reply to, and manage Usenet news.

NNTP (Network News Transport Protocol)   The standard protocol used to distribute Usenet news between computer systems on the Internet in a form that machines can read and computers can access.

packet-switched network   A message delivery system in which information is broken into small units (packets) and routed through a computer network using the most efficient route available for each. The packets may travel along different paths, but are reassembled into one message by the receiving computer.

parallel search tool   A search tool or service that takes one search expression, submits it to several search services, and returns selected results from each. This is an example of a meta-search tool.

people finder   A Web-based email or telephone directory. See also *white page service.*

personal agent   See *agent.*

personal home page   A Web page used by an individual to give personal or professional information.

PGP   Pretty Good Privacy, the name given to a public key encryption system for exchanging email in a secure, encrypted format. PGP was developed by Philip R. Zimmerman in 1991.

phrase searching   A search feature supported by most search engines that allows you to search for words that usually appear next to each other. It is possibly the most important search feature.

plug-in   A software application that is used along with a Web browser to view or display certain types of files as part of a Web page.

Shockwave from Macromedia is a plug-in that allows the browser to display interactive multimedia.

POP (Post Office Protocol)   The way many email programs retrieve messages from a mail server. Email is delivered on the Internet to the mail server and an email program running on a personal computer retrieves that email through POP.

post   A message sent to an email discussion group or a Usenet newsgroup. Also, to send a message to an email discussion group or Usenet newsgroup.

PPP (Point-to-Point Protocol)   A standard protocol that allows a computer with a modem to communicate using TCP/IP.

proprietary database   See *commercial database.*

protocol   A set of rules for exchanging information between networks or computer systems. The rules specify the format and the content of the information, and the procedures to follow during the exchange.

proximity searching   A search feature that makes it possible to search for words that are near each other in a document.

public key encryption   An encryption method that involves the use of two codes or keys. The two keys, one called the private key and the other called the public key, are assigned to an individual. Using the public key, anyone can encrypt a message or file that can only be decrypted or decoded by the use of the corresponding private key.

reference work   A resource used to find quick answers to questions. Traditionally thought of as being in the form of books (such as dictionaries, encyclopedias, quotation directories, manuals, guides, atlases, bibliographies, and indexes), a reference source on the World Wide Web closely resembles its print counterpart. A reference book doesn't necessarily contain hyperlinks to other resources, although it will often have hyperlinks within the document itself.

relevance   A measure of how closely a database entry matches a search request. Most search tools on the Web return results ranked by relevance. The specific algorithm for computing relevance varies from one service to another, but it's often based on the number of times terms in the search expression appear in the document and whether they appear in the appropriate fields.

relevancy ranking   A ranking of items retrieved from a database. The ranking is based on the relevancy score that a search engine has assigned.

results per page   A feature of some search engines that allows you to designate the number of results listed per page. Search engines usually list 10 results per page.

robot   See *spider*.

router   A device (hardware) that transfers information between networks.

scroll bar   The rectangular area on the right side of a window that allows you to move up or down in an open document. You move by clicking and dragging it or clicking on the arrow at the bottom of the bar.

search engine   A collection of programs that gather information from the Web (see also *spider*), index it, and put it in a database so it can be searched. The search engine takes the keywords or phrases you enter, searches the database for words that match the search expression, and returns the results of the search to you. The results are hyperlinks to sources that have descriptions, titles, or contents matching the search expression.

search expression   The keywords and syntax that you enter into a search form. With this expression, you ask a search tool to seek relevant documents in a particular way.

search form   The rectangular pane or oblong box that appears on the home pages of most search tools. In this space, you enter a search expression.

shareware   Software that you are allowed to download and try for a specified period free of charge. If you continue to use the program after that time, you are expected to pay a (usually modest) fee to continue using the product legally.

signature   An optional portion of an email message consisting of information about the sender such as his full name, mailing address, phone number, etc. The signature is stored in a file and automatically included with each message.

smiley   The emoticon used to denote a smile, a grin, or a joke. Two common forms of this emoticon are :) and :-).

SMTP (Simple Mail Transfer Protocol)   The Internet standard protocol used to transfer electronic mail from one computer system to another.

source file   The text file that contains the HTML tags for a Web page. A browser reads the source for a Web page from this file and then, using the HTML tags, displays the Web page.

spam   Unwanted and unsolicited email. The electronic equivalent of paper junk mail.

specialized database   A self-contained index that is searchable and available on the Web. Items in specialized databases are often not accessible through a keyword search in a search engine.

spider   A computer program that travels the Internet to locate Web documents and FTP resources. It indexes the documents in a database, which is then searched using a search engine (such as AltaVista or Excite). A spider can also be referred to as a robot or wanderer. Each search engine uses a spider to build its database.

status bar   The bar or rectangular region at the bottom of the browser window that shows several items of information regarding the transfer of a Web document to the browser. When the mouse is moved over a hyperlink it shows the hyperlink's URL. When a Web page is requested it gives information about contacting and receiving information from a server. During transmission it tells, in terms of a percentage, how much of the document has been transferred and indicates whether transmissions are being carried on in a secure manner.

stemming   See *truncation*.

stop word   A word that an indexing program doesn't index. Stop words usually include articles *(a, an,* and *the)* and other common words.

streaming media   The method of displaying or playing media such as sound or video as it is being transmitted across the Internet rather than retrieving the entire file before displaying it.

subject category   A division in a hierarchical subject classification system in a Web directory. You click on the subject category that is likely to contain either the Web pages you want or other subject categories that are more specific.

subject guide   A collection of URLs on a particular topic. Most easily found listed in virtual libraries, they are also referred to as meta-pages.

subscribe   To join a discussion group, interest group, listserv list, or mailing list. You use this term when writing commands to join such a group and to list a Usenet newsgroup on your newsreader.

synchronous communication   Communication where the participants participate at the same time. Chat is an example of synchronous communication.

syntax   The rules governing the construction of search expressions in search engines and other databases.

tag   A code used in HTML that identifies an element so that a Web browser will know how to display it.

TCP (Transmission Control Protocol)   A protocol used as the basis of most Internet services. It is used in conjunction (actually on top of) the Internet Protocol. It allows for reliable communication oriented to process-to-process communication.

Telnet   Allows for remote login capabilities on the Internet. One of the three basic Internet services, Telnet allows you to be on one computer and to access and log in to another.

text file   A file containing characters in a plain human-readable format. There are no formatting commands such as underlining or displaying characters in boldface or different fonts. It is also called an ASCII file.

thread   A collection of articles that all deal with a single posting or email message.

thumbnail   A representation of an image in a size that's usually much smaller than its true size. For example, we may represent an image whose size is 100-by-200 pixels as a thumbnail of 25-by-50 pixels.

toolbar   A sequence of icons or items in the window above the content area of a Web browser. Clicking on an icon or item executes a command or causes an action.

top-level category   One of several main subjects in the top of a hierarchy in a directory's list of subjects.

truncation   In the formulation of a search expression, truncation is used when you want to find all endings of a word. It is done by cutting off the end of the word back to the root, and replacing it with a symbol, usually the asterisk (*). When given such a request, a search engine or database will look for all possible ends of the word, in addition to the root word itself.

unified search interface   A meta-search tool that allows searching several search engines simultaneously.

unsubscribe   To leave, sign off from, or quit a discussion group, interest group, listserv list, or mailing list. You use the term when writing commands to end a relationship with a discussion group or to remove a Usenet newsgroup from the list of those you would regularly read.

upload   Transfer a file from the computer system being used to a remote system.

URL (Uniform Resource Locator)   A way of describing the location of an item (document, service, or resource) on the Internet and also specifying the means by which to access that item.

Usenet news   A system for exchanging messages, called articles, arranged according to specific categories called newsgroups. The articles are passed from one system to another, not as email between individuals.

virtual community   A collection of individuals who form a bond through electronic communication.

virtual library   A directory that contains collections of resources that librarians or other information specialists have carefully chosen and organized in a logical way.

virus   A program or executable code that must be part of another executing program. Usually viruses change the configuration or cause havoc with a computer system. The viruses are hidden within some useful or standard program.

visual editor   An application program that is used to edit or create documents or Web pages. It's visual in the sense that the software makes changes that you see immediately. Some examples of visual editors are Microsoft Word (a word processor) and Netscape Composer (used with Web pages).

Web browser   A program used to access the Internet services and resources available through the World Wide Web.

Web page   The information available and displayed by a Web browser as the result of opening a local file or opening a location (URL). The contents and format of the Web page are specified using HTML.

Web presence provider   A commercial service (in most cases) that provides a Web server to host a Web site. Fees often depend on the amount of disk space available, monthly traffic measured in bytes, and types of services that are provided.

Web server   A computer that is running the software and has the Internet connections so that it can satisfy HTTP requests from clients. In other words, it is a properly configured computer system that makes it possible to make Web pages available on the Internet.

white page service   A Web search service that helps locate email or street addresses for individuals. Similar services for businesses and government agencies are called yellow page services.

wildcard   A character that stands in for another character or group of characters. Most search tools use an asterisk for this function. Although a wildcard is most often used in truncation, it can also be used in the middle of words (for example, wom*n).

World Wide Web   The collection of different services and resources available on the Internet and accessible through a Web browser.

INDEX

10-K reports, 316
404 error, 38

A

accessibility
    of a Web page, 429–430
address box (Internet Explorer), 201
Adobe Acrobat, 298
agents, 259–260
all-in-one search tools, 259
AltaVista, 287–299, 333
    image searching, 292
    implied Boolean searching,
        287–289
alternate text, 203–204, 446
Angelfire, 105
annotations, 277
anonymous FTP, 386
antivirus software, 392–393
AOL Instant Messenger, 81–82
APA (American Psychological Asso-
    ciation) style, 340, 347, 348
ARPANET, 22–24
articles, 162, 175–177
ASCII (American Standard Code for
    Information Interchange), 112,
    425, 443
asynchronous communication, 67,
    69
.au, 362
avatars, 74

B

background colors, 467–468
background images, 467–468
Basic Search Strategy: The 10 Steps,
    277–290
BinHex, 112
biography databases, 312
blocking devices, 261–262
bookmark list, 205–206
bookmarks (Netscape), 196, 243
    for citing resources, 349–355
    properties, 353
Boolean operators, 252–253,
    271–273
Boolean searching, 252–253,
    279–280, 284
bots, 259–260
browsers, 186–228
business on the Internet, 20

C

cache, 220–221
capturing and using text, 366–371
capturing data, 371–373
capturing images, 366–371, 374–377
case sensitivity, 275
CataList, 152
CAUCE (Coalition Against Unsolic-
    ited Commercial Email), 96
cellpadding, 469